FAMILY THERAPY OF DRUG AND ALCOHOL ABUSE

Edited by
Edward Kaufman
and
Pauline Kaufmann

Editorial Assistant
Leo J. Mailman

Foreword by
E. Mansell Pattison

GARDNER PRESS, INC., NEW YORK

GARDNER PRESS, INC.
19 Union Square West
New York 10003

Library of Congress Cataloging in Publication Data:
Main entry under title:

Family therapy of drug and alcohol abuser.

1. Drug abuse—Treatment—Addresses, essays, lectures. 2. Alcoholism—Treatment—Addresses, essays,
lectures. 3. Family psychotherapy—Addresses, essays,
lectures. I. Kaufman, Edward. II. Kaufmann,
Pauline.
RC566.F36   616.8'6'06   78-9346
ISBN 0-89876-026-7

Printed in the United States of America

*To the families we came from
and
the families we created*

CONTENTS

CONTRIBUTORS

David Berenson, M.D.
Faculty, Family Institute of Westchester, White Plains, New York

Doug Bond, M.A.
Genesis House, Monterey, California

Donald A. Cadogan, Ph.D.
Formerly: Assistant Director, Alcoholism Treatment Center, Bergan Pines County Hospital, Paramus, New Jersey
Presently: Private Practice, Pasadena, California

Sandra B. Coleman, Ph.D.
Director, Research and Evaluation Achievement through Counseling and Treatment (ACT), Philadelphia, Pennsylvania
Private Practice, Newtown, Pennsylvania

Donald I. Davis, M.D.
Assistant Professor, Department of Psychiatry and Behavioral Sciences, George Washington University School of Medicine, Washington, D.C.

G.G. DeAngelis, Ph.D.
Program Director, Pride House, Van Nuys, California

Eloise Kates Julius, M.S.W., A.C.S.W.
Associate Director, Family Institute of Westchester, White Plains, New York

Edward Kaufman, M.D.
Associate Clinical Professor of Psychiatry, Chief, Psychiatric Services, Director of Family Therapy Programs, University of California, Irvine Medical Center, Orange, California

Pauline Kaufmann, M.S.W.
Director of Family Therapy, Phoenix Foundation
Consultant in Family Therapy, Bellvue Hospital Social Service Department, New York, New York

Lilly M.
Writer and Recovering Alcoholic, New York, New York

Salvador Minuchin, M.D.

Professor of Child Psychiatry and Pediatrics, University of Pennsylvania
Director, Family Therapy Training Center, Philadelphia Child Guidance
Clinic, Philadelphia, Pennsylvania

Peggy Papp, M.S.W.

Philadelphia Child Guidance Clinic, Philadelphia, Pennsylvania

E. Mansell Pattison, M.D.

Professor of Psychiatry and Human Behavior, Social Science, and Social
Ecology, Acting Chair, Department of Psychiatry and Human Behavior,
University of California, Irvine Medical Center, Orange, California

Dennis M. Reilly, M.S.W., A.C.S.W.

Southeast Nassau Guidance Counseling Center, Wantagh, New York

M. Duncan Stanton, Ph.D.

Director, Addicts and Families Program, Philadelphia Child Guidance
Clinic
Associate Professor of Psychology in Psychiatry, University of Pennsylvania
School of Medicine
Director, Family Therapy Program, Drug Dependence Treatment Center,
VA Hospital, Philadelphia, Pennsylvania

Peter Steinglass, M.D.

Associate Professor, Department of Psychiatry and Behavioral Sciences, The
Center for Family Research, George Washington University School of
Medicine, Washington, D.C.

Tomas C. Todd, Ph.D.

Chief Psychologist, Harlem Valley Psychiatric Center, Wingdale, New York
Research Psychologist, Addicts and Families Program, Philadelphia, Pennsylvania

David Wellisch, Ph.D.

Assistant Professor of Medical Psychology, UCLA Neuropsychiatric Institute, Los Angeles, Claifornia

Genevra Ziegler-Driscoll, M.D.

Chief of Psychiatry, Coordinator of Family Therapy, Eagleville Hospital
and Rehabilitation Center, Eagleville, Pennsylvania

Foreword

This is a valuable book that makes a timely clinical contribution to the *treatment* of alcohol and drug abuse problems. In retrospect, there has been little interest in the treatment of alcohol and drug abusers during most of the twentieth century (5). And despite increased scientific and professional concern, my most recent analysis of professional attitudes turned up little change in the prevailing hostility and negativism toward this group of troubled people (3). So the contributors to this book are unusual in their willingness to plunge ahead in developing new and more effective treatment methods.

It would be premature to conclude that family therapy is the only treatment or the best treatment for addictive behaviors. Our empirical data are still far too sketchy to suggest such conclusions. However, I believe that family therapy as we know it today is headed in the right clinical direction—that is, we have moved beyond a simplistic and atomistic approach to human behavior. We see that behavior is the product of social systems, and that change in behavior, in part, results from changing social systems. This book describes clinical methods for changing certain social systems: marriages, parent-child systems, nuclear family systems. I believe the clinical data presented in each chapter clearly illustrate how change in these social systems may in turn affect the addictive behavior of the target patient. Furthermore, the clinical data from these chapters repeatedly show that the addictive behavior is in a real sense a secondary problem, and a manifestation of the primary problem of social dysfunction in the social systems of these people's lives.

Although the attention of each chapter is focused on clinical issues of family evaluation, diagnosis, and intervention, the book as a whole bears out certain fundamental assumptions about the clinical enterprise. These are so important that it is worth emphasizing them in this foreword.

First, this book assumes that alcohol and drug addiction are behavioral problems—that is, that people learn to use alcohol and drugs, and that continued use and abuse are conditioned and reinforced through social interaction with significant others in one's life. In the light of the extant research, I believe this is the most tenable scientific position (7).

Second, this concept of addiction leads us to consider treatment methods that will "unlearn" the conditioned behavioral patterns and change the patterns of social reinforcement. Some of the clinicians in this book report success with changing very small units of social reinforcement, such as in marital therapy; whereas some units of social reinforcement change are much larger, as in multiple family therapy. We do not yet have reliable clinical indicators of when small or large social units will require change for an individual case. Yet the treatment principle involved here is the same.

Third, the contributors to this book employ a similar model of illness. They do not consider alcohol and drug abuse as a "thing" that one contracts like a cold. Rather, they use a "syndrome" model of illness. That is, addiction is a constellation of behaviors which together constitute a self-destructive pattern of abuse. This syndrome of behavior we conviently and appropriately term the illness of addiction.

Fourth, as a corollary to the above, the clinicians in this book do not get caught in the trap of considering the "sick" addict as helpless. Nor do they make the addict the passive recipient of "help." Rather, these clinicians appropriately emphasize that, although we may employ the model of illness, that does not exclude assumption of responsibility for one's own behavior, and active participation in the change of one's own life repertoire and one's social systems. Treatment, then, is a mutually active process.

Fifth, the concept of addiction as a syndrome of behavior allows us to naturally consider the social system within which the learning of addictive behavior has taken place. We turn to the family. In various chapters we find evidence that addictive behavior is *nonspecific*—that is, whether a family generates addiction to alcohol, heroin, sleeping pills, or marijuana may be relatively dependent on social style, availability, and peer practice, rather than on any intrinsic differences in families. In fact, it is striking that the same family may produce different target drugs of abuse.

Sixth, the nature of the family comes under examination at several places in the book. Those chapters which deal with intergenerational family structure, extended kinship, and multiple family relations demonstrate the growing clinical awareness that when we speak of the family and family therapy, we need to extend our vision and our treatment methods beyond the nuclear family.

In our own basic research on family structure, we have shown that the nuclear family is but part of a larger social network. In fact, the family with whom we live is part of a larger "intimate psychosocial system" which comprises the basic social unit of existence. Thus, when we speak of "family," we need to consider this larger "psychosocial family" (6). This leads to appropriate consideration of larger social units of treatment and social change, as indeed several of the chapters describe.

Seventh, this book contains a number of excellent descriptions of clinical technique addressed to social system change. As our concept of family has been necessarily enlarged, so too must be our concept of therapeutic method. I suggest that family therapy, as described, is part of a larger conceptual approach to behavior change, namely social system change. Elsewhere, the theoretical and conceptual detail of social system therapies is examined (1,2,4). Finally, we have a number of very apt descriptions of the therapist working with families and related social systems. Again, this is part of the restructuring necessary to the clinical enterprise. The model of the passive interpretive psychotherapist who is nonintrusive works well for a specific type of psychotherapy with specific types of patients with specific problems—namely, the socially functional neurotic. However, that model of behavior for the therapist is not appropriate for therapeutic problems involving major social dysfunction, and in work with other than individual patients. The therapist of social systems must learn how to function as a catalyst, as a system intervenor, and as an agent for system change. Many chapters in this book describe these functions clearly and correctly.

Although the therapists who contribute to this book have described exciting, rewarding, and often successful treatment methods, we should not conclude that the treatment of drug and alcohol problems is easy. It can be hard, frustrating, and disappointing. These are not simple treatment problems. But for too long professionals in mental health have taken on the easy cases and left the difficult therapeutic problems neglected in the dusty corners of our society. This book stands as a sturdy signpost, pointing toward appropriate and effective treatment of drug and alcohol abuse problems. The authors are pioneers who have staked out new land and established a viable treatment community. They invite us to join them.

E. Mansell Pattison, M.D.

REFERENCES

1. Pattison, E.M., Social System Psychotherapy. *American J. Psychotherapy* 17:396-409, 1973.
2. Pattison, E.M., Psychosocial Systems Therapy. In R.G. Hirschowitz & B. Levy (Eds.), *The Changing Mental Health Scene*, New York: Spectrum Publications, 1976, pp. 127-152.

3. Pattison, E.M., Ten Years of Change in Alcoholism Treatment and Delivery Systems. *American J. Psychiatry* 134:261-266, 1977.
4. Pattison, E.M., A Theoretical-Empirical Base for Social System Therapy. In E.F. Foulks et al. (Eds.), *Current Perspectives in Cultural Psychiatry*, New York: Spectrum Publications, 1977, pp. 217-253.
5. Pattison, E.M., Bishop, L.A. & Linsky, A.S., Changes in Public Attitudes on Narcotic Addiction. *American J. Psychiatry* 125:160-167, 1968.
6. Pattison, E.M., DeFrancisco, D., Frazier, H., Wood, P.E., & Crowder, J., A Psychosocial Kinship Model for Family Therapy. *American J. Psychiatry* 132:1246-1251, 1975.
7. Pattison, E.M., Sobell, M.B., & Sobell, L.C., *Emerging Concepts of Alcohol Dependence*, New York: Springer, 1977.

Introduction

Edward Kaufman, M.D.

Pauline Kaufman, M.S.W.

This book is about families, families of origin and nuclear families; second chance families and therapeutic families. The coeditors, in the process of their work with families, and colleagues, have become deeply and closely related. The families we have worked in and with have taught us the pain and love of intimacy, the longing for and fulfillment of closeness, as well as the need for individuation and distance.

Our work in Therapeutic Communities has shown us the need in families for rational authority, competence and mutual respect based on performance, not assigned titles or academic degrees. Much of what we have learned we owe to our non-academic colleagues, whose rich albeit painful experiences have become integrated and "professionalized," as they have worked in Therapeutic Communities.

In the solution of common treatment problems distance marked by academic titles has disappeared. Therapeutic treatment families have developed and continued to monitor themselves as they worked and grew. We have been part of this experieince, and we invite you to share this with us.

This book was initially titled "From Enmeshed Enemy to Ally: The Family Therapy of Drug and Alcohol Abusers." Then the titles were reversed and finally "From Enmeshed Enemy to Ally" was totally dropped. This shift in the title happened for a number of reasons. As we continued our work in the field, it became apparent that not as many workers, originally as we thought, were familiar with the term "enmeshed." Even as we began to talk to experienced workers in the field, we became aware of the varying ways the term was defined. We had liked the title because it conveyed a multitude of meanings which were relevant to our work. The first of these was the transition, particularly in drug free therapeutic communities, from viewing the family as an enemy to be totally excluded from treatment to including the family as a vital part of treatment. Although this movement toward including the family is growing, it is still doing so all too slowly and we had hoped and still hope that this book will facilitate the process. In addition, in outpatient settings, the family of the substance abusers was an enigma, thus, the family was frequently excluded from treatment, because of not knowing what to do with them. We hope to clarify this enigma by discussion of family treatment for substance abusers in outpatient as well as other treatment settings.

1

The other major meaning which we felt was conveyed by "From En-meshed Enemy to Ally" was the transition which occurs in families in treat-ment from enmeshed enemies to ally. However, as is obvious from most of the chapters in this book, many families do not begin treatment as en-meshed enemies. Some begin as disengaged, some as psychologically en-meshed, but geographically distanced and some as not at all involved. Most families begin therapy with some enmeshed relationships and some dis-engaged ones. As we thought further, even the goal of the family being an ally is not always valid. In some cases, our goal is for family members to be-come disengaged from each other. Although this is best done within the family milieu, it may have to be done with a family in absentia because of geographical problems, deaths, or inability to locate family members.

Frequently, this individuation and disengagement is enacted with con-comitant release of intense anger, pain and sorrow. A state of mourning en-sues as childhood hopes, yearnings and fantasies are measured against reality. This happens most typically in separating addicts from their fami-lies of origin or spouses from alcoholic partners. In these families, the tran-sition would be from enmeshed enemy to appropriate disengagement. Some families should begin and stay disengaged, others should move from a disengaged state to mutuality. In addition, the subtitle implies that this book's approach is Structural Family Therapy. Although we certainly stress this system of therapy, our approach is too eclectic to be limited to any in-ference that this is our only method. "From Enmeshed Enemy to Ally" was dropped, for all these reasons, despite its catchy and paradoxical flavor.

We define abuse as any use of a substance which impairs an individual's social or vocational functioning or physical health. Addiction or depen-dence is always evidence of abuse. The prevailing picture of substance abuse has changed greatly in the past two decades. Although every few years there is a new substance of concern, what we frequently see is the abuse of, or dependence on, many chemicals simultaneously. These so called "polydrug" abusers have brought with them a higher incidence of in-dividual and familial pathology than seen in previous years.

Twenty years ago the adolescent delinquent was involved with car theft, fire setting, petty thefts, and out-of-wedlock pregnancies. Crime against the person in the adolescent population was comparatively rare. Mugging, murdering and other acts of violence were the exception. Drugs and alcohol were rarely a reason for placing an adolescent in a therapeutic setting.

With growing traffic in drugs and billions of dollars involved in the legal and illegal marketing of drugs, more and more young people coming from every level of society have become involved with drugs. So that currently, almost every adolescent who requires residential care is problematically in-volved with the abuse of drugs and/or alcohol.

Similarly, adult heroin addicts did not commit violent crime in the early 1950's. They were schooled in such non-violent activities as shoplifting, con games, and pocket picking and used these skills to earn the money for their drugs. The available heroin at that time was sufficient to absorb their aggressive energies. Presently, heroin addicts are much more violent and therefore, more likely to be apprehended and institutionalized. When they are in institutions, their families become more available for treatment. Optimally, this treatment should take place in community based residential settings rather than correctional institutions.

Treatment of the family with a substance abusing member is a complicated process. Treatment takes place simultaneously on many levels. In meeting the needs of the family as an entity, the spouse sub-system, the sibling sub-system, and the individual needs of each person in the family must be considered. These three areas must interlock and work in harmony. Teaching and demonstrating effective parenting is an important aspect of treatment. Encouraging and enabling families to form positive social networks aids in the total treatment. Part of family therapy is the problem-solving process that goes on. Hopefully, these techniques become internalized so that the family maintains them throughout its lifetime. While family therapy and change in family structure is not a societal panacea, it can help families to have a richer life and have a positive impact on their offspring as well as the communities of which they are a part. In order to insure effectiveness of the family in the community, the therapist may have to enter the community network as a facilitator. He/she may have to involve vocational guidancě or educational specialists, intervene with the school or employer directly or deal with other members in the individual's extended network. In some cases, a new network may be provided through MFT. In other words, we do not believe that we can solve all problems through family therapy. In many cases, family therapy alone is not enough. In some cases it is a valuable or essential adjunct to other modalities. However, the wider therapy ranges into the individual's network in an adaptive way, the more likely the treatment will succeed.

The techniques in this book are appropriate whether the index patient is abusing or dependent on substances. It is of interest, but no surprise, that most of the chapters on drug abusers deal with families or origin and most of the chapters on alcoholics deal with nuclear families. The major reason for this is that alcoholics tend to be older than drug abusers. However, as Dr. Ziegler-Driscoll points out, these differentiations have become more and more blurred of late, as alcoholics and drug abusers have become progressively similar in every way, including age. Certainly, in our work with the families of younger alcoholics (and many of these abuse other drugs as well), we have seen no differences between their families and the families of drug abusers. The final chapter of the book spells out basic therapeutic techniques which are functional with all types of substance abusers.

Dr. Minuchin's chapter is the only one in this book which is not specifically directed towards substance abusers. We have included it because his way of looking at a family and his therapeutic techniques are the cornerstone of successful therapy with drug abusers. We will not explain or individually justify our choices of the other chapters. They speak for themselves. We selected individuals who have worked as family therapists for many years with substance abusers and who provide a variety of approaches. We asked them to utilize a format which clearly states what the family patterns are and/or what to do to change them. We emphasized that the authors present the specifics of how to use their therapeutic modality in such a way as to be available to the reader for testing and tasting and incorporating into his/her own treatment system. In general, very few therapeutic techniques can be learned from a book. We feel that this book contains an unusual number of such "pearls." We hope the reader will evaluate them, try out those that seem to fit and incorporate those that do. Obviously, in some cases, consultation and evaluation will be helpful or necessary before techniques can be used successfully. We welcome you as readers of these chapters and hope that you can learn as much from reading them as we have from writing them.

Constructing a Therapeutic Reality

Salvador Minuchin, M.D.
PROFESSOR OF CHILD PSYCHIATRY AND PEDIATRICS
UNIVERSITY OF PENNSYLVANIA
DIRECTOR, FAMILY THERAPY TRAINING CENTER
PHILADELPHIA CHILD GUIDANCE CLINIC

Psychotherapy has been handicapped by the nineteenth-century concept of man as a hero. Individual psychotherapy emphasizes a psychological constructs inside the individual and elaborates contrapuntal relationships between the individual and his context. This concept of the patient as a carrier of his psyche surrounded by the boundary of his skin required in complimentation the figure of therapist as objective observer. The relationship between the therapist and the patient is organized according to rules that maintain both the therapist and the patient in parallel orbits while developing in fantasy transferential intimacy.

Pathology inside the patient is related to fixation or dysfunctional learning at some point in early life. In all therapies there is the assumption that it is essential to correct the early dysfunctional learning in order to produce growth and change.

This has created an orientation in therapy that involves the search for psychopathological dynamics. We have created a generation of sleuths who are looking for psychodynamic clues to an emotional crime. A generation of psychopathologists has been schooled in the search for the weakness in people's experience. This group of experts is objective, benevolent, and optimistic. They understand that they are only explorers of subterraneous rivers that exist, that they are not adding to or subtracting from life; therefore, they are not responsible for change, only for discovery.

Family therapy operates on the theoretical assumption that man is part of his context and that individual changes require a change in the reciprocal relationship of man in his context. Family therapy searches for pathology in the loop between the individual and his social network. The therapist joins the family in the therapeutic system and becomes part of the circumstances of the family members; as such, he intervenes, modifying the family members' experience and organizing and constructing their own reality.

This concept is troublesome because it means that a family's reality in therapy is a therapeutic construct. We have detoured comfortably around it in theoretical analysis of therapy by adhering to the concept of insight, so the therapist's task can be seen as merely exploration of the truth. The concept of therapeutic reality puts a heavy responsibility on the therapist. He must recognize that his input organizes the field of intervention and changes the family's reality and his own. The freedom of the therapist as a constructor of reality is limited by the finite reality of family structures, in general, and by the idiosyncratic way in which they are manifested in the patient's family.

With this conceptualization of therapy, it is essential to make explicit our map of normal family functioning as well as our ideas of therapeutic change.

Concepts of the Family

The Matrix of Identity

Family therapy is a product of the twentieth-century philosophies that approach human beings as members of social groups which govern their behavior. This is a departure from the body of thought which has handicapped individual dynamic therapy by putting the whole of the individual's life inside him, as though man remained constant in spite of his circumstances. In fact, family therapy has gone too close to the opposite pole, sometimes approaching the human being as a mere respondent to field pressures.

Effective therapeutic techniques depend on a broad view of the human experience. While it is certainly correct to locate people's behavior in the feedback loops of social group processes, it is also important to recognize that the individual has a range of responses to these processes. Within the family transactions, each family member has a number of choices. The wider the range of choice, the greater his or her experience of freedom within the system. This experience of freedom, or autonomy, is essential for the individual. Equally important is a sense of belonging—of coming from a certain reference group. Indeed, the individual's sense of well-being depends on the proportioning of these two ingredients. Dependency and autonomy are complementary, not conflicting, characteristics of the human condition. Their proportioning is negotiated in the development of the system and crystallized by the current social context.

Families mold and program the child's sense of identity early in the socialization process. The sense of belonging comes with the child's accommodation to the groups within the family and his assumption of the transactional patterns which form the family structure. The sense of autonomy occurs through participation in different family subsystems in different contexts, as well as through participation in extrafamilial groups. A psychological and transactional territory is carved out for each person, determined by the contrapuntal relationships of individual and system.

The family, then, is the matrix of its members' sense of identity of belonging and of being different. Its chief task is to foster their psychosocial growth and well-being throughout their life in common. This is the first element of a therapist's schema of a family.

The family also forms the smallest social unit which transmits a society's demands and values, thus preserving them. Therefore, the family therapist must see the family as the link between the individual and larger social units. The family must adapt to society's needs as it fosters its members' growth, all the while maintaining enough continuity to fulfill its function as the individual's reference group.

The Family as a System

The family therapist must also recognize that the human family is a social system that operates through transactional patterns. These are repeated interactions which establish patterns of how, when, and to whom to relate. When a mother tells her child to drink his juice and he obeys, this interaction defines who they are in relation to one another in that context and at that time. Repeated operations build patterns, and these patterns underpin the family system. The patterns which evolve become familiar and preferred. The system maintains itself within a preferred range, and deviations which pass the system's threshold of tolerance usually elicit counter-deviation mechanisms which reestablish the accustomed range.

The System Develops Over Time

In his early development within his family context, the child develops certain parts of his biopsychological potential, and this is what he becomes familiar with as being himself. In the measure in which the child encounters other social groups and develops in another context new areas of competence and interpersonal skill, certain aspects of his personality are activated in his complementary relationship with significant people. The potential of the individual is developed and restricted at the same time as certain types of transactions become more available and familiar. These responses tend to be identified as *self* while other aspects of self remain potentially available, and some hardly available because of disuse.

A reciprocal interplay develops by which the individual determines the range of his responses. Certain aspects of his personality are confirmed more frequently by significant people as self, and that reinforces the continuous use of certain alternative behavior and modalities of being.

When people marry they must develop a number of common transactional patterns. Each spouse has his own behavior patterns and value system, including expectations of how people should and will relate to him. These patterns clash and mesh in the small events of daily life, and each spouse changes in accommodation to the other.

Areas of autonomy and complementarity are defined. The range of choices narrows, and after some period of life together, the range is reduced to the preferred patterns. The spouses become predictable to each other. In areas of narrowed experiential range, the spouses develop implicit or explicit contracts, with value overtones. Even dysfunctional patterns can become preferred, and the couple will maintain them as long as possible. If the patterns are violated, each spouse may feel betrayed, though neither may remember the origin of the pattern.

But family circumstances change through time, and the family must be able to change. Other transactional patterns are activated, and new structures develop in a balanced process of morphostasis and morphogenesis. Alternative transactional patterns always exist within a system, though these are hidden from the observer by the dominant preferred patterns. But when change becomes necessary, the functional family activates the alternative patterns of the system.

The Differentiation of the System

Family systems are differentiated; they carry out tasks through subsystems. Individuals are subsystems within a family, as are dyads such as husband and wife, and larger subgroupings formed by generation, gender, or task. People accommodate kaleidoscopically in different subsystems to achieve the mutuality necessary for human intercourse. A child has to act like a son so his father can act like a father, but he may take on executive powers when he is alone with his younger brother.

The rules defining who participates within a subsystem, and how, are the subsystem boundaries. The functioning of these boundaries is an important key to the system's viability. They must be defined well enough to allow the subsystem members to carry out their functions, but they must not isolate the subsystem from the rest of the system.

The nuclear family has at least three subsystems: spousal, parental, and sibling. These subsystems are units with differentiated functions. They offer and demand the exercise of specific social skills in different contexts. For example, in the parental or executive subsystem, parents and children negotiate decisions from positions of unequal power. In the sibling subsystem, children interact more as peers, negotiating issues of competition, defeat, accommodation, cooperation, and protection. The spousal subsystem is an arena of complementarity, of learning how to give without feeling that one has given up.

Each subsystem must keep negotiating boundaries that protect it from interference so it can fulfill its functions and resolve its problems. But the boundaries' selective permeability does not preclude the possibility of summoning other family members to resolve specific subsystem problems.

The family is a differentiated social unit structured by transactional patterns. In some areas the system is quite flexible, offering a broad range of choices. In other areas, preferred patterns are tightly maintained. Alternative patterns exist but are not used. The family is constantly subjected to demands for change, sparked by developmental changes in its own members and by extrafamilial pressures. Responding to these demands from within and without requires transformation. The positions of family members toward each other and the external world change, as they must. But the system must also maintain the continuity to protect its members' sense of belonging.

Stresses are inherent. All families are subject to crises when a member enters a new developmental stage, a new member joins, a former member leaves, when the family is making contact with social institutions, and so on. In general, families respond to these periods of existential crisis by marshalling their resources. If necessary, alternative transactional patterns are mobilized, and new ways of responding to changes in circumstance are evolved.

Family Pathology

Sometimes families respond to demands for change by increasing the rigidity of their prefered transactional patterns. The range of choices narrows, and family members develop stereotyped responses to each other and to the extrafamilial environment. The family becomes a closed system, and family members experience themselves as controlled and impotent. At this point, a family comes to therapy. The stereotyping process often leads to labeling one family member the deviant. Or the family may enter therapy because of "lack of communication" or "inability to cope."

Difficulties in a family are not an indicator for therapeutic restructuring. The difficulties of performing a family's tasks in modern society are real and intense, and stress in a family system is anything but abnormal. Family therapists may minimize the real problems inherent in the processes of adapting while maintaining continuity just as individual dyanmic therapists have minimized the difficulties in the individual's social context. A family in transition should not be labled pathological. That label should be reserved for families who increase the rigidity of their transactional patterns in the face of stress, avoiding or resisting any exploration of alternatives.

A couple in therapy began to contemplate divorce seriously when the husband's union was engaged in a bitter strike. The husband's position was, "You refuse to take my needs into consideration. You have always exploited me because of my sense of responsibility and duty. I will not give in to you any longer. I have begun to realize that I have rights, and my dignity as a human being is paramount." The wife's position was, "You are selfish. You have stopped considering the family's needs and are only concerned with your own. You are so wrapped up in yourself that you don't see me. If you want to leave, you can go now instead of asking me to do things for you like a typical male chauvinist." The therapist read the decision to consider divorce as the effect of massive intrusion from an extrafamilial context into a spousal conflict, resulting in increased stereotyping. He strongly advised them not to come to any decisions until the strike was over, and he pointed out to the couple how much the husband's position resembled his union's stance in the strike negotiations, and how much the wife sounded like the management. Two weeks after the settlement of the strike the couple wanted to stay together and work on the problems of the family.

The Family in Therapy

The family therapist's definition of a pathogenic family, then, is a family whose adaptive and coping mechanisms have been exhausted. Family members are chronically trapped in stereotyped patterns of interaction which are severely limiting their range of choices, but no alternatives seem possible. In this time of heightened rigidity of transactional patterns, conflict overshadows large areas of normal functioning. Often one family member is the identified patient, and the other family members see themselves as accommodating his illness. The family has gone through a reification process that gives priority to dysfunctional areas.

It is not essential to explore the development of these dysfunctional patterns in most cases. The family's history is manifest in the present, and change can only be achieved in the present. It is possible to explore any family member's past or open up alternative modalities of being with the family of origin, but it is not necessary. The exploration of the "hows" of our previous relationships can be significant in understanding how we became what we are, but it is usually not necessary for changing the present family context. The therapeutic process will be that of changing family members' psychosocial positions vis-á-vis each other. The therapist may or may not try to help his patients understand their narrowed reality. But he will always address himself to the actualization of possible change. He may tell a family member that he is dependent, angry, or depressed. But he will know that this focus can reinforce the already crystallized interactions. He may or may not explore the family members' feelings, but he will always explore the system of complementarity that elicits those feelings. This approach emphasizes the transactional nature of experience and simultaneously suggests the possibilities of change.

Of course, any description of therapeutic technique presupposes that the therapist has begun to join the family in such a way that family members trust him, even if they do not agree with him. The therapist must know how to affiliate with the family and support it through the sense of dislocation its members will experience as change develops.

Challenging the Patients' Reality

The first step in the process of change is a challenge to family members' self-perception and experience of reality. Challenging reality is a prerequisite for change common to all therapeutic processes. In psychoanalysis, the analyst challenges the patient's experience of reality on the basis of an expanded self. The patient is taught that the psychological life is larger than the conscious experience, and he learns to free-associate in order to block the usual screening processes with which he organizes his reality. The analyst organizes the data the patient presents according to psychoanalytic constructions.

In family therapy, the challenge is based on the axiom that family members have alternative ways of transacting. The family therapist does not challenge his patients, only their patterns of interaction. What we call "reality" is the reality of the most preferred or available experiences. The purpose of therapy is to activate certain aspects of the individual and the system that render available new modalities of transaction. For example, in a family where the husband was overly central, the therapist paid special attention to the wife's feeble efforts to communicate, conveying the impression that her inputs were more meaningful than her husband's. In a family whose identified patient was a college dropout who had been diagnosed as schizophrenic, the therapist supported the mother, who was willing to consider her son lazy, and snubbed the father, a very competent physician who preferred a crazy son to a failure. In other words, the therapist joins the family in ways that make it possible to activate the alternatives whose presence he postulates.

A family with an identified patient has gone through a reification process which overfocuses on one member. The therapist reverses this process.

He enters and joins the family by paying attention to the family-evolved reality: the symptoms of the identified patient. He expands his focus to the symptom bearer, and then abandons the symptom bearer to move toward family interaction. This sequence may occur in the first session, or it may develop over a number of sessions.

In a family with a bright seventeen-year-old boy who was failing in school, the parents and a younger sibling spent much of the first session discussing the identified patient's school performance. He remained silent, acting uncomfortable when attacked, but for the most part was lost in his own thoughts. The mother said to the father that if the boy went to a private school where he could be challenged, his performance might improve. The father said this was unrealistic, for it would involve great financial sacrifice for the whole family. He added that the mother was blind to the boy's laziness. Finally, he said that if the boy did go to private school, it would have to be her responsibility, but if she wanted to deprive the whole family, he would consent.

The therapist talked with the identified patient about his school, his friends, his areas of difficulty and interest, his teachers, and his plans for next year. He challenged him for letting his parents make such an important decision for him. He suggested that the boy was acting like an 11-year-old; only thus was it appropriate for his younger brother to discuss him with his parents while he remained silent. He also pointed out that the boy was manipulating his parents to control him by acting younger than he was. Then the therapist challenged the parents for taking decision-making power away from the boy. He then moved away from the identified patient to the parents, and explored the coalition between mother and son that left father feeling excluded. The mother's plight then came into focus: how the family made her the center for decisions, overburdening her, and how her own orientation towards serving her family facilitated this overcentralization.

The third session was held with husband and wife alone. Then the focus went back to the older boy's problems in school, but now the utilization of these problems in the family was very much part of the picture.

The speed of the movement from symptom to patient to family will depend on the nature and intensity of the symptom, the flexibility of family interaction, and the therapist's style. When a symptom is serious, the family system is extremely rigid. In such a case, the therapist must stay with the symptom of the identified patient for a while. Moving away from it will increase the pressure within the system, increasing the symptom's intensity until the therapist responds to the family's reality. When the identified patient's symptoms are milder, the therapist can move faster.

Psychotherapy as an Experimental Field

How does the therapist become acquainted with a family's range of possible interactions, challenge the present straitened reality, create the possibilities for alternative interactions, and still support family members while maintaining himself in a position of expert leadership? This is the artistry of therapy, no doubt, but it is buttressed by the therapist's map of his goals and by the planned flexibility of the experimenter.

The therapist meets a field of stabilized family interactions. He becomes involved with the family members as he observes how they interact. He tracks the content of their communications and the ways they communicate. He tests the limits of family flexibility, requesting the family members to interact in a different way.

He lets himself be organized by the family's response to his inputs. This way, his inputs can challenge family interactions without going beyond the thresholds the system can tolerate. When he suggests a modification of the way family members interact, he is introducing an experiemntal probe. The responses will give him information about unmapped areas and directions for his next intervention. Some discussions of therapeutic strategies make it seem that the therapist's strategies are organized regardless of the family's feedback. In the reality of therapy, however, family responses modify the therapist's behavior, and the therapist must be alert to these responses to confirm his hunches or change his strategies.

A newly married couple with a twelve-year-old child from the wife's previous marriage came to therapy because of the child's crippling asthma. He had asthma since the age of two, and had always slept with his mother. With the mother's remarriage, his asthmatic attacks had increased, especially at night. He now had his own room, but usually his mother or stepfather slept in his room to allay his fear and monitor his wheezing. The therapist directed the parents to shut the door of their bedroom, not to go to the child's bedroom unless it was absolutely necessary, and never to sleep with him. He explained that the family was in a transitional situation, and everyone would have to adapt to the new circumstances. The task was unsuccessful. The mother was convinced of the necessity for change, but she was unable to ignore her son's calling her for fear of precipitating a serious attack. The therapist learned that this route to change was closed.

In the next session, he asked the boy for the names of two close friends at school. The boy, a loner, took almost three minutes to give two names. The mother tried hard to attract his attention so she could prompt him, but the boy, acting on a suggestion the therapist had made earlier, did not look at her. The therapist got up from his chair to give the boy a handshake. He labeled the three minutes' thinking for himself a triumph of autonomy, and discussed how difficult the task was for the mother. He further discussed, with the boy and the stepfather, what kinds of things they could do to respectfully block mother's unnecessary interventions. An exploratory task had indicated a closed pathway. Another had indicated a new and promising direction.

Constructing the Therapeutic Reality

A therapist never deals with a family's whole reality. He never knows the dynamics of the total situation, and he begins his therapeutic challenge before he has learned a great deal about the family. The only purpose of the beginning interventions is to shake the ridigity of the field. If the alternatives that the therapist indicates feel right to the family members, the process of change has begun. But even when the therapist and family are well into the therapeutic process, the therapist is operating in terms of "partial constructs." His position in the therapeutic system allows him to organize his own reality and program his experience of the patients' reality. The therapist will dismiss many elements of the family's life as "not part of the therapeutic reality." In effect, the therapist selects partial constructs to be the reality of therapy, in accordance with his goals.

To change the reality of a patient, we need to change the reality of the relationship between the patient and his context. The therapist finds himself in the position of a "constrained changer." The family has the capacity to control him by determining his complimentary responses. The family may also activate his rescue fantasy and induce him to supplement a system's needs. The therapist, then, is in and out of a system that he has to change. He can operate as an active participant transacting with family members, as part of a dyad or triad, or as a creator and director of family scenarios. In both situations he will facilitate the experiencing of alternative reality. In every situation he has the limitation of his own life experience, his value system, and his esthetic sense; nonetheless and paradoxically, the more real the therapist's involvement, the more objective and experimental he becomes.

Sometimes the therapist is simply picking one point in a circle and calling it the beginning. For example, a man and woman who have been married for twenty years are discussing their sex life. For as long as then can remember, they have agreed that the wife should close the door when she wants sex. The husband is unhappy about this, because he feels he should initiate the act. The wife claims he does initiate: she closes the door when she sees that he wants sex. The husband says that she initiates it: whenever the wife looks at him in ways that indicate she is wondering if he wants sex, he indicates that he does. The feedback process can be elaborated further and further back. The therapist picks any point of entry that seems promising.

The following examples show how a therapeutic construct can also be a new causal linking for the family, one which allows them to reorient their positions in relation to one another. In one session a younger girl attacked her 13-year-old sister, the identified patient, by deriding her for letting their stepfather bathe her. The therapist challenged the mother for "allowing her daughter to tattle about family situations." The actual event was that the younger daughter talked and the mother was silent. The therapist's construction, "you allowed her to talk," connected two events in a statement of casuality that shifted the mother's anger, which for the first time was directed at the younger daughter instead of the older girl.

A young husband described a situation in which he had been very depressed. He said that his wife suggested that she return to her parents in order to protect him in this situation. The wife had transformed an event in her husband's life to an interspouse problem. The therapist went one step further and challenged the ease of the wife's move from wife to daughter, including the extended family in a therapeutic construct.

The father of a fourteen-year-old educable retarded child picked up a ball the boy had dropped and put it in his lap. Later in the session, the boy dropped the ball again, and this time the therapist put it in his lap. Clearly he had been induced by the family's organization around the boy, which had rendered this child almost helpless. If the therapist had instead challenged the parents for immobilizing the boy, the slender event could have generated sufficient emotional intensity to further therapeutic change.

The first session with a family with an anorectic daughter finished with the whole family experiencing the child as protecting her mother from loneliness of her relationship with her busy, aloof husband. The anorexia at the center of the family's life receded, to be replaced by the therapeutic highlighting of the distance between the spouses.

A Family Therapy Grammar

With this view of family therapy as a construction of reality, it is useful to derive certain ad hoc rules which form an intermediate step between the basic steps of therapy and the therapeutic reality. Rules can help an inexperienced therapist operate with some level of competence while he still feels ignorant. They can also direct an experienced therapist through the beginning stages of therapy with a family he does not know.

The rules discussed below are instructions the author finds himself repeating to different therapists who are treating families. They have a certain universality because they spring from generic ideas about the family and the therapeutic process, but they are rules only in the sense of something that is repeated. They will probably be correct about sixty percent of the time—that is, they are better than chance. But their usefulness diminishes as the idiosyncracies of each therapeutic system appear.

Creating the Therapeutic System

The therapist must establish himself as the leader of the therapeutic unit; this is a sine qua non of therapy. To assume leadership, he must join the family and accommodate himself to its transactional patterns. This process of joining is essential before and at the time that the therapist introduces restructuring maneuvers.

His restructuring interventions are directed toward making alternative transactions available. He directs the family to explore these alternatives by entering into alliances and coalitions with different family members. In these processes the therapist moves from a position of proximity in which he interacts with other members of the therapeutic system, to a disengaged position from which he directs family members to enact certain transactions, creating interpersonal scenarios that become the experiential field of the family member.

Some family therapists suggest that the therapist must be indirect in his goals because family members will resist direct leadership. While this position is sometimes correct, it is frequently unnecessary. When properly joined by the therapist, family members cooperate with him in the therapeutic process. When the therapist is enabling, his inputs will not be resisted.

The therapist organizes the process in terms of what is possible. If a diagnosis creates a solution that does not help, the "beginning of the circle" can be set at another point. The therapist will construct the truths of therapy according to what is most possible and least painful for the family. Every technique/strategy is measured only insofar as it is goal related. These strategies are good or bad because of how they work. Being correct has nothing to do with relevance. The therapist must learn to focus on that which is relevant. "Truth" needs to be relevant.

Supporting the Family's Functions

Other middle-range concepts of therapy can be derived from concepts of normal family dyanmics. The family system supports individuation and differentiation. It also supports a sense of belonging. The therapist will support both.

Rules That Support Individuation. Family members should speak for themselves. They should tell their own story. Family members should not tell what other members think or feel, though they should be encouraged to ask the speaker questions. Two members should not discuss a third who is present without his participation. Family members should be discouraged from asking each other for data they should know, or from consistently checking, verbally or nonverbally, for approval of statements or actions. Competent acts should be signaled whenever they occur and family members should be encouraged to transact competently.

Dealing with an identified patient, the therapist should avoid crystallizing the symptoms by discussing other positive and negative aspects of the symptom-bearer and of other family members. Broadening the focus to the complementary underpinnings of the symptom—who elicits it, what its function is—is also helpful. If two members of the family have labeled a third the deviant, the therapist should not address himself to the identified patient immediately. He should go to another family member to try to elicit different data, so the identified patient does not experience the therapist as joining in the process of labeling him. However, the therapist will usually avoid joining with the scapegoated family member against the other family members because of the danger that the more powerful members will attack the therapist through his vulnerable ally and intensify the scapegoating. The therapist determines the success of tasks because success is defined by the therapist's punctuation. The end of a transaction can be longer or shorter depending on the therapeutic goal.

Rules That Support System Functioning. The therapist will often work to clarify or reinforce functional subsystem boundaries. For example, he will almost automatically support the boundaries which define the executive subsystem. If the spouses elicit a child's support when discussing a husband-wife issue, this will be blocked. When spouses and therapist discuss a couple's sexual life, other family members should be asked to leave the room. It is preferable, if the identified patient is a child, not to enter the conflicts of husband and wife before the therapeutic system is established well enough for the family members to know that they can depend on the therapist. Spouse conflicts, in such cases, may appear early in therapy, but the therapist does not explore the area until he knows the family trusts him to defend them.

The functions of each subsystem will be rewarded. For example, if a member of a family is doing well, the therapist can praise the other person's role in facilitating the change in behavior; e.g. parents may be complimented when a child improves.

When members of a subsystem are defined as unequal, the therapist may relabel the definition of power (for instance, by saying to a supposedly weak spouse, "How do you get your wife to organize your actions?"). The exploration of complementarity moves members away from accusation and stereotyping.

When working with a subsystem, the therapist may ask members who do not belong to that subsystem to leave the room or move their chairs back to define their noninvolvement.

The therapist can use subsystems to define problems or change moods. If the adolescents of a large family are experiencing difficulty negotiating issues of independence, separate sessions can be held with the parents and adolescents, with the younger children excluded. When working in a hostile atmosphere between spouses, the therapist can promote mood change by bringing in the children, moving the spouse subsystem to the parental subsystem.

These are ad hoc rules, to be discarded as each therapeutic system develops and its elements become clear.

Family therapy has come to a point of development at which it may be profitable for its practitioners to make their philosophies explicit; this chapter has been written in this spirit. In conclusion, it should be pointed out that family therapy is not a tool for humanistic revolution; in fact, it is often the opposite. One of the family's tasks is to provide continuity with a society which the family therapist, in his own value system, may consider restrictive. Family therapy is the active process of changing dysfunctional patterns of transaction and eliciting available alternative patterns. It is a process in which therapist and family members, working together, search for and enact an alternative reality that expands the possibilities for the family and its members.

The Similarities in Families of Drug Dependents and Alcoholics

Genevra Ziegler-Driscoll, M.D.
CHIEF OF PSYCHIATRY AND COORDINATOR OF FAMILY THERAPY
EAGLEVILLE HOSPITAL AND REHABILITATION CENTER
EAGLEVILLE, PENNSYLVANIA

In the earlier literature more is written about the families of alcoholics than of addicts. In most cases, the viewpoint is different, reflecting mainly the typical difference in age. Barr (1) noted that the reports of the families of alcoholics have usually been concerned with the families they have established (families of procreation), in which they are husbands or wives and parents, while studies of the drug addicts havs been concerned with families in which they are the children.

In the Eagleville Family Study, which was recently completed as one part of the Combined Treatment Demonstration Grant, this difference in the nuclear families was not substantiated in the sample of ninety families who entered the research project. Instead, the distribution of the families of origin and families of procreation is similar for both substance groups.

Barr also proposed that we would find similarities between the families of alcoholics and drug dependents in the study. She suggested that the "myths" would be similar, that their identified roles in the family would be much alike, that the family dynamics would, likewise, be similar, and that alcohol abuse would be prevalent in both groups of families of origin.

This chapter describes the findings that have corroborated these hypotheses and the changes that occurred through family therapy, either conjoint family therapy or relatives' groups.

Eagleville and the Family Study

A brief description of Eagleville Hospital and Rehabilitation Center and a profile of the patient population may be helpful in orienting the reader to the setting in which this study took place. Men and women in the first phase of hospital treatment are called residents. Our private institution admits both alcoholic and drug dependents, treating them together in an abstinent therapeutic community with emphasis on the group process in psychotherapy, recreational activities, community and unit meetings, rap groups, Alcoholics Anonymous, and Narcotics Anonymous. Opportunities for remedial education, graduate equivalency degree attainment, and vocational testing are also provided.

The ratio of drug dependents and alcoholics is approximately 1:1. Women are in the minority, ranging in proportions of 4:1 to 6:1 in a resident population of 130. The distribution by race (black and white) is approximately equal. Most of the residents come from working-class families and have less than 12 years of education.

Although the residents were admitted into the family study[1] as randomly as possible during the period from October 1974 until December 1975, this process was modified by events such as early irregular discharges. Most of the men and women in the final sample, therefore, had completed the first stage of treatment, i.e., the in-hospital phase of 45 to 60 days. The 90 residents are evenly distributed by substance abuse, 51 percent drug dependents, 49 percent alcoholics; 69 percent black, 31 percent white. The proportion of men and women is approximately the same: 86 percent to 14 percent in the drug dependent group and 85 percent to 15 percent in the alcoholic group.

Following an initial audiotaped research interview, the families were again randomized into one of three subgroups: conjoint family therapy, relatives' group, and a control group. Therapy continued for a period of 10 to 20 weeks. A second research interview was scheduled 6 to 8 months following the close of therapy.

The Similarities in the Families

Family Patterns and Roles of Substance Abusers

The first finding, and one that we had not originally anticipated, is the approximately similar distribution of the families of origin and of procreation in the two substance-abuse groups (Graph 2-1). Despite the age differential—26 years for the drug dependent and 33 years for the alcoholic—59 percent and 48 percent respectively entered the family study with only their parents or surrogates; another 9 percent and 14 percent presented with members of both their families of origin and procreation; i.e. with their parents as well as their spouses, current or prospective. Thus the residents participated in the study as sons and daughters in 64 percent of the total sample: 68 percent drug dependent and 62 percent alcoholics.

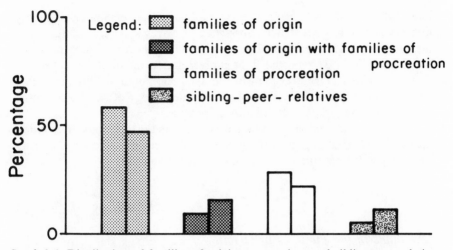

Graph 2-1. Distribution of families of origin, procreation, and sibling-peer relatives who participated in the family study with respective alcoholic or drug-dependent member (the subject).

Substance Abuse

The second similarity that was noted in the families of the two groups was the high rate of substance abuse, primarily alcohol, among the family members: 59 subjects, or 66 percent among the total sample of 90 families. In the drug group the incidence was 29 out of 46 or 63 percent; in the alcoholic group, 30 out of 44 or 68 percent. (Table 2-1). Over half were fathers: 62 percent and 57 percent in the drug and alcoholic groups, respectively. Only 10 percent of the relatives in both groups who were reported to

Table 2-1
Incidence of substance abuse, primarily alcoholism, in the families of the alcoholic and drug dependent subjects in the family study.

	Subjects with Substance-Abusing Relatives		Fathers		Mothers		Other Relatives		Total Number of Relatives
	#	%	#	%	#	%	#	%	#
Drugs (N = 46)	29	63	18	39	3	7	10	22	31
Alcohol (N = 44)	30	68	17	39	3	7	28	64	58
Subtotal	59	66	35	39	6	7	38	42	89

have substance-abuse problems were mothers. The remainder of family members exhibiting substance abuse were primarily spouses, siblings, cousins, uncles, and grandparents. Twenty-nine out of the 59 (35 percent or approximately 1 in 3) reported 2 or more relatives involved in substance abuse, a finding more prevalent in the alcoholic families. This factor is a concern not only as it may relate to the epidemiology of substance abuse, but also as it may affect the treatment process.

In subsequent sections of this chapter, the major divisions of families, i.e. origin, procreation, and sibling-peers, are discussed separately in order to highlight the specific issues presented in each group.

Families of Origin

Dynamics in the Families of Origin

As we discuss the dynamics and the treatment process in the families of origin, a further subdivision into three subgroups as follows is not only useful, but also critical: (1) two-parent families in which both parents attended the initial research interview or family treatment sessions or both; (2) two-parent families in which the father failed to attend any of the sessions, and (3) one-parent families, usually including a mother (Table 2-2). Here a dissimilarity between the two substance-abuse groups becomes apparent. Two-parent families are more highly represented in the drug families whereas single-parent families of alcoholics outnumber those of the addicts, 2:1.

Despite the parental composition, however, two characteristics were common in these families. The first was a high level of reactivity to the sub-

Table 2-2
Distribution of subgroups according to family structure in the sample of families of origin of the alcoholic and drug-dependent subjects in the family study.

	Two-parent		Two-parent (Father Absent)		One-parent		Total	
	#	%	#	%	#	%	#	%
Drug	15	26	8	14	8	14	31	53
Alcohol	6	10	5	9	16	28	27	47
Subtotal	21	36	13	23	24	42	58	100

stance-abuse problem in conjunction with a relative lack of understanding about addiction and the nature of its role in the life of their addicted member. The second was an overly dependent relationship of the younger substance abuser, whether an alcoholic or addict, with the parent figures. Separation from such involvement was only one among several adolescent tasks that they had not resolved. With substance abuse beginning so often at this adolescent stage, completion of these tasks can seldom proceed successfully so that the individual is ill-equipped to make the transition into adulthood. Furthermore, the role of substance abuse in maintaining the dependent/independent struggle is a familiar one. Passage into healthy autonomy, therefore, may be postponed indefinitely unless some crisis or intervention precipitates a break in the vicious cycle. Approximately half of the subjects in the family study admitted that they had been "spoiled" or "overprotected" as they were growing up.

At third characteristic found in more than three-fifths (37 out of 58 or 64 percent) of the families of origin in the study was either an absent or peripheral father figure, more commonly in black families than white (5 to 1). Even in four of the families presenting with two parents, the father's role was peripheral because he had relegated major responsibility for child rearing to his spouse. This characteristic of lower-class organization (especially of some lower-class minority groups) is described by Minuchin and other family investigators (9). As indicated in the previous section, the rate of alcoholism among the parents, primarily the father, was higher in these single-parent groups. Although this difference in itself may not be significant, the separation associated with the alcoholism occurred during the childhood of more than half of the substance abusers in this one-parent group.

Another syndrome related to the dependence and more commonly found in the families with the peripheral father or the single parent is the parental child. In one single-parent family the alcoholic son had taken on the responsibility that his alcoholic father had failed to assume and was ineffectively trying to set matters straight for his mother and siblings. In another family not in the study, the parental child had completely missed experiencing his adolescence in the usual manner because he had carried the father's role from his early teens and, in addition, had established his own family in his late teens. His drug addiction, with its onset in his thirties, appeared to be a manifestation of a belated adolescence and provided a way to extricate himself from the yoke of mounting responsibilities.

In the three-generation families, which include the parents and children of the substance abuser who is also a parent, other generational boundary problems are present. These issues will be discussed later as we look at the families in which the substance abuser is a parent.

Goals of Treatment[2]

As we have described some of the characteristic dynamics which these families present, we can now outline some steps in treatment. Establishing rapport with each member of the family, or "joining" is essential. During this initial phase another goal is to decrease the overreactivity of the family to the addiction and to clarify mutual expectations. In the next stage, the therapist will move to facilitate the individuation/separation process, to help the parents let go, and to support the substance-abuser in leaving. Parents are aided in becoming more adequate in their parenting roles; they are guided in setting more realistic limits more effectively. The siblings are helped to move into more appropriate roles for their state of development. Simultaneously the substance abuser is supported in assuming more responsibility for the consequences of his or her substance use, for becoming more self-sufficient, and for an eventually moving toward greater autonomy.

As the family is able to shift its focus of concern from the substance-abusing member, other issues may emerge. Problems of other siblings may have been masked by the subject's addiction. These may worsen as the addict's or alcoholic's problems are resolved. In other instances, when actual separation has been facilitated, the subject may move out of the family, only to have the vacancy filled by a younger sibling. The parents may then need further help to work effectively with that child's increasing independence before he begins to use drugs as one way to cope with his conflicts. The parents' ability to facilitate the disengagement of the next adolescent sibling is thereby reinforced. Independence per se is not the goal for these families, but rather a healthier interchange in the family system that will allow the members to have some flexibility between autonomy and interdependence, which in turn will facilitate their development toward greater self-actualization.

A further goal in therapy is to help parents consider their marital problems, which can no longer be set aside with the excuse that they are preoccupied with the problems of their children. Those family therapists who were experienced and comfortable with sexual and marital counseling were able to help parents look at these areas. Others met resistance and did not push couples to pursue these issues, but would leave the door open for further therapy when the parents felt ready.

In those families with the peripheral father, an early goal is to bring that parent into a more central position in the family but at the same time support the wife in finding other satisfying outlets to replace the mother-child attachment.

In families with the parental child the goal is to realign the roles, if possible, so that other members share some of the responsibility where such rearrangement is appropriate. The therapist further reinforces the parental child's competence while also encouraging outlets for healthy regression and relaxation.

Treatment Approaches

In the earlier description of the family study we mentioned the two treatment groups: conjoint structural family therapy in which the entire family, including the subject, was seen together, and group therapy with members of the subject's immediate family, either spouse or parent groups. The research proposal postulated no hypothesis that one type of family intervention would prove better than the other. Rather the aim was to explore the relative merits of each to reach desirable goals for the families.

The initial steps in both relatives' groups and conjoint family therapy sessions were similar and proceeded as follows:

1) Establishing rapport with each family member ("joining");

2) Defining expectations of the group or family sessions;

3) Distancing emotionally to replace overreactivity (Education about addiction to correct misunderstanding was helpful at this point.);

4) Formulating an appropriate course of action for the family with consensus of all participants if the subject returned to substance abuse;

5) Detaching the parent, or other participating relative from the subject's addiction problem and placing responsibility for the consequences of the addictive behavior upon the substance abuser.

Since overdependence was so frequently a presenting problem in the families of origin, the next steps were designed to facilitate the individuation of the family members. Sometimes this necessitated establishing clear boundaries between parents and children in families where a breakdown of the generational boundaries had occurred, frequently by an alliance of mother with son or father with daughter. The very structure of the parents' group advanced this process of individuation and separation. When the subject was concurrently involved in some peer group therapy or treatment program, this process was further facilitated. Both generations were thus reinforced in their roles with the support of their respective group members. In this atmosphere, as trust developed and cohesion occurred, the parents could begin to share and look at their own conflicts, which the addiction of the offspring had tended to disguise or enabled them to avoid.

Outside the group sessions the relatives maintained contact by telephone and provided support as crises arose. This type of support is not available with conjoint family therapy but falls upon the family therapist until the members can use other systems, e.g. extended family, or groups, such as Al-Anon or Alcoholics Anonymous.

The obvious shortcoming with the relatives' groups, however, is the absence of the subject and other siblings or significant family members who live under the same roof or relate regularly to each other. This absence presents various disadvantages. First, when the alcoholic or addict is in a separate therapeutic setting, lack of coordination of the two processes may precipitate crises if communication between therapists fails to corordinate their respective efforts. For example, a young female addict was discharged from the treatment facility before the family therapist was notified; he was unable to prepare the family for the event. In order to avoid such a breakdown in communication, a preferable arrangement is to designate one or the other therapist as leader of the treatment team. Who gives up whose treatment leadership prerogative, however, is not always readily resolved. At Eagleville, while we achieved an improved level of cooperation among the therapists, this fell short of our goals.

A second disadvantage with the subject's absence is the inability to initiate interactions by role playing or restructuring tasks in the actual sessions. In a family with a peripheral father, for example, one of the goals of structural family therapy is to help move the father into a more central position. In a conjoint family session, the therapist might begin by placing the father next to the subject so that they can easily talk to each other while the mother listens. The therapist might also decide to engage the mother in a conversation while the other two are talking together. Such tasks, of course, can be assigned to the parents in the group setting, and they can then try them at home with other family members. The live practice during the therapy sessions, however, may be more productive.

A way of overcoming the shortcomings of the separate approaches is some flexible arrangement whereby parent groups are interspersed with conjoint family therapy sessions. Thus can be derived the value of both therapeutic thrusts. This combination did in fact prove effective with one parents' group which met regularly throughout the study.

Outcome in Families of Origin

The tendency to measure the success of treatment of substance abusers primarily on the basis of the subject's progress toward abstinence and improvement in psychosocial adjustment is an understandable approach for agencies concerned with the problem of addiction. This emphasis, however, may fail to realistically assess areas of progress in subjects who have a chronic, relapsing disorder of drug dependence or alcoholism. Also, evaluations within the narrow time span of the followup (6 and 12 months) taps only a segment of the total recovery process, which is usually a gradual and more prolonged one. Furthermore, for the purposes of the family study this approach tended to overlook the benefits that may accrue to the "other victims" of substance abuse through family intervention.

In the family study we tended toward this shortsighted approach. The outcome ratings were determined by data from the subjects who were interviewed at intervals of 6 and 12 months following discharge. The hypothesis that family therapy, in addition to the regular inpatient treatment, would result in better outcome among the subjects, according to the criteria briefly described above, failed to be substantiated by the data in the family study. Clinically we knew that significant changes were occurring with some subjects and their families. We also suspected that there must be other valuable information from the study that needed to be extracted and interpreted. A more careful analysis, therefore, led to the development of this chapter. Once we recovered from the discovery that family therapy was no panacea, we could become more objective and look for further meaning in our experience.

Could we distinguish factors that augur well for family therapy with these families of origin? Does the presence of the father in the family affect the outcome? Is the age of the subject or of the parents a factor in prognosis? Why do some families seem receptive to the structural approach in resolving family problems while others do not? Whether or not from the family study data answer some of these questions, further clinical experience and study will be necessary to corroborate our impressions or provide other answers.

The more favorable outcomes occurred in those families of origin in which both parents were involved in the process; with subjects who were younger, i.e. under 30 years of age (11), and also presented with younger parents. The degree of flexibility in the parents is probably the more crucial factor rather than a cut-off age of 50. Regrettably no comparison of outcome of subgroups of subjects was built into the analysis of the family research project; therefore, whether these subjects involved in family therapy have done better than similar subjects and families without family therapy cannot be stated at this time.

The following case excerpts illustrate these prognostic factors.

Case 1. The elderly parents of a 21-year-old white male with mixed alcohol and drug addiction were unable to utilize optimally the parents' group to which they had been assigned. Their rigidity prevented them from shifting their old behaviors and attitudes and interfered with the progress of the other group members. The family therapist moved them from the group into conjoint family therapy with the son. Even in this setting progress was limited.

Case 2. A 33-year-old black heroin addict was in conjoint family therapy with his mother, two sisters, and brother. After his discharge from Eagleville, he returned to live with his two sisters; the mother lived nearby. As the therapist encouraged the subject to develop more responsibility for his life, she met more resistance from the family members. As much as they seemed to want to see their brother stop using drugs, they could see no relation to the suggestion that he pay some reasonable rental fee to them. They flatly rejected this proposal and discontinued therapy.

Case 3. This dramatic case not only demonstrated the intensity of the dependent/independent struggle but also represents some of the better prognostic elements. This 21-year-old white male was primarily addicted to Dilaudid but was also abusing alcohol. His father was a heavy weekend drinker. Following his discharge from Eagleville, the subject returned to live with his parents and sister. They participated in conjoint family sessions during the course of the study.

In the beginning the family struggled to establish a more acceptable pattern of living together. The parents had vacillated in the past between tolerating their son's addictive behavior and kicking him out of the house. On the one hand they would protest and extract promises and on the other hand, with frustration, would say, "Out!" In response to this gesture, the son would take his parents on a guilt trip: "See, you don't love me." In family therapy they were helped to set up realistic expectations with the son's participation and reluctant agreement. Although he soon returned to drug use, the parents were supported in deciding that the son quickly be readmitted to Eagleville. This second hospitalization began three months after the first discharge.

During this second inpatient phase the son seemed to make more progress in developing better self-esteem and moving toward more appropriate plans to separate from his family. By planning to enter a halfway house following his second discharge, he was shifting dependence to another institution. Our subject, however, left this setting within a few days and returned to his parents' doorstep. They now had to face a crucial test. All the family had shared in the decisions that had been made to that point. One of these was that the son could not return to live with them if he failed to live up to his part of the contract. Staying at the halfway house until he was ready to support himself in the community was part of that contract. But here he was, in the middle of the night, banging on their door, screaming to be admitted, threatening to break in if the parents refused! Nevertheless they withstood the barrage. Despite many wavering moments they persevered, with the family therapist, who was readily accessible, supporting their every move. The parents even threatened to call the police. But the son finally desisted and went away. That crisis was the turning point. Soon thereafter the young man obtained a job, established himself in an apartment, and began to date. He was about to be married as the family study was terminating. That he will enter a marriage in which he transfers his overdependence from his parents to his wife remains a possibility.

Other problems seem inherent in the families with a single parent or a peripheral father. In the family study most of the single-parent families were black; 31 out of 37 or 86 percent. Substance abuse, primarily alcoholism, was slightly more prevalent among these parents and was often related to the separation of the father from the family when the subject was young. As described in an earlier section, the dynamics in these families do not appear race-related, but cultural factors may add dimensions that require special consideration. In regard to the prevalence of single-parent families in the black community, Eleanor Holmes Norton (10) was quoted as reporting to the Urban League in Atlanta that the percentage of black households headed by black women had increased to 35 percent by 1975. By the age of 16, two-thirds of all black children have spent some years without a father. The psychological and economic penalties, she argued, are immense and destructive to the long-standing loyalty of the black family. Boszormenyi-Nagy (4) also described loyalty as a significant characteristic of black families. Important as it is for the family, such loyalty may also intensify the bond between mother and son and increase the conflict as pressures push him toward separation. To help these young people attain healthy autonomy requires careful and sensitive handling.

In the family study our results with these subjects and their families were not impressive. A group of mothers began to provide support for each other and to develop some alternatives for meeting their emotional needs. Unfortunately the group suffered a premature demise when the therapist was hospitalized and then convalesced for an extended period of time. This group modality with young single black mothers, however, has been demonstrated to be effective in the Community Mental Health Program of the St. Francis General Hospital in Pittsburgh (6).

Since a relatively high number of subjects accepted the opportunity to participate in the family study, there may be a message for us. If these participants are, in fact, indicating a need for help, we, as workers in the field of human services, should be prompted to continue our search for more effective solutions.

If the outcome of this therapy with the addicted subject seems to place a negative value on family therapy, a look at the changes that occur in the subjects' families provides a positive note. Boszormenyi-Nagy (3) has noted that change in a family can occur on three levels: in an individual member's habitual behavior; in the nature of dyadic or other subgroup interactional patterns (conditions or alliances, displacements, etc.) and in the overall style of the family. He further states that changes observed on each of these three levels will have to be evaluated in terms of long process considerations.

In the family study we proposed the possibility of an etiologic factor in the family interaction. An alteration in this interaction, however, does not guarantee recovery of the alcoholic or drug addict; it may just remove one contributing factor. Other factors may still be affecting the course of the addiction, e.g. peer influence and other secondary gains derived from the addiction. Intrapersonal and other interpersonal conflicts may also be unresolved. Hence change in the subject's behavior does not rule out the possibility of change on other levels within the family.

What can we say about changes that occurred in the families? Some parents learned to shed their useless guilt and refuse to be tryannized; they also learned how to be better parents, and set some reasonable limits not only for their addicted children, but also for their others. One mother exclaimed how much more comfortable they were with their son and how they wished that they had this kind of help before their daughter had become addicted. Some parents also developed a more satisfying marital relationship. Parental children began to shift into appropriate peer roles and became able to move toward healthier psychosexual development. Two of the study fathers, who had been heavy drinkers, began to look at their own substance-abuse problems. Such were a few of the changes that occurred in individuals, subgroups, and family behaviors. Thus, treatment of the family as part of a total approach offers an opportunity for the addicted member and the family to take a new step, together or apart, with better understanding and less conflict.

Sibling Peer Group

In this small group of subjects who included only their siblings, and in one case a cousin, the alcoholics outnumbered the drug subjects 7 to 2 (78 percent and 22 percent). Furthermore, most (8 or 89 percent) of the group was black. The parents were either deceased or divorced and out of contact with the subjects. Brothers of two of the male alcoholics were recovered alcoholics. The only white subject in this group was an addict whose sister was also a drug user. Their parents were living, and the addict wanted to involve his parents somehow. At that time, however, he did not see them as receptive to family sessions.

Families of Procreation

Families of procreation, those families in which the substance abuser is the parent, represent the second large group in the family study, 37 percent and 36 percent of the drug and alcohol subjects respectively (Graph 2-1). Ten subjects—4 (9 percent) drug and 6 (14 percent) alcoholic—also brought their parental figures into the initial family interviews. Two of these subjects included their children and their parents. These three-generational families will be discussed in this section as a special problem situation for family treatment with addict parents.

The total number of families of procreation (33) was evenly divided according to substance abuse. Three subjects in each substance category were assigned to the control group. Of the remaining 27 families assigned to therapy, 15 (8 drug dependent, 7 alcoholic) actually attended one or more sessions, i.e. either conjoint family therapy or relatives' groups.

Subgroups of Families of Procreation in Family Study

Further division of these families of procreation into categories according to their composition becomes helpful as we analyze the inherent problems that they present in family therapy and that may also provide some indicators for outcome (Graph 2-2).

These primary divisions are (1) the subject and spouse, with or without children, (2) the subject with without spouse and members of the family of origin, and (3) one-parent subject with children (Graph 2-2). At this point some differences begin to emerge in the respective representation of drug-dependent and alcoholic families in these subgroups, but the numbers are too small to assume statistical significance.

Subject and Spouse (with or without children). In the first subgroup of families, 23 entered the family study; 18 were assigned to treatment (11 drug subjects and 7 alcoholic). Only 7 drug-dependent (64 percent and 2 alcohol-dependent families (29 percent) attended at least one family session. In these families the presenting problems for therapy were greatly dependent upon two factors: the presence of active substance abuse in the spouse, and the status of the subject and spouse relationship at the time of treatment contact.

SPOUSE SUBSTANCE ABUSER. One-third (6 of the 18) of the subjects in this total subgroup (of subject and spouse) were married to partners who were also substance abusers; four spouses were actively using, and two were inactive. Of the two inactive spouses, the alcoholic wife had obtained sobriety through the program of Alcoholics Anonymous; the addicted spouse had been in drug treatment elsewhere.

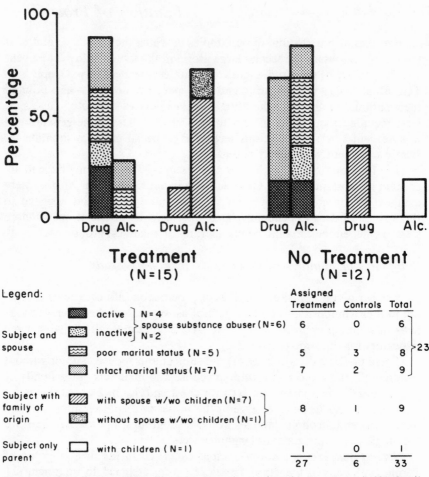

Graph 2-2. Distribution of families of procreation assigned to treatment in the family study according to composition, characteristics, and participation in family treatment.

The subsequent course in the families with the active spouse was stormy. Two of the drug subjects were incarcerated soon after their discharge from the Eagleville Hospital and Rehabilitation Center on new drug charges. Both of their wives entered drug treatment facilities. One came to Eagleville and also continued in conjoint family therapy with her parents. The third drug subject's wife began to drink more heavily after his discharge, but they refused to enter family treatment. The fourth subject, an alcoholic, entered the family study with his own agenda: to bring his estranged wife into treatment for her drinking problem. She attended the initial research interview but refused further overtures of help involving either individual or group counseling. The spouse lived with her mother, who seemed to support her daughter's decision.

SPOUSE NOT SUBSTANCE ABUSER. Poor Marital Status: In the second category, 12 subjects (7 drug-dependent, 58 percent; 5 alcoholic, 42 percent) presented with a spouse who was not a substance abuser. The marital status in five (42 percent) of these families, however, was very poor. All had either been separated or were in the process of doing so at the time of admission to Eagleville. Two men assigned to treatment saw family therapy as a possible route for reentering the marital relationship. One control subject had been divorced twice and was hoping to effect a reunion with his first wife. Here again were obstacles to family treatment. Only one of these families continued in therapy after an initial family session. The progress in that family was one of repeated crises and intermittent drinking bouts. Separated at the time of admission, the subject and his wife reconciled. After struggling through drinking sprees and suicidal attempts, they were still together at the one-year followup.

Intact Status: Only seven subjects with nonsubstance-abusing spouses— 58 percent of this subgroup, 5 (71 percent) drug-dependent subjects and 2 (29 percent) alcoholics—came into family treatment with intact relationships. Only 3 (43 percent) of these families continued in family therapy. This last group of subjects, therefore, represented a low proportion of families in the family study, but on the basis of the unit's ongoing experience, this group has represented families that benefit from the types of family therapy offered in the family study. Their characteristics are as follows:

1) Children present;

2) Intact families, not too hostile, but contacts pseudoemotional; expression of feeling frequently indirect or camouflaged while underlying feelings emerge during bouts of substance abuse;

3) Spouse overreacting to the substance abuse;

4) Spouse with minimal understanding of addiction;

5) Spouse attempting to control husband (subject) and family; also often in alliance with one child;

6) Parenting problems;

7) Marital problems.

Subject, Family of Procreation, and Family of Origin. This last subgroup of 8 subjects represents approximately 30 percent of the families of procreation assigned to treatment in the family study. They entered not only with a member of their own family (usually the spouse) but also with one parent or both. In only 2 of these families did the children of the subject also participate in the family therapy sessions. Such three-generation families present a unique situation as the subjects come with problems in relating as children to their parents as well as with problems in regard to being parents to their own children. The unit has had most experience with families of this type. Characteristically the grandparents care for the subject's children while the addict or alcoholic parent is actively addicted and/or in treatment. The role of the latter is then one of another child or a peripheral parent.

FAMILY THERAPY WITH THE FAMILIES OF PROCREATION. As with the families of origin, conjoint family therapy and relatives' group therapy were provided to these subjects and their families by random assignment.

Only one spouse group was organized, and its existence was brief. The husbands (subjects) were programmed to attend an outpatient group at the same time as the spouses were meeting in the same facility. One of the addict subjects refused to attend his group and threatened to harm his wife if she continued after her first group meeting. Not surprisingly, she dropped out. Too few members were recruited, no cohesive feeling developed, and the group soon expired.

As indicated elsewhere,[3] the family therapists had minimal experience in treating the alcoholic and addicted parents and their families during the life of the family study, but since the termination of that study, they have been seeing more and more addicted parents and their spouses. Interestingly the ratio has also been reversed from that of the family study so that the number of families of procreation is approximately double that of the families of origin.

The goals in the conjoint family therapy sessions with these parent-addicts or alcoholics are as follows:

1) Reduce overreactivity by educating the spouse about addiction; the aid of the addicted parent in this process may be helpful in lessening the fears and apprehensions that arise from misunderstanding (2).

2) Appropriately place responsibility for drinking or drug behavior on the addict or alcoholic thereby reducing self-blame and guilt in the spouse (8).

3) Improve parenting skills of both parents; restructure family if alliances between the parent and child are present.

4) If the addict father is peripheral, help him become more central. This may require role-playing during the sessions to involve him in problem-solving discussions with his wife, or conversations with his children while the wife is encouraged to listen actively or become engaged in a simultaneous interchange with the therapist. She may resist the move to shift more responsibility to the father. Support in helping her develop other areas of

competency and interest to replace the one she is relinquishing may aid this process. Sometimes redefining her changes as a way to help her husband is useful. One-to-one sessions and Al-Anon are also important aids to the spouses during this period of adjustment. Some wives may profit by entering employment or involvement in outside activities.

5) As parenting issues are resolved, work on the couple's intimate relationship is encouraged but may be resisted.

THREE-GENERATIONAL FAMILIES. In the three-generational households, the role of the mother-parent subject was like that of a dependent child. A realignment of these generational roles was necessary if the subject was to assume more responsible behavior. To accomplish this goal in conjoint family therapy was a gradual process which required (1) increasing the adequacy of the subject as a parent, (2) shifting the grandparents from their parental role with the subject's children to other acceptable and satisfying activities, and (3) helping the grandparents and subject develop mutual respect and support for each other and become more like peers. With this clearer delineation of roles and better functioning in the family, behavioral problems in the children tend to decrease, but some children may need attention for such specific needs as learning disorders and physical problems.

OUTCOME OF FAMILIES OF PROCREATION. By now it has become quite evident that few of the families of procreation who entered the family study represent a group with good prognostic characteristics so that the outcome of subjects in family therapy mentioned earlier becomes more understandable. With the termination of the family study and the shift to an open-admission policy of referrals, however, more of the intact, two-parent families have entered family therapy and evidence of better results in both the subjects and their families has been noted. A more careful study, however, will be necessary to corroborate this impression.

In those families of procreation which do improve with treatment, many changes occur whether or not the substance-abusing parent stops using drugs or alcohol. As with the families of origin, the spouse is helped to understand addiction. The lessening of self-blame and guilt in the spouse promotes a shift in behavior to more appropriate interactions among the family members. The spouse becomes able to deal with a recurrence of the partner's substance abuse more effectively. Her self-esteem is enhanced as she begins to see herself as less powerless and develops other areas of her life with the support of the family therapist, as well as with members of Al-Anon or other groups that she is encouraged to join. In the intact family the parent subject is aided in being reinstated to a more central role in the family as the spouse is assisted in relinquishing some control. Parenting and communication skills are areas amenable to improvement; work on intimate areas may be subject to more resistance but invariably is indicated.

With some addict families who did not live with their parents, extended family sessions were at times indicated to help resolve the conflicts between the two generations, rather than let them continue to impede the progress in the work of the couples. Marriage provides no magical resolution to the influence and attitudes that marital partners carry from their own family backgrounds into their present relationships.

Changes in the children of these families are sometimes quite dramatic. In one family the truancy and aggressive behavior of the children decreased and the school grades improved as the subject became abstinent and with his spouse developed better parenting skills.

In another family, one child had become a parent substitute for the malfunctioning parent. Through family therapy this parental child was freed to be a child and relate more with his peers, while the parents received support and learned to function more adequately.

The following case history is an example of what takes place in therapy, and shows the progress made within a three-generational family:

The mother was a 28-year-old heroin addict with two children of elementary-school age. All three were living with the subject's mother and stepfather, who had cared for the grandchildren during the subject's hospitalization. In the course of conjoint family therapy, the subject (mother) was helped to assume a more responsible parental role with her children and to relate to her own parental figures on a more adult level. Likewise, the grandmother was supported in making this shift and allowing her daughter to take on a more active mothering role as the subject demonstrated increasing interest and capability. Simultaneously the therapist aided the grandmother in relinquishing this central role, in bolstering her self-esteem, and supporting her involvement activities with her husband or in outside pursuits. Changes occurred in the children with these parental role shifts. In school their grades went up, and their lying and stealing diminished as the family improved during the course of eight months of family therapy. The school counselor reported, "The grandmother and mother appear to have learned consistency in their discipline and how to show feelings more appropriately. While this family is far from 'out of the woods,' it is on the right path."

One-Parent Family The one-parent family involved a divorced father and his teenage son and daughter. They attended the initial research interview but rejected family therapy. The father was recently divorced and lived with his parents, while the children resided with their mother. The subject father expressed satisfaction after the three had met together for the research interview and seemed to feel no need for further services of a family therapist.

The Effect of Addiction Upon Children

Up to this point we have focused on parental relationships, but more attention to the effect upon children by intervention in these families is in order. We have noted in passing some alliances of children with parents or grandparents. In all the families, except one in the unit's present experience, the behavior of the children was noted to be an accurate barometer of the state of the parent substance abuser. With the parent's return to alcohol or drugs, the children exhibited more antisocial behavior and did poor academic work. It becomes important to determine factors that enable some children to handle better than others the anxiety and stress induced by their parent's addiction and frequent separation from the family, or by longitudinal studies to discover whether they internalize the conflict only to exhibit its effects at a later date. Two possible variables that may be crucial are the age of the children at which the effects of the parental addiction are most intense, and the manner in which the nonaddicted spouse is able to cope with the stress of the other parent's addiction.

Because the effects of parental addiction on the offspring raise the question of whether there is a higher risk of the children becoming substance abusers, prevention becomes a priority consideration (7). El-Guebaly and Offord (5) recently completed a critical review of the offspring of alcoholics, and concluded that they are more likely to suffer from emotional disturbance, particularly antisocial behavior, compared to various control groups of children. We propose that similar dynamics are also at work in the families with drug-dependent parents. El-Guebaly and Offord also concurred that factors both across and within families of alcoholics which do not result in children having apparent increase in vulnerability to psychosocial illness should be carefully studied.

Conclusion

A research project with substance-abusing subjects and families has been recently concluded at Eagleville Hospital and Rehabilitation Center.

One hypothesis of this family study, that the families of drug addicts and alcoholics are similar, was substantiated on the basis of the following findings:

1) The 90 subject families consisted of a similar distribution of family types—families of origin and families of procreation—despite the age difference of the alcoholic and addicted subjects.

2) A similar high rate of alcoholism or problem drinking was present in the families of ths subjects in both substance-abusing groups.

3) Similar dynamics were characteristic of both groups of families.

In the families of origin these dynamics were further influenced by the parental structures, i.e. the presence of two parents, of one parent with the other parent absent or peripheral, or of only one parent. Here one dissimilarity between the two substance groups appeared in the higher number of alcoholics, primarily black, who had parent families.

In the families of procreation—that is, those in which the subject is a parent—the dynamics, problems to be worked on in family therapy, and outcome were associated again not only with the family structures, but also with the status of the relationship between subject and spouse at the time of admission to the Eagleville treatment facility.

In a third subgroup—i.e. subjects who entered the family study with their siblings or other peer relatives—another dissimilarity between the two substance groups is noted. Most of these subjects were black alcoholics.

The possible goals for family therapy are outlined and the steps for moving toward these goals are described for two modalities: conjoint structural family therapy and relatives' groups. The advantages and disadvantages of each modality were noted.

The outcome of family therapy was reviewed on the basis of changes not only in the alcoholics and drug-dependent subjects, but also by changes in the family, their individual members, and subgroups. We also enumerated some prognostic indicators that appear to augur well for family therapy. We propose, however, that the treatment of the family is part of a total approach that offers an opportunity for the addicted member and the family to take a new step, together or apart, but with better understanding and less conflict.

Treatment of the families of procreation with "high-risk" children was posited as one approach to primary prevention.

We also reiterate an oft-heard plea for further studies to corroborate some of the concerns we have expressed in this chapter and which we hope will lead to more effective approaches to the families of drug addicts and alcoholics.

REFERENCES

1. Barr, H., The Role of the Family in Addiction. Combined Treatment Demonstration Grant, H81-DA-01433-01.
2. Berenson, D., A Family Approach to Alcoholism. Personal circulation.

3. Boszormenyi-Nagy, I., The Concept of Change in Conjoint Family Therapy. In A.S. Friedman et al. (Eds.), *Psychotherapy for the Whole Family*, New York: Springer, 1965, pp. 305-317.
4. Boszormenyi-Nagy, I., Loyalty Implications of the Transference Model in Psychotherapy. *Arch. General Psychiatry* 27:374-379, 1972.
5. El-Guebaly, N. & Offord, D., The Offspring of Alcoholics: A Critical Review. *American J. Psychiatry* 134:357-365, 1977.
6. Kane, R., Report presented at the Pennsylvania Psychiatric Society Meeting, Hershey, Pennsylvania, April 15-17, 1977.
7. Kellerman, J.L., A Guide for the Family of the Addict, Torrance, California: Families Anonymous, Inc.
8. Kellerman, J.L., A Guide for the Family of the Alcoholic, New York: Al-Anon Family Group Headquarters.
9. Minuchin, S., Montalvo, B., Guerney, B.G., Rosman, B.L., & Schumer, F. *Families of the Slums,* New York: Basic Books, 1967.
10. Novak, M., The Family Out of Favor, *Harper's*, April 1976.
11. Stanton, M.D., Structural Family Therapy with Families of Heroin Addicts. Paper presented at Society for Psychotherapy Research, San Diego, California, June 16-19, 1976.

FOOTNOTES

1. A more complete report of this research design of the study is available in *Family Process*, 1977, *16* (*2*), 175-189.

2. The overall goal of structural family therapy is to mobilize and support the strengths of the family and help the members develop new skills so that the family can better cope with present tasks and move on to the next stage of the family's development.

Part I
DRUG ABUSERS

From a Psychodynamic Orientation to a Structural Family Therapy Approach in the Treatment of Drug Dependency

Edward Kaufman, M.D.

ASSOC. CLINICAL PROFESSOR OF PSYCHIATRY
CHIEF, PSYCHIATRIC SERVICES, DIRECTOR OF FAMILY THERAPY PROGRAMS
UNIVERSITY OF CALIFORNIA, IRVINE MEDICAL CENTER
ORANGE, CALIFORNIA

Pauline Kaufmann, M.S.W.

DIRECTOR OF FAMILY THERAPY, PHOENIX FOUNDATION
CONSULTANT IN FAMILY THERAPY
BELLVUE HOSPITAL SOCIAL SERVICE DEPARTMENT

Drug abuse and dependence do not occur in isolation; they afflict a particular member of a specific family living in a community that is part of a larger society. If drug abuse is seen from the vantage point of these four concentric circles, intervention tends to be ecological, sociological, and familial, as well as psychological. An individual psychodynamic approach can not stand alone. Nor can any approach which ignores one or more of these circles.

The growing number of addicts[1] in the last ten years is a result of many interwoven determinants. It is frequently difficult to find which factor is primary. However, the most important causes over the past decade are societal, involving community and familial dysfunction.

A survey was made of 20 young women who were residents in a drug-free therapeutic community. By means of in-depth interviews it was revealed that 18 of them had been sexually abused before the age of eleven by their father, father-surrogate, or older brother. Although it was tempting to come to certain conclusions based on this information, further questioning revealed that all of these young women came from inner-city families where bedrooms and beds were shared by two or three other members of the family, and sleep space was allocated on the principle of first-come, first-served. It was not unusual for sisters and brothers to share a bed, and sometimes children and one or other of the parents did so.

We have a "chicken and egg" dilemma here. Which came first, the socioeconomic or the psychodynamic factors? The following two sets of observations deal with the addict and his family. They are the result of twenty years of therapeutic work with addicts of varied ethnic and socioeconomic origin, and have proved valid regardless of the social class, race, sex, or drug of choice. Other observations which differ according to these variables will be described later in the chapter.

Common Features of the Addict

1) Drugs are used to facilitate or obliterate concern with sexual performance, communication, and assertion. In neurotics they are used to alleviate symptoms and in psychotics to provide an internal homeostasis (4,5).

2) Social factors are important in all classes and ethnic groups. In ghettoes and other areas where poverty is concentrated, drugs may be the only available means to an exciting and seemingly fulfilling life. In the middle and upper classes, use of drugs represents an attempt to deal with a lack of meaning in one's life, emotional sterility, and the absence of intimate relationships (4,5).

3) The more out of keeping from an individual's social background and cultural norms a pattern of drug abuse is, the more likely it is that the user is suffering from severe underlying mental illness (4,5).

4) There is no orderly progression from dependence to independence, and pseudoadult stances are common.

5) Identification with quasi-parenting older delinquents, peers, and siblings is common.

Common Features of the Family with an Addict Member

1) The drug addict is the symptom carrier of the family dysfunction.

2) The addict helps to maintain family homeostasis.

3) The addicted member reinforces the parental need to control and continue parenting, yet he finds such parenting inadequate for his needs.

4) The addict provides a displaced battlefield so that implicit and explicit parental strife can continue to be denied.

5) Parental drug and alcohol abuse is common and is directly transmitted to the addict or results in inadequate parenting.

6) The addict forms cross-generational alliances which separate parents from each other.

7) Generational boundaries are diffuse—there is frequent competition between parents. Frequently the crisis created by the drug-dependent member is the only way the family gets together and attempts some problem solving, or is the only opportunity for a "dead" family to experience emotions.

The histories of hundreds of addicts with whom these writers have worked are characterized by circularity and replication. The nuclear families of addicts tend to replicate the pattern of the family of origin. Therapeutic communities have seen two and three generations of families with addict members. When family therapy becomes part of the treatment of the adult addict or part of his reentry process, new family patterns are learned, and the cycle of dysfunction which produced an addict member in the family is interrupted. In E. Kaufman's early work with addicts (4), families presented by the patient through fantasies, distortions, and in some cases, accurate reportage, but the families themselves were most often not included in the diagnostic or therapeutic process.

It is only with a knowledge of the structure of the total family unit that the family can be understood and its potential as a therapeutically developed. Although our knowledge of the family structures of addicts has developed over twenty years of working in this field, we did not approach the formal study of family structures until about five years ago. Presented below is a quantitative study of family structures based on Kaufman's work (6) with 61 families of former heroin-dependent individuals housed in Su Casa, a residential treatment setting located in the ethnically diverse Lower East Side of Manhattan, and with 14 families of heroin addicts at The Awakening Family, a Synanon-derived program in Los Angeles County.

Studies of addicts from one social class or ethnic group and generalized to all addicts account for many of the differences cited in the literature about the family structure of addicts. The author's previous work has emphasized the vast differences between addicts from different ethnic, social, and cultural groups (5). The multiplicity of ethnic groups at Su Casa and the Awakening Family permit some generalizations about addict families, as well as hypotheses about ethnic-specific patterns. However, selection of these populations had also contained some biases which prohibit us from making sweeping generalizations about all addict families. The families evaluated constituted less than one-fourth of the families of clients who entered residential treatment. Thus, families who were geographically distant or emotionally disengaged tended not to participate and were not a part of the sample. This led to a strong bias towards involved and perhaps enmeshed families. The dynamic patterns were derived mainly from observations in multiple family therapy rather than from individual family

interviews. This setting may provide further bias through overidentific-
ation, as families too readily recognize patterns in themselves that they see
in others.

The ethnoracial breakdown of the 78 patients[2] in this study is shown in
Table 3-1.

Italian and Jewish families of origin tended to be involved in family
therapy in a high proportion of cases. The spouses of Hispanic residents attended more readily than the families of origin. Blacks, who constituted a
third of the residents, did not become involved despite the constant presence of a black cotherapist at Su Casa. Sixty-two patients (79 percent) were
males, and 16 (21 percent) were females. The average age of both patient
groups was 25 years.

Eight (10%) families consisted of mate only. Sixty-seven (86 percent) of
the families contained at least one member of the family of origin. Twelve
mates of residents whose family of origin also attended were part of the
group, so that there were 20 mates (26 percent) in all.

The author observed that the 14 families at The Awakening Family
were sufficiently similar to those at Su Casa to warrant combining the two
samples. Although the Mexican-American California group had some similarities to New York City Puerto Ricans, there were also marked differences.

Structural Patterns

The basic patterns of familial interaction were analyzed structurally
using the concepts of Minuchin (9). Thus, parent-child relationships were
designated as enmeshed, clear, or disengaged, terms which will be defined
below. Most families were observed for over six months. In addition to
post-group discussions of patterns, verbatim transcripts of all sessions were

Table 3-1

	Number	Percent
Hispanic		
(2 Mexican-American)	18	23
Italian	15	19
White Anglo-Saxon Protestant	14	18
Jewish	10	13
Black	8	10
Irish	7	9
Greek	1	1
Mixtures	5	6
(two with one Italian parent each)		

recorded and later analyzed to confirm initial impressions. Several months' of sessions were recorded on videotape and presented to several experienced family therapists who reviewed the structural patterns with the therapists. Nevertheless, all of the observations were quite subjective.

Fifty-six of 64 (88 percent) mother-child relationships were considered enmeshed, as were 23 of 57 (40 percent) father-child relationships[3]. Two mothers were disengaged, as were 24 fathers (42 percent). Seven fathers and one mother died at a time which was crucial to the onset of drug abuse. Many parental divorces also occurred at the onset of drug abuse and appeared causally related. No relationship between an addict and his parent was designated as having clear boundaries. However, in the case of 6 mothers and 13 fathers, their relationship to their addict child was equivocal or varying, or insufficient information was available to classify these relationships as either enmeshed or disengaged. The mother or stepmother was present in all but one of the families of origin who participated. A total of 23 fathers did not participate in the family therapy, but 16 of these were classified by hearsay mainly as disengaged.

Of the 17 mates of male addicts, 11 (65 percent) women and one homosexual mate were quite passive and submissive. Three female mates were dominant and two relationships were too egalitarian to be so classified. All three male mates who attended were former addicts receiving methadone treatment who were quite dominant. One male mate who was talked about extensively in therapy had died traumatically shortly before his wife entered treatment. Although the woman to whom he was married was quite a strong person, their relationship was apparently balanced.

Siblings tended to fall equally into two basic categories: one group was composed of fellow addicts whose drug dependence was inextricably fused with that of the resident, and the other consisted of older siblings who were either the parental child who assumed an authoritarian role when the father was disengaged, and/or were themselves highly successful. Some of these successful siblings had individuated from the family, but many were still enmeshed. A third, smaller group of siblings was quite passive and not involved with substance abuse. Enmeshed addicted siblings buy drugs for each other, inject the other, set the other up to be arrested, or pimp for one another. At times a large family may show sibling relationships of all these types. When addict siblings vary widely in age, their drug abuse may not be enmeshed but is rather a product of similar parental and societal factors. Three addict sibling pairs were treated simultaneously in residence and, in the two cases where the families attended regularly, with beneficial structural shifts. One sibling who was not in residence, but who attended multiple family therapy regularly, showed great progress, as did the resident. Many successful siblings were quite prominent in their fields, and in these cases the addict sibling withdrew from any vocational achievement rather than compete.

Mothers tended to be enmeshed with addict children in all ethnic groups. Six of 10 Jewish and 7 of 13 Italian father-child pairs were enmeshed. Puerto Rican, black, and white protestant fathers tended to be disengaged or absent from the therapy. The black and Greek samples were too small for generalization. However, most of the black families had strong, involved mothers, and the Greek family consisted of three totally enmeshed generations.

According to Minuchin (9), enmeshment and disengagement refer to a preference for a type of transactional interaction. Enmeshed family subsystems are frequently handicapped in that a heightened sense of belonging requires a major yielding of autonomy. Thus stresses in one family member cross over to the other (9). Disengaged systems tolerate a wide range of individual variation but lack a feeling of loyalty, belonging, or the ability to request support when needed (9). Narcotic addiction in a family member places such a great stress on the family that secondary enmeshment or disengagement can be expected. However, the authors' impressions are that these patterns, particularly mother-child enmeshment, antedated—and indeed led to—abuse of and dependence on narcotics.

The most frequent pattern observed was that of a male addict enmeshed with his mother, thereby separating her from her spouse, who retaliated with either brutality to the addict and/or disengagement from the family. The extent of what was considered pathologic enmeshment was quite variable. Extremely enmeshed mothers may become psychotic or suicidal when their sons act out or individuate themselves. In one case, a mother who was chronically psychotic and who had repeated psychiatric hospitalizations was symbiotically tied to her addict son during her psychotic episodes. Early in their family therapy the addict helped provoke an overt psychotic episode in his mother in order to reestablish their symbiotic tie. When this pattern was demonstrated in the family sessions, the cycle was interrupted. After the mother emerged from her psychosis, she poignantly told her son in the group, "I will not hold you to me any more." Another extremely enmeshed mother made a suicide attempt when her son left the program. Enmeshed mothers think, act, and feel for everyone in the family, but more so for their addict child. Several mothers regularly ingested prescribed minor tranquilizers or narcotics which were shared overtly or covertly with their sons. Many mothers suffered an agitated depression whenever their son or daughter "acted out" in destructive ways. Mothers who received prescription tranquilizers or abused alcohol frequently increased their intake whenever the addict acted out. The mother's psychosomatic symptoms are frequently blamed on the addict. In a Puerto Rican family, the addict's brothers told him that if their mother died from asthma, they would kill him.

The relationship between mothers and daughters tended to be extremely hostile, competitive, and at times chaotic. Half the mother-daughter relationships were also severely enmeshed. When her mother committed suicide, a daughter also made a serious suicide attempt. One father committed suicide after his wife ordered him out of the house for his brutality. The son assumed a parental-child role and did not use heroin until shortly after his mother remarried (to a man with addicted twin sons). A third of the fathers were alcoholic, though all but four of these had abandoned their families or died from alcoholism and were not a part of treatment. The one father who had himself been a heroin addict raised five of his six children as addicts. In the majority of Italian and Jewish families the entire family was quite enmeshed. Frequently both parents collaborated with the addict to keep him "infantilized" under the guise of protecting him from arrest or other danger. The pattern of father-son brutality was quite common although it was seen in fathers who were enmeshed as well as disengaged. With disengaged fathers, brutality was frequently their only contact with their children. However, enmeshed fathers do beat their sons thereby pushing the sons into strong coalitions with the mother against the father. Physical brutality was common between Italian fathers and their sons. However, this was a multigenerational problem which was a part of enmeshed intimacy. In these Italian families, physical beatings did not seem to be traumatic in and of themselves. It is much easier for a father to hit a child once or twice than enforce a discipline over hours and days. In a Mexican-American family, the father was described as disengaged by his son, this before the father was seen in therapy. However, he attended every family session and after a while his machismo relaxed so that he could tell his son that he frequently worried about him so much that it impaired his functioning at work. Although the mother was the family "switchboard" through whom all communications went, the father was the family spokesperson who made the final decisions and stated them, a common pattern in Mexican-American families. This particular father was "too equivocal" to be classified as enmeshed or disengaged.

Overt incest was reported in only one father-daughter pair but was suspected or experienced covertly in many parent-child and sibling pairs. This is a much lower incidence of incest than is reported in most recent studies of female addicts, including the survey quoted earlier in this chapter. It may be a function of the predominant use of a group setting which did not condone discussion of this sensitive issue.

The addict acts as a barometer of family functioning, even when in treatment, so that his disruptive behavior is a symptom of familial dysfunction. There may be an extended period of familial difficulty during which the addict's abuse of drugs is denied by the entire family. Alternately, the addict is the scapegoat upon whom all intrafamilial problems are focused. Often the family's basic interactional pattern is dull and lifeless and only becomes alive when mobilized to deal with the crisis of drug abuse (12). Guilt is frequently used to manipulate and may be induced by the addict to coerce the family into supporting the maintenance of a habit or by parents to curb individuation. Many mothers had severe psychosomatic symptoms which were blamed on the addict, thereby reinforcing the pattern of guilt and mutual manipulation. Mother's drug and alcohol abuse and suicide attempts were also blamed on the addict.

Most of the fathers who were present in the therapy were very hard workers who had become supervisors, and who set very high performance standards for their sons which were not met or even approached. Many sons, particularly Italians, worked directly for their fathers, frequently in the construction field. They were protected in this way from having to meet the usual demands of employment. Several fathers suffered disabling physical injuries after the onset of their son's drug dependence which prevented them from continuing to work.

Physical expressions of love and affection are generally either absent or used to deny and obliterate individuation or conflict. Anger about interpersonal conflicts is not expressed directly unless it erupts in explosive violence. Anger about drug use and the denial of its expression is seen quite frequently and is almost always counterproductive. All joy has disappeared in these families, as lives are totally taken up with the sufferings and entanglements of having an addict child. However, in many cases, the joylessness preceded the addiction. As Reilly (12) noted, communication is most frequently negative, and there is no appropriate praise for good behavior. There is a lack of consistent limit-setting by parents, and deviance may be punished or rewarded at different times (12). This may even occur when there is no splitting of the parental alliance as described earlier. As in delinquent behavior related to drug abuse, there is vicarious parental gratification derived from the "risqué" aspects of the addict's life.

Discussion

The basic structural pattern in the families we have observed in this group is compatible with observations about other families of drug abusers, as well as those of alcoholics and schizophrenics (1,8,10,12). That is, the mother and son are symbiotically tied to each other prior to the onset of drug abuse, and the father is excluded and reacts with disengagement and/or brutality. However, several of our observations concern other factors which have not been sufficiently developed in the literature.

The family patterns of narcotic addicts vary in different ethnic groups. The father may be disengaged in white Protestant and black families but enmeshed in Italian and Jewish families. Larger samples of families from each ethnic group must be studied, and more rigorously, to clearly delineate these patterns. In addition, there should be a study of "normal" families in each ethnic group to determine what if any differences there are from addict families in these ethnic groups. Our preliminary observations on the relationship of the female addict to her family must also be documented by further studies. The communication patterns of these families are less distorted than those of schizophrenics. Double binds are clearer, and more overt, but frequently the adolescent's only escape route is through drugs.

Siblings are of crucial importance either through their own addiction, which is enmeshed with that of the identified patient, or in their role as a parental, authoritarian child, or as an extreme success with which the potential addict cannot compete. Addicts may themselves have been parental children who have no way of asking for relief from responsibilities except through drugs. More commonly, an addict is the youngest child, and his addiction maintains his status as the baby. Addict spouse pairs frequently duplicate roles with each other which they have developed in their families of origin and which may not be correctible unless work is done with the original family as well as the newly created nuclear family.

It is of interest that several, but not all, of the hypotheses about the families of addicts based on our earlier work with individuals has been supported by more recent work with families. The conclusions made in 1970 based on these psychoanalytic interviews were:

The fathers of these addicts were reported as intelligent, accomplished, cold, distant, sadistic, sexually and aggressively competitive with their sons and seductive with their daughters. Mothers were perceived as either distant or overtly seductive. There were many mothers who were psychotic and several who were themselves drug and alcohol abusers. Repeated masturbatory fantasies about mother as well as overt sexual attraction to her were common in male patients. Several siblings were also opiate dependents and in most of these cases there was a symbiotic tie between the addict siblings (4).

Thus, siblings and fathers were seen quite similarly to their counterparts in the family studies. However, many alternative roles were not revealed. The importance of mothers was grossly underestimated as described in these psychoanalytic interviews.

Families who do not participate voluntarily in treatment must also be studied to determine their role, if any, in the etiology of drug abuse in the identified patient. Alexander and Dibb (1) have stated that "a minority of opiate addicts maintain close emotional and financial relationships with their parents." However, this statement was based on a retrospective study of records of patients in methadone treatment in British Columbia. Methadone-maintenance patients, in the author's experience, tend to insulate their families from therapy more than addicts involved in any other form of treatment. In the 18 families studied (1) they noted that the father was dominant when present, as he was in 11 of the cases. However, their treatment sample was limited to Caucasians. Noone and Reddig (10) found that a majority of drug abusers and addicts maintain close ties with their families of origin. They observed that such families frequently undergo "mock separations" through overdoses or institutionalizations which ultimately strengthen loyalty bonds. In a study of 85 addicts, Stanton (14) noted that of addicts with living parents, 82 percent saw their mothers and 58 percent saw their fathers at least weekly while 66 percent either lived with their parents or saw their mothers daily. In 1966 Vaillant (15) reported that 72 percent of addicts still lived with their mother at age 22, and 47 percent continued to live with a female blood relative after age 30. Interestingly, Vaillant also noted that of the 30 abstinent addicts in his follow-up study, virtually all were living independently from their parents. This may be evidence of how strong an enemy the family is if it is not made an ally through treatment. That only one-fourth of the residents at Su Casa and The Family were involved in family treatment is as much a reflection of limited outreach and treatment resources as it is a true indication of family involvement. Since multiple family groups frequently were composed of over 40 individuals, further outreach would have been counterproductive.

The symbiotic tie between mothers and sons has been consistently noted in the literature. Fort (3) noted that such mothers were "overprotective, controlling and indulgent" and resembled the mothers of alcoholics and schizophrenics. "They were willing to do anything for their sons, except let them alone." In a comparison of mothers of drug addicts, schizophrenics and normal adolescents, the mother's symbiotic need for the child was highest in the mothers of drug abusers (2). Fort (3), in a group comprised mainly of ghetto addicts, noted the "frequent virtual absence of a father figure" and that in the rare instances where there was a prominent father figure, "he was most frequently a severe dominating person" who demanded that his son "grow up" but who desired to keep him an infant so that he would not be threatened by him. More recent studies of middle-class families have noted the presence of a strong father (1). Kirschenbaum et al. (7) noted that "the father's position as strong leader of the family seemed to be a fiction ... needed and nourished by the mother as the 'real head of the family.'" Schwartzman (13) also noted that fathers were either "strawman" authoritarian figures or distant but clearly "secondary to the mother in terms of power."

Several authors have noted recently that drug use is essential to maintaining an interactional family equilibrium that resolves a disorganization of the family system which existed prior to drug taking (9,10). The "addictor" in the system may be the parent(s) or the spouse as noted by Pearson and Little (11). Wellisch et al. (16) noted that one partner, usually the male, is supported or taken care of by the other and so becomes an "easy rider" throughout the relationship. Our experience is that the male addict dominates either the addicted or nonaddicted spouse to take care of him in much the same way he related to his mother. This pattern was particularly clear in Puerto Rican addicts.

We hope this material will stimulate further family work and the development of precise research instruments so that these ideas and hypotheses can be validated. The dynamics and structural sets described in this chapter should certainly be looked for by anyone who works with addicts and their families. It is hoped that the therapist will seek out these maladaptive sets, validate them, and begin to change them in addict families, for it is only when these changes occur that addicts returning to their families are not drawn back into patterns which inevitably lead to readdiction.

REFERENCES

1. Alexander, B.K. & Dibb, G.S., Opiate Addicts and Their Parents. *Family Process* 14:499-514, 1975.
2. Attardo, N., Psychodynamic Factors in the Mother-Child Relationship in Adolescent Drug Addiction: A Comparison of Mothers of Schizophrenics and Mothers of Normal Adolescent Sons. *Psychotherapeutic Psychosomatic* 13:249-252, 1965.
3. Fort, J.P., Heroin Addiction Among Young Men. *Psychiatry* 17:251-259, 1954.
4. Kaufman, E., The Psychodynamics of Opiate Dependence: A New Look. *Am. J. Drug & Alcohol Abuse* 1:349-370, 1974.
5. Kaufman, E., The Abuse of Multiple Drugs: Psychological Hypotheses, Treatment Considerations. *Am. J. Drug & Alcohol Abuse* 3:293-304, 1976.
6. Kaufman, E., The Therapeutic Community and Methadone: A Way of Achieving Abstinence. *Intern'l J. Addictions* 14, 1979, in press.
7. Kirschenbaum, M., Leonoff, G., & Maliano, A., Characteristic Patterns in Drug Abuse Families. *Family Therapy* 1:43-62, 1974.
8. Klagsbrun, M. & Davis, D., Substance Abuse and Family Interaction. *Family Process* 16:149-174, 1977.
9. Minuchin, S., *Families and Family Therapy*, Cambridge, MA: Harvard University Press, 1975.

10. Noone, R.J. & Reddig, R.L., Case Studies on the Family Treatment of Drug Abuse. *Family Process* 15:325-332, 1976.
11. Pearson, M.M. & Little, R.B., Treatment of Drug Addiction: Private Practice Experience with 84 Addicts. *Am. J. Psychiatry* 122:164-169, 1975.
12. Reilly, D.M., Family Factors in the Etiology and Treatment of Youthful Drug Abuse. *Family Therapy* 2:149-171, 1976.
13. Schwartzman, J., The Addict, Abstinence and the Family. *Am. J. Psychiatry* 132:154-157, 1975.
14. Stanton, M.D., Some Outcome Results and Aspects of Structural Family Therapy with Drug Addicts. National Drug Abuse Conference, San Francisco, California, May 5-9, 1977.
15. Vaillant, G., A 12-year Follow-up of New York Narcotic Addicts. *Arch. General Psychiatry* 15:599-609, 1966.
16. Wellisch, D.K., Gay, G.R. & McEntee, R., The Easy Rider Syndrome: A Pattern of Hetero- and Homosexual Relationships in a Heroin Addict Population. *Family Process* 9:425-430, 1970.

FOOTNOTES

1. After a brief crusade to change the term "addict" to "drug dependents" or "drug-dependent individuals," the authors frequently resort to the former term because it is clearer. "Addict" means someone who has been dependent on drugs for a substantial period of time—in this sample, generally for over six years.
2. There were 3 sibling pairs in residence, thus 78 patients and 75 families.
3. Parents of the sibling pairs were considered separately here because relationships differed.

4

Structural Family Therapy with Drug Addicts*

M. Duncan Stanton, Ph.D.
PHILADELPHIA CHILD GUIDANCE CLINIC
UNIVERSITY OF PENNSYLVANIA
PHILADELPHIA VA HOSPITAL

Thomas C. Todd, Ph.D.
HARLEM VALLEY PSYCHIATRIC CENTER

While there is an increasing body of literature on the nature and importance of family factors in drug addiction (5, 6, 11, 13, 15), not a great deal has been written on the actual methods for family *treatment* of addiction (13). Thus the family-oriented therapist was left to his own resources if he wanted to progress from an "understanding" of addict families to the adventure of bringing about change. It is the purpose of this chapter to present some strategies and techniques which we hope will not lessen the adventurous nature of the trip but will help the therapist keep from getting lost or discouraged as he sails these newly chartered waters.

Our experience has primarily evolved within the context of a research program on the effectiveness of family therapy with drug addicts (14, 16, 17, 18, 20). It gained impetus in 1972, when we undertook a survey of family contacts of 85 addicts at the Philadelphia Veterans Administration Drug Dependence Treatment Center (DDTC). Results showed that of those with living parents, 82 percent saw their mothers and 59 percent saw their fa-

*Funding for this work was provided through grants from the National Institute on Drug Abuse (DA 1119) and the Attorney General of Pennsylvania's Public Health Trust Fund (56772). Research and clinical support was provided by the Philadelphia V.A. Hospital Drug Dependence Treatment Program.

Other project staff, who contributed substantially to the development of this treatment approach, included Henry Berger, M.D., Gary Lande, M.D. (therapy supervisors), Gerald Hawthorne, David Heard, Ph.D., Sam Kirschner, Ph.D., Jerry Kleiman, Ph.D., David Mowatt, Ed.D., Paul Riley, Alexander Scott, M.S.W., Samuel M. Scott, Peter Urquhart, (therapists), Esther Carr, John M. Van Deusen (research associates), Elton Hargrove, Charles P. O'Brien, M.D. and George Woody, M.D. (Philadelphia V.A. Hospital Drug Dependence Treatment Program).

thers at least weekly; 66 percent either lived with their parents or saw their mothers daily. The figures become more striking when one realizes that the average age of these men was 28 and all of them had previously been separated from home and in the military for at least several months. The data also corroborate other studies (reviewed in [17]), such as Vaillant's (19) follow-up study of New York addicts in which he found that 72 percent of the total sample, or 90 percent of those with living mothers, still resided with their mothers at age 22.

This made us recognize how intensively involved the addict is with his family of origin. At this point, we have seen these close entanglements so often that we are skeptical when any addict, especially one under age 35, tells us that he does not see his parents regularly. Such knowledge has helped us to insist that the parents be involved in treatment, even when the addict tries to persuade us that the "real problems" are with his wife or girlfriend.

The therapeutic aspects described in this chapter are based primarily upon more than 60 families seen in family treatment within the research program, although we also had less systematic experience with drug-using families prior to the project. Much of the work in the early stages was exploratory, and part of our goal here is to help others to learn from our mistakes. At this writing, 33 of the families have been followed up six months after treatment, and the results are dramatically better than for a matched group of clients in the DDTC methadone/individual counseling program (14, 16). Family therapy more than doubled the average number of days free from heroin and opiates during the six months (80 percent vs. 36 percent), with similar results for most other outcome criteria.

The family therapy model employed in the project had two major influences. Many of the treatment concepts derive from the work of Minuchin (7) and colleagues of the Philadelphia Child Guidance Clinic, particularly a psychosomatic research project, in which one of us participated.[1] Since structural family therapy is described at length in the present volume, only the highlights will be presented in this chapter. Structural therapy has been shown to be effective with a variety of problems and different kinds of therapists. A case in point is one of the major outcome studies to date with this approach (9), in which 50 cases were seen by 16 therapists with widely ranging levels of experience and who came from 4 different disciplines. Our own work with addicts has involved 9 different therapists from 4 professions, most of whom had modest clinical credentials; 3 of them were "paraprofessionals" and did not have academic degrees.

A second major source of our ideas has been Jay Haley, who served as a major consultant to our project. Haley introduced ideas originally worked out with families of schizophrenics, first in Palo Alto, later at the Philadelphia Child Guidance Clinic,[2] and more recently at the Family Therapy Institute of Washington, D.C. with Cloe Madanes. In addition to having helped develop structural family therapy, Haley contributed many ideas to the project that are uniquely his own. Some can be found in Haley (3, 4), but most have not yet appeared in print. A summary of his therapy approach with this problem will be offered in the section on "Course of Therapy."

Structural family therapy typically focuses upon patterns of family interaction and communication within the session and attempts to influence these patterns directly and actively. Tasks or "homework" are assigned to consolidate changes made during the sessions. In this approach, past history and insight are deemphasized, with the major stress placed on changing current interaction. The therapist usually attempts to set boundaries and restructure the family, often by reinforcing generational boundaries between parents and offspring.

Clinical Context

The major part of our work has been done with patients who initially enrolled for methadone treatment at the Veterans Administration DDTC. Most of them were male, under age 35, and had been addicted to opiates for at least two years. Half were black and half, white. To be selected for our project they usually had to have contact weekly with one parent or parent-substitute (e.g. stepmother, mother's boyfriend) and at least monthly with the other. The majority of the patients had been treated previously for drug addiction.

Upon admission, their eligibility for our program was determined. If a treatment opening existed, eligible clients were then assigned to a family therapist. If not, they went the regular methadone treatment route and were assigned to a drug counselor for individual counseling and monitoring of medications. The family therapist served as the client's drug counselor for those in family treatment. It was his responsibility to meet with the client and discuss bringing his family into treatment. This often led to a lengthy process in which the therapist contacted the parents and other family members and encouraged their participation (18, 20). It usually necessitated a number of telephone calls and in a few instances, home visits. In 71 percent of the cases, the family was successfully brought into treatment.

Family therapy proceeded as an adjunct to the DDTC program and was accompanied by at least weekly urine testing (randomly scheduled) and other administrative linkages. In general, however, family therapy evolved into the major mode of treatment for those who participated in it.

Family Characteristics

Families in our project exhibit many of the patterns described in the earlier literature (1, 5, 6, 8, 10, 11, 13, 15). For example, there is a very close, dependent, mother-son relationship paired with a distant, excluded father (although in at least two of our cases the roles were reversed and the father was the parent closest to the children). Approximately 50 percent had a parent with a drinking problem. Furthermore, in most cases the fathers were observed to be most upset by their son's addiction, as the mothers tended to minimize it. This differs from typical child or adolescent problems, where the mother is more likely to voice the complaint.

There is usually a lack of constructive pressure for change in these families. The addict is discounted as a person, the family feels powerless, or the family blames outside causes (peers, neighborhood) for his problem. In some families, the addict's drug problem is the focus for all family problems. Further, the addict is often overprotected by the family and treated as a helpless and incompetent person. In these families, drugs are viewed as an all-powerful force that he cannot resist.

The special role that the addict plays within the family is particularly important. His actions help to maintain family stability—largely at his own expense.[3] Thus he serves a "noble," sacrificial purpose (12).

Course of Therapy

In the remainder of the chapter, we will present basic principles drawn from our work with the families of addicts.[4] Obviously, not all apply equally well to all families, nor do all families move through these stages with equal speed. Our usual length of treatment is 10 to 12 sessions, but some families have required fewer, and several, as many as 18.

Before discussing the treatment in more detail, its general approach can be understood by this summary from Haley's forthcoming book on therapy with problem young people.[5]

There are certain assumptions that improve the chance of success with young adults who exhibit mad and bizarre behavior, or continually take illegal drugs, or who waste their lives and cause community concern. For therapy, it is best to assume that the problem is not the young person but a problem of a family and young person disengaging from one another. Ordinarily, an offspring leaves home by succeeding in work or school and forming intimate relationships outside the family. In some families, when a son or daughter begins to leave home, the family becomes unstable and in distress. If at that point the young person fails by becoming incapacitated, the family stabilizes as if the offspring has not left home. This can happen even if the young person is living away from home, as long as he or she regularly lets the family know that failure continues. It can also exist even if the family is angry at the offspring and appears to have rejected him. Family stability continues as long as the young person is involved with the family by behaving in some abnormal way.

A therapist should assume that, if the family organization does not change, the young person will continue to fail year after year, despite therapy efforts. The unit with the problem is not the young person, but at least two other people: these might be two parents, or a mother and boy friend or sibling, or a mother and grandmother. It is assumed that two adults in a family communicate with each other by way of the young person and they enter severe conflict if the young person is not available to be that communication vehicle. The therapy goal is to free the young adult from that triangle so that he or she lives like other normal young people and the family is stable without the problem child.

This therapy and its premises has no relation to a therapy based on the theory of repression where an individual is the problem. Therefore, there is no concern with insight or awareness and there is no encouragement of people to express their feelings with the idea that this will cause change. Therapists accustomed to experiential groups or psychodynamic therapy have difficulty with this approach.

The therapy should occur in the following stages:

1. When the young person comes to community attention, the experts must organize themselves in such a way that one therapist takes responsibility for the case. It is better not to have a team or a number of separate therapists or modes of therapy. The one therapist must be in charge of whether the young person is to be in or out of an institution and what medication is to be given, and when. Only if the therapist is in charge of the case can he put the parents in charge within the family.

2. The therapist needs to gather the family for a first interview. If the young person is living separately, even with a wife, he should be brought together with the family of origin so that everyone significant to him is there. The goal is to move the young person to more independence, either alone or with a wife, but the first step to that end is to take him back to his family.

There should be no blame of the parents, but instead, the parents (or parent and grandmother, or whomever it might be) should be put in charge of solving the problem of the young person. They must be persuaded that they are really the best therapists for the problem offspring (despite past failures in trying to help him). It is assumed that the members of the family are in conflict and the problem offspring is expressing that. By requiring the family to take charge and set the rules for the young person, they are communicating about the young person, as usual, but in a positive way. Certain issues need to be clear:

a. The focus should be on the problem person and his behavior, not on a discussion of family relations. If the offspring is an addict, the family should focus on what is to happen if he ever takes drugs again. If mad and misbehaving, what they will do if he acts bizarrely in the way that got him in the hospital before. If anorectic, how much weight she is to gain per day, and how that is to be accomplished.

b. The past, and past causes of the problem, are ignored and not explored. The focus is what to do now.

c. The therapist should join the parents against the problem young person, even if this seems to be depriving him of individual choices and rights, and even if he seems too old to be made that dependent. After the person is behaving normally, his rights can be considered. It is assumed that the hierarchy of the family is in confusion. Should the therapist step down from his status as expert and join the problem young person against the parents, there will be worse confusion and the therapy will fail.

d. Conflicts between the parents or other family members are ignored and minimized even if they bring them up, until the young person is back to normal. If the parents say they have problems and need help too, the therapist should say the first problem is the son, and their problems can be dealt with after the son is back to normal.

e. Everyone should expect the problem person to become normal, with no suggestion that the goal is a handicapped person. Therefore, the young person should not be in a halfway house, a day hospital, kept on medication or on maintenance methadone. Normal work or school should be expected immediately, not later. Work should be self-supporting and real, not volunteer.

3. As the problem young person becomes normal (by achieving self-support, or successfully going to school, or by making close friends) the family will become unstable. This is an important stage in the therapy and the reason for pushing the young person toward normality. The parents will threaten separation or divorce or one or both will be disturbed. At that point, a relapse of the young person is part of the usual pattern, since that will stabilize the family. If the therapist has sided with the parents earlier, they will lean upon him at this stage and the young adult will not need to relapse to save them. The therapist must either resolve the parental conflict, or move the problem young person out of it while it continues more directly. At that point, the young person can continue to be normal.

4. The therapy should be an intense involvement and a rapid disengagement, not regular interviews over years. As soon as positive change occurs, the therapist can begin to recess and plan termination. The task is not to resolve all family problems but the ones around the problem young person, unless the family wants to make a new contract for other problems.

5. Regular follow-ups should be done to ensure that positive change continues.

Our approach to the families of heroin addicts is based upon the above principles and, as previously mentioned, shows considerable evidence of success. While other family therapy approaches may yield insightful observations about these families, we are interested in what *works* rather than what is interesting or "true" at some level of interpretation. This statement may seem obvious, but we have seen others become so enamored of family dynamics that the means for effecting change escape them. Furthermore it has not been characteristic for most other programs to evaluate their degree of success in any objective fashion. We have made an effort to monitor our own effectiveness in order to further develop our techniques.

Initial Phase

Given the general approach, a more detailed description can be offered of the steps in the therapy. The initial contact with the addict and his family (to get them into treatment) may demand considerable time and effort by the therapist (18, 20). Our research design required that we get at least the addict and both parents or parent-substitutes together before proceeding.

When we encounter resistance from the addict, particularly protestations of independence from his parents, we generally stress our need for the perspective that only his parents can provide. Once we are given permission to contact the parents, we stress the need for help from everyone and studiously avoid any implications of blame. We also emphasize that this program differs in one significant way from programs that have failed in the past: we involve the parents actively, rather than excluding them (18, 20).

It is necessary to emphasize the importance of a *nonblaming stance* in this treatment. We find that the confrontative techniques which may be useful in group therapy with drug abusers generally do not work with these families. Instead such approaches tend to foster massive family resistance and counterattack. This is not to say that we do not challenge families, but that we try to express our points in nonpejorative ways. We typically *ascribe noble intentions* to the behaviors we observe in the families. ("He's defending the family like any good son would." "You are trying your best to be a good mother.") This serves to lessen overt resistance, and allows therapy to proceed more smoothly and rapidly.

Early sessions typically focus on setting common goals for treatment. At this stage all goals should relate directly to helping the index patient stay off drugs. If the family brings up other issues, their relevance should be questioned—the family should have to justify them as pertinent to the primary goal. To keep therapy focused and productive, it is often appropriate to establish a date for detoxification and then to help the family prepare for it. At all times the therapist should avoid a power struggle with the parents or the addict, for he will always lose in the end and treatment will falter.

The major goal of the therapist in the early stages is to form an alliance with both parents, so that they can take an effective stance toward the addict. It is critical that the therapist keep the parents working *together* in the early stages. He should not allow them to get into their own marital difficulties, as this will divide and deter them from the task at hand. One way of facilitating this in cases where the addict and mother are overinvolved is to get father to take charge of his son.

Usually the experience of father and son relating must first come about in the session before it can be generalized to the home situation. It may be possible to get them engaged in discussing some common interest such as work or fishing. The mother should be present during this exchange and may need the therapist's subtle support while her husband and son are engaged.

Other tactics may also be used, depending on the specific clinical situation. When it appears that the mother endorses the drug behavior of the addict, with the father consistently more punitive, it may be possible to force the mother to deal with the negative behavior of the addict, thus breaking the alliance with him. Alternatively the therapist may meet only with the parents to formulate a strategy to which both parents will adhere.

Middle Phases and Crises

As change starts to occur and the addict stops or curtails his drug-taking, a family crisis can be expected. It normally happens three or four weeks into treatment. Most commonly it will revolve around the parents' marital relationship, with them talking about, or taking steps toward, separation or divorce. This puts tremendous pressure on the addict to become "dirty" again in order to reunite his family. At such times the therapist will need to devote considerable time and energy to resolving the crisis. He will have to be accessible and perhaps constantly on call. His goal is to get the parents to hold together in relation to the addict and not let them separate, at least until this storm is weathered. If the transition is handled skillfully, treatment is usually on the way to a successful outcome, for succeeding crises will be easier for the family to cope with; a previously recurrent pattern has been broken and real change has occurred.

After an initial improvement, it is not uncommon for other problems to crop up in family sessions. The therapist must beware of getting thrown off the track by these difficulties, as they sometimes are introduced to avoid the primary goal of treatment. One approach the therapist can use is to deal with such problems only if the family can justify their relevance to drug-taking; e.g. "He can't get off drugs if he doesn't first have a job to replace them." Should the therapist find himself lost by these side issues, he can always reorient the therapy by returning to the primary symptom. It is important for him to raise the question, "How does this relate to his drug problem?" before the family does.

In instances where drug taking by the addict has recurred, the question of responsibility arises. Who is responsible for his drug use? Often there is a good deal of squirming in response to this question. Conventional drug treatment programs get around it by either taking responsibility themselves or thrusting it on the index patient. However, when seen in a context where addiction serves a clear family function, the conventional view has shortcomings. It should be remembered that the addicted individual was raised by, and in most cases is still being maintained by, his family of origin. It is thus with the family that responsibility rests, and the therapist should help the family either to accept it or to *effectively* disengage from the addict so that he must accept it on his own.

At the suggestion of Jay Haley, we have recently begun to explore a variation on the responsibility theme, in which the family takes charge of the detoxification process in the home. Our aim is to have the family help the addict detoxify "cold turkey." It might be done over a weekend, and preparation with the family is required to anticipate such problems as the addict getting out of the house, a sibling or friend bringing him drugs, parents relaxing their vigilance, etc. "On call" medical and therapeutic backup are available to the family throughout. It appears wise to negotiate a contract beforehand to undertake the process a second time, in case the first attempt fails; if the family members know they might have to go through it twice, they are more likely to succeed the first time. Normally detoxification takes place at the drug treatment center, so if it fails, the family does not feel responsible. However, if family members are themselves involved in the process, they are not going to take subsequent drug use by the addict so lightly. They will be angry with him and may in this way be able to establish appropriate distance from him. In addition, the therapist can use either success or failure of the first attempt to his (and their) advantage. Obviously, a successful home detox has the family doing just what it should do, and getting credit for it, as well. Conversely, failure can serve a disengaging function.

Final Phase

It should be remembered that we are dealing here with a brief-therapy model. One advantage of this model is that it catalyzes and compresses into a time span of three to five months a process which may otherwise be prolonged with questionable effectiveness. The short-term, contractual arrangement forces more rapid change. If the therapist can maintain the family as an ally in this process, it can be quite effective.

Treatment may evolve toward other issues if freedom from drug taking has been maintained for a month or more. Two topics which often arise are gainful employment or schooling and, where appropriate, getting the addict out of the home. Underlying both topics are issues of separation: either physical separation or separation through increased competence and the resulting independence of functioning.

There are a number of ways of dealing with these issues. They can sometimes be approached through the assignment of small, unchallengeable tasks, such as having the addict look up two jobs or two apartments in the classified section of the newspaper. It is ideal for the parents to participate in these tasks, so that they feel some sense of participation in the addict's eventual success. Another approach is to shift the roles of the parents, to, for example, either those of grandparents (rather than overinvolved parents), or of parents to any younger children they might have—"You can let him go because you have these other kids to worry about." Further, if the parents are retired or near retirement, the therapist may want to work with them on planning this stage of their lives.

Another subject which may emerge in later stages is the parents' marriage. If the index patient is stabilized and clean, it may be possible to deal with this. It is crucial to keep the addict from getting involved in the parents' problems once they start to deal with marital issues. In fact, it is rather common for the addict to attempt to reenter their relationship after he has been clean for a while, so the therapist must be prepared to help the parents resist him. If the therapist can orchestrate treatment so that the parents vocally tell their son to stay out of their marital discussion, a reasonable outcome can probably be expected.

Termination difficulties will not generally arise if adequate change has occurred and been maintained long enough for the family to feel a sense of real accomplishment. Otherwise the family will be fearful and may generate crises or other problems in order to keep the therapist involved. In any case, it is probably advisable to space final sessions further apart and perhaps to tentatively arrange for a kind of innoculatory follow-up session two to four months after termination.

Special Issues

There are certain aspects of this treatment which deserve additional discussion. Most of them pervade the total treatment process and have been arrived at through the pain of experience. Although the bulk of the material herein deals with heroin addicts, we do not feel that the principles set forth are necessarily limited only to this group. Heroin addicts are perhaps the most intractable of drug abusers, but our feeling is that if a therapist can be successful with *these* cases, others will be comparatively easy.

Administrative Support and Flexibility

Without clear commitment and support from the administrative arm of the overall drug treatment program, this treatment will flounder and probably fail. It is a truism to say that drug addicts are manipulative, and we have found that changes in administrative procedures are often necessary to plug loopholes and adapt to particular family situations. For example, we encountered instances in which the index patient approached the DDTC medical director to get him to talk to his parents about treatment; this "flanking move" would have succeeded had the medical director not contacted the family therapist and let him take charge of the issue. In another case, the therapist put the father in charge of his son's methadone, so that all raises or decreases were to be cleared with father. Without administrative support, this process could have been undercut and the father's authority nullified.

A similar issue is the amount of control the therapist has over management of the index patient's overall program. When we started our research program, each client had both a drug counselor and a family therapist. With such an arrangement the addict's interpersonal skills surfaced, and he could often succeed in getting his two helpers to struggle over his treatment and their respective turfs; he played them off against each other. We changed this by having the therapist wear both hats—family therapist and drug counselor—thus eliminating the triangulation. It also gave the therapist control over medications by making all changes go through him. This eliminated a lot of undermining and also allowed him to deal with crises more effectively. We do not think this treatment will succeed unless the therapist has such control.[6]

A practice which we would advocate, and which exists in at least 40 drug treatment programs across the country (2), is that of *requiring* the family to come in either at, or immediately after, intake and before any treatment whatsoever begins. In situations where this is practiced, it engenders only a slight increase in dropouts and saves much of the effort expended in recruiting families. If clients know there is no other way to get treatment or methadone without bringing their families in, they can usually find a way to do it.

Urinalysis Results

The results of weekly urine tests have been quite helpful in our family treatment. They give a tangible indication of progress and do not allow family members (or the therapist) to sidestep this issue. They can also serve as aids in getting the family to take responsibility and put pressure on the index patient to remain clean. It usually helps to negotiate the ground rules for failure with the family at the outset of treatment. The idea is to get advance agreement that they will believe the urine tests. If the addict protests that someone has switched or will switch urine samples with him, the therapist should get them to agree on the number of times they will accept this story before they can finally trust the urinalysis results.

Parental-Addict Triad

It has become clear to us that family treatment must first deal with the triad composed of addict and both parents before proceeding further. If this step is skipped, therapy will falter and possibly fail. In some cases with married addicts, we started with the marital pair and found that it only served to strain or dissolve the marriage; thus the addict would end up back with his parents. However, families will differ on the rapidity with which the transition from family of origin to family of procreation can be made. In some cases, the parents can be eased out of the picture within a few sessions, while in others they have to be involved throughout treatment. The key is to start with the parental-addict triad and to move away from it in accordance with parents' readiness to release the addict.

We attempt to include all siblings living at home or in the immediate vicinity. Again, the rule of thumb is to see how family members interact before concluding that any member is not needed in the sessions. Siblings may serve a number of functions in the sessions. They may act as allies to the addict and help to get him to assert himself more appropriately. Often they provide a useful alternative focus and prevent exclusive attention from being given to the addict. It is not unusual to find siblings who are also addicted or have problems as severe as those of the addict. Finally, siblings always provide additional data on family interactions, which the therapist may use to advantage.

Other Systems

It would not be accurate to view our treatment approach as always limited just to the addict and his immediate family. This may be the primary system involved, but other interpersonal systems are also engaged as appropriate. We deal with them if they are particularly relevant to the case and can serve to facilitate or hinder therapeutic progress. Such systems might include friends, important relatives, vocational counselors, employers, school or legal authorities and, of course, the staff of the drug treatment program itself.

Single-Parent Families

Because of the restrictions of our research design, most of our work has been with families in which two adults of different sex were involved, either as parents or in quasiparental roles. In cases where only one parent is available—usually the mother—the process differs somewhat. Here the therapist may have to at least temporarily fill a parental role toward the addict, and at other times, must assume an almost spouselike role toward the parent. Often the latter is a way of substituting for a role which has been played by the addict. The next step is to develop alternative structures and supports for the parent through inclusion of relatives, friends and so on—in other words, to establish or build on the natural support system. In this way the parent will be less dependent on the addict and able to move toward greater disengagement. When applicable, another approach is to help the parent get a job or develop more outside activities. Still another, stated earlier, is to transfer some of the attention from the addict to any younger siblings remaining in the family. Again, joining with the parent is a crucial part of the process, and under no conditions should the therapist become engaged in a direct power struggle with the parent over separation of him/her from the index patient.

Female Addicts

We have worked only with a few families in which the index patient was female. Our impression is that the dynamics are similar in many ways to those for males, as are the therapeutic strategies. However, this is an area that needs further exploration.

Therapists

As a closing note, let us mention some qualities and behaviors in therapists which appear to contribute to successful treatment. The ability to be active is important and is a cornerstone of structural therapy in general. Passive, reflective styles usually do not work well. On the other hand, the therapist must be able to be supportive, concerned, accessible, and enthusiastic. Flexibility is also essential, as drug addicts' families are very skillful and will "trip up" an inflexible therapist. Finally, since these families can be very demanding and draining—especially in a brief-therapy context—we would not recommend that a therapist carry more than three or four such cases at a time, particularly while learning these techniques.

REFERENCES

1. Alexander, B.K. & Dibb, G.S., Opiate Addicts and Their Parents. *Family Process* 14:499–514, 1975.
2. Coleman, S.B., & Stanton, M.D., An Index for Measuring Agency Involvement in Family Therapy. *Family Process* 17:479–483, 1978.
3. Haley, J., *Uncommon Therapy*. New York: Norton, 1973.
4. Haley, J., *Problem-solving Therapy*. San Francisco: Jossey-Bass, 1976.

5. Harbin, H.T. & Maziar, H.M., The Families of Drug Abusers: A Literature Review. *Family Process* 14:411–431, 1975.
6. Klagsbrun, M., & Davis, D.I., Substance Abuse and Family Interaction. *Family Process* 16:149–173, 1977.
7. Minuchin, S., *Families and Family Therapy.* Cambridge, MA: Harvard University Press, 1974.
8. Reilly, D.M., Family Factors in the Etiology and Treatment of Youthful Drug Abuse. *Family Therapy* 2:149–171, 1976.
9. Rosman, B.L., Minuchin, S., Liebman, R., & Baker, L., Input and Outcome of Family Therapy in Anorexia. In J.L. Claghorn (Ed.), *Successful Psychotherapy*, New York: Brunner-Mazel, 1976.
10. Schwartzman, J., The Addict, Abstinence and the Family. *American Journal of Psychiatry* 132:154–157, 1975.
11. Seldin, N.E., The Family of the Addict: A Review of the Literature. *International Journal of the Addictions* 7:79–107, 1972.
12. Stanton, M.D., The Addict as Savior: Heroin, Death and the Family. *Family Process* 16:191–197, 1977.
13. Stanton, M.D., Family Treatment Approaches to Drug Abuse Problems: A Review. *Family Process* 18(3), 1979, in press.
14. Stanton, M.D., Some Outcome Results and Aspects of Structural Family Therapy with Drug Addicts. In D. Smith, S. Anderson, M. Buxton, T. Chung, N. Gottlieb, & W. Harvey (Eds.), *A Multicultural View of Drug Abuse: The Selected Proceedings of The National Drug Abuse Conference—1977.* Cambridge, MA.: Hall/Schenkman, 1978.
15. Stanton, M.D., Drugs and the Family: A Review of the Literature. *Marriage and Family Review* 2(1):1–10, 1979.
16. Stanton, M.D. & Todd, T.C., Structural Family Therapy with Heroin Addicts: Some Outcome Data. Paper presented at the Society for Psychotherapy Research, San Diego, California, June 1976.
17. Stanton, M.D., Todd, T.C., Heard, D.B., Kirschner, S., Kleiman, J.I., Mowatt, D.T., Riley, P., Scott, S.M., & Van Deusen, J.M., Heroin Addiction as a Family Phenomenon: A New Conceptual Model. *American Journal of Drug & Alcohol Abuse* 5:125–150, 1978.
18. Stanton, M.D., & Todd, T.C., Engaging "Resistant" Families in Treatment: II. Some Principles Gained in Recruiting Addict Families. In press.
19. Vaillant, G.E., A 12-year Follow-up of New York Narcotic Addicts: III. Some Social and Psychiatric Characteristics. *Archives of General Psychiatry* 15:599–609, 1966.
20. Van Deusen, J.M., Stanton, M.D., Scott, S.M., Todd, T.C., Engaging "Resistant" Families in Treatment: I. Getting the Drug Addict to Recruit His Family Members. In press.

FOOTNOTES

1. Psychosomatic project staff, besides Minuchin and Todd, included Lester Baker, M.D., Ronald Liebman, M.D., Leroy Milman, M.D., and Bernice Rosman, Ph.D.
2. Members of the PCGC schizophrenia project were Charles Billings, M.D., Harold Cohn, M.D., H. Charles Fishman, M.D., Paul Gross, M.D., David B. Heard, Ph.D., David Hunt, M.D., Gary Lande, M.D., Lawrence Miller, M.D., David T. Mowatt, Ed.D., Lee Petty, M.D., Alberto Rish, M.D., Meyer Rothbart, M.D., and Frances Ziegler, M.S.W.
3. The role of the addict in family homeostasis is elaborated in a recent paper from our project (17).
4. A more detailed presentation, including specific cases, is given in our forthcoming book, *The Family Therapy of Drug Addiction.*
5. Haley, J. *Leaving Home: Therapy with Disturbed Young People,* New York: McGraw-Hill, 1979, in press.
6. Haley has emphasized similar issues in his work with severely disturbed young people, and makes it a general rule only to work with therapists who have overall control of the case.

Family Therapy With Adolescent Substance Abusers

Pauline Kaufmann, M.S.W.
DIRECTOR OF FAMILY THERAPY
PHOENIX FOUNDATION, NEW YORK CITY

The very title of this paper is antithetical to a basic assumption about adolescence. From the more conventional point of view, family therapy for adolescents is contra-indicated. If we assume that adolescence should be the beginning of separation from from the family of origin as part of establishing one's identity, then family therapy runs the risk of antithetically bringing the family closer together.

It is difficult, if not impossible, to separate ourselves from something we have not experienced. For many of the adolescents who have had or are having problems with substance abuse, living in the family has not been a nurturing experience. If we assume that fixation at an early stage of development occurs because of deprivation on the one hand or indulgence on the other, we can understand that many of these adolescents are stuck. They are literally hanging around, mouths open, waiting to be fed. If they are not fed by human means within the context of a familial setting, they will frequently resort to the use of chemicals to give them the illusion that their needs are being met pharmacologically.

It is not surprising that separating these adolescents from their families and placing them in a conventional therapeutic community has not met with much success. The family has demonstrated graphically its problem in dealing with the adolescent's drug abuse and acting out. It is apparent that rehabilitation is not a spontaneous growth process. It is our experience that many adolescents and their families work out their problems and free the adolescent for the completion of his growth tasks when family therapy is an intrinsic part of the total treatment.

Within the structure of a nine-to-six therapeutic community, we see family therapy as the primary treatment modality. New York City, like many large metropolitan areas, has a growing population of young people between the ages of 12 and 18 who are multiple substance abusers. The families they come from have been bombarded by poverty, inadequate housing, disease, unemployment, and the problems of one-parent families.

The adolescent is not only a product of his family's difficulties but frequently of the curriculum of poverty. Part of that curriculum in the inner city consists of early experimentation with drugs and alcohol in an attempt to have some illusion of joy. The family's precarious homeostasis involves every member of the family. The adolescent is frequently scapegoated when he attempts to act out and in any way upset the balance. When these adolescents are admitted to a therapeutic community for drug addicts, they replicate their problems and roles in their family of origin. They find themselves in the role of scapegoat in the therapeutic community, of being isolated and eventually ejected. They go home, and once more the cycle is started. The home is not able to contain them. They often land in the courts, training schools, and holding institutions. At best, they complete this cycle and are out on the streets again around the age of 18, surviving in a way that is destructive to themselves and to the society in which they live.

To have an impact on this problem, we had to have a treatment design that included the total family. This design not only had to take care of the needs of the adolescent within his family, but of the total family within the community. We saw the tasks of the adolescent as being these: attending school, dating, establishing peer relationships, forming trial vocational plans, defining roles and generation boundaries, beginning gradual individuation, and forming new dyadic and triadic relationships within his immediate community. In order for the adolescent to achieve this, we saw the need to restructure the total family, so that recidivism would be curtailed. For the adults in the family, we had to be immediately useful if we were to enlist their aid: we had to provide them with a support system. This was even more mandatory when there was a one-parent family. This support system included various community agencies where they could get adequate housing, monetary assistance, day care for children of working mothers, employment training, and other services. We had certain levers that were extremely useful. The family invariably came to us at a point of crisis. This would be through a court referral when the adolescent had broken the law, from school personnel who found the adolescent "uneducable;" from the family when the acting out of the adolescent had so disrupted family functioning that general anarchy prevailed.

We offered the family an alternate school that was part of the Board of Education school system and where their adolescent could be between 9 and 6, six days a week. The family had to agree to be involved in therapy a minimum of once a week with the total family attending. They also had to agree to be available by telephone in case of emergency or to come in for additional sessions if and when they were indicated. Most families, because of the crisis, were very willing to go along with any of the demands or any part of the contract that we articulated. We had difficulty in some cases when the crisis had abated in getting families to keep their part of the contract. Some of the usual problems were: parents competing with the setting, fear of losing control over the adolescent, some fear—especially in one-parent families—of abandonment by the children, and some need to indicate that their failure was not their fault and that the new setting had to fail also. We undercut much of this by being of continuing usefulness to the parents. When there was a dramatic change in an adolescent's behavior—for instance, if he had been doing well in school and suddenly there was a series of failures—we arbitrarily made the assumption that something was happening at home that was interfering with our student's success. We would call the home and invite the entire family in. Frequently, it took a great deal of planning and support to get the family to come. Without exception, we found our assumption was correct, with a family crisis reflected in the failure of the adolescent or in his acting out within the 9 to 6 environment. We would then institute a series of intensive family sessions. Sometimes we worked with the adults in the family alone, particularly if there were a mother and a father or father-surrogate. If the crisis were such that the adolescent was invariably pulled into the difficulty and could not free himself, we would offer to have the adolescent live in for a short period of time so that the parents would have time to work out their problems. They would have to agree to come at least three times a week until the crisis was resolved. With few exceptions, the family experienced this as giving and helpful, and as evidence of our concern for the parents in the family, as well as the adolescent. We would have the entire family meet before the adolescent was returned to it. Aside from dealing with the particular crisis, much time was spent with parents to help them understand the necessity for restructuring the family. They were supported while they tried out new ways of relating to each other, and helped to set appropriate boundaries between themselves and their children.

A typical family who came to us for help consisted of Debby Marks,[1] age 45, divorced with husband's whereabouts unknown; Carl, her oldest son, age 23; Sam, age 18; and Marcie, the identified patient, age 15. Debby Marks applied to have Marcie admitted to our day treatment program at the point where Marcie had been expelled from her second residential treatment home. Marcie had been considered untreatable by these two residential centers and unmanageable by two foster homes. She had been brought back to court by the social agency and faced the possibility of being sent to a training school. Debby, the mother, was in a state of acute anxiety. She was given an appointment and came in with Marcie. The mother did all the talking. She presented the history of Marcie's stay at various places and kept finding fault with her, alternately crying and yelling. Marcie smoked incessantly during all this, looked at no one, and answered questions belligerently and monosyllabically. The first contact with these two members of the family involved presenting Marcie with her choices and making it clear that the day center was a possibility but had certain basic regulations that she would have to accept as part of the contract. We also made it very clear to Debby that the total family would have to be involved. We took Marcie off the hook by stating that Marcie's behavior was very diffiuclt but the problem was that the entire family was in trouble, and we saw Marcie as only one aspect of that problem. Marcie tried to intervene and use what had been said to fault her mother and her brothers. We suggested very strongly that we end the session and that we have another one the next day with the entire family present.

When the family arrived for the second session, they seated themselves in a manner which was a graphic representation of the relationships and the structure of the family. Mrs. Marks and Carl, age 23, sat together and immediately talked with each other while waiting for the director of the center to join the family therapist and the family. Marcie sat by herself and Sam was the furthest away from the center of the circle that the group formed. Carl tried immediately to take the session over by criticizing Marcie in terms of how much misery she caused her mother. This was interrupted, and we directed ourselves to the mother as the executive of the family. We asked her to tell us how she experienced life at home with her three children. She informed us immediately that Sam was an alcoholic and she needed some help in finding placement for him. Marcie was responsible for her mother's ulcers, she said. She was forever worried about Marcie and could have no life of her own. Marcie had not only been thrown out of every place Debby had taken her, but she had also had an abortion and played around with drugs and alcohol. She smoked incessantly. Carl added that she smoked marijuana most of the time. According to Debby, Carl never gave her a moment of trouble. He ran the house, supervised Marcie when the mother wasn't around, and attended college. Further questioning elicited the information that he was taking one course at a community college and was unemployed. He depended on his mother for whatever money he had. Carl did not date, had no friends, and spent his time looking at television and doing a few tasks around the house. He was obviously a depressed, passive young man.

In a subsequent session we obtained the additional information that Sam was on probation, having been brought to court because he participated in a mugging and stealing in his neighborhood. He had been in a hospital for a short period of time to "dry out." However, he denied being an alcoholic and would not voluntarily become part of any program to deal with his drinking. We felt, and the mother agreed, that Sam needed to be placed in a structured environment where liquor would not be obtainable and where he would have an opportunity to find some satisfaction in living other than drinking.

In these two sessions we had addressed most of our questions to the mother. We were careful to demonstrate that we saw her as the adult in the family who was responsible for making decisions about her two younger children. We addressed Carl directly when it came to his own plans. We had very little success in getting him to look at his life. He obviously saw himself as a parent, and was unwilling to consider playing any other role. In the third session, with the entire family present we began the restructuring that we thought should take place. As a result of our previous work and the discussion in the third session, the family agreed that Marcie would attend the day center from 9 to 6, and go home each night. Sam would be put in a residential treatment house of the same program in a different area so that he would have a chance to deal with his drinking and begin to establish some goals for himself. We posited the idea of a parenting team. At home, Debby was responsible for what happened. In the day center, the team would be responsible for Marcie from nine to six, and would be in communication with Mrs. Marks so that both the home and the day center would have similar limits and goals for Marcie. We would be avaialble to Debby by telephone and by personal contact. The parenting team would consist of Mrs. Marks, the family therapist, the director of the day care center, and the director of the residential treatment center where Sam would be staying.

The treatment team agreed that during the next week Sam would be placed in one of the residential treatment centers of the program, that Marcie would be admitted to the day care program, and that several sessions would be held with the mother alone in an attempt to get her to create workable boundaries between her and Carl so that he could be freed to look for a job or attend school and could begin to form appropriate peer relationships. In the next few weeks the entire family had three stormy sessions around Carl's relationship with his mother and his abuse of his parenting role within the family. The family was helped to restructure its operations. With our help, the mother limited Carl's role in the family. He was seen as having more time than the others and so was given certain duties around the house. He was limited and prevented from acting as a surrogate parent with Marcie and also as the conveyor of information from the siblings to his mother. Mrs. Marks was encouraged and helped to form direct relationships with all of her children, and not to go through Carl when she had something to say to them.

In the ensuing three weeks, the reports from the school on Marcie were very positive, and her interaction within the day center was appropriate. Sam had settled in, had not had a drink and seemed to be working well. Carl still stayed home most of the day and would occasionally try to direct Marcie's activities in the evening. The mother intervened with this and seemed to have a degree of success. At the end of the third week, Carl called to say that his mother was sick with the flu and that the family could not come in. This was checked with Marcie, who said that her mother was indeed sick and that Carl was running the house once more. In the ensuing week Marcie's behavior underwent a dramatic change. She slept during classes, was extremely irritable, fought with her peers in the residence, and was late four out of five mornings in getting to school. Sam seemed not to show any effects from his mother's illness. At the beginning of the fifth week, Mrs. Marks called, in tears. She felt that everything had fallen apart. Marcie and Carl had had a fist fight and had broken furniture. She had been unable to intervene effectively and she was becoming desperate. We scheduled a meeting of the total family for the next day. When they arrived, the old seating arrangment was resumed, with Marcie and Sam on the outside and the mother and Carl together; Debby looked quite ill. She cried during the entire session. She felt that things had been better before and that she just couldn't handle what was happing with Marcie. Carl had been very helpful to her while she was sick and Marcie was back to her old behavior. We pointed out that when Debby became sick, Carl went back to the role that he had played before, and this was impossible for Marcie to accept. We suggested that Marcie move into the residence on a twenty-four hour basis for a limited time until Mrs. Marks felt better. Marcie used this as a way of striking out at her mother and saying that she never wanted to live at home anyway. Thus started again the cycle of mutual faulting, crying, and withdrawal. Once more the therapist intervened and suggested that Marcie do this for herself, that it was important that she continue with the gains that she had made. In the meantime, her mother would have to agree to come in for two sessions by herself and one with Carl. The family agreed. During these sessions, boundaries between the mother and Carl were established once more. Debby agreed to make certain demands on Carl. She also suggested that perhaps it would be better if he went to stay with his maternal grandparents for a while. They wanted him to live with them, and the grandfather was very anxious to have him work in the family construction business. We pursued this further, and Mrs. Marks stated that she had a friend whom Carl objected to her dating and she felt it would be a relief if Carl were out of the house for a while. We encouraged her in this and asked her if she would bring this up and discuss it with Carl when both of the other children were present. She seemed much relieved at this suggestion and said she really wanted to do this. At the final session held with Carl, Marcie, Sam, and their mother, they agreed that Carl would stay with his grandparents and begin to work in the grandfather's business until he was making enough money to live on his own. Marcie would stay in the day care center but would come home each night, and Sam would stay in the residential treatment center. Mrs. Marks brought up her dating. Marcie liked the whole idea, liked the man and thought it was "neat." Sam said it was all right with him. Carl thought it was ridiculous that a woman his mother's age should date. He got very little support from anyone, including the therapist, who suggested that perhaps it would be important for Carl to start his own dating life and that what his mother did would be something that she herself decided. With this support, Mrs. Marks became very definite, saying she had every intention of dating, that it was her own business and that she was very glad that Marcie like the man she was seeing. Marcie returned home after a two-week stay in the residence. The family had been in treatment for six months. The two children, Sam and Marcie, continue to use the facilities. Carl is slowly beginning to move away from home and Debby is still seeing the same man. The mother and Marcie are developing an appropriate relationship. They seem to be enjoying each other, and conflicts that arise are generally able to be resolved through some discussion—if not at the time that they occur, then at least several hours later.

In the treatment of the adolescent substance abuser within the context of the family, we have found certain techniques effective and useful. We have helped the family and the staff to see the therapeutic community as an extension of the home and the home as an extension of the therapeutic community. Thus, any possible manipulation by the adolescent is undercut. This approach is experienced as supportive by the parent or parents. During crises when the acting out of the adolescent overloads the family strucutre, the adolescent is invited to live in at the residence, thus giving the total family a chance to heal and restructure itself. During this period the entire family and/or individuals within the family are seen on an intensive basis. When the crisis is resolved, the adolescent is returned home.

We have found that if we are to be successful, our help to the family must be concrete and immediate. Our efforts frequently concern the economics of the family, housing, schooling, clothing, and other circumstances or problems of everyday living. Our overall goal to restructure the family in such a way that each individual has a chance for optimal development within the family. Thus boundaries between family members are made clear and consistent. Children are helped to have direct access to the adults in the family. Spouse transactions are helped to be clear and unambiguous. Where there is a parenting child, his or her duties are limited and clarified. Coalitions within the family are open and flexible. Boundaries around a marital pair or the heterosexual dating pair are made consistent and delineated. Where there is an extended family, the role and authority of the generations are clarified.

Frequently family therapy ends with a focus on the therapy of the marital pair or the heterosexual pair who are living together or planning to do so.

The family we have presented is part of a day care program entitled Step One of the Phoenix Programs of New York City, now in its third year.[2] One of the project's most dramatic results is the greatly improved educational functioning of the adolescents who are in this program. Ninety percent of the adolescents who come to Step One have a history of school failure. They have been labeled uneducable, emotionally disturbed, delinquent, and truant. Over 70 percent are sent to the courts for delinquent behavior, and the majority of these children come from one-parent families in which the mother is generally present. There are two teachers supplied by the Board of Education for 40 children in two classrooms. The teachers report that they have less than 10 percent truancy and 10 percent lateness. Approximately 90 percent of the students' skills have improved sufficiently so that they will be able to graduate from high school before they reach 18. This is a dramatic contrast with the general achievement of this group within the public school system.

There are a growing number of reports of the failure of large urban school centers in dealing with the inner-city adolescent. Step One, and our experience in this day care setting, may well be a model for a more successful way of educating the troubled adolescent in the large cities. Certainly such a plan, characterized by the following, is economically feasible: having smaller institutions instead of large, expensive, impersonal buildings; 20 children in a class; a school that is open from nine to six with hours when teachers are not there occupied by group activities related to the facility within which the children spend most of their time; a rich recreation program; evening sessions in which parents and children are together in family therapy and family educational sessions. Family and community stresses on the family are frequently reflected in the behavior of the adolescent who is striving for some identity. He is programmed for failure by the very community in which he lives, and frequently his only escape is into a world of fantasy aided by drugs and alcohol. The Phoenix program, although it is limited, has had a degree of success that augurs well for replication within the larger school system.

REFERENCES

1. Kaplen, S.L., Structural Family Therapy for Children of Divorce: Case Reports. *Family Process* 16:75–83, 1977.
2. Minuchin, S., *Families and Family Therapy*, Cambridge, MA: Harvard University Press, 1974.
3. Minuchin, S., Montalvo, B., Guerney, B.G., Jr., Rosman, B.L., & S.Chumer, F., *Families of the Slums*, New York: Basic Books, 1967, pp. 352–378.

4. Narceso, J. & Burkett, D., *Declare Yourself: Discovering the Me in Relationships*, Englewood Cliffs, NJ: Prentice-Hall, 1975.
5. Sager, C.J., *Marriage Contracts and Couple Therapy*, New York: Brunner/Mazel, 1976.
6. Sager, C.J. & Kaplan, H., *Progress in Group and Family Therapy*, New York: Brunner/Mazel, 1972.
7. Wairond-Skinner, S., *Family Therapy: The Treatment of Natural Systems*, London: Henley and Boston, 1976.

FOOTNOTES

1. All names have been changed to preserve anonymity.
2. This project operates under NIMH grant #1 H80 MH 01049.

Multiple Family Therapy with Drug Abusers*

Edward Kaufman, M.D.
ASSOCIATE CLINICAL PROFESSOR OF PSYCHIATRY
CHIEF, PSYCHIATRIC SERVICES,
DIRECTOR OF FAMILY THERAPY PROGRAMS
UNIVERSITY OF CALIFORNIA, IRVINE MEDICAL CENTER
ORANGE, CALIFORNIA

Pauline Kaufmann, M.S.W.
DIRECTOR OF FAMILY THERAPY
PHOENIX FOUNDATION
CONSULTANT, FAMILY THERAPY
BELLVUE HOSPITAL SOCIAL SERVICE DEPARTMENT

Multiple family therapy (MFT) is a technique which is particularly useful and applicable to drug abusers and their families. This type of therapy can be used in any treatment setting for drug abusers, but is most successful in residential settings where the family is more available and accessible. MFT was initiated as a modality by Laqueur (6) in an inpatient unit of a state hospital but as used by the authors, it has many other roots. These include social network intervention (13), multiple impact therapy (12), the ward or town meeting concept of both the psychiatric and Synanon modes of the therapeutic community, and a host of group and family therapy techniques. Group techniques run the gamut from psychoanalytic through psychodramatic, existential, gestalt and encounter. Family techniques include sculpting or choreography (10), structural (8), and systems (3). All of these are described in detail in other chapters of this book.

Group Composition and Environment

The greater the motivation and involvement of the patient, the easier it

---

*Based on material included in Multiple Family Therapy: A New Direction in the Treatment of Drug Abusers. *American Journal of Drug and Alcohol Abuse*, 1977, *4* (*4*), 467–478 and the 1974, 1975, 1976, 1977, 1978 National Drug Abuse Conferences.

is to initiate the family into therapy, particularly in MFT. Thus it is extremely difficult to generate MFT in low intervention programs such as most methadone maintenance programs or outpatient psychotherapy clinics. It becomes progressively easier to do so in day programs and inpatient settings. However, the setting which most readily lends itself to the establishment and continuance of a successful MFT group is a residential therapeutic community (TC). One reason that families come to groups in this setting is that they may be required to do so if they are to visit the resident. Also, since the identified patient (IP) is now drug-free for the first time in years, he or she can be related to without chaos and with trust and warmth. It is best to have the IP invite the family to come in, but the therapist may send a form letter or call. The last may be necessary in order to involve a reluctant family or family member.

One of the authors recently finished four years' work with a patient in a methadone maintenance treatment program (MMTP). Therapy was unsuccessful despite the use of an ancillary mental health clinic and several group psychotherapy experiences. During this time the patient consistently refused to have his mother or any family member involved in treatment, although he lived with his mother throughout the treatment. Federal guidelines about confidentiality, particularly as they are applied to MMTP, and a noncoercive attitude on the part of the New York City agency sponsoring the treatment, prohibited insisting that the family be involved. Finally, after several drug overdoses and detoxifications, the patient agreed to enter a therapeutic community. After two weeks in residence, the patient and his family appeared at the first MFT to which they were invited. The mother's crucial role in treatment was immediately apparent. However, two involved aunts and an older brother, none of whom had ever been mentioned previously, attended regularly. This extended family was found to be necessary for restructuring the family system and changing this difficult patient.

In a residence the group may be composed of all of the families in the TC or separated into several groups of three or four closely matched families. Our experience is with the former, partly because there is a lack of primary therapists, as well as because we view the group of families as one community.

There are generally as many as 40 to 50 individuals in the weekly multiple family group, including 10 to 15 families. The group includes identified patients and their immediate families as well as any relatives who have an impact on the family. Friends and lovers are included if they are an important part of the addict's network and are drug-free. If they are abusing drugs or alcohol, they are excluded from the group until they can control this symptom, which is disruptive or destructive to the group. When there are no rigid guidelines about excluding family members and friends, a good deal of meaningful material is produced. One client's drug-abusing boy-friend arrived with his "only drug-free friend," who happened to be the client's former husband. Although she was able to ask them to leave before the group began, the feelings which were stirred up between her and her ex-husband recreated old unresolved problems which were dealt with in MFT. Families should be oriented and interviewed prior to entering the group. A genogram can be made and a family map begun during the initial eval-uation. Once it becomes apparent in the group that a troubled family re-quires them, individual family sessions are provided. Some family secrets may have to stay within the family, but generally participants are encour-aged to bring the content of these individual sessions into the multiple fam-ily group, as this remains the primary modality of family therapy. An experienced family therapist works with counselors in the program as coth-erapists. The total group frequently functions as adjunctive family thera-pists. Usually family members take their cues from primary therapists and will be approriately confronting, reassuring, and supportive. At times the family's own needs prevent this, and their anger at their child or their pos-sessiveness will spill over to all the former addicts in the group. Families share experiences and offer help by acting as extended families both to each other and to the residents outside the time they spend together in therapy. Residents who accompany each other on visits serve as supports in the home and behavioral reporters in MFT groups. Supporting residents may help the IPs with their family "homework" on visits as well as in the MFT.

The group is seated in a large circle with cotherapists distributed at equal distances to provide observation of the total group. We do not use a "fish bowl" with the primary family in the center of the group because this discourages the participation and identification of the other families. Fami-lies sit together, and their seating arrangements are carefully observed, as they usually follow structural patterns. They may be asked to separate if there is a great deal of whispering or disruption. The group begins with ev-eryone introducing himself, giving name and role. A group member will de-scribe the purpose of the group, generally stressing the need for families to communicate honestly and to express their feelings openly. At times this description emphasizes the importance of understanding and changing the familial forces which have led to drug abuse. The first family is frequently worked with for about an hour.

The conflicts focused on set the emotional tone and influence the topics discussed in the entire group. Many other families will identify with these conflicts, express feelings, offer support, and work on similar conflicts. Gen-erally three or four families are worked with intensively in a night. Almost all families participate verbally, and usually all families are emotionally involved.

The informal contacts which take place before and after group are crucial. Therapists should mingle and interact during these pre- and post-group sessions. Many pre-session contacts are excellent grist for the therapeutic mill. Post-group interaction may either confirm insights and validate feelings or undermine therapeutic work if it is not monitored. Families of "splittees" are encouraged to continue to attend to maintain their structural shifts and to facilitate the IP's return to treatment.

The Therapeutic Team

A prerequisite for the therapeutic team is a primary therapist who is experienced in group and family therapy and comfortable in large groups. There must also be several cotherapists who are an integral part of the treatment program and can provide feedback from the group to the program and input from the program to the group. The group should be used to train counselors in the dynamics of families and the techniques of family therapy. All too frequently, younger counselors in TCs tend to overidentify with their client's hostility to parents because of their own conflicts. Similarly, counselors who are themselves parents may overidentify with the parental system. Thus, counselors should have supplementary training experiences which focus on their own family of origin. Counselors should also have supplementary didactic courses and assigned readings, particularly if they are to become primary therapists. Cotherapists should work together as a team which agrees to disagree so that there is a unity which allows room for individual differences. This provides a role model for a parental system which is unified but not rigid.

Speck (13) has cited qualities of a good network leader which are also important in an MFT primary therapist. "A sense of timing, empathy with emotional high-points, a sense of group moods and undercurrents and some charismatic presence... along with the ability to dominate, the leader must have the confidence that comes with considerable experience... the ability to efface himself, to delegate and diffuse responsibility... rather than collect it for himself." The role of the MFT therapist, like the network leader, is similar to that of the good theatrical director, but with a greater concern for the therapeutic than the dramatic. Interestingly, Papp (11) also emphasizes the therapeutic aspects of theatricality in MFT, particularly as seen in sculpting. "True theatre strips aways superficiality to the bare bones of meaning, reveals a hidden truth, shares a universal experience." Minuchin (9) also notes that the therapist functions "like the director of a play, setting the stage, creating a scenario, assigning a task and requiring the family members to function within the new sets that he has imposed."

MFT is a stimulating and rejuvenating experience for the therapist and treatment program as well as the family. The therapist becomes the paternal and/or maternal figure for a host of families who become a single family network and, in many ways, a single family. The therapist assumes temporary parental control of all of these families at the same time as he or she is the child of all of them. Thus the therapist gives and takes in a multitude of parental and childlike roles. At the same time the therapist must step away from this emotional entanglement and be objective. A therapist may even say to his cotherapists and the group, "I am going to join this family system to experience it. Pull me out if I'm getting too involved." The primary therapist must always keep in mind that one of his primary functions is to be considered a supportive ally by every member of the group. He must also feel capable of and correct in interrupting any communication which is destructive or disruptive.

Family Dynamics and Techniques

These will be discussed in detail in other chapters of this book. Only those dynamics and techniques which are most applicable to MFT will be discussed here. Generally those techniques which are most familiar to the treatment system are most readily used in MFT. Thus in MFTs and TCs, confrontation and encounter are used in the service of structural changes. The therapist must join the treatment system as a whole as well as each family. New techniques can be gradually introduced to MFT and thence to the overall program, or vice versa.

In the early phases of treatment, the families support each other by expressing the pain they have experienced in having a drug abuser in the family. The family's sense of loneliness and isolation in dealing with this major crisis is greatly attenuated by sharing the burden with other families. The means by which the family has been manipulated are quite similar and form the beginning of a common bond. The addict son or daughter has lied to and stolen from his or her family. Many families have given the addict money for his habit to keep him from stealing and risking incarceration. Group members express commiseration for the family's suffering. The family is strongly encouraged not to repeat this pattern. The family learns to see its covert hostile aspects rather than its apparent benevolent ones. Many addicts who have difficulty with the demands of a TC will try to convince their families to take them back once again and protect them from its "evils," just as the families had protected them from jail. Intervening in this system helps prevent many from quitting the group early on. We call this "closing the back door." Many families are able to do this merely through group support. Others must learn to recognize and reduce the addict's ways of provoking guilt and enmeshing them in his problems before they can close the door to the cycle of symbiotic reinvolvement. An initial period of ventilation of anger and resentment may be necessary before strategies for change can be introduced. An atmosphere is created in which all families are encouraged to be open and express everything about everyone. This does not give the family permission to hurt sadistically under the guise of honesty.

The giving of food may be utilized as an important family transaction. Food may also be limited gifts to the entire group. This helps create a sense of the group as one family. It may also alleviate the families' guilt and permit them to gratify their need to give without "infantilizing" the IP.

As the therapy progresses, the role of the family in producing and perpetuating the abuse of drugs is identified. Patterns of mutual manipulation, extraction, and coercion are identified and negated. The family's need to perpetuate the addict's dependent behavior through scapegoating, distancing, protection, or infantilization is discouraged, and new methods of relating are tried and encouraged. Families tend to feel guilty when the addict confronts them with their role in the addiction cycle. This has occurred in the home and reoccurs in the early phases of multiple family therapy. If the therapist does not intervene, the family will retaliate by inducing guilt or undermining growth, and may ultimately pull the addict out of treatment. Drug dependence is viewed as a family problem in which there can be no scapegoats. Parents must be given a great deal of support in family sessions because of their own guilt and the tendency of patients and even counselors to attack them. For some parents, even the admission in public that there is a family problem leads to shame and reactive hostility. Such parents require individual family therapy sessions where they can receive individual support. When they can overcome their embarrassment about expressing feelings in "the public" of the group, they have taken a valuable step toward the overt expression of feelings in general. Counselors in the program and families frequently lead the group away from working with the family system to the IP and his problems in the TC. When this occurs the group must be refocused on the family program. Counselors will often similarly focus on other individual drug-abusing family members and should be helped in redirecting the focus to the family system. Frequently material is revealed in MFT which could lead to severe setbacks and punishments for residents. It is important that the family therapist have input into the program's use of such disciplines lest they undermine the family therapy or recreate destructive family patterns within the program.

Multiple family therapy groups help residents actualize insights about their family which they have achieved in their own therapy. Many families learn to express love and anger directly for the first time in these groups. Deep emotional pain is expressed when appropriate, and other family members are encouraged to give support to such expressions rather than nullify or deny them. Frequently the entire group is in tears or applauds appreciatively. Kissing, hugging, and rocking are ways that families tend to obliterate pain under the guise of giving comfort. In situations where families are emotionally isolated, encouraging the mutual exchange of physical affection is helpful.

The identified patient acts as the barometer of the functioning of the total family. When his behavior becomes maladaptive or disruptive, it is assumed that the family is under increased stress and may be reverting to former destructive patterns. This is particularly true in adolescent day programs when there is frequent parental contact. The identified patient's behavior is viewed as part of the family stress at the same time as it is handled as his individual responsibility by his peers in encounter groups within the TC. As an extension of the TC, peers can be quite supportive of each other yet hold each other responsible and challenge each other more effectively than can adults. Therapeutic homework is frequently assigned to reinforce the family's structural changes. Not only are family tasks assigned, but different family roles are also allotted in restructuring the family. Weak ties between family members are strengthened by either suggesting joint activities which build closeness and/or identifying the fears and patterns which have led to weak ties. Strengthening such ties will diminish other enmeshed ones. Overwhelming family members may be asked not to attend sessions for several weeks to strengthen other ties. The family pain at having an addicted member can be used to motivate overinvolved family members to begin to separate.

Any number of other therapeutic strategies may be useful in restructuring the family. Much will depend on the individual therapist's style. We consistently focus on dysfunctional communications. We delineate individual boundaries by not permitting family members to speak or feel for each other. We point out nonverbal coercive communications which tend to overwhelm family members, inhibit expressiveness, or produce double binds. We ask that messages be stated clearly with underlying meanings made explicit. We also assign tasks to family members to promote individuation. It is most important for mothers who are single parents to find pleasure in their own lives and for couples to learn or relearn to enjoy each other. Frequently grandparents must be brought in and intergenerational patterns demonstrated before parents can change. Interpretations which simultaneously focus on the responsibility of both parties are effective and diminish guilt provocation and scapegoating. they also help maintain the therapist's position as an ally of every family member.

We have found that psychodramas dealing with negotiation and·resolution of disagreements, formation of positive subgroups, changing communication styles, teaching verbalization of anger, affection, or friendship, are all helpful in changing the dysfunctional system. The "empty chair" technique can be used to tap deep feelings—generally anger at the withdrawl of the member or anguish at loss—about family members who are not present. Family sculpture (10) is a technique which is very valuable in MFT with drug abusers. Its use with alcoholics is described in detail elsewhere in this book.

In the latter phases of MFT, families express intense repressed mourning responses which are essential to a healthy family adaptation. Feelings about a sibling who has died from an overdose come out most easily. In still later phases a lost parent can be mourned. Family secrets and myths are also revealed in the later phases of MFT. When anxiety stirred up by early shifts has been resolved, more advanced tasks can be assigned. In the final phases, the family and IP are separated from the group.

A knowledge of the specific dynamics of a family permits further "family" therapy with the individual alone and also provides crucial material for individual and group therapy. Frequently we learn of the resident's overwhelming anger toward a parent. At times it is obvious that this anger is too destructive to be expressed in the presence of the parent, even in a moderate way. The resident is then encouraged to express the anger in his own therapy before expressing it to his family.

Videotape can also be used to confront family members with emotions which are denied. By repeated replays it is possible to have family members recognize such patterns as guilt induction and infantilization through enmeshing affection and denigration. Videotapes of MFT are excellent teaching devices and are available from the author.

As noted earlier, families in MFT act as supports for each other outside the session, and may continue to do so after therapy has been terminated. These families frequently replace the entire network of the addict with a new, therapeutic one.

Sample Group

We would like to describe a typical multiple family therapy session to illustrate these family dynamics and therapy techniques.

The ten families and three therapists were grouped in a circle which included over 40 individuals. The group began with everyone introducing himself by stating his name and role in the group. A group member was asked to describe the purpose of the group. He emphasized communication and confrontation of feelings. In this group, four families were worked with intensively, but the remaining families identified strongly with them.

The first family worked with consisted of the identified patient (IP), a 27-year-old Italian male, his older brother, mother, father, and wife. The mother dominated the family and their communications. The father was crippled and unable to work so that the mother has assumed the financial support of the family. It emerged that the father did not take care of his physical health because of his worry over his addict son. The group then pressured the father to make a dental appointment, and when he was vague, they exerted pressure on him to make a commitment, which he did. The son experienced his guilt and began to cry, stating that he still needed his father. His mother cried in response to her son's tears and the three of them embraced. We learned that the IP, his wife, and son ate most of their meals at the mother's house prior to treatment. They were continuing this pattern on weekend passes and the wife and child were eating their meals there during the week. The wife and child were given the task of eating most meals at home during the week and the nuclear family was asked to eat in its own home three out of four weekends. The mother and father readily agreed to reinforce this individuation. The IP and his wife embraced, bringing tears to the eyes of most group members.

The next family on which we focused consisted of a 23-year-old resident, his mother, and father. This family was also Italian, as were two others. (One cotherapist was Sicilian.) We worked with them to consolidate an insight from a previous session. They had devastatingly insulted their son and denied doing so. They had been shown the sequence on videotape to break through their denial. They accepted that they had devastated him and in getting in touch with their anger at him, they were able to refrain from putting him down in this session. The group also pressured them to involve their drug-abusing daughter in therapy.

A third family consisted of the identified patient, a 34-year-old Irish male, a younger sister and brother. The mother had been quite active in MFT but did not attend this session because the family had moved away. The father had never been present but was frequently discussed because of his pattern of severe withdrawal. The father had not left his bedroom in three years and never came out when his son visited. In this session the son realized how much he had identified with his father's emotional isolation, even to a point of duplicating his posture. He was helped to recognize and experience this rigid control system. His anger toward his father would be a subject for future group work. He also realized how he had attempted to be a father to his younger siblings to the point of neglecting his own needs. The sister reached out to him and partially broke through his isolation with her poignant plea. Another resident who was attending the group with his mother identified heavily and sobbed about not being closer to his own sister. He was asked to talk to the first resident's sister as if she were his own. In doing so, he reached a deep level of yearning and anguish. His mother reached out to him and began to rock him. To diminish the infantilization, the therapist asked the mother to not rock him. Freed from his mother, he was able to sob heavily about missing his sister and his guilt in pushing her away. We returned to the Irish family, but were still unable to break through the IPs emotional isolation. It was pointed out that it was difficult for him to express feelings because of his identification with his father and his need to stay the big brother who had no weaknesses.

Discussion

We would like to summarize the literature on MFT which has influenced our work, and discuss it in the context of our experience. Laqueur's (6) objectives with schizophrenics are identical to our own with drug abusers i.e. "improvement of communication between all members of the family and achievement of better understanding of the reasons for their disturbing behavior toward each other." Laqueur reminds us that MFT "affords the families an opportunity to learn from each other indirectly, through analogy, indirect interpretation, mimicking and identification"; thus "the resources of all family members tend to be exploited more successfully when several families are treated together in one group than when each family is treated as a separate entity." He points out that schizophrenics (like drug addicts) are helped to transfer the energies of early symbiotic relationships to external objects in such groups. Laqueur emphasizes how important it is for the therapist not to be caught up in the multiple double binds set up by patients and parents in order to demonstrate that emotional distance from these patterns can be developed; thus the therapist is a role model for individuation. Likewise the IP may identify with another individuating family member and separate with much less anxiety than is usually associated with such learning.

Leichter and Schulman (7) conduct MFT in an outpatient setting and, like Laqueur, choose three to four families in a manner that creates a homogeneous yet balanced group. They insist that the entire nuclear family be included, and have at times expanded the group to include the extended kinship where relevant, i.e. grandparents or divorced spouses. They cite types of families for whom MFT is preferable to working with one family. Such families include those who are isolated or whose system is circulatory and rigidified, especially when symbiotic. MFT is also helpful when there is a missing parent (usually the father), since the group provides parental substitutes. Leichter and Schulman also have found that particular dynamics lend themselves to resolution in MFT. Reality testing is strengthened as distortions within a family are readily apparent to other group members, who point them out in a manner which is readily accepted. In turn, others can correct the reality of their own family. Likewise, transferences to nonfamily members in the group can be traced to the person's own family. The degree of distortion can be quickly pointed out as the person who has caused overreaction is present in the group in his own reality. Another goal in these groups is to bridge intergenerational alienation and isolation through experiencing the universality of human needs and emotions. Adults can provide conflict-free parenting to the children of others in MFT, and parents and children alike can gratify their own need to be parented. The unreality of the "good" child in the family can be pointed out, as can the price such a child pays for this position in the family. At times even the addict can be the "good child." In general it is easy for one family to perceive another family's malfunctioning, learn to think in such terms, and then apply their new thinking to their own family. Leichter and Schulman (7) note that MFT provides a particularly fertile ground for the emergence of spontaneous and unexpected attitudes and insights" which occur almost as a "byproduct" of ongoing processes.

Papp (11) has learned that "hopeless" families do better in groups. After six months of trying to match families, she assembled a group composed of the last three families in a waiting list. Thus she "learned by default that there are no barriers of race, religion, culture, education, psychiatric diagnosis, politics or prejudice which cannot be transcended in a group and used to therapeutic advantage." Papp's pioneering use of sculpting has been very helpful to these authors and is quite useful in MFT. Family sculpting, or choreography as she later termed it, can transform a group from an inhibited, intellectualized, or anxious rambling body into an "active, alive, highly involved, purposely focused entity."

The literature on the specific use of MFT with drug abusers is quite sparse. A very early paper was written by Hirsch (5), which discussed a therapy group composed of parents of adolescent drug abusers at the Riverside Hospital in 1958. This group did not include complete families, but these parents were encouraged to share their mutual difficulties. Since 1958, parent groups which excluded the addicted child have not been uncommon, particularly in therapeutic communities. We have not found that including the total family in any way reinforces unwholesome defenses or leads to a deterioration of communication. However, these parent groups have been more educational than therapeutic and have not dealt with resolutions of underlying conflicts. Berger (2) and Bartlett (1) have led MFTs with addict families. Berger's groups met only monthly in association with the therapeutic community of the Quaker Committee on Social Rehabilitation in New York City. His groups had a code in which they sought to elicit truth in order to examine the past and present without blaming or provoking guilt. They focused on patterns which contribute to self-hate and hurting oneself by hurting one's parents. Another emphasis is on those nonverbal behaviors of members who are not initially aware. They become conscious of them through the observations, interpretations, and reactions of others. Berger also uniquely focuses on "crisis creators," "help rejecting complainers," preachers, and placaters. A small family group within the larger group is used, with two residents assigned as advocates of the "truth," one for the family and one for the resident.

Bartlett (1) writes of an MFT on a detoxification ward; this group is of necessity short term. In the first session or two, the family denies underlying problems. By the third group the therapist confronts the family with its behavior and underlying dynamics and structure, particularly stressing the family member as "pusher" and the addict roles as scapegoat, interpreter, go-between, and emotion-supplier. In the fourth through sixth sessions, it is decided that a treatment plan will be implemented. This is obviously not a simple decision, and underlying issues such as assertions of parental authority and the addict's power to maintain anxiety in others must be dealt with. The therapist supports the parents' capacity to exert change in their own home and accept the hypothesis "that change is possible."

Bartlett (1) reports a follow-up study of a group of seven families treated by Kaufman in which 5 patients remained drug-free a year after termination, and no siblings became addicted. A later study by Kaufmann showed that of a group of 45 adolescent substance abusers at Phoenix House, the rate of recidivism after twelve to eighteen months of treatment was over 50 percent. When the entire family had been part of treatment in another group of 45, the recidivism rate dropped to 20 percent. Recidivism was evaluated by a one-hour indepth interview with the family in addiction to a cross-check with school and/or employment. Hendricks (4) compared a group of male narcotic addicts who received multifamily counseling with a control group who did not. He found that one year after release, 41 percent of the treatment group remained in outpatient status compared to 21 percent of all male outpatients.

Our belief is that drug addiction is a symptom of family stress exacerbated by societal stress. We are primarily involved with the forces in the family that produce and maintain the symptom, as well as those forces within the therapeutic community that serve to maintain these symptoms. The staff and residents constitute their own family system. These also can be dealt with in ways that are similar to those used to deal with family dysfunction. The MFT group frequently acts as a barometer which reveals the overall functioning of the TC and underlines problems or cohesion in the TC family.

Middle-class families, particularly Italian, Greek, Irish, and Jewish, tend to be quite enmeshed. Puerto Rican and black mothers tend to be over-involved with sons who are drug addicts. These family structures are described in detail in Chapter 3. Enmeshed families tend to be the ones that come regularly to therapy, and distanced families come rarely, if ever. Thus in MFT it appears that most, if not all, families of addicts are enmeshed. The multitude of cultures and languages in our families is frequently bridged by the universal aspects of the problems, but it also presents many difficulties despite the use of therapists from several ethnic groups.

In some cases, distance between family members is a necessary goal. In many families the goal is a restoration of the family homeostasis. Certainly an intact family of origin with appropriate mutuality is curative and can prevent drug abuse. Similarly, so is a healthy nuclear family composed of the addict, nondrug-abusing spouse, and their own children.

Multiple family therapy is unique in contemporary society in that families expose themselves to one another and try to have a significant effect on each others' way of life. MFT enriches and stimulates the totality of any therapeutic program which utilizes this technique.

In our experience MFT reduces the incidence of premature dropouts, acts as a preventive measure for other family members, builds a subculture that acts as an extended "good family," and creates and supports structural family changes which interdict the return of drug abuse.

REFERENCES

1. Bartlett, D., The Use of Multiple Family Therapy Groups with Adolescent Drug Addicts. In M. Sugar (Ed.), *The Adolescent in Group and Family Therapy*, New York: Brunner/Mazel, 1975, pp. 262–282.
2. Berger, M.M., Multifamily Psychosocial Group Treatment with Addicts and Their Families. *Group Process* 5:31–45, 1973.
3. Fogarty, T., Evolution of a Systems Thinker. *The Family* 1:26–43, 1974.
4. Hendricks, W.J., Use of Multifamily Counseling Groups in Treatment of Male Narcotic Addicts. *Intern'l. J. Group Psychotherapy* 21:34–90, 1971.
5. Hirsch, R., Group Therapy with Parents of Adolescent Drug Addicts. *Psychiatric Quarterly* 35:702–710, 1961.
6. Laqueur, H.P., La Burt, H.A., & Morong, E., Multiple Family Therapy: Further Developments. In J. Haley (Ed.), *Changing Families*, New York: Grune & Stratton, 1971, pp. 82–95.
7. Leichter, E. & Schulman, G.L., Multi-family Group Therapy: A Multidimensional Approach. *Family Process* 13:95–110, 1974.
8. Minuchin, S., *Families and Family Therapy*, Cambridge, MA: Harvard University Press, 1974.
9. Minuchin, S., Structural Family Therapy. In S. Arieti (Ed.), *American Handbook of Psychiatry* (Vol. 2), New York: Basic Books, 1974, pp. 178–192.
10. Papp, P., Sculpting the Family. *The Family* 1:44–48, 1973.
11. Papp, P., Multiple Ways of Multiple Family Therapists. *The Family* 1:25, 1974.
12. Ritchie, A., Multiple Impact Therapy: An Experiment. In J. Haley (Ed.), *Chaning Families* New York: Grune & Stratton, 1971, pp. 36–44.
13. Speck, R.V. & Attneave, C.L., Social Network Intervention. In J. Haley (ed.), *Changing Families* New York: Grune & Stratton, 1971, pp. 312–332.

From Multiple Family Therapy to Couples Therapy

Pauline N. Kaufmann, M.S.W.
DIRECTOR OF FAMILY THERAPY
PHOENIX FOUNDATION
CONSULTANT IN FAMILY THERAPY
BELLVUE HOSPITAL SOCIAL SERVICE DEPARTMENT

Edward Kaufman, M.D.
ASSOCIATE CLINICAL PROFESSOR OF PSYCHIATRY
CHIEF, PSYCHIATRIC SERVICES,
DIRECTOR OF FAMILY THERAPY PROGRAMS
UNIVERSITY OF CALIFORNIA, IRVINE MEDICAL CENTER
ORANGE, CALIFORNIA

The literature of family therapy is replete with stereotyped assumptions that lose their usefulness when they become dogma. For example:

1) The identified patient is the symptom carrier for the total family. (Why not the family as the symptom deliverer?)
2) The identified patient helps maintain the family homeostasis (a destructive one at best, so why maintain it?).
3) The identified patient must solve his problems within the family context.

We have found that the health of the family is directly related to the quality of the relationship between the authoritative adults in the family.

Our experience has been in a day care treatment center for adolescent drug abusers[1] and in two residential settings for adults[2]. Our interest is in the detoxification of the entire family and the return of the previously addicted client to his or her family and community.

Couples who were part of our multiple family therapy groups began to ask for couples sessions. The frequently stated rationale was that they had problems that related only to the couple and could not be resolved with adolescents present. A number of couples had difficulty assuming responsibility for the family's dysfunction with the children present.

With the adult addicts, a primary focus was frequently on the couple relationship between the addict and spouse or potential spouse.

Su Casa and The Family have been described elsewhere in this book. The Phoenix Foundation's House Center has a population of 45 adolescents ranging in age from 11 to 17. The center operates six days a week from nine to five. A school program manned by the New York City Board of Education is an integral part of the day-care program. Approximately 2/3 of the population is male. Sixty percent are black, 25 percent, Hispanic, and 15 percent, white. Many of the adolescents are on probation and sent to us by the court. They are referred because of truancy, petty theft, and possession of narcotics. Frequently they come to us under a Petition for Persons in Need of Supervision. A smaller number of adolescents are brought by their parents after they have been expelled from school because of violence in the classroom, gross infractions of rules and possession of dangerous weapons.

Contact is generally initiated by the mother's telephone call. At the time of the initial contact, the parents are usually in a state of crisis. They feel they have nowhere to turn and are ready to accept any kind of help that is offered. We make it clear that the first appointment must be attended by both parents or parental surrogates as well as all the siblings living in the house. If there is a grandparent or relative living in the house, we insist that he or she come too. In this first interview, the family is encouraged to talk about the problem of the identified patient, his abuse of drugs and subsequent delinquent behavior. No other information is deemed important. The operation of the day center is explained. It is made very clear that the identified patient will not be accepted unless the parents are an integral part of treatment. We require that they be available by telephone and that they contact us when regulations at home or school are broken. Also the parents must attend multiple family therapy once a week at the center with their other children as well as the identified patient. School Attendance is stressed, with the parents held responsible for getting their child to school on time. The school notifies parents whenever a student is late or does not come to school. It is the parents' job to see that the school is notified in case of illness or any other problem that may keep the identified patient from attending school. The therapists are supportive and reassuring to the family. We tell them that as long as parents are involved in the program, take responsibility for coming to all the family therapy groups, and seeing that their son or daughter attends school, there is usually no recurrence of ongoing destructive behavior. Most parents, perhaps because of the crisis they have been through, agree to participate actively in the program. Generally we find that their enthusiasm tends to diminish as their son or daughter begins to fit into the program. At this point we call a family meeting and once more reinforce the terms of the contract. We make it quite clear that we cannot help their child unless the parents participate actively in the program. Usually it takes one or two such reminders. On rare occasions, the student is expelled until he can come back with his parents. This has been done when there was no other way of getting the parents to attend family therapy sessions.

These sessions are open-ended multiple family therapy groups. Parents are assigned to one of the two existing groups as their child is accepted into the program. The new family introduces itself to the group and states its reason for being there. Within a very short time, group members who have been in family therapy for a while orient the new parents. An entire social network is created by the group. It is used for socializing and support, as well as sharing sources of information with the new members. In the beginning, all discussion is related to the problem of the drug-abusing identified patient (IP). Thus, the spouse system is looked at from the IP's vantage point, as is the sibling subsystem; generational boundaries, as well as alliances within the family, are examined from this same focus.

It is not unusual to have a student do very well in the first two or three months and then lose all interest in the program and begin to be late and cut classes. When this happens, we assume that something has gone awry in the family, and call the parents in for an individual session. We generally discover that there has been a crisis in the relationship of the marital pair or the parental surrogates, and the identified patient has been used as the battlefield. If this is the case, we will suggest that our student become a twenty-four hour resident for a week or two, at most, and that the parents receive intensive couple therapy until the crisis is resolved. When the parents think they are ready, we have a final session with all the siblings and our resident, and once more restate the terms of our initial contract. We find that by taking the student out of the house, the parents become available for working on their relationship, so that treatment of the total family can continue.

As the family continues to attend the multiple family sessions, the parents and the children become assistant therapists for the new families coming in. This is generally the point at which drug abuse is no longer the problem for the identified patient, and other siblings in the family are doing well. Up until this point, the group has been concerned with the problem of drug abuse. When other matters have been introduced, they have been related to the central problem. When the presenting problem of drug abuse and school attendance have been resolved, the content of multiple family therapy sessions concerns marital problems. It is at this point that parents are invited to the couples group and leave the multiple family therapy group. In the couples group procedures are reversed. Couples may not speak about their children; they must focus on the relationship between themselves. If material is brought up about the children, it is allowed only if it is relevant to the problems the couple are having. Invariably, three issues are discussed: money, sex, and intimacy.

Generally money, particularly its use as a power ploy, is the first problem to be discussed. It is the easiest issue on which to focus. Many of these couples have had little or no experience in the lover-spouse role. Their courting rarely lasts very long; sometimes it never existed at all. It is not unusual to see people who have been married twenty years or longer evince a great deal of shyness in the group. They are encouraged by other group members to touch, hold hands, and set up "dates" when they go out together. Much of this is a learning situation, and couples frequently are uncomfortable during this phase.

In a number of cases, the husband or the lover, when he has become angry and frustrated, has beaten his mate. This is noted, but not specifically examined. Instead the group helps the couple "exhume" tender feelings that may have existed but have been buried in the family strife. Couples are taught how to fight creatively in the present rather than relive past conflicts, and how to go about resolving problems. The more experienced group members encourage the others to talk about their sexual life. For many couples, sex has become an abortive experience and a source of pain rather than pleasure.

A number of divorced parents have attended the couples group with their new husband, wife, or lover. When this occurs, the divorce becomes a reality during the group experience, and both parents are free to make a more lasting commitment to their new partners. As the couples begin to get pleasure from their own relationship, the use of the children as a battlefield diminishes. The couples are able to solve their problems between themselves. The generational boundaries between them and their children become appropriate and realistic. The parents begin to be able to separate themselves from their own families of origin. Crises are dealt with by all members of the family in a problem-solving manner. Couples attend the couples group for ten to twenty-five sessions. When they leave, they know that the center is available to them for consultation. We ask couples to come back after a three-month period for a "check-up" on a one-time basis. By this time, their children, who have been attending our day care center, have graduated and are back in the community, either in a community school or in a job, and are living at home. An informal survey of some 100 families two years after having been in multiple family therapy and couple therapy indicates that approximately 75 percent of the families are doing well. There is no recurrence of a drug problem, and the parents are apparently enjoying each other.

The movement from multiple family therapy to couples therapy was a natural evolution in this setting. Once we made the assumption that when an adolescent who had been doing well in the day care center started cutting school or experimenting with drugs and was having trouble at home, we called the parents in for a couple session.[3] We began to incorporate couples therapy into our design. When we removed the identified patient from the home we prevented the recurrence of the old dysfunctional pattern. Parents had to resolve their couple problems, for the identified patient could no longer be used as the battlefield if he was not there. In the few sessions of intensive couple therapy with the children not present, we began to see that the couple, as they resolved their own problems, took responsiblity for the identified patient and asked for his return.

It was from these crisis experiences that we began to understand the need for seeing couples without their children. As they talked about themselves in the couples group, the pronoun "we" began to be used more and more. The couple experienced their "we-ness" when they dealt with the children in the family. They expressed some amazement at how easy it seemed to be when they were in agreement. From this they developed ways of talking to each other about the children and the problems they presented. Couples spoke about generational boundaries in terms of their many different ideas about distance and closeness. Occasionally, a mother wanted to see herself as her daughter's friend, or a father wanted to be a pal to his son. Other members of the couple group talked about parenting and that distance between the generations which was necessary and good. As the partners began to invest more in each other rather than in the identified patient, the child had fewer crises. Members of the couples group made each other aware whenever a couple would form a covert alliance with the identified patient or one of his siblings. The members of the couples group became increasingly aware that the parenting people were the center around which the family revolved. Sibling problems were minimal when these two felt good about themselves and each other. In the group sessions, the couples monitored each other and shared experiences. They also alerted each other to "slippage." Sexual problems which could not be discussed in the multiple family therapy group were the subject of many couples sessions.

The identified patient and other siblings were rarely mentioned. If a couple was asked about a particular child, the answer was usually short, and they frequently said, "When we're doing fine together, the kids have no problems." Occasionally they would add with some amazement that they were really having fun with their kids. The couples group reinforced the fact that the parents were the foundation for the structure of the family, with much of the family dependent on the parents' stability.

After the final session in the couples group, the entire family had its last session with the family therapist. In this last session, gains were noted and fears expressed. There was frequently an easy kind of affection among the family members, as well as some anxiety about how the family would function when it was not coming to the day care center. At this point the therapist informed the family that it had an appointment in three months for a check-up, and that its members were free to call the day care center at any time. Things were not ended, they were just being changed.

It has been our experience that this movement from multiple family therapy to couples therapy was growth-inducing. Parents reported that they felt they could begin to take the responsiblity for their children as a couple. One other interesting development occurred in the couples group: the members formed a social network, and many of them saw each other on weekends, went to movies or dances together, and frequently visited each other's homes. They exchanged services and babysat for each other or had the older children come to the house of a mother who was not working on a particular day. On the whole, they found each other helpful and supportive. Many of the couples continue to use the day care center as a resource for problem solving, not only for the family but for neighbors and relatives. They not only share problems but also celebrations such as marriages, births, and birthdays.

Another type of couples group evolved with the adult addicts. This group was composed of addicts and their spouses, and included in-house couples. The MFT group was used as a screening device to evaluate the viability and therapeutic potential of the relationship between the addict and spouse. If no member of the family of origin was available and the addict-spouse dyad was felt to be such that it would be conducive to a drug-free, healthy state, then the pain would be added to the couples group after four to ten sessions in MFT. When the family of origin was available, then a great deal of work was done with the addict in that system before or concurrent with the couples group. (Unfortunately, at Su Casa, the MFT and couples group met at the same time. At The Family, this was not the case). We never worked directly with the spouse's parents, though in some cases, she or he was coached in how to deal with her or his family of origin. If there are ample trained staff, then direct work should certainly be done with the spouse and his own family. Another issue that can be dealt with in the MFT prior to couples group is the parenting function of the addict. MFT is an excellent opportunity to help the addict to become a parent again as well as to develop a united parental subsystem with his spouse.

Thus a couple has worked together in MFT to control their disruptive eight-year-old. Likewise a divorced father whose teenage sons attended the MFT achieved a level of self-esteem which permitted him to ask his drug-free children not to smoke (cigarettes) as a step towards establishing himself as a loving, limit-setting father.

In the couples group, many of the principles which Berenson describes in this book are applicable, although many others are not. This is because in groups with residential clients, present drug abuse is not as much of a problem as the spouse's attitude toward drug intake, and if his behavior contributes to or provokes drug abuse, this behavior is identified and shifted. In most cases, the couples who have reached the stage of couple therapy have a relationship which is evaluated as potentially constructive. Thus the spouse is not encouraged to detach emotionally or physically, but the major purpose of the group is to establish a mutual, loving relationship between partners.

Couples groups are an excellent way to deal with newly established in-house couples or the ex-addict's relationships as he moves out into society. At The Family, any in-house couple that wants to build a relationship is asked to meet with the cotherapists of the couples group to evaluate their relationship and its potential suitability for work in that group.

Many of the techniques described in this book are used with couples, particularly structural, communication, and systems approaches. Some techniques, such as examining and shifting triangulation, are particularly suited to a couples group. The therapist must be aware that couples will suck him into a triangle, replacing issues such as children, money, power, drugs, alcohol, and affairs with their relationship to the therapist. An important technique with couples is to examine their hidden agendas and rule-governed behavior (2). One rule to remember is that partners tend to balance each other and that balancing may be more important than what the couples feel is a fixed attitude on their parts. The sterotype of female spendthrift and male tightwad is frequently reversed in couples where there is a male addict. However, if he gives up spending money on drugs, he rapidly becomes the tightwad, which may push the spouse into becoming a spendthrift. Another rule (2) is that spouses tend to provoke each other into escalating quarrels which can only be abated by pulling in a third party (in-law, child, therapist). In the addict-spouse pair, there is frequently competition over who is the sickest and most needy. This may be a source of many quarrels and continues when the addict is drug-free.

Spouses tend to communicate through a third person (2). This can be dealt with even if that person is not a member of the group, as couples who are used to this pattern will find someone in the group to communicate through. Frequently the problem a couple presents is not the real problem at all. The presenting problem may be a protective device that keeps the marriage going, such as an affair to provide needed distance, tapping anger to alleviate depression, or provoking substance abuse (2). Substance abuse may be provoked or supported in the potential addict because of the spouse's need for self-punishment, to control someone who is weak, to have someone to punish, or out of a need for love which is so desperate that the love object must be rendered so helpless that he is incapable of leaving (7).

The therapist must take great pains to ensure that he is not unknowingly the object of the couple's triangulation. Likewise he must not join one side lest he became a part of the problem rather than its solution (2). The therapist must also realize that despite similarities, all couples are different and, in particular, different from his own coupling relationships. (2)

A critical period in every relationship occurs when one partner gives up substance misuse, for the nonusing partner must find an entirely different way of relating. There are totally new expectations and demands, and for the first time there is communication, an art which neither may have ever learned. Thus, couples must support each other in learning the basic tools of communication. Sex has been used for exploitation and as a means for asking total forgiveness to the extent that it becomes nonexistant. This too must be slowly redeveloped; in many cases the ex-substance abuser has sex "on the notch"[4] for the first time in her or his life. Difficulties also arise because the recovering abuser has given up the most precious thing in his life (drugs or alcohol) and expects immediate rewards. The spouse has been "burned" too many times and is not willing to give the substance abuser the rewards he feels he deserves. We encourage spouses to begin to trust and reward at the same time as we ask ex-abusers to reevaluate their expectations. The ex-substance abuser may go through a period of mourning for months or years after giving up the precious substance-love object: This depression should be alleviated. If it is not, it can lead to a homeostasis which is dependent on it and as crippling for the couple as substance abuse. When and if the depression lifts, it also causes new conflicts which must be resolved.

In-house couples are in a situation much like summer camp. There are a limited number of partners available in a closed environment, and if any of them make the slightest move towards each other, they are designated as a couple by the entire house. A couples group should permit them some distance and give them permission to separate if they choose. An advanced couple which has worked out many of its problems can be an excellent role model for newer relationships. At The Family, any couple which develops a relationship is asked to write a paper on what a relationship is, which they read to the entire house. This provides a model for mutual relationships.

Cotherapist pairs should be a man and a woman who are able to disagree within the group to establish a model for healthy conflict resolution. This type of balance in the cotherapy team also helps prevent unhealthy coalitions and triangulation. Couples groups in either an adult or adolescent program provide a natural means for structural shift and subsystem support. It is critical that the shift not be made simply because such groups exist, but with the full knowledge that such a group will support certain systems and weaken others. If this is always kept in mind, then such specialized couples groups can be extremely helpful and, in some cases, essential.

REFERENCES

1. Framo, J.L., Rationale and Techniques of Intensive Family Therapy. In I. Boszormenyi-Nagy & J.L. Framo (Eds.), *Intensive Family Therapy*, New York: Hoeber, 1965.
2. Haley, J., *Problem Solving Therapy*, San Francisco, CA: Jossey-Bass, 1976.
3. Haley, J., Marriage Therapy. *Arch. Gen. Psychiatry* 8:213-234, 1963.
4. Laqueur, H.P., General Systems Theory and Multiple Family Therapy. In J.H. Massermass (Ed.), *Current Psychiatric Therapies* (Vol. VIII), New York: Grune & Stratton, 1968.
5. Minuchin, S., Montalvo, B., Guerney, B.G., Rosman, B.L., & Schumer, F., *Families of the Slums*, New York: Basic Books, 1967.
6. Minuchin, S., *Families and Family Therapy*, Cambridge, MA: Harvard University Press, 1974.
7. Whalen, T., Wives of Alcoholics: Four Types Observed in a Family Service Agency. *Quarterly J. of Studies on Alcohol* 14:632-641, 1953.

FOOTNOTES

1. Day Care Center of the Phoenix Foundation funded by NIDA Grant No. 1 H80 MH01049
2. Su Casa, New York, N.Y. and The Awakening Family, Norwalk, California
3. In single-parent homes, the authority couple could be a mother and grandmother, a mother and older sibling, a relative, or anyone functioning as an ongoing authority figure in the family.
4. off of drugs

8

Family Treatment of the Homosexual Adolescent Drug Abuser: On Being Gay in a Sad Family

David Wellisch, Ph.D.
ASSISTANT PROFESSOR OF MEDICAL PSYCHOLOGY
UCLA NEUROPSYCHIATRIC INSTITUTE
LOS ANGELES, CALIFORNIA

G.G. DeAngelis, Ph.D.
PROGRAM DIRECTOR
PRIDE HOUSE
VAN NUYS, CALIFORNIA

Doug Bond, M.A.
GENESIS HOUSE
MONTEREY, CALIFORNIA

The issue of the integration of the gay individual and gay subculture into the mainstream of our society is one of great currency. The conflict over gay rights has become front-page news, with the two sides polarized into distinct and often angry positions. The issue of homosexuality permeates most human structural elements, and the position and role of homosexuals in basic societal structures such as the nuclear family unit is constantly challenged. These challenges are not only offered at the nuclear family level, but unfortunately are common elements in the discussion of adolescent rights and problems in state and federal legislatures, as well as the Supreme Court.

This chapter addresses the problem of adolescent drug abuse combined with adolescent homosexuality. The major issues discussed include issues pertinent to the adjustment of the gay adolescent drug abuser to our adolescent residential drug treatment program, Pride House, and, conversely, the adjustment of the program (by staff and residents, both heterosexual and homosexual to the gay resident. Thus these two family units, the nuclear and the created (Pride House is referred to as a "family" by the staff and residents alike), potentially represent a manageable and observable microcosm through which insights into the larger, societal level conflicts of homosexuality may be obtained. This chapter will also consider issues presented in individual and multiple family therapy by nuclear families, some of whose members are gay adolescent drug abusers.

Issues Presented at Pride House

In some sense, it is easier to unravel the Gordian knot of the gay adolescent drug abuser by beginning with what we know from daily observation of this group in family therapy sessions versus what we "understand," speculate, or fantasize. Thus the interface between the treatment program and the resident becomes the starting point in this chapter.

Pride House is a 75-bed residential center for adolescent drug abusers located in the San Fernando Valley of Los Angeles. This area is a bedroom community for Los Angeles. Residents are referred to the program by a large number of private and public sources. In the case of the gay adolescent drug abuser, the referral source is rarely private. These residents are almost always sent at the request of the Juvenile Court of the juvenile justice system. This system is frequently very hard-pressed to find placements for this subgroup of juvenile drug abusers, as most other residential programs specifically screen out gay adolescents. The gay adolescent thus arrives at the door of Pride House with a conflictual emotional set beyond that of his or her heterosexual counterpart. If this conflict could be verbalized, it might sound like, "Well . . . I guess you're stuck with me, because people think I'm weird and no other placement wants me, and I sure can't go home." This emotional set leads directly to the same behavioral theme for the gay adolescent as for the straight adolescent in the initial phase of treatment. The name of that theme, of course, is testing the limits. The form of the theme is frequently quite different from the heterosexual resident for the gay adolescent, whose testing usually assumes the form of outrageous behavior and sex roles in the form of grooming and dress. This is in contrast to boasts of omnipotence in the form of drug "war stories," or threats of violence, both of which are more frequently made by new nongay residents. The staff and residents tend to use the term "flaming" (short for "flaming queen") to confront this vigorous and persistent homosexual behavior. Two cases serve as examples. In the first instance, the adolescent was a Latin male, S.S., who wore purple nail polish, gaudy lipstick, and ultrafeminine blouses that left his midriff bare, in the early phase of residency. His dress tended to become less obtrusive, as did his hand movements and walk, and he stopped calling other males "honey" as his integration into the program family proceeded beyond the entry phase. All of his ornamental and behavioral armor surfaced once again with the entry of a second homosexual, C.D., into the program. This individual was another "flaming" gay adolescent determined to introduce his distinctive identity and influence into the family milieu. Sibling rivalry, so predictable in the nuclear and treatment family, assumes its own form within the gay subculture of Pride House. The internal sense of powerlessness and lack of influence upon the group is a universal dread that is initially fought by all new residents. For all adolescent drug abusers, the need to have an identity and to exert some perceptible influence upon the group is very strong. In the homosexual resident, caricaturing the opposite sex becomes the path of least resistance. He often acts out by having angry outbursts, attempting to bring drugs into the house, or forming a heterosexual relationship even though such a relationship is not encouraged by the program.

In the second case, A.A., a 16-year-old Asian male went as far as wearing a bra stuffed with toliet paper to gain a reaction from the Pride House family. The reaction of his nuclear family during his stay at Pride House was total nonresponsiveness, uninvolvement, and unconcern. When called on the phone, A.A.'s brother indicated: "We know of no one by that name." The denial of A.A.'s very existence and the lack of nuclear family support could not have been more obvious. It was clear that any behavioral change evoked in this adolescent would have to be the result of Pride House interaction. When confronted by the chief counselor about his stuffed bra, A.A. flew into a rage but wouldn't leave the room (as is the usual pattern with new residents who become enraged when they are confronted by staff), choosing instead to hold his ground and escalate the confrontation, which is so satisfying at a covert level. In actuality this program represented the first real interest in A.A.'s behavior in quite some time. Testing this interest and the real level of staff concern is common at this stage of the program.

All of the residents of the Pride House family are expected to participate in a very intensive program of group therapy. As with well-known adult programs in the field (Synanon, Daytop, Odyssey House, Tuum Est, and others), the group modality is important in Pride House's treatment regimen although individual and family modalities are also utilized extensively. The issues of power, identity, and control become sharply focused when gay and straight residents attend groups together. It is here that the frequently described nuclear family processes of forming alliances, subgrouping, triangulating family projection process (6) and family scapegoating(1), reach their apex for the residential family. It has been our repeated observation that the gay residents in covert unconscious collusion with the nongay residents will promote an extensive focus on their homosexuality, on being different, on their bitchiness, and on their bizarre behavior as a group defense against the discomfort of discovering similarities, and especially against the possibility of allowing their pain as gay adolescents to emerge in regard to the massive rejection they have experienced in the context of their nuclear families. The straight adolescents can relate to such pain but would really rather not, if at all possible. Another difficulty is the reluctance of heterosexual group members to identify and share common adolescent problems with gay group members. When it is examined, it seems that this fear stems from a conviction that if one shares feelings with gays and identifies with them in any way, it will cast doubt on one's own sexual identity. This fear of homosexuality and the concomitant threats to the perceived heterosexual self are well known in adolescents (7). It becomes entirely possible to block all of this with discussions characterized by name calling, sarcastic denigration, and general uproar. The notion of "invisible loyalties" (5) is quite obvious with the gay residents. It is at this point that the staff has tended to feel most helpless, confused, and unable to proceed with effective treatment. If this group defense can be breeched, in the vast majority of cases the unconsciously threatened gay adolescent drug abuser then arranges to be dropped from the program or leaves it in a rage.

S.S. (the 15-year-old Latin male previously referred to) was virtually unsurpassed at providing the kind of stimuli which kept a group chaotic and unfocused, especially when it came to issues relevant to his pain. Finally the program's psychological consultant and its chief counselor, both of whom were able to see and cope with this process as it unfolded, limited the group and S.S. to material relevant to S.S.'s family history. This was the first (and ultimately the only) time S.S. dealt with his feelings about his family in any depth. He revealed that his mother had died of leukemia when he was 10, after the usual horrifying, depriving course of this illness. The family, including S.S. and eight siblings (all male, three of whom were also gay), was left to the ambivalent guidance of the father, who was never home and not interested in the family. Approximately one year after the mother's death, the father was shot and killed, leaving his sons completely alone. The older siblings established an appearance of pseudoresponsibility for the family such that the authorities did not send all of the brothers to foster homes. S.S. was able to say with feeling that he missed his mother greatly, but after watching leukemia take its toll upon her, felt relieved that she had died. The interpretation was made that one way not to deal with separating from her was to essentially become her in behavior and dress, thus never giving her up. This made him cry for the first time since entering the program. The next day S.S. picked a fight with a female resident who was pregnant, attempted to stab her in the abdomen with a fork, and ran out the front door, never to return to the program.

Another excellent example of the adeptness of the gay adolescent resident at blocking conflict resolution through offering himself as scapegoat/sacrificial object, came during a meeting of the entire Pride House Family (all the staff and residents together). The meeting took place immediately after the family had watched "Roots," the dramatic TV series which focused on issues such as separation, loss of identity, racial conflicts, impotence in the face of external sources of power, and, most of all, impotent rage on the part of the adolescent protagonist in the drama. Needless to say, the adolescent residents deeply and emotionally identified with Kunta Kinte. Subsequent to viewing the program, racial tensions within the multiracial Pride House family were predictably very high. The designated purpose of the meeting was to deal with an alleged racial slur which was directed from a new staff member (Caucasian) to a resident (black). The actual content of the family discussion quickly went beyond racism into the area of dealing with helplessness in the face of omnipotent authority. The bulk of this discussion was carried on by the residents, not the staff. At the point where feelings were highest, with most people feeling frustrated, one gay resident, C.D., made himself obtrusive by being silly and then sarcastically "bitchy" when confronted about it. The entire family, with the emphatic participation by the staff, came down heavily upon C.D., with the net result that the tension and frustration engendered by the previous issues dissipated almost immediately. The rest of the meeting was spent in calling C.D. a "tramp." Both he and the community could easily handle this. The relief to the collective family caused by the offering and acceptance of the gay sacrificial object is so great that changing such a process in midstream, even if it is understood, is quite difficult. As Bion (4) and Bennis & Shepard (2) have noted, dealing with group avoidance in such situations is the key, but it is elusive in situations which involve such an attractive, energetic, and obtrusive scapegoat as the gay adolescent drug abuser.

Gay Adolescent Abusers and Their Nuclear Families in Therapy

The focus of the second section of this chapter will be on the nuclear families in treatment at Pride House. Three cases will be discussed, two of which were in a multiple-family therapy context, and one in individual family therapy. In agreement with Kaufmann & Kaufman (8), we have come to treating families of drug abusers in the multiple-versus individual-family therapy mode. We have reached this position not solely out of necessity, but also truly out of choice. We now feel change can be more rapid in the multiple mode because of the added weight of the group which we feel we can utilize.

It has been our observation, as it has that of the Psychoanalytic Research & Development Fund Study on Sexual Deviation (1) headed by Mortimer Ostrow, that the gay adolescent's images of parental roles and identities have been unusually unclear and inconsistent, much more so than that of their straight counterparts. These families have functioned in a way which has offered rigid external, overt roles and identities, which, when examined more closely, gave way to concealed and "mysterious" (13) family systems characterized by ambivalence, seductiveness (especially toward our residents), passivity, and, most of all, very intense aggression.

The M. family personified these issues in their interactions around T.M., their daughter, a 17-year-old heroin-addicted female resident. T.M. entered Pride House via court order after several nearly fatal car accidents while high on heroin, with T.'s father always fixing her car (and thus "fixing" her to proceed with her addiction). The family was upper class socioeconomically; the father was a successful physician. The mother was a housewife, and the three other siblings all seemed to be doing well, or so it appeared on the surface. It was later revealed in therapy that T.'s younger brother was becoming quite involved with drugs. T.'s behavior in the program was initially sullen and provocative, with her image that of a "butch"; i.e., as masculine and unattractive. She soon became interested in B.G., another female resident with a long history of degrading, explicitly masochistic homosexual relationships with older females. The pair announced they were "in love" but remained in Pride House for several months with the understanding that they could not become sexually involved, as no resident is allowed to have sexual relations with another resident.

The choice of this relationship by T. did not make sense to the staff until the dynamics of her family system were revealed in multiple-family therapy. The relationship of Dr. and Mrs. M. was presented as clearcut, with Dr. M. the authority, the effective family manager, and the competent parent. The family emotional system was less clearcut in terms of Dr. M. who emotionally isolated himself. The marital relationship was a study in parent-child relating when reviewed within a transactional analysis grid (3).

In the process of therapy, the father attempted to keep himself in the position of go-between described by Zuk (15), becoming the semipermeable membrane standing between the group and the family. It was evident that the family covertly cooperated with this, and Dr. M. assumed the role of family counselor versus family member. He and Mrs. M. portrayed a sadomasochistically-oriented parent-child union characterized by incessant verbal humiliation by Dr. M. of Mrs. M. They had no intimacy beyond this perverse involvement, although it was revealed that T. and her father did share a more physical intimacy. Dr. M. gave T. pelvic examinations "just to see if she was pregnant" from time to time; neither of them saw this as unusual, and were surprised at the troubled group reaction. T. had effectively taken her mother's place and had identified with her father to the point of having her own relationship with a masochistic, childlike, visibly meek female figure, B.G.

Family therapy with the M. family reached a point where these dynamics were visible and were being presented to the family. In one session Dr. M. was urged to really be "one-up" in relating to his wife and was told to stand on a chair when relating to her and to lecture her. Rather than being ego-dystonic or inducing self-consciousness, this was totally comfortable stance for the couple and personified the level of their resistance.

As the pressure mounted in group and family treatment, T. became more angry at her parents and especially at her father. She then decided that she and B.G. needed to leave the program to set up their life together. They did so for approximately five months, with T.M. beating B.G. and humiliating her by drinking and resuming heroin use. B.G. presented herself for more treatment after their breakup, while T.M. went on to her career in opiate addiction.

The G. family was in individual family therapy for seven sessions. B.G. (the previously mentioned lover of T.M.) was an 18-year-old alcohol and barbiturate user, an attractive young woman characterized by the chief counselor as "a scared puppy, always afraid of being hurt." As the staff came to understand, her real fear was of her fascination for and attraction to being hurt. Being hurt had come to symbolize love for her and had become an eroticized form of attachment.

The individual family therapy sessions were held with B.G. and her mother alone. There was a brother who lived in another city, and no father presently was in the family. Mrs. G. had been married three times. Her first two husbands had been violent alcoholics. B.G. had frequently witnessed her real father and first stepfather beating her mother. These were predominant scenes in remembrances of her childhood.

In the sessions, Mrs. G. appeared irritated and angry about everything. She was angry at men in general, angry at B. and her problems, and angry at her own inability to deal with the problems in the family. B. responded by withdrawing, being timid and passive, and never facing her mother frontally, instead always talking to her facing sideways.

The family therapist proceeded on the assumption that the anger and withdrawl syndrome displayed by the two was really an effective way of preventing each from finding out what the other really felt, thought, or needed. It became evident that neither had ever gone beyond this limited sphere of interaction. This led to a final session (not final by the therapists' choice) at which the mother and daughter hugged and cried. Both appeared frightened by this. Immediately after, B.G. got drunk, and was terminated from the program, thus returning the family situation to its previous state.

The J. family was seen in multiple family therapy. A.J., a 16-year-old very effeminate male who was minimally involved with drugs, was the identified patient. He, his mother, and stepfather were involved in the treatment. The only other family member, Mr. J.'s natural son, lived away at college.

A.J. was a virtual mirror image of his mother: pretty, smartly dressed, and "bitchy." He sat between his mother and stepfather unless otherwise requested, and this structural change was the first request made of his family in therapy. We attempted to develop a less intense fusion between A.J. and his mother while strengthening the bonds between A.J. and his father along the lines developed by Minuchin (10). This required use of a psychic crowbar, but was proceeding satisfactorily until Mr. and Mrs. J. began to explore their own marital situation more fully. Mrs. J. had "seduced" Mr. J. away from his sexually slumbering first marriage of twenty-three years. Mr. J. stated: "She gave me back my manhood and got me interested in living again." Their marriage was followed by A.J.'s incessant acting out, which made Mrs. J. "too depressed and too nervous" to satisfy Mr. J. sexually. When the acting out quieted down after A.J.'s admission to Pride House, Mrs. J. developed back trouble and had a small growth removed from her face, all of which became "unbearable and made me so depressed that I could not pay much attention to Mr. J." The difficulty this couple had in their relationship, coupled with Mr. J.'s disappointment and Mrs. J.'s depression, set off another round of acting out on the part of A.J., who stole his mother's car and went gay bar-hopping with another gay resident. This led A.J. to be terminated from the program and placed in Juvenile Hall. He was soon back home with Mr. and Mrs. J., and once again general uproar within the family became the way of life. The program was frequently consulted, and finally A.J. was readmitted, pending his admission to another program in Connecticut, 3,000 miles away from both the nuclear and Pride House family.

This geographical separation, suggested by the program director, became a viable solution to part of the problem. A.J. remained there for more than a year and has not returned to live with his parents. The parents have continued to keep in contact with Pride House with Mrs. J. still looking depressed and Mr. J. still looking frustrated. Suggestions that they have marital counseling have not been accepted.

Conclusions

We have now worked with twenty gay adolescents in our program. While success is not achieved easily with our heterosexual adolescent residents, it has been even more elusive with this group. Most of the gay clients do not go beyond the therapeutic cooperative group impasse of staying focused on homosexual behavior. Resolution of other issues is seldom, if ever, reached. A handful of homosexual adolescents has stayed in the program once this impasse has been resolved. They have made impressive gains in terms of abstinence from self-destructive involvement with chemicals, cessation of self-destructive prostitution (the usual means of support for this group), and the ability to face significant others without suffering humiliating fears and anxiety. Generally this smaller subgroup (of an already small subgroup) has had more effective parenting and is slightly more mature than those gay clients who do so poorly and bolt in the face of self-confrontation.

We have learned that the parents of these homosexual clients present with their own problem set which centers around their own conflicts. Similar conflicts exist for the parents of heterosexual residents, but the quality of such conflicts is greater for the parents of the gays. Perhaps most sobering, as illustrated by the situation with B.G. and T.M., is the potential of these gay adolescent drug abusers to recreate in vivo the psychosexual misery of their families of origin. Unfortunately the only way which can be found to tolerate such misery is with generous doses of analgesia, a form of self-medication which, if nothing else, does palliate the underlying pain and confusion found in this population.

This is a problem which also perplexes our staff and it is in this area that work can be done. The potentially healing interface between any adolescent drug abusers and a residential staff exists but demands constant attention. We have found in a recent study (14) that staff and gay residents focus on psychosexual issues to the significant exclusion of other material *not* excluded in therapeutic work between the same staff and heterosexual, but closely matched, residents. Homosexuality can be a seductive defense in its complexity, one which can spread far beyond the individual to become a stagnating defense for the group. The unwillingness to work through this defense and denial system ultimately becomes the central issue of concern in family and group treatment of the gay adolescent drug abuser.

References

1. Ackerman, N. W., *Treating the Troubled Family*. New York: Basic Books, 1966.

2. Bennis, W. & Shepard, H. A theory of Group Development. *Human Relations* 4 415–457, 1956.

3. Berne, E., *Games People Play*. New York: Grove Press, 1964.

4. Bion, W. R., *Experiences in Groups*. London: Tavistock Publications, 1961.

5. Boszormenyi-Nagy, I. & Spark, G. M., *Invisible Loyalties*. New York: Harper & Row, 1973.

6. Bowen, M., Family Psychotherapy with Schizophrenia in the Hospital and in Private Practice. In I. Boszormenyi-Nagy & J. Framo (Eds.), *Intensive Family Therapy*, New York: Harper & Row, 1965.

7. Freedman, A. & Kaplan, H., *Comprehensive Textbook of Psychiatry*. Baltimore: Williams & Wilkins, 1967.

8. Kaufmann, P. & Kaufman, E., Multiple Family Therapy with Drug Abusers. Paper presented at the National Drug Conference, San Francisco, May 6-9, 1977.

9. Laufer, M., A View of Adolescent Pathology. In S. C. Feinstein & P. Giovacchini (Eds.), *Adolescent Psychiatry*, New York: Jason Aronson, 1977.

10. Minuchin, S., *Families and Family Therapy*. Cambridge, MA: Harvard University Press, 1974.

11. Ostrow, M. & the Psychoanalytic Research and Development Fund Study. *Sexual Deviation: Psychoanalytic Insights*, New York: New York Times Book Co., 1974.

12. Stanton, M. D. & Todd, T., Some Principles for Family Therapy with Drug Addicts. Paper presented at the National Drug Conference, San Francisco, May 6-9, 1977.

13. Stoller, R., *Perversion: The Erotic Form of Hatred*, New York: Pantheon, 1975.

14. Wellisch, D., Peternite, C., & DeAngelis, G. G., Staff Interaction with Homosexual Adolescent Drug Abusers: A Controlled Study. Unpublished.

15. Zuk, G., *The Go-Between Process in Family Therapy*, New York: Behavioral Publications, 1971.

9

Drug-Abusing Families: Intrafamilial Dynamics and Brief Triphasic Treatment

Dennis M. Reilly, M.S.W., A.C.S.W.
SOUTHEAST NASSAU GUIDANCE COUNSELING CENTER
WANTAGH, NEW YORK

Introduction

Since 1972, the Southeast Nassau Guidance Center has maintained an ambulatory, drug-free treatment program for youthful drug abusers and their families. This program, a branch of SNG's community mental health center, serves a suburban, largely white, middle class Long Island population within commuting distance of New York City. The majority of our drug-abusing clients are between the ages of twelve and twenty-five. The most common drugs of abuse are, in descending frequency of use, marijuana and alcohol, barbiturates and minor tranquilizers, amphetamines, cocaine, and hallucinogens. Only about 12 percent of the population abuses heroin, methadone, or other opiates. Most are polydrug abusers.

The findings reported in this study are based upon our five years of experience with this population. We believe that much of what we have noted concerning the functioning and treatment of drug-abusing families can be generalized to other treatment populations. However, this should be done with caution as our observations rest upon a rather restricted sample, one that is geographically limited and racially and economically homogenous.

As a result of our work with youthful drug abusers and their families, we have come to see the family as the interface between the individual and his society. The family is the fulcrum, the pivot point, the mediator, and the interpreter between its members and their culture. As such, it is particularly influential in the socialization of its members, whether into "prosocial" or "antisocial," roles. It is a semipermeable membrane which regulates the flow of either prosocial or delinquent influences from the outside world of peers, class and group interests, media, social values, and so on. It is a social lens mechanism which may either selectively magnify and focus socially

115

deviant influences upon its individual members, or screen and filter them out. It is the disturbed family system which creates in its individual members—the identified patients or "symptom bearers"—a vulnerability to antisocial or "prodrug" influences of peers, media, or subcultures. It is the disturbed family system's need for a delegated family black sheep, scapegoat, or deviant which makes a young person particularly susceptible to the adoption of delinquent or drug-abusing values and behavior. It is the disturbed family system which "pushes" the black sheep into the arms of a drug-abusing peer group. This helps to explain why one young person may choose to "differentially associate" (26) with a drug-abusing peer group, while another chooses a prosocial one. Finally, it is the disturbed family system which "nominates" the drug abuser and "elects" him to his scapegoat office.

Characteristic Interactions in Drug-Abusing Families

As we have noted previously (22, 23), our experience makes it possible to construct a tentative profile of a family system which tends to produce drug-abusing behavior in its members. Such a profile must remain, however, something of an "ideal type" as no one family will manifest all of its characteristics in real life. It is a type that must remain "culturebound" to the extent our research sample is unrepresentative of the general population. It is a profile which is relative, a matter of degree. Drug-abusing families carry trends moderately extant in all families to a pathological extreme. With these points in mind, we can move on to an examination of some of the common interactional themes manifested by the drug-abusing families under study.

Negativism

Drug-abusing families often describe family life as dull, deadened, alienated, lifeless, and shallow. They feel isolated from one another, encapsulated, out of touch. Communication occurs in primarily negative ways via criticism, complaints, blaming, nagging, and corrections. In such families, members quickly learn that the only way to introduce a modicum of "life" or excitement into the system is to precipitate a crisis. Children swiftly learn that the only way they can consistently gain attention is to make trouble or create problems—"the squeaky wheel gets the oil." Acceptable behavior is rarely praised or recognized, indeed, it is generally ignored, whereas "bad" behavior is unfailingly reinforced with attention and a surge of heightened excitement and involvement, rare and treasured commodities in such households. By the time the children are old enough to enter the adolescent subculture they are already primed to discover an enormously convenient and sure-fire means of stimulating family system excitement and provoking negative adult attention: drug-abuse.

Parental Inconsistency

Parents in many of these families seem incapable of setting clear and consistent rules or limits to govern their children's behavior. The same unit of behavior which they ignore one moment, they may punish or reward the next. They often disagree as to whether and how to discipline. Children get very confused and ambivalent messages concerning what is right or wrong, acceptable or unacceptable. This situation creates in the children an enormous hunger for clarity and structure and they tend to engage in behavior designed to provoke either the parents or parental substitutes into taking a definite stand. Drug abuse often serves this function admirably. The young person will, sometimes even half-consciously, flaunt his drug involvement in a cry for help, attention, and concern. He will leave drugs around the house in places easily accessible to his parents, or she will advertise her drug abuse in front of teachers at school or police on the streets.

Parental Denial

As the young person escalates his attempts to "set himself up," "incriminate" himself, and get caught, his parents often respond by escalating their denial of what is occurring. They manage "not to see" the drugs "hidden" in obvious places, not to notice their children's altered behavior. Often this denial persists until outside authorities are forced to intervene. And even then, even at that late date, the parents' response is often, "No, you're mistaken, it can't be my child!"

Vicarious Parental Behavior

Often parents have a vested interest in "not seeing," and therefore not stopping, their children's drug abuse. These are parents who, despite conscious disapproval and verbal condemnations, unconsciously envy the hedonistic freedoms they attribute, rightly or wrongly, to today's youth. Though they may not be able to indulge themselves in these "forbidden pleasures," they are able to gain a great deal of second-hand gratification by covertly licensing them in their children. They clearly convey to their children this morbid fascination, whether it relates to drugs, sexuality, violence, or general life style. Finally, their messages concerning drug use are ambivalent in the extreme, usually taking the form, "Don't let me catch you using drugs," with the emphasis upon not getting caught or not letting the parents "know" that they are using drugs.

Miscarried Expression of Anger

These families have problems expressing feelings in general, positive as well as negative, with open expressions of anger considered as especially dangerous. Family members already feel deprived of love, affection, and attention, and this state of emotional deprivation creates an enormous sense of rage and frustration. However, this very rage is suppressed and repressed for fear that it will lead to further rejection and loss of love, or to complete loss of control over potentially murderous impulses. Instead of expressing it directly, a youth in such a family comes to discharge anger indirectly. Drug abuse is an excllent vehicle for misdirected rage. It allows one to express it passive-aggressively through spiting one's parents. In such a case the drug abuse (and, more important, getting caught in the drug abuse) is a hostile and rebellious act. For some the drug abuse is symbolically murderous, a kind of parenticidal gesture. This is illustrated by the numbers of young people who say, "If my parents knew I used drugs, it would kill them," and who then promptly arrange to get caught using drugs in a manner designed to be as embarrassing as possible to their parents. Drug abuse is also an excellent way to misdirect anger in an intropunitive way, to take it out on oneself. Such an adjustment is quite common among drug abusers and leads to a more or less chronically depressed state, a poor self-image, a self-defeating life style, a tendency to be accident prone, occasional suicidal ideation or attempts, and a number of masked suicides disguised as overdose deaths.

Self-Medication

As has been commonly observed, the youthful drug abuser is usually not the only person in his family to ingest mood-altering substances. Often the entire family defends against unpleasant effects and seeks pleasurable sensations and experiences via taking something to relieve anxiety or depression, to bolster self-esteem, or to feel "alive" or "human." Whether this something is a mild tranquilizer prescribed by a doctor, an over-the-counter sedative, alcohol, coffee, cigarettes, or junk food, the message is clear: if life is hard to swallow, then swallow something to make it bearable.

Pathogenic Parental Expectations

Parents in such families often manifest extremely unrealistic expectations of their children. When these are too high, love is made conditional upon success, and a young person will often turn to drugs, which serve a double function, for they not only allow one to spitefully revenge oneself upon demanding parents, but also provide a tailor-made excuse for every failure—"What can you expect of me? I'm just a junkie," or pothead, or speed-freak. In other cases parental expectations are unrealistically low: almost from birth the parents predict that the youth will fail. They expect the worst, and the child learns to fulfill the self-fulfilling prophecy, to play out his negative life-script in an attempt to live down to his parents' expectations; to give them what they want.

Underlying Family Themes

We have described several interactional patterns rather characteristic of drug-abusing families. However, the question remains as to why the families behave in this unfortunate manner. We believe that the answer lies in two related underlying themes usually present in the family system: impaired mourning and homeostatic collusion in the symptomatic behavior.

Impaired Mourning

The families of drug abusers are, in our experience, intensely preoccupied with the issues of attachment and separation, fusion and individuation, dependence and autonomy, loss and restoration, and death and rebirth. The parents of youthful drug abusers have often suffered profound emotional losses within their own families of origin. They have a strong sense of having lost their own parents via death, divorce, rejection, or neglect. The conflicts over this loss have never been worked through; mourning is incomplete and the love/hate ambivalence so characteristic of such relationships is never resolved. The ties to the lost love objects of the family of origin are never given up, and the individual is never able to transfer affections fully to new love objects (such as the spouse and children in the family of procreation).

Traditional psychoanalysis describes how such impaired mourning can lead to melancholia, a condition in which the ego is identified with the lost object; by castigating itself, via intropunitive depressive symptoms, it symbolically punishes the ambivalently loved object by proxy. This simultaneously accomplishes object conservation (keeping the object alive within oneself) and revenge (12).

The parents of drug abusers handle their impaired mourning in a different way (22). Often they manage to avoid the painful experience of melancholia or reactive depression, to defend against the pains of loss and abandonment, by projecting their conflicts over loss and separation onto their present-day families. Their unresolved grief survives intact and contaminates their families of procreation. It creates the dull, deadened, negativistic, lifeless, and loveless atmosphere so characteristic of drug-abusing families.

In order to achieve object conservation, in order to guard against loss and the recognition of loss, the parent will reincarnate his ambivalently loved and lost object in first one, then the other, of his current family members. He will recreate a lost parent or sibling in a spouse or a child. Children who are the object of such "irrational role-assignments" (11) are "parentified"; often their roles are "chosen for them before they are born" (10). They are turned into revenants, ghosts from the past. The hostility originally felt against the abandoning object is then displaced onto the child, who serves as designated proxy (3). In our experience it is often the drug-abusing child who has been selected to reincarnate or stand in for his parents' lost objects. He is named after or seen as taking after or resembling the lost objects. His family role is to function as the black sheep or scapegoat whose bad behavior both provokes and justifies his parents' ambivalent attachment to him and their hostile overinvolvement with him. Identifications are confused with relationships, ego boundaries are weak, and ego fusion and diffusion are high. And since the parents have never adequately mourned or accepted the loss of their own parents, they are quite unable to tolerate the loss of their children, particularly the child who has been selected as proxy for the lost object. Thus, despite a deceptive facade of encapsulation and noninvolvement, all family members are covertly enmeshed in sticky, ambivalent ties and snared by a high degree of reciprocal separation anxiety. Finally, as Paul (21) points out, families which have failed to cope with losses suffered early in their life cycles often develop a family style characterized by "a relative paucity of empathy," a "lack of respect for individuality," attempts to "deny the passage of time," and the tendency to unwittingly keep a family member "in an inappropriate dependent position." This is an excellent description of a typical drug-abusing family.

Familial Collusion

Drug-abusing behavior within a family system operates as a homeostatic regulatory device. As we have seen, it serves to rationalize the parents' hostile overinvolvement with the drug abuser, thus maintaining him in the ambivalently-regarded revenant role. Consequently it makes possible object conservation, revenge, and the deferment of long overdue mourning. The obstacles posed by the drug abuse, its inertia and its drag, are sufficiently powerful to prevent the youthful drug abuser from achieving the escape velocity necessary for departing from the family's orbit. Achievement of separation and autonomy is forestalled and the parents need not suffer the pains of an empty nest. The drug abuse may serve as a means of saving the marriage, as it conveniently distracts the parents from having to deal with personal or marital problems. Also it serves to precisely equilibrate the emotional distance between the parents—when they drift too far apart and greater closeness is desired, it can unite them in a joint rescue mission to save the drug abuser's soul; when things get too close for comfort and increased distance is sought, the drug abuser can come between his parents to give them breathing space (24). Drug abuse also conveniently provides the nondrug-involved well siblings with a handy negative role model, allowing them to feel successful against the backdrop of the identified patient's failures. Finally, the drug abuser's symptoms often operate as a cry for help from the entire family; they serve a flagging or signal function, an SOS from a family begging for outside assistance.

Our findings concerning the collusive involvement of the family system in drug abuse are in line with the reports of other researchers in related works. Boszormenyi-Nagy and Spark (4) see delinquent adolescents as "loyal traitors" fulfilling a negative loyalty commitment to their families. Stierlin (25) has described troubled youth as "bound delegates" sent out on "delinquent missions" by vicarious parents. Alexander and Dibb (1, 2) point out the central role played by dependency/autonomy struggles in drug-abusing families and allude to the failure of the parents to support movement towards adult responsibility on the part of the drug abuser. Harbin and Maziar (16), in a comprehensive review of literature dealing with the families of drug abusers, note widespread support for the idea of intrafamilial etiology. Noone and Reddig (20) utilize Jay Haley's (15) concept of a symptom as a signal that a family has become stuck at a crucial point in its life cycle. They see drug abuse as a sign that the family has failed to cope adequately with the normal adolescent separation crisis and task. For them, drug abuse is a way for the adolescent to remain rebelliously dependent upon his parents, a way of staying at home without losing face. Cannon's (6) study of drug-abusing families noted a parental tendency to "infantilize" the drug abuser, to perceive him as weak, and to encourage him to escape frustrations rather than overcome them. Finally, it is interesting to note that a recent poll (13) reports that adolescents throughout the country perceive drug abuse as "the biggest problem facing their generation," with "the inability of parents and children to communicate and 'get along' with each other" a close second.

Treatment

We have found a course of brief, triphasic, and time-limited conjoint family therapy to be most effective with our client population. We try to limit the treatment course to fifteen sessions and state this limit clearly at onset of treatment. We find that the time limit is extremely helpful in maintaining focus and motivation, that it aids in specification of goals, and that it makes possible a timely crisis intervention. In addition, the time limit forces the family to confront the issues of separation, loss, and abandonment in vivo as part of the treatment process and in the person of the therapist. The limit provides a timely reassurance to family members who resist initial involvement (this too shall pass) and those who fear that therapy will be interminable. Our strong expression of confidence that meaningful change really can occur in as few as fifteen sessions provides a powerful placebo effect, a potent therapeutic use of suggestion, and a strong dose of hope to people who may have seen the situation as hopeless. Finally, it serves as a living challenge to the myth of mutual helplessness which surrounds a long-standing drug-abuse problem.

Early Phase

In the beginning we concentrate on redefining the problem as the family system, rather than as the drug abuse iteself. We challenge the myth of the designated patient, the idea that the drug abuser alone is, as Bowen (5) says, the sick one. We ask all family members both what they like about the family and each other, and what they would like to change. Blaming is discouraged, and negative comments are often relabeled (15) or reframed (27) as positive signs of concern or caring. The emphasis is upon how the situation can be changed rather than on how things got this way. The therapist teaches and models communication skills, the use of behavioral contracts, mutual exchange contingencies, and reciprocal positive reinforcement. Bargaining and compromise are encouraged. The family is confronted about its tendency to reinforce negative behavior with attention; expressions of affection are encouraged, and the family is helped to praise, attend to, and reward "good" behavior and to withdraw attention from "bad" (18). The family is helped to identify specific everyday family events which serve to cue or reinforce drug-abusing behavior. Once identified, the family is encouraged to stop this offending behavior and find a substitute mode of interaction. Initially anger is handled by helping the family members to express it openly, to render it overt rather than covert. Once they are capable of this, the therapist shifts gears and, in a seemingly paradoxical way, relabels the anger as a positive demonstration of concern and involvement. This is done to defuse the situation and to render it more amenable to compromise and the use of behavioral contracts. During this stage our focus is overwhelmingly upon restructuring the family; on establishing or strengthening generational or subsystem boundaries (19); on extricating the children, particularly the drug abuser, from enmeshment in the parents' marital conflicts; and in "remarrying" the parents.

Often this focus upon restructuring the family, improving the marriage, emphasizing the positive, and changing the contingencies of social reinforcement for everyday behavior, is enough to bring about the desired changes. When a family seems to be responding well to this approach and when, by the fourth session or so, we see a diminution of drug abuse and an increase in positive family interaction, we maintain this strategy for the duration of treatment, with little recourse to alternate techniques. We find that this approach is extremely effective with our working-class, blue collar, or action-oriented families who often appreciate a present-centered, process-focused, and enactive (19) approach.

However, some families seem to bog down in this initial stage, and by the fourth session still show no willingness to relinquish their old negativistic patterns of interaction. When this occurs, we move into a secondary treatment phase in which we concentrate more upon the past and its effect on the present. At this point we focus on the issue of impaired mourning. This is often necessary for middle class families, and especially for excessively intellectual and insight-oriented families who refuse to make any progress until therapy bestows upon them the obligatory eureka, the depth insight into past traumas they have come to expect from treatment.

Secondary Phase

In this phase we help the family to work through their conflicts concerning impaired mourning, attachment, separation, and loss—conflicts which are at the root of the family's scapegoat system and collusive investment in the pathology. We ask, in effect, "Who are the ghosts haunting this family? Whom do they possess and how can we exorcise them?" We seek to identify the projections, identifications, and displacements contaminating the family. We ask about parental losses and try to determine whether impaired mourning has led to reincarnation of a lost object in a scapegoated spouse or child.

We explore the family naming process, since family names present valuable clues in our attempt to trace family identifications. We ask who the parents and the children are named after. How were the names chosen? By whom? Which names were discarded? What are the family nicknames? Whom do parents and children seem to take after? Of whom do other family members remind them?

The Romans had a proverb, *nomen est omen.* They saw a predictive, prognostic, and prophetic quality in names. They were right. In the uncon- cious, names are magical and powerful. Naming often confers not only an identity upon a child, but also an identification.

When a father named Stephen names his son, Stephen, Jr., we might suspect that he may have a greater than usual investment in his son func- tioning as a surrogate, as an extension of himself. We may suspect further complications should he name a daughter, Stephanie. Names may also re- veal fixed parental expectations, directives, and role allocations, thus func- tioning as self-fulfilling prophecies. Thus parents may name a daughter Eve because they need her in the role of temptress or seductress; or they may name her Virginia because they need her to remain viginal. They may name her Dawn because, in shared subconscious fantasy, they see her as a savior who will alleviate a depression and bring hope, light, and a new day to a failing marriage and a bleak life. A weak, emasculated, and ineffective father may name his son Lance or Victor, or another name that has a strong masculine, phallic, or heroic ring. A mother who has recently lost her own father may quickly arrange to have a baby as a replacement, naming it af- ter the deceased in an attempt to effect a reincarnation, a literal renais- sance.

Thus, by asking how the parents and children were named and by ex- ploring the implications of that process, we can help the parents to better understand they ways in which they are tragically burdening themselves and their children by confusing identifications with relationships and births with reincarnations.

Throughout this phase the parents are encouraged to discuss their fami- lies of origin in detail; they are helped to recognize the ways in which they have been attempting to gain belated mastery over archaic relationship pat- terns arising in their families of origin within the inappropriate context of their family of procreation.

Haley's (14, 15) and Watzlawick's (27) paradoxical techniques of "pre- scribing the symptom" or encouraging patients to deliberately produce heretofore spontaneous behavior can be adapted for use in this phase. Par- ents can be directed to keep lists of all the ways in which the identified pa- tient resembles or reminds them of the lost love object. Within the session they are encouraged to engage in role playing by relating to him as if he really were the lost object. Forcing them to do overtly what they have been doing less than consciously all along is frequently far more effective in stop- ping the inappropriate behavior than is an intellectual interpretation.

As this phase concludes, our goal is to help the parents to finally and be- latedly complete their griefwork in relation to their lost love objects. We en- courage the emergence of the previously blocked affective constellations— feelings of abandonment, disappointment, anger, and guilt; and later sad- ness, longing, forgiveness, tenderness, and hope.

Final Stage

Once the parents' regressive attachments to their own lost objects are loosened via mourning, they become better able to let go of their children, to allow them to separate and individuate. Since they no longer require that their children stand in as reincarnations or revenants, since they no longer need them to be possessed by the ghosts of lost objects, they can now afford to be less possessive (22). They become better able to treat their children like real people in their own right, and are less likely to cast them in fixed, stereotyped, and ambivalent roles.

In the final sessions, both the treatment course and the gains made by the family are reviewed. The therapist helps everyone to work through their feelings concerning termination of treatment and separation from the therapist. Confidence is very strongly expressed in the family's ability to make it on its own, to function independently, to maintain gains, and to resolve future problems without ever necessarily needing further treatment. Should a return to treatment ever be indicated, it is not defined as a failure or a relapse. Rather, it is reframed as a sort of a booster shot, check-up, refresher course, or reinforcement designed to help the family help itself through a difficult period.

Case Illustration

Throughout most of this paper we have concentrated upon the unmarried drug abuser living at home with his parents. However, our technique can be adapted to other situations, including that of a married drug abuser living with his spouse in his own household. Discussion of such a case will help to illustrate an array of treatment interventions.

Bill, 21, and his wife Dierdre, 22, had been married for one year. Bill had smoked marijuana and gone out drinking with his friends several times a week since his early teens. Dierdre was aware of this when they married. However, recently Bill had increased his smoking and drinking, and had begun using amphetamines rather heavily as well. Dierdre insisted Bill apply for treatment and both were assigned to conjoint marital therapy.

Bill was the oldest of several siblings. Both his parents were alive, and the father was an alcoholic. The mother was the dominant spouse and, according to Bill, often treated the father like one of the children. She was very strict and controlling with the children. Dierdre was an only child. Her mother had also been the dominant spouse, the father having been "kindly, but weak and sickly all his life."

In the first treatment phase, the therapist redefined the problem as the marital relationship rather than Bill's substance abuse. The therapist had the couple review what they liked about one another, all the good times they had in the past, and the tender and happy moments they still shared. That they had entered counseling the therapist indicated was a sign of their mututal concern and proof of their maturity, courage, and foresight.

Dierdre complained about Bill's drug and alcohol abuse. Bill objected that Dierdre was exaggerating and felt that she was being "contaminated" and "recruited" by his own mother, who had gotten her to join his mother's Al-Anon group.

The therapist explored the situations which cued Bill's substance abuse, his binges. Invariably they began rather harmlessly with both Bill and Dierdre having a social drink in a restaurant or smoking a small amount of marijuana at a party. The problem would begin with Dierdre's attempts to control Bill. While they were both in the middle of their first drink, for ex-ample, she would start to warn him that he should not get drunk. He would grow resentful and begin to drink just to spite her. She would escalate her warnings and he would escalate his drinking until he could hardly stand.

The couple was helped to see that Dierdre's attempts to control Bill merely provoked the undesired behavior. Dierdre was instructed to ignore Bill's drinking or drug use at the next party they attended; controlling him-self would be his responsibility, and if he failed the unpleasant results would be his problem, not hers. She was successful in doing this, despite Bill's attempts to provoke her into resuming her strict mother role. After a few unpleasant mornings after, Bill spontaneously reduced his drinking and drug use at parties.

The directive to Dierdre not to reinforce Bill's substance abuse with at-tention resulted in a reduction in his alcohol and marijuana use to subcult-urally normal, social levels within four weeks. He ceased all amphetamine use by the fifth week. In the seventh week, following an argument with Dierdre, he took several uppers in a highly theatrical and ostentatious fash-ion. He was, he admitted later, "trying to get Dierdre's goat." She remained calm and he abandoned the attempt. Following that incident there were no recurrences of amphetamine abuse.

However, an interpersonal problem remained. Bill feared Dierdre wanted to trap him with commitments; he saw her as overly demanding, draining, and as a crybaby. Dierdre felt he was aloof, insensitive, and un-caring. She wished he would not avoid her as much as he seemed to, that he would spend more time with her. A reciprocally reinforcing behavioral con-tract (8, 17) was set up in which Dierdre would allow Bill a specific amount of time "out with the boys" in exchange for his guaranteeing her a specific amount of conversation and closeness each night.

In the second treatment phase, which was considered necessary because of this couple's difficulties with intimacy, the therapist concentrated upon the naming process and upon unresolved grief in the spouses concerning events in the families of origin. Dierdre said she had been named after a fictional folkloric character, "Dierdre of the Sorrows"—or at least that was her mother's association with that name. Her middle name, Veronica, was a character in a soap opera her mother used to listen to before her birth; it was also, her mother told her, the name of the grieving woman in the New Testament account of Christ's crucifixion. When Bill heard how Dierdre chad been named he joked, "Boy, that's really you! With names like those, no wonder you're a crybaby! You're a walking soap opera; everything's a tragedy to you." Throughout her life, Dierdre had been a worrier, especially concerning her father's health. He had died two months before the couple entered treatment. It emerged that Dierdre had begun to worry about Bill's health and his alcohol and drug use right after her father's death. It was then that she first began to see Bill as weak, needing her and her help as her father had. By selectively attending to the weak parts of Bill's personality, she unwittingly reinforced them and thus succeeded in reincarnating her father in Bill. Now she could worry about Bill and sacrifice for him as she had for her father.

Bill was a junior, named after his father. From birth, he was seen as the family black sheep, as taking after his father. His mother was especially fearful that he would become an alcoholic like her husband. Consequently she was stricter with him than with the other children, often taking special care to warn him away from the evils of drink. Naturally this approach resulted in precisely the opposite of what she consciously intended. Bill was clearly convinced that he would turn out like his father; however, his response was "what the hell, I might as well enjoy it since it's inevitable anyway." In his late teens he described himself as a "hell raiser." However, after his marriage, he settled down. When Dierdre's loss of her father precipitated her attempts to rescue and control him, he began to develop an "allergic" reaction to her. She began to remind him more and more of his controlling mother. Part of him enjoyed being mothered again—it gave him an excuse to abdicate responsibility: "It was as if I'd never left home; I didn't have to look out for myself because my mother or Dierdre would do it for me." But another part of him resented the outside control, feeling trapped, annihilated, and swallowed up; this part rebelled. If his mother or Dierdre wanted him to drink less, "by God, I'd drink more." His ambivalent response to Dierdre's attempts at control not only exacerbated his substance-abuse symptoms and his tendency to avoid and distance himself from her, but it also reinforced her own counter-productive attempts to rescue him. Both were caught in a vicious cycle.

The therapist helped Dierdre to become more consciously aware of her lifelong role as sorrower, rescuer, and martyr, and assisted her in belatedly mourning her father. This freed her to see Bill as a real person, distinct from her father; it also permitted her to regard his drug and alcohol use more realistically, as being essentially nonproblematic unless he and she colluded to make it a problem. It also gave her the security to let go of Bill a bit, to allow him the breathing space he seemed to need in the marital relationship if he was not to feel trapped. The therapist helped Bill to confront his lifelong role as a black sheep and a stand-in for his alcoholic father. He came to realize that he need not necessarily follow the script his parents had unwittingly written for him. He was helped to mourn that his mother's love was ambivalent, and to come to terms with it, so that he no longer needed Dierdre to reincarnate his controlling, intrusive mother. This simultaneously freed him to show an increased degree of closeness and tenderness towards Dierdre.

At the conclusion of therapy Bill and Dierdre's relationship was markedly improved, and substance abuse was no longer a problem.

Assessment

We have been very encouraged by the success of this brief triphasic conjoint family therapy approach. As the family's investment in the drug-abuse symptom falls away, the drug use itself occasionally shows a complete cessation. More often, it decreases in frequency, or a switch from the harder to the softer, less dangerous drugs occurs. Simultaneously there is a notable improvement in family communication and relationship patterns.

Of course the extent to which this technique can be confidently generalized to other socioeconomic or treatment populations is undetermined. However, it does seem potentially adaptable, at least to a variety of youthful populations. One of its virtues, at least in our eyes, is that it is a rather eclectic and flexible method. Depending upon the case at hand, one might utilize techniques borrowed from the structural family therapy school or the communications theorists in one phase, and the insights of the object-relations school in another. The freedom to do so is refreshing. Too often internecine rivalry between the varying family therapy schools (7, 9) blocks the creative synthesis of diverse approaches so necessary if our field is to remain viable and if we are to remain vital and helpful as therapists.

REFERENCES

1. Alexander, B.K. & Dibb, G.S., Opiate Addicts and Their Parents. *Family Process* 14:499–514, 1975.

2. Alexander, B.K. & Dibb, G.S., Interpersonal Perception in Addict Families. *Family Process* 16:17–28, 1977.
3. Boszormenyi-Nagy, I., Intensive Family Therapy as Process. In I. Boszormenyi-Nagy & J. Framo (Eds.), *Intensive Family Therapy*, New York: Harper & Row, 1969.
4. Boszormenyi-Nagy, I. & Spark, G., *Invisible Loyalties*, New York: Harper & Row, 1973.
5. Bowen, M., Family Psychotherapy with Schizophrenia in the Hospital and in Private Practice. In I. Boszormenyi-Nagy & J. Framo (Eds.), *Intensive Family Therapy*, New York: Harper & Row, 1969.
6. Cannon, S.R., Social Functioning Patterns in Families of Offspring Receiving Treatment for Drug Abuse, Roslyn Heights, NY: Libra Publications, 1976.
7. Ferber, A., Mendelsohn, M., & Napier, A., *The Book of Family Therapy*, Boston: Houghton Mifflin, 1973.
8. Fischer, J. & Gochros, H., *Planned Behavior Change*, New York: Free Press, 1975.
9. Foley, V., *An Introduction to Family Therapy*, New York: Grune & Stratton, 1974.
10. Framo, J., Rationale and Techniques of Intensive Family Therapy, In I. Boszormenyi-Nagy & J. Framo (Eds.), *Intensive Family Therapy*, New York: Harper & Row, 1969.
11. Framo, J., Symptoms from a Family Transactional Viewpoint. In C. Sager & H. Kaplan (Eds.), *Progress in Group and Family Therapy*, New York: Brunner/Mazel, 1972.
12. Freud, S., Mourning and Melancholia. In *S. Freud, Collected Papers* (Vol. 4), New York: Basic Books, 1959.
13. Gallup, G., Drugs, Parent Relations Are Top Problems. *Newsday*, May 18, 1977.
14. Haley, J., *The Power Tactics of Jesus Christ*, New York: Avon, 1969.
15. Haley, J., *Uncommon Therapy*, New York: Ballantine, 1973.
16. Harbin, H. & Maziar, H., The Families of Drug Abusers: A Literature Review. *Family Process* 14:411–431, 1975.
17. Knox, D., *Marriage Happiness: A Beahvioral Approach to Counseling*, Champaign, IL: Research Press, 1971.
18. Liberman, R., Behavioral Approaches to Family and Couple Therapy. In C. Sager & H. Kaplan (Eds.), *Progress in Group and Family Therapy*, New York: Brunner/Mazel, 1972.
19. Minuchin, S., *Families and Family Therapy*, Cambridge, MA: Harvard University Press, 1974.
20. Noone, R. & Reddig, R., Case Studies in the Family Treatment of Drug Abuse. *Family Process* 15:325–332, 1976.
21. Paul, N., The Use of Empathy in the Resolution of Grief. *Perspectives in Biology and Medicine* 2:153–169, 1967.
22. Reilly, D., Family Factors in the Etiology and Treatment of Youthful Drug Abuse. *Family Therapy* 2:149–176, 1975.
23. Reilly, D., Legislative Testimony. In *Anomalies in Drug Abuse Treatment*, State of New York Legislative Document #11, New York: New York State Legislature, 1975.
24. Reilly, D., Theory of Family Therapy. Panel presentation at National Drug Abuse Conference, San Francisco, CA, May 7, 1977.

25. Stierlin, H., *Separating Parents and Adolescents*, New York: Quadrangle/New York Times Book Co., 1974.
26. Sutherland, E. & Cressey, D., *Principles of Criminology* (5th Ed.), Philadelphia, PA: Lippincott, 1955.
27. Watzlawick, P., Weakland, J., & Fisch, R., *Change, Principles of Problem Formation and Problem Resolution*, New York: Norton, 1974.

10

Siblings in Session

Sandra B. Coleman, Ph.D.
DIRECTOR, RESEARCH AND EVALUATION
ACHIEVEMENT THROUGH COUNSELING AND TREATMENT
PHILADELPHIA, PENNSYLVANIA

Introduction

Substantial evidence from recent data (2, 5) indicates that there is a repetitive pattern of drug and alcohol abuse within families of adolescent drug users. A frequent interpretation of this intergenerational occurrence is that for such families, drugs and alcohol become ways of coping with stress. These learned addictive behaviors offer a legacy which is given to each new generation, each time increasing the probability that there will be abusing offspring. Although there is adequate support for the idea that addictive behavior can be "transmitted" from grandparent to parent to child, little has been written about the "infectiousness" of drug use from sibling to sibling. In general, even the ever-widening group of professionals who are using family therapy to treat drug addicts have failed to give much attention to the effect of siblings on drug-using behavior.

This chapter focuses on a project designed for siblings of drug addicts as a means of augmenting the important work accomplished in more traditional therapy with the whole family. The concept of a sib group evolved from several years of doing family therapy with middle-class, Caucasian families who had at least one adolescent member recovering from drug abuse (largely heroin) at a therapeutic community. During family therapy sessions the following observations led to the development of a sibling therapy group.

A major issue was the manner in which attention-getting behavioral strategies were used by family members. From the time a child's drug addiction was discovered, parents were steeped in the conflict and resolution of the problem. Primary focus was placed on the addict, and younger (latency age) sibs were often forced to handle responsibilities for which they were ill-prepared. Although they were given little attention, many demands were placed on them. Because they did not present overt problems of their own, they became passive agents in a process in which their personal trauma was overlooked. Even within family therapy sessions where therapists modified structural positions and interactions within the entire family system, the younger children were most difficult to reach. They developed attachments to the therapists but were resistant to revealing much of themselves. It was easy to speculate that such rigid defenses and the suppression of their dependency needs in juxtaposition with the modeling effects of an older drug-using brother or sister made the chances for their future addiction quite high. It seemed all the more likely in some cases where families already had two or more youngsters using drugs.

The most typical family pattern found the mother in a dyadic relationship with her addict son. In our experience, the second drug user was often a female who was in alliance with her father. This left the other youngsters on the periphery to fend for themselves. Direct observation of these sibs indicated that when there was more than one child who was younger than the drug user(s), they were often in a coalition with each other. This is consistent with Caplow's (3) observation that sibling coalitions arise as a consequence of other parent-child conditions.

Beyond being in therapy sessions with parents and older sibs, the younger siblings were asked to attend a session at least once without parents. When alone it became apparent that these children were very much aware of the covert family transactions and understood the ways and means in which they were reinforced. They knew the secrets and why they were concealed, and they further controlled this protection by using power tactics on each other. This led them to acquiesce to the actions of others when they were in sessions with their entire family. Beyond their family loyalty these youngsters had a special feeling for each other which was strengthened by the family drug crisis. They identified strongly with one another, and this created a powerful force. It was felt that although such a subsystem might have only a slight influence on the other family members, it had considerable influence on the sibs. Thus if one of them started to take drugs, it was likely that the other would follow. Conversely, if one were to reject drugs, the other might yield to his or her influence. In addition to the dyadic bonds formed by the younger sibs within a given family, there existed a network of sibs from multiple families. This resulted from the fact that three of the families lived on the same street, while most of the others were from the same community. These children attended the same schools and had been playmates since early childhood. In a similar fashion, their older brothers and sisters had often been initiated into drugs together. Thus there were extra familial dyadic coalitions and interfamilial sibling alliances. Since a loosely contrived sibling group was already in existence, creating a formal structure seemed both logical and timely.

It was felt that the group's exposure to therapy would lead to more open and constructive communication among members of the same age. Therapists could then help the sibs to incorporate the new behavior into their respective families. The basic focus of the group was threefold: 1) to encourage expression of feelings within the group; 2) to use group process as a means of reflecting interpersonal reactions, behaviors, and the like; and 3) to provide a trusting milieu within which stresses and problems about family, school, and peers could be discussed and guided toward resolution.

There were eighteen youngsters who attended the group during its two-year existence. The constellation of youngsters included six sibling pairs and six nonrelated individual siblings. Among the family dyads there were three pairs of brothers, one pair of sisters and two pairs of brother/sister dyads. The remaining sibs were all female. Although a few more youngsters were to attend for brief periods of time, the basic group that convened in the beginning remained relatively stable. Sessions were held once a week and lasted for 60 to 75 minutes. In addition to the sib therapy sessions, there were periodic group meetings with parents to exchange information regarding the youngsters' behavior at home and in school. Sibs requested that they not be required to attend. Group confidentiality was upheld so that parents were given a progress report rather than a direct account of therapeutic material. Family therapy was held concurrently, and more than two-thirds of the siblings were in treatment with their families either before or during the time when sib group was held.

Process

Although the initial response on the part of parents and sib group members was one of enthusiastic acceptance, the early months proved difficult. The sibs were unusually anxious, and expressed their tension by becoming physically abusive with each other. Attempts to direct this hyperactive behavior into a constructive, acceptable form failed. The environment was one of diffuse chaos which often did not subside when the group ended. The general destructiveness among members frequently prevailed to the extent that they attacked each other after leaving the therapy room and at times one member, singled out as a scapegoat, received a beating by several others. Those who did not participate directly contributed to the behavior by passively watching. Their behavior was similar to that of the youths in *Lord of the Flies* (4). Therapists became wardens and agents of control rather than the supportive counselors they had purported to be.

In an attempt to channel the excessive motor activity, several techniques were adapted. During the warm months, groups were organized into teams.

Outdoor races, tag, and even softball games were held. Although far from the original plans drafted, this "recreational" therapy proved to be an effective release. Gradually the group was moved back into the therapy room, where rules for respecting others and a "hands-off" policy were developed.

At this point, physical tension was channeled into the use of "sculpting" techniques and "collages." These methods derive from group and family therapy models which use nonverbal "pictures" to symbolically represent family and group dynamics. Each member had an opportunity to arrange the other group members in a tableau that demonstrated perceived roles, emotions, and conflicts as projected by the "arranger." Frequently such methods tapped rigidly defended processes and led to disclosure of problems that might normally take several months to unfold.

Shortly before Thanksgiving members were relaxed enough to portray their expected holiday dinners by sculpting group members into family roles. This led to the first spontaneous discussion of feelings related to family members, particularly grandparents. One highly verbal girl reflected that she really hated the holiday because her mother became upset every time the maternal grandmother arrived at their home. She said she didn't like to see her mom get so upset and wondered why her grandmother spoke to her mother as if she were still a young child.

Although this apparent breakthrough in group behavior made the therapists optimistic about the future of the group, the acting-out behavior seemed to abate only temporarily. Poor impulse control again became overwhelming and sessions were disappointingly tense. More structured activities were obviously needed, and several proved successful. One particularly useful method of channeling hostility was the use of the "Slip Group," a model patterned from that used in the agency's residential program. In order to help recovering addicts learn to delay their impulse gratification, they are required to refrain from immediate expression of hostility and to record their anger toward another resident or staff member on a piece of paper, or "slip," and present that directly in group therapy. There the person who has written the slip faces and confronts the individual who is the object of the anger. The two parties sit in the center of the group circle while the others observe. No physical contact is permitted but heightened verbal release is encouraged. This method of confrontation was adapted by the sibs and was useful and always available to those who needed it. In one particularly climactic session, each group member entered the therapy room with a brown lunch bag filled with slips "dropped" on each member of the group, including the therapists.

Spontaneous methods of facilitating group communication always seemed more useful than preplanned activities. Group drawings and poetry provided an immediate vehicle for expression when members were uncomfortable with each other and could not yet handle direct contact unless they were very angry. An example of a poem composed by the group just six months after its inception follows:

Joe is a moe
Sue is an ass
Dina feels woe,
The group feel woe.
Bob is a slob
We act like a mob
Serene is a queen
Gail raises Hell and Jon belongs there.
Loren gives hickeys
Nel sure smells and can go to Hell.
Kirk is a jerk...
He eats a pack of certs
Dale is a Jew
Hal sucks on his toe.
Jeff loves Kim
Rita is a pizza
Mike is cool
Our group is real cool when we swim in the pool.

Such a "nonsense" rhyme contains important insights reflecting attitudes, feelings, and roles of individual group members. Two of the most significant lines in this poem are, "Dina feels woe,/The group feels woe." This part of the jingle points to what became the pivotal point in the outcome of the group's very existence. From the first day, 12-year-old Dina exhibited more diffuse anxiety and impulsivity than any of the other sibs. She demanded maximum attention from all, and each week seemed to arrive in group with a new means of getting it. Although mature, she presented herself as a sexually-enticing young woman whose every movement suggested promiscuous behavior in the not-too-distant future. Her charisma had a rippling effect such that the group action seemed to ebb and flow with her whims. She was always in the center, and no amount of intervention on the part of the therapist effected any change. She chewed gum, knitted unidentifiable garments, and, had uncontrollable relentless outbursts with a verve that influenced and rocked the group's tenuous foundation. That she was threatened and unable to cope with the situation was obvious, but no amount of support or control proved effective. The group at times ignored her, yet she had uncanny wit and ability to manipulate the flow of the sessions to the extent that she always became the focus of rage or laughter. Small group interventions that attempted to unlock existing dyads helped others, but not Dina. All her partners succumbed to her influence. When others cooperated in a sentence completion sensitivity exercise, she drew pictures of hostile animals.

When it seemed that her regressive behavior could not in any constructive way be dealt with in the group, she was asked why she wanted to be there. Her answer was, "I don't, but my mother won't let me quit." Previous attempts to question her motivation for group attendance had resulted in her denial of any desire to leave, but finally the stress must have become too great and she was honest. When she was reassured that her leaving would be supported by the therapist and that she could return when ready, she acquiesced. As if clairvoyantly, the free associations in the poem point to what seemed to be the embodiment of the group's early character and near demise.

The absence of the Lolitaesque member produced an immediate and amazing change. In the earlier phase it was necessary at all times to have a bag of techniques with which to orchestrate order out of what seemed like ceaseless cacophony. The second phase was markedly different. There was a quieting down and the need to impose mechanisms for successful group functioning diminished. Members spontaneously brought problems to the group. A circle was formed and the group topology at least became traditional. At last it even looked like group therapy. No more physical violence occurred, the subgroups merged into the larger mass, and the group became cohesive. One of the most exciting developments took place one day when the therapist arrived late and found the group settled and functioning on its own.

The rationale for this change is not fully explainable. Possibly Dina's leaving set some kind of example. Seemingly based on her own decision, it may be that at some level the group forced her out. Did they identify enough with her impulsivity to fear their own destruction if she stayed? Does this indicate that the therapy represented an important dimension of their lives that they wished to preserve? Certainly Dina's impact on the group was profound. It may be that her departure served as a symbolic representation of possible group destiny, which suggests these youngsters really opted for survival. References to Dina were rarely made after she left, though one general statement was that without Dina, group was much better. When someone occasionally attempted to report on her current behavior (learned via the neighborhood or school grapevine) the group members quickly reminded each other "We don't discuss people who aren't here." Perhaps the calm was a result of normal group process and development, or maybe everyone simply became exhausted, but whatever the reason, the shift was surely welcome.

Content

The sib group sessions provided a fascinating excursion into the minds and lives of its members. The scope of the therapeutic material was widespread and rich, and the themes—too frequently—tragic.

Death, either symbolic or real, was the most familiar recurring theme. It always left a sobering effect on the members. The first such experience after the group's formation took place when Rita's 23-year-old brother was the victim of a robbery-homicide in the home he shared with several students in Philadelphia. Ironically this brother was the only member of Rita's family who was not addicted to drugs, alcohol, or food. (Rita, her mother, and a married sister were all very obese; her father was an alcoholic who, as a result of family therapy, became sober for the first time in over a decade; another brother was drug-addicted; and a sister was a pothead.) Rita and her family came for family therapy immediately after the murder. In addition, upon learning of her brother's death, Rita, who had been away from the group for several months, sobbingly said that she wanted to return to sib group. Several group members became tearful when Rita recounted the sad episode. She cried a great deal, and the group in general was quite responsive to her. Each member related a personal experience with death. Considering their ages they had suffered some rather unusual losses, including one boy's four-year-old sister who had died of leukemia several years before. An interesting result of Rita's tragedy was that in contrast to her previous peripheral position in the group, she became an integrated and accepted member.

Several months later, another 13-year-old broke into sobs. Her older brother, a diabetic since childhood, had returned to using drugs. In the past the combination of his physical illness and heroin had so threatened his life that he was given last rites three times. Sue told the group that she feared this time would surely be fatal. Again the group talked seriously about their past experiences with death. They suggested that Sue disclose her fears to her brother, which she was subsequently able to do. Although she doubted that this would change his behavior, she admitted that she felt considerable relief in having faced him so honestly.

One of the youngest members, Margo, dropped out of the group before the first spring. She said she could not tolerate the stress and acting-out of the others. A rather quiet child, she was too determined for us to be able to reverse her decision. In midsummer her pet dog was killed by an automobile. A week later Margo was back in group. She cried profusely and told everyone how angry she was toward the careless driver, an ornery, insensitive neighbor. Margo had considerable difficulty overcoming the loss, even though her parents bought her a new puppy. There was little change in her affect until it was suggested that the new dog be brought to group. Following the puppy's much-approved visit, Margo's mourning subsided. For several subsequent sessions other sibs arrived at group with a variety of pets in tow.

Sexual functioning and behavior were also important concerns. Despite initial giggles and whispers, discussions proved frank and informative. Most youngsters felt their parents did not accept the idea of premarital sex for their daughters, but allowed their sons greater sexual permissiveness. Attitudes were amazingly mature in this area, and most agreed that responsibility was the major determinant regarding sexual expression.

Sex-role conflict also presented problems for the sibs. One 11-year-old boy complained of unfair quantities of housework, which he felt should be shared by his sister. He had difficulty assessing how much of his anger was due to the fact that "women's work" was imposed on him. Another member was conflicted about her pattern of catering to her older brother, who always wanted "BLT's just as I sit down to watch TV." His bribes irritated her, yet fear of rejection prevented her from confronting him. The group helped her to summon the courage to talk to him, and positive results were reported.

These examples point to the constructive nature of the group. However, serious problems began to surface at the end of eighteen months. Two concurrent repetitive topics bear attention. One was the emergence of drug use. Smoking and drinking among members became central issues. Boastingly one girl talked of having gone to a beer party where she became ill from drinking her own six-pack. She stated that although vomiting was not fun, she really liked the feeling of being high and claimed that she was not hesitant about trying it again. Her story prompted others to share equally "thrilling" encounters with alcohol. One member said that she consumed her can of beer with parental permission. This 11-year-old youngster had a father recovering from alcoholism, an alcoholic brother who was a former drug user, and another sib who was a rehabilitated heroin addict.

When therapists confronted the group with the implications of their behavior, the general response was one of denial and rationalization, but emotionally they were detached. As sense of braggadocio prevailed. This was also seen in regard to cigarette smoking. Two girls, both 13 years of age, had been given parental permission to smoke. It was suggested by a nonsmoking sib that those with permission should smoke in group. Without hesitation the two members removed cigarettes from their pockets and prepared to light up. Therapeutic intervention provoked a discussion centering on the attitudes and concerns of all with regard to the issue of permitting smoking during group. Although two boys said that they felt they did not want their lives endangered by breathing smoke-filled air, many sibs opted for smoking. A week to think it over was suggested. Several sibs directly told the therapists, "You're not supposed to be parents, so you have to let us decide." The following week, the two abstainers held their ground but all the others, including the ones who previously were undecided, voted in favor of granting permission.

The second problem was that of school. Truancy, school suspension, and behavioral difficulties requiring disciplinary action by school officials increased. One girl, a former high achiever with ambitious career goals, announced that she was suspended for disobeying a teacher's order to change her seat. Another youth was suspended for smoking, while another's repetitive truancy became a major issue which led to his mother's decision to place him in another school district where he would live with his father, from whom she had recently separated.

Although this deterioration seemed to be spreading among all the sibs, there were really only four youngsters in the foreground of the mounting rebellion. One of the four was Dina's brother, who unlike his sister had always been one of the group's "straightest" members. It was interesting that this small subgroup included only the sibs who resided on the same suburban street.

Concern about the potential invasion of similar acting-out among the other youngsters led to the therapeutic decision to use a multiple family approach (6). The rationale for this intervention was that the upheaval occurring in the smaller sibling network might reflect an unrecognized family problem. In addition, conjoint parental cooperation in limit-setting was mandatory. Due to office space limitations the multiple family therapy sessions were limited to the four siblings from the group, Dina, and their parents. Older sibs were not included since most of them were either away at school, in the service, or in some way successfully coping with their own lives. None were using drugs. It is important to note that each of the three families had been in family therapy and had made many changes in their structural patterns and affective relationships.

The G family included Mr. and Mrs. G. and their four children. Rita, their 13-year-old daughter, was the only family member attending sib group. Rita had always been an excellent student and athlete, and had never been a discipline problem. A 15-year-old sister had recovered from polydrug and alcohol abuse; a 17-year-old brother was "straight"; and the eldest brother, 20, had recovered from heroin addiction. Mr. G. had been an alcoholic for most of his adult life, but as a result of family therapy had joined Alcoholics Anonymous and had been sober for two years. Mrs. G., the daughter of an alcoholic father, had recently won a long struggle to lose more than 40 pounds of excess weight. She and her husband were enjoying considerable marital satisfaction at this time.

The R. family included Mrs. R., who was separated from her husband. He had been described as a heavy drinker. The two sons in sib group were Kirk, 12, and Michael, who was 14. There were also two daughters aged 16 and 10. Seven years previously a four-year-old daughter had died of acute leukemia. This was the only family seen at the drug program that did not include a drug-using adolescent. It had been accepted for family and sib therapy because of Mrs. R.'s fear that the neighborhood friends would adversely influence her own children.

The M. family consisted of Mr. and Mrs. M., who separated from each other after family therapy allowed them to cooperatively disengage from an unrewarding union. Their children included a 20-year-old son, a former heroin addict; an 18-year-old daughter who had recovered from heavy polydrug use; Dina, 13, and Jonathon, 12. Jonathon still attended sib group, and Dina had not returned when multiple family therapy first began. Neither Mr. nor Mrs. M. was addicted, but Mrs. M.'s father was an alcoholic, and there were several other alcoholics in her family ancestry.

These three families were all quite willing to participate in multiple family therapy, and the only parent who did not attend was Mr. R.

The results of multiple family therapy were encouraging. In three months the disruption in sib group came to a halt and the acting out was significantly reduced. With the exception of Dina, the youngsters seemed to embrace the parental controls. Two issues emerged as major factors in the recent sibling upsurgence. The first was that parents were not paying much attention to what their children were doing. When they sent them to bed they assumed that was where they went. They did not know how little it took to sneak out a back window and summon buddies to a series of midnight escapades. All the parents were employed, which meant there was no guidance after school hours. In short, controls were lacking. Even if one household attempted to set limits, there was no neighborhood consistency, so the children could always find leverage somewhere. Instead of manipulating one hesitant parent against the other controlling one, it was one family system's loose structure that was pitted against another household's attempt to be effective. The disorganization of the neighborhood reinforced the youngster's chaotic, destructive behavior. The second element of the tension was Mrs. M.'s alleged affair with a black man, Mr. W., who was becoming an increasingly frequent visitor at the M. home. Neither Dina nor Jonathon were ready to accept their mother's new interracial liasion. They turned to their friends for support, which generated mass sibling disapproval. Since Dina was the most distressed, she once more overpowered the group. This was easy to do, as Mr. M. was the youngsters' favorite parent and the one who had always helped repair their bikes and bruises. It took Dina little time to have others acknowledge that her father's position was being usurped and abused. Although there were other minor issues that emerged, the evidence all pointed to the anxiety about Mr. W. In one session Jonathon said apologetically that he felt that the sib's recent delinquency had influenced their parents. "People always think that the kids copy their parents," he said. "I think that we've done the opposite and that our parents are acting just like us." He went on to cite an incident in which several sibs had absconded to the woods to spend the night without getting approval. It became quite clear that most of these youngsters felt quite guilty.

The problems were resolved by introducing consistent rules which were enforced by all neighborhood parents. Communication among parents was considered tantamount to approving all children's requests. There was an increase in supervision and guidance. Adults took turns offering a helping hand and each one "on duty" became a counselor and trouble shooter. In addition there was a rigidification of generational boundaries. Children were given group understanding for their loyalty to Mr. M. but were asked to respect his estranged wife's right to her own life. Mr. M. did not feel threatened or vindictive, and he wanted the children, in short, "to mind their own business." Mrs. M. did learn how to continue her new relationship more discreetly, and she began to spend more time with Dina and Jonathon alone.

Multiple family therapy was clearly successful in resolving the crisis which flared in the sib group. Its rapid acceptance was largely due to the fact that all members had previous therapy experience and valued it as a vehicle for attaining personal goals. The effect of multiple-family therapy on the sib group was almost immediately apparent. The sessions were calmer and the subgroup became integrated with the other members. A major event was Dina's return. Although it was questionable whether or not she could sustain her reasonably subdued behavior, it was important to give her the opportunity.

The sib group continued to meet for approximately three months after multiple family therapy sessions ended. No further difficulty arose, and it was soon evident that the group was ready to terminate. Its purposes had been achieved and the youngsters were doing well. A final party was held and promises were made by both therapists and sibs that continued contact would be possible if difficulties were encountered. This has not yet happened. More than one year later it appears that most of the children are doing well. The only known exception is, unfortunately, Dina. For a period of time she was using drugs, was truant in school, and spending time with many boys several years her senior. From the last phone contact with her mother it was learned that she was going to a local clinic for individual therapy. Her brother Jonathon was on firm ground and has consistently been an honor student. Rita G. is concentrating on scholastic achievement and has slightly reduced her somewhat chubby figure. The K. brothers are also doing well.

Conclusions

The sib group was an exploratory attempt to apply group therapy techniques to siblings as a complement to therapy with their addict families. It was an effort to concentrate on younger, preadolescent siblings from the viewpoint that they were an influential system in the family, and in combination perhaps even more powerful among their peers. It was hoped that a therapeutic group of such youngsters would prevent what seemed to be their inevitable inheritance of addiction.

The early experience with the sibs was one of disruption and anxiety. As the group became cohesive, its focus became constructive and therapeutic. The original goals were being met when some serious problems surfaced. These were not resolved until a smaller subgroup of siblings and parents attended weekly multiple-family therapy sessions.

This was not a systematic study with a tightly conceived research design and methodology. The interventions grew from need rather than a plan. A post hoc analysis, therefore, is all that can be offered.

The siblings were not well integrated with their families. The older sibling subsystem initially took over the parental functions vis-a-vis acting out with drugs (7). Major family conflicts were centered on separation/individuation issues which seemed to be resolved in family therapy for the parents and the older sibling subsystem. But apparently the younger sibling subsystems were somehow overlooked. Perhaps in an attempt to keep them from becoming mediators between the parents and older sibs, therapists moved them too far from the family in a case of "overexile." The notion of sibling "exile" was discussed by Bank and Kahn (1), who suggest that the well sibling is used to keep the family "in uneasy but stable balance." The therapist's task is to shift the sib from this position. Also, our family therapy with addicts may not have modified the system substantially enough for parents to incorporate behaviors used with older sibs when younger ones developed similar conflicts. Regressive behavior might explain what occurred later.

The sibling group became a vehicle for anxiety release. The acting-out behaviors occurred in the group, where sibs trusted the therapists to help. Family systems then were restructured on a neighborhood network level.

During the multiple family therapy sessions parents learned to be more efficient in their executive functions by using their neighborhood family network as an important resource.

Banks and Kahn (1) feel that family therapists may have overlooked the importance of "sibling interaction and sibling therapy." Ten years ago Minuchin (7) noted that sibs often consult each other during periods of conflict. This project demonstrates that there was therapeutic value in putting siblings in their own sessions. Similar projects with systematic evaluative measures of process and outcome are necessary. Such groups may well be preventive, since today's siblings are the parents of the future. Thus, if we can incur positive change when a sib's development is interrupted by family trauma, the sins of their brothers and sisters may not be visited upon them.

REFERENCES

1. Bank, S. & Kahn, M., Ssiterhood-brotherhood is Powerful: Sibling Subsystems and Family Therapy. *Family Process* 3:311–337, 1975.
2. Blum, R.H., *Horatio Alger's Children*, London: Jossey-Bass, 1972.
3. Caplow, L., *Two Against One: Coalition in Triads*, Englewood Cliffs, NJ: Prentice-Hall, 1968.
4. Golding, W., *Lord of the Flies*, New York: Coward-McCann, 1962.
5. Jessor, R., Graves, R., Hanson, R., & Jessor, S., *Society, Personality, and Deviant Behavior: A Study of a Tri-Ethnic Community*, New York: Holt, Rhinehart & Winston, 1968.
6. Laqueur, H.P., chapter in A Ferber, M. Mendelsohn, & A. Napier (Eds.), *The Book of Family Therapy*, New York: Science House, 1972.
7. Minuchin, S., Montalvo, B., Guerney, B.G., Rosman, B.L., & Schumer, F., *Families of the Slums*, New York; Basic Books, 1967.
8. Von Bertalanffy, L., *General Systems Theory: Essays in Its Foundation and Development*, New York: Braziller, 1968.

Part II
ALCOHOL ABUSERS

11

Family Therapy with Alcoholics: A Review*

Peter Steinglass, M.D.
ASSOCIATE PROFESSOR DEPT. OF PSYCHIATRY AND BEHAVIORAL SCIENCES, AND
THE CENTER FOR FAMILY RESEARCH
GEORGE WASHINGTON UNIVERSITY SCHOOL OF MEDICINE
WASHINGTON, D.C.

It is generally accepted that there are presently nine million adults in the United States who abuse or are addicted to alcohol. The American public has recently become aware that alcohol is once again the drug of choice of the American teenager. Financial estimates indicate that alcohol abuse exacts a staggering toll on American industry via absenteeism, interference with performance, and interference with sound judgment. These dramatic "tips of the iceberg" indicate that alcohol abuse in our culture carries with it staggering social and psychological consequences.

The pervasiveness of alcohol use and abuse in the United States is of such proportions as to guarantee that any mental health professional practicing in this country will be working with a significant number of patients whose use of alcohol has reached abusive proportions. For family therapists, who traditionally work with groups of two or more adults in conflict either with each other or with their adolescent children, the likelihood that one member of this group abuses alcohol becomes even greater. It seems clear, therefore, that treatment techniques for alcoholism should be of primary concern to the family therapist.

Whereas previously alcoholics were conceptualized as homeless, jobless, physically ravaged individuals with meager psychological resources, it is now clear that this "end stage" alcoholic is most unrepresentative of the patient population that abuses alcohol. A significant, if not major, proportion of the alcoholic population continues to function within nominally intact and stable family systems, which makes it a natural clientele for the family therapist. Therefore, whether or not the family therapist feels alcoholism

*This chapter is based on material previously published by Dr. Steinglass in Family Therapy in Alcoholism, in B. Kissin, & H. Begleiter (Eds.), *The Biology of Alcoholism* (Vol 5), New York: Plenum, 1977, and in Experimenting with Family Treatment Approaches to Alcoholism, 1950–1975: A Review, *Family Process*, 15(1), 97–123, 1976.

per se is a condition appropriately treated by family therapy techniques, the symptom itself is so pervasive as to be virtually unavoidable. As we shall see in our review of the literature, however, alcoholism therapists have come relatively late to the family field, and family therapists have only recently begun to view alcoholism as an area of interest. This mutual disregard is frankly not at all surprising.

From the perspective of the traditional establishment in the alcoholism field, the priority issue has been the transformation of alcoholism from a moral problem into a medical problem. This conversion has been seen as a necessary prerequisite for the transfer of responsibility for alcoholism treatment from the judicial system into the medical establishment. With this goal in mind, the emphasis has been on the medical model. Alcoholism is viewed as a disease process with an etiology, a set of symptoms, a typical course, and a predictable prognosis. However, the medical model is designed primarily to describe disease processes as they affect an individual. Hence family therapy feels strange and foreign.

From the perspective of the family therapist, on the other hand, clinical interest has focused on disturbed communicational patterns and structural dissonance within the family. Although these phenomena are hardly absent in the family with an alcoholic member, the abusive consumption of alcohol and its attendant behavioral and physical consequences appeared at first glance to be so overwhelming that it was hard to imagine successful treatment being achieved in any way other than intensive work with the individual who was doing the drinking. Despite these obstacles, family therapy techniques have been used with increasing enthusiasm in alcoholism treatment. In recognition of this trend, the Second Special Report to the U.S. Congress on Alcohol and Health (47) called family therapy "the most notable current advance concerning alcoholism in the area of psychotherapy."

Family Therapy as a Treatment Modality

The recognition that disturbed family life may play a significant etiological role in the genesis of psychopathology dates back to the earliest psychoanalytic notions of human behavior. All psychodynamic theories of human functioning have viewed family relationships as the emotional substrata out of which the adult personality is formed, and disturbed family relationships therefore are thought to increase the likelihood of adult neurosis, psychosis, and personality disorder. The notion of simultaneously interviewing two or more family members as part of a psychotherapeutic intervention, however, did not occur until the mid-1950s, and only became firmly established in the decade of the 1960s. Nevertheless, although relatively slow in starting, family therapy has rapidly established itself as an exciting and innovative therapeutic approach, and has become part of the standard repertoire in most community mental health centers and residential treatment programs.

Family therapy developed in response to two fundamental clinical observations. The first was the repetitive experience of mental health professionals working with psychotic patients that despite the intensity or format of their therapeutic work with the individual patient, abnormal functioning invariably reappeared when the patient returned home and resumed his preexisting family life. The second clinical observation, long known and understood by playwrights and novelists but not as well appreciated by clinicians because of their concentration on the individual patient, was that each family member has a unique and often disparate version of family events and family relationships. The first clinical observation suggested that progress for the individual patient might only be secured if simultaneous and complementary progress also was achieved in the individual's social environment—namely, his or her family. The second observation suggested that individual differences in perceptions of family life could only be resolved for the clinician if he or she observed the family directly. That meant bringing the entire family in for a simultaneous interview.

These clinical observations received considerable support from concurrent research findings regarding the relationship between schizophrenia and family life. This work, especially the notions of Bateson et al. (8) on the "double bind," the notion of "pseudomutuality" proposed by Wynne and his colleagues (79), Wynne and Singer's (67, 68, 80) work on thought disorder, and the family "skew" notion of Lidz et al. (52), all suggested that schizophrenia seems to develop in conjunction with a particular pattern of disturbed family functioning. The critical implication of these theoretical notions was that in certain instances it may be more profitable to view the family rather than the individual as the basic unit of pathology. A short additional step brings us to the conclusion that therapeutic interventions should be directed toward the whole family rather than its symptomatic member alone. This evolution from individual to family is summarized by Ackerman (3) as he contrasts psychoanalytic and family treatment methods: "Psychoanalytic treatment focuses on the internal manifestations of disorder of the individual personality. Family treatment focuses on the behavior disorders of a system of interacting personalities, the family group."

At its present stage of development, family therapy is a term used to describe a wide variety of therapeutic techniques. Bowen (14), for example, in his review of the first decades of family therapy, lists 12 distinct therapeutic approaches or modalities all qualifying as bona fide forms of family therapy. Foley (30) narrows these approaches down to four basically distinct types: conjoint family therapy, multiple-impact therapy, network therapy, and multiple-family therapy.

This diversity in form and structure of the therapeutic setting led the GAP Committee (37) on the family to conclude in their report, *The Field of Family Therapy*, that family therapy is "not a treatment method in the usual sense." Pointing out that there is "no generally agreed upon set of procedures followed by practitioners who consider themselves family therapists," they conclude that the shared base is the common conviction about the relationship between individual and family psychopathology, and the belief in the therapeutic benefits of seeing the family together.

In other words, despite the continuing debate over the structural components of the therapeutic situation (for example, who should the therapy be addressed to: the parental couple, the whole family, the extended family, the social network; or what schedule should be adopted for the sessions: the traditional weekly sessions of conjoint therapy, the intensive two-week schedule of multiple-impact therapy, the marathon quality of network therapy), family therapists share a body of core concepts that apply to all family therapy approaches.

As we shall see in our review of family approaches to alcoholism, most of the popular family therapy techniques have at one time or another been applied to families containing alcoholic members. These techniques, however, have often been implemented by therapists who are relative novices to the family field. The result has been a somewhat haphazard application of poorly understood techniques, resulting in confusion about outcome and significance of the therapeutic venture.

Let us therefore spend a few moments reviewing six key concepts that differentiate family therapy from other therapeutic modalities. Although a unified or comprehensive theory of family functioning, family pathology, and therapeutic change has yet to be developed, the following core concepts have gained widespread acceptance and deserve our attention.

The Family as a System

Drawing on concepts from general systems theory, family therapists have found it profitable to think of the family as an operational system. This view treats the whole family as the primary organizational unit. Individuals within the family represent component sybsystems of this primary organizational unit. The emphasis is on patterns of interrelationship between these component parts, hence the focus on interactional behavior, structural patterning within the family, and the balance or stability of the system as a whole. Any single piece of behavior for the family systems therapist has to be understood first in terms of how all the component parts (individuals) are contributing to or making the behavior possible, and secondly, how the behavior is affecting all the individuals in the family. Pathology becomes redefined as a structural or functional imbalance in the family rather than as difficulties being experienced by any single individual within the family. Therapy is focused on the improved understanding of the structure and patterns of functioning within the family, and on correcting these imbalances that have led to stress or strain within the "system."

The Concepts of Homeostasis

First introduced by Don Jackson (41), this concept utilizes a term introduced by Cannon to describe regulatory mechanisms in physiological systems and applies it to family systems. The notion is that families tend to establish a sense of balance or stability, and have built-in mechanisms to resist any change from the predetermined level of stability. This stability does not necessarily imply a healthy state of affairs. The family, for example, might include as part of this stabilization pattern a piece of chronic psychopathology such as chronic alcohol abuse. But Jackson's notions imply that regardless of the quality of stabilization, families have built-in mechanisms to restore their specific sense of balance whenever events occur that tend to disrupt this balance.

The "feedback loop" is the primary mechanism for the maintenance of homeostasis. In physiology, the "negative feedback loop" was a term coined by Cannon to describe the pituitary-endocrine gland axis controlling hormonal levels in the body. As the hormone product of one component part of the axis increased, the hormonal product at the other end of the axis decreased, and vice versa. In family terms, the negative feedback lopp is most frequently used to describe two interrlated aspects of behavior usually carried out by two or more individuals in the family. The behaviors are interrelated but conflict with each other in that each one's presence tends to inhibit the other's. A pattern is established in which behavior A is invariably followed by behavior B, which in turn inhibits or prevents the further expression of behavior A. The end result is a return to the prior level of functioning (the homeostatic level) of the family. A clinical example of such a negative feedback loop is the spouse who encourages socializing or brings alcohol into the home or demands to be taken to a restaurant where drinks are ordered, every time the alcoholic member of the family makes a try at abstinence.

The feedback loop is one of a series of mechanisms postulated by family therapists to explain the intricate series of checks and balances they observe occurring in families, the end result of which is the remarkable stability of interactional behavior exhibited clinically by most families. *Cybernetics*, a term introduced by Norbert Wiener (77), has become an attractive theoretical model utilized to explain this process of self-regulation in family systems. Although originally intended to explain processes of control in physical systems, and utilized most profitably to develop concepts of logic in computer science, Wiener's concepts have proven highly adapatable to the field of human interactional behavior. Cybernetic regulation is the key concept that attempts to explain the perpetuation or maintenance of chronic patterns of behavior in family systems. In this sense, it becomes the key concept when family theorists attempt to explain interactional factors maintaining chronic alcohol abuse in families.

The Concept of the "Identified Patient" or "Scapegoat"

Perha'ps the most revolutionary impact of family therapy on psychiatry has been the redefinition of psychopathology in family terms. The schizophrenic individual becomes the schizophrenic family. The alcoholic individual becomes the alcoholic family. The antisocial individual becomes the antisocial family. This transformation occurs via the concept of the identified patient. According to his concept, the symptomatic member of the family—be he or she schizophrenic, alcoholic, or psychopathic—is not merely a disturbed individual who would be clearly symptomatic in his own right regardless of the behavioral setting. Instead he or she is the labeled or identified patient selected by the family system of which he or she is a member to express for the entire family the particular disturbance represented by the symptom selected.

For example, the antisocial adolescent is viewed as acting out antisocial fantasies shared by all family members, and the schizophrenic individual is seen as manifesting the stresses and stains created by the psychotic pattern of interaction within the family as a whole. An extension of this concept implies that the selected individual might, through his or her symptom expression, be protecting or stabilizing the level of functioning of other family members. In this view the alcoholic member of the family might, through his or her drinking, be protecting the family from overwhelming depression or intolerable levels of aggression. Such a model would be used to explain, for example, the clinical appearance of significant depression in a nonalcoholic spouse when the alcoholic stops drinking.

Communication Patterns

Family therapists have focused on communication patterns within the family with the same enthusiasm that analysts have reserved for dream material. Communications, both verbal and nonverbal, are viewed as reflecting the basic structural and interactional patterns governing the family's behavior, and therefore frequently become the primary focus of attention during therapy sessions. Some family therapists even contend that improvement in patterns of communication should be the only therapeutic goal. According to this view, once the family employs healthy channels for communication, it will be able to tackle and resolve any conflicts that may come its way.

In alcoholism, interest in communication has focused on the nature of communicational patterns during intoxication. An appreciation of the contrast between sober and intoxicated interaction of the entire family has been viewed by some family therapists as critical to their understanding of the dynamics of the alcoholic family.

Behavioral Context

A cornerstone of individually oriented dynamic psychiatry has been the role of conflict as a determinant of behavior. Behavior is seen as internally motivated, resulting from the conflict between individual wishes and external reality. Although motivating factors may be outside of conscious awareness, the process leading to the final expression of behavior is a process that resides in the individual and is therefore under individual control. The behaviorist model, although postulating a different mechanism for behavior, also views the process as internal to a single individual.

Family therapists, because they work with more than one individual, have been interested not only in internal processes but also in the relationship between individual behavior and the interactional field within which the behavior is expressed. This relationship has been called the "context" for behavior. The context, which is usually thought of as a combination of the setting and its cast of characters, can predetermine the behavior of any single individual in that contextual field by limiting the possible choices or range of behaviors the individual can successfully or appropriately express. The family therapist is particularly interested in combinations of behaviors and contexts for behavior which occur repeatedly in a particular family. These combinations often evolve into characteristic patterns of interaction. These patterns of interation, if potentially destructive to the family unit as a whole, may then become primary targets for investigative work in the therapeutic setting.

Describing drinking behavior to the family therapist is therefore inadequate if only the quantity and frequency of alcohol consumption is considered. The drinking must also be examined in terms of the behavioral context within which it occurs, and the characteristic pattern of relationships between family members that emerge when alcohol is present.

Boundaries

Because family therapists are interested in interactional *fields*, they must also pay attention to the quality of the boundaries separating participants in the field, and the boundary surrounding or separating the entire field from the outside world. Family therapists are therefore concerned both with the nature of the boundaries separating individual members of the family (e.g. generational boundaries) and with the relationship of the nuclear family to the outside world. Rigid and impermeable boundaries between the family and the outside world tend to isolate the family, preventing it from utilizing extrafamily resources to benefit individuals within it. Excessively permeable boundaries, on the other hand, destroy the family's sense of group integrity and connectedness, often preventing it from behaving as an effective unit. Alcoholic families have been characterized as having extremely rigid boundaries, leading to a characteristic sense of isolation within the community. Therapeutic interventions might therefore involve intensive examination of such boundary phenomena.

Family Therapy in Alcoholism

Phase I: Early Interest in Family Issues and Alcoholism

In 1937 Robert Knight (49) published a classical paper which raised, for the first time, curiosity about the role of family factors in the etiology of alcoholism. Based on his intensive psychoanalytic case-history work with chronic alcoholic men, Knight's report hypothesized that alcoholism arises in a family constellation composed of a domineering mother and a passive father, a notion that subsequently gained widespread acceptance. The following year Chassell (19) published another case report. He also postulated a two-generational model leading to the production of an identified alcoholic. But in contrast to Knight, Chassell emphasized the presence of an abusive and domineering, but somewhat capricious, father as the key element.

These early papers continue to be of interest to us because they established a particular framework for exploring family factors in alcoholism. This framework incorporated perspectives which, in retrospect, actually retarded the growth of family therapy as an acceptable treatment approach for alcoholism at the same time that it focused on family factors as etiological agents. Since these perspectives are still very much with us, they deserve brief mention.

First, for Knight and (Chassell) family factors were of interest only from the etiological perspective. The behavior demanding explanation was the abusive drinking of the alcoholic individual, and little attention was paid to interactional behavior or object relations. As a result, family factors were viewed as the germinative medium nourishing the alcoholic's psychopathological development. The logical conclusion was that knowing the family helps to understand the individual, but treatment remained individually oriented. Second, the emphasis on a specific family constellation associated with the production of alcoholism presages the notion that alcoholic individuals are more alike than different, that a specific alcoholic "personality" can be demonstrated to exist, and that families should consequently be lumped together and dealt with by "alcoholism" professionals rather than family experts in general family treatment centers. Third, the emphasis on family constellation led inevitably to an emphasis on structural components of family life rather than communicational styles or functional components of family living. This emphasis also later isolated alcohol therapists from developments in the family therapy field which tended to be oriented toward issues of interaction and communication.

So even though the family therapy field didn't really develop until the decade 1955–1965, existing notions and already established orientations in alcoholism therapy left alcohol therapists unprepared to adopt or experiment with these new techniques.

Phase II: The Alcoholic Marriage

In the 1950s interest turned to the clinical study of marriages between male alcoholics and their wives (5). The primary concern centered on the role of the wife initiating and perpetuating her husband's drinking. A debate arose between two factions. One was represented primarily by psychiatrists and psychiatric social workers who viewed the wife of the alcoholic as a person with severe, long-standing psychopathology antedating marriage, which led her to choose an alcoholic husband as a way of satisfying and stabilizing intrapsychic needs (9, 31); the other faction was represented primarily by sociologists who explained the behavior of these wives as directly resulting from having to deal with the repetitive pressures and stresses placed upon the marriage by the husband's drinking (44, 45, 46, 50). In retrospect this debate was probably artificial. The most recent review of this literature (22) concludes that no convincing evidence has emerged suggesting a single personality "type" characteristic to wives of alcoholics, or a theoretical explanation of their behavior.

In any event, although interactional models were being proposed to explain behavior in an alcoholic marriage, most of the clinical data stimulating these ideas come from individually-oriented therapy or research. For example, a clinician would be impressed with repetitive stories of inconsistent behavior on the part of his alcoholic patient's wife in which the wife is described as keeping the liquor cabinet well stocked, pouring drinks for her husband, and making excuses for him in his work situation, at the same time that she is complaining bitterly about his excessive drinking and threatening to leave if he doesn't stop. Only rarely were these clinical data verified via a clinical interview with the wife as well (53, 76). Sociologists, on the other hand, obtained much of their data directly from wives, and had little opportunity to substantiate these reports via direct observation or collateral interviewing (44, 50).

However, these studies were important in providing a changing focus for therapy. Whereas earlier studies focused on family issues only from a historical perspective, in the alcohol marriage they stressed the here and now. As long as the alcoholic individual was viewed in isolation, and explanations for his or her abusive drinking were related only to individual psychodynamics or pathophysiology, then the only logical treatment approaches would be individually oriented. If, however, questions were raised about the extent to which an interactional relationship between a husband and wife might either cause or perpetuate abusive drinking, then logic would dictate that a place had to be found for the spouse in the treatment plan. As Joan Jackson (46), has noted, "Once attention had been focused on the families of alcoholics, it became obvious that the relationship between the alcoholic and his family is not a oneway relationship. The family also affects the alcoholic and his illness. The family can either help or interfere with the treatment process." Jackson therefore concludes that significant family members must be taken account of, if not actively involved, in treatment in order to achieve success.

Phase III: Concurrent Therapy for Alcoholics and Spouses

In 1954 a project was instituted in the outpatient department of the Henry Phipps Psychiatric Clinic at the Johns Hopkins Hospital involving concurrent group meetings of male alcoholics and their wives (34, 35). This project represented the first attempt to adapt the most successful psychological therapy approach to alcoholism—group therapy—to a family orientation. Nine male alcoholics and their wives were recruited and placed in two separate groups, one for the alcoholics, one for the wives. Thus once they had volunteered for the study, husband and wife went their separate ways and entered into a group which developed its own schedule, therapy format, rules, and group process issues. Although the intent was to involve the marital couple concurrently in the treatment process, Gliedman and his associates assumed that different therapeutic issues would exist for alcoholic husbands versus wives. Each spouse would therefore need a different group in order for appropriate therapy to occur. For example, the wives' group was envisioned as "the usual analytically oriented therapy group," while the alcoholics' group was viewed as more structured, with specific techniques adapted to control anxiety levels in the group.

Despite the very small patient sample, this study is pivotal in the development of family techniques for the treatment of alcoholism. Although the specific results of the study were equivocal (marginal but not convincing improvement in most of the patients treated), ground was broken in a number of important areas that have subsequently become characteristic of family approaches. Perhaps the most important of these areas is the issue of outcome variables.

Most treatment programs have focused almost entirely on a diminution of drinking as the sole outcome variable of merit. Although the wisdom of this approach has been questioned on occasion, the majority of treatment programs continue to be judged against a standard of percentage of patient population abstinent within a specified time frame. Gliedman, by including wives as potential clientele for the treatment program, significantly expanded the scope of appropriate outcome variables against which successful treatment was to be judged. Symptom reduction, for example, applied to the wife as much as it applied to her alcoholic husband. If symptoms such as depression are applicable for the spouse, then they must also be applicable for the identified alcoholic. Thus reduction in depression is added to reduction in drinking as an acceptable criterion for successful treatment. Secondly, the concurrent treatment of both members of a marriage naturally leads to an examination of marital satisfaction and marital interactional behavior as target criteria for therapeutic change. Although Gliedman is primarily a group therapist who explains his technique as an extension of group therapy to a natural collateral group, a subtle change has begun in which the marriage itself has become an appropriate focus for the therapist's attention.

Patients were evaluated before and after treatment by means of four measures: (a) a drinking checklist to measure the severity of drinking; (b) a symptom checklist to indicate the amount of distress from psychological symptoms; (c) the mutual satisfaction or dissatisfaction experienced by the alcoholic husbands and their wives with each other during sobriety as contrasted with intoxication; and (d) a social ineffectiveness scale.

Within this widened perspective, Gliedman and his associates found that although there was some reduction in drinking behavior, the greatest changes in behavior resulting from the concurrent group-therapy technique were in the areas of "marital milieu" (defined as satisfaction of alcoholic husband and his wife with each other) and "personal morale" (the alcoholic individual's satisfaction with himself). A significant change also was felt to occur in reduction in psychological symptomatology, especially irritability and depression, on the part of both alcoholic husband and nonalcoholic wife. The least change seemed to occur in the area of social effectiveness, which was judged to be poor at the start of therapy and showed little improvement as a result of the group experience. Gliedman's conclusion was that his concurrent group-therapy technique was most effective in its ability to improve or elevate self-esteem in a patient group that tended to be demoralized prior to therapy.

Following the Johns Hopkins study, several clinical papers appeared in the literature describing group techniques for working with spouses of alcoholics (15, 53, 60, 63, 75). These papers indicated a growing interest in the development of techniques for changing the treatment focus from the alcoholic individual alone to the alcoholic individual in a marital context. It also reflected the conviction that the inclusion of the nonalcoholic spouse in the treatment of those alcoholic individuals who retained a stable marriage was a necessary prerequisite for successful therapy. Pixley and Stiefel (63), for example, state, "There is no question at this point that if psychotherapy is to be effective for a larger proportion of the alcoholic population the wife must also be treated."

The most ambitious study of concurrent group psychotherapy was carried out by Ewing and his colleagues (27) at the University of North Carolina School of Medicine. For a period of four years, starting in 1955, a program was established offering an optional concurrent group therapy program for spouses of alcoholic individuals already in treatment. Although the program was offered to male and female alcoholics alike, only wives of male alcoholics volunteered for the program.

During the first 18 months of the program's inception, 32 still-married alcoholic men were accepted into the group therapy program offered by the Department of Psychiatry for alcoholism treatment. Of these 32 men, 16 wives volunteered to participate in concurrent group psychotherapy sessions. In contrast to the Johns Hopkins group, similar schedules were adopted for the husbands' group and the wives' group. Both groups met weekly in different rooms in the same building.

Although the basic technique was described as "dynamically oriented group psychotherapy," Ewing concurs with Gliedman in noting the particular needs of alcoholic patients for more structured experiences stemming from a lower capacity to withstand tension and anxiety. However, in contrast to Gliedman, Ewing noted considerable resistance in the wives' group to traditional psychotherapeutic technique, and an unwillingness to develop any real therapeutic orientation. Their clinical description of group process

Family Therapy with Alcoholics **159**

in the wives' group indicates a general resistance to any discussion of intragroup feelings, but a much greater facility in talking about attitudes toward alcohol and drinking and their feelings about their husbands' abusive use of alcohol (extragroup feelings).

Long-term follow-up data provided by Ewing's group are impressive on two scores. First is the finding of a significantly greater persistance in therapy for those male alcoholics whose wives were attending a concurrent group psychotherapy session (see Table 11-1). Second, long-term follow-up (a minimum of three years after the inception of group therapy) indicated significantly improved control of drinking and considerable improvement in marital harmony for those men engaged in concurrent group therapy with their wives, as opposed to men coming alone to the therapy program. The question of whether this improvement was due to the specific working through of marital issues in the therapy sessions, or merely to the increased longevity of treatment (because the engagement of the wives assisted in keeping their alcoholic husbands in treatment for a longer period of time), is raised but left unanswered by this study. However, since engagement of alcoholics in long-term therapy has in and of itself been a major obstacle to successful treatment, the results of the Ewing study have to be viewed as impressive.

Table 11-1
University of North Carolina Concurrent Therapy Study[a]

Comparison of Length of Attendance of Patients on the Basis of Wives' Participation in Group Meetings[b]

Patients	Attended less than 6 months	Attended more than 6 months	Total
Married men			
Coming alone	13	3	16
Coming with wife	7	9	16

Comparison of Improvement in Patients on the Basis of Wives' Attendance in Group Meetings[c]

Patients	Totally sober or very much improved	Only slight or no improvement	Uncontacted at follow-up	Total
Married men				
Coming alone	3	7	6	16
Coming with wife	8	3	6	16

[a]From Ewing et al. (1961).
[b]Chi square = 4.80; p 0.05.
[c]Chi square = 3.46; p 10 0.05.
Steinglass, P., Kissin, B. & Begleitee, H. (Eds.) in *The Biology of Alcoholism* (U.S.), New York: Plenum, 1977 Family Therapy in Alcoholism

Ewing's findings were strongly supported in a study carried out by Smith (69) at the University of Edinburgh. Despite the fact that the treatment program was radically different (alcoholics were hospitalized for up to six weeks, as opposed to being treated on an outpatient basis in the Ewing study), the institution of a separate therapeutic group for wives of alcoholic men led to a significantly greater rate of improvement as contrasted with men whose wives did not attend.

These clinical papers have therefore been largely enthusiastic about the concurrent group psychotherapy technique. Although the emphasis remains on the effectiveness of the technique as an adjunct to the treatment of the alcoholic husband, wives are reported to be engaged in treatment for their own needs, having demonstrated independent issues of concern which could benefit from therapeutic examination.

A pessimistic note, however, is sounded by Pattison and his colleagues (60) in their work with lower-class families. Attempts to involve such families troubled by alcoholism problems in family-oriented treatment programs have been infrequent. Alcoholism in these families tends to present as just one of a wide range of social and psychological problems. Since alcohol abuse is often a socially acceptable norm in this socioeconomic group, the notion of alcoholism as a distinct disease process is alien, and such families are resistant to treatment approaches specifically directed at alcoholism as a symptom.

Pattison attempted to involve wives of male alcoholics referred to the Cincinnati Alcoholism Clinic by the courts and social agencies in an "orientation class" which was viewed as an adjunct to the husbands' treatment program. In contrast to Ewing and Smith, the Cincinnati program was viewed as only marginally effective in involving the wives, and of undemonstrated value in facilitating the husbands' treatment. Yet Pattison's conclusion is not that family approaches should be abandoned. In fact, he argues strongly that in lower socioeconomic groups, just as in middle-class groups, alcohol problems often exist in a family context and may be aggravated by the family context, as well as impacting on the family's ability to cope with its multiple problems.

But therapeutic approaches must be adapted to social realities. He therefore specifically suggests using the public-health nurse (58) and making visits as appropriate techniques of intervention with alcoholic families. Such a program contrasts dramatically with more traditional public health approaches to alcoholism, in which the lower-class alcoholic is usually isolated from his or her family, treated in a residential setting with a heavy emphasis on detoxification and individual rehabilitation, and then returned to a socioeconomic situation usually totally out of the awareness of the therapists who have been working with him or her.

Phase IV: The Adaptation of Family Theory to Alcoholism Therapy

The studies discussed up to this point, although taking cognizance of family factors in alcoholism, were by and large adaptations of existing individual and group therapy techniques. During this same time period, however, a body of clinical theory dealing with family pathology, family concepts of symptom formation, and family-oriented therapeutic interventions was being developed. The strong clinical orientation of these notions separated these emerging theoretical ideas from earlier social scientific approaches to the family. Whereas earlier sociological and anthropological approaches had concentrated on family structure, cultural influence, and role theory, clinically oriented theorists such as D. D. Jackson (42, 43), Bowen (12), Ackerman (4), Minuchin et al. (56), and Boszormenyi-Nagy and Framo (11) concentrated on general systems theory, communications theory, cybernetics, and game theory, as well as the familiar foundations of psychodynamic-psychoanalytic theory.

Since most of these clinical thinkers were psychiatrists, their attention was naturally drawn toward new explanations for traditional psychiatric conditions such as schizophrenia, psychosomatics, and adolescent dysfunction. Although somewhat puzzling in retrospect, alcoholism and drug abuse was almost totally ignored, both theoretically and clinically.

In the late 1960s and early 1970s some cracks began to appear in this wall of indifference. The first marriage of family theory and alcoholism therapy appeared in an article by Ewing and Fox (26), in which they adapted theoretical concepts associated with both Bateson's (7, 8) and Jackson's work with families, especially Don Jackson's notion of homeostasis in family systems (41). The alcoholic marriage is viewed as a "homeostatic mechanism" which is "established . . . to resist change over long periods of time. The behavior of each spouse is rigidly controlled by the other. As a result, an effort by one person to alter his typical role behavior threatens the family equilibrium and provokes renewed efforts by the spouse to maintain the status quo (4)."

Specifically addressing marriages between male alcoholics and their wives, they suggest a process in which these two people strike and elicit an "implicit . . . interpersonal bargain," a marital "quid pro quo," to use Jackson's (42) terminology, in which the male alcoholic's passive dependency needs implicitly encourage his wife's protective nurturing ones. A sexual bargain is also struck engaging an undemanding alcoholic husband in a behavioral pattern which complements the behavior of his sexually unresponsive wife. Both of these interactional pacts are played out within the context of a cyclical system, in which the alcoholic marriage alternates between periods of sobriety and periods of intoxication. "By alternating between suppression of impulses and direct expression of them, he can maintain the conflict surrounding impulse gratification for a lifetime."

Ewing and Fox (26) recommended family therapy for such families for two reasons: it increases the likelihood that a drinking problem will be acknowledged by a patient population (middle-class, gamma-type male alcoholics) who are ususally resistant to such self-labeling procedures, and it stimulates motivation toward change within the alcoholic himself.

As has already been mentioned, the specific therapeutic modality suggested is concurrent group therapy. Separate husband and wife groups meet at the same time, but in different rooms and with different therapists, for dynamically oriented group psychotherapy adapted to the shared life experiences and problematic interests of the group members. Both groups are seen as going through an initial resistance phase in which they attempt to pin the rap on their spouse as the trouble-maker in the marriage, followed by a period of insight into their own role in the maintenance of marital homeostasis. Of particular note, are clinical examples from the wives' groups underscoring their ambivalence about their husband's achieving sobriety. Although sobriety brings with it the desired goal of behavioral stabilization, it often carries with it seemingly undesirable aspects for both husband and wife, such as unfamiliarity with the new pattern of the marital relationship, new demands for intimacy, and increased depression.

Based on their extensive clinical experience, Ewing and Fox conclude that "alcoholism can no longer be seen purely in terms of intrapsychic dynamics.... It is the family emotional homeostasis which seems to perpetuate the drinking and it is this behavior which must be changed if the drinking is to be controlled." Their therapeutic approach emphasizes the need for reciprocal work with husband and wife in order to coordinate change in both halves of the homeostatic dyad. The corollary prediction is that working within an individual framework might increase the drive to change in the individual but would also increase the pressure toward resistance on the part of the spouse. Therapeutic efforts in one direction are therefore countermanded by resistances in the other direction, minimizing the opportunity for a positive therapeutic outcome. The author and his coworkers (21, 70, 71, 72, 73, 78) have incorporated many of the same concepts (homeostasis, marital bargain, complementary role functioning) in a more comprehensive interactional model of alcoholism, developed in response to clinical observations of family interaction made during states of experimentally induced intoxication. These observations suggested that interactional behavior during intoxication is highly patterned and often dramatically different from the behavior predicted by the family during sobriety. As one example, a family that claimed drinking by their "identified alcoholic" caused depression, fighting, and estrangement was observed to show increased warmth toward aach other, increased caretaking, and greater animation when the "alcoholic" was permitted to drink.

The interactional model proposed by this author is based on general systems concepts of family functioning. These concepts posit that families are operational systems, obeying laws general to all systems, including the importance of organization, drive toward homeostasis, circulatory of casual events, and feedback mechanisms as factors determining the quality of interaction between the component parts of the systems (in this case members of the family plus alcohol).

Alcohol ingestion and intoxicated behavior is then viewed from the perspective of the extent to which and the manner in which it affects the interactional life of the members of the family. The author also suggested that alcohol, by dint of its profound behavioral, cultural, societal, and physical consequences, might assume such a central position in the life of some families as to become an organizing principle for interactional life within these families, and labeled such a family an "alcoholic system." In it the presence or absence of alcohol becomes the single most important variable determining the interactional behavior not only between the identified drinker and other members of the family, but between nondrinking members of the family as well.

This model implied that an intricate and delicate balance exists between drinking and the day-to-day functioning of the family. In fact, it was suggested that in certain instances alcohol might be unconsciously viewed by the family as a stabilizing, rather than a disruptive, influence on their interactional life. Although superficially disruptive, from a different vantage point, the abusive use of alcohol seemed to produce extremely patterned, predictable, and rigid sets of interactions which dramatically reduced uncertainities about the family's internal life and its relationship to the external society.

The opportunity to directly observe intoxicated interactional behavior led not only to unique theoretical proposals but also to quite different conclusions about therapuetic intervention. If, in fact, alcohol might be aiding "system maintenance," which in clinical terms means serving some important dynamic function in the interactional life of the family, then the first role of the therapist dealing with the drinking symptom in a family context is to gain an appreciation of the relationship between alcohol and family life. In certain situations it seems clear that the identified patient's drinking behavior emerges de novo in a family situation at a time of stress or strain. In these situations the drinking behavior might well be viewed as a signal or symptom reflecting this stress or strain, and crisis intervention is called for. On the other hand, if alcohol consumption is part of an ongoing interactional pattern within the family system, then the traditional therapeutic

TABLE 11-2
Major Studies Employing Family Therapy Techniques for Alcoholism

Investigator	Treatment location	Principal mode of therapy	Goals of treatment	Number of patients treated
J. Ewing, V. Long and G. Wenzel	University clinic	Concurrent therapy. for alcoholics and spouses	Reduce drinking behavior via involvement of spouse in therapy	32 alcoholics 16 spcuses
L.H. Gliedman, D. Rosenthal, J.D. Frank, and H.T. Nash	University hospital outpatient clinic	Concurrent therapy for alcoholics and spouses	Improvement of the couples' marital relationships through the use of group treatment	9 alcoholic men and their wives
C. Smith	Community hospital	Concurrent therapy for alcoholics and spouses	Education on the process of alcoholism. Better understanding of marital relationship. Overcome rivalrous feelings about therapy of spouse.	22 alcoholics and their wives
P.H. Esser	Community clinic	Family therapy	Reduction of drinking behavior and improved family functioning via involvement of family as a whole in the treatment process.	14 families
D. Meeks and C. Kelly	Posthospital clinic	Conjoint family therapy	Improve family communication and problem-solving ability.	5 families
G. Burton and H. Kaplan	University clinic	Multiple-couples group therapy	Improvement in the area of marital conflict with focus on excessive drinking only to the extent that it had a role in the conflict.	39 couples
D. Cadogan	Posthospital clinic	Multiple-couples group therapy	Reduction in drinking behavior via emphasis in therapy on marital communication, family equilibrium, dormant conflict, and pathological family interaction.	20 couples— controls 20 couples— therapy
B.F. Corder, R. Corder, and N. Laidlaw	State alcoholism clinic	Multiple-couples group therapy	Improve interaction between spouses. Encourage participation in follow-up services offered in patient's community. Improve existing program without spending more money.	20—alcoholics— controls 19 alcoholics and spouses— therapy
D.M. Gallant, A. Rich. E. Bey, and L. Terranova	State alcoholism clinic	Multiple-couples group therapy	Improvement of the marital relationship. Abstinence for the alcoholic.	118 couples
P. Steinglass, D. Davis, and D. Berenson	State hospital	Multiple-couples group therapy	Improvement in family functioning through emphasis on examination of the relationship between alcohol use, intoxicated behavior and interaction.	10 couples

TABLE 11-2 Continued

Follow-up time	Outcome measurements	Critical Results

Follow-up time	Outcome measurements	Critical Results		
6 months and 3 years	Effect of wife's attendance at group therapy meetings on the length of time in treatment and amount of drinking of her alcoholic spouse.		Coming Alone	Coming with Wife
		Six-month follow-up		
		Attending less than 6 months	13	7
		Attending more than 6 months	3	9
		Three-year follow-up		
		Abstinent/Decreased drinking	3	8*
		Slight/No change in drinking	7	3
		Uncontacted	6	5
Immediately following treatment	1. Drinking checklist. 2. Symptom checklist: Assesses patient's psychological difficulties. 3. Adjective checklist: Assesses satisfaction and dissatisfaction alcoholic and spouse receive from sobriety and intoxication. 4. Social ineffectiveness scale: Rates alcoholic spouse on interpersonal ineffectiveness.	**Greatest changes:** Satisfaction of patient and spouse with each other Satisfaction with self **Least changes:** Social ineffectiveness		
16 months	Statistical measurement of the relationship between patient's social stability, treatment outcome, and group attendance of wife. Abstinence was rated optimal and death was worst outcome.	Patient's social stability and wife's attendance at a spouse's meeting related to favorable treatment outcome. Patient's social stability not found to be related to attendance of wife.		
4 months to 2 years	Evaluation of general family integration and functioning of each family member and amount of drinking by alcoholic.	Abstinent—satisfactory home life 9 No change 2		
Evaluated during various points in treatment	Evaluated progress by reviewing selected tape recordings on an ongoing basis and focusing on changes in: (1) drinking behavior; (2) family interaction and equilibrium; (3) family involvement in treatment; (4) "identified patient" effects; (5) therapist involvement.	All families involved showed improved relating, healthier communication, and increased mutual support. Two of the alcoholics maintained their sobriety and the other three reduced their drinking substantially.		

9 to 77 months	Questionnaire given before and after treatment measured changes in (1) drinking amount; (2) family pathology (areas of considerable disagreement between the couple); (3) social deterioration (consequences of alcoholic's drinking, i.e., hospitalization, etc.).		Decreased	No change	Increased
		Drinking changes	20/36	10/36	6/36
		Family pathology	18/24	3/24	3/24
		Social pathology	18/38	20/38	—

6 months	Before and after treatment—administration of Primary Communication Inventory (PCI) and the Conjugal Life Questionnaire (CLQ) to measure communication in marriage and how much trust and acceptance there is in the marriage; assessment of the amount of drinking.		Drinking Behavior	**Decreased**	**No change**	**Increased**
		Therapy group	9	4	7
		Control group	2	5	13
		In the therapy group, spouses of patients who were still drinking had significantly lower scores on the CLQ than spouses of abstinent patients, implying greater difficulty with acceptance and trust.				

6 months	Determined current drinking pattern; treatment, marital and employment status, and compared the two groups by means of Fisher's Exact Test applied to the resulting contingency table for each category.		Therapy	Control
		Resumed drinking	8	17
		Improved treatment status	15	4
		Unemployed more than 1 month	1	10

2 to 20 months	Success: improvement in the marital relationship and abstinent or no more than 2 drinking episodes. Failure: unhappy home life, problems with drinking. Unknown: discontinued treatment	53 definite successes 41 failures 24 unknown

6 months	1. Contextual drinking history 2. Individual assessment (SCL 90, Connors, SSIAM) 3. Dyadic Interaction Assessment (Olson & Ryder, IMC, Drewery & Rae Interpersonal Perception Technique, Ravich Interpersonal Game/Test) 4. Marital Satisfaction Inventory 5. Structured interview evaluating individual, marital, family, and social functioning	**Drinking behavior** Decreased 5 No change 2 Increased 2 Marked improvement clinically in marital interaction. Analysis of formal testing of interaction not yet completed

intervention aimed toward abstinence is totally inadequate to the task.

A logical extension of this theoretical model is to view family therapy not so much from the point of view of involving family members as a mechanism for improving treatment with the identified alcoholic, but rather to view the entire family, or the marriage itself, as the patient. Therapeutic intervention becomes interactionally rather than intrapsychically oriented, and goals for treatment center around an improvement in the functioning, flexibility, and growth potential of the family system as a whole rather than the more limited focus on reduction in drinking on the part of the identified alcoholic.

A paper by Davis and others (21) expands on this theoretical model in two signficant directions. First, it incorporates behavior theory; second, it underscores the importance of focusing on maintenance factors rather than etiological factors at this very primitive stage of our understanding of chronic alcoholism. Pointing out that historically there have been two major premises underlying therapeutic approaches to alcoholism—the notion that excessive drinking is maladaptive and the belief in the existence of ultimate causes as explanations of why alcoholism develops—Davis notes that these premises have given rise to a wide variety of therapeutic approaches. These range from moralistic exhortations and aversive behavioristic approaches deriving from the maladaptive premise to the uniform psychodynamic or psychobiological approaches based on ultimate-cause theories. Clinical experience, however, suggests that alcoholic behavior is more profitably thought of as a final common pathway. Incorporating behavioral concepts into the systems model allows for clinical diversity while at the same time suggesting new therapeutic strategies.

Davis et al. (21) postulate the following: (a) the abuse of alcohol has certain *adaptive* consequences; (b) these adaptive consequences are sufficiently reinforcing to serve as the primary factors maintaining the habit of drinking, regardless of what underlying causation there may be; and (c) the particular adaptive consequences or "primary factors" for each individual may differ and might be operating at a number of different levels including intrapsychic, intracouple, or on the level of maintenance of homeostasis in a family or wider social system, but the final common pathway is the reinforced chronic abuse of alcohol.

Two major implications for therapy are suggested. First, it is necessary for the therapist to determine the specific manner in which drinking behavior is serving an adaptive function for an individual or family. The maladaptive consequences are obviously readily apparent. Search for the adaptive consequences requires more clinical skill. Second, it is suggested that once the adaptive consequences of drinking have been ascertained, therapy may be structured around helping a patient to manifest the adaptive behavior while sober instead of only during drinking, and to learn effective alternate behaviors.

Davis and his colleagues have gone on to develop a second-generation model incorporating many of these earlier theoretical notions, a model they call the "alcohol maintenance model" (71). The model was structured around three concepts: the notion of interactional behavior cycling between two different states, the sober state and the intoxicated state; the notion of patterning or predictability of behavior that has reached a steady state; and the hypothesis that alcohol use in the "alcoholic family" has become incorporated into family problem-solving behavior.

The model proposed that one could think of any family group as facing three basic problems. The first is a significant psychological disarray in a single member to which the family must make some adaptive response (the individual–psychodynamic behavioral determinant). The second is a serious impasse which arises between two family members but cannot be attributed to disarray in either (the family–interactional behavioral determinant). The third is a serious difficulty the family, as a group, faces in making some kind of adjustment to its immediate social environment (the family–societal behavioral determinant). The model further proposed that problems in any of these three areas can build until they reach an emergency level threatening fundamental disruption of the family itself. At that point the family seeks a reequilibration or stabilization, and for the alcoholic family, that stabilization has become associated with the change from sober to intoxicated interactional states.

It was postulated that the stabilizing effect of alcohol is made possible by two features of the behavior it induced. First, the new behavior pattern associated with intoxication becomes immediately available for stabilization (related to the rapid change in behavior associated with the physiological effect of alcohol). Second, the behavior is stylized, stereotyped, and contains few surprises. The last quality is especially useful for stabilization. This proposed maintenance model was diagrammed as follows:

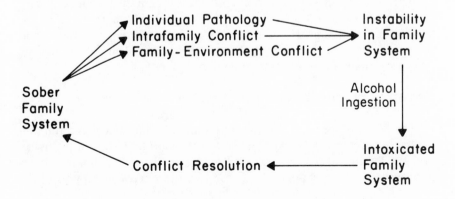

Figure 11-1

As can be clearly seen in the diagram, the major emphasis in this model is on the association between chronic drinking patterns and problem solving. The alteration in individual and interactional behavior that occurs when alcohol is introduced, was proposed as being specifically geared to the needs of the particular family. For example, in some families, equilibrium might be thought of as being restored by increasing interactional distance (drinker goes off to drink in the basement), or diminishing physical contact (no sex with someone who is drunk), or reducing tension in the family (familiar patterns of behavior are less tension-provoking than unique patterns); whereas in other families alcohol might be associated with closer interactional distance (making contact by fighting after the alcoholic spouse has been drinking), disinhibition (alcohol permits ritualized sexual behavior), or maintaining distance from the social environment (fights with neighbors when drunk).

Bowen (13), using similar concepts, also views alcoholism as potentially explainable in the language of family systems theory. Pointing out that alcoholism is one of the common human dysfunctions, Bowen contends that as a dysfunction, alcoholism must "exist in the context of an imbalance in functioning in the total family system." In this context, every family member is seen as contributing to the dysfunctional behavior of the alcoholic member. In fact, Bowen would contend that the dysfunction of the alcoholic can only continue with the support of his or her family. Therefore treatment that alters the behavior patterns of these other family members will by definition eliminate the necessary substratum for the existence of alcoholism. Bowen therefore states that "when it is possible to modify the family relationship system, the alcoholic dysfunction is alleviated, even though the dysfunctional one may not have been part of the therapy."

Bowen's statement represents the most undiluted justification for family therapy of alcoholism currently in the literature. At this stage, it is probably too strong a pill for most alcoholism therapists to swallow. A more integrative approach, particularly one that takes into account the profound behavioral consequences of alcohol consumption, is probably more useful at this point in our knowledge. However, insofar as they represent the interest and concern of an influential family therapist in the problems of alcoholism, Bowen's views deserve our close attention.

Phase V: Conjoint Therapy with the Alcoholic Family

The previous section has reviewed the growing *theoretical* literature on family therapy for alcoholism. The literature reporting results of the use of conjoint family therapy for alcoholism has to date been limited to infrequent clinical papers describing case histories offered in support of the use of family therapy techniques. By conjoint family therapy, we are now talking about techniques involving conjoint interviewing of both members of a marital pair, or conjoint interviewing of two or more members of a nuclear or extended family. Concurrent interviews occurring in separate locations or therapy techniques involving multiple families in a group format are discussed later, as well as in other chapters of this book.

The state of the literature, however, is in all likelihood unrepresentative of the extent to which family therapy techniques are actually being utilized for the treatment of alcoholism. In many alcoholism treatment centers it is routine for therapists to insist on the inclusion of other family members in the initial evaluation, and conjoint interviewing techniques are often included as one option available to the treatment team. However, it is not yet the case that family treatment centers routinely view the treatment of alcoholism as within the scope of their expertise. Traditional family agencies will often refuse to work with families containing an identified alcoholic member, even when the families present themselves because of problems other than alcoholism. This is paticularly true with agencies working with lower-middle-class and lower-class families where a rapid referral to the "alcohol" center is the preferred disposition regardless of the nature of the presenting complaint.

An interesting study by Meeks and Kelly (54), evaluating the efficacy of family therapy techniques introduced during the recovery phase of the treatment of the alcoholic member of the family, is the most representative and influential of the clinical studies of conjoint family therapy. Although only five families were treated and studied, as a pilot study this report is of considerable interest to us.

Meeks and Kelly adhere firmly to the theoretical orientation of the family therapist and proceed to apply treatment techniques developed by one of the founders of the family therapy movement, Virginia Satir. They accept a "basic premise" common to all family therapists that the family itself, rather than its individual members, is the unit of treatment, and that the family as a psychological unit has internal processes which help to establish an emotional balance characteristic of the family as a whole. They also accept the premise that dysfunctional behavior on the part of one family member may actually be viewed as functional by the family as a whole insofar as this behavior helps to restore the critical psychological balance or equilibrium that the family desires.

In their study, conjoint family therapy was begun following an intensive seven-week program of individual and group psychotherapy in a day treatment program. During this program, family members were seen separately from the "alcoholic patient." At the beginning of the aftercare phase, however, family members were seen in conjoint interviews only; the alcoholic member was never seen separately from his or her family during the after-care phase. Families were seen for periods ranging from ten to twelve months.

The treatment techniques employed were modeled on guidelines estab-lished by Satir (65). The focus was on the traditional family therapy interest in interaction, communication, role performance, and redefinition of prob-lems in family rather than in individual terms. Therapeutic goals were de-rived from Ackerman (4), another family therapy pioneer, and included achievement of a clearer definition of interactional conflicts, improved and more open communications about these conflicts, a greater understanding of intrapsychic determinants of interpersonal conflicts, and an improved level of complementarity in family role relations. Treatment evaluations in-cluded an interest in the drinking behavior of the identified alcoholic, but focused more intensely on issues of improved family interaction and family equilibrium. Such issues as problem definition, communication, patterns of relating, and methods of problem solving, are included as possible variables indicating improved family functioning. The study also attempted to assess the extent of the family involvement in the treatment process, the extent to which the therapists were able to remove the alcoholic member from the "identified patient" status, and issues of therapist involvement.

Although Meeks and Kelly underscored the exploratory nature of their report, they were enthusiastic about their experience. They concluded that techniques geared toward redefining alcoholism issues in family terms are quite profitable. The more drinking behavior can be seen as merely one as-pect of family interaction, the greater the likelihood that the "alcoholic" member of the family will be able to shed his or her label and establish new patterns of interaction within the family.

Esser (23, 24, 25) reached similar conclusions in reports stemming from his experience with conjoint family therapy in the Dutch city of Haarlem. Once again the emphasis is on the recovery, or aftercare, phase of treat-ment. Family therapy is seen as potentially expanding the scope of treat-ment from hospitalization and clinical care for the identified alcoholic, to a more sociotherapeutically oriented approach to the entire family. The fam-ily of an alcoholic is viewed as a "group under stress," but this stress is re-lated as much to disturbed interactions as it is to the behavioral effects of alcohol. Restoration of communication, concentration on role conflicts, and the removal of the alcoholic from the role of the "identified patient" are again seen as the central issues that the therapist must approach.

These clinical reports can be best characterized as promising but un-substantiated, enthusiastic but primarily impressionistic. They seem to re-flect the level of optimism attached to family therapy for alcoholism, e.g. the alcohol and health statement, by Keller (47), and Chaftez et al.'s look at alcoholism (18), but leave unanswered questions about the verifiable efficacy of these techniques.

Phase VI: Multiple Couples and Multiple Family Group Therapy Approaches

Multiple couples group therapy is a particularly popular form of family therapy currently being utilized in alcoholism treatment. This technique uses the group setting and group process to assist couples in examining marital interaction patterns and the relationship between these patterns and drinking behavior. Its increasing popularity as a treatment modality in alcoholism treatment programs is perhaps related to the assumption that it represents the "best of all possible worlds." It retains, in format at least, a group therapy structure and is therefore attractive to many alcoholism therapists who have viewed group therapy as the treatment of choice. However, it also acknowledges the importance of family factors in the exacerbation of alcoholism and is responsive to the growing feeling that alcoholism treatment is less effective if significant family members are not involved in therapy.

In the family therapy field, multiple couples group therapy has evolved as a specialized form of multiple family therapy (51), in which anywhere from three to twenty families are convened for therapy sessions which involve not only the adult generation, but also children, and at times three-generational extended families. Multiple couples groups, from the point of view of the family therapist, represents an attempt to work within a group setting, with the working relationship between husband and wife having profound effects on all relationships within the family.

In the alcoholism field, in contrast to the historical trend in family therapy, multiple couples groups stem primarily from the desire to include spouses in group therapy, as opposed to working with couples in a group context. This distinction, although perhaps subtle at first glance, has significant implications for the type of therapy that evolves. If the therapist's primary training and orientation are in group process and group therapy, then this emphasis on the group as a whole in multiple couples groups will be retained. If the therapist's training is in family therapy, however, the major focus will be on the couple as an interactional unit, and the relationship between the couple and other couples in the group will be seen as a model of the couple's interface and interactions with the outside world. Since alcoholic couples and families are often socially isolated, especially as abusive drinking increases, the multiple couples group offers a unique setting to work on problems of social isolation and interaction with the outside world.

A growing body of experimental and clinical literature now exists concerning multiple-couples group therapy approaches to alcoholism. This literature includes traditional treatment outcome studies (17, 20), reports of experimental treatment techniques (11), and summaries of clinical experiences (10, 32, 64). We will examine three reports more extensively: an outcome study of multiple couples therapy based on group techniques (17), an experimental study based on family therapy principles (71), and a clinical report of the extensive use of multiple couples groups in an operational alcoholism treatment program (32).

Cadogan presented the first controlled study in the literature of multiple-couples group therapy in alcoholism treatment. Forty alcoholics (both men and women) and their spouses were recruited while the alcoholics were still inpatients at a traditional alcoholism unit, and asked to volunteer for a "new and effective method of treatment" in which "an attempt would be made to improve family problem-solving patterns, to encourage the expression of feeling in marital communications and to develop a new awareness of the effect of their behavior on others." The study group represented the first 40 couples who volunteered for this new outpatient multiple couples group therapy program. Subjects were then randomly assigned to one of two groups: an immediate treatment group, or a waiting list. Those in the latter category continued with the traditional treatment program but did not engage in the outpatient multiple couples group. Ultimately 20 couples were assigned to each group. Groups proved to be comparable in age, socioeconomic status, severity of alcoholism, and involvement with other treatment programs (especially AA).

The treatment group engaged in open-ended multiple couples group therapy sessions (ninety-minute sessions on a once-weekly schedule). The average group was composed of five couples and membership was fluid, with dropouts being replaced by newly interviewed recruits. Follow-up evaluation occurred six months after the couple was recruited for the study. Follow-up results were striking. At six months, 9 alcoholic members in the therapy group remained abstinent, 4 were doing some drinking, and 7 had relapsed completely. Among the control group, however, only 2 were abstinent, 5 were drinking moderately, and 13 had completely relapsed.

Gallant et al. (32) have provided a report of the most extensive application to date of multiple couples group therapy as an integral phase or component of an ongoing alcoholism treatment program. Their program, the New Orleans Alcoholism Clinic, is comprised of two integrated units, a 36-bed inpatient unit, and an outpatient alcoholism clinic. Gallant has been routinely assigning every discharged married patient who is returning home to live with his or her spouse to a multiple couples therapy group in the outpatient clinic as the major form of ongoing treatment. These therapy groups, composed of 4 to 7 couples meeting every two weeks for a two-hour session, have a traditional alcoholism treatment goal of total abstinence for the alcoholic combined with an interpersonal goal of improvement in marital interaction. Treatment techniques combine both family therapy orientations toward analysis of interactional behavior, and group therapy techniques of encouraging direct exchange and feedback between all members of the group.

Gallant has reported the results of 118 couples assigned to the clinic's multiple-couples groups. Follow-up data were not systematically gathered, but most couples were contacted following treatment, and drinking history and quality of family life were explored. (The follow-up period varied from two to twenty months.) Fifty-three of the 118 couples were considered to be definite successes at the time of follow-up (either complete abstinence or no more than two brief drinking episodes, and having a "reasonable" marital relationship), and 41 were considered definite failures (unhappy family life, frequent drinking episodes, or sobriety felt by the treatment team to be temporary and without satisfaction or contentment). Twenty-four couples were lost to follow-up. Based on these findings Gallant et al. "conclude that marital couples group therapy is the treatment of choice at this time for married alcoholic patients. The denial and projection mechanisms, exaggerated in the alcohol-marital problem, are more easily approached and treated in a group."

The author and his colleagues (70, 71) have carried out work with multiple couples therapy groups as part of their research studies examining interactional behavior in alcoholic families. An experimental treatment program was established at the National Institute on Alcohol Abuse and Alcoholism (NIAAA) Laboratory for Alcohol Research in which couples with one or two alcoholic members were placed in an intensive, six-week multiple couples group therapy program. Although the treatment program was conceptualized of a rich clinical field allowing for the examination of interactional behavior, the treatment process itself was highly unusual and proved to be quite fascinating in its own right. In contrast to Cadogan's work, where the emphasis was on the desirability of involving the spouse in a group process, the NIAAA group was firmly based in family therapy.

The experimental treatment program was divided into three phases: an initial two-week outpatient phase in which groups met for three sessions per week; a ten-day inpatient phase during which three couples were simultaneously admitted to an inpatient facility; and finally a posthospitalization three-week outpatient phase with two group meetings per week. Following the six-week intensive treatment program, groups reconvened at six-week intervals for follow-up sessions over a six-month follow-up period.

The core of the program, and clearly its most innovative feature, was the hospitalization period. The hospital setting itself was a redesigned inpatient unit in a traditional state hospital. This unit was described by the research team as a "simulated apartment setting" which was supposed to provide a homelike atmosphere for the couples, allowing them to reproduce as accurately as possible their usual interactional behavior. Of greatest importance, however, was the fact that alcohol was made freely available during the first seven days of the hospitalization period and couples were asked to engage in their usual drinking patterns while they were on the ward. This last feature of the treatment program was an extension of the use of experimentally induced intoxication as a potential adjunct to therapy, and was based on theoretical notions about the role alcohol can play in maintaining fixed interactional patterns within families. (These notions are discussed in Phase IV.) The specific rationale provided to the couples for this free availability of alcohol was that the therapist, by being able to directly observe intoxicated behavior, could gain a better understanding of the role that alcohol consumption was playing in the couples' lives.

The treatment program utilized a variety of techniques to examine patterns of interaction exhibited by each couple, and to contrast the difference between interaction during sobriety versus interaction during intoxication. These techniques included videotape recording and feedback, role-playing techniques, use of one-way mirror observation and feedback from observers, analysis of speech and communication patterns, emphasis on nonverbal behavior and postural analysis, and use of three-generational family genograms. All of these techniques have been used extensively by family therapists in more traditional settings.

The multiple couples groups were conceptualized by the researchers as a societal system composed of three distinct elements or levels: individuals, couples, and the whole group. This type of group was therefore viewed as an excellent vehicle for observing the relationship between individual dynamics and intracouple dynamics, while at the same time giving therapists an opportunity to observe the couple's behavior in negotiating its position in a group of strangers (this perhaps analagous to the relationship between the family and the outside society). However, the therapeutic target was always the couple, and individual dynamics or whole group behavior was viewed from the vantage point of its relationship to each of the three couples.

Although this NIAAA program obviously represented a radical departure from traditional alcoholism treatment, it also is the purest example in the literature of an approach to alcoholism treatment based on family principles. Let us therefore summarize the main features which made this program unique. First, the program recruited middle-class, intact couples who displayed a substantial degree of economic and interactional stability despite the chronic abuse of alcohol by one of its members. Second, the program not only did not insist on the usual abstinence model of treatment; it actually suggested that intoxicated behavior can be utilized by the therapist as an adjunct to treatment. Third, instead of viewing the individual alcohol abuser as the "problem," therapy was directed at the couple. Fourth, both drinker and spouse enjoyed similar status as inpatients in a psychiatric hospital, and treatment goals and techniques were based on examining the relationship between alcohol use, intoxicated behavior, and interaction. And last, the therapists insisted on improved family functioning rather than a reduction of drinking behavior as the primary target. Because each of these features represented a natural extension of family theory into alcoholism treatment, they have profound implications regarding potential consequences of the more generalized application of family therapy techniques in alcoholism treatment. These implications will be more fully discussed at the close of this chapter.

Although the author and his colleagues have advised caution regarding outcome results from this experimental study, emphasizing the highly experimental, pilot nature of the program, it was found that couples responded quite positively to the treatment approach. Although only ten couples were treated, they all completed the study despite its strenuous demands, and reported feeling a profound emotional impact deriving particularly from the in-hospital experience. The enthusiasm of patients for the therapeutic work was particularly impressive to the therapists in light of the fact that all couples had failed repeatedly in previous therapeutic efforts. The therapists were also most enthusiastic about the in-hospital experience as a mechanism facilitating the rapid clinical understanding of the relationship between drinking behavior and interactional life for each of the couples worked with.

Two additional studies, although not focusing specifically on multiple-couples therapy, will be mentioned here because they also involved simultaneous work with spouses in a traditional hospital setting. Corder and his colleagues (20) carried out a pilot project at a residential alcoholism treatment center. Wives of male alcoholics were included in a four-day intensive workshop which followed a traditional three-week inpatient program. The workshop program included group therapy and videotape analysis of the sessions, didactic lectures, group discussions of "game playing" and role playing, recreational activities, and AA and Al-Anon meetings. A six-month follow-up performed on the pilot group of 20 alcoholics indicated a significant reduction in drinking for the experimental group as compared to a control group which had gone through the traditional treatment program alone.

Paolino and McCrady (57) have been experimenting with the "joint admission" of an alcoholic and nonalcoholic spouse, the latter being a "guest" of the hospital. The couple lived on a psychiatric ward that includes patients of all diagnoses and ages over twelve. The nonalcoholic spouse participated in ward activities as much as possible while retaining his or her job. The patient and spouse also participated in three types of weekly therapy groups: a group for problem drinkers only, a group for spouses of problem drinkers only, and a group for couples in which one member is a problem drinker and the other member does not have a problem with alcohol. These groups all continued after the couples left the hospital and were considered an essential part of the treatment program.

Paolino and McCrady conceptualized the goals of such a joint admission as follows: (a) to give the staff the opportunity to observe the couple's interactions, (b) to provide comprehensive feedback for the couple about their patterns of interacting, (c) to integrate the spouse into the milieu so that the spouse has the same opportunity as the problem drinker to experience the closeness and caring of the unit, (d) to integrate the spouse into the milieu so that the spouse may incorporate the approach to handling problems which is taught in the milieu. The researchers plan extensive experimental studies based on this treatment approach.

Al-Anon Family Groups

Al-Anon is an indigenous self-help movement which arose spontaneously as a parallel but separate movement to Alcoholics Anonymous in the late 1940s. Over five thousand Al-Anon Family Groups now exist worldwide.

Al-Anon Family Groups are modeled after Alcoholics Anonymous; that is, as a group fellowship of peers sharing a common problem. In the case of Al-Anon the peers are spouses, children, and close relatives of alcoholics who are usually but not necessarily part of an AA group. The typical member is the wife of an alcoholic man in an upper-middle-class family with a strong religious orientation. Although infrequently studied systematically by social scientists, Al-Anon Family Groups have been characterized as "a remarkable, self-help, non-professional modality of group therapy and group education" (1).

Al-Anon closely parallels AA in structure and function. It exists for the most part outside the traditional medical or social service framework within which alcoholics are usually "treated" by the community, with members recruited through word of mouth, newspaper advertisements, and church group support. The group meetings correspond to AA in their religious flavor, their emphasis on anonymity, and their structured format for achieving self-help. The operational philosophy of the program includes the Twelve Steps, adapted from AA, supplemented by the Twelve Traditions, a series of policy statements that outline the nature of Al-Anon and the goals and limitations of a particular group (see Table 11-3). The group meeting itself follows a semistructured format, is chaired by a group leader, and usually centers around ways in which different group members can adapt or incorporate the Twelve Steps into their lives.

Ablon (1) has attempted the most comprehensive analysis of the group process that occurs during Al-Anon meetings. She feels that all successful Al-Anon members must accept one basic didactic lesson and three principles for operating in the groups themselves. The fundamental didactic lesson is to accept AA's concept of alcoholism, which is "an obsession of the mind and an allergy of the body." This concept implies that the alcoholic member is behaving neither out of irresponsibility nor out of a perversity toward other family members. Instead, he or she has a disease which is totally outside of the alcoholic's control, and in this sense other family members are advised that they should not "take it personally." A disease analogy is usually made, with the Al-Anon family member told that the alcoholic can no more control his or her drinking than the cancer patient or diabetic can control the organic changes associated with his illnesses.

The three operational principles stressed by Ablon are, first, a "loving detachment from the alcoholic," in which the family member accepts the fact that he or she has control only over his or her own behavior and must accept the idea that only the alcoholic can work out his or her own solutions; second, the reestablishment of self-esteem and independence; and

Table 11-3
The Twelve Steps of Al-Anon

1. We admitted we were powerless over alcohol—that our lives had become unmanageable.
2. Came to believe that a Power greater than ourselves could restore us to sanity.
3. Made a decision to turn our will and our lives over to the care of God as we understand Him.
4. Made a searching and fearless moral inventory of ourselves.
5. Admitted to God, to ourselves, and to another human being the exact nature of our wrongs.
6. Were entirely ready to have God remove all these defects of character.
7. Humbly asked Him to remove our shortcomings.
8. Made a list of all persons we had harmed and became willing to make amends to them all.
9. Made direct amends to such people whenever possible except when to do so would injure them or others.
10. Continued to take personal inventory and when we were wrong, promptly admitted it.
11. Sought through prayer and meditation to improve our conscious contact with God as we understand Him, praying only for knowledge of His will for us and the power to carry that out.
12. Having had a spiritual awakening as a result of these Steps, we tried to carry this message to others, and to practice these principles in all our affairs.

third, a reliance on a "higher power," a religious emphasis that of course also closely parallels AA.

Although it is difficult to compare Al-Anon Family Groups with traditional therapy groups, they would probably be most appropriately characterized as supportive or introspective groups analogous to other religiously oriented meetings such as the Quakers. The group member is encouraged to find himself or herself in the many similar stories shared by other group members, and adjust or adapt his life to the operational principles followed by the group. Interpersonal interaction is for the most part discouraged, and direct confrontation between group members is usually strictly censured. In this last regard, the groups tend to be more gently supportive than their AA counterparts.

Although Al-Anon Family Groups have often been dismissed by professional therapists because of their quasi-religious framework and their anti-intellectual and antiscientific tradition, they currently comprise the single largest "treatment" program involving families with alcoholic members. Although for the most part they fly in the face of theoretical notions that underlie the family therapy movement (the view of the alcoholic as the helpless victim of a disease process is the most flagrant example), several of the operational principles bear a remarkable resemblance to principles advocated by many family therapists. For example, the principle of "loving detachment" is quite similar to that advocated by many family therapists who insist that families will show movement or growth only when individual members concentrate on changing their own behavior rather than attempting to manipulate or change others in the family system.

Most studies of Al-Anon Family Groups to date have included enthusiastic anecdotal reports of favorable clinical outcomes for the families involved. The one study that carried out more systematic assessments (6) concluded that most Al-Anon members were more satisfied with this experience than any other therapy contact they had had, and these members related this feeling particularly to their new and changed understanding of alcoholism. Parenthetically, male alcoholics involved in AA were found to have an easier time achieving and maintaining sobriety if their wives were simultaneously attending Al-Anon fellowship meetings.

Discussion

Our review of the existing literature leaves us with a sense of guarded optimism about the application of family therapy techniques in the treatment of alcoholism. Although every study we have mentioned concludes with an enthusiastic statement encouraging greater use of family therapy, it is also apparent that very little hard evidence exists at this point demonstrating either the efficacy of family therapy by itself or the comparative value of family therapy versus more traditional forms of therapy in the treatment of alcoholism.

Considerable controversy exists concerning the adequacy of methodologies currently available for psychotherapy research. However, even using existing standards for research, the studies reviewed in this chapter are problematic. In fact, virtually every study should be viewed as a pilot or exploratory venture, rather than as a definitive attempt to validate a treatment method. Nevertheless, despite the absence of solid experimental data to support their clinical convictions, therapists in the alcoholism field seem increasingly convinced that family therapy techniques represent a powerful new addition to the therapeutic armamentarium. We therefore should anticipate that the use of these techniques will increase dramatically over the next decade.

It is less clear, however, exactly what form these family therapy techniques will take. Our survey of the existing data indicates that no single family therapy technique has gained a dominant position or demonstrated superior credentials regarding treatment of alcoholic families. Instead, for alcoholism therapy, just as for family therapy in general, a wide variety of approaches is currently being advocated and should be deemed supportable. We can think of these family approaches to the treatment of alcoholism as falling into the following categories: (a) "pure" family therapy, based on a family systems theoretical formulation of alcoholism; (b) group or individual approaches designed specifically to fulfill criteria suggested by a family theory of alcoholism; (c) techniques involving concurrent therapeutic work with other family members in addition to the identified alcoholic, but using a more traditional, individually oriented, psychodynamic theoretical base; (d) specialized techniques developed for working with spouses of alcoholics, usually eclectic in nature; and (e) supportive approaches geared to assist spouses and children of alcoholics in dealing with common difficulties they face as a result of having an alcoholic member in their family.

It also seems clear that family approaches have not been confined to one particular location, such as an outpatient clinic. The fact that several investigators have been experimenting with the simultaneous admission of alcoholic and spouse to an inpatient setting indicates that virtually every therapeutic setting can be adapted to incorporate family issues. In fact, the only generally agreed upon prerequisite for family therapy in alcoholism is the presence of an intact family.

If the current enthusiasm for family therapy continues, it is not unlikely that future therapy programs for alcoholism will be split into two distinct approaches: a family-oriented psychosocial approach applied primarily to middle- and upper-class alcoholics with intact families, and a biomedically oriented approach combining pharmacotherapy, behavioristic techniques, and group therapy applied primarily to single alcoholics. The former approach would structure itself on a family systems theoretical framework, while the latter approach would remain within the more traditional framework of the medical model of alcoholism.

Although from one vantage point the incorporation of family therapy techniques into alcoholism treatment programs represents a logical, commonsensical extension of clinical experience, it is important to recognize that certain aspects of the family therapy movement have radical underpinnings. Therapists not aware of these underpinnings often move somewhat naively into work with families rather than individuals, only to discover much later the long-term implications of their change in therapeutic focus. Therefore, although it certainly seems warranted to encourage the continuing expansion of family treatment techniques in the alcohol field, we also need to discuss potential implications of this trend.

Three major implications must be underscored. The most basic, although not necessarily the most obvious, implication is a shift in theoretical thinking and conceptualizations, what Bateson (7) has called an "epistemological" change. This change, embodied in the theoretical notions connected with family therapy, redefines notions of disease processes, dysfunctioning, casual relationships, motivation and so on. The most obvious consequence of this change in thinking is the redefinition of alcoholism in family terms discussed in the Phase IV section. These notions, logically extended, have led several psychiatrists to postulate the existence of a subpopulation of families in which the use of alcohol actually stabilizes interaction for the family and is therefore viewed as adaptive rather than dysfunctional (21, 73). At the very least, however, the theoretical underpinnings of family therapy suggest that the alcoholic is merely the labeled victim, set apart by his family as a scapegoat and protecting his family through the repetitive cycling of intoxicated behavior from the family's difficulties in coping with each other and with the outside world.

The second major implication of the increased use of family therapy techniques is the changing definition of the patient population. This aspect not only involves the obvious change that nonalcoholic family members are also to be actively involved in the treatment process; it also means that, since the family therapist sees the whole family as his patient, therapeutic efforts are directed equally toward alcoholic and nonalcoholic patients. The shift toward family therapy has also meant a significant change in the socioeconomic status of the patient population. Whereas in previous years traditional alcoholism treatment centers were working with lower-middle-class and lower-class alcoholics, many of whom were already separated from family and work, while AA and Al-Anon provided services for middle-class and upper-class individuals and families, family therapy techniques have usually been applied to the intact, middle-class family.

In addition to the change in the socioeconomic level of the patient population, there has been a change in the timing for intervention in what must be thought of as a chronic disease process. The availability of family therapy techniques has increased the likelihood that therapists will intervene at a much earlier stage in the alcoholic process. In fact, many families seek therapy, not because of a devastating alcohol problem, but because of a devastating problem in family communications, parent-child conflict, sexual difficulties, or the like. The existence of a pernicious drinking pattern in one or more members of the family might only emerge as history-taking proceeds.

The third implication arises from changing outcome goals. The traditional goal of abstinence as an isolated behavioral change makes very little sense in the context of family therapy (59). Substantial clinical evidence now suggests that abstinence as an isolated behavioral change often carries with it attendant increases in pressure on the family system, frequently including dissolution of the marriage. It was the recognition that family members other than the identified alcoholic had to be actively involved in the treatment process and undergo change in order to successfully reduce drinking while maintaining the family structure, that has led to the increasing use of family techniques. Although most of the studies reported in this chapter retained a reduction in drinking as a primary indication of successful treatment outcome, increasingly such family variables as communication, social functioning, relationships with extended family, and evidence of symptomatology in children were used as alternative outcome variables.

If one looks at families with alcoholic members being treated in family therapy clinics, then the shift is perhaps even more dramatic. Traditional family therapists might even view alcoholism as a symptom of secondary importance, with treatment goals being primarily directed toward issues of family functioning and a reduction in drinking viewed as a desirable secondary gain following the primary change in the quality of family life.

These implications add up to a striking shift in one's concept of alcoholism. In family therapy terms, alcoholism is merely one of a wide range of behaviors used by families in their ongoing functioning. Although it obviously is dramatic and highly visible behavior, it is the tip of the iceberg. The important issues, the family therapist would maintain, exist in the structure, communicational style, and relationship system of the family. Any typological or diagnostic system should be based on these latter qualities, rather than on the existence or absence of a drinking problem. Alcoholism, by this analogy, is the equivalent of fever, or adolescent delinquency. Whereas it makes some sense to view such a symptom or piece of behavior as primary in the diagnostic and treatment process (the fever work-up or the therapy group for adolescent runaways), increasing knowledge directs us toward the antecedents of this behavior.

The logical extension of family theory therefore argues against the artificial grouping of families by behavioral symptoms such as abusive drinking. Extended further it means that families with alcoholic members who view themselves as dysfunctional and seek help should be seen in family centers rather than alcoholism treatment centers. Furthermore, if family therapy proves to be the treatment of choice for middle-class and upperclass alcoholics with intact families (as suggested in a still very preliminary way by the studies described in this chapter), then our task will be to integrate such families into family therapy programs and eliminate entirely the separate alcoholism treatment program that has up to this point claimed such families as part of its natural clientele.

All of these issues underscore the importance of our gaining a clearer understanding of family techniques before we make sweeping claims about their applicability. The initial enthusiasm for family therapy approaches to alcoholism, although clearly worth supporting, must continue to be evaluated objectively rather than embraced in an uncritical fashion. Although this is obviously sound advice regarding any new treatment technique, it is particularly relevant here because family therapy carries with it the potential for radical changes and shifts in our approaches to the treatment of alcoholism.

REFERENCES

1. Ablon, J., Al-Anon family groups. Impetus for Change Through the Presentation of Alternatives. *Am. J. Psychother.* 28(1):30, 1974.
2. Ablon, J., Family Structure and Behavior in Alcoholism: A Review of the Literature. In B. Kissin and H. Begleiter (Eds.), *The Biology of Alcoholism* (Vol. IV), 1976, pp. 205–242.
3. Ackerman, N.W., Family Psychotherapy and Psychoanalysis: Implications of Difference. *Family Process* 1:30, 1962.
4. Ackerman, N.W., *Treating the Troubled Family*, New York: Basic Books, 1966.
5. Bailey, M., Alcoholism in Marriage: A Review of Research and Professional Literature. *Q.J. Stud. Alcohol* 22:81, 1961.

6. Bailey, M., Al-Anon Family Groups as an Aid to Wives of Alcoholics. *Social Work* 10:68, 1965.

7. Bateson, G., *Steps to an Ecology of Mind*, New York: Ballantine Books, 1972.

8. Bateson, G., Jackson, D.D. Haley, J., & Weakland, J.H., toward a Theory of Schizophrenia. *Behav. Sci.* 1:251, 1956.

9. Bergler, E., *Conflict in Marriage*, New York: Harper & Row, 1949.

10. Berman, K.K., Multiple Conjoint Family Groups in the Treatment of Alcoholism. *J. Med. Soc. N.J.* 65:6, 1968.

11. Boszormenyi-Nagy, I., & Framo, J.L. (Eds.), *Intensive Family Therapy*, New York: Harper, 1965.

12. Bowen, M., The Use of Family Therapy in Clinical Practice. *Compr. Psychiatry* 7:345, 1966.

13. Bowen, M., Alcoholism as Viewed through Family Systems Theory and Family Psychotherapy. *Ann. N.Y. Acad. Sci.* 233:115, 1974.

14. Bowen, M., Family Therapy after Twenty Years. In S. Artieti (Ed.), *American Handbook of Psychiatry*, New York: Basic Books, 1976.

15. Burton, G., Group Counseling with Alcoholic Husbands and Their Wives. *Marriage and Family Living* 24:56, 1962.

16. Burton, G., Kaplan, H.M., & Mudd, E.H., Marriage Counseling with Alcoholics and Their Spouses. *Br. J. Addict.* 63:151, 1968.

17. Cadogan, D.A., Marital Group Therapy in the Treatment of Alcoholism. *Q.J. Stud. Alcohol* 34:1187, 1973.

18. Chafetz, M., Hertzman, M., & Berenson, D., Alcoholism: A Positive View. In S. Arieti & E.B. Brody (Eds.), *American Handbook of Psychiatry* (Vol. 1), York: Basic Books, 1974, pp. 367–392.

19. Chassell, J., Family Constellation in the Etiology of Essential Alcoholism. *Psychiatry* 1:473, 1938.

20. Corder, B.F., Corder, R.F., & Laidlaw, N.L., An Intensive Treatment Program for Alcoholics and Their Wives. *Q.J. Stud. Alcohol* 33:1144, 1972.

21. Davis, D.I., Berenson, D., Steinglass, P., & Davis, S., The Adaptive Consequences of Drinking. *Psychiatry* 37:209, 1974.

22. Edwards, P., Harvey, C., & Whitehead, P.C., Wives of Alcoholics: A Critical Review and Analysis. *Q.J. Stud. Alcohol* 34:112, 1973.

23. Esser, P.H., Conjoint Family Therapy for Alcoholics. *Br. J. Addict.* 63:177, 1968.

24. Esser, P.H., Conjoint Family Therapy with Alcoholics—A New Approach. *Br. J. Addict.* 64:275; 1970.

25. Esser, P.H., Evaluation of Family Therapy with Alcoholics. *Br. J. Addict.* 66:251, 1971.

26. Ewing, J.A., & Fox, R.E., Family Therapy of Alcoholism. In J.H. Masserman (Ed.), *Current Psychiatric Therapies* (Vol. 8), New York: Grune & Stratton, 1968, pp. 86–91.

27. Ewing, J.A., Long, V., & Wenzel, G.G., Concurrent Group Psychotherapy of Alcoholic Patients and Their Wives. *Int. J. Group Psychother.* 11:329, 1961.

28. Ferber, A., Mendelsohn, M., & Napier, A., *The Book of Family Therapy*, New York: Science House, 1972.

29. Finley, D.G., Effect of Role Network Pressures on an Alcoholic's Approach to Treatment. *Social Work* 11:71, 1966.

30. Foley, V.D., *An Introduction to Family Therapy*, New York: Grune & Stratton, 1974.

31. Futterman, S., Personality Trends in Wives of Alcoholics. *Journal of Psychiatric Social Work* 23:37, 1953.
32. Gallant, D.M., Rich, A., Bey, E., & Terranova, L., Group Psychotherapy with Married Couples: A Successful Technique in New Orleans Alcoholism Clinic Patients. *J. La. State Med. Soc.* 122:41, 1970.
33. Gliedman, L.H., Concurrent and Combined Group Treatment of Chronic Alcoholics and Their Wives. *Int. J. Group Psychother.* 7:414, 1957.
34. Gliedman, L.H., Nash, H.T., & Webb, W.L., Group Psychotherapy of Male Alcoholics and Their Wives. *Dis. Nerv. Syst* 17:90, 1956.
35. Gliedman, L.H., Rosenthal, D. Frank, J.D., Nash, H.T., Group Therapy of Alcoholics with Concurrent Group Meetings with Their Wives. *Q.J. Stud. Alcohol* 17:655, 1956.
36. Gray, W., Duhl, F.J., & Rizzo, N.D. (Eds.), *General Systems Theory and Psychiatry*, Boston: Little Brown, Boston, 1965.
37. Group for the Advancement of Psychiatry Report, The Field of Family Therapy, Vol. 7, Report No. 78, 1970. New York: GAP Publications.
38. Haley, J., *Strategies of Psychotherapy*, New York: Grune & Stratton, 1963.
39. Haley, J. & Hoffman, L., *Techniques of Family Therapy*, New York: Basic Books, 1967.
40. Howells, J.G. (Ed.), *Theory and Practice of Family Psychiatry,* New York: Brunner/Mazel, 1971.
41. Jackson, D.D., The Question of Family Homeostasis. *Psychiat. Q. Supplement* 31:79, 1957.
42. Jackson, D.D., Family Rules: Marital Quid Pro Quo. *Arch. Gen. Psychiatry* 12:589, 1965.
43. Jackson, D.D., The Study of the Family. *Family Process* 4:1, 1965.
44. Jackson, J.K., The Adjustment of the Family to the Crisis of Alcoholism. *Q.J. Stud. Alcohol* 15:562, 1954.
45. Jackson, J.K., Alcoholism and the Family. *Annals of the American Academy of Political and Social Science* 315:90, 1958.
46. Jackson, J.K., Alcoholism and the family. In *Society, Culture and Drinking Patterns* D.J. Pittman & C.R. Snyder (Eds.), New York: Wiley, 1962, pp. 472–492.
47. Keller, M. (Ed.), Trends in Treatment of Alcoholism. In *Second Special Report to the U.S. Congress on Alcohol and Health*, Washington, D.C.: Department of Health, Education and Welfare, 1974, pp. 145–167.
48. Kelly, D., Alcoholism and the Family. *Md. State Med. J.* 22(1):25, 1973.
49. Knight, R., The Dynamics and Treatment of Chronic Alcohol Addiction. *Bull. Menninger Clin.* 1:233, 1937.
50. Kogan, K. & Jackson, J., Stress, Personality and Emotional Disturbance in Wives of Alcoholics. *Q.J. Stud. Alcohol* 26:486, 1965.
51. Laquer, P., Mechanisms of Change in Multiple Family Therapy. In C.J. Sager and H.S. Kaplan (Eds.), *Progress in Group and Family Therapy* New York: Brunner/Mazel, 1972, pp. 400–415.
52. Lidz, T., Fleck, S. & Cornelison, A.R., *Schizophrenia and the Family*, New York: International Universities Press, 1965.
53. MacDonald, D.E., Group Psychotherapy with Wives of Alcoholics. *Q.J. Stud. Alcohol* 19:125, 1958.
54. Meeks, D.E. & Kelly, C., Family Therapy with the Families of Recovering Alcoholics. *Q.J. Stud. Alcohol* 31:399, 1970.

55. Minuchin, S., *Families and Family Therapy*, Cambridge, MA: Harvard University Press, 1974.
56. Minuchin, S., Montalvo, B., Guerney, B.G., Rosman, B.L., & Schumer, F., *Families of the Slums*, New York: Basic Books, 1967.
57. Paolino, T.T. J. & McCrady, B., Joint Admission as a Treatment Modality for Problem Drinkers: A Case Report. *Am. J. Psychiatry* 133:222, 1976.
58. Pattison, E.M., Treatment of Alcoholic Families with Nurse Home Visits. *Family Process* 4:75, 1965.
59. Pattison, E.M., A Critique of Abstinence Criteria in the Treatment of Alcoholism. *Int. J. Soc. Psychiatry* 14:268, 1968.
60. Pattison, E.M., Courless, P., Patti, R., Mann, B., & Mullen, D., Diagnostic Therapeutic Intake Groups for Wives of Alcoholics. *Q.J. Stud. Alcohol* 26:605, 1965.
61. Pattison, E.M., DeFrancisco, D., Wood, P., & Frazier, H., A Psychosocial Kinship Model for Family Therapy. Presented at the American Psychiatric Association Annual Meeting, May 1975.
62. Pittman, D.J., & Tate, R.L., A Comparison of Two Treatment Programs for Alcoholics. *Q.J. Stud. Alcohol* 30:888, 1969.
63. Pixley, J.M., & Stiefel, J.R., Group Therapy Designed to Meet the Needs of the Alcoholic Wife, *Q.J. Stud. Alcohol* 24:304, 1963.
64. Sands, P.M. & Hanson, P.G., Psychotherapeutic Groups for Alcoholics and Relatives in an Outpatient Setting. *Int. J. Group Psychother.* 21:23, 1971.
65. Satir, V., Conjoint Family Therapy, Palo Alto, CA: Science and Behavior Books, 1967.
66. Singer, M. Wynne, L., Thought Disorder and Family Relations of Schizophrenics: II. Classification of Forms of Thinking. *Arch. Gen. Psychiatry* 9:199, 1963.
67. Singer, M. & Wynne, L., Thought Disorder and Family Relations of Schizophrenics. II. Methodology Using Projective Techniques. *Arch. Gen. Psychiatry* 12:187, 1965.
68. Singer, M. & Wynne, Thought Disorder and Family Relations of Schizophrenics: IV. Results and Implications. *Arch. Gen. Psychiatry* 12:201, 1965.
69. Smith, C.J., Alcoholics: Their Treatment and Their Wives. *Br. J. Psychiatry* 115:1039, 1969.
70. Steinglass, P., An Experimental Treatment Program for Alcoholics Couples . *J. Stud. Ac.*, in press.
71. Steinglass, P., Davis, D., & Berenson, D., Observations of Conjointly Hospitalized "Alcoholic Couples" during Sobriety and Intoxication: Implications for Theory and Therapy. *Family Process* 16:1, 1977.
72. Steinglass, P., Weiner, S., & Mendelson, J.H., Interactional Issues as Determinants of Alcoholism. *Am. J. Psychiatry* 128:275, 1971.
73. Steinglass, P., Weiner, S., & Mendelson, J.H., A Systems Approach to Alcoholism: A Model and Its Clinical Application. *Arch. Gen. Psychiatry* 24:401, 1971.
74. Weiner, S., Tamarin, J.S. Steinglass, P., & Mendelson, J.H., Familial Patterns in Chronic Alcoholism: A Study of a Father and Son during Experimental Intoxication. *Am. J. Psychiatry* 127:1646, 1971.
75. Westfield, D.R., Two years' Experience of Group Methods in the Treatment of Male Alcoholics in a Scottish Mental Hospital. *Br. J. Addict.* 67:267, 1972.

76. Whalen, T., Wives of Alcoholics: Four Types Observed in a Family Service Agency. *Q.J. Stud. Alcohol* 14:632, 1953.
77. Wiener, N., *Cybernetics* (2nd Ed.), Cambridge, MA: M.I.T. Press, 1961.
78. Wolin, S., Steinglass, P., Sendroff, P., Davis, D.I., & Berenson, D., Marital Interaction during Experimental Intoxication and the Relationship to Family History. In M. Gross (Ed.), *Experimental Studies of Alcohol Intoxication and Withdrawl*, New York: Plenum Press, 1975.
79. Wynne, L. & Singer, M., Thought Disorder and Family Relations of Schizophrenics: I. Research Strategy. *Arch. Gen. Psychiatry* 9:191, 1963.
80. Wynne, L., Ryckoff, I., Day, J., & Hirsch, S., Pseudomutuality in the Family Relations of Schizophrenics. *Psychiatry* 21:205, 1958.

12

Marital Group Therapy in Alcoholism Treatment

Donald A. Cadogan, Ph.D.
FORMERLY ASSISTANT DIRECTOR
ALCOHOLISM TREATMENT CENTER
BERGAN PINES COUNTY HOSPITAL
PARAMUS, NEW JERSEY

PRESENTLY
PRIVATE PRACTICE
PASADENA, CALIFORNIA

It is widely accepted that the attitudes, beliefs, and needs of our parents form the backdrop of our family relationships and are prime determinants in the development of our human relations concepts. Also, our family relationships and interactions appear directly linked to the development of our emotional makeup. Interpersonal relationships and emotional states are ostensibly part of a feedback system that influences both. Feelings and human relations cannot be conceptually separated without producing a loss of understanding. Alcoholism can be seen as resulting from the emotional condition associated with human relations difficulties and as part of a feedback system that perpetuates its existence. Because of this, the family or at least the spouse of the alcoholic should be included in treatment if it is to be effective and enduring. One of the modalities that includes the spouse, and which appears effective in the treatment of alcoholism, is marital group therapy (6).

Essentially marital group therapy consists of working with four to six couples in a group. The procedure utilizes group dynamic and problem-solving principles in a group therapy format. Much of the focus of therapy is on interpersonal relations as manifested in the marriage and in the group, with efforts to help members generalize beyond the therapy setting. Efforts are also made to clarify the link between human relations problems and emotional difficulties. Marital group therapy is a variant of group therapy proper and is effective for corresponding reasons. However, marital group therapy appears to enhance many of the therapeutic factors found in group therapy (7). Most notably, by virtue of including the spouse, marital group therapy makes family problems and pathological family interaction patterns more apparent, more pertinent for group discussion, and gives the discussion greater impact.

Problem Solving

As in group therapy, marital group therapy affords an opportunity to learn about problem solving and provides practice in the rational discussion of problems. Members generally find it easier to see solutions to the problems of other members even when the problems are similar to ones with which they have struggled in vain. When members offer such solutions, their feelings of worth tend to increase. These members, in turn, have the opportunity to consider options and alternatives offered to them to solve their own difficulties. In this manner much information is exchanged. The offering of solutions or help by group members instills a sense of caring in the group. Marital group members sometimes indicate that feeling the group cares is more important than the solutions reached.

For example, in one group a very dependent woman alcoholic presented a problem that had troubled her for years and had caused her husband much consternation. However, she discounted all the suggestions the group offered. When the group finally became angry she confessed that she didn't want a solution so much as a feeling that someone was concerned. Group members should be made aware of this so that their frustration levels remain tolerable when group suggestions are not followed.

Group work includes examining the reasons that valid group suggestions were not followed. The resistances offered by members to following good advice often point to underlying pathological motives and can usually be seen as part of a process that keeps them troubled. Emphasis on this process provides the group with a course of action when their solutions are rejected. This further reduces potential group frustration. It should be stressed that discovering the processes involved in problem solving is a more important part of the marital group's work than finding the solutions themselves. The group's emphasis on the process of problem solving rather than the problems themselves allows for greater generalization on the part of its members. Let us return to the woman just mentioned. The group informed her that she was avoiding a solution in order to obtain care from her husband. However, her refusal to overcome her difficulties was frustrating her husband, producing resentment, and thus increasing her need to feel cared for.

It is well known that alcoholics tend toward overdependency. Also they tend to demean themselves because of this, and usually come to resent those upon whom they are dependent. Emphasis on process thwarts the development of excessive dependency on the group by enabling members to discover what barriers or obstacles they have set up to keep from helping themselves. Although many options and alternatives are offered in the marital group, group members are not really there to have their problems solved for them.

The problem-solving tasks of discovering options and alternatives, and obtaining needed information or encouragement, appear enhanced by the marital group therapy format. The problems discussed are usually relevant to family life. The individual's problems are often of interest to all the members because these problems can usually be seen as part of the couple's relationship. A group composed of couples minimizes the difficulty sometimes found in mixed groups when such problems relevant to marriage as child-rearing, in-law intrusion, and financial sharing, might dominate the discussion, but be of little interest or value to unmarried members. Also, the commonality of interests associated with the mutual circumstance of marriage, as well as the alcoholism that is potentially destroying it, lends itself well to the development and maintenance of group cohesiveness.

Problems Are Purposeful

The problem-solving function of the marital group is viewed by some as threatening to family life. Just as the alcoholic's problems can serve a purpose for him, so also can the alcoholic's family derive benefit from his difficulties.[1] For example, in a family where the bonds of cohesiveness are loose, or where its members' positions are vague, the introduction of a problem such as alcoholism can strengthen family bonds and clarify positions. The family rallies together for the purpose of helping the "sick" member, and thus is provided with what it lacks: a sense of meaning, purpose, and importance. In this manner the family of the alcoholic restructures and adjusts to the alcoholism. Equilibrium is then established and further change, opposed. The alcoholic's behavior and his family's efforts to help him become part of the family's pattern of functioning. Therapeutic efforts to take these patterns away are often met with resistance, for problem resolution at this point would create an uncomfortable state of disequilibrium in the family. The family's *raison d' être* is derivied not from the solution, but from the problem. Meeks and Kelly, in a study of family therapy with the families of alcoholics, state:

It has been frequently observed that, in response to the treatment of a single family member other members tried to sabotage, or become part of his treatment, as though they had a stake in his illness; hospitalized patients often got worse after visits from family members, as though family interaction had a direct bearing on symptoms; other family members got worse as the patient got better, as though sickness in one of its members [was] essential to the family's way of operating (11).

When a family's only purpose is to help a troubled member, family existence is threatened when the member is no longer troubled. It is understandable, therefore, that a family held together only by its problems would seek to maintain them, and covertly work against treatment. However, if a new purpose is developed, family unity can be strengthened without needing a troubled member. It thus becomes one of the tasks of therapy to help the family find a new sense of purpose if treatment sabotage is to be avoided.

Let us return once again to the alcoholic woman mentioned earlier. Although dependent, she was also gregarious and fun-loving, and appeared to move easily in social situations. Her husband, by comparison, was a compulsive, hard driving executive who felt socially awkward and who envied her easy sociability. He often felt she contributed more to their relationship than he did. Her dependence on him was the one factor that gave him a sense of importance and belonging in the marriage. Consequently, at the least request he would obtain alcohol for his wife. This increased the likelihood of her drinking and tended to undermine her recovery efforts. Confrontation of this by the marital group led to the development of a mutually beneficial, interdependent relationship where each recognized the value of his contribution to the family. This couple reported, as have others, a renewed family purpose in their united efforts to stave off alcoholism and maintain sobriety.

Although some families need a problem in order to function, some also feel guilty because there is a problem. Spouses of alcoholics often report feeling guilty. They tend to feel that they have done something wrong, have in some way contributed to their mates' problem, or have failed to help when help was needed. They seem to know that their mates' difficulties are in some way gratifying. However, guilt is an uncomfortable emotion that presses for reduction and often produces resentment against those who point to its justification. Therapists and alcoholics, by virtue of their roles, tend to remind spouses of this failure. Thus they often become the focal point of spousal resentment. Some spouses perceive psychotherapy as an indictment and actually block the alcoholic's efforts to obtain help. If the problem is not resolvable, however, the family cannot be blamed for failing to correct it. For this reason, therefore, as well as those previously mentioned, many families who seek or encourage treatment for their alcoholic members have a secret desire for treatment to fail. These factors often present major, sometimes insurmountable, obstacles to treatment success. However, an open, but supportive, discussion in the marital group about these barriers to treatment is one of the most productive therapeutic tactics. The object here is not to increase spouses' feelings of guilt and resentment, but to elicit their cooperation and include them in the search for better alternatives.

Interpersonal Anxiety

It is not only the feelings and familial relationship patterns of alcoholics that contribute to their drinking; it is also their feelings and patterns with people in general. Underlying the gregarious facade of many alcoholics is often a deep-seated and feared introversiveness. Their self-esteem is easily threatened, and results in feelings of hostility that often leaves them tense and anxious in social situations. Yet the prospect of withdrawing from others is often experienced as equally, if not more, unpleasant. Alcoholics, however, tend to interpret their fear of isolation as further evidence of weakness and unacceptability. Many alcoholics are confused about their affectional needs and interpret them as additional evidence of an underlying inadequacy. Though hungry for affection and acceptance, some alcoholics confuse the good feelings associated with comradery as evidence of latent, but fundamental, homosexuality. Many feel that closeness to others might lead to exposure of these unacceptable qualities and will result in rejection and isolation. These fears and conflicts leave many alcoholics feeling stiff and awkward in social situations.

Alcohol tends to decrease anxiety associated with interpersonal interaction. As such, moderate alcohol intake is experienced as pleasant by many people. Indeed, only the simplest and most basic societies have not had a drug for the purpose of altering moods and reducing the anxiety and stress of everyday life (10). Many alcoholics find alcohol profoundly rewarding or desirable because of their heightened social anxiety and because of the anxiolytic effects of alcohol. The disclosures of alcoholics in therapy have corroborated this assertion. Alcoholics often claim they need to maintain a gregarious facade in public, but they also resent it. Some also are afraid that their facade is transparent and insist that alcohol greatly reduces the anxiety associated with this feeling.

To reduce the attractiveness of alcohol use, alcoholics need to deal with and overcome their human relations anxieties. Therefore this becomes one of the important functions of therapy with alcoholics and is part of the marital group therapy process. Through the operation of feedback, i.e. confrontation and discussion by group members of the expectations and emotional impact members have upon each other, marital group therapy helps the couples as units, as well as individually, to learn about maladaptive behavior which may have been undermining their socializing efforts. Feedback also enables members to develop a stable and more accurate sense of identity, and to check the reality of their influence on others. The anxiety asssociated with anticipated rejection can be greatly reduced by these experiences.

Socialization

Alcoholics often complain that their difficulties are compounded by their deteriorated social life and by loneliness. Social isolation, through an emotional incubation process, seems to increase alcoholics' fear of others and further reduces their ability to function socially. For some couples the marital group fills the social void in their lives. The gratification of social and affiliative needs by the group reduces the pain of its absence. However, it also reduces the pressure to assuage the loneliness and seek extra-group friendships. One of the functions of the marital group is to help its members develop and sharpen their social skills. It is not intended to satisfy their social needs. This author does not believe it is part of the therapist's mandate to forbid the development of friendships between group members. However, it is appropriate to warn members of the marital group of this potential complication and to encourage them to utilize the socialization skills acquired in the marital group to expand their social contacts.

When intragroup friendships do arise, members are encouraged to discuss in the marital group any feelings about group that they share with each other outside of group. This reduces the likelihood that feelings about the group will be dissipated through catharsis and left unresolved. It also decreases the likelihood that cliques or alliances will develop. The marital group is especially prone to the development of alliances because it is composed initially of many subgroups, i.e. married couples.

Communication

Communication difficulty is another important factor to consider when treating alcoholics. Taciturn people who keep their feelings secret and are socially inhibited often drink to reduce their inhibitions. However, drinking tends to socially isolate these individuals, which further impairs their ability to communicate. Alcoholics' communication difficulties and social inhibitions foster alcohol abuse, which in turn exacerbates their difficulties, thus pulling these individuals into self-perpetuating vicious cycles.

Hanson and his associates claim that one of the major problems in the alcoholic's marriage is lack of communication (9). They say that meaningful communication flows mostly from spouse to alcoholic, but rarely in the other direction. The author has found this to be true in the families of many alcoholics. However, the discussion of problems, self-disclosures, and sharing of feelings with or in the presence of one's spouse as it occurs in the marital group greatly improves marital communication, which in turn helps to clarify misconceptions about the marital relationship. These misconceptions can usually be seen as the progenitors of undue pressure or stress in the relationship. They tend to result in feelings of anxiety, or of failure and depression. Clarification of these misconceptions can quickly relieve these feelings.

However, with some couples there are problems getting the marital group process started. Some people are so threatened or so intimidated by their spouses' presence in group that they refuse to speak. For example, one alcoholic who came for treatment had been locked in a struggle for dominance with his wife. He refused to disclose any weaknesses or inadequacies in front of her for fear she would use them to her advantage. He was correct. His wife had a similar fear which was also warranted. This resulted in a home atmosphere that consisted of icy silences, manipulations, and power ploys. Drinking was one of the weapons used in this marital war. This couple refused to communicate openly and was therefore unwilling to enter the marital group. It was necessary to see them separately in individual therapy. Individual sessions helped them to realize that their attempts to dominate each other were destructive to their relationship. In time, though with reservations, they were willing to try marital group therapy. Although they agreed it was self-defeating, they continued to compete with each other in group. Repeated confrontations of their destructive patterns by group members as they were manifested in group led to greater awareness of these patterns and increased agreement about their folly. It should be noted that group confrontations also pointed to the underlying dynamics of these patterns. In time this couple became more trusting, caring, and supportive of each other, and more open in their relationship. Drinking also stopped and was correlated with their improved marital relationship.

This illustration supports the notion that intellectual understanding needs to be supplemented by in vivo or group experiences before real cognitive and behavioral changes take place. It also points out that it is sometimes necessary to see spouses separately. However, the author believes that this should be temporary, and its goal that of enabling the couple to communicate openly and together in their attempts to resolve marital and personal problems.

As indicated earlier, one of the therapeutic factors that appears most helpful to alcoholics and their spouses is the aid the group offers in discovering self-defeating beliefs and in correcting misconceptions. Indeed, some would argue that this is the most important therapeutic factor (4, 8, 14). These discoveries and corrections usually lead to changes in the attitudes, feelings, and behaviors that had been destructive to their relationships and to their lives. One example of this process is the quick turn-about in feelings that results when sexual fears, expectancies, or beliefs are frankly discussed by the marital couple. Discussions about sexual beliefs and feelings are especially pertinent for alcoholics in a marital group since many report sexual problems. These difficulties usually involve fear of impotency or frigidity, an inability to please their spouses, fear of a diminishing sexual drive, and fear of the emergence of a presumed underlying homosexual condition. They usually come to discover, among other things, that anxiety is the principal nemesis of their sexual difficulties. The therapeutic effect of such a discussion is enduring and is also experienced by other couples in the group who have similar misconceptions, but had been afraid to discuss them.

Pathological Family Interaction

Another important function of the marital group lies in its ability to expose and help resolve pathological family interaction. Sometimes spouses are selected in an attempt to satisfy pathological needs. Unfortunately, the attempt to satisfy these needs often has a reverse effect and serves only to perpetuate the need for satisfaction. According to Ackerman, neurotic conflict can be destructive to a relationship, but it can also hold a bad relationship together (1). The pathological traits of some alcoholics are complemented or neutralized by the pathological traits of their spouse. Improvement in one partner's disorder could have a deleterious effect on the relationship in that the pathological needs of the other partner would no longer be satisfied by the relationship.

However, the pathological patterns in a marriage are usually the product of both partners. Some marital unions are formed by immature individuals who are not ready for a meaningful and adult relationship. These marriages are based on a desire on the part of both members to parentify each other. As a result the anxiety-producing features of the original parent-child relationship are often reproduced and reexperienced, and the self-defeating coping mechanisms used in childhood are again utilized.

Despite the anxiety experienced in these relationships, there remains a need to recreate them, return to them, or in some way reexperience them. The need to be again subjected to disordered relationships may be the product of a propensity to resolve anxiety by again facing it, thus developing a sense of mastery, success, or power. Unfortunately, by using the same inadequate coping mechanisms, the experience of defeat, failure, and weakness tends to be reproduced.

Alcoholics in group often tend to select strong and controlling spouses' to depend upon in order to satisfy a need for security or safety. However, they also indicate a dislike of needing others, and usually resent their marital partners' strength. They then tend to act out by drinking in an attempt to assert their independence and to defy and weaken their partners' control. These maneuvers are usually destructive to their marital relationships, leave these relationships tenuous, and result in the return of their feelings of insecurity. The spouses in such relationships tend to be angry, controlling people who are looking for reasons to justify preexisting hostile feelings, and find in their mates' behavior much justification for martydom, scorn, self-pity, and controlling behavior. This behavior engenders further hostility in the alcoholics. Thus alcoholics are often attracted to partners they covertly resent in an effort to resolve conflict produced by disordered early family interaction. The partners, on the other hand, appear attracted to the behavioral manifestations of the alcoholics' resentment, i.e. their drinking, neediness, irresponsibility, and violence. In this manner spouses often attempt to rectify their own disordered human relations experiences.

In the marital group these patterns become apparent. The alcoholic woman and her husband mentioned earlier are examples of this. The group helped to expose her pathological need to feel cared for, and her tendency to function inadequately in order to obtain her husband's care. He, in turn, had a pathological need to feel needed, which he gratified by keeping his wife needful. The marital group helped to expose this and pointed to its destructiveness. Initially this couple was not aware of such a pattern and instead felt innocent of any responsibility for the difficulties in their relationship. They therefore felt they had many justifiable reasons for hostility and for acting out. It is important to note, however, that they were able to see these patterns quite clearly in other group members. This author believes that seeing these patterns in other people helped this couple understand its own pathological needs and to more readily accept group confrontations directed toward them.

Group Attractiveness

There are other aspects of marital group therapy that help it to function effectively. If the group is to have an impact on the maladaptive attitudes, beliefs, needs, and human relations patterns of alcoholics it needs to be viewed as important. The attractiveness of the group to its members adds to their willingness to see the group as important. In general, single people prefer the company of single people, and married couples tend to associate with other married couples. Marital group therapy should therefore appear more attractive to its members who are married because of its compostion.

Groups composed of married couples appear to enhance feelings of affiliation. According to Powdermaker and Frank (13), feelings of affiliation increase the therapeutic potential of the intragroup relationships. Alcoholics and their spouses, as well as other people in therapy, have verified these assumptions. Couples, when given a choice between marital group therapy and group therapy, tended to choose the former. Some people are quite enthusiastic about the prospect of meeting other couples, discussing their difficulties with them, and discovering what other marital relationships are really like.

However, some people do not find the marital group therapy format initially attractive. For example, one alcoholic came to treatment with feelings of failure which were reinforced by his wife's conviction that he was in fact a failure. He was the son of a wealthy professional whom he wanted to emulate. Yet when success was in sight he would drink and sabotage his efforts. His wife had married him partially because of his professional potential. Although he resented this, he also believed that his value as a person came from his professional status. This couple did not want close emotional contact with a group comprised of alcoholics or people with emotional problems. Instead they wanted therapy to cure his alcoholism so he could rise farther above such people.

They eventually came to see their social climbing as contributing to the superficiality of their relationship and as fostering underlying resentment. The husband's resentment, in turn, was resulting in a desire to fail as an act of angry defiance. As the couple put aside these goals, they became more self-accepting, and came to see the group as comprised of "real" people. For this couple, group importance seemed corrolated with self-acceptance.

Feelings of self-acceptance and affiliation are also enhanced when members discover that they are neither unique nor alone in the world. Ohlsen claims that when group members find that other members in the group have problems similar to their own, it gives them a greater sense of belonging and a feeling that they will be better understood (12). Alcoholics often report a comforting feeling of oneness with others when they discover that other group members have or have had similar problems. Alcoholics Anonymous has long known this and facilitates the experience by encouraging its members to openly discuss in the group their problems with alcohol. This discovery appears to help many alcoholics realize that their difficulties are less the result of being defective than that of being human. This helps them to believe that their problems can be mastered or at least coped with. It also appears to enhance feelings of self-esteem when alcoholics know that their spouses are coming to similar realizations.

Hope

In addition to feeling oneness with others, alcoholics need to know, and need their wives to know, that their problems are resolvable. The very existence of a group of people with similar life circumstances and similar problems coming together for the purpose of resolving their difficulties, and sanctioned by the authority of a professional therapist, lends hope to its members. The instillation of this hope is an important therapeutic factor that the group offers through its positive attitude toward problem resolution, and is added to by the degree of importance attributed to the group by its members. Statements by members of the group to other members about how they have benefited from the group encourage other members to keep trying even in the face of failures, set backs, regressions, or slips in sobriety. One alcoholic who came to therapy with a history of anxiety attacks accompanied by severe depression claimed he had tried many things to overcome these feelings. His last report was always alcohol. He flatly told the group that what he needed was hope that the group could help. The group members responded by indicating how the group had helped them. One member who also experienced anxiety and depression and drank to obtain relief explained the process in group that had helped him. He insisted his group experiences had greatly reduced his desire to drink.

Statements such as these help new members develop the kind of commitment often essential to successful therapy. However, the author has found it unnecessary to elicit such statements, for group members usually want their efforts to be effective and readily proselytize their new discoveries. It should be noted, however, that exaggerated claims produce unrealistic expectations and passivity, and set members up to be disappointed. The alcoholic just mentioned was encouraged by the group's statements but also needed to know the group's limits. The marital group creates an atmosphere that facilitates therapeutic change, but it does not create this change.

Therapist Openness

In any description of therapy or discussion of therapy techniques, something should be said about the therapist. His behavioral style, manner of approach, and attitudes add a vital dimension to the therapeutic process and have a direct bearing on the outcome of treatment. Many therapists believe that effective therapy can only occur when the therapist remains aloof, objective, and more of an expert observer than a participant. However, this concept is being questioned in many quarters. Aronson believes that the person of the therapist is the potent agent for change (3). The therapist's belief in himself as a consistent and stable person communicates courage and vitality to the group. Aronson also claims the patient comes to know these facts about the therapist. Knowledge about the nature of the therapist facilitates the therapeutic process. It seems clear that self-disclosures by the therapist would facilitate this knowledge. Apter (2) claims that therapist disclosures help the patient to form an identification and encourages reality testing. Yalom (16) believes that therapist self-disclosures help to demystify therapy and in turn aid the group in developing autonomy and cohesiveness. Yalom also claims that such therapist transparency requires that the therapist have a less analytic, and more humanistic, attitude toward therapy. In this manner the alcoholic can become more of a collaborator in the therapy process. This style is also grounded in the Alcoholics Anonymous philosophy. Incorporation of this attitude appears to facilitate the marital group therapy process for alcoholics.

It seems to greatly enhance feelings of self-esteem when alcoholics can see their own feared weaknesses and inadequacies in, and comfortably handled by, their therapist. This experience can only take place if the therapist is willing to share some of his own difficulties. If the therapist has struggled with personal problems and has resolved them or has learned to cope with them, he presents a positive and realistic model with which alcoholics can identify and then emulate. Such disclosures produce feelings of comfort and closeness in therapy. Alcoholics often report that their therapists' self-disclosures produce in them greater feelings of trust and acceptance of their therapists and greatly enhance the alcoholics' willingness to discuss their problems in group. Many alcoholics come to see that weaknesses and inadequacies are part of the structure of meaningful relationships.

This author is firmly convinced that awareness of our weaknesses in others allows us to bridge the space that separates us emotionally. The experience of this paradox leads us to reverse the belief that our inadequacies will cause rejection. It should be noted, however, that the proper timing of these disclosures by the therapist is important.

Current Research

Overall, much current research points to the importance of spouse involvement in treatment. Hanson and his associates claim that including the spouse in treatment can "help the alcoholic husband become less of a mystery to his wife and to 'let her in' ... help the wife become aware that her negative evaluation of her spouse is creating distance, not only in her own perception of him, but in making it more difficult for her to become more open about her own feelings and thoughts" (9). Trotter and her associates (15), concurring with previous researchers that no specific alcoholic personality has yet been described, found that wives' involvement in treatment correlated positively with the completion of inpatient hospital treatment. These researchers claim that the wife's involvement in treatment leads to increased understanding and support of her alcoholic husband, and allows for behavioral changes in her that correspond to changes occurring in her husband, who is also in treatment. Burton and Kaplan state at the conclusion of their research:

The hypothesis that improvement in the area of marital conflict is associated with improvement in drinking behavior has been supported. This is sufficient to conclude that counseling which focuses on the family pathology of alcoholics may be therapeutic not only with respect to the family and marriage problems, but with respect as well to the drinking problem (5).

Summary

In general, alcoholism appears to be the product of disordered experiences of human relationships that are part of both the past and present. Alcoholism appears to be a response to these experiences, and needs to be viewed as a symptom of troubled interpersonal relationships or as an attempted solution to these troubles. The alcoholic's interpersonal matrix should be carefully considered and should be part of the treatment focus. The family of the alcoholic provides him with his most important, and potentially his most destructive, interpersonal contacts. Family therapy appears to be the most reasonable' approach to treatment of the human relations dysfunction associated with alcoholism, with marital group therapy as one variant of this approach that appears most effective. Clinical and experimental evidence supports the view that marital group therapy is an effective form of treatment for alcoholism. However, more research on marital group therapy in the treatment of alcoholism, with treatment focused on the important progentiors of this disorder, is needed.

REFERENCES

1. Ackerman, N.W., *The Psychodynamics of Family Life,* New York: Basic Books, 1958.
2. Apter, N.S., Breaking the Rules. In J.G. Gunderson & L.R. Mosher (Eds.), *Psychotherapy of Schizophrenia,* New York: Jason Aronson, 1975.
3. Aronson, G., Crucial Aspects of Therapeutic Intervention. In J.G. Gunderson & L.R. Mosher (Eds.), New York: Jason Aronson, 1975.
4. Beck, A.T., *Cognitive Therapy and the Emotional Disorders,* New York: International Universities Press, 1976.
5. Burton, G. & Kaplan, H.M., Marriage Counseling with Alcoholics and Their Spouses: II. The Correlation of Excessive Drinking Behavior with Family Pathology and Social Deterioration. *Brit. J. Addict.* 63:161–170, 1968.

6. Cadogan, D.A., Marital Group Therapy in the Treatment of Alcoholism. *Quarterly J. Stud. Alcoholism* 34:1184–1194, 1973.

7. Cadogan, D.A., *Marital Group Therapy*, Behavioral Science Tape Library, Leona NJ: Sigma Information, 1977.

8. Ellis, A. & Harper, R.A., *A Guide to Rational Living*, Hollywood: Wilshire Book Co., 1972.

9. Hanson, P.G., Sands, P.M., & Sheldon, R.B., Patterns of Communication in Alcoholic Marital Couples. *Psychiatric Quarterly* 42:538–547, 1968.

10. LaBarre, W., Anthropological Perspectives on Hallucination and Hallucinogens. In R.K. Siegle & L.J. West (Eds.), *Hallucinations, Behavior, Experience and Theory*, New York: Wiley & Sons, 1975.

11. Meeks, D.E. & Kelly, C., Family Therapy with the Families of Recovered Alcoholics. *Quarterly J. Stud. Alcohol* 31:399–413, 1970.

12. Ohlsen, M.M., *Group Counseling*, New York: Holt, Rinehart & Winston, 1970.

13. Powdermaker, F.B. & Frank, J.D., *Group Psychotherapy*, Cambridge, MA: Harvard University Press, 1953.

14. Raimy, V., *Misunderstandings of the Self*, San Francisco, CA: Jossey-Bass, 1975.

15. Trotter, A.B., Gozali, J., & Cunningham, L.J., Family Participation in the Treatment of Alcoholism. *Personnel and Guidance J.*, 140–143, October 1969.

16. Yalom, I.D., *The Theory and Practice of Group Psychotherapy*, New York: Basic Books, 1975.

FOOTNOTES

1. To avoid confusion, the author will be using the masculine pronoun to refer to the alcoholic and the feminine to refer to the alcoholic's spouse. However, although the majority of identified alcoholics are male, alcoholism is an insidious and destructive problem for both sexes. For female alcoholics the gender identity ascribed by these pronouns can often be interchanged.

13

Family Choreography:
A Multigenerational View
of an Alcoholic Family System

Eloise Kates Julius, M.S.W., A.C.S.W.
ASSOCIATE DIRECTOR
FAMILY INSTITUTE OF WESTCHESTER
WHITE PLAINS, NEW YORK

Peggy Papp, M.S.W.
PHILADELPHIA CHILD GUIDANCE CLINIC

Over the past two decades research has broadened clinical perceptions of alcoholism so that the alcoholic is viewed within the context of a total family system. Chafetz and his colleagues (3) state that "alcoholism is now seen not as a result of one person's pathology, but as a result of interaction among all family members in a behavior program that maintains family homeostasis."

Alcoholism is responsible for homeostasis in specific ways. A fairly constant drinking pattern stabilizes a family system. A change in alcohol intake can function as a distress signal indicating upset in some part of that system; or it can serve to accommodate stress and later reestablish equilibrium at another level. When alcohol has thus assumed the central position in a family's social, cultural, emotional, and physical life, it functions as the organizing principle in what can be labeled an alcoholic family system (10).

Members of such alcoholic family systems, as well as outside observers, may be under the impression that family interactions are chaotic, tumultuous, free flowing, and operating with erratic disorganization. Quite the opposite is true. Beneath the external disorder there is a methodical and systematic internal program. The process might be more accurately described as organized chaos.

Family members are locked into fixed roles centering around alcohol intake. Drunken stages trigger automatic reactions which include specific behavior and dialogue; sober stages are equally predictable. Roles are fixed in complementary opposition so that the irresponsible rascal when drunk becomes the overly responsible "pillar of the family" when sober. These drunk/sober behavioral cycles appear to be quite rigidly determined, leaving the participants little or no flexibility in using alternate methods for problem solving.

Family members also seem to be locked into ruminating excessively about alcohol. While the labeled alcoholic plots and schemes and is totally organized around when to take a drink, when not to, and whether one will be available, the nondrinking member, in a parallel process, is preoccupied with whether there will be liquor available as a temptation, whether to hide the bottle, how much the drinker will consume, how to avoid an unpleasant situation—and other unpleasant factors. The family worrier becomes reactive, sees alcohol as anathema and organizes around being on the alert for the smell of alcohol on the family drinker's breath, especially ut parties and other social occasions. The worrier's watchfulness and emotional toxicity to liquor is as real, as powerful, and as stabilizing a force in the alcoholism triangle as the drinker and the drink. Alcohol serves as the mechanism for maintaining an emotional distance in interpersonal relationships.

People trapped in these circumstances rarely understand them. It is difficult for them to become detached from the process and gain sufficient perspective on what is going on, to identify their roles in the program, and then implement a strategy to extricate themselves.

Family Choreography

The authors found that family choreography provides an orderly, sequential overview for persons caught in predictable alcoholic family systems. Traditional verbal therapies, when applied to these systems, often seem to perpetuate the characteristic problems of denial, projection, and blame. Family choreography, rather than concentrating on words, shows the progress of family continuity through physical movement and emotional experimental processes. It illustrates and traces various stages of a family's development. This is particularly useful in the alcoholic family system since it enables the people taking part to perceive of the drinking problem across multigenerational family lines, to observe and experience the similarities of behavior of those surrounding the alcoholic in times past and present, and to realize that while the actors may have changed from grandfather to father to husband to brother to son, the roles and situations have remained exactly the same.

The authors began using family choreography with alcoholic families while they were working together on a project funded by the National Institute on Alcohol Abuse and Alcoholism. The three-year project was designed to prevent alcoholism in children of families having a history of drinking, to develop innovative community presentation programs on alcohol, and to conduct time-limited family education workshops and individual and multiple therapy groups. Many of the techniques developed are still in use in the authors' work with alcoholic families. Family choreography enabled single- and multifamily therapy groups to trace the repetitive interactional patterns and roles assumed in situational family scripts. It helped group members to perceive themselves and other family members in less personal and less threatening metaphors.

The term "family choreography" emanated from "sculpting," a nonverbal action technique developed by David Kantor (5); he used it as a concrete experiental process to explore family systems and conceptualize individual roles and effective relationships in spatial arrangements. He called this process "family sculpturing." Satir (9) and Papp (8) devised prescripted sculptings as participatory/experiential demonstrations for educational and community workshops to illustrate dyadic and triadic relationships. Family sculpturing—or sculpting, as it is more widely known—has been employed with single- and multifamily groups, with groups of schizophrenic patients (6), and as a training technique for students of family therapy. Papp (8) named the process choreography, noting: "since emotional relationships are always in motion, sculpturing is an instrument of movement. It choreographs transactional patterns, alliances, triangles and shifting emotional currents and projects them outward like a silent movie" (8).

This action-oriented technique focuses rapidly and graphically on the ways in which the alcoholic family system is organized. The choreographic process is dramatic and complete within itself, having a beginning, a middle, and an end. It centers on a process which is developed, staged, experienced, and examined, all within one session or occasionally two. Because the action is in pantomime and essentially nonverbal (and therefore uncluttered with the defensive barriers provided by words), it becomes a mix of concrete, emotional, and illustrative experiences for the person involved.

Choreography helps families move beyond an emotional and behavioral impasse; acting out a problem tends to clarify it as well as the relationships involved. After the scene has been repeated several times, the participants begin to assume some responsibility for the problem rather than blaming someone else, and try to resolve it instead of perpetuating it. Choreography can be used with a disorganized family as a concrete and simplified process for getting its members to focus on an issue and work together for change. By tracing their family's history, by enacting its multigenerational life cycles from birth to death, the members can begin to view parents, grandparents, and other relatives in new perspectives: as children, as yearning adolescents, as infatuated lovers, as ill-prepared adults, as persons who have loved, wept, failed, or succeeded, with identities other than merely those of father and mother.

All choreography consultations were videotaped so that the families could review their choreographies at a later date with their therapist and, if they chose, with other family members.

Case Illustration and Discussion

The following excerpts from a consultation illustrate the use of family choreography as a tool for identifying behavioral patterns from one generation to another.

Mary Tracy, 29, requested therapy for problems she and her husband were having because of his drinking. She was unhappy, worried about the future, and concerned with his unreliability. Her husband Kevin, 34, also saw the therapist, denied that he had drinking problems, and was generally late or missed appointments completely. Mary had been in therapy for four months and was working on her reaction to the alcoholism in both her nuclear and extended families.

As the genogram indicates, Mary and Kevin had been married for six years and had a 5-year-old daughter, Kathleen. Both parents were of Irish descent and had indicated an extensive history of alcoholic abuse in their families. The multigenerational drinking patterns are noted, with the alcoholic members labeled by Mary.

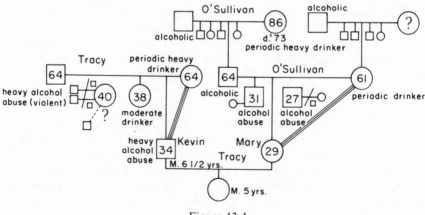

Figure 13-1

The family choreography consultation brought Mary's family experiences alive for her. In tracing family patterns across generational lines Mary highlighted her role. Her life had been organized around protecting and pleasing her mother and assuming responsibility for the family drinkers. That role continued into her marriage, with the triangle being represented by Mary, her husband, and the bottle. The choreography pinpointed her total involvement: she had committed almost all of her time to thinking and talking about who would be drinking what and when, and what would happen.

The consulting therapist (Papp, who will be designated as Th in the following) asked Mary (who will be called M) what she hoped to get out of the family choreography experience.

M: I'd like to see where I fit in, where I am in my family. Does that make sense? I've always felt very pulled. If not by my mother, then by my father. I've always felt very responsible for everyone.
Th: So if you had a label what would it be?
M: Oh, I was the worrier. I worried all the time about what was going to happen. That was my way, I guess. I would worry what my parents would be doing ...what my brothers were doing... if they were going to get in trouble... if they were going to be late. That's the way I was. As a child I couldn't go to sleep unless my brothers were home. I can remember waiting for their footsteps through the alley. This is the way I've always been.
Th: Let's begin with that.

Staff members volunteered to act as family members for Mary's choreography. She was told to choose someone to play her part while she functioned as director. This enabled her to remain one step removed from the emotional interactions she would be describing, thereby helping her maintain perspective.

Th: Now, would you show us a time when you were worrying about everyone ...where they would be and what they would be doing?
M: Usually when we were out. I was worrying, like when I was at a party.

Mary was instructed to show the actors what to do rather than describe it. She told them where to stand and how to look. Then she placed herself near her father but remained alone. Her father and her brothers were all acting silly and happy. The actors portrayed the family's merrymakers while Mary watched them carefully.

M: So the only ones that are serious are my mother and I. My mother is always very serious, watching the three of them. *I'm always very serious, watching what my mother is doing.*

Th: What have the three of them been doing that your mother would be watching?

M: They're laughing and having a good time.

Th: Okay, and what concerns her about that? Why can't they laugh?

M: My mother is a very... oh, you have to realize they were at a party. And my father might be drinking. My brothers are laughing, silly, all the time, usually telling jokes. My father too.

Mary looked on intently as the actors moved through the party scene. Her eyes darted rapidly from her mother to the laughing men and back again to her mother. The therapist pressed her to be more specific, to examine her mother's behavior.

Th: What is your mother worried about?

M: She doesn't like them when they're silly.

Th: What would be your mother's worst fear?

M: That my father would get drunk... that he'll stagger and fall.

Th: Is that what your mother is worried about, that he'll fall?

M: Yes, all the time. My father is the party one. You know, good times and all that. My mother is the worrier, the serious one... always worried about what he is going to do

Th: Is she worried that he's going to embarrass her? Or hurt himself? Or what?

M: Yes, hurt himself. I think, uh... probably by falling.

The group was directed to continue being silly, laughing, drinking, and staggering. The person playing Mary's father was directed to get drunker and eventually stumble and fall on the floor.

Th: What would you do?

M: Usually watch my mom, because she's upset. And because my father's smiling.

Th: What are you afraid will happen to your mother? Let's carry that into some kind of fantasy nightmare, like if she got terribly disturbed. What might happen to her?

M: She might start to yell at my dad. And I'd be bothered and not want yelling. She'd make her point to my father in a vicious way... and my father would just look up, but he wouldn't pay any attention.

Mary would try to hide her discomfort by talking to someone else at the party or going into the kitchen for some tea, but mostly by staying as far away from her family as she could. Finally her mother would assemble the children and tell them it was time to take father home. They would help him into the car, with her mother beside him yelling all the time as he drove home. The family would form a cavalcade of cars to be sure that he got there. Mary and her husband would bring up the rear.

M: I'd be in another car, probably with my husband. Usually way behind, because it upsets me and I can't take it the way my brothers do. Acting funny. It isn't funny to me. So I have to try to calm myself... somehow. I really cry.

The drama continued along its ritualistic course. The mother continued yelling; the father was put to bed.

M: My mother is annoyed at both my brothers. She's screaming at them. And, uh, I come in and I'm upset so I don't say much. And my mother is ranting and raving about how he's embarrassed her, how he could have hurt himself. ..and my brothers are still laughing.
Th: What happens between you and your mother now?
M: Well, my mother and I go into the kitchen while my husband stays outside with the boys. She talks about my father. Not anything bad, but she'll just say, "You know, I'm worried about your father... what if he got hurt?"

Mary's mother is adhering to a predictable pattern in the alcoholic family system. She isn't relating directly to another member of the family; instead she forms a triangle by discussing the all-important third person, the alcoholic. This triggers Mary.

M: Of course I'm yelling. Now, at this point I'm very angry. Because I feel like ...why does he constantly do this?
Th: You're yelling at whom?
M: My mother. Because she's always concerned with my father. If he falls down, if he's going to hurt himself. Everything is my father, my father, my father. Everybody takes over everything he does. How's my father ever going to do for himself? And, of course, like, when I try to talk, to say this or that too her she just closes me off. She shuts me off. (Weeping.) And if I say it to my brothers, well, they just laugh it off and say he wants to have a good time.
Th: So how does this end?
M: Well, usually by me crying. Because I can't get it into my mother's head. That if she would only let my father grow up and do what he has to do. If he gets drunk and he falls... he falls. Just leave him alone. He's... it's him... it's not her or I... yet we all feel it.

The staff participants in the choreography reported to Mary later that they experienced a sense of inevitability about the action. They felt that the people they portrayed had a major investment in keeping the focus on the father and his drinking, and that if he stopped drinking, or the mother stopped worrying and yelling, every member of the family would be deprived of a familiar role and the familiar interactions that went with it. They were a well-organized alcoholic family system.

Mary had an opportunity to experience her role and its limited possibilities for interaction in two ways. First, she directed the scenes; later, she replaced the person acting her part so that she could play the role herself.

Choreography helped Mary clarify her predicament. The next stage was designed such that Mary would experience the impossibility of fulfilling the task she had established for herself and would open her mind to the possibilities for change. She was instructed to replay the scenes, including one that showed an end to her mother's pain and another showing an end to her father's drinking.

In the scene with her mother, Mary moved forward and then drew back. She looked uncomfortable and unhappy. The therapist urged her to try harder, "to save your mother." Mary found herself unable to move. Finally she whispered, "I can't." To test the emotional fusion, and assess her capacity for change, the therapist asked her if she could walk away from the family scene. Mary left the room and closed the door behind her, only to open it immediately and stand in the doorway crying.

Th: Are you upset because you try to stop them and you are unable to?
M: I've tried so many times ... but I really have no control over it. It's so frustrating, no matter what I do. I've tried to cut away from them. But still I go back to the same thing again and again. I can't reach any of them. My brothers don't hear me ... my mother is all wounded ... and my father, he's just there. I want to say something to them, but I can't. I can't even say, "I love you." I hoped to be different, but I couldn't. I wanted to say, "Please I love you. Don't do it." I once said that to my dad and he just said, "I love you too." I can't say that to my mother. I can't say it. I can't make her pain go away.
Th: That's true. And what impresses me is that you want to, so terribly. And how frustrating it must be.
M: It's terrible. I feel like I should do something but I can't.

The therapist asked Mary if she could turn her back on her family.

M: They'd just go on and on ... doing the same thing.
Th: So if you're not able to do anything about it, what would be different if you weren't there?
M: It would be better for me.
Th: What about your brothers?
M: When we're alone with each other, it's fine. I don't feel that nervous or anxious. I feel that we treat my dad like such a baby. We all do it.
Th: Yes ... and you know, I was thinking, you also treat your mother that way too.
M: We don't treat them like parents. The last time we went out my mom said, "Who's going to drive us home?" And I said, "Mom, you're the parents and we're the children. It's not our responsibility." And then she didn't say anything. So I said, "It's not my responsibility to take care of you. I've got my responsibility to my own child."
Th: I'm wondering ... what would it take for you to really let go. To say to them, "I'm not going to be in this scene anymore. I'm going to treat you like adults. Which means that you're responsible for your life and I'm responsible for mine. I'm just not going to be able to see you any more."

M: What would I do?

Th: Well, I guess, just not go to the parties with them.

M: Right. That's what has happened over the past six months. Because I couldn't handle it. But then they say to me, "Why don't you want to be with us? Don't you love us?"

This question is characteristic of the "pull of the system." It is used on any member of the family who tries to initiate change.

Th: Nobody appreciates what you're trying to do.

M: They all say, "Who do you think you are?" But you know . . . you can't change them . . . my mother's worrying. I always thought she was so grown up. I thought my mother was probably the smartest person . . . and a very strong person.

Th: She probably is. You see, my feeling about it is that it's like they're playing a game. I don't mean it's superficial, because we all play games in life . . . we all follow certain patterns again and again. If you were to withdraw from that game, they would have to set up a different one. And they'd have to find different rules to play by. There's no way they can keep on with that game once you withdraw from it. In some way or other they would really have to do something different. Particularly your mother.

M: They'd just keep going on. Even if I let go.

Th: Well, maybe they'd find someone else to play your part. Do you want to keep it?

M: No. I don't. Because it hurts me so much . . . and because it's such a responsibility for me. Always . . . even toward my brothers . . . it was like, "Don't let them run," or "Watch this," or "Look out."

Th: Your brothers seem to be quite carefree. Did you ever feel that way?— carefree?

M: Yes, when I'm away from them. You know, with my friends. I like to have a good time and laugh a lot.

As an encouragement to Mary to alter her role as the "responsible one" and the "worrier," the therapist invited her to explore the other side of the coin, i.e. Mary's carefree attitude when she's with friends—the role she envies in her brothers but cannot play at home becasue of her alliance with her mother.

Th: I think it's interesting, sometimes, to have people change roles. So they can get a sense of what it's like to be somebody else. I'd like you to see what it would be like for you to be one of your brothers. Would you try it? Tell some jokes . . . have some fun.

The party scene was replayed with Mary attempting to assume the role of one of her brothers. This meant restructuring the dysfunctional mother-daughter and father-sons alignments, creating a generational boundary, and leaving her parents to join her sibling system. Despite considerable support and coaching from the therapist, Mary was constrained, awkward, and wary throughout the scene. Her discomfort in getting into the spirit of her brothers was a measure of her resistance to changing her family role and alliances. Nevertheless, the reenactment did serve to further her understanding of the dilemma. She concluded the scene with the comment, "See, I really think I have to change."

At that point the therapist decided to track themes and patterns from Mary's family of origin to her nuclear family so that Mary could clearly see the role she played in perpetuating the dysfunctional process. The choreography again focused on her family system's external organization and its internal rumination.

Th: What I think would be helpful is if you could show us when you get caught up like that in a present situation. When you feel pulled apart or responsible for something you can't solve. When do you feel like that?
M: Almost every day.
Th: Would you show us a scene of something going on in your life today?

Mary chose one of the staff/actors to play the part of her husband, and another to play her daughter, Kathleen. She cast herself as Mary.

M: I feel like I'm always angry when my husband is near me. It starts as soon as he opens the door. I'm usually waiting in the kitchen, waiting for the door to open. Or the phone to ring.
Th: What are you thinking as you do this?
M: Oh, why isn't he on time? He's about half an hour late. Why does he have to do this? He said he'd be home on time and he isn't. If he's only half an hour late, then I'm not that mad. But if it's more, I get mad. I'm always talking to myself, saying things like, "Why can't he be on time? What's the big deal?" And I'm wondering if he's coming home.
Th: Say it's about an hour and here he comes. What does he look like when he comes in?
M: He smiles. And then he says, "Are you mad?" Usually I don't look at him, but as soon as I do... he knows.

Mary describes the familiar sequence. She attempts to hide her frustration and rage by walking away from Kevin; he follows her and tries to apologize, she rebuffs him, and then he leaves her alone, joining their daughter in front of the television, saying, "I guess Mommy's mad because I didn't call."

Not only were Mary and Kevin acting out predictable scenes, but so was five-year-old Kathleen! She was playing waiting-for-daddy along with her mother. One could speculate that if this process continued for another twenty years, Kathleen could say what Mary said as she began the choreography consultation. "I've always felt very pulled. If not by my mother, then by my father."

Th: I'm trying to figure out what makes this similar to your family of origin. The thing that is similar is that you're trying to change someone and find that you can't.

M: Exactly.

Th: Well, let's see you really change him. Really get across to him that he has to be home on time. Show me the way you would do that.

Mary refused to try. She wept as she explained that she *had* tried to act differently, first by being kinder, then by threatening. Nothing worked. She had, just prior to consultation, decided to try a separation.

M: When he calls I try to be nice. I try not to let him know that I want to be with him. But I can't live with someone who doesn't want to come home. In a lot of ways I'd rather live alone. That's scary. Over the years it has gotten progressively worse. Every four or five days he'd go and get drunk. Then there'd be car accidents and he'd be in the hospital. Or we'd go somewhere and he'd say, "I'm only going to have a few." I can't live ... waiting. I'm waiting all the time. It's like all I do is wait for the doorbell to ring. I wait for him to do this, I wait for him to do that. I expect so much from this person. He's never going to do it ... that's what I have to learn.

Th: Are you still waiting? Even though you're alone, are you still waiting?

M: Yes, I'm still waiting for something to happen, for something to change. The only thing that can change is me!

Mary spoke of her attempts to live alone and how others reacted to it. Her mother alternated between telling Mary she never should have married Kevin and trying to persuade her to return to him. Mary got an entirely different reaction from her old high school friends:

M: It didn't matter to anyone. For the first time I felt they liked me whether I was with him or not. I felt like they accepted me. I never thought anyone accepted *me* ... rather than *his* being so special, that he was more important than I was. Yet when I told them about the separation they said, "That's good, we're glad you decided to do something."

Mary began to realize how much of her experiences with Kevin were similar to those between her mother and father. She was encouraged to talk about her problems with her mother, to tell her how hard it was to change someone else.

M: Well, I try ... but even though we talk about it she goes right on doing the same thing. She won't change ... my mother treats him like a baby. She'll say to me, "Your father has to go down to the Social Security office. You or your brothers will have to go with him." Daddy's a man, he doesn't need anyone to go with him.

When the consultation ended Mary was asked how she felt about the choreography experience.

M: Very sad. But now I know there are things I can change.
Th: Like what? How would you change yourself?
M: I'd start to live. I care about people, but I'm going to have to come before everyone else. If I don't I'm going to destroy myself in a lot of ways. Until maybe six months ago I felt I had to do something or else I was just going to die. I don't mean die a death, I mean die inside . . . be like this forever and accept it. Then something happened: I just said, "You want to change, *you* got to do it." And I'm going to. But I have to remember that I can't rush into anything, I have to take my time. All my life I've been rushing, trying to touch something or reach something. And it hasn't happened because I've been in such a rush. I never took time to sit down. I get so fearful at times.

Follow-Up

Mary decided not to review the video tape of the consultation until a year later. Seeing it at that late date reminded her of many changes she had made in her life. She noted that communications between herself and the rest of her family were being carried on in a more adult manner. She had stopped being the mediator between her mother and father. She was able to visit them or not, as she wished, but she didn't feel that she either had to be with them or get away from them. In the meantime she filed for separation papers and worked part time in a local shop.

Even though she was not living with Kevin, she was still unable to change her attitude toward him, nor Kevin toward her. He continued to behave like Peck's Bad Boy and she continued to treat him as such. When she got angry he became contrite and gave her money for child support. When she was calm and considerate, he ignored her and withheld payment. Her attraction to him remained strong. She still couldn't give up her fantasy that he would change and they would live happily together. Nevertheless, she decided to press her appeal for assistance in family court. Since the choreography focused primarily on the family-of-origin interactions one could speculate that Mary might benefit from experiencing another choreography focusing on her nuclear family patterns.

Kevin viewed the video tape three weeks after Mary's consultation, without Mary present. He cried as he watched it and then requested some individual therapy sessions. He met with the therapist a few times, then dropped out of treatment. During the following year he was hospitalized once for a car accident and twice attended detoxification programs sponsored by his employer. He continues to deny that he has a drinking problem.

REFERENCES

1. Berenson, D., Alcohol and the Family System. In P. Guerin (Ed.), *Family Therapy: Theory and Practice*, New York: Gardner Press, 1976, pp. 284–298.
2. Bowen, M., Family Therapy and Family Group Therapy. In H. Kaplan & B. Sadock (Eds.), *Comprehensive Group Psychotherapy*, Baltimore: Williams & Wilkins, 1971.
3. Chafetz, M.E., Hertzman, M., & Berenson, D., Alcoholism; A Positive View. In S. Arieti (Ed.), *American Handbook of Psychiatry*, New York: Basic Books, 1974, pp. 367–399.
4. Davis, D.I., Berenson, D., Steinglass, P., & Davis, S., The Adaptive Consequences of Drinking. *Psychiatry* 37:209–215, 1974.
5. Duhl, F., Kantor, D., & Duhl, B., Learning, Space and Action in Family Therapy: A Primer of Sculpture. In D. Bloch (Ed.), *Techniques of Family Psychotherapy*, New York: Grune & Stratton, 1973, pp. 48–63.
6. Julius, E., A Pilot Program for a Schizophrenic Group. *J. of Marriage & Family Counseling* 4:19–24, July 1978.
7. Minuchin, S., *Families and Family Therapy*, Cambridge, MA: Harvard University Press, 1974.
8. Papp, P., Family Choreography. In P. Guerin (Ed.), *Family Therapy: Theory and Practice*, New York: Gardner Press, 1976, pp. 465–479.
9. Satir, V., *Peoplemaking*, Palo Alto, CA: Science & Behavior Books, 1972.
10. Steinglass, P., Davis, D.I., & Berenson, D., Observations of Conjointly Hospitalized "Alcoholic Couples" during Sobriety and Intoxication: Implications for Theory and Therapy. *Family Process* 16:1–16, 1977.

14

Therapeutic Strategies in Conjoint Hospitalization for the Treatment of Alcoholism*

Donald I. Davis, M.D.
ASSISTANT PROFESSOR
DEPARTMENT OF PSYCHIATRY AND
BEHAVIORAL SCIENCES
GEORGE WASHINGTON UNIVERSITY
SCHOOL OF MEDICINE
WASHINGTON, D.C.

Peter Steinglass, M.D.
ASSOCIATE PROFESSOR
DEPARTMENT OF PSYCHIATRY
AND BEHAVIORAL SCIENCES, AND
THE CENTER FOR FAMILY RESEARCH
GEORGE WASHINGTON UNIVERSITY
SCHOOL OF MEDICINE
WASHINGTON, D.C.

Introduction

Although alcoholism is usually thought of as a socially disruptive, chronic, debilitating disorder, most alcoholics in our society still live in intact families. The search for cases of incipient alcoholism probably should be directed primarily toward the family. Family therapy, although a late arrival to the field of alcoholism treatment (12), has garnered a rapidly in-

* This work was supported in part by a Career Teacher Award in Drug Abuse and Alcoholism (Dr. Davis) under Grant No. TO1-AA-07003 and in part by Grant No. RO1-AA-01441 (Dr. Seinglass), both from the National Institute on Alcohol Abuse and Alcoholism. The authors wish to give special thanks to Ms. Lydia Tislenko for her assistance in the selection and preparation of the clinical material from therapy sessions used in this manuscript.

creasing group of proponents. A small but growing field of family interaction research on alcoholism and other drugs of abuse provides a strong
theoretical basis for applying such a family approach to alcoholism treatment (7). Our own research, which has included some of the earliest alco-
holism-related family interaction studies (14), had led us to the study of the
function of alcohol abuse in a family unit and to a concept which we have
applied to both research and therapy, which we have termed "the adaptive
consequences of drinking" (4).

In this chapter we shall focus specifically on the therapy conducted during a ten-day experience with conjoint hospitalization of husbands and
wives, as an adjunct to therapy for alcoholism in one or both spouses. This
was a component of a pilot experimental treatment program we have been
studying. Experimental findings from observations of couple interaction
during this program have been described elsewhere (13). Our goal here is to
illustrate the special ways in which conjoint hospitalization was used to
therapeutic advantage.

A few scattered reports have appeared in the literature describing experiences with conjoint psychiatric hospitalization of family members. The
programs reported fall into two major categories: research-oriented programs designed around an experimental treatment approach, and treat-
ment-oriented programs attempting to explore new techniques. Investigators working in the former type of program have reported serious
reservations about conjoint hospitalization as a treatment technique. Investigators in the second type of program have been enthusiastic about conjoint hospitalization.

Bowen's work (2, 3) with schizophrenics and their families is the first
major study involving conjoint hospitalization of family members. Bowen
initially admitted mothers of schizophrenics as "normal controls" to a psychiatric ward. Observations of the mother-patient dyad left such powerful
impression on him that Bowen moved on to hospitalize whole families.
Bowen's description of this work, especially in terms of the impact of direct
observational material on emergent theoretical concepts, is strikingly similar to the experience we shall report in this paper. "The research," he contends, "revealed striking 'new' characteristics of the mother-patient relationship not clearly 'seen' in the previous work" (3).

The family implication of schizophrenia, Bowen feels in retrospect, became obvious in this new setting, not only because the intensity of the relationship was heightened by the experience of conjoint hospitalization, but
because the new design established a totally different observational set for
the investigator. The information was always there, but it was not "seen"
because of the "observational blindness" of the investigator.

Bowen's enthusiasm for his relationship with the hospital adminis-tration, however, was far more reserved. Despite its overall support of the research project, the hospital administration, by Bowen's account, was unable to overcome its traditional "individually oriented" approach to medical practice. Such issues as diagnosis, administrative privileges, orders, record keeping, and physician responsibility were handled administratively as individual rather than family issues. The therapeutic orientation of the program—namely the view that the family rather than the individual was the patient—was in conflict with the official administrative view of the hos-pital. Bowen also voiced an important reservation about the program from the treatment point of view: "a live-in environment is not the most favor-able for change in family psychotherapy. It was possible for families to as-sume a fairly good level of responsibility for the psychotic family member, but the parents became over-dependent on hospital resources available to them, which precluded development of their own resources" (3).

In contrast to Bowen's view, two more recent studies of conjoint hospi-talization, carried out primarily for treatment rather than research, strongly endorsed hospitalizing family members as a critical feature in a treatment program. The most enthusiastic report in this regard comes from Abroms and his colleagues at the University of Wisconsin Medical School (1). They have presented a clinical report of their experience treating one hundred patients and their families on an inpatient basis. Both clinical vignettes and impressions of the therapists indicate dramatic breakthroughs in previously intractable treatment situations following a decision for conjoint hospi-talization.

In the field of alcoholism, Paolino and McCrady have recently pub-lished a preliminary report of a treatment program for alcoholics involving conjoint hospitalization of spouses (9). Their initial clinical impressions are also optimistic, and they plan to do a controlled study of their program.

In contrast to these earlier or concurrent experiences, our treatment pro-gram used conjoint hospitalization as one component in a three-phase in-tensive short-term treatment experience that included both inpatient and outpatient phases and was centered around multiple couples group therapy.

In addition, conjoint hospitalization was only one of two major depar-tures from traditional treatment approaches undertaken by the program. The second was the application of "experimentally-induced intoxication" to a family-oriented treatment approach. Our couples were allowed to freely consume alcohol during their hospitalization, and were included in therapy sessions whether they were sober or intoxicated.

Design of the Program

The overall design of the program was as follows: therapy began with 90-minute, outpatient multiple-couples sessions meeting on the research ward three times a week for two weeks. These first two weeks were followed by the whole group spending ten days in the hospital (one work week and two long weekends), during which formal multiple-couples sessions were held daily. During the immediate post-hospitalization work week, there were three outpatient group sessions. Finally, over the next two weeks, the group met twice weekly. Thus the groups met intensively for a total of six weeks. Subsequently there were once-a-month meetings for six months, and then six-month, one-year, and two-year research interview follow-ups.

The ten-day conjoint hospialization occurred on a ward that had been remodeled to provide a living room and kitchen and three small two-room suites for couples. Hence groups could not be larger than three couples. We shall be reporting our experiences with four treatment groups: two groups of two couples each and two groups of three couples each, a total of ten couples. (The two-couple groups resulted from the last-minute need to drop couples just prior to therapy for reasons of acute medical complications from alcohol.)

The couples represented a wide range of occupations and cultural backgrounds. Though it was not the intent of the program, all couples were white. No blacks were referred. All but one of the couples volunteered for the study out of a sense of desperation at the failure of all previous treatment efforts. The one exception was a couple who indicated they volunteered out of curiosity and a willingness to assist a scientific effort.

These four groups were treated by two principal therapists, both psychiatrists with training in family therapy. Each worked with one three-couple and one two-couple group. One worked with a staff nurse as cotherapist: the other worked without a cotherapist. The reader will find more complete details regarding ward conditions, use of alcohol, and measurement of blood levels associated with the study in a recent journal article by Steinglass, Davis, and Berenson (13).

Use of Videotape

The research ward was extensively equipped with video recording equipment; and the use of videotape feedback, especially regarding intoxicated interactional behavior, was a critical feature of the therapy program. Interest in the use of videotape self-confrontation techniques with alcoholics dates back to work by Paredes and Cornelison (10) in the sixties. Their emphasis, and that of subsequent studies which amplified the use of self-confrontation techniques as an adjunct to behavior modification, was on the aversive quality of the experience of watching oneself intoxicated. However, in the laboratory in which the current study was done, a prior, exploratory study (15) had indicated that the self-confrontation experience tended to produce profound depression and, if anything, greater intake.

Attempting to avoid these earlier pitfalls (11), but also drawing heavily on the experience of family therapists with videotape techniques, the current study utilized a unique approach to self-confrontation techniques of intoxicated behavior. The following are its important aspects:

1) The growing experience of family therapists in using videotape as an adjunct to family therapy indicates that a trial exposure to viewing oneself is a necessary prerequisite if one is to profitably view one's own *interactional* behavior. Subjecting oneself to the process is necessary not only to overcome the novelty effect, but also because of the startling and complicated effect of viewing one's own family in action.

2) A particularly valuable aspect of videotape techniques is reproducibility. Stop-action, replay, and editing techniques all heighten the sense of patterning in interactional behavior and can be used to underscore target behaviors with whichever one is working.

3) Videotape may be considerably more successful as a positive reinforcer, than as a punishment.

Examples of our use of videotape in conjoint hospitalization will be given in the next section.

Context of the Program

The decision to hospitalize couples was made as a logical next step in the study of the systems function of alcoholic behavior, our long-range research interest. Our immediate need was a setting that would permit observations of interactional behavior with and without intoxication. Why did we focus on couples rather than families? The hospital in which the research ward was located would not permit nonalcoholic minors to be admitted. Hence it was decided to admit married couples to the study. In order to observe interaction of the marital unit with other people, as well as individuals and intramarital interaction, it was also decided to admit more than one couple at a time.

The subjects were all in need and desirous of help, and clearly a major inducement for them to take part in the research was that their participation was intended to be therapeutic. Thus, for both ethical and practical reasons, the research was carried out in the context of (a necessarily innovative approach to) therapy. The theoretical and clinical orientation of the staff was toward family therapy. The developing literature on multiple-family (8) and multiple-couples therapy (6) was also drawn upon. Thus, an experimental therapy for alcoholism was developed which was made up of general systems and structural and problem-solving approaches to family therapy, using a brief, intensive multiple-couples format. Direct observation of interactional behavior during intoxication was also a unique feature of our work with these couples and will be highlighted in the clinical illustrations.

The Clinical Experience

In-Hospital Course

Behaviorally the inpatient phase roughly divided itself into two sections: an initial three- to four-day period characterized by significant drinking, and a subsequent five- or six-day period when drinking diminished to a trickle.

In all cases identified alcohol abusers consumed alcohol while on the ward, but the distribution of consumption varied from subject to subject. Patterns of alcohol consumption during the initial four-day period coincided with important parameters of each individual's chronic drinking pattern. Solitary drinkers at home were also solitary drinkers on the ward; tavern or party drinkers tended to drink in the common room with other subjects present. Subjects who reported drinking bouts ending in verbal battles engaged in the same behavior on the ward, whereas other couples who reported drinking often associated with lovemaking were noted to have retired to their private bedrooms after drinking had started.

The subsequent period, during which time drinking usually diminished dramatically, was a time of intense therapeutic effort. The capacity of the couples to immerse themselves in this work far exceeded that of the staff. It was not unusual, for example, for the group to convene in the living room during the evening to view videotapes of therapy sessions or common-room activity. These viewing sessions might last as long as five hours, during which time couples were actively interacting around shared issues of concern, repeating sections of videotape for emphasis, or following particular suggestions of the therapist, such as paying careful attention to differences in affect or physical contact during intoxication versus sobriety. A major initial staff concern, that the time spent on the ward would be too unstructured and that couples would react negatively to being cooped up in a research ward of a state hospital, proved to be totally unfounded.

The mood of both patients and staff during the inpatient week was optimistic. Although in part this positive mood stemmed from the vacation-like atmosphere of the ward, in which couples were able to experience a moratorium from concerns with children or work, patients were enthusiastic about the inpatient week as a therapeutic experience. There was often renewed optimism about the marital relationship and the sense that they were taking positive action to alter their lives.

Separation at the end of the week was difficult. There were many jokes along the lines of "If you can't get someone else for your next study, we will be happy to come back." Both patients and staff acted as if they would either never see each other again or were undergoing a long separation, even though they knew there would be an outpatient session the following day.

The Impact of Conjoint Hospitalization

What did conjoint hospitalization do for multiple-couples therapy? Although the answer is surely complex, its most important aspect was the provision of a vastly increased clinical data base to the therapists. Rather than having to rely on self-report, interactional data were available by direct observation. Both therapists *and* other group members could draw upon the data in making a point or carrying out a strategic intervention. Such data were also available to the nursing staff and served a similar purpose in their many informal discussions with the couples.

We shall illustrate the impact of conjoint hospitalization by providing some extended clinical examples.

Clinical Vignette 1. F. (husband, nonalcoholic) and M. (wife, identified alcoholic) first presented themselves to the group as having no problem but her drinking, which leads her to act suicidal, disregard the needs of the children, and drive F. away. F. had been "fed up" and "about to leave" M. for quite some time. In the couples group, other couples spent much of a session recalling to F. how surprised they were at how very solicitous and concerned he had acted once M. had begun drinking the night before. Although it came out then that M. had been sexually responsive with F. when she had been drinking, and they had stopped having sex other than when she was drinking, the impressions of others were generally rejected at that time. Staff and other couples viewed this behavior of his as reinforcing her drinking, both positively by giving her caring responses when drinking, and negatively by allowing her to avoid his unsupportive behavior when she was drinking. They pressed F. to reverse the timing of his two different patterns of relating with M. Two days later, in another group session, the conversation centered around how M. tends to push F. away. Calling upon more direct observation from another evening, another group member observed,

Well, last night, though, you [F.] didn't go near her [M.] and you stayed in the living room. She kept calling you, repeatedly. She kept calling down, F., F., where is he? over and over again. Then when you finally did go in and then you came back out, she started calling again [inaudible]. I mean, you were trying not to go in, after talking with Dr. B. He said, "Do what's best for yourself," and yet you did go in many times. So maybe she rejects you one way and then she's [inaudible] in another, it seems.

The couple about whom these repeated observations were made found them useful in shifting out of an increasingly desperate individual problem orientation, into a new, still highly conflictual, but less despairing interactional frame of mind.

Clinical Vignette 2. B. (husband, alcoholic) came to a morning couples-group session, while his wife, J. (also alcoholic), did not. Because both husband and wife were on the ward, the group felt there existed the real option of going to get the absent spouse. As will be seen from the following example, which is not unique, the possibility of getting the spouse provides the opportunity for gaining a better understanding of the process leading to one spouse being absent.

The session begins with the therapist (T) saying that someone has gone to awaken J. so that she can attend the therapy session. A brief discussion ensues.

B.: Yeah, she's sleeping. I think she ought to be left alone.
T.: We'd like to have her join the group if she can.
B.: I would like for her to be left alone.
T.: Yeah?
B.: Yeah.
T.: You sound [inaudible] pretty strong.
B.: Yeah, I was there two minutes ago. She's sound asleep. I don't want her woken up and brought in here.
T.: What would happen if she comes in here?
B.: I'll send her back into her room, that's what will happen.
T.: You look angry with me.
B.: Yes, I am. I think, uh, that you, you should ask me, whether I want my wife woken up.

Before J. can come, B. goes out to talk with her. He soon returns without her. Everyone in the group takes part in a discussion, first about B. being angry with T. for making a decision about B.'s wife, then about others wondering if B. has really conveyed to J. that he does not want her to come, and finally about the sense that B. himself is reluctant to stay with the group and if pressed to expose himself and his wife J., who may still be acting intoxicated, to the group, he might get angry and leave the group. B. finally responds:

Well, let me, you know, we're kind of in an uptight situation. Let's uh, let me just make a statement, M., I'm not trying to be a bastard. My feeling in this situation is again the same, is that I have an obligation to J. as a husband. And J. is sound asleep. I've been in to talk to her. She's still under the influence of booze. I don't feel that I want her to make an a—, an exhibition of herself. Not in this group. I would probably put up with it, but with a half a dozen people I don't even know are there, you know, my wife is incoherent. I don't feel, I feel it's undignified. Uh, I don't feel it's dignified. And I think, you know, I'm not a specimen under a microscope and neither is my wife . . . .

After several other comments:

T.: But, but M. is saying that in the same situation she would want to be in here, right now.

B.: No, I discussed that with J., and I said, look, I'm not. J.'s reaction, that she's still pretty loaded, was, maybe you're trying to keep me out because you'll say something and I won't be there to hear it. I'm worried about that. I said, "Look, you make your own decision, you come or you stay in your room. I'm just telling you, you have the choice. If you want to come, come. If you don't, don't. She said, "Well, I'd rather sleep. I'd rather sleep than be in that session." I said, "Then sleep." I think we have a choice, and if you decide someday that you don't want to sit in on a session, you've got a headache or you're bombed, I'm not going to sit here saying, "I'm being cheated because she's in there asleep."

M.: I do feel that way, I still feel I'm being cheated. And I also feel, B., that you didn't give her a choice, because I've observed that J. reads you very well.

The discussion then goes back and forth for a while between the last issue and the former one of who should make a decision about B.'s wife. The focus then returns to wanting J. present.

B.: Well, let's put it this way. J. is willing to come. Let's discuss it. Let's not put it under the carpet. J. is willing to come. She was in the room, trying to get dressed and not in very good shape. And I said, "Look now. I, I want you to understand something. That, as your husband, I'm telling you. You have a choice. You've been told to come. But you don't have to come. And you make up your mind." "Well, you may talk about me if I don't come." I said, "Well, I don't think you should worry. I don't think that's a very important thing. I don't really think you're in shape that would . . .

T.: [interrupting] B., this morning, you, H. [a man in the group], and I were talking in here. One of the things we were talking about is that you're communicating other than your words with L. out in the kitchen. We talked about how your second glance to her must have communicated, I think you agree, probably communicated, "What the hell are you doing here?"

B.: Hm, hm.

T.: Only you did not say the words.

B.: Right.

T.: And, I have the feeling that you communicated to J. something of "what the hell are you doing getting ready to come to this session." That's sort of, maybe I'm overreading, but that's what I'm picking up.

Soon B. asks F. (a woman in the group) to go ask J. if she wants to come in. F. at first agrees, then spends quite some time conveying that she feels she will incur animosity from B. for doing it. Finally, F. tactfully suggests how B. might go to J. and tell her the group would like her to reconsider; B. agrees to go.

J. does come in and later in the sessions summaraizes how she felt about coming, saying:

J.: I don't, I didn't mind it at all. In fact, when they knocked on the door and said, "Come," I said, "Yes, I'll be there." And B. said, "are you going to go in there and make a fool of yourself? You're putting yourself in a vulnerable position."
T.: Can you tell B., then,
J.: [interrupting] And I wondered, what vulnerable position am I going to be in, the fact that you passed out on our bed last night and I couldn't get any [sleep].

Thus it evolved, and because of the conjoint hospitalization could be verified, that in fact it was B. who had been drinking heavily to the point of passing out the night before, and J. had had only a little to drink but (aided by her fatigue) had been acting drunk and had agreed not to come into the session which clearly served the protective function of neither exposing B.'s weakness nor J.'s anger at him before others. In this way, their social isolation of recent years had been perpetuated and an interactional pattern had set in that was made up mainly of a repeating sequence of mutually abusive, verbal fights.

Subsequently B. and J. agreed that their fights were always on the same issue. He spends all of his time at work and treats his secretary better than he treats her, so that she doesn't want to be seen socially because of embarrassment and anger at how poorly he treats her. She is liable to be drunk and screaming at him, and does not dare make any social plans. Although both agreed that their arguing and drinking seemed to begin some years ago during a period that happened to include the death of significant female figures in J.'s family, neither B. nor J. had emphasized these losses during sobriety or expressed an awareness of their mutual depression.

During the period of conjoint hospitalization, however, the importance of these losses, the couple's sense of isolation from a supportive extended network, and their profound sense of mutual depression were demonstrated in dramatic fashion.

The therapist concluded that his primary task was to break into the mutually accusatory pattern the couple exhibited when intoxicated, while at the same time preserving the couple's increased affective display. By interrupting the destructive pattern, the therapeutic process might heighten both husband's and wife's awareness of their own and each other's underlying depression. Exploring these issues in the multiple-couples group, a goal of decreasing the couple's self-perceived need for social isolation might also be achieved.

During the second half of the inpatient phase, therefore, the therapist concentrated on these issues with considerable success. As a result, husband and wife again reviewed their feelings surrounding the death of Mrs. B.'s aunt. This time, however, Mr. B. was able to express his considerable fondness for this woman and his profound sense of loss at her death. In contrast to an earlier intoxicated episode, when he concentrated his attention on a devastating attack toward his wife, this time he revealed his own loneliness and began to sob.

At six-month follow-up the couple was found to have only minimally decreased their alcohol intake but reported far less abusive behavior associated with drinking. The quantity of their social life also seemed improved. They continued to exhibit sexual dysfunction, however, and, although aware of their mutual depression, had not yet worked through their continuing sense of loss.

Clinical Vignette 3. The next case concerns W. (a chronic alcoholic husband) and F. (his obese wife). Their marriage was basically structured around overfunctional/underfunctional role distribution, with F. playing the overfunctional role (consistent wage earner, high-status job, prime decision maker, etc.). This role structure, however, resulted in a sexual and affective demarcation that tended to dampen emotional displays and reduce aggressive or assertive behavior on W.'s part. Sexual behavior in particular suffered as a consequence.

F. quickly established herself in the couples group as a self-righteously proper, stiffly relating, competing woman who joined in discussion only in a limited way and to serve certain moralistic purposes in furthering the therapy of the alcoholics in the group. However, by living and eating with the others, her characteristic stances came under considerable pressure for change. F.'s moralism was appreciated and seemed warranted when it became apparent that she was contributing little to the well-being of the group, while her husband was quite competently cooking for everybody. The group also took note of W.'s competence and his greater assertiveness when drinking than when sober. They put pressure on W. in formal therapy sessions with his wife, to do what they had observed him capable of in everyday living.

Similarly, by the middle of the conjoint hospitalization week, the therapist was able to establish as his primary task an adjustment in the role relationship of this marriage. This end was accomplished by focusing the couple's attention on their interaction when W. was drinking. The therapist challenged both their assumption that W. could only be assertive with the help of alcohol and also F.'s assertion that she had to be strong and all-powerful in order to keep the marriage afloat. With group support, W. was helped to be more direct and assertive while at the same time learning to tolerate his wife's expression of feelings of helplessness and dependency. F. was encouraged to lean on her husband and other group members, and to define appropriate limits for her responsibilities to the marriage and family.

At six-month follow-up, W. reported occasional social drinking of not more than two drinks and no episodes of intoxication. He had obtained an appropriate job within one month of finishing the treatment program, and had worked steadily since that time. He was also in the process of building a new home, the culmination of years of planning, and the couple was to move shortly to their new community. F. remained highly successful at work, had received unsolicited gratitude for increased receptivity to problems of her supervisees, and had been given new responsibilities. Both husband and wife expressed a greater satisfaction with their marriage, although significant sexual difficulties remained. F. had experienced a modest weight loss. Both husband and wife were considerably more relaxed in their dealings with their daughter. Although the daughter continued to have significant difficulties in her own marriage, both W. and F. seemed able to define the limits of their responsibility toward their child.

Therapy Techniques

Several general techniques of therapy were prominent enough in our work with all of these couples that they deserve special attention here before we summarize our experience with conjoint hospitalization. These techniques were developed to achieve several general objectives of our treatment approach. The first objective is to focus on behavior that seems to improve during states of intoxication. The second objective is to attain the competent performance of the same, or an appropriate competing, behavior, without alcohol. The third objective is to restructure roles between spouses where indicated.

In describing techniques, we shall begin with our use of videotape, since its role was ubiquitous in the inpatient program. We shall then mention four nonvideo-dependent strategies which were also emphasized in our efforts to achieve the above objectives.

Videotape feedback. An approach to the use of video self-confrontation techniques was developed which emphasized the recognition of specific patterns of interactional behavior occurring in marital couples when one or both members of the couple were drinking. The emphasis was specifically on the patterns of interactional behavior, not on the behavioral effects of the alcohol per se. Subjects were therefore instructed specifically to ignore such behavioral consequences of alcohol ingestion as slurring of speech, staggering, unkempt dress, and so on, and to concentrate instead on the quality of the interaction. If a particular couple was having difficulty in ignoring the intoxication itself, they were instructed to watch the videotape playback, initially without sound. Turning off the sound tended to amplify instead the behavioral aspects of the interaction, and patterning often jumped out where only drunken chaos previously could be noticed.

Emphasis was placed on the basic theoretical model underlying the therapeutic approach, namely, an understanding of the perceived "adaptive consequences" of drinking (4) for the particular couple. The couples were therefore encouraged to contrast sober and intoxicated behavior; if this contrast was difficult conceptually, editing was done to place side by side behaviors from different time periods of the study. Behavior was selected because it seemed to represent subjectively positive behavior, thereby highlighting the "adaptive" flavor of the behavior. For example, one couple was instructed to note the increased physical contact they demonstrated during intoxication as contrasted with sobriety. Another couple might be instructed to note the extent to which they were able to challenge the therapist constructively during intoxication as opposed to their more passive acceptance of interpretations during sobriety.

Once this training had been completed, the entire library of videotapes currently available on that particular study group was opened up to the couples for their use on a voluntary basis. Although it was anticipated they would use the tapes only sparingly (because of the previous reports of the aversive quality of the self-confrontation experience), in fact their capacity to view these tapes was astounding. It was not unusual, for example, to have a study group watching four consecutive hours of videotapes during one evening.

Curiosity. This required learning to delay responses long enough to explore another's intent, reasoning, or feelings, and reach shared understandings. An effort was made to restrict this curiosity to what was happening *in the present*, among the people interacting. It was stressed that *nonverbal communications* were not to be ignored in this process.

Shifting the focus of attention and efforts at change from the drinker to both spouses and from the individual to the relationship. For example, when early discussions of one couple were limited to the problems of the chronic alcoholic husband, attention was shifted first to his wife's problem of being chronically obese, and then to the problem of chronically constricting rigid roles in their relationship.

Finding and highlighting the *positive* aspects of a conflictual interaction sequence. To give an example from a multiple-couple session, we shall take the particularly difficult situation of B. and J. (referred to earlier in Clinical

Vignette 2), chronic, daily-using alcoholics locked into a constant argumentative interaction. The therapist was doggedly holding to the task of finding caring in the midst of shouting. To quote from midsession:

T.: But J. [wife], I don't believe you. You know why?
J.: No, why?
T.: Because you didn't come to the session. You did what you thought he wanted you to do. And you've been doing that for years.
J.: That's exactly right.
T.: So you must be getting something out of it.
J.: No, I'm not.
T.: You're not? Then B. [husband] is doing the same thing, because he's staying around and keeping things going and doing some things the way you want, too
J.: He's not doing anything the way I want.
T.: I'm terribly—
B.: [inaudible]
T.: That you're outraged, terribly angry about the, the mixed messages that he gives you, and yet, you act according to what he wants you to do.
J.: I'll tell you why. I'm terrified of him. I'll look you in the face—I'm terrified of you.
T.: You don't—
J.: I say I could kill you. But I know that you would; I wouldn't. But I know goddam well you would kill me. I, I say I could kill you. It's verbal.
B.: Yeah.
J.: And I know damn well I wouldn't. But I have no reassurance that you wouldn't. Even when I'm opening up the garage door, ten, twenty years ago, and you keep revving up the motor, like you'd drive it straight right through me. I have no feeling that you wouldn't kill me. I can talk about feeling like killing you, but I know I couldn't.
T.: J., it sounds like you're really—
B.: [interrupting] It's an odd feeling—
J.: It's a terribly odd feeling, B., to know that somebody might murder you.
B.: I'm not a particularly violent person. I don't know why you'd—
J.: [interrupting] You're not?
B.: No.
J.: You're a very violent person.
T.: J., again, I'm trying to tune to, it sounds to me like you're saying that you couldn't kill him. You care about him. Now can you tell him that?
J.: Yes, I care about people.
T.: Him, you.
J.: Yes, I do. I care about our lives. And the feeling of wanting to kill you is the way you've wrecked our lives. The way you ruthlessly, just absolutely stamped on me, kicked me, beat me, bounced me, like I'll beat you into submission.
T.: J.—
J.: I'll beat you into my way of life.
T.: J.—Again, let's stop here because—
[J. crying] you did say that you do care about him, and—
J.: What else do I have to care about except him and my children?
T.: Okay.
J.: There's nobody left in my life.

T.: You care about him. Now I don't think he's heard that from you in a long, long time. And I think the other side—
J.: What else—except that I care. Why the hell would I be ... if I didn't care.
T.: Okay, but I don't think he did know that, because I think you sounded frightening ...

Modeling is the last of the general strategies which we shall single out for (brief) special mention. At its best, modeling was used to increase a couple's skills at solving shared problems or resolving conflicts between one another.

Discussion

We believe the conjoint hospitalization experience was a positive one for both patients and therapists and we have attempted to show the ways in which we found conjoint hospitalization to serve an enabling function in our efforts to conduct multiple-couples psychotherapy. For the therapists, rapid evaluation of interactional dynamics was facilitated. For the patients, the period of hospitalization allowed them to redefine alcoholism as an interactional problem and allowed them to absorb and integrate feedback about their interactional patterns. Conjoint hospitalization was a great asset in the observation of intoxicated interactional behavior as well. Whether the opportunity for intoxicated behavior was critical to our positive attitude toward conjoint hospitalization we cannot know for sure, but it did not seem to us to be a prerequisite for making good therapeutic use of the conjoint hospitalization experience.

Despite these generally positive feelings about the period of conjoint hospitalization, significant administrative difficulties arose in our attempt to carry out the program. Although these difficulties were partially attributable to our use of experimentally-induced intoxication, conjoint hospitalization itself proved to be a thorny issue. In our review of previous experiences with conjoint hospitalization, we have noted the marked differences reported by other programs regarding their relationships with hospital administration.

Our experience regarding conjoint hospitalization was closer to Bowen's (2, 3) than to the Wisconsin group's (1). We too encountered major obstacles in attempting to work with the hospital administration of a traditional psychiatric hospital. Nursing staff found it extremely difficult to accept the need for hospitalization of a nondrinking spouse. A number of staff members were themselves overfunctioning spouses married to chronic alcoholics, and although intensive training alleviated this difficulty with the nursing staff working directly on the project, genuine support from nursing administrators was not forthcoming. A myriad of minor and petty difficulties seemed to plague the study. For example, since we were unable to obtain parking spaces for subjects' cars during the hospital phase, a couple might leave the hospital, fresh with new insight and enthusiastic recommitment to their marriage, only to find their cars covered with parking tickets.

From an administrative standpoint, it seems clear from our experiences and those of others discussed in this chapter that enthusiastic reports about conjoint hospitalization occur when there is a genuine meeting of the minds between the treatment staff and the hospital administration, whereas conflicts between these two groups can create endless frustrations even when well-meaning support is intended. Both the current study and Bowen's study, for example, received genuine support and approval from research advisory committees and top-level administrators. But middle-level administrators had a skeptical attitude, and thereby diverted staff energies from treatment to administrative issues. In other words, these programs received their initial support because they were labeled as research, and overt principles and values dictated support for experimentation; but covert attitudes, especially the traditional medical model, led to experiencing the notions of conjoint hospitalization as conflictual. Those programs, on the other hand, which advertised conjoint hospitalization as treatment rather than research seem to have received more genuine support from hospital staff. We might speculate that the greater enthusiasm voiced in the reports of these studies is a direct consequence of this support.

The "treatment" programs (1, 2) integrated conjoint hospitalization into an existing psychiatric treatment service. Married couples and family members participated in the ongoing activities of the ward, and the unique aspects of their hospitalization were adapted to ongoing administrative organization, rather than imposing a totally new structure on the existing treatment service. The "research" programs (3, 13), on the other hand, established a separate treatment service specifically designed to suit research needs. The task of integrating such a program into existing hospital structure has clearly proven problematic. In the future such programs might more profitably be carried out in a setting in which the researchers control administrative as well as experimental design decisions.

Summary recommendations are threefold: 1) conjoint hospitalization is worth pursuing; 2) it is critical to identify the primary motive for hospitalization as either interaction research or experimental treatment; and 3) it is essential that, if interaction research is the primary motive, the experimenter be able to control administration of treatment as well as research.

Since we have also given special attention to our extensive use of videotape during conjoint hospitalization, we should summarize our experience with that tool of therapy in this discussion as well. The experience with videotape playback is illustrative of a technique that has proven difficult to implement in the past (11), but was utilized by the therapists during the in-hospital week with relative ease. Whereas previously individuals were unable to meaningfully integrate direct observations of their intoxicated behavior via videotape playback, the emphasis on finding positive behaviors to view, and the supportive yet intensive therapeutic atmosphere associated with conjoint hospitalization, seemed to evoke a totally different response from subjects watching themselves on tape. The experience was viewed as both profound and positive by all couples who went through the study. It would, therefore, appear to have considerable clinical promise.

A final word about our experience with conjoint hospitalization of couples for alcohol treatment is in order. Most alcoholics do not need in-patient treatment, even for detoxification (5). The couples in our clinical illustrations had had extensive outpatient alcoholism therapy, had rejected Alcoholics Anonymous, and several individuals had been briefly admitted to inpatient psychiatric and alcohol detoxification units. In each case, the alcoholics were still actively drinking and experiencing problems with their drinking at the time of admission to our program. For these rather desperate, but still intact, marriages conjoint hospitalization offered a unique opportunity to take time out from despair, an opportunity in which change for the better becomes conceivable just because both husband and wife see the avenues for change and know that their spouses have also seen them. It is also possible that brief conjoint hospitalization, with its potential for rapid identification of interaction patterns, will turn out to be a useful adjunct to the therapy of less treated, less despairing alcoholics in intact marriages. This will be true particularly if the costly hospitalization occurs near the outset of treatment and can be proven cost-effective by shortening the usual length of outpatient care for alcoholism.

REFERENCES

1. Abroms, G.M., Felinger, C.H., & Whitaker, C.A., The Family Enters the Hospital. *Amer. J. Psychiat.* 127:1363–1370, 1971.
2. Bowen, M., A Family Concept of Schizophrenia. In D.D. Jackson (Ed.), *The Etiology of Schizophrenia*, New York: Basic Books, 1960, pp. 346–372.
3. Bowen, M., Family Psychotherapy with Schizophrenia in the Hospital and in Private Practice. In I. Boszormenyi-Nagy & J.L. Framo (Eds.), *Intensive Family Therapy*, Maryland: Harper & Row, 1965, pp. 213–243.

 4. Davis, D., Berenson, D., Steinglass, P., et al., The Adaptive Consequences of Drinking. *Psychiatry* 37:209–215, 1974.
 5. Feldman, D.J., Pattison, E.M., Sobell, L.C., et al., Outpatient Alcohol Detoxification: Initial Findings on 564 Patients. *Amer. J. Psychiat.* 132:407–412, 1975.
 6. Gottlieb, A. & Pattison, E.M., Married Couples Group Psychotherapy. *Arch. Gen. Psychiat.* 14:143–152, 1966.
 7. Kalgsbrun, M. & Davis, D., Substance Abuse and Family Interaction. *Family Process* 16:149–173, 1977.
 8. Laqueur, H.P., Mechanisms of Change in Multiple Family Therapy. In C.J. Sager & H. Singer (Eds.), *Progress in Group Family Therapy*, New York: Brunner/Mazel, 1972, pp. 400–415.
 9. Paolino, T.J., & McCrady, B., Joint Admission as a Treatment Modality for Problem Drinkers: A Case Report. *Amer. J. Psychiat.* 133:222–224, 1976.
10. Paredes, A., Ludwig, K.D., Hassenfield, I.N., et al., A Clinical Study of Alcoholics Using Audiovisual Selfimage Feedback. *J. Nerv. Mental Dis.* 148:449–456, 1969.
11. Schaefer, H.H., Sobell, M.B., & Mills, K.C., Some Sobering Data on the Use of Self-confrontation with Alcoholics. *Behav. Therapy* 2:28–39, 1971.
12. Steinglass, P., Experimenting with Family Treatment Approaches to Alcoholism, 1950–1975: A Review. *Family Process* 15:97–123, 1976.
13. Steinglass, P., Davis, D., & Berenson, D., Observations of Conjointly Hospitalized "Alcoholic Couples" during Sobriety and Intoxication: Implications for Theory and Therapy. *Family Process* 16:1–16, 1977.
14. Steinglass, P., Weiner, S., & Mendelson, J.H., A Systems Approach to Alcoholism: a Model and Its Clinical Application. *Arch Gen. Psychiat.* 24:401–408, 1971.
15. Weiner, S., Steingalss, P., & Mendelson, J.H., Videotape Self-confrontation and Free Choice Experimental Intoxication in Chronic Alcoholics: A Preliminary Report. *World J. Psychosyn.* 3:32–35, 1971.

15

The Therapist's Relationship with Couples with an Alcoholic Member

David Berenson, M.D.
FAMILY INSTITUTE OF WESTCHESTER
WHITE PLAINS, NEW YORK

In previous publications, I have presented an overview of an approach to alcohol problems that integrates Bowen's Family Systems Theory with Alcoholics Anonymous and Al-Anon (1, 2). The purpose of this chapter is to address specific issues that arise in the therapist's relationship to couples in the "wet" phase of alcoholism and to begin to place the therapeutic approach that has been developed so far into a wider general systems theory context. In general systems theory the word "isomorphism" means the same form or, for our purpose here, the same pattern. It indicates that there is a tendency of systems to replicate patterns or that there is redundancy of systems. At all levels within the system the same process is going on, although there may be a difference in surface manifestation. (Isomorphism carries a contextual or holistic connotation and is a stronger term than analogy or homology. It does not mean identity, "identical with," in a content sense. For example, transference is a specific example or content within the context of isomorphic therapeutic relationships.)

For the purposes of this chapter, we will be talking about how the relationship between the therapist and an individual or family with an alcohol problem replicates, or is isomorphic with, what is happening within the family. An example illustrates the point: the spouse of an alcoholic might fluctuate between trying to save the drinker and persecuting him, similar to a pattern some therapists will follow when they first allow the alcoholic to do almost anything, perhaps even come drunk to sessions, and then switch to a more punitive position, telling him to go to AA and get sober before they will treat him. What is similar in both situations is being caught within an emotional system and reacting automatically, rather than having a clear view of how the system operates and being self-determined in one's own behavior.

Therapists historically have had difficulty treating alcohol problems because of their reliance on words or content. We are taught as therapists to interpret, point out, and clarify problems verbally. This, again, may replicate patterns within the alcoholic family. The spouse of the alcoholic may have been pointing out to the alcoholic for years how self-destructive his behavior is and how it is also harming her.[1] The alcoholic becomes a master at seeming to agree with the words and then, by his behavior, demonstrating or dramatizing his disagreement. When therapists interpret, they may think that they are clarifying the situation, but from the point of view of the alcoholic family system, they are only continuing to perpetuate the existing pattern. Thus, in treating alcoholism as well as other problems effectively, the therapist must pay attention to the total condition or pattern that exists within the family and within the treatment situation. He must allow himself to get sufficiently involved or pulled in to have some relationship with the family and must remain sufficiently uninvolved or outside the system that he can modify the system, a continuum referred to by Minuchin as "joining" and "restructuring (6)."

The first thing a therapist needs to do in approaching an alcoholic family is to establish a situation where he has a clear view of the family patterns, analogous to the surgeon maintaining a clean operating field. There are a number of steps or techniques that a therapist can use toward this end. The first is to structure the treatment in such a way that he has maximum leverage with minimum chaos. For example, the tendency among most therapists is to try to first treat the alcoholic, since he is obviously the one with the problem. In attempting to do that, the therapist is replicating or being isomorphic with the pattern within the family. Fogarty has developed the terms "pursuer" and "distancer" (5). Within the family, this means that wife has become a pursuer who is forever moving in to tell the alcoholic how he must change, and the alcoholic has become a distancer who is always moving away and is more expert at looking at the spouse's behavior than his own. No matter how skillful the therapist, the mere fact of approaching the alcoholic directly will be isomorphic with the wife's behavior, and any content or process interpretations that the therapist attempts to use will be ineffectual since the alcoholic will be continuing to play his role as the distancer and will define the situation as one where he can win by continuing to drink, frustrating spouse and therapist. The first move, therefore, in restructuring or recontextualizing alcoholic systems is not to pursue the alcoholic.

The therapist then has two other choices: to work with the couple or with the spouse alone. The focus is on keeping the problem within the couple. Throughout any treatment for alcoholic problems, the therapist needs to make it clear that it is not his problem he is treating, but that he is being a consultant to the family. Thus, in conjoint sessions or with spouse alone the therapist points out transactional patterns and does not get very involved in interpreting content. The goal is to cool down the emotional entanglement or fusion within the system to allow both spouse and alcoholic to get some perspective on their automatic patterns.

By seeing couples, one immediately protects oneself from the problem of what to do when the alcoholic comes drunk to a session. In the session, the therapist defines it as the spouse's problem rather than his own and may proceed to do a session while the alcoholic is drunk, pointing out either in the session, or by means of videotape after the session, how the drinking affects the interaction within the couple. One always has the right to end sessions if the alcoholic is too disruptive. The therapist is absolutely responsible for the structure of the therapy and is not responsible for what happens within the couple.

Frequently the alcoholic will seek to sabotage the therapy by refusing to come to conjoint sessions. The spouse will then adopt a position of pseudo-hoplessness and helplessness and say, "If he doesn't come, what can I do?" At this point the therapist has the opportunity to see the spouse rather than the couple in therapy and in fact can often attain better results in treating a "wet" system by using this modality. Now the structure of therapy is such that what goes on between spouse and therapist replicates what is happening between alcoholic and spouse. The alcoholic says to the spouse implicitly or explicitly, "I can't be responsible for myself, so you be," which is exactly what the spouse is saying to the therapist. Thus, in clarifying the situation and taking an "I-position" with the spouse, the therapist is modeling behavior which the spouse can then find useful in resolving her problems with the alcoholic. ("I-position" is a term developed by Bowen (3) that refers to being self-determined in one's behavior rather than reacting to the forces within a system. In taking an I-position, one accepts responsibility for one's behavior rather than attributing blame to someone or something else.)

There are a few specific steps which are essential for the therapist to take in starting therapy with the nonalcoholic spouse. He must first calm down the emotional intensity within the sessions and then within the family. While in chaos or extreme conflict, few systems can stabilize enough to move to another level. Seeing one member of the family is a first step toward calming down the system and getting some clarity. The next step is to create a support system for family members so that the emotional intensity is not all channeled into the individual therapy sessions. If the family has social problems such as jobs and housing, the therapist will need to provide support, either through a natural support system such as extended family and friends, or through an artificial support system such as social agencies or vocational training. However, in the majority of families with alcohol problems the lack of support is more emotional in nature, and there the therapist can suggest other support that will essentially give the same message as the therapy does. One obvious resource is Al-Anon, with the nonalcoholic spouse attending Al-Anon meetings as well as therapy sessions. Following a suggested policy of nonreactive behavior seems reasonable and obvious in therapy sessions, but at home in the middle of chaos, many people have difficulty remembering and acting on the therapeutic suggestions. Having an Al-Anon sponsor a phone call away is extremely useful in providing emotional support and in calming down the situation. Thus, I will often refuse to take phone calls between sessions from clients who are calling about a crisis and have refused to go to Al-Anon meetings. If they are in Al-Anon and have attempted to reach a sponsor who is not available, then I am quite willing to take phone calls. The message is that people are responsible for their own lives and that therapy provides an opportunity to look at and take responsibility for their lives, not a place to receive sympathy.

Another resource which provides remarkable emotional support without sympathy and is a safe place to experience helplessness and powerlessness is the *est* training. Recently, I have been suggesting that some nonalcoholic spouses take the est training, and this shows considerable promise of speeding up the entire therapeutic process.

It is essential for the therapist as well as the spouse to have an emotional support system. Frequently the alcoholic transfers his anxiety to the spouse, and the spouse transfers it to the therapist. Therapists must then carefully distinguish between consciously keeping the responsibility in the family to allow them to deal with the problem and reactively letting the anxiety touch off something in him or her, amplifying the total anxiety within the therapy system, and then adding it to the family system. Thus, consultation or supervision on an as-needed basis is essential for the therapist to maintain some clarity or objectivity. There are a couple of mechanisms for doing this. The first would be to audio- or videotape sessions, with review either by the therapist alone or with the consultant. The second would be to discuss with the consultant whatever emotional reactions are triggered off in the therapist in dealing with these types of systems. The two reactions that most often come up are getting pulled in or overinvolved with the system and, conversely, protecting oneself against overinvolvement by withdrawing or being rejecting. Again, the purpose is to look at the entire structure or pattern of the therapy rather than its content or "facts."

An option which is absolutely necessary to support the therapist in structuring or being responsible for the therapy is to allow the possibility of not seeing the individual or family in therapy. Within the mental health field, we tend to make it a duty or obligation that we must see whoever walks into our office, and a usual practice is to initially give people a once-a-week appointment for an indefinite length of time. When the therapist subsequently gets sufficiently frustrated at the lack of progress, the individual or family is frequently discharged with what I call a farewell curse, in which the client is told that he or she is unmotivated or borderline or narcissistic. The therapist must keep for himself or herself the option of not automatically treating clients in two situations. The first is when the therapist realistically recognizes that he is incapable of handling a particular problem. This situation will occur either when the therapist is professionally inexperienced or when he has unresolved emotional patterns in his own nuclear or extended family which are similar to patterns within the client family. If that is the case, the therapist can then refer to another therapist but has the responsibility of clearly informing the client(s) that the referral is being made because the therapist lacks the necessary skills, not through any fault of the client(s). The second situation occurs when, in the therapist's accurate professional assessment, therapy at a particular time would not be useful toward resolving a particular problem. For example, if the client is given the recommendation of Al-Anon in addition to therapy sessions, does not take advantage of the suggestion, and continues in therapy for a number of sessions with no improvement, the therapist can point out that until the client is willing to take this additional step it is very unlikely that the situation will improve. This is analogous to an internist prescribing penicillin for pneumonia, the patient refusing to take the medicine, and then repeatedly coming back and asking the physician to keep trying to treat the pneumonia. It is important initially to communicate clearly to clients what is being prescribed or suggested; one must also be willing to resume therapy when the client subsequently either follows the suggestion or demonstrates an equally viable alternative. Many clients will come into therapy in order not to change or not to resolve problems, and the therapist has the responsibility of not maintaining the illusion that people are resolving problems when they are really reinforcing and perpetuating them.

The isomorphy here with what happens within families is that the alcoholic and spouse are forever debating what the problem is, coming up with new ideas on how to resolve it, and never quite succeeding in making any progress. Thus, for the therapist to interpret content, or hope that if he says just the right thing in the right way, people will change, is likely to be as futile as the spouse of the alcoholic thinking, "If I just say or do the right thing to him this week, I can change the situation." Thus, as a general principle, a clear, nonreactive position will have more of an impact in resolving alcoholic problems than brilliant words or interpretations.

Once the therapist has the spouse in therapy with a clear contract to work on her contribution to the process which maintains dysfunctional drinking, I have found it useful to outline three options for the spouse which can serve to resolve the drinking problem. They are:

1) Keep doing exactly what you are doing.
2) Detach or emotionally distance yourself from the alcoholic.
3) Separate or physically distance yourself.

The first option does not seem as if it would do much to resolve the drinking problem. If someone could do exactly what he was doing and chose to do so, rather than attributing blame to other people or resisting the pattern, the problem could be resolved. In this author's experience, few people have been able to use this as a way of resolving an intense alcohol problem. The main advantage of this option is that one can immediately get down to work in therapy. Most clients, when given the choice between changing and not changing, will choose not to change, but in a covert way. By first prescribing doing exactly what you are doing, the therapist can undercut this entire gambit. Specifically, what the therapist might say is, "You've been putting up with it for ten years. I don't see why it can't go on for another ten." A statement like this defines the responsibility as existing within the family, not with the therapist, and supports the creation of a therapeutic context. Over and over again, in therapy, clients will avoid options two and three, and then the therapist can tell them that they are in reality choosing option one.

Clients quickly say that keeping the situation just the way it is would be intolerable and that they want to move on to the next option, which involves emotional detachment or distance. This entails not criticizing the alcoholic's drinking but just accepting it, continuing to live with him, and being responsible for one's own reactivity about the drinking. This is a difficult goal and in drinking systems with a high degree of emotional intensity, almost impossible. Here again there is an isomorphic trap that therapists and Al-Anon sponsors can fall into. AA talks about the alcoholic needing to accept his powerlessness over alcohol and repeatedly points out that one cannot stop drinking alcoholically by using will power. Al-Anon then teaches this powerlessness over alcohol to the spouse of the alcoholic. Its goal is to get her to stop asking the alcoholic to control his drinking. However, many Al-Anon members, as well as therapists, ask the spouse to detach or emotionally distance herself by using will power, by controlling her emotions. This is as impossible as asking the alcoholic to stop drinking by using self-control. Thus, when giving the choice of emotionally detaching or distancing, the therapist has no expectations or illusions that the spouse will immediately be able to do so. Again, option two turns out to be an "impossible" choice for most people.

Option three entails getting a physical separation. The spouse usually will first think about getting the alcoholic or drinker to move out of the house because "I don't want too leave him with all the things I've worked for so hard for so many years." As a general rule in handling alcohol or any other problem, if one is not prepared to go every step of the way by oneself, one will repeatedly get defeated. Thus, the alcoholic can easily find ways to frustrate attempts to get him out of the house. He can flatly refuse to go or can give lip service to obeying orders of protection and then return home, basically maintaining the apparent power of the drinker. Again, the therapist must allow the spouse to consider this (option 3a) and find out that it is often practically unfeasible. What I call option 3b would be to have the spouse move out of the house. The spouse will initially consider this an impossibility. It means directly facing all the problems or issues of independence that she has tried to avoid by getting married, as well as formidable logistical difficulties.

In summary, then, the therapist has presented the spouse with three impossible options. The problem can be resolved by either choosing one of these courses of action and following through, or by experiencing helplessness, hopelessness, and powerlessness because these situations will be repeated and clarified. This is a crucial point of therapy. The therapist must at the same time repeatedly clarify these as being the only options available to the client. He should also not have any expectations that the client will necessarily adopt any one of them right away.

The next part of therapy consists of allowing the client to share her feelings of emptiness or despair at the impossibility of achieving any of these solutions. The goal is for the spouse to "hit bottom" and focus on being responsible for herself rather than continuing to try to change the alcoholic. Many people will become terrified at this prospect and seek to run away from it. I have found it useful at this point to say something such as the following to clients: "I can understand how scary this is. If you can find any other way of resolving the situation, I encourage you to do so. In my experience there is no other way of getting out of this situation, and eventually you will have to choose one of the options we have outlined. To get through it, you will have to experience quite a bit of emptiness, hopelessness, and despair. When you feel ready to confront the situation, please call me up for another appointment."

The isomorphy here is that the therapist can fall into the trap of asking the spouse to change for him or her, much as the spouse has been asking the alcoholic to change for her. Once the therapist defines the possible choices, he must allow the spouse some time to choose one of the alternatives. The fundamental principle is that one can never change anyone else; one can only create a context in which another person is allowed the possibility of changing.

The isomorphy for option two for the therapist is to continue to work with the spouse on other issues besides her reaction to the drinking, stating clearly to the spouse that you have no illusions that such work will resolve the drinking problem. This resembles the spouse continuing to live with the alcoholic while detaching from the drinking. Option three for the therapist is to interrupt the therapy, giving the client the opportunity to return at such a time that he or she is ready to work in therapy. This is much like the spouse physically separating from the alcoholic without making any decision about divorce. Many therapists fall covertly into option one, continuing to do whatever has been making the situation unworkable. It is crucial that the therapist not fall into this trap.

During this phase of therapy, the therapist can use systems concepts such as pursuer/distancer and triangles as a way of providing perspective on the situation for himself and for the client. By seeing the process connected with drinking as oscillating over time and as occurring in a wider family context, perhaps over generations, the client begins to get outside her own viewpoint. She begins to see the functioning of the entire family system and then to accept some responsibility for it.

The therapist will need to be beware of getting involved in a triangle where he is overly close to the spouse, with the alcoholic in the distant position. A triangle may be defined as an automatic emotional system operating with three people (4). One way to visualize it is by imagining a rubber band connecting you and two other people, or you, another person, and a thing. Each time someone moves, the rubber band maintains the same amount of tightness. For example, if you feel closer to your father, you will feel distant from your mother. In a threesome, as distinguished from a triangle, each member has freedom to move freely with the other two. Thus you can feel closer to your father without feeling more distant from your mother, or you can feel close to both at the same time or simultaneously distant from both. Seeing a spouse individually can create a triangle with the alcoholic in the distant position feeling persecuted, left out, and as though people are conspiring against him. Conversely, if the therapist is not triangled into the system, the alcoholic may have a sense of support even if therapy sessions are held without him and may not do much to undermine the situation. (It must be recognized that in a chapter of this nature, triangles can only be presented conceptually, and that clinical and personal experience are necessary to understand it experientially.)

Some specific techniques to minimize triangulation are to invite the alcoholic to sessions, letting him know that he can choose to come or not to come. One can make a point of keeping him informed about what is happening by telephone, or one can call him up and tell him that the therapist and his wife are conspiring against him. The point to be made is that there is no particular form that distinguishes between triangles and threesomes; rather it is the context or way one controls the situation that is relevant.

A crucial phase of the therapy comes at the point when the spouse begins to focus on herself, observes her functioning within the system, begins to accept responsibility for her contribution to the system, and starts to modify her behavior. It is essential that the therapist point out that at this juncture, the alcoholic will usually get worse. In attempting to avoid the hoplessness or emptiness of hitting bottom that goes along with the recognition of his own responsibility, the alcoholic will do whatever he can to get the spouse back into the fusion or entanglement. This may include losing his job, getting hospitalized, threatening suicide, and increasing his drunken driving, which may kill other people. The anxiety is transmitted from alcoholic to spouse to therapist. The relationship between spouse and therapist is isomorphic with the relationship between alcoholic and spouse; the spouse is trying to manipulate the therapist into taking over her responsibility, much in the way she has been manipulated into taking over the alcoholic's responsibility. It is crucial for the therapist to predict this situation in order to not precipitate a crisis before spouse is ready for it.

The alcoholic will, in fact, commit suicide only when it is not all right with the spouse for him to do so. If the spouse can say something such as, "I prefer you not to kill yourself or kill me, but I am powerless to stop you from doing so," it is extremely unlikely that the alcoholic will damage himself or someone else. Similarly, if the therapist says, "It is perfectly okay with me for you to live with this drinking problem in your marriage for the rest of your life," it is unlikely that the spouse will do so. The trap here, of course, is using the words as a manipulation or gimmick rather than truly creating a context where it is acceptable for the therapy to be either a failure or success. Thus, if either the spouse or the therapist is using these words sarcastically or as a way of trying to cover up his or her true feelings, a disaster may result. Extending the isomorphism to another level, it must be acceptable for therapists to choose not to treat alcohol problems and for supervisors not to insist that they do so. Choice cannot be imposed externally.

Once the spouse has hit bottom and accepted responsibility for herself and for any outcome of that responsibility, the alcoholic will then be more accessible and will hit bottom. He can get sober in therapy and/or in Alcoholics Anonymous. The trap that will come up here is that now that success is almost achieved, therapist, spouse, and other family members and friends tend to rush in with encouragement to get the alcoholic to stop drinking. This can undo all the progress that has been made. It is necessaary for the alcoholic to be truly hopeless and powerless in order to stop drinking. This touches off emotional resonances within family members, friends, and therapist who then try to give the alcoholic hope.

If one has become a therapist as a way of attempting to control unresolved problems of one's own, it will be impossible to treat people at this phase, since what we are describing is acceptance or surrender rather than control or manipulation. One is empowered only when one accepts being powerless. If the therapist has not personally experienced powerlessness or hopelessness as a liberation, he will reactively impede the system from hitting bottom with his helpful suggestions, which is isomorphic with the spouse stopping the alcoholic from hitting bottom with her well-intentioned concerns. The est training may serve as a resource for the therapist to get in touch with his helplessness and hopelessness and unrealized power, isomorphic with Al-Anon for the spouse, and Alcohlics Anonymous for the alcoholic.

If the alcoholic has truly hit bottom, the system will now move into the "dry" phase or, in rare instances, directly into sobriety, the integration and transcendence of wet and dry behaviors and feelings. There are then new specific issues for the therapist to handle but the principles of creating a therapeutic relationship or context remain the same.

REFERENCES

1. Berenson, D., A Family Approach to Alcoholism. *Psychiatry Opinion* 13:33–38, 1976.

2. Berenson, D., Alcohol and the Family System. In P. Guerin (Ed.), *Family Therapy: Theory and Practice*, New York: Gardner Press, 1976.

3. Bowen, M., Principles and Techniques of Multiple Family Therapy. In P. Guerin (Ed.), *Family Therapy: Theory and Practice*, New York: Gardner Press, 1976.

4. Bowen, M., Theory in the Practice of Psychotherapy. In P. Guerin (Ed.), *Family Therapy: Theory and Practice*, New York: Gardner Press, 1976.

5. Fogarty, T., Marital Crisis. In P. Guerin (Ed.), *Family Therapy: Theory and Practice*, New York: Gardner Press, 1976.

6. Minuchin, S., *Families and Family Therapy*, Cambridge, MA: Harvard University Press, 1974.

FOOTNOTE

1. For ease of presentation and because of some clinical differences between the husband and wife as the alcoholic, I will refer to the alcoholic as "he" and the spouse as "she".

16

A Recovering Alcoholic Speaks and Her Family Therapist Introduces Her

Pauline Kaufmann, M.S.W.
DIRECTOR OF FAMILY THERAPY
PHOENIX FOUNDATION,

Lilly M.
WRITER AND RECOVERING ALCOHOLIC

Introduction

My introduction to Lilly was through a book of her short stories. On the book's jacket was a full-sized portrait of Lilly. She had a stark face; her eyes were open wide with fright and frozen with the expectation of pain. I picked the book up several times only to find that I could not get past the portrait: a cry for help, a face surrounded by fear, a person forever pursued by her own devils.

In the following weeks I read the book. I shared with Lilly sensitive segments of a life beautifully and poetically described. The theme of a "lost child" permeated the stories, frequently understated and written from inside the child's world. I found myself wondering about the writer: had the face on the jacket finally broken into tears; had the scream come from her lips? Later the book and Lilly were stored in my head and I thought no more of her.

Many months later one of my students told me about a young woman who desperately needed help and urged me to see her. The woman was Lilly.

Lilly appeared with the same frozen, wild, starved look and quivering mouth. She spent her first session being a good little girl and trying to please me. I disregarded her need to be good and to please, and we went on to talk of why she was here.

In the ensuing weeks we dealt with her ghosts: the cold bitter undemonstrative mother who said, "Children are a nuisance and a burden"; the absent father and the brother who would hit and threaten her. She described the only childhood resolution she knew for this pain and deprivation—to get sick and run a fever. Then mother would be nice to her.

Despite the fact that Lilly and her family (mother, brother, and half sister) were separated by hundreds of miles, the family continued to occupy all of Lilly's psychological space. In the beginning, therapy dealt with her family in absentia. The ever-recurring themes were fear of abandonment, the need to be a very good girl in order to gain acceptance, the feeling that boys and men beat you and threaten you, and the sense that any expression of anger and opposition were dangerous and bad. In her child's mind her anger and bad behavior had caused suffering and death.

In therapy the family was reconstructed. Lilly came to see the family structure as one that caused pain to all of its members. It was at this point that Lilly began to visit her mother and rework their relationship. At present the relationship between Lilly and her mother is characterized by mutual support and caring. Lilly can laugh with her mother at the parental idiosyncracies. Lilly and her brother have become good and affectionate friends who share a common concern for their mother. Lilly's half sister has visited her and also brought her two children and husband.

Despite the easing of family tensions and the discovery of her mother and brother as people with whom she shared a large part of her childhood and who are her friends, Lilly has much to do in her current living. Still, many of the old ghosts have been laid to rest. New relationships are less frequently burdened by old sterotypes. She reports a growing freedom and spontaneity and she continues to be sober.

Lilly's Story

Before I say anything about my own life and recovery from alcoholism. there are two things I must stress. The first is that there is no indication that the roots of alcoholism are entirely emotional. If this were so—if the basis of the disease were psychological—it would follow that therapy could "cure" the alcoholic and allow him to drink again, and this is simply not conceivable. However, it is quite clear to me that the emotional factor is a large part of the package. In my own recovery, the most important priority is maintaining sobriety, and this has included therapy to deal with the problems over which I once drank and over which I will drink again, I believe, if these problems are dealt with as they were in the past. The second point is that whatever I say is from my own experience; I am speaking for myself and not for AA as a whole.

In the four years that I've been sober, one of the changes that has taken place is my attitude toward my childhood and family. I am now thirty-five, and have a brother, thirty-nine, and a half sister from my father's second marriage who is twenty-eight; we are just getting to know each other. My mother is still lviing, but my father died about fifteen years ago. While I was drinking I laid the blame for my failures squarely at my mother's feet and tried in various ways to scare or coerce her into showing love. It was convenient to use her, my parents' divorce, and my brother's hostility when we were children as an excuse for my insanities. I did not seem capable of seeing my mother as a separate person who also happened to be my mother and who had a life and problems of her own. This attitude of self-pity and blame has changed to a better evaluation of where my own sickness lay; I have been able to extract from the past just where my confusions were and find out how to begin to sort them out. Whatever anger I have is confined to the present; I do not see my family as the villains I once did, nor myself as the victim.

In fact, I have come to really like my mother. As an adult I had constructed as many barriers against affection as she had; and often, now, just being with her and letting her know I care about her has allowed us both a measure of love and even respect. She told a friend of mine recently that she no longer worries about me or feels guilty about having "ruined my life." Although she did not feel free to tell me this directly, it still made me very happy. It also made me very aware that while drinking and yelling at her I had not considered what a terrible burden this was to lay on a parent. I no longer feel so bound up with her, so ready to jump with guilt, or to apologize and defend myself. And when I do occasionally fall into these old patterns, I can see them as just that—an old familiar way of reacting which I can talk to my therapist about and try again to change. As soon as I began to learn through AA and therapy, that I have something to say about how I feel or react, I could begin to gain some detachment from my mother. It has not been easy and I have worked as hard at trying to establish a reasonable relationship with her as I have worked at anything else in sobriety. My therapist has been invaluable in letting me see that I cannot go looking for a mother who never existed, but must accept her as she is. I think I have a great deal of sympathy for her now, an understanding of the kind of depression she has lived with, of the handicaps of her own life, and have a real desire to get to know her.

I can better remember now the ways in which my mother was supportive of me as a child, and recognize that she always let me know that I was important to her. Until I got sober, I could only remember the signs of her disinterest, could only see my childhood negatively. In therapy as I have learned to take responsibility for how I feel or what I do, and the anger has fallen away. I have been able to draw on some of the positive things from my own life, strengths I did not know I had, interests Ihad long since given up. I had felt cut off from my own life before and during the drinking, and I now feel connected to it, to my family and the place where I grew up. And it has been a nice thing to share with my mother.

Much of my relationship with my brother, as adults, was based on me as his little messed-up sister, with him as reliable big brother. He was very kind to me during my drinking and at a difficult time in his own life, and I accepted our relationship on that level—insisted on it really. I was not able to imagine his life outside of his usefulness to, and support of, me. I do not say this to condemn myself, but to point out the awful inwardness of alcoholism; I could not afford to see people as anything other than means to my own safety. It has been with some grief that I have put together the pieces of what he must have been going through in his own life while I was drinking.and oblivious. We do not see much of each other now, for geographical reasons, but when we do it is with affection and as equals. I think I have let him know that I care about him, and he has been able to ask advice and tell me his troubles as often as I have been able to do the same with him. I have a lot of respect for the way he has put together his life considering his own very real unhappiness; and I can tell him this now. We talk often about how to get along with our mother, sharing our difficulties, or making decisions about responsibilities. My mother has recently retired and been more depressed and needy than she has seemed in a long time, and I have found that trying to help her with little things—accompanying her to the doctor, doing an errand for her, bringing her a present—cheers her up and makes our relationship more viable; and these are the kinds of things my brother and I can discuss and decide about.

I suppose the process—the change in attitude toward my family—has been one of realizing that I am not fixed in my old relationships with them; and in gaining some freedom or detachment from them, I feel freer in my life with other people. I do not have to make other people into criticizing mothers, absent fathers, hostile brothers, or jealous sisters. (I have not talked about my sister because we are just getting to know each other, but there has been a lot of jealousy between us in the past). I can begin to see other people on their own terms, and not as extensions of my fears and needs, and without the hatred and suspicion with which I once viewed the entire world. This process began when people in AA accepted me without judgment, without my needing to prove myself. It began when I saw that I was not so different from others, and that by taking responsibility for my place in the world I could be free of the delusion that I was a victim and the world was hostile. And the process continued when I began therapy, after I had been sober for a year and a half; the therapist did not condemn me but instead helped me to sort out my confusions and to begin to deal with problems on a daily basis, letting go of my childhood and the attendant need to place blame. So at this point I would like to say something about that childhood, but not without stressing again that although the atmosphere was conducive for my alcoholism, I cannot find the whole story there.

My parents were not alcoholics, although my father's father was, but as I did not know him there was no example set for me of using alcohol. Nonetheless, at the age of thirteen I very consciously wanted to get drunk. I had one good friend at the time, and I clung to her until I began to annoy and burden her with my possessiveness. She tried to explain this to me, and I certainly heard everything she said since I can still remember it, but I was incapable of addressing myself to it. Instead I sulked and acted hurt, became depressed and avoided her which, as I had intended, caused her enough guilt that when she approached me again she did not dare broach the subject. I was in terrible pain, afraid I would lose her friendship, but I could not conceive of taking a look at what I was doing, or of what her point of view was, or of what could be done. Instead I suggested we get drunk. We bought two bottles of Listerene; she took two sips and stopped. I drank my bottle and the rest of hers, and although I got quite sick, I also had a sense of tremendous relief. I see this first drunk as typical of my way of dealing with things all through my life. Blaming others for hurting me, as I saw it, even when they were trying to help; blackmailing them emotionally; needing to ease the pain—this need for relief was to be a determining factor in my drinking long after the alcohol ceased to bring it about. But my need for it did not abate.

After my parents married, they moved from their home state to live in the country. I did not know my grandparents, but do know that my mother's mother had some, if not many, nervous breakdowns during my mother's childhood; and that her father, to whom she was very close, died in her teens. She had spoken of running away from her family to marry my father. My father had many jobs, before and after this marriage, and was described by my mother as irresponsible and indifferent to her. I have a brother three years older than me; and when I was four, my father and mother separated and subsequently divorced. My father remarried and had a daughter seven years younger than me, but as they lived in another country I did not know her, nor did I see my father more than a handful of times after the divorce. I have been told by friends of my mother that it was she who wanted the separation, that my father was the more attentive to us children, and that he was affectionate. But I have only their word to go on. I remember him at home just once, when my brother and I annoyed him and he yelled at us and locked us in the cellar. His visits after the divorce were infrequent and had special meaning for me, but he was a stranger also. I had no conscious feeling of anger for his seeing us so rarely, and in fact until his death in my twenties, I managed to give him little thought. I could go for a year without remembering his existence. At nineteen I received a letter from him and was stunned at the idea that I actually had a father. My control, or denial, of feelings was always strong, as I have learned to my dismay in sobriety. After his death, I did go into therapy for the first time but was not able, until I got sober, to make any use at all of professional help.

My mother was not a demonstrative woman. She said many times that having children was a nuisance and warned me against growing up to be burdened with them. She has been quoted as saying: "I can't give them [the children] affection, but I can see that they get to the dentist." When I have seen her, now that I am an adult, with little children, she is self-conscious and very stiff. She may not have become as bitter as I remember her until after the divorce, but that is how I remember her: bitter, resentful, and down on everything. Although my brother and I did a lot of work around the house—more, I was told by other parents, than most children—we were criticized a lot with the specific implication that we could do more, or better. I was always nervous about these chores, whether I could do them well enough or fast enough, and I know that well before adolescence I was beginning to drag my heels, compounding the problem by being sullen and reluctant to help out. My brother stood up to my mother, and made many choices in direct opposition to her and her values, and so brought on more of her anger than I did. I tried to stay in her good graces and ape her opinions; my only opposition was sullenness. She often said with pride that I never cried as a baby.

We never talked about anything; I remember that. My mother was often depressed, and the tension in the house was terrible; other people have commented on how my brother or I would seem to come to life as soon as we were away from home. I learned to read my mother by her moods and voice inflections, and guessed wrong, I suppose, as often as right, but in any case came to believe that people communicated by implication and not with words. A common situation which occurs to date unless I make the effort not to fall into it, has her haranguing bitterly about everything and everybody and the misery of her life, and when I would fall silent—feeling, as a child, helpless and hopeless—she would say: "And what's the matter with *you*?" I felt that she was at fault for depressing me, but that I was meant to feel guilty for being depressed; and this acceptance that I was in the wrong, this belief that other people *made* me feel whatever I felt, was to stay with me.

I remember one time when I went to her for reassurance, and, not receiving it, never went again. We had moved to the city when I was eight and I had nightmares about her abandoning me; when I went into her room, she kicked me out. I kept all my fears to myself after that, acquiring that paradoxical combination of isolation and dependency, clinging to her without ever telling her anything. I did learn to get things I wanted by sulking or crying in my room and later by playing sick to get out of anything I didn't believe I could do, like homework. She was quite nice to me when I was sick, and this trick worked for years.

My brother and I did not get along in childhood. My mother would get angry at him, and then he would hit me or just threaten me. I always managed never to incur her direct anger, so I felt some compassion for him. There was one time during a storm when he took hold of my arm all the way home as though to protect me. I felt defensive on his behalf when she criticized him, but did not defend myself when she criticized me. Her criticism of me was not delivered with anger but with bitterness and disappointment. Once, after I had failed, again, to do the dishes on my own initiative, and had been told, again, about my selfishness, I went outside and beat up my cat. The cat died a year later, and in no way as a result of my having struck her—and I knew at the time that I had not caused her death—nonetheless I felt terribly guilty, not for her death so much as for her having suffered at my hands during her life. It seemed to me crucial not to incur anger and not to get angry.

The stiff upper lip was a virtue. I steeled myself against tears or pain of any kind. Nonetheless my mother complained about her life a lot, and this contradicted my idea of what a stiff upper lip involved. Were my brother and I to be stoic, when she did not have to be? If duty was so important, where was *her* duty, if not in some small part to her children? Or were we merely "duty" and not wanted? I began to see life as a loathsome moral obligation I could not meet. Comfort was her greatest pleasure: a nap, a trip, a hot meal. But I did not feel comforted *by* her; on the contrary, I was told about the starving Armenians if I was hungry rather than given something to eat. I denied myself many meals, many warm socks, and came into adulthood with a deep disregard for myself at every level. I simply did not figure out, until I was 33, that to avoid being cold one dresses warmly. I reported, after I grew up, to physical and mental illnesses to punish others, I suppose, for not taking care of me, but just as often as an excuse to let up on myself.

I do not remember my mother ever praising me, and this has been corroborated by some of her friends. She did, however, tell me whenever one of her friends complimented me, and I would hang around waiting for her to pass on these tidbits. But I came to believe that she made them up to please me (I did know that she wanted to please me). All this second-hand praise made my "image" very important to me—or the weight I gave to it made it so. I sifted out what qualities were most praised, and modeled myself on this: very quiet, a good listener, pretty but waifish. A photograph of myself that I treasured, because others did, was of me standing up on the sides of my feet with shyness, my face turned aside.

My mother did not encourage our interests and successes, and at some point I made this lack of encouragement my own, sabotaging myself at every step. But the one constant in my life was books which were to remain my main consolation, if not my only source of identification with the human race.

Because he stood up to her, my brother appeared tougher and more self-assured. I was certainly self-sufficient as a child and unafraid of the physical world. But I was often nervous, unable to sleep or eat, and became depressed over any changes: the end of the school year, the end of vacation, the departure of a visitor. It may be that I was regarded, and regarded myself, as oversensitive and frail. The first fantasy I remember was of a doctor coming to take care of me.

My mother was an intelligent, witty, and very able woman. She had many friends who loved her, drawn by some magnetic quality of melancholia. I was intimidated and impressed by her. True to her word, she was not affectionate and she did take us to the dentist, but she also had a kind of camaraderie with us on occasion, and these occasions were important. It is strange but I felt privileged that she was my mother, and I think this reflects my fear of her as well as my clinging, abject need. I was so terrified of the bitter and contemptuous running commentary she made on life, that I would do or say anything to keep it from being directed at me, while all the time convinced that in fact she was telling me, by parable and story, that it was—every bit of it—directed at me, that her anger was a reflection of my failure to meet her standards. And at the same time that I imitated her opinions, I did not feel any real sharing with her, could not ask her what any feelings—my own or hers—meant. I became very secretive and ashamed of emotion, and by adolescence had very little sense of myself; I was full of self-criticism.

I was very homesick for the country and felt superior to and alienated from city children. At age eleven I began to steal compulsively, without pleasure. Because my mother often complained about having to cook for us (she may not have complained as often as I thought, but I chose to believe she loathed this task), I would often throw out my dinner when she was not looking and survive on candy bars and canned peaches that I stole. I began to beg at a friend's house for breakfasts and treats, usually sugar, and to mooch desserts off of friends' school lunches, for which I did not have a meal ticket, preferring to believe that my mother was denying me this ticket rather than to figure out that she simply did not know I needed one, which was the case. I wore the same dirty blouse for weeks, hiding it under a sweater at home, but revealing it at school so people would feel sorry for me and think my mother did not take care of me. My favorite teacher, who had encouraged my skill at drawing, one day criticized some outlandish inaccuracies in a painting I had done, and I retaliated by pulling some tricks on her which befuddled her and made her say that she was getting too old to teach. I began to cheat in school. I was envious of my schoolmates for being friends with each other but made no attempt to join them after school and turned down invitations. There were some years of real antagonism between me and my mother; nothing was said, but neither one of us was considerate of the other. My brother by then had gone off to a boarding school for disturbed children, and then to college. He did not, even in retrospect, seem very disturbed, but he was stubborn and angry and, I believe, had been in some kind of trouble in school. I saw very little of him during this time.

In high school, as schoolmates were beginning to do grown-up things like go to parties and get summer jobs, I withdrew more and more and began to court my mother, as I had done as a child, aping her and sentimentalizing our life together and spending more and more time with her. This was to last, along with an unusual dependency, well into my drinking, when I at last began to punish and retaliate and to marvel at her hurt and anger.

By mid-adolescence I was a depressed, inward-turned girl. Life just seemed to "happen" to me; I felt powerless and blameless. Everything was everybody else's fault. I was always on the defensive, an adversary stance masked by good behavior and sentimental attachments; I really had no sense of other people's existence, much less my own. I felt as though my head were packed in cotton wool, and I had to check mirrors all the time to be sure I was still there. I was frequently very depressed; at seventeen I stopped menstruating for a year and a half, for no organic reason. Every time I started something new I hoped it would be the answer and save me, and when it was not, I dropped it. This included schools, jobs, friendships, men. It never occurred to me that I was in any way responsible. The lid was on very tight, and whenever anything broke through this control and denial, I turned to alcohol. Throughout my adolescence my control was so good that I needed alcohol rarely—for one-night drunks, attended even at this stage by blackouts;—but as I got older, the controls worked less and less well, and I drank more. The drinking initially increased because I needed it more and more, and then it increased under its own momentum because I was addicted. At this stage I no longer drank because I had problems, but because I was an alcoholic.

It was only by being defeated at the hands of alcohol that I was able to stop the denial and self-justification that characterized most of my life; not to stop it in a flash, but to begin to make some chinks in the wall. By the time I got sober, I had not stayed with any particular job or maintained more than one friendship for any length of time; I had been depressed or anxious for most of my adult life, alternating with brief bouts of extreme self-adulation and cockiness; I was divorced with no children, and I only knew how to deal with people through coercion, seduction, and dependency. I rode roughshod over my family and friends, not, I believe, through any real cruelty, but simply because, my own feelings being so distorted and anesthetized, I could not believe that other people could suffer either. As soon as I got sober, I was willing, in extremes, to take a different look at myself and my life. It has been a slow process, and in the beginning it had to be a very gentle one; the extreme self-loathing I felt would have sent me back to alcohol, I believe, if the process were not begun so simply as it is in AA, through identification with other people who have been over the same route, and with their patient, tough-minded, and generous support.

In my own experience, the very real strain of early sobriety did not permit introspection or therapy in any depth. The whys of the drinking did not matter at this stage. I knew I was sick; I needed to know that I was merely human.

My fear and subsequent need for control of feelings needed time to subside. I was willing to listen in meetings, to begin to reverse old opinions and self-justifications bought at so high a price, but I had to begin slowly and at my own pace. The first thing that had to be established for me, and which I believe is the basis for any willingness to change, is this: I wish to remain sober at all costs, regardless of how I feel or of what happens around me. With sobriety as the guideline, there is not too much room for quibbling with life or blaming others. These were the very attitudes that I drank over, and so I must let go of them in order to stay sober.

I do not claim that every alcoholic needs this time in early sobriety just to be sober, but I needed it. And when I was ready for therapy, I knew I was ready. I was sober a year and a half when I began to recognize that I felt better and safer, but the same old problems still plagued me, even though I could not blame alcohol for my behavior. It was admitting that I had to deal with these things that sent me to therapy. This need is provided for in AA by the twelve steps, but I felt that I needed extra, or complementary, help. It is safe to say that almost all my ideas before sobriety—about myself, about others, about what was going on in my own head or between myself and other people—were held in the light of such misapprehension that it was almost like starting from scratch in order to live a life that now makes sense. I no longer see my life as a list of grievances, and have been willing and more and more able to stop looking at the "wrongs" other people have done me and take a look at my own difficulties in getting along with myself and others. I have needed the intervention of the therapist and people in AA, needed to be shown how to take a look at myself without at the same time indulging in further self-loathing and guilt. I know that the help I have received in learning to get along with my family and to put the past behind has been one example of how, if I deal with the things which I once would have gotten drunk over, sobriety is that much easier. The desperation to remain sober changed to a desire to be so—a choice for life, maybe, or just the conviction that I could now live it.

17

The Application of the Basic Principles of Family Therapy to the Treatment of Drug and Alcohol Abusers

Edward Kaufman, M.D.
ASSOC. CLINICAL PROFESSOR OF PSYCHIATRY
CHIEF, PSYCHIATRIC SERVICES, DIRECTOR OF FAMILY THERAPY PROGRAMS
UNIVERSITY OF CALIFORNIA, IRVINE MEDICAL CENTER
ORANGE, CALIFORNIA

The chapters in this book have focused on the multitude of therapeutic approaches which can be helpful in working with the families of substance abusers. The editors have emphasized their utilization of a synthesis of many approaches. We would also like to stress that each therapist should choose those systems of family therapy that best suit his or her personality, making use of those techniques which can be grafted onto one's own individual syle and family background. The better we as therapists understand ourselves and our own families, the better we are able to choose and utilize appropriate therapeutic techniques.

In this final chapter we would like to present a review of the major approaches to family therapy and apply them to the treatment of substance abusers. The five basic approaches have been described by Anderson (2) as psychodynamic, structural, communications, experiential, and behavioral. Although these five approaches have borrowed greatly from one another to a point where there is substantial integration, there are nevertheless discrete differences which, at times, have led to conflict between them.

If the substance abuser is habituated to drugs or is unable to attend sessions without being under the influence of a chemical, then the first priority is to get him off the substance, at least temporarily. Most therapeutic changes in dysfunctional families cannot be initiated until the regular use of chemicals is interrupted. Thus the first goal is to persuade the family to pull together to initiate detoxification. Generally this must be done in a hospital. In some cases it can be done on an an ambulatory basis, such as outpatient detoxification from narcotics with methadone or using benzodiazepines with alcoholics. If after detoxification the chemical-free state is not maintained, then a drug-aided measure to keep the client from abusing chemicals can be initiated. Antabuse, narcotic antagonists, or short-term, low-dose methadone maintenance can be used in this way. Some individuals will require longer hospitalization, a day program, or a residential therapeutic community to ensure sufficient abstinence from chemicals to enable family therapy to occur. Therefore, the second step is to help the family to initiate and support these modalities. Berenson, in his chapter, has described a system for working with the drinking alcoholic. We know of no such approach to families with a drug addicted member.

Psychodynamic Treatment

This approach is taken by many different theorists, among whom there have been considerable differences. These include Ackerman (1), Bowen (5), Nagy (4), Zuk (18), and Paul (12). Since this author is psychoanalytically trained, his own ideas about the contribution of this discipline will also be included.

The basic principles of the psychodynamic approach are first, using history to uncover past actions which are inappropriately applied to the present (transference); and second, creating change through insight. This insight is achieved by cognitive or affective reencounter with the past (2). In Bowen's systems approach the cognitive is emphasized, and every attempt is made to eliminate the use of affect (5). Systems theory examines triangulation and uses of the genogram and family chronology. Triangulation implies that whenever there is emotional distance or conflict between two individuals, these tensions will be displaced onto a third party, issue, and/or substance (e.g. alcohol, drugs).

The genogram has become a basic tool in many family therapy approaches. A genogram is a pictorial chart of the people involved in a three-generational relationship system which marks marriages, divorces, births, geographical location, deaths, and illnesses (7). All significant physical, social, and psychological dysfunctions may be added to it. It is used to examine relationships in the extended family complex. The genogram is the first step for a therapist to take in understanding his or her own family as well as families in treatment. The genogram uses the following symbols (7) to illustrate these relationships (Figure 17-1).

Once the names, ages, and dates of the above crucial events are filled in, other relevant facts can be added, including "the family's physical location, frequency and type of contact, emotional cutoffs, toxic issues, nodal events, and open/closed relationship index (7)."

Recently, I was requested to conduct a case conference at an alcoholism treatment program. I had asked to see a family that was receiving treatment at the clinic. Although the therapists there saw many couples, they had only

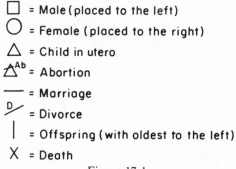

☐ = Male (placed to the left)

◯ = Female (placed to the right)

△ = Child in utero

△^Ab = Abortion

— = Marriage

╱ = Divorce

| = Offspring (with oldest to the left)

X = Death

Figure 17-1

one "family" in therapy, which they presented in absentia. One of the counselors asked the question, "Why should we do family therapy?" and then proceeded to give the family history, which is depicted below in genogram format. The identified alcoholic patient was Jim, a 46-year-old ex-marine. He married June, age 48, in 1975. It was the second marriage for both and we learned that June's first husband, Joe, had also been alcoholic, and that they had been divorced in 1973. Jim had been married to Betty in 1946, and

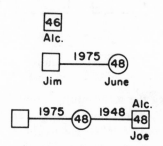

Figure 17-2

divorced in 1973. One son from each first marriage was involved in treatment, and June's eight-year-old daughter also lived in the family. However, one therapist reported that Jim had two other children from his first marriage. June's therapist stated that June's father was an alcoholic, but no information was known about any of the other parents. This points to another function of the genogram, uncovering gaps in information. The genogram also focused on a very crucial, but as yet unemphasized, aspect of this family, that both of June's husbands were alcoholic, as was her father, a critical issue in the treatment of June as well as the rest of this family. We also learned that Steve, a brother whose relevance had been minimized, had frequently drunk with his father and had been brutalized by him.

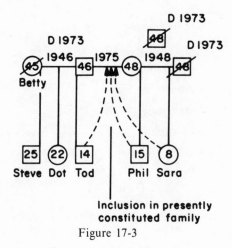

Inclusion in presently
constituted family
Figure 17-3

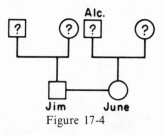

Figure 17-4

One session involving the reconstituted family of Jim, June, Tod, Phil, and Sara had been held. The family scapegoated Jim and ganged up on him about his drinking and brutality. He accepted this passively in the session, but retaliated against everyone as soon as they arrived home. June was held responsible for giving Jim his daily Antabuse, which he stopped taking after a few weeks. The family refused further joint sessions, but June, Tod, and Phil continued to be seen individually. Jim, who was described as a racist and sexist, had been assigned a black female therapist, which helped account for his reluctance to continue therapy. June should have been helped to become disinvolved from Jim's alcoholism, and assigning her the responsibility for the Antabuse was antithetical to this. I suggested that she be referred to a group at the clinic for the "significant others" of alcoholics. Tod had already begun to abuse drugs and alcohol, but avoided any discipline by pretending to behave responsibly and setting Phil up as the guilty culprit whenever his father appeared. Thus Phil would be inappropriately punished, a situation to which he reacted by becoming truant and engaging in an enmeshed, protective relationship with his mother. Each son was thereby participating in a triangle with the parents which separated the parental bond. It was suggested that a white male recovered alcoholic be assigned as Jim's individual therapist, with the hope that after Jim had received a few supportive sessions, the staff could utilize the knowledge gained from examining the genogram such that the family could resume conjoint sessions.

Another helpful diagnostic tool which has been developed by systems theorists is the family chronology which is a time map of the major family events and stresses. The chronology enables the family and therapist to understand the evolution of family patterns over time (7). The chronology, together with the genogram, "elicits the facts about the structural characteristics, membership, nodal events and toxic issues in a family." One of the major benefits of this approach is that many important conflicts and stresses are learned about in the first session or two which otherwise might not come out until much later. The genogram and chronology emphasize another aspect of the systems approach, which is to deemotionalize and objectify data. This is not to deny that strong affect will be released in the early phases of this type of therapy. However, further attempts to achieve insight should be suspended until the initial affect is resolved.

Systems theory emphasizes that family therapy can be done even if only one individual is personally available. This is done in five phases: engagement, planning, re-entry work, the work, and follow-through (6). This approach is also very helpful in training family therapists to understand their own families but will not be reported here. It should be emphasized that individuation achieved by physical distancing is not real and requires further insight.

My personal experience in the use of past history is that it is extremely helpful if it can be utilized without blaming, guilt induction, and dwelling on the hopelessness of long-standing, fixed patterns. A family chronology of each individual in family treatment is thus extremely helpful in providing information which can be used to enhance change. A psychoanalytic interpretation can be used directively to accomplish immediate shifts in the family system. An example of this technique was used with a family I recently saw in consultation. The 17-year-old son had lost his driver's license as a result of being in an accident while intoxicated. Immediately after disciplining the son for driving in a car where beer was consumed, the mother embraced and kissed him. When she was given the task of disciplining him without embracing him, she was asked to remember that discipline did not necessarily mean being held by her feet and dipped head first into a bucket of water, which she had been subjected to as a child. Another mother who could not ask for support from her husband, was reminded that she was not an Army officer as her father, with whom she had indentified, had been.

Structural Family Therapy

Although I have used a variety of family therapy techniques for many years, it is only since I have incorporated structural treatment into my methods that I have felt the family treatment of substance abusers has fallen into place. There are two articles on structural family therapy (SFT) in this book, one is by Minuchin, the founder of this system; the other is by Stanton and his colleagues. Stanton is the associate of Minuchin who has focused on heroin "addicts." Still, since many basic principles of the theory and practice of SFT have not been developed in these chapters, nor applied to substance abusers in the existing literature, I have provided the following material so that the reader may better utilize this relevant therapeutic system with substance abusers.

Family structure refers to the invisible set of functional demands that organizes the ways in which family members interact. The goal of SFT is a more adequate family organization achieved through manipulation and rearrangement of present patterns of interaction (sets) (10). Once the genogram has been developed and understood, a family can be examined by mapping boundaries and subsystems. Boundaries are the rules defining who participates in a family and how. These may be represented as (10):

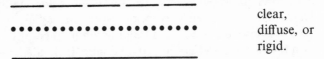

clear, diffuse, or rigid.

Subsystems may be formed by generation, sex, interest, or function. The two most common subsystems are executive (parental) and sibling (10).

The relationships between family members may be designated as

affiliation or overinvolvement.

Conflict is designated as disruption ——/⊦—— . A coalition is depicted as } . Conflict frequently results in detouring to a third party, hence "detouring." ⊲⊦⊳

The "ideal family" could be mapped as: (M mother, F father, C child)

```
         |
     M   |   F          M ====F
    -----+-----  or  -----+-----
     C   |   C          C  |  C
         |                 |
```

with clear boundaries between all individuals, affiliation between parents, and separation of the executive and sibling subsystems. The family therapist functions as a boundary maker who clarifies diffuse boundaries, opens rigid ones, and helps establish generational lines, particularly separating the spouse subsystem from the demands and needs of their own parents as well as those of their children. Frequently probes, which are described later, are used too help delineate these boundaries and their resilience.

The spouse subsystem must have sufficient complementarity and mutual accommodation to implement tasks. If it is dysfunctional, the therapist challenges the process without challenging motivation, and with a complementarity which focuses on the contribution of both parties, i.e. if a husband is controlling, the therapist might focus on the wife for letting herself be controlled. Depending on the family structure, the therapist might ask the husband to make all the decisions and the wife to not undermine them, or the wife to make all the decisions and the husband to support them. The child should have access to both parents but be excluded from spouse functions. Parents cannot protect and guide without controlling and restricting. Children cannot grow and become individuated without rejecting and attacking (10).

Therapeutic Tactics

The starting point is always the diagnostic family map, as described earlier, which helps to organize material and set goals. Therapeutic tactics are generally divided into two major categories, coupling or joining, which consists of those tactics which are used to enhance the therapist's leverage within the family, and change production, which is composed of strategies designed to change dysfunctional sets (11).

Coupling or Joining In coupling with the family, the therapist alternates between existential engagement and disengaged expert. The therapist must be capable of joining each sub-system, including the siblings. He must enable each family member to feel his respect for each one of them as an individual as well as his firm commitment to healing. The therapist must make contact with each family member so that they are following him even when they sense he is unfair. There are three types of coupling techniques: maintenance, tracking, and mimesis. *Maintenance* requires supporting the family structures and behaving according to the family's rules. The therapist may initially speak to the family through the family spokesperson or "switchboard." When a family is being pushed beyond its ability to tolerate stress, maintenance techniques can be used to lower stress. Other maintenance operations include supporting areas of family strength, rewarding, affiliating with a family member, supporting a threaented member, and explaining a problem (11). *Tracking* involves adopting the content of family communications and using the family's own special language to offer the therapist's ideas. As in hypnosis, if the patient refuses the therapist's suggestions, the refusal is manipulated into a form of obeying the command (11). The therapist enters the family as a supporter of family rules but makes the rules work in the direction of his goals for the family. *Mimesis* involves the therapist's adopting the family's style and affect as reflected by the members' actions and needs. If a family uses humor, so should the therapist, but without double binds. If a family communicates through touching, then the therapist should also touch. The therapist might join an isolated father by sharing pipe utensils or a cigarette or by removing his tie or jacket at the same time as the father. Mimesis is frequently done unconsciously and is readily used here in contrast to individual psychoanalytic psychotherapy where it is generally contraindicated, as are most joining techniques. Sharing food in multiple-family therapy (MFT) encourages a joining of all the families present as well as uniting the therapist with each family.

Change Production or Restructuring. Unlike coupling, change production involves a challenge to the families' homeostasis and takes place through restructuring the family sets. In restructuring, the therapist uses expertise in social manipulation, with the word "manipulation" being used in a positive rather than a pejorative sense. Techniques used for change production include the contract, probing, actualization, marking boundaries, assigning tasks, utilizing symptoms, manipulating, mood and support, education, and guidance (10). Frequently a single therapeutic intervention will utilize many of these techniques. Families are motivated to change in three ways. They are challenged in their perception of reality. They are given alternatives that make sense. Alternative transactions provide new relationships which are self-reinforcing. The reader is reminded that joining is necessary as a prerequisite and facilitator for change production, and that the therapist may alternate between joining and restructuring.

1. THE THERAPEUTIC CONTRACT. A prerequisite for change is the therapeutic contract. (10). This is a decision to concentrate on mutually agreed-upon, workable issues. The contract should always promise help with the problem that brought the family in, before it is expanded to other issues. Goals should be mutual. If there is disagreement about them, then work on resolving disagreements should be made a part of the contract. If family members are seen individually, a contract that everything will be shared with the entire family is preferable, but not essential, as necessary information may only be revealed if there is confidentiality. The length of time that treatment will require should be included in the contract but can be extended at a later date.

2. PROBING. The therapist affiliates with the family system and feels its

pressures. Thus the therapist's spontaneous responses will probably be syntonic with the family system. If not syntonic, the therapist's responses will challenge the system and thus be valuable as theraputic probes (10). All therapeutic maneuvers are probes in that they test the family's resilience and ability to change. Probes may be repelled or may elicit three types of positive responses:

A. Assimilation without difficulty, leading to learning, but not necessarily to growth.

An example of this is a family in which the alcoholic father was deceased and three of the four siblings who were drug abusers, were still liviing with their mother. The fourth was in residential treatment, and the family was in MFT. Two of the drug abusers came to MFT but did not participate because they arrived intoxicated. The oldest daughter did attend MFT and described how she had extricated herself from extreme parental-child responsibilities by disengagement. As a probe, it was pointed out to her that with her pulling out, the drug abusing siblings had all moved in and were being taken care of by their mother in a way which was perpetuating their drug abuse and causing the mother to disorganize.

When she next returned to the group, the daughter related that her drug-abusing sibs would have to function on their own as she was taking her mother to her house and putting her furniture in storage. The sister had reassumed her parental-child role in order to extricate her mother from a bad situation and force her sibs to sink or swim. Although she stated that this would only be until her mother could reestablish herself, she had assimilated the probe and made changes without any personal growth. However, her shift could eventually lead to growth for the family.

B. An accommodation which expands transactional patterns and activates alternative patterns. This is seen when, without causing stress, probes lead to a decrease of infantilized enmeshed cross-generational ties and begin to build ties between distantiated parties.
An example of this is when mothers are readily pulled away from their addict sons and given tasks which build the relationship with her husband or unaddicted children; e.g. buying a wedding dress with a daughter, taking a vacation with the husband.

C. An increase in stress, which, only after it unbalances homeostasis, leads to transformation. This is a basic principle of all reconstructive therapies. In order to accomplish this, the therapist must have the respect of every family member and may have to unbalance the system in a way which may seem unfair.

A common example of this is disengaging a severely enmeshed mother. This may seriously stress and unbalance a family. In some cases, the family may have to weather the storm of the mother's psychosis, depression, or psychosomatic illness. Excluding members from directly attending sessions or by having them sit outside the family circle or behind a one-way mirror is a powerful tool which generally is a stressful probe.

This kind of family crisis may occur when the addict stops using drugs while living within the family. If the crisis is not anticipated, the family may leave treatment. If it is resolved, the prognosis is quite good.

3. ACTUALIZING FAMILY TRANSACTIONAL PATTERNS (ENACTMENT). Patients frequently direct their communications to the therapist. Instead they should be required to talk to each other. They should be asked to enact and relive transactional patterns rather than describe them (10). They should show how they deal with substance abuse and other family problems rather than talk about them. It is our experience that role playing facilitates actualization of patterns (as well as changes them). Manipulating space is a powerful tool for generating actualization. Seating arrangements reveal much about alliances, coalitions, centrality, and isolation. Changing seating may create or strengthen boundaries. Asking two members who have been chronically disengaged and/or communicating through a third party to sit next to each other, by removing their "switchboard" or "blockade" can actualize strong conflicts and emotions. Enactment minimizes intellectualization and changes boring family sessions into exciting, dynamic ones. It is only when directly observing family patterns "in vivo" that the therapist can accurately map the family, begin to restructure it and ultimately evaluate the effects of interventions.

4. MARKING BOUNDARIES. This is achieved by delineating individual and subsystem boundaries (10). Individuals should not answer for others, should be talked to and not about, and shold listen to and acknowledge the communications of others. Family members should not feel for each other or read each others' minds. Nonverbal checking and blocking of communications should also be observed and, when appropriate, pointed out and halted.

The parental subsystem should be protected from intrusion by children, as well as by other adults in and outside the family. Frequently, in order to strengthen the executive, parental system, sessions which exclude everyone but the parents should be held. Tasks (described below) to build closeness are suggested.

5. ASSIGNING TASKS. Tasks may be assigned within the session or as homework (10). As Stanton and Todd point out in this book, it is preferable for a task to be accomplished in the session before homework can be given. Talking clearly to each other is a frequent early task. Asking a central figure to be quiet for five minutes or a quiet member to conduct a monologue are simple in-session tasks which build shifts based initially on briefly maintained changes. A distantiated couple can be asked to explore each other and the space around them for five minutes.

Therapeutic homework assignments permit the therapist and the therapeutic work to "live" with the family until the next session. A father who had neglected his medical and dental care because he was worried about his son's drug abuse was asked to make an appointment with a dentist. Sons who always shop with their mothers have been asked to shop with their fathers or by themselves. Parents are frequently asked to take a vacation or to go out dancing or to dinner together. A husband and wife might be asked to plan a pleasant surprise for each other without telling about it. In response to this task, a wife planned remarriage in a church and the husband planned for a set of new wedding bands. Disengaged fathers and sons are asked to do something that brought them close in the past. Fishing, attending sporting events, or even watching television together can help bridge gaps. After there is some common experience, a more intimate assignment such as taking a walk or talking alone for thirty minutes a day can be used.

6. UTILIZING THE SYMPTOM. Paraphrasing a frequently quoted statement of Freud's, Minuchin finds that the symptom of the identified patient (IP) is "the royal road to family structure" (10). Thus, this symptom is in a very special position and the first goal should be to influence the rest of the family to help the identified patient with it. The symptom is not dealt with directly by the therapist. If the symptom of some other family member is focused on before the IP's symptom is alleviated, the family will very frequently leave treatment.

The symptom may be exaggerated in order to emphasize the family's need to extrude it. A behavior which I have frequently exaggerated is encouraging a family to continue the "glories" of overindulging an addict at home. This type of technique, also called the use of paradox, is well illustrated by Minuchin (10) in dealing with a family where the presenting problem was the child's stealing. He instructed the child to continue stealing and to steal from his father. This relocated the antisocial behavior in an immediate situation which mobilized the family to deal with it directly. This task would rarely have to be given to any addict who is enmeshed with his family, as when this is the case, he invariably steals or "borrows" from every family member. Frequently purses and wallets are left around to be plucked at the addict's will. However, even when this is the case, overtly instructing the addict to try to steal from the family can mobilize its members to deal with him.

Relabeling the symptom may be very helpful, as when drug abuse is termed an attempt to bring divorced parents together or to alleviate parental child responsibilities. Relabeling can be used to gradually broaden the focus of treatment.

7. MANIPULATING MOOD. The family's affect can be taken in as a joining operation and then manipulated or exaggerated to achieve change (10). After several sessions with a family in which the adolescent son had been

truant and smoking pot constantly, the father came in furious, depressed, and ready to quit therapy and leave the family. The son and mother were both quite depressed. My cotherapist asked me to play the son's "alter ego"[1] to facilitate communication between the son and the father. I stated that the family's mood had made me feel too depressed to try to communicate, as I felt that the son had subtly undermined the therapeutic contract in order to bring his father's anger back upon him and his mother. I reluctantly agreed to serve as alter ego as a way to shift this apparently stuck family. In doing so I became in touch with the son's anger at having lived up to so much of the contract and not yet receiving any support and "strokes" from his dad. The mother, in her traditional role in the family, tried to cheer me up by pointing out to me and the family all the gains they had made. We were then able to focus on the father and his need to perpetuate his angry state at the residue of the unhealthy coalition between his wife and son. The father then shared with us the fact that his anger at his son was similar to his anger at his brother, who had constantly "ripped him off" and had been supported by their mother in doing so. By then I was out of my depression. I gave the family the task of involving the father in the first step of decision making instead of the last step, where he was the bad guy if he refused and felt ripped off if he agreed. When they returned the following week, they reported that father and son were able to communicate in an open way, which was unique for them. The alter ego is a powerful technique for manipulating mood. In this case, my use of my own "depression" was one way of shifting the family's mood, and the alter ego, still another. A therapist reported to me that he became so depressed in dealing with a disengaged, ungiving family that he began to cry, as he had done with his own similar family. When he shared this experience the rigid family system opened up.

8. SUPPORT, EDUCATION AND GUIDANCE. The support and nurturance that a family offers its members must be understood and encouraged (10). Since most addict families do not know how to give these "strokes," they must be taught and enhanced with embers of support kindled like sparks into a fire. The therapist may have to assume executive functions as a model and then step back so the family can assume them. Ex-addicts who have "made it" are very valuable in teaching addicts how to reintegrate in the straight world with straight friends. In MFT, parents teach other parents to "close the back door" and help their children individuate. Families are taught how to recognize when their child is using drugs and how to not support it. This concludes the section on structural techniques. These techniques are not used as discrete separate entities as most interventions simultaneously use two or more change modalities.

Jay Haley has utilized and developed many systems of family therapy which bridge several of the five general categories we have described. He began with important works on communications before he teamed up with Minuchin and SFT. He has evolved his own system of therapy which includes many behavioral techniques as well. His *Problem Solving Therapy* (8) is highly recommended to the reader, particularly chapters 1 and 2, which cover the first interview and giving directions. Haley describes four stages of the first interview: a social stage, in which the family is greeted and made comfortable; a problem stage, in which the presenting problem is stated; an interaction stage, in which members talk to each other in a way which actualizes the conflict, and a goal-setting stage, when the family spells out the changes it seeks. These stages are deceptively simple. When employing them it must be emphasized that no standard approach works with the wide range of problems which will be presented. With substance abusers, a more authoritative approach is frequently necessary. These stages are a matrix upon which flexibility and spontaneity can be superimposed.

In the social stage, the therapist functions as a host. The therapist should shake hands with each member, introduce himself individually and remember everyone's name. Everyone is made comfortable, and should be given a flexible choice of where to sit so that they can have a full range of seating possibilities. Seating choices are a strong initial key to family structure. Social interaction should take place with each family member before the problem is presented. This initial period of socialization is essential in all therapies. It is particularly important with Mexican-American families, where its omission would be considered gross rudeness on the part of the therapist.

Most families will feel quite defensive, particularly that their being asked to come in implies that they are the problem rather than the IP. At this stage the therapist should gather information but not share it as this could increase the inevitable defensiveness of the family. The family's mood should be noted and matched. The parents who attaches quickly to the therapist may be trying to involve him in a coalition.

The onset of the problem stage is demarcated by a shift in posture and voice tone on the part of the therapist, with responsive shifts by the family. The therapist may state what he or she knows including his position on family therapy, and ask for everyone's ideas about the problem or merely ask what the problem is (8). With substance abusers, the overt problem is obivous and need not be asked for. Thus I frequently begin with, "What's it been like to have Johnny in the family and abusing drugs?" or "How do you handle Sheila's drug abuse and requests for money?" or "What are the problems in this family?" General and ambiguous questions have the advantage of giving the family members room to display their point of view

(8). Haley recommends that "the adult who seems less involved with the problem be spoken to first and the person with the most power to bring the family back be treated with the most concern and respect." It is not a good idea to start with the addict and ask him or her why the family is there as it may appear as if the therapist is blaming the IP for everyone being there. Some therapists start with the least involved child. I find that this child can frequently provide an objective view of the family but is too passive and reticent to be put in the spotlight at the beginning of the session. The therapist should attempt to define the problem clearly so that the dysfunctional family sets can be changed by using that problem as a lever (8). Everyone should have a turn, i.e. "by preventing an overtalkative parent from being the only one who talks, the therapist is actually helping him or her" (8). Although one can assume that a child's problems are a reflection of marital problems the therapist should not verbally connect these at this stage. Likewise, the therapist should not comment directly on indirect communications such as nonverbal messages at this stage. While focusing on the IP, the family should be led to begin to look at the problem in broader terms.

The interaction stage has been described earlier in the section on actualization in SFT. Haley adds some important points here; including the idea that when two people are talking, a third should be introduced into the conversation so that ultimately everyone is talking to one another (8). Actions should be fostered, as they reveal more about the family than words. If the father's role is to be controlling and hostile, he can be asked to act that way so the family can respond to him.

Defining desired changes is important so that it is known what everyone in the family, including the IP, wants from the therapy. This leads to the therapeutic contract, which we also described in the section on SFT. "The clearer the contract is, the more organized the therapy will be." (8). The therapist can center the therapy around the presenting problem while achieving other goals which he feels are essential for families of substance abusers. The presenting and crucial problem is always the substance abuse of the IP but it must be restated in an interactional form which renders it solvable. Thus rigid problems should be made more ambiguous so there is more room to maneuver. An initial goal is frequently to enlist the family's support in initiating detoxification, hospitalization, residential care, or maintenance, when necessary. Once initial shifts provide a return to family homeostasis, the family is essential in helping the IP to stay in treatment as long as necessary. The next goal with the family is to help it set detoxification from methadone maintenance and/or gradual return to society as a priority. When the substance abuse is not sufficiently severe to intrinsically prevent family therapy from occurring, then therapy can begin without requiring a totally drug-free state as an initial goal.

The first interview should end with setting up the next appointment. Important members of the family system such as grandparents, housekeepers, siblings, cousins, aunts and uncles who did not attend should be invited. Other family members who are actively abusing chemicals present a problem. They should be invited to at least one session to understand their effect on the family and to see how the family deals with them. However, if their substance abuse is too disruptive to the family therapy, then they may be excluded from the treatment until their abuse subsides. Future sesssions will also have to deal with the family's efforts to enter that abuser into appropriate treatment. Once that person has achieved a drug-free state (or a level of occasional substance abuse), then the former substance abuser must be included in the treatment, as he or she is invariably crucial to the abuse pattern of the IP. In my experience, two drug-abusing siblings can be treated in the same residence. This is in contrast to a spouse pair, who are extremely difficult to treat in the same residential setting. This problem can be ameliorated if the families of origin of both spouses are seen for their own family therapy.

The therapist may assign homework at the end of the first session, particularly if the family has responded to directives in the session and the therapist has initiated adequate rapport.

Communications Therapy

The proponents of this system include Haley (8), Watzlawick (15), Satir (13), and Bateson (3). However, pointing out and shifting problems in communication is an important aspect of all family therapies. In this system the IP's symptom is viewed as a communication to the family and as evidence that more appropriate forms of communication are blocked (2). Incongruent messages are focused on, particularly when nonverbal communication is at variance with the verbal message (2). One of the earliest·contributions of these therapists was the "double bind" (3) which was initially demonstrated in the families of schizophrenics. The four characteristics of the double bind are: (1) two different messages are given simultaneously, frequently one verbal and one nonverbal; (2) the receiver of the message is intimately involved with the sender and so cannot become detached from the message; (3) the messages are mutually exclusive; and (4) the receiver is not permitted to comment on the double bind or express his or her feelings about it.

Double binds are present in all families, and more in the families of substance abusers than in "normal" or "neurotic" ones. However, double binds are of a different quality in the families of substance abusers than those of schizophrenics. In the former, double messages are clearer, more overt, and less confusing. However, the potential drug abuser may find that drugs are the only way he can leave the field of communication. The retreat to adolescent drug abuse then interferes with the development of alternative ways of dealing with confusing messages.

The goals of communication-centered therapy are to correct discrepancies in communication. This is achieved by having messages clearly stated, by clarifying meanings and assumptions, and by permitting feedback to clarify unclear messages (2). The therapist acts as an objective governor of communication who teaches people to speak clearly and directly in a structured, protected experience.

Experiential Therapy

Most family therapists who work with substance abusers are experiential in that they deal with the immediate moment of experience between themselves and the family. Whitaker (16) describes how involving this approach is for the therapist. "It became clear that my personal growing edge must become my central objective in every relationship if experiential therapy was for my experience, then patient modeling could be for real. If I could change, they might try to." Thus the therapist is involved as a real human being with the use of substantial self-disclosure. The therapist is a genuine, involved person who uses common sense skill and in guiding intimate conversation in order to achieve change.

Behavioral Therapy

Once again, much of the change which is achieved by successful family therapists involves the use of behavioral techniques even when the therapists are not specifically schooled in this theoretical approach. Malout and Alexander (9) and Stuart (14) are leading proponents of a purer behavioristic approach. They emphasize that the parent's responses to the child continue his undesirable behavior. Thus the parent is taught extinction of these responses and how to give positive reinforcement for desired behavior. Paul Wood (17) suggests a modified behavioral approach in which the child is never punished because being punished may be seen by the child as an alternative to desired behavior. He points out that if parents join together and present a clear message to the child with no alternatives, then behavior can be modified.

Conclusion

In closing this final chapter, Minuchin's phrase, "The road is how you walk it (10)" comes to mind. We have provided a variety of techniques from which the therapist can pick and choose those most suitable to his or her needs. However, one should never use a technique that intrinsically runs counter to one's grain. Psychoanalysis was very appealing to me when I was in training, and I was drawn to it largely because of peer pressure. However, I found structural family therapy to be much more suitable to my personal style. It permitted me to be the direct, active, involved person I know myself to be. Still, psychoanalysis provided a body of knowledge which I have found extremely valuable in every therapeutic contact I have ever made. This is particularly true when the past is not used as a "copout," but rather as a facilitator to enable immediate change to occur.

Our own backgrounds influence even the types of families with which we do best. My Jewish, enmeshed, extended family heritage helps me to tune into other similar families, particularly Italian and Greek. Having grown up with blacks helps me to understand their families. I have difficulties in breaking through the defenses of families which are totally disengaged. My background prepares me well for Latin families, but my lack of knowledge of the language and culture is an inhibiting factor. Many elements determine how we walk the road of family therapy.

I hope that the incomplete material in this chapter will stimulate the reader to study the original source material so that these intelligent minds can be experienced more fully. The ideas I have presented are meaningless if one merely reads them. They must be tried and tested before one can decide whether they fit one's personality and approach as a therapist and can be used to change other human beings within the setting of their families.

REFERENCES

1. Ackerman, N.W., *The Psychodynamics of Family Life*, New York: Basic Books, 1958.
2. Anderson, C., Lecture Delivered at Orange County Department of Mental Health, October 6, 1977.
3. Bateson, G., Jackson, D.D., Haley, J., & Weakland, J.H., Towards a Theory of Schizophrenia. *Behavioral Science* 1:251–264, 1956.

4. Boszormenyi-Nagy, I., & Spark, G., *Invisible Loyalties*, New York: Harper & Row, 1973.
5. Bowen, M., Family Therapy and Family Group Therapy. In H. Kaplan & B. Sadock (Eds.), *Comprehensive Group Psychotherapy*, New York: Williams & Wilkins, 1971.
6. Carter, E. & Orfanides, M.M., Family Therapy with One Person and the Family Therapist's Own Family. In P. Guerin (Ed.), *Family Therapy*, New York: Gardner Press, 1976, pp. 193-219.
7. Guerin, P.J. & Pendagast, E.G., Evaluation of Family System and Genogram. In P.J. Guerin (Ed.), *Family Therapy*, New York: Gardner Press, 1976, pp. 450-464.
8. Haley, J., *Problem Solving Therapy*, San Francisco, CA: Josey-Bass, 1977.
9. Malout, R.E. & Alexander, S.F., Family Crisis Intervention: A Model and Technique of Training. In R.E. Handy & J.G. Cull (Eds.), *Therapeutic Needs of the Family*, Springfield, ILL: Charles C. Thomas, 1974, pp. 47-55.
10. Minuchin, S., Families and Family Therapy, Cambridge, MA: Harvard University Press, 1974.
11. Minuchin, S., Structural Family Therapy. In S. Arieti (Ed.), *American Handbook of Psychiatry*, Vol. II, New York: Basic Books, 1974, pp. 178-192.
12. Paul, N.L. & Paul, B.B., *A Marital Puzzle*, New York: Norton, 1975.
13. Satir, V., *People Making*, Palo Alto; Science & Behavior Books, 1972.
14. Stuart, R.B., Behavioral Contracting within the Families of Delinquents. *J. Behav. Therapy & Experimental Psychiat.* 2:1-11, 1971.
15. Watzlawick, P., Weakland, J.H. & Fisch, R., *Change: Principles of Problem Formulation and Probelm Resolution*, New York: Norton, 1974.
16. Whitaker, C., A Family Is a Four-Dimensional Relationship. In P.J. Guerin (Ed.), *Family Therapy*, New York: Gardner Press, 1976, pp. 182-192.
17. Wood, P. & Schwartz, B., *How to Get Your Children to Do What You Want Them To Do*, Englewood Cliffs, NJ: Prentice-Hall, 1977.
18. Zuk, G.H. & Boszormenyi-Nagy, I. (Eds.), Family Therapy and Disturbed Families, Palo Alto: Science & Behavior Books, 1967.

FOOTNOTES

1. In the alter ego technique, each therapist sits beside a family member and speaks for that person. It is used to tap underlying feelings or to help change behavior.

INDEX

J

DATE DUE

RUNNING FOR FREEDOM

Running for Freedom

Civil Rights and Black Politics in
America Since 1941

Steven F. Lawson

Temple University Press
Philadelphia

AJM 5865- 3/3

Temple University Press, Philadelphia 19122

ISBN 0-87722-792-6

Library of Congress Cataloging-in-Publication Data

Lawson, Steven F., 1945–
    Running for freedom: civil rights and Black politics in America since
1941 / Steven F. Lawson.
        p.   cm.
    Includes bibliographical references and index.
    ISBN 0-87722-792-6
    1. Afro-Americans—Civil rights.   2. Afro-Americans—Politics and
government.   3. Civil rights movements—United States—History—20th
century.   4. United States—Politics and government—1933-1945.   5. United
States—Politics and government—1945-   I. Title.
E185.61.L38   1991
323.1'196073—dc20   90-40255

For Nancy Ann Hewitt

About the Author

Steven F. Lawson is professor of history at the University of South Florida in Tampa. He has received fellowships from the National Endowment for the Humanities, the American Council of Learned Societies, and the National Humanities Center. He has served as an adviser to the television documentary series, *Eyes on the Prize,* and has participated as an historical consultant on voting rights cases. His publications include *Black Ballots: Voting Rights in the South, 1944–1969* (1976), which was awarded the Phi Alpha Theta best first-book prize; *In Pursuit of Power: Southern Blacks and Electoral Politics, 1965–1982* (1985); and numerous articles and essays on the civil rights movement and politics.

Contents

Preface

In the more than two decades since the civil rights movement achieved some of the most momentous reforms of the twentieth century, scholars have produced a rich body of literature detailing the battle for racial and political equality. Initially, most of the works focused on the activities of major civil rights organizations and leaders and their efforts to enact national legislation, gain presidential support, and win litigation before the federal courts. In general, they concentrated on the responses of government institutions and officials to demands for social change. More recently, a second generation of scholarly studies has shifted the emphasis away from powerful leaders, interest groups, and agencies to indigenous mass movements, seeking to discover their unique structures, ideologies, strategies, and tactics. From this perspective, black protest and politics are not viewed primarily as a struggle for obtaining civil rights laws in the national arena but for liberating black communities at the grass roots level.

As scholarly inquiry has refocused the vision of this struggle "from the bottom up," it is appropriate to consider how efforts at the local level intersected with those on the national stage. Both national civil rights campaigns aimed at legislation and litigation and community organizing directed toward consciousness raising were part of a larger process of empowerment. In an interactive way, the civil rights movement altered local black institutions and shaped national goals; in turn, the actions of the federal government and established civil rights groups transformed local communities in the process of expanding freedom.

An interpretive synthesis, this book examines the freedom struggle and black political development since the beginning of World War II. Moving along two tracks, the national and the local, this study attempts to gauge the connections between the two.

Pressure from below ultimately pushed the federal government to challenge disfranchisement. Northern blacks, whose votes swung the balance of power in close national elections, demanded that lawmakers remedy the plight of blacks deprived of their rights in the South. The urgency of a response became greater as southern blacks, prevented from registering their discontent at the polls, used nonviolent civil disobedience to spark crises forcing the national government to come to their aid. In organizing against racism, the civil rights movement mobilized blacks for political action and prepared the way for extensive black participation in the electoral process following passage of the 1965 Voting Rights Act.

The franchise figured prominently in the thinking of both white officials and black protesters, though in different ways. White leaders saw the ballot as a means of promoting orderly social change during a period when black protests and hostile white reactions to them threatened civic peace and the legitimacy of democratic institutions. Blacks considered the franchise less as an implement of social cohesion and more as a weapon for destroying racist institutions and encouraging liberation. In pursuit of group power, African-Americans marshaled their forces to elect candidates of their own race, a preference that has highlighted the conflict between proportional representation and color-blind politics, between affirmative action and traditional notions of political equality.

Since 1941, the political system has been opened up to active minority participation, gradually though sometimes dramatically, and black Americans are working through it to acquire the advantages long denied them. Consequently, they have come to rely much less on the tactics of agitation and confrontation employed so effectively during the civil rights struggle and to depend more on the process of bargaining and compromise associated with professional politics. As a result, increased electoral power at the local level and influence at the national level generally have come at the expense of mass-based activism. Many black leaders have made the transition from the civil rights battlefield to the electoral arena, but they have had to heed the realities of practical politics. Furthermore, despite considerable progress, the political system has only partially settled black grievances, especially those related to economic deprivation. Race has not disappeared as a divisive element, and polarization of the electorate often stands in the way of further resolution of critical problems.

Whatever these limitations, the quest for freedom over the past half century released blacks from serving as passive objects of white domination and forged them into active agents striving to shape their own political destinies. Much of this story necessarily focuses on the South, where the civil rights movement originated and tested its most innovative political strategies. Yet the problems of racial inequality and political powerlessness were not confined to any one region, but were national in scope. Though they did not have to reacquire the ballot as was the case in the South, northern blacks nonetheless had to struggle to mobilize their communities to compete successfully for electoral office and obtain political legitimacy. In doing so, they joined black southerners in trying to redefine the meaning of success and to infuse American politics with a greater dose of democratic participation. The words of Jesse Jackson both underscore this point and provide the title for this book:

> Winning is new people running.
> Winning is also new voters.
> Winning is more young voters.
> Winning is providing hope....
>
> We're not just running for an office.
> We're running for freedom.[1]

ACKNOWLEDGMENTS

I would like to acknowledge my debt to the many scholars of civil rights history and black politics upon whose fine works I have drawn. Fortunately these fields have attracted many top-notch researchers, and their insights have contributed greatly to my own interpretive study. The bibliographical essay that appears at the end of the book is not only a guide for students but is also an expression of appreciation to the many authors from whom I have benefited. In addition to reading the works of other scholars, I also had the unique opportunity to listen to their ideas as an adviser to the production of the film documentary series *Eyes on the Prize, I* and *II*. Henry Hampton, the executive producer, gathered together an insightful group of civil rights scholars whose lively meetings turned into the

[1]"Jesse Jackson on Winning," *New York Times*, May 5, 1984, 10.

most stimulating seminars I have ever attended. At those sessions I learned a great deal from Henry and the Blackside staff, and from Professors Vincent Harding, Clay Carson, David Garrow, Darlene Clark Hine, Paul Gaston, Aldon Morris, and the other participants too numerous to name in so short a space.

Books need free time to develop and get written, and I thank the University of South Florida for granting a yearlong sabbatical allowing me to do so. I took my leave as a fellow at the National Humanities Center in Research Triangle Park in North Carolina. There I found more than arboreal splendor and an environment conducive to contemplation and writing; I encountered a resident staff whose hospitality made hard work a joy. My colleagues in the "Horseshoes Seminar"—Jack Greene, Charles Townshend, Tom Cogswell, Phil Mitsis, and Mike Holt—stimulated my thinking and kept me laughing. While in North Carolina I further enjoyed the warm company of Eugene Goodheart, Kate Townshend, Judith Bennett, Cynthia Herrup, Jacqueline Hall, Robert Korstad, Joe Sinsheimer, Val Rogers, Lorna Chafe, and Jean Anne Leuchtenburg. Both in the Tar Heel State and elsewhere I have had the good fortune to spend time with the two Bills: William Chafe and William Leuchtenburg. Besides friendship, they have provided me with models of historical synthesis that combine scholarly breadth with elegance of style.

My return to USF after such a wonderful year was made less difficult through the camaraderie of Louis Pérez, Robert Ingalls, Kelly Tipps, Georg Kleine, Tom Dilkes, Giovanna Benadusi, Fraser Ottanelli, Sylvia Wood, and Peggy Cornett. I am grateful to Mark Stern of the University of Central Florida for sharing the fruits of his research with me. I thank outside reviewers Darlene Clark Hine, Michigan State University; Gary W. Reichard, Florida Atlantic University; and George C. Wright, University of Texas at Austin, who were extremely encouraging and perceptive.

Most of all, I am indebted to Nancy Hewitt. Without her generosity of spirit, sharp intellect, and unflagging patience, this book would have been much more difficult, if not impossible, to write. Reserving a paragraph for her alone only partially expresses my gratitude. I hope I can do more for her in the many years ahead that we spend together.

Steven F. Lawson

RUNNING FOR FREEDOM

Chapter 1

World War II and the Origins of the Freedom Struggle

For African-Americans, the ultimate aim of politics, either protest or electoral, has been liberation. Seeking emancipation from the bondage of white supremacy, disfranchised southern blacks challenged the political system for admission, even as they hoped to transform it by their participation. Civil rights proponents have long believed that blacks could not be free without obtaining the right to vote. At the turn of the century, W. E. B. Du Bois set the standard for rejecting racial solutions that excluded the exercise of the franchise. Attacking Booker T. Washington for his strategy of postponing black participation at the ballot box, Du Bois insisted that the right to vote was intimately connected to first-class citizenship. Without it blacks would never command respect, protect themselves, and feel pride in their own race. To Du Bois, a scholar of the freedom struggle after the Civil War, Reconstruction provided vivid evidence that black elected officials could transform the lives of their constituents. From this experience they derived the historical lesson, summarized by Eric Foner, that "it was in politics that blacks articulated a new vision of the American state, calling upon government, both national and local, to take upon itself new and unprecedented responsibilities for protecting the civil rights of individual citizens."

The long history to obtain the right to vote suggests that reenfranchisement was considered the decisive first step toward political equality. Civil rights proponents expected participation at the polls to yield the kinds of basic benefits that groups exercising the

1

franchise customarily enjoyed. Yet for black Americans, much more was at stake. With their systematic exclusion from the electoral process, the simple acquisition of the vote constituted an essential element of liberation from enforced racial subordination. The political scientist Charles V. Hamilton, who studied the voting rights struggle both as a participant and a scholar, found this passion for the ballot very understandable. "White America had spent so much effort denying the vote to blacks," he observed, "that there was good reason to believe that they must be protecting some tool of vast importance. Perhaps it was reasonable to put so much emphasis on the one fundamental process that clearly distinguished first-class from second-class citizens."

VICTORY AT HOME AND ABROAD

Going off to war in the months after Pearl Harbor, black GIs might very well have pondered the connection between politics and freedom. They had many reasons to wonder about the principles of the democratic creed and their promise of first-class citizenship for all. Like their white counterparts they remembered December 7, 1941, when Dorrie Miller, a black sailor, performed heroic deeds that would win him the Navy Cross; but they also carried with them the memory of Sikeston, Missouri, where on January 25, 1942, a black prisoner named Cleo Wright was taken out of the local jail and cruelly burned and lynched by a white mob. Unlike Japan and its Axis partners, which were eventually defeated on the battlefield and forced to accept unconditional surrender, the killers of Cleo Wright were never brought to justice. Helping to combat fascism abroad, black fighting men and the families they left behind also demanded unconditional surrender from the forces of racism at home. Blacks failed to persuade the American government to wage total war in their behalf, but they did lay the groundwork for continuing the battle in the decades to come.

This determination to stand up for their rights, strengthened by the Second World War, grew out of both disillusionment and optimism. In response to Woodrow Wilson's pledge during World War I to make the world safe for democracy, blacks had followed the advice of Du Bois to "close ranks [and] while this war lasts, forget our special grievances." Rather than freedom, the end of the war pro-

Dorrie Miller receiving the Navy Cross from Admiral Chester Nimitz. Miller was later killed in action. (U.S. Navy, The National Archives)

duced bloody race riots and a continuation of Jim Crow practices. At the same time, African-Americans refused to plunge into despair and experienced instead a heightening of racial consciousness. The Harlem Renaissance and the black nationalist movement spearheaded by Marcus Garvey explored the roots of black identity and helped forge renewed racial solidarity. A. Philip Randolph organized workers into the Brotherhood of Sleeping Car Porters and not only fought for economic benefits from employers but also challenged racial discrimination within the trade union movement. In addition, the National Association for the Advancement of Colored People (NAACP), an interracial organization founded in 1909, kept alive the battle for equal rights by lobbying Congress to enact an antilynching bill and petitioning the Supreme Court to outlaw disfranchisment measures such as the white primary.

The Great Depression provided unexpected opportunities for black advancement. Franklin D. Roosevelt's New Deal extended economic relief to the one-third of the nation that was ill-housed, ill-clothed, and ill-fed, which included blacks as well as poor whites. Blacks profited from these programs because of their poverty, not because of their race; in fact, many New Deal agencies, especially in the South, were administered to preserve prevailing racial practices that maintained blacks in a subordinate position. Despite the perpetuation of racial discrimination and the unwillingness of President Roosevelt to fight for special civil rights measures, African-Americans welcomed federal assistance. "Any time people are out of work, in poverty, have lost their savings," Du Bois remarked, "any kind of a 'deal' that helps them is going to be favored."

Blacks showed their appreciation by abandoning their traditional allegiance to the Republican party of Abraham Lincoln and hopping aboard the Roosevelt bandwagon. This realignment was facilitated by appointments of blacks to federal posts, a sufficient number to convene an informal "black kitchen cabinet" in Washington. Whites sensitive to racial concerns headed several New Deal agencies and worked to see that relief was distributed more fairly. Furthermore, Roosevelt's selections to the Supreme Court after 1937 paved the way for a constitutional revolution that augured well for NAACP attorneys preparing a legal assault upon racial discrimination. Most of all, the President's wife, Eleanor, nurtured the growing attachment African-Americans felt toward the Roosevelt administration. Mrs. Roosevelt's commitment to civil rights was far greater than her husband's, and she served as an ally in the White House to see that complaints of black leaders received a hearing in the Oval Office. This combination of racial gestures and economic rewards led the majority of the black electorate to vote for Roosevelt beginning in 1936.

On the eve of World War II, blacks stood poised to consolidate their gains and press ahead for full equality. Their political agenda included an end to job discrimination, which helped keep black unemployment at a high 11 percent in 1940; legislation to empower the federal government to prosecute lynchers and to abolish the poll tax on voting imposed by eight southern states; the destruction of the lily-white Democratic primary; and the abandonment of the principle of "separate but equal" that actually produced segregated and unequal treatment in the armed forces, public education, and public accommodations. As the prospect of war increased, black aspirations collided with the reality of pervasive discrimination in a country where mobilization for war came first.

National defense took priority over racial equality in the armed services. As the nation inched closer to the side of the Allies and prepared to join them in war, the Army maintained its customary policy of segregation, the Navy recruited blacks only as messmates, and the Marines and Army Air Corps generally excluded them. When pressed by black leaders for integration of the military, in the fall of 1940, President Roosevelt refused to alter practices that had "been proved satisfactory over a long period of years." Instead, he directed the utilization of "the services of negroes... on a fair and equitable basis." To do otherwise, he and his advisers believed, would risk upsetting white soldiers and would lower their morale, thereby jeopardizing the war effort.

The attempt to make the system of racial separation operate more equally failed to solve the problem. Black GIs assigned to military bases in the South encountered segregation both on and off the bases. Conforming to the law and customs of the surrounding communities, the military enforced segregation in recreation clubs, theaters, and post exchanges. In one camp, a sign on a chapel announced religious services for "Catholics, Jews, Protestants, Negroes." When they received passes to travel into town, black soldiers rode on segregated buses and used Jim Crow facilities. With the population of many towns swollen with servicemen, an intolerable strain was placed on public transportation and accommodations. Crowded transit systems often led to pushing and shoving between black and white passengers, frequently ending in violence. In July 1942, a black Army private in Beaumont, Texas, refused to vacate his seat in a section of a bus reserved for whites. After his arrest, he was shot by white patrolmen while in their custody. Racial incidents such as this were becoming increasingly commonplace throughout the South that year, culminating in a riot in Alexandria, Louisiana, in which 28 blacks were wounded and nearly 3,000 arrested.

Among the black soldiers encountering wartime discrimination was Jackie Robinson. Having attended the University of California at Los Angeles before entering the service, Robinson excelled in basketball, track, baseball, and football, a sport in which he was named as a college All-American. However, these accomplishments did not guarantee him an easy time in the Army. When military officials attempted to keep him out of Officers' Candidate School at Fort Riley, Kansas, he successfully complained and gained admission to the program. Despite his athletic prowess, Robinson was barred because of his race from playing on the baseball team at the Army training camp. In protest, he refused to join the football team, which was open to blacks. In 1944, Lieutenant Robinson again challenged unfair racial treatment. While stationed at Ford Hood, Texas, he steadfastly refused to follow a bus driver's order that he sit in the back of the vehicle with the other black passengers. Subjected to a military court-martial for his defiance of local segregationist customs, the former All-American athlete was found innocent.

Black civilians also encountered blatant racial prejudice as they sought employment in wartime industries. Blacks had been especially hard hit by the depression, and as the economy geared up for war production after 1940, they looked forward to taking their places in the booming factories. They had to wait in line, however, behind millions of unemployed white workers who were the first choice of employers. When African-Americans showed up looking for work at aircraft plants, they were informed that "the Negro will be considered only as janitors and in other similar capacities." Of 100,000 aircraft workers in 1940, only 240 were black. In related electrical and rubber industries, black employees constituted a meager 1 percent and 3 percent of the work force. The federal government, which let out war contracts and could have challenged discriminatory hiring practices, collaborated with employers in reinforcing them. According to the policy of the United States Employment Service, "white only" requests for defense labor would be filled in conformity with "the social pattern of the local community."

That whites did not intend the war to alter race relations was demonstrated in several other ways as well. Though the process of storing blood plasma was developed by a black scientist, Dr. Charles Drew, the Red Cross refused to mix donations of whites and blacks in their blood banks. In Tennessee, those blacks who wanted to fight for their country experienced difficulty in getting enlisted by all-white selective service centers. Refusing to appoint blacks to sit on draft boards, the governor of the state explained: "This is a white man's country. The Negro had nothing to do with the settling of America." In neighboring Mississippi, to avoid any suggestion that the war against totalitarianism overseas was meant to affect the status of blacks at home, the state legislature ordered the deletion of all references to voting, elections, and democracy in textbooks used in black schools.

Despite these racist setbacks, most blacks supported the war effort and responded to the global conflict as did other patriotic Americans. One survey revealed that 66 percent of blacks considered that they had a great stake in the outcome of the war and 43 percent felt that they would be better off than before. Though daring victories of nonwhite Japanese over Caucasians early in the war inspired admiration in many blacks, the majority realized what would happen if the Axis powers emerged victorious. "If Hitler wins," the NAACP pointed out, "every right we now possess and for which we have struggled here in America for three centuries will be instantaneously wiped out." At least if the Allies triumphed, black Americans would be free to continue fighting for their democratic rights. Desiring full participation as American citizens, they had no real difficulty choosing which side they were on.

Nevertheless, blacks remained sorely troubled by the discrimination they encountered at home. Their loyalty was not at issue, but as one knowledgeable observer declared, many blacks displayed a "lack of enthusiasm for a war which they did not believe is being fought for true democratic principles." Lloyd Brown, a black soldier stationed in Salina, Kansas, who was refused service at a restaurant that admitted German prisoners of war, poignantly expressed his disappointment: "If we were *untermenschen* [sub-human species] in Nazi Germany they would break our bones. As 'colored' men in Salina, they only break our hearts." That the price of a fascist victory would cost more than an Allied one was acknowledged by African-Americans; yet this awareness did not bring contentment. No greater slogan of despair over the gap between the democratic creed and discriminatory practice existed than in the sardonic statement popular at the time: "Here lies a black man killed fighting a yellow man for the protection of a white man."

Cynical yet hopeful, African-Americans used the war to pursue their own political aims. While blacks sought to defend their country on foreign battlefields alongside other American citizens, they also intended to open up a second front for freedom at home. Wartime ideology extolling the virtues of the "four freedoms" and denouncing the doctrines of Aryan racism was not lost upon blacks. On January 16, 1943, a black newspaper, the *Baltimore Afro-American*, published a "Draftee's Prayer," a poem that tersely summed up the twin goals black soldiers fought for:

So while I fight
Wrong over there
See that my folks
Are treated fair.

Black leaders agreed and seized the opportunity to turn America's
lofty pronouncements to their advantage. Shortly after Pearl Harbor, Walter White, the executive secretary of the NAACP, asserted
that "declarations of war do not lessen the obligation to preserve
and extend civil liberties here while the fight is being made to restore freedom from dictatorship abroad." These sentiments were
echoed in the pages of the *Pittsburgh Courier*, a black newspaper
that mounted a campaign for the "double V," victory at home and
overseas. In this way, the black press not only reflected the increasing militancy of its readers, but also reinforced black support for the
war against the Fascists. Not willing to postpone their egalitarian
demands as they had during World War I, blacks planned to attack
"the principle and practice of compulsory segregation in our American society."

This new assertiveness on behalf of full equality had its most
powerful expression in the March on Washington Movement
(MOWM). Organized by A. Philip Randolph, the militant trade
union leader, the MOWM represented both the exclusiveness of
racial pride and the integration of blacks into the mainstream of
American life. The group barred whites from participation not out
of prejudice but because, as Randolph explained, an all-black
movement would promote "faith by Negroes in Negroes." The
main goals of the movement were the desegregation of the armed
forces and the elimination of discrimination in employment by government contractors. To gain these ends, Randolph proposed a
mass march on Washington by some 75,000 to 100,000 blacks to
take place in June 1941. Though this proposal had the endorsement
of established black groups such as the NAACP, the MOWM derived its power from the black masses rather than middle-class reformers, who generally worked for change through the courts and
legislatures. In this way, the MOWM foreshadowed the successful
protest tactics of the later civil rights movement.

The MOWM timed its efforts well. The prospect of tens of thousands of blacks descending on the nation's capital as the United
States prepared for war disturbed the President. Concerned about

tarnishing the nation's image as well as hampering attempts to rally support for the Allies, Roosevelt tried to get Randolph to halt the demonstration. Unsuccessful, the chief executive agreed partially to meet the movement's demands. Issuing Executive Order 8802, the President created the Fair Employment Practice Committee (FEPC) to investigate and publicize cases of employment discrimination. However, he left the policy of segregation in the military basically unchanged. Not getting all that he wanted, Randolph nevertheless called off the march, convinced that he had won an important political victory and confident that the movement would continue to apply pressure for social change. The MOWM did function throughout the war, but it never reached the same level of influence as it had during this first confrontation with the President.

Rising black militancy stimulated the growth of existing civil rights organizations. Foremost among them, the NAACP kept up the pressure to lower racial barriers along the color line. Although this oldest of civil rights groups had thrown its weight behind the MOWM, it preferred to operate in the traditional arenas of litigation, legislation, and lobbying. The national association's staff of dedicated attorneys prepared suits against white Democratic primaries in the South, segregation of passengers on interstate buses, and unequal educational facilities. The NAACP functioned as a clearinghouse for complaints from black soldiers and civilians experiencing discriminatory treatment and directed them to the attention of officials in Washington. It prodded the Justice Department to investigate and prosecute perpetrators of lynching and other forms of violence and joined with white liberals and labor unions in petitioning Congress and state legislatures to lift poll tax restrictions on the ballot. As a reflection both of its increased activism and the rising expectations of blacks, NAACP membership soared from 50,000 in 1940 to over 450,000 in 1946. Of these new recruits an estimated 15,000 black GIs signed up while they were still in uniform.

In addition, black activism spawned the formation of new protest groups. Most important for the future was the creation of the Congress of Racial Equality (CORE) in 1942. Like Randolph's March on Washington Movement, CORE believed in the tactic of direct action to spotlight racist problems and bring them to an immediate resolution; in contrast to MOWM, however, the group welcomed white participation. Founded in Chicago by pacifists committed to the principle of nonviolence, its interracial membership initiated sit-in and picketing campaigns to desegregate public accommodations in northern cities. These innovative techniques led to the desegregation of restaurants and movie theaters in Detroit, Los Angeles, Denver, and Chicago, and they caught on with black college students, such as those at Howard University, who successfully integrated several restaurants in Washington, D.C.

As blacks actively confronted Jim Crow and pushed for their rights, they often came into sharp conflict with hostile whites. The friction did not result as much from legal battles in the courts and in legislatures and along picket lines as from the increasing daily contact between blacks and whites in the overcrowded communities the war had produced. The influx of blacks into urban areas in search of jobs brought them into direct competition with older white residents and newer white migrants for employment, housing, and recreational facilities. By 1943, 50,000 southern blacks and 500,000 whites had swarmed into Detroit to find work. Instead, many of them found substandard housing and high rates of tuberculosis and infant mortality. These deplorable conditions fell hardest upon blacks, and when attempts were made to provide some measure of relief whites resisted them. On June 20, 1943, this explosive situation finally erupted in a bloody race riot over a fracas at an amusement park, and after the smoke cleared 34 blacks had been killed, 700 injured, and $200 million in property destroyed. Only the intervention of federal troops restored peace to the "Motor City." By the end of the year, another 241 racial disturbances in forty-seven cities had broken out, though none as severe as in Detroit.

With violence spreading throughout American cities, civil rights leaders became alarmed. Following a riot in Harlem, New York City's black newspaper, the *Amsterdam News*, warned that only by making blacks "feel that they are part of this country" would the violence cease. The way to achieve that, most black leaders believed, was to continue to press for the "double V" but to do so through peaceful channels. The NAACP called upon its chapters to step up the campaign for racial equality in the courts, legislatures, and ballot boxes, thereby removing potentially incendiary conflicts from the streets. This preference for seeking social change in a deliberate and orderly fashion diminished support for the tactics of direct mass action. After 1943, the once popular MOWM received criticism from the black press as "just Ku Kluxism in reverse" for its all-black policy, and a poll of black newspaper readers showed that 70.6 percent opposed the March on Washington Movement. Established civil rights leaders and their organizations did not retreat from the goal of securing full equality, but their strategy of measured militancy helped defuse the appeal of more confrontational approaches toward achieving that end.

To combat racial discrimination, they increasingly put a premium on attracting sympathetic whites. Before the war, white liberals thought primarily in economic rather than racial terms. They figured that the New Deal's recovery programs would lift blacks out of poverty along with whites and improve black chances of gaining acceptance for civil and political equality. However, the end of the depression had not significantly extended first-class citizenship. Wartime ideals and the persistence of racism exposed by the 1943 riots persuaded liberal whites to assign a higher priority to civil rights. Fighting Hitler's atrocities abroad shifted the focus of racism at home from an economic to a moral issue, prompting liberals to try to prove that their society did not behave like Nazi Germany. Accordingly, they joined with blacks to set up interracial committees in scores of communities to open up better lines of communication and avoid the type of situation that engendered racial violence. The increasing presence of whites in the civil rights movement after 1943 had a further moderating effect on black militancy and reinforced those who favored the tactics of cooperation over confrontation, legalism over disruption, the ballot over direct action. The most prominent of all white liberals, Eleanor Roosevelt, endorsed this approach in contending that blacks should strive for complete equality but they should "not do too much demanding [or] try to bring those advances about any more quickly than they were offered."

Mrs. Roosevelt's husband had the power to influence the pace of racial change, and he chose to act cautiously. According to the historian Harvard Sitkoff, President Roosevelt held a paternalistic view toward racial affairs, believing that the "Negro" was "an unfortunate ward of the nation to be treated kindly and with charity as a reward for good behavior." Ordinarily preferring gradualism and education to promote racial toleration, FDR felt even more inclined toward those methods at a time when winning the war was his chief concern. Though he disapproved of any racial prejudice that lowered black morale, he also took into account the position of southern white politicians who opposed any change in the racial status quo and whose legislative support for war appropriations he greatly needed. Black voters had joined the New Deal Democratic coalition, but their political clout remained weaker than that of Dixie politicos. In offering encouraging words to African-Americans, "Dr. Win-the-War" Roosevelt never forgot that while the overseas conflict lasted "the long-range problems of racial and minority-majority antagonism cannot be settled. . . . [T]he war must be won first."

The experience of the Fair Employment Practice Committee demonstrated this point. Created by Roosevelt to head off the proposed June 1941 march on Washington, the FEPC was authorized to investigate discrimination in defense-related employment but lacked the power of enforcement. Instead of coercion it relied on publicity and persuasion to expose and alter biased practices. Reflecting the President's philosophy, committee members believed that winning the war should take precedence over the pursuit of racial equality. One commentator summed up their thinking: "For the government to terminate an important war contract by reason of the contractor's indulgence in discriminatory employment would be highly impractical."

Unable to compel compliance and unwilling to alienate powerful employers, the FEPC achieved mixed success. Of 8,000 complaints submitted to the committee, two-thirds were dismissed without merit and only one-fifth were settled in the South. Employers and unions, which were also covered under the executive order, ignored 35 of 45 compliance decrees. For example, the railroad brotherhoods and southern railway lines signed an agreement restricting employment opportunities for blacks and then disregarded an FEPC order against it. The government did not dare take action that might provoke a crippling strike by a powerful union and also antagonize the white South. In contrast, the President sometimes backed the committee when the political risks were not so great. In Philadelphia, a strike by a dissident union faction in protest of an FEPC ruling upgrading black jobs on streetcars triggered President Roosevelt's decision to send in federal troops to resume normal operation of the transit system. In this instance, a stronger rival union supported the black position, and the residents of the "City of Brotherly Love" did not threaten a political revolt over the settlement. Even the lukewarm record of the FEPC proved too much for southern members of Congress, who succeeded in 1944 in enacting a provision that paved the way for the committee's legislative funding to be cut off two years later.

Although blacks did obtain some benefits from the FEPC, their main economic gains resulted from labor shortages during the war. As millions of whites marched off to battle and industrial production expanded, blacks helped plug the labor-power holes on the home front. Black employment rose by over 1 million; the number of unemployed dropped from 937,000 to 151,000; union membership doubled; and the percentage of blacks in defense work climbed from 4.6 to 8.3. African-Americans found jobs in factories where employers had initially resisted hiring them. Under the strain of war, the number of black employees increased from 6,000 to 14,000 in shipyards and from zero to 5,000 in aircraft plants. The federal government itself gave black employment a big boost, increasing its rolls from 60,000 to 200,000 Afro-American workers. On the down side, most of the blacks entering the labor force took jobs at low levels as janitors and custodians. Consequently, blacks made up only 3.6 percent of craftsmen and foremen; 2.8 percent of clerical and sales personnel; and 3.3 percent of professional and technical staff. Concentrated in low-paying jobs, black families on the average earned about half the income of whites. Nevertheless, the improvements in their economic condition whetted black appetites for more and raised expectations that opportunities would continue to grow once the war ended.

African-Americans also beefed up their political muscle as a force for freedom. In the North, where voting booths were open to blacks, both the Democratic and Republican parties courted them. In 1940, the GOP presidential candidate, Wendell Wilkie, campaigned hard for the black vote and made slight inroads in a losing effort. In lining up behind Roosevelt's third-term bid, the black electorate moved the victorious President to grant them concessions. Black support spurred FDR to add an antidiscrimination clause to the Selective Service Act, appoint Colonel Benjamin O. Davis as the first black (brigadier) general, select blacks as civilian aides in the War Department and Selective Service, and establish an Army Air Corps training school at Tuskegee Institute. Four years later, though the Democrats did not draft a strong civil rights plank for their platform, FDR personally called for a permanent

FEPC and elimination of restrictions on the ballot. Again, the black electorate responded enthusiastically.

Because black support for the President was much stronger than for the Democratic party as a whole, the minority vote seemed very much up for grabs once the popular chief executive was no longer a candidate. In 1940, 67 percent of Afro-American voters had backed the President, though only 42 percent considered themselves Democrats. After the election in 1944, both Democrats and Republicans took note that a shift in the black vote in eight states would have defeated Roosevelt's reelection for a fourth term. Given their strategic location in major urban centers in northern states rich in Electoral College votes, blacks looked forward to wielding the balance of power in close presidential races in the future.

Meanwhile, in the South, where blacks remained largely disfranchised, wartime developments lifted hopes for change. In 1944, the Supreme Court's *Smith v. Allwright* decision struck down the Democratic white primary. Victory in these preliminary contests ordinarily determined the winners in subsequent general elections in the one-party South, and hence the destruction of the white primary would remove a major obstacle to black participation in the region. The assault on the primary had begun two decades earlier. In 1923, after the Texas Legislature officially barred blacks from participating in Democratic primaries, the NAACP mounted a legal challenge that had great significance for blacks in the Lone Star State as well as for those in the rest of the South where the exclusionary practice also flourished.

Initially, the NAACP convinced the judiciary of its argument, but these triumphs neither settled the issue nor did they gain for blacks the right to vote. In 1927 and again in 1932, the Supreme Court ruled that a state could not officially authorize racial discrimination in the fashion of Texas without violating the Fourteenth Amendment of the Constitution. However, in a pattern that would become increasingly common in the face of rising black protest, southern officials resisted attempts to dismantle segregation and disfranchisement by countering with measures purporting to conform with the law while at the same time managing to evade it. In this instance, the Texas Legislature obeyed the court's pronouncement by repealing its white primary regulation, thereby leaving the state Democratic party free to adopt rules denying blacks access to its internal affairs. Previously the high tribunal had struck down the white primary because the state had deliberately created and maintained it, but the court had left open the question of whether a political party, operating as a private association, could deny blacks participation in its activities. Presented with another case in 1935, the Supreme Court decided that a political party had the constitutional right to fix its own qualifications for membership and therefore could legally exclude blacks if it so desired. In *Grovey v. Townsend* the justices argued that the conduct of a primary was strictly a private party matter and was immune from the guarantees of the Fifteenth Amendment, which forbade interference with the right of blacks to vote in general elections open to the public.

Before they could overcome this judicial blow to reenfranchisement, blacks first had to settle some differences that had hampered their legal battle. The main problem concerned the conflict for control of the case between local blacks and the NAACP, headquartered in New York City. Run in a hierarchical manner, the national association insisted on maintaining tight supervision of its programs from the top down. This style irritated some black attorneys and other leaders in Texas, who believed they should play a greater role in shaping policies and legal strategies directly affecting their community. They also wanted the NAACP to make a greater effort in recruiting black lawyers whenever possible to try suits and to rely less heavily on whites. These tensions had produced unfortunate results. Against the wishes of the NAACP, which considered the attempt premature, a group of black Texans had initiated the *Grovey* case and suffered a severe setback to the cause of black voting rights.

Following this debacle, the NAACP sought to remedy the difficulties. Under the leadership of Charles Houston, the dean of Howard Law School, and his protégé, Thurgood Marshall, the national association assembled a talented staff of black attorneys and labored to work more closely and harmoniously with blacks in the local areas from which the legal challenges arose. This interaction between national and grassroots forces became the hallmark of the burgeoning civil rights struggle. In the wake of *Grovey*, the NAACP organized black Texans into a mass movement for first-class citizenship. Its state convention created a Democratic Primary Defense Fund, which galvanized black churches, civic leagues, fraternities, and business groups behind a fund-raising campaign to finance a new court suit. "Brother, have you spared that dime for your liberation and freedom?" asked a black newspaper, and the response was generous. As Darlene Clark Hine has observed: "The white primary became a rallying cry for black Texans and assisted them in developing black solidarity." In addition to contributing money and generating publicity, local blacks furnished the plaintiff to contest the white primary. Represented by Marshall, a Houston dentist and NAACP member named Lonnie Smith filed litigation against S. E. Allwright, a state election official who had refused to allow him to cast a ballot in the 1940 Democratic primary.

On this fourth attempt to wipe out the offensive and highly resilient discriminatory electoral procedure, African-Americans finally triumphed. Drawing upon a recent opinion in a case brought by the federal government against voting fraud in a Louisiana primary, on April 3, 1944, the Supreme Court reversed *Grovey*. The justices held that where a primary was an integral part of the electoral process, as was the circumstance in Texas, blacks were entitled to the protection of the Fifteenth Amendment, which sheltered their right to vote from racial discrimination. Smith not only won for himself the right to participate in the crucial Democratic primary, but he greeted his victory as a second emancipation for blacks throughout the South. The Houston dentist gleefully commented that this ruling would affect the political history of the country more than any case since the infamous *Dred Scott* decision before the Civil War. If the joy of victory caused this happy plaintiff to exaggerate somewhat, many could still agree with the assessment of an NAACP attorney that the "Supreme Court released and galvanized democratic forces" which one day would transform the political life of the South and the nation.

Toward this end, suffragists had also aimed their attack at another troublesome obstacle to black voting: the poll tax. Confined to the South, this financial requirement differed from state to state but generally discouraged the poor of both races from going to the polls. In fact, it worked a greater hardship on whites than on blacks, as long as the white primary and the racially biased administration of literacy tests operated to chase southern blacks away from the ballot box. Encouraged by Roosevelt's New Deal, progressive southerners tried to find ways of extending economic and political democracy to the region. Consequently, in 1941 they formed the National Committee to Abolish the Poll Tax, composed of labor, liberal, and civil rights groups. Actively cooperating with the

NAACP and the Congress of Industrial Organizations (CIO), the anti-poll-tax alliance lobbied national lawmakers to enact a measure repealing the restrictive levy in federal elections.

America's entry into World War II provided proponents of abolition with fresh ammunition for their attack. Reformers claimed that the disfranchising effects of the tax hurt public morale, and they compared the decline of free elections in Fascist-dominated Europe with the shrinking of the electorate in the poll tax South. Twice during the war, the repeal advocates convinced the House of Representatives to support their proposal, only to suffer defeat in the Senate. Though whites stood more to gain than did blacks from elimination of the tax, southern foes warned their constituents of the dangerous racial consequences of legislative repeal. "If the [anti]poll tax bill passes," Senator Theodore Bilbo of Mississippi contended, "the next step will be an effort to remove the registration qualification, the educational qualification of the negroes. If that is done we will have no way of preventing negroes from voting."

Despite such fears, pressure from the progressive, interracial coalition encouraged Congress to take some limited but positive action to soften the burden of the poll tax. In 1942, lawmakers exempted soldiers from having to meet poll tax requirements to vote in national elections. Reformers also made some progress at the local level. In 1945, Georgia abolished its franchise tax entirely, and at the war's end most of its neighbors in the region released their returning veterans from having to pay for casting a vote. Even with these wartime changes, most blacks remained disfranchised. Southern officials discriminated against black soldiers seeking to claim their poll tax exemption, and the majority of blacks continued to encounter insurmountable suffrage barriers, such as literacy tests. Yet the easing of poll tax restrictions, together with the Texas white primary ruling, had a liberating impact. Between 1940 and 1947, the proportion of southern blacks enrolled to vote climbed from 3 percent to 12 percent.

Taking advantage of these opportunities, blacks marshaled their forces at the local level to convert votes into power. To stimulate both greater registration and political involvement, grassroots organizations offered citizenship classes, conducted poll tax payment drives, and initiated challenges to discrimination within state Democratic parties. In one imaginative move that would be copied in the 1960s, black activists in South Carolina, in cooperation with the

NAACP, formed a statewide Progressive Democratic Party (PDP), which attempted to unseat the regular Democrats at the 1944 national convention. Though unsuccessful, the PDP still managed to stimulate political activity, and by 1948, more than 35,000 blacks voted in the regular Democratic party primary, a figure ten times greater than the turnout four years earlier.

The South Carolina campaigns received the enlightened guidance of three members of the state's black middle class. Segregation had produced unequal treatment and inferior public facilities for nonwhites, but it had also provided blacks with opportunities to develop separate religious, economic, and civic institutions under their exclusive control. Having achieved a measure of independence within their business and professional spheres, some of them attempted to gain for the majority of blacks the right to participate in governing their own communities. The Reverend James Hinton held a managerial position with Pilgrim Life Insurance Company, a black-owned enterprise, and headed the Palmetto State's NAACP Conference. He was joined by Osceola McKaine, a native of Sumter and a World War I veteran who had established a successful restaurant business in Belgium before returning home shortly after the onslaught of Hitler's army. Rounding out the trio, John McCray provided valuable leadership as editor of the *Lighthouse and Informer*, a black newspaper in Columbia that editorialized against racial injustice and for first-class citizenship. As Hinton, McKaine, and McCray showed, middle-class blacks did not have to confine their egalitarian impulses to seeking change exclusively through the courts. They worked tirelessly to organize South Carolina blacks behind a variety of grassroots activities to regain the precious ballot snatched away in the late nineteenth century. McKaine, also an editor of the *Lighthouse and Informer*, saw the black masses aroused by the war against fascism and responsive to the renewed efforts to advance their political fortunes. In his view, the creation of the PDP marked a revolutionary beginning "to give the disinherited men and women of both races in South Carolina some voice in their government, [and] some control over their destinies."

To reinforce their local drives, black leaders requested federal assistance. They usually met with disappointment. An organizer of the South Carolina PDP held the national Democratic party "as responsible as the state party for the denial of membership to Negroes in that it tolerates discrimination in the South." This policy would not change so long as white voters constituted the foundation of the Democratic party in the South and their elected representatives played a key role in determining the outcome of legislation desired by the President. Based on this political calculation, Roosevelt's Justice Department refused to follow up *Smith v. Allwright* with criminal prosecutions against suffrage violators. When Senator Lister Hill of Alabama, a legislative ally of President Roosevelt, heard that such legal action was contemplated in his home state, he warned the White House that it would "be a very dangerous mistake." Worried about a political revolt at the polls in Dixie and concerned about getting along with the southern-influenced Senate Judiciary Committee, the Justice Department backed off with the President's blessing. For similar reasons the chief executive declined to give more than lip service in favor of congressional measures designed to repeal the remaining poll tax requirements in the South.

While Roosevelt attempted delicately to balance the political wishes of southern whites and blacks, demographic forces were in motion that would eventually upset that equilibrium. During the war southern blacks voted with their feet and migrated northward, more than doubling the number of their race living above the Mason-Dixon line. Increased urbanization was propelled by changing labor patterns on the farm. The extension of mechanized agriculture, especially the use of the tractor, during the decade of the 1940s pushed blacks off the farm and sent them to northern cities in search of jobs. Remembering the plight of friends and relatives left behind, they intended to use their unfettered ballots to select candidates favoring civil rights measures. Some 750,000 blacks journeyed from rural areas to cities within the South, and there they usually encountered a less restrictive application of suffrage requirements. Moreover, the urban environment afforded wider social space to develop racial solidarity and community organizations for political and economic emancipation. Away from the tight regulations imposed by the plantation economy, they were more readily exposed to the wartime promises of democracy and became more determined to challenge enduring forms of racial discrimination. These demographic changes were a precondition for the building of a movement to transform race relations in the postwar South.

The tempo and direction of that change would be determined by the interconnected efforts of federal officials and local black communities across the South. Civil rights groups, including national associations and their local chapters, as well as civic, fraternal, and religious organizations initiated the struggle to eradicate racial barriers, mobilize the black masses to confront these obstacles, and apply ongoing pressure on white officials to demolish them. In cities and towns throughout the region, blacks were joining together to transform their own lives economically, politically, and psychologically, seeking to liberate themselves totally from the bonds of oppression. The process of struggle could free blacks spiritually and forge racial pride and solidarity, but their liberation would not be completed without allies in Washington helping them crack potent southern white opposition and enacting their goals into law.

World War II was the seedtime of the racial and legal metamorphosis that was to sweep over the South. The war propelled a growth of racial consciousness and a burst of militancy that foreshadowed the assault on Jim Crow. It provided new economic and political opportunities and at the same time underscored the failure of the nation to allow African-Americans to take full advantage of them. Having caught a glimpse of a better life and frustrated by the resistance to achieving it, blacks did not intend to retreat. They had already seen some of the old hurdles tumble in the courts, and their nascent political influence had pressured the President into supporting limited reforms. By V-J Day, black troops had fought together with whites on an emergency basis in the European theater of war, and planning for integration had begun in the Navy. Surveys showed that the more contact whites had with blacks in the military and in the workplace the more likely they were to oppose segregation. Buoyed by these initial advances and imbued with egalitarian wartime ideology, African-Americans looked ahead with great expectations for the future.

A TROUBLED PEACE

Black veterans marched at the forefront of those demanding unconditional surrender from the forces of fascism at home. Having fought for their country and demonstrated their worth on the battlefield, they returned to their communities intent on challenging the racist practices they had temporarily escaped from. On May 19, 1945, before shipping out of Okinawa, Private Herbert W. Seward expressed the view of many of his black buddies in a letter to the *Pittsburgh Courier*:

Our people are not coming back with the idea of just taking up where they left off. We are going to have the things that are rightfully due us or else, which is a very large order, but we have proven beyond all things that we are people and not just the servants of the whiteman.

By reading black newspapers and letters from home they had kept track of the many incidents of racial discrimination and abuse that blacks experienced during the war. The "majority will return home," Walter White of the NAACP predicted, "convinced that whatever betterment of their lot is achieved must come from their own efforts."

One such veteran was Jackie Robinson. Having played on an integrated baseball squad in college, Robinson was determined to crack the color line that barred blacks from the major leagues. While playing professional ball with the Kansas City Monarchs in the Negro Leagues in 1945, he was spotted by the Brooklyn Dodgers' owner, Branch Rickey, who wanted to integrate the country's national pastime. Displaying the same fierce pride that pushed him

World War II veteran Jackie Robinson integrated major league baseball and became a star with the Brooklyn Dodgers. (UPI/Bettmann Newsphotos)

to protest wartime discrimination, Robinson readily accepted the challenge. "I'm ready to take the chance," he declared in anticipation of his task. "Maybe I'm doing something for my race." After playing a season in the minor leagues, in 1947, Robinson joined the Dodgers and succeeded in opening up one of America's most cherished institutions to blacks. Indeed, Robinson served as an enormous source of pride for all African-Americans looking for expanded opportunities and equal rights in the postwar years.

At the same time, black southerners directed much of their energy toward extending the right to vote, which they considered the essential weapon in gaining and protecting the rest of their civil rights. Many black GIs had barely taken time to remove their uniforms before they marched to local courthouses to register to vote. In Birmingham, Alabama, about a hundred ex-soldiers paraded in double file through the main street of the city, ending up at the registrars' office. Veterans like these reasoned that as long as blacks did not determine who governed them, they would continue to be victimized by racial discrimination. One discharged soldier from Georgia thought that conditions would be better in the future. "Now that the war has been won," he wrote, "the most difficult job ahead of us is to win the peace at home. 'Peace is not the absence of war, but the presence of justice' which may be obtained, first, by becoming a citizen and registered voter. If you become a registered voter we may be able to win the peace." Black leaders concurred. The *Pittsburgh Courier* predicted "that once Negroes start voting in large numbers...the jim crow laws will be endangered and the whole elaborate pattern of segregation threatened and finally destroyed."

Southern officials tried to block this chain of events at the first step, resorting to a variety of racist subterfuges to perpetuate black disfranchisement. Even after the destruction of the white primary, registrars were able to exclude blacks from the suffrage by administering literacy tests for prospective voters. In the hands of bigoted clerks these examinations were manipulated to prevent qualified black applicants from enrolling and were interpreted to allow illiterate whites to pass. White registrars accomplished this biased feat by asking only blacks the meaning of highly technical clauses in state and federal constitutions or by asking them such absurd questions as "How many bubbles are there in a bar of soap?" One Mississippi official frankly admitted that he "didn't care which way the

[Negroes] answered those questions, it wouldn't come up to his satisfaction."

Mississippi had long been a leader in reducing blacks to second-class citizenship. Combining the white primary, literacy tests, and the poll tax, with terror and coercion thrown in for good measure, the Magnolia State had created a "closed society." Blacks lived at the bottom of a rigid caste structure, held down by a separate and unequal educational system, dependent upon white-controlled economic institutions for survival, and disciplined to remain in place by official and private acts of violence. Generations of white supremacists had sternly taught Mississippi blacks that participation in civic life was folly. Not surprisingly, in 1944, out of 350,000 adult black Mississippians only 2,500 had managed to register to vote.

However, for several years after World War II the idea that "politics is white folks' business" was challenged by a small but determined group in the Magnolia State. In 1944, a small circle of middle-class blacks from Jackson, led by T. B. Wilson, the secretary of the local NAACP chapter, formed the Mississippi Progressive Voters League. Designed to stimulate black enrollment, the league attempted to educate black citizens to recognize the importance of the suffrage. This task was made a bit easier after *Smith v. Allwright.* Until that ruling, Wilson explained, blacks "were indifferent, disinterested, but when we worked up this case of registering and voting them because the Supreme Court decision gave us to understand that we could vote, then they began to register." In addition, like most other southern states, Mississippi exempted veterans from payment of the poll tax for voting. Their racial and political consciousness heightened by the war, black veterans in Mississippi attempted to exercise their franchise rights.

In doing so, they ran up against Senator Theodore "The Man" Bilbo. An outspoken bigot whose storehouse of invectives was plentiful enough to smear racial, religious, and ethnic minorities alike, Bilbo had few peers to match the virulence of his antiblack tirades. In the midst of his reelection campaign in 1946, he encouraged white Mississippians to keep the ballot boxes shut to the growing number of blacks who were seeking to register. "The Man" unabashedly suggested to the registrars that if "there is a single man or woman serving...who cannot think up questions enough to disqualify undesirables then write Bilbo or any good lawyer, and there are a hundred good questions which can be furnished." Bilbo was confident that the Magnolia State's brand of racial justice would not pose a hazard to these biased attempts. "How many registrars do you think can be convicted here in the state of Mississippi?" he asked rhetorically. If such chicanery did not do the trick, the senator informed his audiences: "You and I know what's the best way to keep the nigger from voting. You do it the night before the election. I don't have to tell you more than that." Apparently getting his not too subtle message, one county clerk refused to register a black veteran because "niggers don't vote in this county." To add injury to insult, the rejected ex-GI was abducted and flogged by white vigilantes as he left the courthouse. Given these potent lessons in repression, fewer than 1 percent of adult blacks registered to vote, and a majority of white electors cast their ballots to return Bilbo to the Senate.

Meanwhile, Bilboism did not go unchallenged. Aided by the NAACP and sympathetic whites in the North, the Progressive Voters League compiled affidavits documenting the racist nature of the senator's demagoguery. Sufficient evidence was accumulated to convince the Senate to send a special committee to conduct public hearings in Jackson on the charge that Bilbo's election was tainted with fraud and corruption. Because the five-member investigation team contained a Democratic majority including three southerners, and because it was chaired by Allen Ellender, an avid defender of white supremacy in Louisiana, blacks did not expect a favorable report. Instead, they hoped to expose how disfranchisement operated in Mississippi and to arouse northern senators to block Bilbo from taking his seat.

On December 2, 1946, blacks journeyed from all over the state to puncture the myth of their contentment with race relations in Mississippi. They jammed the hearing room to testify before a mixed gallery of friends, hostile whites, and the national press. With veterans in the forefront, they braved the danger of possible retaliation from angry whites resentful of the unfavorable publicity the proceedings trumpeted throughout the country. An observer compared the plight of the black witnesses to that of a "pedestrian in any typical American city or community, attempting to cross the street with a green light and the law in his favor but who, nevertheless, is seriously injured or killed in the process."

For three days courageous black veterans recounted their frustrated attempts to enroll and vote. They detailed stories of threats, beatings, and police brutality. The testimony revealed that the registrars misused the literacy exam to prevent them from qualifying to vote. Amazingly the registrars themselves corroborated the damaging testimony. One official admitted that he had told a black not to cast his ballot, because "in the southern states it has always been a white primary, and I just couldn't conceive of this darkey going up there to vote." The candor of this testimony prompted an NAACP representative on the scene to remark: "Sometimes I think Jesus Christ must be ill at ease in Mississippi."

Although these revelations proved that blacks were disfranchised on racial grounds, the Ellender committee voted to exonerate Bilbo of any personal guilt. Instead, the Democratic majority blamed the blacks' failure to vote on the white primary tradition and on lethargy. However, the challenge was not over. As the NAACP had hoped, when the matter reached the Senate floor, in early January 1947, a bipartisan coalition of Republicans and northern Democrats succeeded in postponing consideration of Bilbo's credentials. Suffering from jaw cancer, the Mississippi senator agreed temporarily to withdraw his claim to his seat while he sought treatment for his ailment. This solution turned out to be permanent: on August 21, "The Man" died.

Incipient black militancy in Mississippi yielded limited short-run returns, but it raised promising expectations for the long run. Although Bilbo had departed, the white supremacist system lived on. When John Stennis replaced Bilbo, only the cruel rhetoric and not the underlying policy of disfranchisement changed. Behind the Magnolia Curtain, blacks continued to encounter most of the old difficulties and a few new ones in trying to vote. Yet blacks benefited from having stood up to Bilboism. The public hearings demonstrated rising political awareness, especially among younger blacks. Despite persistent obstacles in front of ballot boxes, nearly 20,000 blacks added their names to registration lists in the decade after the war's end. This modest increase revealed the development of tiny chinks in the armor of the closed society. White politicians who justified their racial policy on the basis that African-Americans were content with their lot had that explanation graphically disputed by black veterans and their friends who defied white hostility to appear in Jackson. As a matter of fact, the Senate investigation documented only part of the rising tide of black protest. A former soldier not called to testify about his own encounter with Bilboism,

Medgar Evers later became state field secretary of the NAACP and worked tirelessly to organize blacks against racial discrimination and disfranchisement. In that capacity, working alongside a new breed of blacks, he helped breathe life into the civil rights movement in Mississippi until additional recruits and allies were mobilized.

Black Mississippians were not alone in their struggle to obtain the franchise. Throughout the postwar South, blacks campaigned to break down suffrage barriers. The NAACP, while concentrating its energies in the courts, was among the groups promoting the use of the ballot. After *Smith v. Allwright*, many of its branches created citizenship schools to teach blacks how to fill out registration forms properly and to answer typical questions that the clerks posed. The national association made cash awards to those who took up this work; in 1947, for example, the organization presented a prize to its chapter in Monroe, Louisiana, for having conducted a drive that added over 600 names to the voter lists. Assistant secretary Roy Wilkins expressed the value to blacks in creating these voter education classes: "The issue of civil rights is politics. If we are to win the fight for civil rights we must use our political strength."

African-Americans also organized voter leagues to supplement the efforts of the NAACP. These groups solicited support from various organizations in the black community—civic, fraternal, religious—and thus they recruited many individuals outside of the national association's orbit of influence. In 1946, an Atlanta All Citizens Registration Committee was formed because "previously NAACP registration drives had failed to reach the masses." Within four months, this committee assisted in bringing out some 18,000 blacks to sign up to vote. In Winston-Salem, North Carolina, an alliance of blacks and organized labor succeeded in electing a black to the city council. In Richmond, Virginia, a similar coalition supporting the election of a black veteran to the state legislature only narrowly failed. Elsewhere, in union halls, business establishments, farm groups, and small county associations, men and women gathered to plan suffrage crusades. Joining them, representatives of the Southern Conference for Human Welfare (SCHW), an interracial group of New Deal liberals formed in 1938, carried on voter registration drives throughout Dixie. In addition, from church pulpits ministers urged their congregants to go to the polls. During the Atlanta registration drive, the Reverend Martin Luther King, Sr., preached for the cause of enfranchisement, thereby providing a role model for his son to follow.

The situation in Winston-Salem especially illustrated new possibilities for black political advancement stirred by the war. A drive by Local 22 of the Food, Tobacco, Agricultural and Allied Workers, a CIO affiliate, to gain a collective bargaining agreement with R. J. Reynolds Company boosted union membership among blacks and stimulated efforts to challenge racial discrimination within their community. This interracial union chapter, with Communists actively in the lead, mobilized working-class blacks to take part in the freedom struggle that had been waged haltingly in the past by a small middle-class segment of blacks associated with the NAACP. By 1947, CIO and NAACP voter registration campaigns had succeeded in enrolling ten times the number of blacks eligible to vote three years before. "I didn't take registration seriously until the union came in and we began to talk about...the importance of voting," one newly signed-up registrant commented. In 1947, Kenneth Williams, a black minister, won election to the Winston-Salem Board of Aldermen largely on the strength of this emergent Afro-American electorate. The efforts of Local 22 and its allies in heightening racial and political consciousness greatly impressed a visiting black journalist, who reported: "I was aware of a growing solidarity and intelligent mass action that will mean the dawn of a New Day in the South. If there is a 'New Negro', he is to be found in the ranks of the labor movement." Ultimately, however, much of the hope for this trade union path toward racial equality was dashed by the rising anti-Communist reaction that gripped the United States during the Cold War era (see Chapter 2).

Attempts to increase black political involvement throughout the South produced substantial dividends. Within a decade after *Smith v. Allwright*, over 1 million blacks, about four times the number in 1944, had qualified to vote. As Everett C. Ladd, Jr., noted, blacks were transformed "from 'blanks' to participants in city politics." Black voters sometimes held a balance of power in close elections and increasingly helped defeat the most racist of candidates. Commentators noted that where blacks voted in sizable numbers treatment by police improved; black patrolmen were hired; and health, education, and recreational facilities were constructed. Streets in black neighborhoods in those areas were paved. Osceola McKaine, who after the war served as a field representative of the SCHW, reported from his travels: "The Negro masses are becoming keenly aware that the questions of jobs and schools are essentially political questions and these are the things that interest them most." The greater turnout at the polls also encouraged blacks to seek political office in the South, and for the first time in the twentieth century nearly a dozen blacks in the South were elected to posts as aldermen, county supervisors, and members of city councils.

SEEDTIME OF REFORM

The struggle to expand the vote following World War II was a prelude to the civil rights struggle that mushroomed in the years after the landmark *Brown v. Board of Education* school desegregation case. The blatant discrimination in registration procedures that had

Blacks in Charleston lining up to vote in the 1948 Democratic party primary. (UPI/Bettmann Newsphotos)

been shockingly revealed to the public and a virtual reign of terror to preserve disfranchisement underscored the need for a second reconstruction in which the national government intervened in the South. As one black journalist explained: "Each time the United States Supreme Court outlaws one of these 'Negro stoppers' a new one is invented. It is clear that sooner or later the federal government will have to step in." It would not be too long before politics combined with principle: In a little more than a decade Washington lawmakers would enact four civil rights measures to extend the suffrage to southern blacks.

Just as vital as federal intervention was local assertiveness. Voter registration activities at the grassroots level paralleled the development of the "new Negro," the African-American unafraid to stand up for his or her rights in the face of grave danger. The over 1 million blacks who registered to vote demonstrated that politics was no longer for whites only. Enrollment drives often brought suffrage reformers into direct confrontation with representatives of the racist system in the South and sustained a protest tradition upon which more militant action would be built in the future. It required courage, pride, and emotional strength for blacks living in Dixie to enter courthouses and run the gauntlet of registrars likely to reject their applications and sheriffs anxious to punish them for having made the attempt in the first place. The lessons learned by the civil rights workers of the late forties and early fifties proved valuable to the "new abolitionists" of the 1960s. They taught that the right to vote could be obtained if the federal government intervened to destroy the white stranglehold over the registration process and civil rights groups rallied the mass of blacks behind the ballot. By virtue of this interdependent relationship, the national government changed the law while the civil rights movement erected a support network emboldening blacks to transform their local communities. Although suffragists were only slightly successful in the 1940s, most of them were still around to see a majority of southern blacks enfranchised within a generation.

The World War II era furnished the staging ground for the black revolution. It revitalized black solidarity, tested innovative protest tactics, and moved the federal government closer to the side of racial equality. Wartime urban migration and improved economic opportunities laid the basis for later social and political changes. The war loosened some of the old chains of subservience imposed by the southern caste system and freed blacks in hundreds of locales throughout Dixie to join together to overthrow Jim Crow. What the historian Nancy J. Weiss concluded about Franklin D. Roosevelt and the New Deal should be extended to the years that followed: "The growing interest of blacks in politics, their involvement in the Democratic party, and their new sense that the political process could be responsive to their needs became essential underpinnings of the drive for civil rights." Along two fronts, black soldiers and veterans and their families and friends steered the United States toward living up to its democratic political principles.

Chapter 2

Ballots, Boycotts, and the Building of a National Agenda

While black southerners struggled to clear racial obstacles in the path of the right to vote, their allies in the North applied increasing pressure to move the federal government behind the cause of civil rights. The Supreme Court had taken the lead in beginning to dismantle barriers blocking equal access to public education, housing, and the ballot box, but neither the President nor Congress had taken very firm steps in that direction. Roosevelt's FEPC lacked the necessary administrative authority to combat discrimination in employment, and during World War II the chief executive generally refrained from engaging in controversies over racial issues that would offend white segregationists and threaten national unity. Similarly, southern lawmakers succeeded in strangling congressional attempts to punish lynchers, repeal the repressive poll tax requirement for voting, and preserve the Fair Employment Practice Committee. The anti-Fascist rhetoric of wartime notwithstanding, in the absence of sufficient political leverage, appeals to moral conscience were not enough to guarantee first-class citizenship for African-Americans.

The proponents of civil rights did not lack political resources. Though a majority of black southerners remained disfranchised in the decade following *Smith v. Allwright*, northern blacks could exercise the franchise as a strategic weapon to combat racial discrimination. Precipitated by World War II, the migration of blacks to the urban centers of the North and Far West in search of defense jobs placed them in a favorable position to tip the balance of power in tight elections. Where this critical mass of voters existed, even blacks themselves managed to win election. This incipient strength placed two blacks in the House of Representatives—Adam Clayton Powell of New York City and William Dawson of Chicago—as well as a sprinkling of officials in local positions. Yet black influence derived from something more than actual minority-group representation, which was meager. Rather it rested in its potential to sway white politicians—to reward friends and punish enemies, the most basic axiom in politics.

THE TRUMAN ADMINISTRATION AND CIVIL RIGHTS

President Harry S. Truman had to factor in such political calculations in finding the right political equation for dealing with African-Americans. The successor to FDR, Truman inherited the New Deal's black converts to the Democratic party. However, in 1945, it was not clear whether this newfound partisan allegiance of blacks was a personal or an institutional one. Would it survive Roosevelt's death or would the black electorate return to its historical Republican mooring? Though the majority of blacks remained faithful to the party of Roosevelt in the November 1946 midterm legislative elections, the GOP recaptured some of FDR's black followers on its way toward securing control of the Eightieth Congress. Charles Houston, the noted attorney and legal adviser to the NAACP, expressed the disaffection of many blacks several months before the elections: "The president may do this and he may do that as leader, but if he cannot produce, well, there is no such thing as gratitude in politics." In December 1945, Houston had evidenced his own frustration with the lack of presidential leadership in civil rights by resigning as a member of the increasingly ineffective FEPC.

A practical politician, President Truman was prepared to heed these warning signals. Much of his early attitudes toward race were grounded in political considerations. As a border-state senator from Missouri during the late 1930s and early 1940s, Truman had supported, without much enthusiasm, abolition of the poll tax and passage of an antilynching bill. About the latter, he admitted to a southern colleague and opponent of the measure: "All my sympathies are with you, but the Negro vote in Kansas City and St. Louis is too important." At the same time, Truman backed legislation to fund the FEPC and spoke out for giving "the Negroes the rights that are theirs." His moderate positions on race made him acceptable to both southern and northern Democrats as the compromise candidate to replace the more controversial Henry A. Wallace as Roosevelt's running mate in 1944.

As President, he quickly received an education about racial injustice that deeply affected his thinking. In 1946, vicious attacks on returning black servicemen in the South generated widespread notoriety. "My God! I had no idea that it was as terrible as that!" the chief executive exclaimed after learning that Isaac Woodward, still in uniform, had been severely beaten and blinded while passing through South Carolina en route home. Together with a bloody race riot in Columbia, Tennessee, and mounting violence and threats of attack against blacks who sought to exercise their newly won suffrage rights, these events shocked Truman.

He responded by appointing a special committee to investigate the deteriorating condition of civil rights and devise remedies for its improvement. The moral concerns that prompted the formation of this group were reinforced by sound political considerations. The defeat of the Democrats at the polls in the 1946 congressional election charted the President's declining political health and brought a prognosis of doom for the party's presidential nominee two years hence. The once robust Roosevelt coalition appeared to be dying in the wake of Truman's inability to solve the postwar reconversion problems of inflation, shortages, and labor conflict as well as growing racial tensions. The establishment of the President's Committee on Civil Rights provided one way for Truman to resuscitate the ailing Democratic alliance in time to achieve a reelection victory.

This strategy was put to a stiff test after the committee issued its report in October 1947. *To Secure These Rights* urged greater federal involvement in promoting racial equality. It endorsed removal of the poll tax and other discriminatory obstacles to voting, creation of a Civil Rights Division in the Department of Justice, and desegregation of the armed forces, interstate transportation, and government employment. These suggestions broke new ground in establishing a reform agenda and alarmed southern white politicians. Already troubled by their perception that Roosevelt's New Deal had tilted the axis of Democratic power away from the rural South to an urban North teeming with ethnic and racial minorities, many southerners resented the Truman committee's assault upon the racial status quo.

Their complaints forced the President to move circumspectly. Despite delivering an unprecedented special message on civil rights to a joint session of Congress in February 1948, Truman failed to press lawmakers to consider particular measures based on the committee's recommendations. He did not want to provoke a southern revolt in the upcoming presidential election, and the prospect of a southern filibuster against any civil rights legislation would prove even more divisive to party unity. Furthermore, southern legislative support for his Cold War economic and military policies toward the Soviet Union commanded a higher priority than did passage of civil rights bills, however worthy they might be.

Yet the Cold War offered a double-edged sword for racial advancement. Having recognized the difficulties in challenging the white South, Truman could not afford to risk the political consequences of ignoring rising black militancy. Since World War II, blacks in and out of the South had begun mobilizing for first-class citizenship, prepared to force the United States to live up to its democratic ideals. This also came at a time when the country was venturing into a fierce propaganda battle with the Soviet Union for allies in global struggle. Committed to the United Nations, President Truman did not want domestic racial conflicts to diminish his diplomatic efforts in the international arena. In this context, the attempt by Mississippi blacks to unseat the racist Senator Theodore Bilbo not only demonstrated a growing collective consciousness against oppression at the local level, but also focused national and world attention on the gap between democratic pronouncements and the reality of bigotry. Recognizing such predicaments, the President's Committee on Civil Rights declared in 1947: "An American diplomat cannot argue for free elections in foreign lands without meeting the challenge that in sections of America qualified voters do not have access to the polls."

Black protest leaders sought to exploit Truman's vulnerability on this point. In its traditional, legalistic manner, the NAACP petitioned the United Nations to consider a list of grievances against American racial practices. In a less conventional way that prefigured future campaigns against racial discrimination, A. Philip Randolph called upon blacks to apply pressure through civil disobedience. In early 1948, the "father" of the March on Washington tangled with Truman over an issue he had first brought up with Roosevelt seven years earlier and had failed to resolve: desegregation of the military. During a period when Truman sought increased military measures to combat Soviet aggression, Randolph urged the President to promulgate an executive order abolishing segregation in the armed forces or he would counsel black youth "to resist a [Selective Service] law, the inevitable consequences of which would be to expose them to un-American brutality so familiar during the last war." Although black leaders divided over Randolph's threatened action, a survey revealed that 71 percent of draft age blacks supported the proposed boycott.

The danger of black insurgency was not confined to Truman's defense program; it menaced the political fortunes of the President. The black electorate gave some indication of rallying around the candidacy of Henry Wallace, who criticized Truman for responding too aggressively in seeking to contain the Soviet Union in foreign affairs and for not acting forcefully enough to repel racial discrimination at home. As early as May 1946, a poll showed that 91 percent of black voters favored Wallace as the Democratic nominee in 1948. Since then the President had appointed a pioneering civil rights committee and presented Congress with a pathbreaking legislative reform agenda. Nevertheless, Wallace carried a strong appeal for black voters. In late 1947, he campaigned throughout the South, audaciously addressed integrated audiences that included many of the region's newly enfranchised blacks, and spoke out in favor of racial equality. Up North, a special congressional election in a Bronx district in New York City with a large black population resulted in the victory of a pro-Wallace candidate.

These political rumblings did not exactly catch Truman by surprise. In November 1947, one of his key advisers, Clark Clifford, had counseled the President to concentrate on appealing to the liberal elements of the Democratic coalition, particularly blacks and labor union members, to ensure his reelection the following year. "Unless there are new and real efforts," Clifford predicted, "the Negro bloc...will go Republican." A strong civil rights stand might disturb the Democratic South, but Clifford suggested that the former Confederate states would not bolt the party of their forebears.

Initially, however, Truman responded cautiously to this advice. Unwilling to confront the southern wing of his party any further, the President backed away from pressing his bold civil rights initiatives in Congress. True, the chief executive had some very good tactical reasons for backing off, given the likelihood that a southern filibuster would kill reform bills as well as stall passage of those pertaining to Cold War remilitarization. But Truman did not face the same legislative hurdle with respect to desegregation of the armed forces. In that case, he could have dealt with the matter by executive decree; this he refused to do. Moreover, he displayed excessive timidity in failing to endorse his own committee's civil rights recommendations as part of the Democratic party's platform. Instead, he planned to run on the Democrats' mild 1944 plank vaguely worded in support of granting minorities equal rights under the Constitution.

Once again, strong political forces knocked the President off dead center and moved him to the left. At the Democratic National Convention in July 1948, party liberals engineered an end run around the Truman-controlled Platform Committee and won a floor fight for a stronger resolution on civil rights. Though stopping short of pledging an end to segregation in the military, it did promise "equal treatment in the service and defense of our nation" as well as "the right to equal opportunity of employment." Hubert H. Humphrey of Minnesota, a leader of the liberal upstarts, eloquently captured the spirit behind the proposals: "The time has arrived for the Democratic Party to get out of the shadow of states' rights and walk forthrightly into the bright sunshine of human rights."

Embracing the revised platform rhetoric was not sufficient. With Randolph still intending to lead a mass draft-evasion movement and with Henry Wallace running on an independent Progressive party ticket, Truman took the kind of concrete action on civil rights he had hesitated to implement previously. Shortly after the Democratic convention adjourned, the President signed two executive orders establishing a nondiscriminatory fair employment policy for the federal government and creating a committee to promote equal opportunity in the armed forces, with the ultimate aim of eliminating segregation. He also convened a special session of Congress to act on his party's civil rights proposals, but southern lawmakers succeeded in blocking them.

These assorted efforts precipitated a revolt by white southerners, contrary to Clifford's predictions. After staging a walkout

Protesting discrimination in the military, A. Philip Randolph heads a picket line at the 1948 Democratic National Convention. (UPI/Bettmann Newsphotos)

from the Democratic National Convention, a band of southern dissidents formed the States' Rights party and nominated Governor Strom Thurmond of South Carolina for President. These Dixiecrats condemned federal tyranny and reaffirmed their allegiance to the principle of racial segregation. Rather than pushing Truman to mend his political fences in the South, this uprising produced the opposite effect. It reinforced the President's determination to secure minority backing in the North. According to this line of thinking, the "Negro votes in the crucial states will more than cancel out any votes he may lose in the South."

Not only might this strategy neutralize southern losses, but it could also undermine black support for Truman's main rivals in the North. The Republican nominee, Governor Thomas E. Dewey of New York, ran on a platform that declared its opposition to racial segregation in the military, a declaration omitted from the Democratic manifesto. Furthermore, Henry Wallace's Progressive party denounced all forms of segregation and gained the endorsement of such prominent blacks as Charles Houston, W. E. B. Du Bois, and Paul Robeson. To secure black votes against his opponents, Truman emphasized his civil rights accomplishments during his first term and, in a symbolic gesture, swung his campaign through Harlem, the first President to do so. He hammered away at the Republican-controlled Eightieth Congress for doing nothing to pass his civil rights proposals. At the same time, he attacked Wallace for permitting Communists to collaborate with his Progressive party, a charge designed to appeal to black civil rights leaders wary of Communist infiltration of their own organizations.

Truman's maneuvering paid off in his reelection. As his counselors had forecast, the loss of five deep South states to the Dixiecrats was more than offset by the huge margins Truman piled up among black voters in the urban North. He captured 69 percent of the black ballots cast in twenty-seven major cities, and in California, Illinois, and Ohio, black votes made the critical difference in his victory. Indeed, his share of the black electorate exceeded that of FDR, and as Nancy Weiss has pointed out, Truman managed to use the civil rights issue "as a means to transform black Roosevelt supporters into black Democrats." The incumbent's pro-civil-rights record along with Dewey's lackluster campaign and the unwillingness of most blacks to "waste" their votes on a Wallacite third-party bid, especially one tainted with the stigma of Red radicalism, solidified black fidelity to the New Deal coalition.

The cementing of black loyalty to the Democratic party as an institution, rather than to a single leader, depended on more than the attraction to civil rights. Though the vote of the cohesive black bloc grew out of racial concerns, class issues also shaped it. In casting a ballot for the Democratic presidential nominee, blacks were endorsing the party that brought economic relief from depression, sponsored measures to increase employment, and defended labor unions from restrictive assaults. The scant evidence that exists for the New Deal era suggests that lower-income blacks, like their white counterparts, were more inclined to back the Democrats than were those higher on the economic scale. This pattern persisted during the Truman years. Donald R. McCoy and Richard T. Reutten have noted that whereas nearly all black newspapers supported Dewey in 1948, reflecting the higher socioeconomic status of their publishers, the lower-income readers of these publications sided overwhelmingly with Truman. For most African-Americans, who were still not afforded equal economic and citizenship rights, race and class interests coincided.

The election of 1948 established civil rights as a key issue on the agenda of presidential politics. Three out of the four political parties had endorsed the extension of racial equality. Black delegates attended the Democratic convention in comparatively small but record numbers and contributed to passing the minority civil rights plank. Blacks were also represented in prominent ways in the Progressive party campaign, and the GOP, the former home of the majority of the black electorate, created a National Council of Negro Republicans to lure them back.

Yet the growing visibility of the civil rights issue did not mean that black Americans, especially those residing in the South, were about to achieve their goal of first-class citizenship through electoral politics. Southern segregationists continued to retain key positions within the Democratic party and in Congress, ready to shred any legislative proposal on civil rights that appeared. Though the chief executive owed blacks a big debt for his reelection, he lacked the substantial commitment necessary to tackle powerful conservative congressional forces against civil rights. For Truman, the Cold War and national security took precedence over domestic reform, and he hesitated to antagonize the southern lawmakers whose support he needed. Besides, Truman's policy of global containment fueled excessive anti-Communist sentiment in the United States. Zealous "Red baiters" equated any challenge to the status quo with un-Americanism. Even liberal and labor organizations such as the NAACP and the CIO hunted for suspected Communists in their ranks. No matter how hard they tried to achieve the requisite purity, civil rights groups still came under attack from segregationists who considered advocates of racial equality soft on communism. This fear of social change and the attempts of politicians to capitalize on it created an inhospitable environment for civil rights activism.

To crack the entrenched opposition to racial equality required a public zeal that did not yet exist. In fact, the majority of whites did not embrace the cause of civil rights. In March 1948, a Gallup Poll that asked whether Americans favored Truman's moderate civil rights program found out that 56 percent did not. Northerners were more likely than southerners to express sympathy, but most of them remained poorly informed about the issue.

THE ELECTION OF DWIGHT D. EISENHOWER

The election of Dwight D. Eisenhower in 1952 did not place a forceful advocate of civil rights in the White House, yet neither did it bring in someone totally unsympathetic to the principle of deseg-regation. The Republican President did not intend to turn back the civil rights clock to the days before the Truman administration. However, events were pushing ahead the timetable for racial equality and creating new standards of measurement to gauge pres-idential performance. Faced with this accelerated schedule, Eisen-hower moved forward, but did so too cautiously to keep in step with the quickened rate of black expectations.

President Eisenhower began his first term in office without hav-ing accumulated any political debt to blacks. The overwhelming share of the black vote, 73 percent, had gone to Eisenhower's Democratic rival, Adlai E. Stevenson. The former Illinois governor exceeded Truman's ratio of the minority vote by recovering the backing of black Wallacites. The newly expanded southern black electorate in Louisiana, South Carolina, Kentucky, and Arkansas provided the margin of victory for Stevenson in those states. The majority of blacks stuck with the Democratic party even though its platform did not retain the strong language of 1948 and its vice presidential nominee was Senator John Sparkman of Alabama, who had opposed Truman's civil rights program.

Unlike 1948, the black vote did not save the Democrats from de-feat. The popularity of General Eisenhower among whites throughout the nation more than canceled out the impact of the black vote. The black electorate could play a decisive role in swinging the outcome of elections only when, as the *Pittsburgh Courier* noted, "the balance between the two major political parties is so even." Such was not the case in 1952. Eisenhower captured 55.2 percent of the popular vote and 442 electoral votes. His winning electoral column included 57 votes from the South, 18 more than the Dixiecrats had gathered four years earlier.

Despite the fact that Eisenhower had made inroads into Dixie and gained endorsements from popular figures such as Governor James F. Byrnes of South Carolina, he entered the White House with a civil rights agenda in mind. The Republican platform had differed from the Democrats' chiefly in its unwillingness to propose federal measures to combat employment discrimination, preferring instead to rely on state authority. Otherwise, the GOP advocated federal action to eliminate lynching, poll taxes, and segregation in Washington, D.C. Eisenhower had also assured black leaders that he would strive to end discrimination in federal employment under his direct control, continue desegregation of the armed forces, and in a campaign address in Harlem, he invited blacks to join his crusade "based upon merit and without respect to color or creed."

However, there were definite limits to Eisenhower's plans for obtaining racial equality. Committed to a view of government that emphasized persuasion over coercion in shaping social and economic relations, Eisenhower wanted to give state, local, and private sectors broad discretion in resolving conflicts in public policy. He believed that problems of race were deeply embedded in the fabric of southern society and could not be easily removed. Still, he considered white southern politicians as law abiding and responsible, and he had faith in their willingness over time to abandon discriminatory racial practices. Consequently, the chief executive would not compel white southerners hastily to change their long-standing racial customs. Gradualism rather than speed characterized his approach. Eisenhower consistently declared in public what he confided to his personal diary at the beginning of his term: "I believe that Federal law imposed upon our states in such a way as to bring about a conflict of the police power of the states and the nation, would set back the cause of progress in race relations for a long, long time."

COMMUNITY MOBILIZATION AND THE MONTGOMERY BUS BOYCOTT

While the cause of civil rights inched along slowly under Truman and Eisenhower in the national arena, southern blacks and a hand-

ful of sympathetic whites in their home communities struggled to
set themselves free. Civil rights leaders viewed electoral politics as
a prime instrument for achieving racial gains. Political exclusion
had pinned a twentieth-century badge of subordination on black
southerners, which enfranchisement promised to remove. Without
a free and unfettered right to vote, the constitutional guarantee of
full citizenship would remain elusive. Given the history of their official exclusion from the governing process, indeed their legitimacy
as participants in government denied, blacks sought to enter politics as a fundamental act of liberation. The vote could be wielded as
a tool of protest, a means of asserting dignity and pride, a source of
personal and group autonomy. "There's one thing the Negro has
that the white man wants but can't get unless you give it to him,"
a black Floridian remarked. "That's your vote. He can offer you a
million dollars for your vote, but he can't get it unless you give it to
him."

These symbolic qualities were not the only rewards attributed
to the suffrage. The ballot had a practical side that offered a way
to improve the daily living conditions of those deprived of basic
public services most white Americans took for granted: paved
streets, regular sanitation disposal, adequate police and fire protection, and access to recreational facilities. The vote would convert
blacks into constituents, providing them with an opportunity to
elect representatives whom they could hold directly accountable
at the polls for delivering material benefits. This classic view of
civic democracy did not take into account the pervasiveness of
race and caste as features that would retard black political influence, but it did conform to the conventional American creed of
self-help and equal opportunity for advancement. In sharing and
promoting this ideal, black suffragists attached their cause to republican principles and portrayed their foes as undemocratic and un-
American.

Whatever the merits of their argument, black southerners still
had to overcome numerous barriers to their entry into politics.
Federal law had eliminated the white primary, but poll taxes, literacy tests, intimidation, and fear induced by centuries of discrimination kept most blacks disfranchised. With federal involvement growing but unreliable and southern resistance firm, blacks
assumed increased responsibility for marshaling their resources
against discrimination. According to Henry Lee Moon, an NAACP

official who closely monitored this heightened political activity, "the real drive to register and get out the vote is essentially a grass-roots movement with local Negro leadership."

The postwar voter and citizenship education campaigns, discussed in Chapter 1, demonstrated the need for collective action. Civil rights groups in concert with voter leagues and sympathetic labor union locals, especially those in the CIO, waged intensive efforts to sign up black registrants and bring them out to the polls on election day. These organizations were necessary to arouse black consciousness to the efficacy of voting, counsel blacks on how to meet the suffrage requirements they faced, and sustain encouragement and support for those willing to break from the past when politics was the exclusive domain of whites.

These endeavors initially worked best in urban areas of the South. In the cities blacks had greater access to education, economic opportunities, and cultural institutions, all of which encouraged civic participation or preparation for it. Even the barriers that still existed there were not erected as high as in the rural black belt where African-Americans were isolated, economically dependent on whites, and vulnerable to reprisals. In 1947, when Richmond, Virginia, blacks mounted a successful voter registration drive, the city's leading newspaper acknowledged: "We do have a democratic tradition which holds that American citizens are entitled to vote and to hold office. So we may as well accustom ourselves to [it]." In Atlanta, Georgia, blacks extended their political influence by forming a coalition with wealthy businesspeople to elect a white mayor, William B. Hartsfield, in 1949. Four years later, this biracial alliance, which cut across class lines, succeeded in electing Dr. Rufus E. Clement, the black president of Atlanta University, to the board of education, turning aside his white opponent.

However, other attempts at forging interracial coalitions based on shared economic experiences ran into trouble. Issues of political ideology divided people with common class grievances, as the situation of tobacco workers in Winston-Salem revealed. Following the Second World War, the R. J. Reynolds Company undertook to roll back the gains that Local 22 of the CIO had made in unionizing black and white workers. In 1947, after management refused to agree to demands for a wage increase, the union went out on strike. The company, supported by the local newspaper, attempted to undermine the walkout by shifting the focus from collective bargaining to Communist infiltration of the union. Indeed, Communists did occupy top positions in Local 22, which left the organization susceptible to charges that it was operating as an agent of a foreign power and using blacks to foster subversive aims. In the highly charged Cold War climate, the company succeeded in attacking the union for its Communist affiliations, but it could not triumph without assistance from the national CIO, which was also engaged in eliminating Communists from its ranks. Whereas the company was attempting to squelch unionization, the CIO merely wanted to establish a non-Communist affiliate. However, "if purging communist leadership also led to a destruction of the legitimate battle to organize the unorganized and achieve social justice," William H. Chafe has argued, "any victory would be hollow." Arrayed against the combined forces of union and management, Local 22 collapsed.

Its defeat under this anti-Communist assault seriously affected the shape of the black freedom struggle in Winston-Salem and in other areas to which progressive unions might have expanded. Blacks continued to play a role in the political life of the North Carolina city, but they lost the kind of civil rights militancy that the union had energized during its heydey in the 1940s. As Nelson Lichtenstein and Robert Korstad have shown, Winston-Salem became a "model of racial moderation." Politics consisted mainly of registering to vote and turning out at the ballot box on election day, with a deemphasis on protest activities and community organizing. Even the NAACP felt the negative effects, as its membership dwindled during the 1950s to less than 500. Political affairs were run by a select group of white and black leaders, with the mass of black residents increasingly relegated to the background in vital decision-making.

Nevertheless, civil rights activism did not disappear from the South. As a matter of fact in cities such as Montgomery, Alabama, the expanding political clout of the black electorate raised expectations for the possibilities of social change. In the "cradle of the Confederacy" blacks counted for between 7 and 8 percent of the registered voters by 1955, a figure slightly above the statewide average. Even with this relatively small ratio of voters, in 1953 blacks had helped ensure the election of a white city commissioner running against the political establishment. This victory encouraged blacks to make demands on local officials, and several individuals who had actively engaged in political organizing following the demise of the white primary led the way. Edgar D. Nixon, a representative of the

International Brotherhood of Sleeping Car Porters and a driving force in the NAACP, obtained a noteworthy 42 percent of the vote in a losing contest for a seat on the county Democratic Executive Committee. Jo Ann Robinson, an English instructor at Alabama State College, headed the Women's Political Council, which served not only to get out the black vote but also to petition the city commission to redress black complaints. Nixon and Robinson were often joined by Rufus A. Lewis, a businessman who chaired the Citizen's Steering Committee.

Buoyed by their growing political confidence, black leaders met with modest success. With the lone commissioner blacks had helped to elect in their corner, they persuaded white officials to increase the number of black police officers and improve bus service in black neighborhoods. Civil rights proponents also pressed demands for appointment of a black to the Parks and Recreation Board and for the elimination of certain humiliating policies related to bus transportation. Particularly irksome were the requirements that black passengers first pay their fares at the front door and board through the back door and that they remain standing when seats were available in the white but not the colored area. The limits of their political strength became manifest when the city rejected their requests for change, and in 1955 their white ally on the commission went down to defeat for reelection, beaten by an opponent who injected explicit racial appeals into the campaign.

Thus, black progress remained at a standstill and black political influence appeared on the decline when Rosa Parks was arrested on December 1, 1955. A seamstress, a former secretary of the local NAACP branch, and a recent participant in interracial workshops at the Highlander Folk School in Tennessee, Mrs. Parks refused to vacate her seat for a white passenger on a crowded bus. A spontaneous action only in the sense that the exact details were not planned in advance, her defiance reflected long-standing personal involvement in civil rights activities as well as the natural extension of political efforts by fellow blacks to challenge racism in Montgomery. Consequently, Parks turned to E. D. Nixon for assistance in bailing her out of jail, and he, along with Jo Ann Robinson, hatched plans for a boycott of the buses. The Women's Political Council took the lead in spreading word of the proposed strike by cranking out some 40,000 handbills on a mimeograph machine borrowed by Robinson.

Once plans for the boycott were set in motion, black ministers, including Dr. Martin Luther King, Jr., were tapped to assume direction of the protest activities. The recruitment of the clergy brought an important dimension to the struggle. A network of independent churches provided a base from which to mobilize the black masses in a way that middle-class–oriented civil rights groups, civic leagues, and political clubs had failed to accomplish. Though ministers like Dr. King's father in Atlanta had used their pulpits on behalf of voter registration drives, they had rarely before undertaken a project that rallied blacks on such a large, community-wide scale against racial discrimination.[1] So long as most black Montgomerians were barred from participating in the electoral process as voters, they resorted to mass protest to achieve their political aims.

Blacks who participated in the yearlong boycott were transformed by the struggle. Reverend King and the Montgomery Improvement Association (MIA), which he directed, came to realize the intransigence of the segregationist forces opposing them and modified their demands accordingly. Originally they had accepted the concept of segregation on the buses and merely sought more courteous treatment and a system that did not force them to relinquish their seats to whites when the black section was filled. Then, the city refused to negotiate, black leaders were arrested, and King's home was dynamited. These acts of resistance stiffened the MIA's resolve, and the organization decided to settle for nothing less than complete desegregation of the buses. Mass meetings sustained the minister-leaders and their congregants behind this evolving goal. The inspiring sermons of the charismatic Dr. King and the singing of gospel songs filled with messages of freedom reinforced group solidarity and the determination to persevere. Nevertheless, collective action alone was not enough to destroy Jim Crow, and victory came only after the Supreme Court, on November 13, 1956, voided segregation on public buses.

The lessons that emerged from the Montgomery bus boycott had profound significance for the battle to obtain civil and political rights. Indeed, it showed that the two were inextricably linked. Acquisition of the ballot by itself did not bring power, nor did the piecemeal dismantling of the limbs of Jim Crow. Even after the buses were desegregated blacks in Montgomery faced sporadic vi-

---

[1]In 1953, the Reverend T. J. Jemison had led a seven-day bus boycott in Baton Rouge, Louisiana, which ended in a compromise. A small number of seats were reserved for whites in the front and for blacks in the rear of the buses, but those in between were open to all.

The Montgomery police fingerprint Rosa Parks after her arrest for failing to vacate her seat on a segregated bus. (AP/Wide World Photos)

olence against their enjoying this right, and most continued to meet obstacles in enrolling as voters. Unless black southerners devised new techniques in mounting grassroots protest, thereby dramatically exposing their plight to the rest of the country, the white South would not voluntarily yield. As J. Mills Thornton has observed: "In the end, the bus boycott teaches that segregation could have been disestablished only in the way in which it was disestablished: by internal pressure sufficient to compel intervention from outside the South." The Supreme Court set the lead in this direction; it remained for the President and Congress to follow.

MASSIVE RESISTANCE AND EISENHOWER MODERATION

The high tribunal's monumental decision in *Brown v. Board of Education* (1954) presented new opportunities for and challenges to the quest for black political equality. Though the ruling applied to the desegregation of public schools, it carried far-ranging implications. Richard Kluger has written that the opinion "represented nothing short of a reconsecration of American ideals." The Court removed the legal sanction a prior bench of justices had conferred on the doctrine of white supremacy in *Plessy v. Ferguson* nearly sixty years before. "Separate but equal" no longer bore legitimacy, and blacks could pursue their full rights of citizenship armed not only with morality but with the law. Yet racial justice did not arrive so simply. The Supreme Court left implementation of *Brown* in the hands of southern federal judges and instructed them to proceed with "all deliberate speed." Whatever that phrase signified, it did not mean "soon." Given some leeway, the southern states attempted to push compliance back for as many tomorrows as possible.

The South embarked on massive resistance to preserve segregation in the schools and black subordination in political affairs. State legislatures passed interposition resolutions "nullifying" *Brown* and enacted pupil placement laws assigning students and teachers to segregated schools according to nonracial criteria. Members of Congress from Dixie issued manifestos denouncing the landmark judicial opinion as unconstitutional and pledging to seek to reverse it. Organizations calling themselves "White Citizens Councils" arose to buttress the efforts of politicians to concoct supposedly legal means to preserve the status quo. However, this middle-class group of solid citizens—the "uptown Ku Klux Klan"—frequently resorted to illegal or extralegal methods of keeping blacks in their place. As employers they fired "uppity" blacks; as creditors they denied loans to blacks or foreclosed their property; and if all else failed the "uptown Ku Klux Klan" retaliated physically.

White supremacists also waged a fierce battle to destroy the NAACP, the group that had successfully litigated the *Brown* case. Charging the organization with subverting the established system of segregation, southern lawmakers tried to drive it from the region. In 1956, Alabama demanded that the NAACP register with the state as an outside corporation and turn over its membership lists. When the association refused to do so for fear of subjecting its members to racial intimidation, Alabama prohibited the NAACP from operating and tied it up in the courts for nearly a decade before the group legally could function again. The South hatched a variety of additional schemes to put the organization out of business. Virginia passed antibarratry legislation aimed at hindering the NAACP from initiating or sponsoring lawsuits against segregation. Louisiana barred teachers from advocating integration of the schools, and South Carolina banished NAACP members from public employment. States such as Florida wielded the weapon of anti-Communism against the association, targeting the NAACP as a subversive organization and establishing a legislative committee to investigate its activities. Although managing to survive, the group suffered considerable damage. In order to defend itself from attack, the NAACP had to divert precious resources away from the main battle against Jim Crow and disfranchisement.

Under this counterassault the drive toward racial equality sputtered. School desegregation moved ahead at a trickling pace and was mainly confined to a handful of cities around the southern periphery; the deep South shouted "never!" White opposition had a similarly chilling effect on the advancement of blacks into electoral politics. Though the rate of black voter registration had begun to slow before *Brown*, new recruits were harder to sign up as tensions escalated over the segregation issue. The White Citizens Councils in Mississippi and Louisiana did their best to keep black applicants off the voter rolls and connived to purge many of those who had managed to get on. In Ouachita Parish, Louisiana, of the 4,000 blacks who had registered through September 1956, only 1,000 remained after Council-inspired challenges. The head of the Mississippi Council facetiously explained the thinking of the disfranchisers: "Why, it'd be like giving the vote to these children of mine, you give the vote to my children and you know who they'd elect for President? Elvis Presley!" Not surprisingly, between 1952 and 1956 only 215,000 additional blacks succeeded in enrolling to vote in the South, leaving 75 percent without the ballot.

Southern blacks had fallen short of reaching their registration potential for several reasons. The voter leagues and the NAACP had merely skimmed the surface. Blacks located in the urban areas of the upper South and in the largest cities in the heart of Dixie made up the biggest proportion of the new voters. However, in rural sections of the black belt, African-Americans with little schooling and money were unable and unwilling to register. In these areas they had trouble developing independent leadership because the tiny group of professionals remained tied to white purse strings.

School boards threatened to fire teachers who exhibited signs of militancy, and banks refused to extend credit to businesspeople and farmers who tried to organize suffrage drives. If economic pressure did not work, registrars managed to apply literacy tests in such a biased manner that hardly any blacks could pass. And whites were not hesitant to use old-fashioned brute force.

Although the issue of school desegregation became the storm center of political controversy between white and black southerners following *Brown*, the acquisition of the suffrage continued to loom large as a source of contention between the races. Each side saw much at stake in the outcome. White extremists raised the bugaboo of racial amalgamation that supposedly would follow black political participation. Blacks "desire a much shorter detour, via the political tunnel," Judge Tom Brady, the founder of the White Citizens Councils, claimed, "to get on the intermarriage turnpikes." Whether or not most white southerners actually feared racial politics entering into their bedrooms, they were concerned that black ballots would lead to a basic rearrangement of power and prestige in society. This view received support from blacks themselves. One commentator declared: "... desegregation would be much further along if Negroes in the South could vote more nearly in proportion to their potential voting population." In effect, both groups exaggerated the importance of the suffrage as a springboard to equality, but each correctly understood that without the extension of the franchise blacks remained vulnerable to rulers not of their own choosing and whites could not be held strictly accountable for the racist policies they imposed.

The key question was how to achieve enfranchisement. As black southerners struggled against resistance from below, they looked to the federal government for support. Once before—during the Reconstruction period following the Civil War—the national government had provided protection for the right to vote from racial discrimination, but ultimately retreated in the face of southern obstructionism. This time African-Americans called for a Second Reconstruction with staying power. During the 1950s they had to rely on a President whose views on race were paternalistic and who preferred to keep Washington out of the internal affairs of the states. This left the job to Congress, a body dominated by a conservative coalition in which southerners routinely pounced on reform measures. Thus, the prospects for assistance from above appeared dim, but they were not hopeless.

Most civil rights leaders and scholars have disapproved of President Eisenhower's handling of racial affairs. Roy Wilkins, the executive director of the NAACP during the Eisenhower years, summed up the perspective of his colleagues: "President Eisenhower was a fine general and a good, decent man, but if he had fought World War II the way he fought for civil rights, we would all be speaking German today." This judgment has been echoed by nearly every historian who has studied this period: "Eisenhower and his subordinates," Robert F. Burk concluded, "had displayed a consistent pattern of hesitancy and extreme political caution in defending black legal rights."

The strength of this criticism lies primarily in the failure of the President to take a firm moral stand in support of *Brown*. When asked whether he endorsed or merely accepted the desegregation ruling, Eisenhower replied: "I think it makes no difference whether or not I endorse it," though he added that he would "do my very best to see that it is carried out in this country." Yet for southern black children it made a critical difference whether the President, especially one as popular as Eisenhower, affirmed their moral, as well as legal, right to attend desegregated schools. The chief executive delayed that possibility by refusing to throw his considerable weight behind the integration process, which, in turn, allowed the momentum to pass to those advocating massive resistance in the South. Ironically, he repeatedly preached the value of education in changing the hearts and minds of individuals, but he distinctly failed to use his presidential pulpit to instruct white southerners about their moral duty to obey the law. Furthermore, he offered scant encouragement to blacks who struggled peacefully to persuade white segregationists to abandon Jim Crow according to the voluntaristic principles Eisenhower espoused. Thus, despite the urging of Martin Luther King, Jr., the President remained silent during the yearlong Montgomery bus boycott.

Even with these failings, Eisenhower's record was not without significant accomplishments. He fulfilled his campaign pledge to work for desegregation of the nation's capital in a variety of ways. Without much fanfare, the White House facilitated the desegregation of local movie theaters, hotels, and municipal agencies. The chief executive placed Vice-President Richard M. Nixon in charge of the President's Committee on Government Contract Compliance, and although this agency, like the FEPC before it, lacked enforcement power, it persuaded the transportation company serving the District of Columbia to hire more black bus drivers and street-car operators and convinced the local telephone company to end segregation in its offices. Moreover, following *Brown*, Eisenhower pressed the District of Columbia to desegregate its schools and likewise ordered several southern military bases to desegregate their educational and service facilities.

These deeds reflected a growing working relationship between the White House and one of black America's premier politicians, Adam Clayton Powell. Along with William L. Dawson of Chicago, Powell sat in the House of Representatives, occupying the highest national elected office held by blacks since Reconstruction. Whereas both belonged to the Democratic party, they displayed very different styles. A product of Chicago's political machine, Dawson usually placed organizational interests above racial goals. For example, in 1952, he assumed a major role in working out a compromise on the civil rights plank of the party platform that represented a weaker version than that of 1948. In contrast, Powell had been an active protest leader in New York City, had a well-deserved reputation as a political maverick, and had voiced sharp criticism of party leaders, particularly Adlai Stevenson, for hedging on civil rights during the 1952 campaign.

With Eisenhower installed in the Oval Office, Powell aimed his sights at the Republicans and found a receptive target. The New York congressman brought the issue of segregated military installations to public attention, and he met with presidential counselors to arrange a satisfactory settlement. Powell added to his influence within GOP circles by the publication in *Reader's Digest* of his highly complimentary article about the President's civil rights achievements. Writing in 1954, he lavishly praised Eisenhower for quietly launching a "revolution" that would mean "an era of greater promise for Negro citizens." Nor did Powell's flattery diminish because the chief executive refused to support the congressman's periodic attempts to attach desegregation riders to school construction bills. This rejection did not smart so much, for Powell did not find any stronger support for his amendment among Democratic leaders.

Powell further manifested his independence by bolting to Eisenhower for President in 1956, opening the possibility of large numbers of blacks following him. Some of Eisenhower's advisers recognized the political dividends to be earned from closer administration identification with Powell and the cause of civil rights.

Congressional representatives William L.
Dawson, on the left, and Adam Clayton Powell,
standing in front of the nation's Capitol, were
known for contrasting styles of political
leadership. (UPI/Bettmann Newsphotos)

They rewarded the congressman with donations to defray the costs
of his campaign for reelection. In a less pecuniary vein, Republican
officials believed that their party had a "wonderful story to tell,"
and recommended publicizing more extensively to black audiences
the President's favorable record on civil rights.

The possible payoff from doing so was high. In 61 legislative districts outside the South, blacks held the balance of power in the
1954 congressional elections that produced thirty-two Democratic
and twenty-nine Republican victories. In 25 of these constituencies, GOP candidates won with a ratio of less than 55 percent of

the vote, while in 14 of those districts the Democrats triumphed in similar fashion. An exchange of fifteen seats from the Democratic to the Republican side would furnish the GOP with a majority in the House. A shift of two seats in the Senate would achieve Republican dominance of that body. With the political importance of this in mind, in 1956, Vice-President Nixon told a campaign audience that he awaited the day "when American boys and girls shall sit side by side, at any school... with no regard paid to the color of their skin."

Eisenhower weighed these considerations against the potential for boosting Republican votes in the South. He hoped to build upon the four southern states he had garnered in 1952. The *Brown* decision, identified with Chief Justice Earl Warren, an Eisenhower appointee, posed a dilemma for a GOP southern strategy, but the President had reduced this liability by persistently declining to speak out forcefully for school integration. Furthermore, he refused to permit his party's 1956 platform to state more than an acceptance of the Court's desegregation ruling. At the same time, Ike set out actively to court white southern ballots, especially in the states of the upper South, where Democratic attachments were less solid.

These overtures certainly dismayed black voters, but they also had reason to question the Democrats' commitment to civil rights. Concerned with recovering their earlier presidential losses among whites in the South, the Democrats attempted to soft-pedal the civil rights issue. Their nominee, Adlai Stevenson, sounded very much like Eisenhower in offering his opinion that "only 'gradual' means would satisfactorily settle the school crisis and other problems affecting equal rights for all Americans." In fact, Roy Wilkins found little to choose between in either the Democratic or Republican platforms. Expressing displeasure with both, he sarcastically observed: "The Democratic plank smelled to heaven; the Republican plank just smelled." In addition, the prominence of obstructionist southern lawmakers in the Democratic party annoyed blacks. Referring to James Eastland, the powerful chairman of the Senate Judiciary Committee, Clarence Mitchell, the NAACP's Washington lobbyist, called the segregationist senator from Mississippi a "stinking albatross around the neck of the Democratic Party." This appraisal was reinforced by Congressman Powell, who urged black voters to repudiate "Eastlandism."

Bombarded by mixed signals emitted by both partisan camps, the black electorate stuck with the Democrats while displaying some movement toward the Republicans. Though Stevenson received between 60 and 65 percent of the black vote, Eisenhower's portion rose more than 5 percent from its 1952 level. In Harlem, his share climbed by 16.5 percent, and in Chicago it jumped 11 percent. In the South, where the Democratic party stood most strongly for white supremacy, blacks exhibited the sharpest reversal from past form. Eisenhower increased his share of the black vote by 25 percent, thereby allowing him to win Tennessee and Kentucky. In the urban South, where most enfranchised blacks resided, the GOP incumbent won a majority of nonwhite votes in Atlanta, New Orleans, Memphis, and Richmond. Whereas blacks might cast a mild civil rights protest vote by favoring Eisenhower, most stayed with the Democratic party, probably in recognition of the New Deal and Fair Deal economic programs from which they benefited. Nevertheless, Roy Wilkins conjectured that the "Republicans could have wrapped up at least 65 percent of the Negro vote...if they had early and emphatically backed the [*Brown*] decision."

Although Eisenhower succeeded once again without the majority of the black electorate behind him, his improved showing encouraged the Republican administration to proceed with pushing ahead its civil rights agenda. As usual, Eisenhower moved cautiously for both philosophical and political reasons—five southern states, one more than in 1952, supported his reelection bid. But he intended to obtain legislation from Congress, something neither Roosevelt nor Truman had been able to do.

His legislative program centered on expanding the suffrage and drawing blacks into the political mainstream. The chief of the Justice Department's Civil Rights Section, Arthur Caldwell, aptly reflected the President's viewpoint. "The heart of the whole problem of racial discrimination," he asserted, "lies in determined efforts to prevent the Southern Negroes from participation in local government through the use of the vote." In contrast with his attitude toward school desegregation, Eisenhower embraced the franchise as a proper sphere of federal intervention. He considered the right to vote as the foundation of constitutional republicanism, with specific guarantees for its protection from racial bias spelled out in the Fifteenth Amendment. Besides, the chief executive emphasized the suffrage because it suited his gradualistic approach toward racial equality. As blacks gained access to the ballot box, he reasoned, they could quietly and methodically remove the barriers that confronted them. Accordingly, this deliberate process would reduce tensions by allowing time for white southerners to change their hearts and minds slowly but surely. Furthermore, especially in light of the inroads the Republicans had made among the black electorate in 1956, the President and his political aides looked forward to bringing newly enfranchised blacks into GOP ranks.

The vehicle for the Eisenhower administration's designs became the Civil Rights Act of 1957. This measure had originated two years earlier after the attorney general, Herbert Brownell, became alarmed by rising violence against southern blacks. During 1955, two black Mississippians had been murdered while engaging in voter registration activities, and a fourteen-year-old youth, Emmett Till, was kidnapped and killed by two Mississippi whites for allegedly making an improper remark to a white woman. Along with Brownell, sympathetic White House aides worried about a "dangerous racial conflagration" brewing in the South. At the same time, the Montgomery bus boycott indicated the determination of black southerners to wage, albeit nonviolently, a prolonged struggle against Jim Crow. In April 1956, Brownell responded to the potential for disruption caused by black protest and white resistance by proposing to Congress a four-part civil rights measure. This omnibus bill created a Commission on Civil Rights, upgraded the Civil Rights Section into a division within the Justice Department, and empowered the attorney general to initiate civil proceedings to enforce school desegregation and voting rights suits.

The President hesitated to embrace his attorney general's broad proposal. His cabinet divided over the matter, FBI Director J. Edgar Hoover warned about Communist influence in the civil rights movement, and the chief executive appeared reluctant to offend his white southern allies. At first, he agreed to approve only the two least controversial provisions, those establishing a Civil Rights Commission and a Civil Rights Division. However, in the heat of his campaign battle for reelection in 1956, he adopted the entire package as his own. Passed by the House, the bill died in the Senate in the clutches of Senator Eastland's Judiciary Committee.

Following Eisenhower's presidential victory, the administration revived the civil rights measure with all four sections intact. That did not last for long. A combination of presidential moderation and Democratic party factionalism shaped the final version of the bill. Never enthusiastic about the item authorizing the Justice Department to seek court orders for school desegregation, the chief executive virtually withdrew his support for it. In one memorable instance, he publicly confessed that he "didn't completely understand" the proposal. In contrast, he did not waver in his support for the suffrage recommendation. "This was the overriding provision of the bill I wanted set down in law," he told a prominent southern senator, and added: "With his right to vote assured, the Negro could use it to help secure his other rights."

The President found a powerful ally on the Democratic side of the congressional aisle. Majority Leader Lyndon B. Johnson of Texas also wanted a measure restricted to the suffrage that avoided the pitfalls of the more emotionally charged issue of school desegregation. The Texas senator was at the stage of his career when he was trying to shape a national reputation to distinguish himself from his segregationist southern colleagues. Although opposed to civil rights legislation earlier in his tenure as a lawmaker, he was never a diehard segregationist and most recently had refused to sign the Southern Manifesto condemning the *Brown* decision. With presidential ambitions possibly in his mind, he was now ready to advance a step further.

The majority leader sought to fashion a bill that would be acceptable to both liberal and conservative wings of his party, one which northern Democrats could claim as a victory for civil rights and southerners could accept as least objectionable. This last concern was particularly important. Though Johnson hoped to enhance his image in the North he retained strong roots in and affection for the South. In fact, he wished to save the region from its worst instincts, as his legislative aide explained: "The South is now completely without allies. In this situation, the South can stave off disaster only by appealing to those men who wish to see a civil rights bill enacted but who are willing to listen to reason." In serving as a broker between the two opposing camps of congressional Democrats, Johnson would improve his own chances for higher office, build party unity, and strengthen the Democrats for competing in upcoming national elections.

Driven by Johnson's skillful parliamentary maneuvering, Congress produced a moderate civil rights law. After the House passed the original four-part version of the bill, the Johnson-led Senate sliced the school desegregation feature, leaving the sections on the Civil Rights Commission, Civil Rights Division, and voting rights litigation. With these features intact, Johnson made a gesture to keep his fellow southerners from waging a filibuster against them. He engineered passage of a proviso that required voting rights infractions in certain cases to be tried before a jury. Until this point, Eisenhower had approved of Johnson's handiwork, but he balked at adding the jury trial proviso. In this instance he joined liberals in both parties who believed that reliance upon southern white juries for enforcement would severely weaken the bill. In the end, Johnson forged an alliance of southerners, Democratic moderates from the North and West, and conservative Republicans to approve the disputed item. After adopting some modifications acceptable to the President, Congress passed the bill and Eisenhower signed it into law.

The first civil rights act in eighty-two years owed its passage to a variety of sources. The Eisenhower administration sponsored the original measure and then cooperated with Johnsonian Democrats to mold it into a right-to-vote law. Southerners refrained from sabotaging the proposal through a filibuster because they could live with a bill restricted to the franchise. Though liberal lawmakers and civil rights advocates expressed great disappointment in the final outcome for its omission of school desegregation, they still took some satisfaction in securing this "half-loaf." Senator Hubert Humphrey of Minnesota remarked to Roy Wilkins: "Roy, if there's one thing I have learned in politics, it's never to turn your back on a crumb." At the very least, the NAACP and its allies had a bill aimed at expanding black voter registration, which they regarded as a significant advance. Moreover, they had a legislative precedent to build upon for the future.

THE TUSKEGEE STRUGGLE

Ultimately the success or failure of the act would be judged by its performance at the local level. The struggle for enfranchisement in Macon County, Alabama, offers a look at the interrelationship between federal policy and grassroots social change. With a unique history and social structure of its own, the county nevertheless shared many of the same experiences as hundreds of localities throughout the black belt of the South.

Located in the southeastern portion of the state, about forty-five miles from Montgomery, the county had a black population exceeding 80 percent. Its county seat of Tuskegee also had a substantial black majority, many of whom came to teach or study at the famous institute founded by Booker T. Washington in the 1880s. Many of the town's residents were employed at the Veteran's Administration Hospital built in 1923, and some had arrived as soldiers for training at the Army air field during World War II. In the postwar era, the size of the black middle class in Tuskegee swelled, and blacks held a majority of the white-collar jobs in the town. The presence of a rising black bourgeoisie centered in Tuskegee, however, could not obscure the existence of widespread poverty, especially in the rural areas of the county. In 1960, 15 percent of Macon County blacks earned $6,000 or more, a stark contrast to the 64 percent with incomes of less than $3,000.

Since the days of Booker T. Washington, when whites had cooperated in establishing Tuskegee Institute, relations between the races had been paternalistic. Whites and blacks took pride in the school as a model for racial advancement as long as it developed within a rigidly segregated environment. Early in the twentieth century a leading white politician explained how things worked: "The very best representatives of the white race, from its beginnings until now, have controlled the destinies of the town...and by the grace of God, will continue that control to the end." This "model community" depended on accommodation on the part of blacks in return for civility from whites in order to maintain this customary power relationship. Yet the pattern of interaction inherited from Washington's era contained the seeds of its own destruction. Given the space to develop their own educational and economic institutions, to lift themselves up by their bootstraps as Washington had prescribed, black Tuskegeeans demanded the full citizenship rights to which their advancement into the middle class entitled them.

To leaders of this upwardly mobile group no badge of inferiority seemed more irksome than did their exclusion from the ballot. No one had worked harder to achieve the goal of black political enfranchisement than Charles G. Gomillion. A sociologist at the institute, he was one of less than a hundred blacks in Macon County to have registered to vote by 1939. Two years later, he converted the Tuskegee Men's Club into the Tuskegee Civic Association, admitted women, and embarked on a concerted campaign to rally blacks to challenge their treatment as second-class citizens. Gomillion based his approach on the concept of "civic democracy," by which he meant that all citizens, regardless of color, had "the opportunity to participate in societal affairs, and benefit from or enjoy public services, in keeping with their interests, abilities, and needs." Without the chance for color-blind political participation, Gomillion reasoned, blacks would continue to suffer from discrimination in the allocation of resources for essential municipal services, such as health and education. Until black Tuskegeeans exercised the power of the ballot, white officials could afford to ignore their requests for equal treatment.

However cordially white rulers behaved out of a sense of paternalism toward blacks, the whites did not intend to be held politically accountable to blacks. Instead, the whites had devised a series of hurdles to prevent blacks from registering to vote. In addition to the standard poll tax restriction, the three-person county election board administered a harsh literacy test to black applicants that whites did not have to endure. The panel used its discretion to fail blacks no matter how educated they were. If blacks pressed on and refused to give up, they often could not find the board in session to risk another try. When in operation the registrars processed black applications at a snail's pace and confined waiting blacks to cramped quarters, making it uncomfortable for them to show up at the courthouse. According to Alabama law, registrars could require applicants to bring a voucher to identify them as a proper resident of the area, and in Macon County the board insisted that a black could not vouch for more than two registrants per year.

In 1945, the Tuskegee Civic Association, in cooperation with the NAACP, decided to bring the election board to court. William P. Mitchell served as the plaintiff. An employee of the VA hospital and executive secretary of the Civic Association, Mitchell had been doggedly and unsuccessfully trying for years to register. The case dragged on for two years and became moot when local officials belatedly "discovered" that Mitchell had been registered in 1943, though he had never been informed of that fact. The situation improved for a stretch of time in the late 1940s after Herman Bentley, a newly appointed member of the registration board who held a populistic commitment to political democracy, broke from tradition and agreed to sign up nonwhites. After more than 400 blacks added their names to the rolls, the other two members of the board put a halt to further progress by boycotting meetings, thereby hamstringing the panel from functioning.

This upsurge in black political participation frightened white officials. In 1950, blacks, now 30 percent of the electorate, wielded their balance of power to defeat the incumbent sheriff and replace him with a more sympathetic white candidate. The landmark *Brown* decision in 1954 and the bus boycott in nearby Montgomery the following year highlighted the threat that rising black activism posed for white supremacy. In response, Macon County officials fought back. Led by State Senator Samuel M. Engelhardt, Jr., they slowed down black registration by removing Bentley from the board and, in 1957, devised a scheme to eliminate nearly all black voters from Tuskegee. Through an imaginative redrawing of the town's boundary lines, the state legislature carved black neighborhoods out of the city, leaving the black electorate disfranchised in municipal elections and not plentiful enough to exert much influence in the county.

Whatever illusions middle-class blacks in Tuskegee may have retained about the fairness of paternalistic whites operating within a segregated system were shattered by the flagrant gerrymander. In response, the Civic Association organized a boycott—a selective buying campaign—against local white merchants. Though lay political leaders like Gomillion led the protest, ministers played an important role in mobilizing masses of blacks who regularly attended church but remained outside the sphere of Civic Association influence. The protest against the gerrymander succeeded in connecting middle-class blacks in the town with impoverished rural blacks in the surrounding county. Paralleling the situation in Montgomery, the Tuskegee boycott welded a community into a palpable force for political change. Years of voter education and litigation by the Civic Association had paved the way, but the experience of collective action rallied ordinary individuals as well as college teachers and professionals into agents of political participation. Gomillion's civic democracy came alive, as mass meetings provided an inspirational forum to build morale, share information, and maintain discipline.

Also like its Montgomery counterpart, the boycott did not force whites to capitulate to black demands; the federal government did. In 1960, the Supreme Court finally declared the gerrymander unconstitutional and restored black voters to the city's political boundaries. In *Gomillion v. Lightfoot,* Justice Felix Frankfurter denounced Alabama's peculiar "essay in geometry and geography" that impaired black voting rights under the guise "of the realignment of political subdivisions."

Macon County blacks had learned at firsthand that protest had to be reinforced by federal intervention in order to achieve equal citizenship rights. Besides the gerrymander battle, the Tuskegee Civic Association was directly involved with obtaining national legislation to erase suffrage discrimination. During the debate over the 1957 Civil Rights Act, Charles Gomillion and William Mitchell traveled to Washington to tell their stories of voter discrimination by county registrars. New York City's *Amsterdam News,* a black newspaper, declared that "nothing could throw the spotlight so brilliantly on the shame and hypocrisy of southern legislators than the fight the Negroes are now waging in Macon County...for constitutional rights to register and vote." Following passage of the 1957 law, Senator Paul Douglas, a liberal Democrat from Illinois, advised Mitchell to "continue to assemble the facts that will help to make the case for the next forward steps."

This Mitchell did by turning over to the Justice Department the voluminous records of suffrage bias he had carefully compiled over the years. As a result, one of the first suits the federal government initiated under the 1957 law pertained to Macon County. However, the Civic Association suffered a setback in 1959, when a federal judge ruled that the statute did not apply to the situation at hand. Because the members of the registration board had resigned, the government had no party to sue.

In the meantime, county residents themselves provided dramatic testimony of the trouble they experienced in attempting to exercise their political rights. In December 1958, the United States Commission on Civil Rights convened public hearings in Montgomery to investigate franchise abuses. The testimony it heard, which was recorded for broadcast on national television news programs, came across as a vivid morality play. Blacks stepped forward to testify, with both passion and dignity, to the affronts they had suffered in trying to accomplish what should have been a simple act of signing up to vote. Instead, property owners, taxpayers, veterans, college graduates, and VA hospital employees explained how the members of the registration board frequently went into hiding, how they engaged in work slowdowns, and how they failed applicants on the literacy tests without ever notifying them of the reason. "I have come up to the other requirements to make myself a citizen," a black Macon County farmer declared. "I would like to be a registered voter; they ought to give that to me. It's like I want to become a part of the government activity."

In contrast, the civil rights commissioners and television viewers saw local officials refuse either to testify under oath about their behavior or to furnish suffrage files that had been subpoenaed. One of Macon County's registrars, Grady Rogers, invoked his constitutional right against self-incrimination and further denied that the commission had the authority to probe into his activities. Faced with this lack of cooperation, the panel obtained the vital information through a court order. The records its investigators subsequently examined convinced the commissioners that the federal government would once again have to intervene to correct widespread voting discrimination. Released in 1959, the agency's report catalogued the obstructionist practices manipulated by Alabama registrars against black applicants and recommended that Congress empower the President to dispatch federal registrars to enroll qualified black voters in the South.

Though civil rights advocates like William Mitchell wholeheartedly endorsed such a proposal, national lawmakers refrained from going so far. The alliance between the Eisenhower administration and Johnson Democrats that had succeeded in 1957 triumphed again three years later. Despite objections from liberals in both parties and from civil rights lobbyists, in 1960 Congress passed a voting rights law that retained judicial supervision over the suffrage process. Instead of federal registrars, legislators authorized court-appointed referees to resolve difficult franchise cases. This procedure was substantially weaker than the one proposed by the Civil Rights Commission because it continued to rely on litigation that had proven to be slow and cumbersome in furnishing a cure for chronic discrimination.

Nevertheless, a provision of the new law immediately benefited Macon County blacks. Allowed to sue state officials when a county registration board ceased functioning, the Justice Department succeeded in obtaining a federal court injunction against prevailing voter bias in the county. In 1961, Judge Frank M. Johnson of Alabama, whose rulings on race made him one of the most liberal federal judges in the South, reviewed the copious documents gathered by the Justice Department in cooperation with the Tuskegee Civic Association and had no trouble finding ample evidence of bias. Consequently, he ordered the registration board to cease its discriminatory practices and to take positive action to speed up its work schedule, enroll qualified applicants, and report back to him on a regular basis. Within a short period, black registration more than doubled to nearly 2,500. After so many years of determination and frustration, William Mitchell was elated. "We had not even thought of such an all-inclusive decree," he jubilantly remarked.

A MEASURE OF PROGRESS

The struggle to obtain the ballot, the prerequisite for blacks to compete in the electoral system, moved forward with some success during the 1950s. Compared with the more emotional issue of school desegregation, reenfranchisement drew greater support from northern politicians and less opposition from southern officials. By lining up behind two voting rights measures in 1957 and 1960, the Eisenhower administration proferred bipartisan legitimacy to the civil rights agenda initiated by President Truman. Clearly on the defensive, white southerners, particularly in the rural black belt and in some major cities, continued to probe how they could keep black political participation to a minimum. In fact the laws were too weak to overcome all the difficulties that remained, but they did establish a crucial precedent for renewed federal intervention against racial discrimination in the South. Eisenhower also set a pattern that would guide his successors: federal intrusion in state control over racial matters would proceed cautiously, with cooperation rather than coercion the standard. Intervention did not necessarily mean invasion, and only as a last resort, as Eisenhower did in Little Rock in 1957, would a president send troops into the South to enforce federal court rulings.[2] Voluntarism backed up by litigation and administrative pressure were the preferred techniques.

For civil rights activists this approach dictated a strategy that increasingly emphasized confrontation. Only by challenging racism directly could they produce the kind of disorder and crisis that would bring federal intervention on their side. Events had already demonstrated that the civil rights movement needed to operate along two tracks—the national and the local. Without pressure from below neither the stimulus for change nor the group solidarity to propel the struggle would exist. Without assistance from above, the weapons to shatter entrenched local resistance would be missing. Blacks in Montgomery and in Macon County had shown the truth of this proposition. Combining mass action, litigation, and lobbying, African-Americans were defining their goals, mobilizing their communities around them, and drawing in national allies on their side.

[2]After a federal court decreed the desegregation of Little Rock's Central High School, Governor Orval Faubus blocked the order by deploying the Arkansas National Guard to keep out nine black students. Having initially remarked that he could foresee no circumstances that would compel him to send military forces into the South, President Eisenhower changed his mind in order to uphold the primacy of national authority. Consequently, he federalized the National Guard and dispatched paratroopers from the 101st Airborne Division to implement the law and preserve order while the students attended the school.

Chapter 3

Surging Protest, Shifting Politics

The initial ferment of black discontent in the 1950s left white supremacy challenged but unbroken. Although innovative boycotts succeeded in rallying black communities against segregation and disfranchisement, they failed to crack Jim Crow or destroy the virtual white monopoly over public affairs. Along with litigation and lobbying, sustained protests in Montgomery, Tuskegee, and scattered cities throughout the South managed to engage the federal government against racial discrimination. However, the combination of local black activism and national involvement had not yet created sufficient force to overcome massive white resistance to extending political power to blacks. Despite passage of the 1957 Civil Rights Act, by the end of the decade slightly less than three in ten adult black southerners had qualified to participate in the electoral process.

CRUSADERS FOR CITIZENSHIP

The bus boycott struggle had produced a new and potentially powerful institutional weapon to gain first-class citizenship. In 1957, the Southern Christian Leadership Conference (SCLC) was formed to coordinate local black protest movements that emerged to challenge racial bias in the South. Black ministers directed the organization. In the past the clergy had often provided conservative racial leadership, stressing otherworldly rewards for those who patiently suffered their fate in the here and now. Following World War II, a new breed of preacher arose, emphasizing Christian virtues of brotherhood, equality, and justice as principles to be attained on earth as well as in heaven. From pulpits in Montgomery, Birmingham, and Mobile, Alabama; Baton Rouge, Louisiana; Atlanta, Georgia; Nashville, Tennessee; and Tallahassee, Florida, these ministers activated the machinery of the black church and the language and symbols of the Bible to lead their congregants in battles against racism.

In effect, the SCLC functioned as "the political arm of the black church." It attempted to supplement the traditional civil rights work of the NAACP with its own brand of activism. Unlike the older group which preferred to achieve political change through legislation and the courts, the SCLC focused on direct action techniques to obtain that goal. Drawing upon their recent experiences in attacking Jim Crow, the founders of the conference chose nonviolent resistance as their primary means of combating white supremacy. This meant that the black masses would be mobilized in their local communities to confront directly the sources of their oppression. More than any other institution, the black church could provide an independent base from which to stage demonstrations and furnish the moral and social support necessary to nurture collective action. Thus, the SCLC fused religious traditionalism—the cultural heritage of the church—with political progressivism.

Though many strong-willed and independent-minded ministers created the SCLC, Martin Luther King, Jr., stood out to lead it. His compelling oratory and his courage in the face of violence during the Montgomery bus boycott thrust him into the national limelight. He had a special ability to give voice to the immediate concerns of ordinary black folks and to place their goals and aspirations within a larger national and international movement for freedom. As one of those people who sat in the mass meetings in Montgomery and heard him preach later recalled: "I mean, he was talking about what we oughta have, and what we oughta be, and what the situation oughta be in the South, and what kind of country we oughta live in." Along with many others, that listener found inspiration in King's powerful message to his audience: "If you will protest courageously, and yet with dignity and Christian love, when the history books are written in future generations, the historians will have to pause and say, 'There lived a great people—a black people—who injected new meaning and dignity into the veins of civilization.' "

King's political strategy developed from both secular and religious influences. An intellectual with a doctorate in theology from

Boston University, King studied the philosophical tracts of Henry David Thoreau, Karl Marx, Friedrich Hegel, and Reinhold Niebuhr, among others, which provided him with a framework for action in which struggle was necessary to liberate oppressed people everywhere. From Mahatma Gandhi, whose ideas he became better acquainted with through advisers such as Bayard Rustin, Dr. King adopted the philosophy of nonviolent resistance to evil. But, perhaps above all, he owed his personal resolve to challenge racism, actively yet peacefully, to Jesus of Nazareth. In his darkest moments of despair, King turned to Christ for strength in confronting the hardships of racial tyranny. In late January 1956, his arrest and the receipt of numerous threats against his life left him sorely troubled. One evening, in the quiet of the midnight hour in the kitchen of his home, he heard the voice of Jesus consoling him: "Martin Luther, stand up for righteousness. Stand up for justice. Stand up for truth. And lo I will be with you, even unto the end of the world."

This total commitment to nonviolence as a religious and ethical principle did not make King politically softminded. Though often speaking about converting the hearts and minds of white supremacists through the example of Christian love, suffering, and forgiveness on the part of blacks, he always understood that this transformation would not occur merely by persuading whites voluntarily to abandon discriminatory practices. Instead, he backed up his moralistic appeals with practical acts of coercion. Ecumenical arguments alone would never lead blacks to freedom; the application of power was essential to changing racist behavior and the underlying institutions that supported it. "When King spoke of 'converting' the oppressor," Adam Fairclough has argued, "he was thinking of a long-term historical process rather than an immediate personal response."

King and the SCLC aimed one of their first efforts at exerting political pressure on the Eisenhower administration and Congress to pass the Civil Rights Act of 1957. Joined by A. Philip Randolph, the architect of the 1941 March on Washington Movement, and Roy Wilkins of the NAACP, King convened a "Prayer Pilgrimage" in the nation's capital "to give thanks for progress to-date, and pray for wiping out the evils that still beset us." For months the SCLC chief had pressed Eisenhower to condemn racist violence against blacks in a major address delivered in a southern city. Repeatedly rebuffed, King informed him that if "you, our President, cannot come South, we shall have to lead our people to you." On May 17, 1957, in commemoration of the third anniversary of the *Brown* decision, nearly 30,000 people gathered to hear King call for the passage of legislation guaranteeing the ballot, which, he declared, would clear the way for the attainment of the other basic rights blacks sought.

Though the convocation came off smoothly, it took final shape in a manner different from that originally conceived. While King prepared to practice the new politics of mass mobilization, Adam Clayton Powell and leaders of the NAACP implemented the old-fashioned politics of power brokerage. The close relationship between the New York City congressman and the Eisenhower administration paid off for the President. Powell, as well as Roy Wilkins, opposed the march as a means of applying pressure on the chief executive. Rather, they favored the protesters directing their full force at Congress, urging it to pass civil rights legislation. Along with NAACP representatives, Powell succeeded in steering attention away from the President as a target of the demonstration. Administration officials breathed a sigh of relief that they had avoided "the damaging effects of a spectacular effort designed to criticize the president." Consequently, in his address Dr. King denounced the lawmakers of both parties who "so often have a high blood pressure of words and an anemia of deeds."

At this early stage in his career, King had limited effectiveness as a national political leader. However significant the Washington demonstration may have been in rallying tens of thousands of blacks in protest against racial discrimination, it had little impact on the eventual enactment of the civil rights bill. Furthermore, it had no immediate impact in persuading the President to make even a symbolic gesture that would recognize the legitimate concerns of civil rights advocates. In June 1957, the Reverend King managed to meet with Vice-President Richard Nixon, who affirmed his personal support for civil rights; nevertheless, the President himself refused to confer with black leaders despite their repeated requests for an appointment. Not until June 1958 did the chief executive hold his first and only conference with a delegation of black leaders. On this occasion they discussed voting rights enforcement, but reached no agreement on the need for stronger implementation by the federal government of the 1957 statute.

By then, King and the SCLC had launched their own project within the South designed to register the majority of disfranchised blacks. They hoped to build upon the momentum of the bus boycotts and galvanize the black electorate as an active force in regional and national politics. "The time has come to broaden the struggle for Negroes to register and vote," the SCLC declared, "for the simple reason that until this happens, we cannot really influence the legislative branch of government." In the past the NAACP, civic leagues, unions, and the churches had conducted voter registration drives. The SCLC sought to link these traditional efforts with its emerging direct action program. The passage of the 1957 Civil Rights Act offered the prospect of federal judicial support for the suffrage, but King believed the effectiveness of the remedy would "depend in large degree upon programs of sustained mass movement on the part of Negroes." According to the SCLC's president: "History has demonstrated that inadequate legislation supported by mass action can accomplish more than adequate legislation which remains unenforced for lack of a determined mass movement."

On February 12, 1958, the birthday of Abraham Lincoln, the Southern Conference embarked on a project to help emancipate blacks from the "strong fear and deep antipathy toward having anything to do with politics." The Crusade for Citizenship hoped by 1960 to enroll an additional 3 million black southerners as voters, doubling the number already on the books. Toward that goal, it planned to coordinate mass registration campaigns through community-based civic organizations and churches. Workshops, clinics, and rallies were conducted in cities throughout the South— Montgomery, Birmingham, Memphis, Atlanta—where SCLC had strong affiliates. Not only would prospective registrants learn how to satisfy suffrage requirements, but they also would learn about the strategy of direct action that SCLC espoused. At the very least, the Crusade intended to gather specific complaints of voter discrimination and turn them over to the federal government.

These ambitious designs went largely unrealized. As a fledgling organization the SCLC lacked the funds and experience to implement such a massive enterprise. Budgeted for $200,000, the Crusade failed to raise more than a quarter of that amount. Inadequate finances placed an economic burden on the Crusade's overworked staff. Ella Baker, who nearly single-handedly managed the operation, received little support from the agency's ministerial leaders.

Baker did not lack the talent or experience to perform the job, for she had served as field secretary and director of branches for the NAACP. However, she was the lone female on the SCLC's administrative staff, and she suffered from the slights of paternalistic male preachers, who did not view women as equal partners and whose powerful egos made it difficult to impose strict organizational discipline upon them.

Even without these internal problems, the SCLC encountered a nearly insurmountable task. The rise of massive white resistance following the *Brown* ruling, though directed mainly at halting school desegregation, thwarted civil rights activities of any kind. Southern officials employed literacy tests and other restrictive registration methods to retard black electoral participation. In the face of suffrage discrimination and in a hostile environment that punitively discouraged minority voting, the SCLC had little chance of reaching most disfranchised southern blacks. Instead of the 3 million new voters that the SCLC targeted, only 160,000 blacks signed up to vote between 1958 and 1960. Still, the group did compile a list of suffrage grievances and presented them for investigation to the United States Civil Rights Commission and the Justice Department.

In addition, the SCLC received scant help from the NAACP. Under assault by southern state governments, the association's activities were suspended or severely limited in several areas. Besides, the NAACP viewed the formation of the Southern Conference with misgivings, fearful of the competition it would provide for funds and publicity. During this same period the National Association, despite its hardships, inaugurated a campaign to register 3 million southern blacks. It, too, fell far short of the mark. Neither conventional registration drives nor those linked to direct action worked against the firm obstacles erected by the white South. Beset by serious internal and external difficulties, by 1960 King and the SCLC had failed to rally the black masses behind the ballot.

With the efforts of the SCLC and the NAACP stymied, the movement for first-class citizenship needed a boost. Blacks had barely penetrated the wall of white supremacy, and fresh troops and ideas were needed to scale over it. The federal government had provided some welcome judicial and legislative relief, but Washington expected southern blacks and whites to resolve their problems largely at the local level.

Civil rights leaders recognized that they did not have sufficient power to win by themselves; yet, at the same time, they understood the importance of blacks joining together to fight for their own freedom. The adoption of boycotts as a response to discrimination had evidenced this. A useful means of forging collective action, they nevertheless possessed limited political advantages. A boycott had the effect of withdrawing blacks from participation in economic and civic life until white businesses or local officials capitulated. Civil rights proponents needed additional techniques that would actively engage blacks in directly confronting white racist practices, particularly those from which they were excluded. Through such encounters they would dramatically expose the source of their oppression, bring the evil to the surface, and exert moral pressure to eradicate it. In the process, people would have to break laws they considered unjust and go to jail for their convictions. By doing so they would ultimately transform themselves, their communities, and their nation.

On February 1, 1960, southern blacks took a critical step in forging those new tactics. Students in Greensboro, North Carolina, shook up the freedom struggle, provided a powerful nonviolent weapon, and furnished fresh, youthful people to deploy it. By sitting down at a segregated Woolworth's lunch counter that would not accommodate them and demanding equal service, four black undergraduates at North Carolina Agricultural and Technical State University energized a sagging protest movement. Within two months their action sparked similar demonstrations in some 60 cities throughout the South, involving thousands of high school and college students, and by year's end protests had sprouted in over 200 cities. What King's Crusade for Citizenship had failed to do for direct action over a span of two years was achieved virtually overnight. These sit-ins spawned wade-ins, kneel-ins, stand-ins, and freedom rides, all designed to bring together ordinary folks to challenge racial oppression head on. The result of these dynamic efforts did not always lead immediately to integration or equality; however, they did help liberate those who participated in them. "I felt as though I had gained my manhood," Franklin McCain, one of the original Greensboro four, declared, "not only gained it, but had developed quite a respect for it."

Many cities throughout the South proved ready to be ignited by these young activists. In Greensboro, for example, the roots of protest were sunk deep. The NAACP had maintained an active chapter since the 1930s, and in 1943, Ella Baker had established an NAACP Youth Group in the city, an organization two of the original sit-in demonstrators subsequently joined. The local black high school also served as a training ground for black insurgency. Several teachers inspired their students to think about the history and culture of African-Americans as a struggle for freedom and to relate their own lives to that quest. "I had to tell youngsters," one instructor remarked, "that the way you find things need not happen. . . . I don't care if they push and shove you, you must not accept [discrimination]." This lesson received positive reinforcement from the pastor of the Shiloh Baptist Church, which some of the students attended. During the 1950s, their minister had been active in civil rights affairs and only recently had succeeded in leading a drive to double the membership of the NAACP chapter.

Furthermore, the young protesters lived in a city in which blacks had gained a measure of access to the electoral process. The heightened political assertiveness that blacks displayed after World War II surfaced early in Greensboro. In 1949, two black candidates for the city council made it through the primary, only to lose in the general election. Following this contest the Greensboro Citizens Association, a black civic league interested in improving municipal services in their community, mounted a voter registration drive that led to the election of its president, Dr. William Hampton, to the council in 1951. Although Hampton ran reasonably well in white precincts, he scored much more impressively in black districts. In unprecedented fashion, black voters united as a solid bloc behind a candidate of their own race. In previous years they had split their votes among various white contestants, but, as one black politician later explained, "You don't help a black by putting his name on the ticket and then voting for six white candidates because you are scattering your vote."

This modest electoral success did not fulfill rising black expectations. During the 1950s, the single council seat occupied by a black as well as the selection of a black to the school board did not alter traditional patterns of racial inequality. Instead, what William H. Chafe has termed "sophisticated American racism" prevailed in Greensboro. Following the *Brown* decision, white leaders permitted only token desegregation of the schools, closed recreational facilities rather than integrated them, and steered black college graduates away from white-collar employment. They did so with civility, not brutality, thereby projecting an image of progress. Outnumbered by whites, the lone blacks on the council and the school board had no leverage to reverse this course. Ironically, their very presence on these panels served to legitimize the discriminatory policies the majority adopted. Thus, the Woolworth sit-in represented both continuity with the black community's past and a significant departure from the electoral and judicial strategies that had stalled in obtaining racial justice.

The creative energy of the sit-ins flowed into the formation of the Student Nonviolent Coordinating Committee (SNCC). Convening in Raleigh, North Carolina, in April 1960, recent protest veterans sought to establish an organization that offered new political leadership. James Lawson, who had been active in the development of the Nashville sit-in movement, expressed the participants' disdain for "middle-class conventional, half-way efforts to deal with radical social evil." They wanted to replace the NAACP's emphasis on litigation with the nonviolent power of "a people no longer the victims of racial evil who can act in a disciplined manner to implement the Constitution." Toward this end, SNCC founders shared the vision of an interracial beloved community preached by Dr. King and SCLC. Indeed, Lawson and others had been inspired by the Montgomery bus boycott and the exercise of grassroots direct action.

Yet if the iconoclastic committee rejected the tactics of the NAACP, it also eschewed any formal affiliation with the SCLC. Part of this independence resulted from a need for self-preservation, a desire not to become absorbed within another organization, and a preference for retaining maximum flexibility of action. But the choice of autonomy reflected an even deeper wish to break with the style of leadership exhibited by Dr. King. Though SNCC's philosophy of nonviolent civil disobedience dovetailed with the SCLC's, the student group had doubts about organizing a mass movement around a single charismatic personality. It adopted instead a decentralized organizational structure, stressed group decision-making, and encouraged the emergence of leadership from indigenous black communities. In effect, SNCC echoed the criticism of Ella Baker, who had become disenchanted with the SCLC. Miss Baker, as she was affectionately called, argued that a "prophetic leader" like Dr. King ultimately stifled the opportunity for people to tailor unique programs to suit their own particular needs.

The perspectives that separated the two groups did not deter the students from cooperating with Dr. King. The SCLC president had earned a national reputation for his civil rights activities, which gave him contacts with important political figures that they did not have. By the autumn of 1960, King had moved from Montgomery to his birthplace of Atlanta, where he copastored the Ebenezer Baptist Church with his father. In the "City Too Busy to Hate," as the mayor referred to it, black students from Morehouse College, King's alma mater, initiated sit-in demonstrations to desegregate downtown eating establishments. Moderate white and black leaders, including "Daddy" King, disapproved of the continuing protests, but the demonstrators persuaded a reluctant Martin, Jr., to join them. In doing so not only did they receive prominent help for their local struggle, but they also set off a chain of events that reverberated nationally and connected black politics with the White House.

On October 19, 1960, Dr. King joined some seventy-five demonstrators in seeking to integrate the cafeteria at Rich's Department Store, where blacks were welcome to spend their money but not to eat. The protest ended in the arrest of King and the others for trespassing. Detained for several days, all but Dr. King were finally released. Earlier in the year, the Atlanta minister had been arrested for driving without a valid Georgia license, issued a fine, and placed on one year's probation. As a result of his current arrest, a county judge ruled that King had violated his probation and sentenced him to four months of hard labor at the state prison.

Although the harsh sentence was not anticipated, the arrest fitted in with a larger plan the student demonstrators had formulated. The incident came in the midst of the presidential contest between John F. Kennedy and Richard M. Nixon, an opportunity the civil rights forces hoped to exploit. One of the organizers of the protest at Rich's recalled that it was deliberately timed "so as to influence the election." The student activists expected that King's arrest "would create enough of a national uproar in the black community," and they intended to put the candidates on the spot concerning their positions on civil rights. "I did not have a preference, believe it or not, between Nixon or Kennedy," recalled Lonnie King, a student activist who was not related to the imprisoned minister.

This neutral stand was hardly surprising. As a Republican member of Congress, senator, and vice-president, Richard Nixon had antagonized liberals on the issue of anti-Communism, but on racial matters he backed reform. One of the few top-level officials in the Eisenhower administration to endorse the *Brown* ruling, the vice-president strongly supported the 1957 civil rights legislation and used his position as presiding officer of the Senate to assist in passage of the measure. Nixon also chaired the President's Committee on Government Contracts, which investigated charges of racial discrimination in federally related employment and sponsored education campaigns to further equal opportunity. He had conferred with Martin Luther King on a couple of occasions during the 1950s and earned praise from the civil rights leader for making "a real impression on the Negro."

As might be expected of a Democratic senator from Massachusetts, John F. Kennedy had routinely supported proposals to relieve the plight of blacks in the South. He voted for civil rights legislation in 1957 and 1960, and spoke out firmly for acceptance of the *Brown* verdict. Yet, Carl Brauer has noted, Senator Kennedy approached civil rights issues as "a moderate by conviction and design." Unwilling to address racial matters as a category of special concern, he considered them an expression of larger social and economic problems. The senator acted more for political reasons than out of any moral obligation and did just enough to court the black electorate in his home state. At the same time, he spent much effort in wooing the white South. In 1957, Kennedy voted for Lyndon Johnson's jury trial amendment to the civil rights bill, a deed that angered liberals and delighted southern conservatives. His pragmatic approach to civil rights questions won for his presidential bid the early endorsement of Governor John Patterson of Alabama, who thought Kennedy "would probably be more understanding of our situation down here" than any other possible Democratic candidate.

That same practical outlook guided Kennedy in his pursuit of the presidency. As the Democratic nominee he selected Harris Wofford, a white attorney with the U.S. Commission on Civil Rights, and several prominent blacks for his campaign staff. One of them, Louis Martin, the editor of the *Chicago Defender*, convinced the opportunistic Congressman Adam Clayton Powell, who had flirted with the Eisenhower administration for the preceding half-dozen years, to join the Kennedy bandwagon. Along with the perennial Democratic stalwart, Congressman William Dawson of Chicago, Powell very effectively spoke in northern black ghettos on Kennedy's behalf. Wofford also introduced Kennedy to Dr. King, who came away from the meeting with a favorable impression of the Democratic aspirant. Still, King considered Nixon a loyal supporter of civil rights, and he declined to endorse either candidate.

The influential black presence in the Democratic camp partially offset Kennedy's choice for vice-president, Senator Lyndon B. Johnson of Texas. Apparently chosen to appeal to Democratic voters in the South, this grandson of a former Civil War Confederate received a low rating among party liberals and blacks for weakening civil rights legislation. Nevertheless, while Johnson soothed southern audiences with his down-home stories, he also reassured blacks "that I have done my dead best to make progress in the field of civil rights."

Nixon followed a similar route. Like Kennedy he ran on a strong civil rights platform that pledged firm executive leadership, promised new legislation to combat suffrage and employment discrimination, backed legal and technical assistance for school desegregation, and upheld the right of sit-in demonstrators to assemble peacefully. Also like his Democratic rival, Nixon labored to improve his standing with southern whites. The GOP nominee campaigned vigorously in the deep South, where he counseled gradualism and urged justice for blacks not as a moral imperative but as a means of undermining Communist exploitation of racial tensions for propaganda purposes. Furthermore, by not appearing in Harlem, as Eisenhower had done, and by appointing few blacks to important and visible roles in his campaign, Nixon avoided offending the white South. One prominent black who joined Nixon's staff, E. Frederic Morrow, an assistant in the Eisenhower White House, bitterly complained that he did not receive any specific assignment or support.

The political balancing acts of both candidates suffered a severe jolt from the arrest of Dr. King in October, just as the student activists had hoped. The nominees reacted very differently, however. Treading lightly at first, Senator Kennedy decided to work for King's release on bail through Georgia's Democratic governor, Ernest Vandiver, and his state campaign director, Griffin Bell. When negotiations stalled, Harris Wofford and Louis Martin came up with the idea of having Kennedy telephone a worried Mrs. Coretta King to express his concern for her husband's safety. This sympathetic gesture did not free the celebrated prisoner, and the candidate's brother and closest adviser, Robert Kennedy, wrestled with the thorny question of whether to take additional action. Initially he had been angry with Wofford for his attempt to involve the senator directly in the King affair, fearing an adverse southern white response. Also concerned with black ballots, he quickly changed his mind, interceded with the Democratic county judge presiding over the case, and obtained King's release on bail. "I called him," Robert Kennedy told Wofford, "because it made me so damned angry to think of that bastard sentencing a citizen to... hard labor for a minor traffic offense and screwing up my brother's campaign."

In contrast, Nixon remained publicly silent during this episode. Privately he believed that King had received a "bum rap," but that it would be improper for him as a lawyer to communicate with the judge. Perhaps he was more interested in political calculations. Nixon refused to heed the plea of a prominent black Republican in Atlanta to make a statement in support of King, telling him "He [Nixon] would lose some black votes, but he'd gain white votes." Still, seeking to walk a fine tightrope, he had the Justice Department draft a statement for President Eisenhower's release, calling the sentencing of King "fundamentally unjust" and directing the attorney general "to take all proper steps" to free him. When Eisenhower declined to authorize such a statement, Nixon lost the opportunity to neutralize Kennedy's efforts on King's behalf.

The Democrats turned the King incident to their advantage. The civil rights leader commended Senator Kennedy for his courage and remarked: "There are moments when the politically expedient can be morally wise." With less than two weeks before the election, the Kennedy campaign distributed nearly 2 million pamphlets, entitled *The Case of Martin Luther King*, in black communities throughout the nation, publicizing the matter. One of the endorsements Kennedy obtained came from Dr. King's father, a Baptist minister who originally had intended to vote against the Democrat because of his Catholic religion. "I've got all my votes and I've got a suitcase and I'm going to take them up there and dump them in his lap," the Reverend King, Sr., declared. Likewise, the younger King's closest friend and colleague in the SCLC, Ralph David Abernathy, remarked: "I earnestly and sincerely feel it is time for all of us to take off our Nixon buttons."

Approximately 68 percent of the black electorate agreed by casting their votes for Kennedy. The Democrats won by less than

120,000 popular votes, three-tenths of 1 percent of the total, and by eighty-four electoral votes. This razor-thin victory highlighted the significant role played by African-Americans in determining the outcome. In several key northern states rich with electoral votes— Illinois, Michigan, New Jersey, and Pennsylvania—black votes made the difference. In the South, blacks helped put the Kennedy-Johnson ticket over the top in South Carolina and Texas. Nixon carried only three states in the region, Florida, Tennessee, and Virginia, two fewer than Eisenhower did in 1956. Nationwide, Kennedy needed strong black support to offset the 52 percent majority Nixon rolled up among white voters. Had not the senator succeeded in regaining 7 percent of the black vote that went to Eisenhower four years before, Richard Nixon would have entered the White House in 1960.

This key segment of the electorate returned to the Democratic party for a variety of reasons. With the popular Eisenhower out of the race, the proportion of black Democratic support again reached its previously high 1952 level. Because Kennedy's civil rights record going into the contest appeared no stronger than Nixon's, the Democratic nominee's intervention in the King controversy attracted blacks who were inclined to vote Republican or, at the very least, retained the loyalty of black Protestants who opposed Kennedy on religious grounds. But the King incident does not explain the entire matter. In King's home city of Atlanta, Nixon outpolled Kennedy in black districts, though his 54 percent marked a slip of twelve points from Eisenhower's share in 1956. Just as important as civil rights, economic considerations steered blacks into the Democratic column. Kennedy benefited from the recession in the last year of the Eisenhower term. The recession hurt economically vulnerable blacks and strengthened their attachment to the Democratic Party, which promised financial relief from hard times.

THE KENNEDY ADMINISTRATION AND CIVIL RIGHTS

As in 1948, black ballots contributed significantly in electing a Democratic President, but the prospective rewards remained unclear. Kennedy had delivered ambiguous messages during his campaign. His gesture toward King, his appointment of black advisers, and his pledge to exert strong executive action to remove discrimination in such areas as housing suggested that a great leap foward was about to take place on the civil rights front in Washington. Yet Kennedy had also led the white South to believe that, as Carl Brauer has noted, "he would not favor a reinstitution of Reconstruction." These soothing words had aided Kennedy in securing 50.5 percent of the popular vote in the South, a rise of nearly three points from Stevenson's total in 1956. In all likelihood Kennedy would have done even better in this bastion of Protestant fundamentalism had his religion, much more than civil rights, not been an issue. Furthermore, even if President Kennedy desired to push for new legislation to combat racial bigotry, he faced a Congress in which southern Democrats wielded disproportionate influence through their control of potent committees, their deployment of the Senate filibuster, and their alliance with conservative Republicans to thwart reform measures.

Caught between rising black electoral strength and entrenched southern white political power, President Kennedy ventured circumspectly in the field of civil rights. Like his predecessor, the President opted to concentrate on extending the suffrage to blacks and drawing them into the political mainstream. Where African-Americans "are given their rights to participate in the political process," Kennedy asserted, "they do it as free individuals...giving their considered judgment on what is best for their country and what is best for themselves and what is best for the cause of freedom." In the tradition of Eisenhower he placed his faith in the courts to ensure equal voting rights for southern blacks. However, Kennedy instructed the Department of Justice, headed by his brother, Robert, to enforce the Civil Rights Acts of 1957 and 1960 more vigorously than had the previous Eisenhower administration. Combining executive and judicial action, the Kennedys hoped to satisfy civil rights proponents without unduly antagonizing southern lawmakers in Congress.

This approach was threatened by rising civil rights militancy in 1961. In May, "freedom rides," aiming to desegregate interstate bus terminal facilities, encountered vicious attacks by southern white extremists. Integrated buses carrying passengers recruited by CORE and SNCC were assaulted and burned outside of Birmingham, Alabama. In Montgomery, a white mob beat the riders as they departed from their bus. Later a bloodthirsty crowd surrounded a church and menaced its congregants gathered inside to hear Martin Luther King voice his support for the protesters. Despite the fact that the Supreme Court had outlawed segregated terminals serving interstate travelers, the Kennedy administration tried to defuse this crisis by urging a cooling-off period during which the civil rights forces would suspend their offensive against Jim Crow. The White House desperately wanted to avoid sending in federal troops to the South for fear of reviving memories of post-Civil War Reconstruction, but the demonstrators refused to comply. In the end, Kennedy dispatched civilian federal marshals to restore peace in Alabama, and the attorney general worked out an agreement with the governor of Mississippi to provide protection for incoming riders before subjecting them to arrest. Finally, the Justice Department obtained a decree from the Interstate Commerce Commission, banning segregated facilities in interstate transportation.

The Kennedy administration attempted to reduce the possibility of provoking further racial confrontations that would again drag the federal government into a clash with state officials. Seeking to channel black protest in a "safer" direction, the Kennedys encouraged voter registration activities. Suffrage drives were a regular feature of American life and civil rights organizations, such as the NAACP and SCLC, had incorporated them as an essential part of their programs. In contrast to the highly publicized and confrontational sit-ins and freedom rides that often generated violence, voter registration drives promised peaceful, nonconfrontational efforts to place the names of blacks on the suffrage lists. Besides keeping the President from having to dispatch federal troops to Dixie in Reconstruction era fashion, a voter registration strategy might enhance the fortunes of the reformist wing of the Democratic party. Additional black voters presumably would support at the national level the party that enfranchised them, and their ballots would also serve to select more moderate officeholders in the South.

The Voter Education Project (VEP) grew out of this convergence of politics and principle. In the wake of the freedom rides, the Kennedy administration believed that "it would be valuable if some of the present energy were channeled into this vital [registration] work." The Justice Department had already begun to file suffrage litigation and invited civil rights groups to work in this area and collect evidence of ongoing discrimination. Kennedy aides with contacts in liberal philanthropic foundations arranged to obtain financing for nonpartisan voter registration activities. Under the auspices of the Southern Regional Council, a private interracial agency based in Atlanta, nearly a million dollars were raised to conduct voter education projects. The council hired Wiley Branton, a black civil rights lawyer from Arkansas, to direct the enterprise and elicited participation from the major civil rights organizations—the NAACP, SCLC, SNCC, CORE, and the Urban League, an organization specializing in housing and employment programs.

Bringing these groups together was a significant political achievement. Though in agreement with Dr. King's assertion that "if we in the South can win the right to vote it...will give us the concrete tool with which we ourselves can correct injustice," they regarded each other warily. The NAACP viewed itself as the premier organization in the fight for black enfranchisement. Tenaciously guarding its terrain, the national association looked suspiciously at rival organizations that had recently arrived on the scene. The NAACP particularly worried about competition from SCLC, whose president, Dr. King, exhibited considerable success as a fund-raiser and organizer of affiliates throughout the South. Because money was usually a scarce resource for civil rights groups, each agency needed to stand in the center of public attention and earn credit for accomplishments that would attract new supporters and financial contributions. SNCC and CORE posed an additional problem for the NAACP, which feared that their direct-action orientation would foster troublesome, diversionary operations pointed away from the goal of suffrage. Placing its commitment to the ballot first, the NAACP cast aside its misgivings and joined the coalition.

From a different perspective, SNCC also worried about signing up with the VEP. Born out of the sit-in movement and weaned on the freedom rides, the group's members suspected that white liberals and established civil rights leaders wanted to raise the child in their own image. For its part, SNCC was ready to stand among adults and pursue its goals militantly. Though some considered the VEP as a clever means of sidetracking protest, the young activists decided to join the project. The fresh infusion of outside funds for voter registration would save the group the money necessary to continue mass action demonstrations. Moreover, persuaded by Robert Parris Moses, a soft-spoken, intense, and compelling field secretary from New York City, SNCC viewed voter registration as a potentially radical means of transforming the political and social lives of southern blacks and whites. "In many ways," one SNCC staffer explained, "it seems to me that the voter registration project is even more significant than other forms of protest. The problem is being attacked at its core. A new sense of human dignity and self respect is being discovered."

Whatever reservations SNCC, the NAACP, and the rest of their civil rights comrades harbored, they agreed that the federal government would try to shelter them from racist harm. Without spelling out their intentions, Justice Department officials, who helped arrange for the creation of the VEP, pledged the cooperation of the Kennedy administration in implementing the project. The civil rights representatives attending planning sessions in 1961 left thinking that they could turn to Washington for staunch protection against violent attacks and other forms of harassment from white supremacists. Wiley Branton inferred that "the Justice Department would take all steps necessary to protect federal or constitutional rights" which embraced "the elementary matter of protection."

The Justice Department held a different view. Attorney General Kennedy and his staff wanted to keep the federal government out of the law enforcement business for political and constitutional reasons. They hesitated to ship troops or marshals into Dixie for fear of alienating powerful southern lawmakers whose cooperation the administration needed to pass its legislative program. Furthermore, they argued that the Constitution left law enforcement in local hands, and they did not want to discourage local responsibility by taking over police powers. Besides, federal lawyers insisted that the national government did not maintain its own police force and that the Federal Bureau of Investigation did not function in that capacity. They envisioned a cooperative partnership between national and state authorities, based on goodwill and mutual trust, and exercised through voluntary compliance rather than coercion. If disputes arose that threatened the constitutional rights and safety of the voter registration workers, the Justice Department preferred to assist them through the courts, not with armed force.

Robert Kennedy had deliberately chosen his top assistant in charge of civil rights enforcement to reflect this viewpoint. He did not want a crusader in the post, and so picked a negotiator. The attorney general passed over Harris Wofford, who had strong civil rights credentials, in favor of Burke Marshall, who had virtually none. Kennedy did not desire someone for the job who had a passionate commitment to racial equality. He explained that he wanted instead a "tough lawyer who could look at things... objectively." Intending to administer existing suffrage laws more forcefully than before, Kennedy desired the head of the Civil Rights Division to appear neutral and not too closely identified with the civil rights movement. Accordingly, he hoped that the image of evenhandedness would make it easier to deal with southern segregationists, such as James Eastland of Mississippi, who chaired the Senate Judiciary Committee. Marshall fit the bill and said he intended "to make the federal system in the voting field work by itself through local action, without federal court compulsion."

The two-front attack initiated by the Voter Education Project and the Justice Department helped boost political participation in the South. From 1962 to 1964, the VEP accounted for some 287,000 new black registrants, about half of the increase. The Department of Justice supplemented these efforts by filing approximately fifty voting rights suits. Overall, during this period the proportion of southern black registrants jumped from 29.4 percent to 43.1 percent, the steepest rise since 1952 [see Table 1]. The bulk of the new voters generally came from urban areas in which hostility to black suffrage was less than in the rural black belt and the unusually repressive cities like Birmingham, where white extremists resorted to bombs to restrict ballots.

These accomplishments exacted a high price. The failure of the federal government to furnish protection for civil rights workers hampered their effectiveness and engendered their bitterness. Field staff from SNCC and CORE dug themselves into the most hard-core–resistant locales in Mississippi, Alabama, Louisiana, and Georgia and met verbal threats, violence, and intimidation by the police. The supposedly safe act of canvassing potential registrants door-to-door and accompanying them to the courthouse often converted suffrage drives into direct-action confrontations. The local law enforcement officers the Justice Department depended on to keep the peace themselves violated the constitutional rights of registration workers. At the mercy of sheriffs who interpreted the law from the grip of a billy club or the handle of a gun, the suffragists pleaded with the Kennedy administration for assistance.

In response, they received sympathy rather than protection. If the FBI appeared on the scene it was not to make arrests but to jot down their observations. In pursuit of interstate car thieves, kidnappers, and bank robbers, the bureau worked closely with local

Table 1   Black Voter Registration in the South, 1944–1964[a]

	1940	1947	1952	1960	1962	1964
Alabama	0.4	1.2	5.0	13.7	13.4	23.0
Arkansas	1.5	17.3	27.0	37.3	34.0	49.3
Florida	5.7	15.4	33.0	38.9	36.8	63.8
Georgia	3.0	18.8	23.0	29.3	26.7	44.0
Louisiana	0.5	2.6	25.0	30.9	27.8	32.0
Mississippi	0.4	0.9	4.0	5.2	5.3	6.7
North Carolina	7.1	15.2	18.0	38.1	35.8	46.8
South Carolina	0.8	13.0	20.0	15.6	22.9	38.7
Tennessee	6.5	25.8	27.0	58.9	49.8	69.4
Texas	5.6	18.5	31.0	34.9	37.3	57.7
Virginia	4.1	13.2	16.0	22.8	24.0	45.7
Total	3.0	12.0	20.0	29.1	29.4	43.1

[a]Estimated percentage of voting-age blacks registered.

SOURCE: David Garrow, *Protest at Selma* (New Haven, Conn.: Yale University Press, 1978), 7, 11, 19.

law enforcement officials, including those in the South, and did not want to jeopardize this cooperation by interfering with traditional racial practices. "You couldn't find those bastards," Timothy Jenkins, a student activist complained about federal agents in general: "All the force, all the demonstrations of force and intimidation... were on the side of the local authorities who wore badges and suits, and they had the ostensible perquisites of the state. Our part of the state was invisible—the federal state."

The Justice Department's reliance on the courts did not help the situation. The Kennedy administration had appointed to federal benches in the South a handful of judges who steadfastly resisted its efforts to enforce suffrage laws and shield individuals who peacefully engaged in voter registration activities. Judges like William Harold Cox of Mississippi publicly belittled the claims both of Justice Department lawyers and black litigants who appeared before him. These judges won appointment, because the President as a matter of courtesy, had to clear their names with the Democratic senators from their home states. The potential choices were narrowed even further, for the candidates had to pass through the nomination roadblock set up by Chairman Eastland's Judiciary Committee. Not all of Kennedy's selections behaved poorly, but too frequently the obstructionist jurists presided in precisely those areas where registration workers faced the greatest hazards.

SNCC'S ENCOUNTER WITH MISSISSIPPI

The experiences of SNCC in Mississippi demonstrated the challenges to black political development. In the deep South, the civil rights activists struggled to organize blacks in local communities to liberate themselves from oppressive white domination. They saw voter registration not as an end in itself but as the means for black people to obtain power to secure control of their lives. According to Bob Moses, the architect of much of SNCC's suffrage strategy, the real issue was "not only do you gain the right to vote but you begin to change all the other educational values." The ballot could open the way for blacks to determine their own leaders and change the conditions that exploited them. Indeed, to the young radicals politics was the key to rearranging economic and social relations. Lawrence Guyot, a SNCC field-worker in Mississippi, explained his group's message: "There is a relationship between your not being able to feed your children and your not registering to vote."

The key to political organizing in the black belt was first to overcome fear. In the Mississippi delta area, blacks had to muster sufficient courage to make an attempt to register. During the late 1950s and early 1960s, several blacks had been killed in retaliation for their political activities, and their deaths served as a vivid reminder for others who might follow them. Short of murder, white supremacists kept blacks in line through economic intimidation. Plantation owners fired "troublemakers" and stores cut off their credit. In August 1962, Mrs. Fannie Lou Hamer filled out a voter registration form and was fired from her job on a Ruleville plantation immediately after she refused to withdraw her application. The SNCC workers who entered these dangerous areas were also subjected to an array of threats, arrests, and brutality. They grappled with their personal fears even as they joined with those they were trying to mobilize to do collectively what was so difficult to do alone. "To go with friends and neighbors," SNCC field secretary Charles Cobb remarked, "made the attempt less frightening and reduced the chances of physical assault at the courthouse, since cowards don't like to openly attack numbers." Still, the struggle

Bob Moses along with other SNCC workers on a voter registration campaign in Mississippi. (Danny Lyon/Magnum)

against fear, no matter how successful in persuading blacks to defy racial discrimination, did not confer the right to vote.

While laboring to extend political power at the grassroots level, SNCC fully realized that without federal intervention it could not break the hold of white control over local electoral institutions. In addition to its campaigns of community organizing, SNCC fought the interconnected battle of mobilizing Washington on its side. The group's staff operated in the rural sections where voter registration was certain to arouse racial confrontation. SNCC planned the national dimension of its strategy to focus attention on what was happening in this "other America." Amzie Moore, the longtime fighter for civil rights who had first brought Bob Moses to the Magnolia State, sought to "expose the conditions in Mississippi with reference to people voting...to uncover what is covered." The civil rights activists counted on newspaper and television reporters to record their plight and influence public opinion in their favor, thereby pressuring the Justice Department to furnish the necessary protection.

Greenwood, Mississippi, sorely tested SNCC's strategy. In LeFlore County, of which this Delta town was the county seat, blacks comprised 64 percent of the population but only 9 percent of the registered voters. In June 1962, SNCC assigned Sam Block to launch a voter education drive in the area. A native Mississippian, the twenty-three-year-old Block had been deeply influenced by the murder of Emmett Till seven years before, which made him realize that one day he had "to do something." After graduating from high school, he left for college in Missouri, joined the Air Force, and returned home during the time of the freedom rides. He became involved with SNCC through his neighbor, Amzie Moore. Block entered Greenwood alone, without a car, money, or a place to stay. He made contacts wherever people congregated—in pool halls, laundromats, and grocery stores. Through his painstaking canvassing for voter registration he "learned that there were a lot of frightened people in Greenwood. They knew local blacks were being killed in LeFlore County...and nothing was being done about it."

The SNCC organizer began to whittle down some of this fear. He received help from blacks who had been involved with voter education attempts in the past. Holding meetings in fraternal halls and churches, he taught those in attendance freedom songs that "served as a drawing card...that seemed to make people want to come back." A local resident expressed the sentiments of many who participated in these sessions: "We have been living in fear, afraid to do something. It is time to do something. The time is now." Having taken the initial step of rallying ordinary, yet heroic black folks, Block could barely move ahead. The applicants he accompanied to the courthouse failed to pass the literacy tests unfairly administered by the registrars, and the SNCC field-worker was ordered by the sheriff "to pack your goddamn bags" and get out of town. He stayed despite constant harassment, arrests, and violent attacks.

When SNCC sent in reinforcements, white resistance grew even stiffer. In October 1962, county officials cut off the distribution of surplus food to some 22,000 residents, contending that the program was too expensive to operate. Block and his companions correctly viewed this action as a reprisal for their voter registration efforts and worried that without the commodities program impoverished black sharecroppers could not survive. In response, SNCC conducted a national food and clothing drive to help the beleaguered farmers get through the winter. In addition to keeping blacks from starving and suffering cold, the drive stimulated their interest in registering to vote. Lawrence Guyot, who was working with Block, recalled how the county government unwittingly assisted SNCC in graphically demonstrating to disfranchised blacks the connection between politics and economics. "It's easy to sell political involvement," he asserted, "when you have that kind of activity by an identifiable political apparatus."

White supremacists provided more brutal lessons about the dangers of voter registration and, hence, confirmed the importance of the ballot. In February and March 1963, whites initiated a reign of terror against SNCC. Arsonists attempted to burn down its headquarters, and unidentified assailants fired shotgun blasts into a car carrying three voter registration workers, seriously wounding one of them. Vigilantes torched several black businesses, burning them to the ground, and aimed gunfire into the homes of two black youths active in the suffrage drive. These attacks spurred the civil rights troops to launch a series of marches in protest of the violence. Direct action and voter registration, which for many SNCC activists originally seemed unrelated, fused in Greenwood. For two weeks, national television cameras spotlighted peaceful demonstrators under siege by the police and their snarling dogs.

As blacks filled the Greenwood jail, they once again exhorted the federal government to intercede on their behalf. Some approached Washington with ambivalent feelings. James Forman, executive secretary of SNCC and one of those arrested, considered "the presence of the federal government as an instrument to be used over the state governments of the South," and expected the Justice Department to protect voter registration workers. At the same time, he doubted federal commitment and believed that suffrage drives would "expose the dirt of the United States and thus alienate black people from the whole system." In part, SNCC had staged the demonstrations, in anticipation of arrests, to force federal authorities to intervene or else "prove the government was not on [its] side, and thus intensify the development of a mass consciousness among blacks." The VEP, which funded voter registration activities in Greenwood, seconded SNCC's request for federal protection. The agency considered such intervention essential if its projects were to be sustained in hostile southern battlefields.

The Justice Department applied just enough pressure to defuse the crisis, but not with sufficient vigor to satisfy black activists. It stubbornly refused to provide personal protection and relied instead on the preferred techniques of litigation and negotiation. The Justice Department petitioned the federal district court for an order releasing the imprisoned protesters and enjoining local officials from interfering with the suffrage campaign. Behind the scenes, John Doar, an attorney in the Civil Rights Division, persuaded Greenwood authorities to free the jailed demonstrators, and in turn, the department dropped the suit that would have permanently restrained town officials. Having restored some peace to Greenwood, the Justice Department backed off for fear of inflaming white passions anew.

Though the voter registration campaign proceeded, the civil rights forces made little progress in actually enrolling black voters. By mid-1963, some 1,300 blacks in Greenwood had taken the literacy test to register, but officials refused to notify them of the results. Faced with such meager gains and the unwillingness of the federal government to protect the constitutional rights of the field-workers, later that year the VEP reluctantly suspended funding for its projects in Mississippi and concentrated its efforts where the returns were higher. Despite these disappointments, such suffrage campaigns as that in Greenwood had a significant political impact. Many of the blacks who encountered the civil rights activists had taken a crucial step toward liberation. They had moved, as a Georgia SNCC organizer reported, "into freedom of the mind, and it is now theirs for life, even if they should never succeed in their efforts to persuade a semi-literate, hostile registrar to put their names on the roll." She succinctly summed up what the movement meant for the political future of the blacks it touched: "They have learned to live with fear, and to advance."

To underscore this point, the civil rights forces in Mississippi devised a novel strategy to turn disfranchised blacks into active political participants. Since 1962, the Council of Federated Organizations (COFO) had coordinated voter registration activities in the state. The NAACP, SNCC, CORE, and SCLC put aside some of their philosophical differences and organizational rivalries to focus their energies on combating the fierce opposition to black suffrage. Out of this cooperative venture the idea for a "freedom vote" emerged. COFO designed a mock election to accompany the regularly scheduled gubernatorial contest in 1963. The parallel balloting would be open to all black adults, especially the 95 percent who had been excluded from the normal electoral process.

COFO aimed the freedom vote in two directions. By casting ballots in this symbolic election, black Mississippians would send a message to the federal government that they wanted to vote and needed outside help to shatter the racial blockades that hampered them. "The freedom ballot will show," declared Bob Moses, one of the prime movers behind it, "that if Negroes had the right to vote without fear of physical or economic reprisal, they would do so." Yet civil rights activists wanted to achieve much more than Washington's assistance. As director of COFO, Moses envisioned the campaign as part of SNCC's enduring attempt to organize black communities around their perceived needs, in pursuit of their own goals, in behalf of their own emancipation, apart from white control. In holding this independent election, blacks would strike a blow for their political legitimacy. Rejected by white registration officials according to their definitions of political eligibility, black Mississippians intended to demonstrate that they were qualified to vote and seek power on their own terms.

Eighty thousand blacks, nearly four times the number of those registered, vividly staked their claim for recognition as first-class citizens. They marked their ballots in makeshift polling places in locations throughout their communities. In a unified manner they voted for the freedom ticket of Aaron Henry, the black president of COFO who ran for governor, and his running mate, Ed King, the white chaplain at Tougaloo College. Though considered illegitimate by official white standards, these voters and their candidates collectively constructed the machinery to continue agitating for equal political rights and representation. "The Freedom Vote gave Negroes an opportunity to build an organization in every nook and cranny of the State," Henry remarked. "We have an organization now in Mississippi that once we get the vote, we'll be able to direct it."

MARTIN LUTHER KING, JR., THE SCLC, AND THE CRISIS AT BIRMINGHAM

While SNCC strived to mobilize people around the right to vote in rural areas, the SCLC shaped its protest around broader issues of segregation and discrimination in a city notorious for its repression of blacks: Birmingham, Alabama. Over the years, this steel city had been the scene of numerous bombings and acts of violence against civil rights activists and, most recently, the freedom riders. The commissioner of public safety, Eugene "Bull" Connor, ruled the police with an iron fist and believed that civil rights protesters were Communist dupes who deserved the harsh punishment they received.

The local movement for first-class citizenship was led by the Reverend Fred Shuttlesworth, a founding member of the SCLC. Pastor of the Bethel Baptist Church, Shuttlesworth also headed the Alabama Christian Movement for Human Rights, a group that originated in the mid-1950s after Alabama officials banned the NAACP from the state. Under Shuttlesworth's lead, the organization had attempted to desegregate schools, buses, and government offices in Birmingham. In retaliation against these efforts, the Reverend Shuttlesworth's home and church were bombed, and the minister and his family were attacked and beaten by a mob. Undaunted by threats, Shuttlesworth continued to challenge the city's system of racial apartheid. "I always believed that the minister is God's first line soldier," he remarked bravely. "I should say I'm a battlefield type general like Patton, I guess."

Against this pattern of intimidation, Dr. King, the Reverend Shuttlesworth, and their associates used mass-action strategies to bolster growing, but still underdeveloped, black political influence. In 1962, approximately 12,500 blacks had signed up to vote, about 10 percent of those eligible. This small bloc of voters joined with white reformers in an attempt to unseat the reactionary Connor. Businesspeople and other civic leaders believed the racial violence encouraged by Connor and his henchmen had a harmful effect on the city's economic fortunes and hoped to put a stop to it. They arranged for a referendum to change the form of city government from a three-person commission to a mayor and seven-member council, thereby reducing Connor's power. The measure passed with solid black support, and in the spring of 1963, the coalition of white moderates and blacks defeated Connor's mayoral bid. Instead of accepting his loss at the polls, Connor began litigation challenging the validity of the new government and its newly elected officials. Meanwhile, he retained control over the police.

On April 3, the day after the disputed election, the SCLC orchestrated sit-in demonstrations to desegregate downtown eating facilities and to press for the hiring of black store clerks. These protests had a twofold purpose: to win concessions for Birmingham blacks as part of the ongoing community struggle led by Shuttlesworth and to force the federal government to combat Jim Crow throughout the region. King deliberately picked Birmingham because of the potential for its police, under Connor's command, to respond brutally to protests. To arouse the conscience of the nation, the SCLC deployed nonviolent marches to provoke the expected response from Connor's men. King did not seek to create bloodshed so much as he attempted to dramatize publicly, for newspapers and television to record, the vicious white resistance to racial equality. "You see a policeman beating somebody and with water hoses," Reverend Shuttlesworth declared, "that's news, that's spectacularism."

The protests did elicit white violence. High-pressure water hoses and trained attack dogs were turned on peaceful demonstrators, many of whom were children the SCLC had recruited into the movement. Bombs exploded at the hotel where King was lodged and at his brother's home. These blasts sparked outraged blacks to take to the streets in retaliation, hurling rocks and bottles at the police. Before the city fell into this grip of violence, local civic leaders and federal officials had quietly negotiated with King to forge order out of chaos. The President sent Assistant Attorney General Marshall to mediate between a committee of white businesspeople and black protesters. They hammered out a compromise that called for the desegregation of eating facilities and the gradual hiring of black sales personnel, but left intact the segregation of most public accommodations and the criminal charges brought against black demonstrators, including King. Subsequently, the newly installed mayor, whose election had been upheld by the courts, established a biracial community affairs committee, and the city council repealed its municipal segregation ordinances.

Although much remained to be done, Birmingham witnessed significant change. The demonstrations strengthened the local movement by fostering racial solidarity and provided tangible evidence that collective action enhanced the influence of blacks in shaping public affairs. To extend the gains derived from direct action protests, civil rights groups mounted voter registration drives to build up budding black electoral clout. By 1964, the proportion of registered blacks had doubled to 20 percent. However far their struggles carried them, they still needed federal support to overcome Jim Crow and disfranchisement. Like their counterparts in Greenwood, blacks in Birmingham continued to face calculated vigilante violence. The culmination of such brutality in Birmingham occurred on September 15, 1963, with the bombing of the Sixteenth Street Baptist Church and the tragic deaths of four young girls worshiping inside.

Meanwhile, the Kennedy administration had continued to venture cautiously in the civil rights field. The President delayed issuing the executive decree on residential desegregation he had promised during the presidential campaign until November 1962. Even then, he limited the order to homes subsidized by federal loans, which left most of the housing market uncovered. Shortly before, the administration had demonstrated its unwillingness to exercise federal might unless given no other choice. Facing a direct threat to a federal court order admitting James Meredith to the University of Mississippi in September 1962, the President finally mobilized sufficient military force to combat racist interference with desegregation. Like Eisenhower in his handling of the Little Rock crisis, Kennedy hesitated to send federal troops to the South, preferring instead to persuade the state to enforce the desegregation ruling voluntarily. On October 1, only after Governor Ross Barnett refused to negotiate in good faith and failed to guarantee Meredith's safety did the President move in the Army. This intervention came belatedly after a riot had broken out, resulting in two deaths and over 300 injuries.

The following year, Kennedy showed that he could learn from his mistakes. On June 11, 1963, the administration won a well-publicized battle with Governor George Wallace to desegregate the University of Alabama. With the Mississippi disaster in mind, the President acted more firmly in dealing with Governor Wallace. Carrying out a carefully orchestrated plan, the Kennedy administration dispatched Deputy Attorney General Nicholas Katzenbach and federal marshals to escort two black students, Vivian Malone and James Hood, whose admission had been ordered by the federal judiciary. After Wallace blocked their entry by standing in the schoolhouse door, the President federalized the state National Guard. The six-hour standoff ended when the Alabama governor stepped aside and allowed integration at the Tuscaloosa campus to proceed peacefully.

In the end, President Kennedy went further than his Republican predecessor, Dwight Eisenhower, in pursuing racial equality. The political pressure of protest had pushed the chief executive to embrace at least the more moderate goals of the civil rights movement. The disruptive Birmingham demonstrations convinced the chief executive that the racial situation in the South had reached a dangerous phase. The crises provoked by civil rights protesters sparked widespread racial confrontations throughout Dixie and even threatened to consume the North. Worried by the escalating violence and the increasing possibility of black retaliation, the President introduced the legislative program he had postponed since entering the White House. The events of the previous two years compelled him to recognize the morality of the civil rights struggle. On June 11, he informed a nationwide television audience that the extension of equal rights to all Americans was an issue "as old as the scriptures and . . . as clear as the American Constitution." Conflicts in Birmingham and elsewhere, he warned his listeners, required legislation "if we are to move this problem from the streets to the courts." The chief executive's proposals attacked segregation in public accommodations and schools, created a Community Relations Service to mediate racial disputes, authorized cutting off federal funds to local agencies practicing discrimination, and expanded judicial power to speed up voting rights cases. The administration's civil rights measures were timed to restore peace to southern battlegrounds by removing the conditions that had spawned protest. Nonetheless, soothing words alone could not stop violence: only a few hours after the president's address, the NAACP's Medgar Evers was assassinated by a white supremacist in Jackson, Mississippi.

FREEDOM VOTES, FREEDOM SUMMER

The Kennedy administration saw its preferred solution to civil rights controversies taking shape in scattered communities throughout the South. In a number of cities, such as Atlanta, Georgia; Tampa, Florida; and Norfolk, Virginia, businesspeople had responded to civil rights turbulence by seeking ways voluntarily to desegregate public accommodations and municipal facilities. These civic leaders recognized that explosive race relations made poor business sense. Seeking to attract outside investments and commercial enterprises to their areas, they took measures to reduce the kind of negative publicity that would tarnish their cities' images, as it had that of Little Rock and Birmingham. A politician such as Mayor Ivan Allen

On August 28, 1963, following introduction of
the civil rights bill in Congress, approximately
250,000 blacks and whites marched on
Washington to stage a massive rally for jobs
and freedom. The demonstration was
highlighted by two contrasting speeches. An
angry SNCC chairperson, John Lewis,
complained that the progress of civil rights
was moving too slowly, while Martin Luther
King, Jr., pictured above, recited his optimistic
"I Have a Dream" speech for an integrated
America. (UPI/Bettmann Newsphotos)

of Atlanta went so far as to support the Kennedy civil rights bill, but
this kind of expression by local white moderates was rare. More
frequently, they tried to maintain local control over the amount
and pace of desegregation in order to forestall federal intervention.
Consequently, they accepted sufficient changes to keep their cities
relatively quiet and out of the headlines, yet without guaranteeing
full equality for blacks.

Also without much fanfare, blacks followed the electoral path to first-class citizenship. In 1964, in Tuskegee, Alabama, a small group of white liberals joined with Charles Gomillion's Macon County Democratic Club, an offshoot of the Tuskegee Civic Association, to elect a biracial slate to city and county offices. By then blacks constituted a majority of the registered voters in Macon County and split about evenly with whites in Tuskegee. With blacks assuming majority status as voters, Gomillion and his associates favored a gradualist approach in sharing power with whites. They wanted to avoid raising the specter of black domination and hoped to show that the two races could cooperate in governing responsibly. Gomillion hoped this policy would serve as a model for encouraging "whites elsewhere to be willing to appoint or elect qualified Negroes, even in places where Negroes were less numerous than in Macon County." The outcome of elections in his own bailiwick did not disappoint the Tuskegee sociologist. An interracial coalition elected Gomillion to a seat on the board of education, along with three other blacks who won countywide positions. In the city, two blacks gained posts on the municipal council. At the same time, whites retained control of both county and city governments and held the key offices of sheriff and mayor.

This landmark election in Macon County revealed the growing complexity of black politics as the majority of African-Americans obtained the vote. Gomillion's strategy had run into serious opposition from within the black community. A group of younger blacks who had come of age during the birth of the civil rights movement in the 1950s challenged the sixty-five year-old Gomillion and his prescription for racial advancement. These insurgents decried the "pace of social change in Tuskegee [as] unconscionably slow" and argued for the election of as many black candidates as possible. This intraracial split reflected different class as well as ideological perspectives. The Gomillion wing articulated distinctly middle-class values and spoke mainly for the professionals and staff of the Tuskegee Institute and the Veterans Administration Hospital. The challengers, many of whom taught at Tuskegee, also came from the middle class but directed their attention to the problems of lower-income and impoverished blacks in the city and the rural sections of the county.

As long as most blacks experienced racial disfranchisement in common, class divisions remained in the background. Nevertheless, class divisions did exist and had already begun to surface in Mississippi as well. The 1963 freedom vote campaign had encountered opposition from some of the state's 27,000 blacks who had managed to register to vote. They resented SNCC's efforts to develop political consciousness among the masses of blacks, which, if successful, might eventually undermine their own leadership. These middle-class blacks had succeeded by playing according to white electoral rules; they considered voting a privilege that should be extended to those, like themselves, who passed the literacy test, as long as it was applied equally. When members of the black middle class opposed racial discrimination they usually did so through "respectable" civil rights groups like the NAACP, which stressed litigation, and not through organizations like SNCC, which they considered disruptive and likely to stir up white hostility. Thus, as Neil R. McMillan has pointed out, in rallying the black masses against white supremacy, civil rights organizers were also challenging "traditional [black] elites once thought to be the natural leaders of their people by the people themselves."

Because racial oppression was so harsh in Mississippi, the civil rights movement generally had been able to submerge class divisions beneath black solidarity. The NAACP had joined SNCC in designing the freedom vote campaign, and one of its leaders, Aaron Henry, had led the insurgent gubernatorial ticket. Following the 1963 mock election, COFO planned a massive voter registration drive for the next summer, climaxing in a challenge to the state Democratic party delegation at the presidential nominating convention in Atlantic City. The project was fashioned to spotlight national attention on the blatantly racist means by which white Mississippians excluded blacks from the suffrage. The planners of the 1964 "Freedom Summer" invited northern white students into the state to expose them to the dangers blacks experienced every day. White Americans hardly noticed the deaths of black people, Bob Moses candidly admitted, but "they would respond to a thousand young white college students" suffering brutality at the hands of Mississippi racists. Like the nonviolent provocation King practiced in Birmingham, the use of white students did not cause the violence; rather it served to dramatize the terror that already existed. It would take blood spilled by whites, COFO cynically though realistically reasoned, to prompt federal intervention.

Months before Freedom Summer was scheduled to begin, the assassination of John F. Kennedy had placed in the Oval Office a new President, though not a new policy. Upon taking over in November 1963, Lyndon B. Johnson threw his support behind Kennedy's civil rights bill and, together with a coalition of liberal lawmakers and civil rights, labor, and religious groups, had waged a long, fierce struggle that succeeded in obtaining a stronger measure than the one originally proposed.[1] However, the new law did not help the political insurgents in Mississippi. Though it accepted a sixth-grade education as evidence of literacy for the purpose of voter registration, the statute continued to leave enforcement with the judiciary, a procedure that proved cumbersome and inadequate. Furthermore, the act failed to address the improper application of literacy tests, which in the past had allowed illiterate or semiliterate whites, but not blacks, to register. Above all, nothing in the legislation directed the administration to provide protection for civil rights volunteers engaged in Freedom Summer.

The murder of three young civil rights workers, James Chaney, Michael Schwerner, and Andrew Goodman—one black and two whites—on June 21, 1964, finally forced some intervention from Washington. President Johnson ordered the FBI, which previously had been ineffective if not uninterested in pursuing civil rights offenses, to launch an intensive manhunt to apprehend the killers. The bureau set up an office in Mississippi and with assistance from paid informers inside the Ku Klux Klan arrested nineteen men, including a sheriff and deputy sheriff, for commission of the crime. Nevertheless, the Justice Department declined to provide day-to-day protection for the suffragists who remained in the field to suffer the usual assortment of intimidating tactics: beatings, bombings, arson, and at least three additional homicides.

This racist reign of terror against the freedom fighters did not prevent COFO from organizing blacks into a potent political force. Though relatively few managed to register to vote during the sum-

---

[1] In addition to the provisions originally offered by the Kennedy administration in 1963, the 1964 Civil Rights Act prohibited employment discrimination based on race and sex and created an Equal Employment Opportunity Commission to implement it. The law passed after the Senate shut off a filibuster that lasted for fifty-seven days. President Johnson signed the bill into law on July 2.

mer campaign, a great many more participated in the formation of the Mississippi Freedom Democratic Party (MFDP). Protesting their exclusion from the process by which state Democrats selected their delegates to the national convention, the Freedom Democrats erected an alternative structure to challenge them. While predominantly black, the reform organization was open to members of both races and included Ed King, the white clergyman who had run with Aaron Henry in the 1963 COFO mock election. In the style of SNCC, which heavily influenced its creation, the MFDP was the product of grassroots organizing constructed from the bottom up. Unlike the conservative regulars, the group pledged to support Lyndon Johnson as the Democratic party's presidential nominee as well as his liberal Great Society platform.

President Johnson counted on widespread black support for his candidacy. Since his early career as an opponent of Truman's civil rights program and his middle years as a proponent of lukewarm civil rights legislation, the Texan had grown into a staunch advocate of racial equality. As he climbed higher up the ladder of electoral success, away from the constraints of his southern segregationist constituency, he developed an increasing sense of moral obligation to extend first-class citizenship to blacks. His ethical and political convictions meshed with his regional loyalty. A complex man, he believed a resolution of racial problems would liberate his native South, white as well as black, from the burdens of outmoded discriminatory institutions that retarded its economic progress. In the absence of the race issue and the reactionary politics it spawned, Johnson envisioned southern Democratic politicians falling in step behind his reform leadership.

In customary fashion, the President attempted to build a broad consensus for his nomination in 1964. The northern, liberal wing of his party backed him solidly, but the South posed some difficulties. Upset with the passage of the 1964 Civil Rights Act and with the expensive social welfare programs that Johnson was preparing for his Great Society, many white southerners were unenthusiastic about their native son. Instead, they seemed to prefer the Republican nominee, Senator Barry Goldwater of Arizona, who had voted against the civil rights law and whose conservative economic views were more compatible with theirs. To stem these potential losses and achieve the biggest possible electoral victory, Johnson came to the convention seeking unity.

The challenge of the MFDP endangered Johnson's plan for a well-ordered convention. Joseph Rauh, a prominent white liberal attorney with connections to organized labor, presented the case for recognition of the Freedom Democrats as the legitimate representatives from Mississippi. He contended that they had been illegally barred from participation in the selection of delegates by the regular party organization and questioned their lily-white rivals' loyalty to the reform principles of the national party. The Freedom delegation backed up its legal right to the convention seats with powerful moral arguments. The most striking presentation came from Fannie Lou Hamer of Sunflower County, the home district of Senator Eastland. She recounted with great emotion the brutality and pain she had suffered from Mississippi law enforcement officials while working for civil rights. In stirring testimony before the Credentials Committee and recorded by television cameras for a national audience, Mrs. Hamer painted a graphic picture of the outrages happening so frequently in Mississippi and asked her listeners: "Is this America? The land of the free and the home of the brave?"

In this conflict, President Johnson mixed his moral concern for the plight of Mississippi blacks with his political passion for consensus. He hastily arranged a press conference to preempt live coverage of Mrs. Hamer's powerful testimony and put forces in motion to work out a compromise on the Freedom challenge that would appeal to blacks, their liberal allies, and moderate white southerners. He let the reformers know that he would choose Hubert Humphrey, the liberal senator from Minnesota, as his running mate if the latter could settle the dispute without a divisive credentials fight. With the help of Rauh, Walter Reuther, the head of the United Automobile Workers, and Walter Mondale, Humphrey's protege who sat on the Credentials Committee, the Minnesota senator hatched a plan acceptable to the majority of convention delegates. It extended two at-large seats to the MFDP and named Aaron Henry and Ed King to occupy them. The rest of the Freedom Democrats could attend the convention as nonvoting guests. Those state regulars who swore allegiance to the national party would officially represent Mississippi and cast its forty-four votes. Furthermore, looking ahead, the Democrats agreed to draw up guidelines to eliminate racial discrimination in delegate selection to the next national nominating convention.

The compromise preserved party harmony at the convention, but it satisfied neither Magnolia faction. Most of the white regulars refused to sign the loyalty pledge and returned home to vote for Goldwater. The Freedom Democrats also rejected the agreement. Believing that they had morality as well as legality on their side, they would not accept a token assignment of two seats while the regulars controlled the votes of the entire delegation. They had not risked their lives merely for a symbolic victory and further resented the fact that Democratic leaders, not the MFDP representatives, had specifically chosen the two delegates for them. For many of the civil rights organizers, particularly those in SNCC, this whole episode had a souring effect on their relationship with white liberals. They felt sold out by the administration and its allies, who presumed to know what was best for them and to dictate a solution accordingly. They also lost trust in their lawyer, Joseph Rauh, and black leaders, such as Martin Luther King and Bayard Rustin, who favored the arrangement for practical reasons—as a first step toward eventual reform and the best bargain they could get. Despite their loss of faith, most of the Freedom delegation returned home and campaigned for Johnson and future recognition by the Democratic party.

The convention challenge also produced serious internal strains within the civil rights movement in Mississippi. As John Dittmer has concluded, the Atlantic City affair marked "the beginning of the end of the COFO partnership and the emergence of class conflict as a major destructive force." The debate over whether to accept the administration's offer split the MFDP delegation. Urban middle-class blacks, about one-fifth of the group, tended to favor the compromise in opposition to the largely rural, poor delegates who rejected it. The latter contingent won the opening skirmish, but when the Freedom Democrats returned home the feud continued. Within the state, blacks who were associated with SNCC's increasingly radical vision of grassroots organizing struggled with more traditional elements allied with the NAACP for control over the future course of black politics.

THE TRIUMPH OF LBJ

President Johnson may have abandoned the most militant blacks at the convention, but he had no intention of ignoring the black elec-

In 1965, the Mississippi Freedom Democratic party contested the election of that state's congressional representatives. The three Freedom Democratic candidates who journeyed to Washington in hopes of replacing the regulars were, from left to right, Annie Devine, Fannie Lou Hamer, and Victoria Gray. The House denied their claim. (UPI/Bettmann Newsphotos)

torate. With Barry Goldwater enticing white voters away from the Democratic party in the South, the President recognized the growing importance of the black vote in carrying Dixie. After Lawrence O'Brien, a top political adviser, returned from traveling through the region during the campaign, he reported to Johnson that "victory in at least four of the states and possibly in six hinges upon the percentage of Negro voters who go to the polls." Because the chief executive would probably garner at least 90 percent of the black vote, the Democrats had to concentrate on getting out the vote. State party leaders like those in Mississippi had discouraged black participation, so it remained for the national organization to mount a suffrage campaign. Under the direction of Louis Martin, the Democratic National Committee sponsored such drives, which, according to Martin, "are better than they ever have been and better than we thought they ever would be." This effort did not prevent Goldwater from capturing five southern states, including Mississippi, but it did help Johnson win the rest of the former Confederacy. Everywhere else, except Goldwater's Arizona, the President triumphed and racked up huge margins among black voters. They went to the polls in approval, as the *Afro-American* newspaper commented, for one whose record "proves his compassionate concern for people, irrespective of race, creed or color."

Johnson's triumph over Goldwater cemented black voters more solidly than ever before behind the Democratic party. The trend that started with Franklin Roosevelt, was pushed along by Truman, momentarily interrupted by Eisenhower, and renewed by Kennedy reached landslide proportions under Johnson. As the black electorate grew in influence, so too did its success in shoving civil rights to the front of the national political agenda. In the South, where the majority of blacks still could not vote, protest and community organizing served as the most potent weapons for influencing politics. In different ways, Martin Luther King and the more radical activists in SNCC and CORE recognized that mobilizing blacks from below pressured the national government to act from above. This pincer movement had trapped and wounded Jim Crow, which though kicking and screaming nonetheless refused to die.

Chapter 4

Reenfranchisement and Racial Consciousness

THE SELMA MOVEMENT AND THE VOTING RIGHTS ACT OF 1965

The distance between Oslo, Norway, and Selma, Alabama, spanned more than an ocean and thousands of miles. For African-Americans it represented the difference between dignity and degradation. The winner of the 1964 Nobel Peace Prize, Dr. Martin Luther King, Jr., returned to the United States after obtaining his prestigious award in Oslo and journeyed to Selma in hope of eliminating the gap between the honorific treatment he had received abroad and the lack of respect blacks were accorded at home. Specifically, he sought to do something about the continuing denial of their right to vote. Throughout the former Confederate states, approximately 57 percent of eligible blacks remained off the suffrage rolls; in Alabama, the figure was a more shocking 77 percent; and in Dallas County, where Selma was the county seat, only 335 blacks out of a total population of 15,000 were registered. With this in mind, on January 2, 1965, Dr. King told an audience gathered at Selma's Brown Chapel AME Church what was at stake in the demonstrations the SCLC was about to launch. "When we get the right to vote," he predicted, "we will send to the state-house not men who will stand in the doorways of universities to keep Negroes out, but men who will uphold the cause of justice."

King's plans capped the twenty-year struggle to reenfranchise black southerners. Since the outlawing of the white primary in 1944, civil rights groups and the national government had attempted to remove discriminatory barriers impeding black suffrage. Though a combination of litigation, legislation, and voter registration campaigns had yielded much progress, the majority of southern blacks still were disfranchised and were likely to stay so unless state and local officials lost their stranglehold on the enrollment process. Like most of the gains made during the civil rights era, the expansion of black ballots depended upon the power of the federal government in reinforcing the efforts of blacks at the local level, who were already fighting for first-class citizenship.

President Johnson intended to throw his considerable political weight behind renewed efforts to secure the right to vote. The chief executive shared civil rights advocates' faith in the ballot as the ultimate weapon in promoting racial advancement. Once blacks voted in large numbers, he believed, "many other breakthroughs would follow as a consequence of the black man's own legitimate power as an American citizen, not as a gift from the white man." This thinking reflected the willingness of liberals like Johnson to use the federal government to attack racist obstacles in the South, but it also mirrored the more conservative view of the right to vote as a self-help vehicle for uplifting an oppressed group.

In addition to these philosophical considerations, Johnson, the consummate politician, recognized the pragmatic benefits that reenfranchising blacks would bestow. In achieving his landslide victory in 1964, the President had lost the votes of five states in his native South—Alabama, Georgia, Louisiana, Mississippi, and South Carolina. In each of these states, the black enrollment figure was under 39 percent. If the Johnson administration found a way to dismantle discriminatory suffrage procedures, it could boost black registration to offset the Republican inroads Barry Goldwater had made into Democratic ranks in the South. After the election, an official of the Democratic party reported "that the first step toward getting out a big Democratic vote is to increase [black] registration."

Having already succeeded in obtaining passage of the 1964 Civil Rights Act, Johnson could not afford to rest on his laurels. This landmark legislation continued to leave voting rights enforcement in the hands of the judiciary. Previous experience had proven the courts inadequate in repelling white southern obstructionists. Besides, in the past registrars had not been deterred from signing up white illiterates while excluding those who were black, and the force of any criterion that preserved some standard of literacy would fall disproportionately on the thousands of undereducated blacks who remained disfranchised.

To correct flaws in the existing legislation, both federal agencies and civil rights groups recommended a new approach. On several occasions, most recently in 1963, the United States Commission on Civil Rights suggested that Congress grant the President authority to appoint federal enrollment officers to register qualified blacks. SNCC went even further. Based on its efforts in the impoverished, black-belt South, the organization advocated the complete abolition of literacy tests as a requirement for voting. Either the country must eliminate these qualifications or, as Bob Moses argued, provide blacks with "the right to learn how to read and write *now.*" Indeed, in several cases, an unusually progressive federal judge in Alabama, Frank M. Johnson, had ordered the enrollment of black illiterates as voters. Because illiterate whites had managed to register in the past, he decreed that blacks under similar circumstances did not have to prove their ability to read and write in order to qualify to vote.

After his election, in November 1964, President Johnson began seriously to consider his options. Although some White House advisers suggested that the administration forgo proposing any new voting rights legislation for a year, until the South had time to adjust to the recently enacted Civil Rights Law, the chief executive forged ahead. After ordering the Justice Department to prepare a new suffrage measure, on January 4, 1965, Johnson delivered the annual state-of-the-union address and affirmed his desire to "eliminate every remaining obstacle to the right and opportunity to vote."

In the meantime, Dr. King marshaled civil rights forces in Selma to guarantee swift and effective federal action. The unofficial capital of the Alabama black belt, Selma had served as an arsenal and naval foundry for the Confederacy. In 1865, Union forces torched the town, and memories of the Civil War and Reconstruction still burned in the minds of local whites. This section of the state had backed the Dixiecrat challenge in 1948, and the attitude of many white officials toward blacks was summed up by James A. Hare, a Dallas County judge. "Your Negro," he asserted, "is a mixture of African types like the Congolite who has a long heel and the blue-gummed Ebo whose I.Q. is about 50 or 55." James G. Clark, the Dallas County sheriff, practiced the "Bull" Connor brand of law enforcement, showed little patience for civil rights protesters, and seemed genuinely to enjoy roughing them up. Sporting a green helmet adorned with an eagle and a Confederate flag and dressing in the style of the World War II general George S. Patton, Clark led his deputies in poking demonstrators with electric cattle prods, beating them with clubs, and dispersing them with tear gas.

This stronghold of segregation and police-state tactics offered an inviting setting for King and the SCLC to wage a major assault against political disfranchisement. From his previous encounter with Connor in Birmingham, the Nobel laureate had learned that the application of nonviolent pressure would provoke intemperate, racist lawmen to commit acts of brutality. The SCLC's strategy depended on blacks behaving with restraint in the face of such vicious attacks and on television cameras and journalists recording the confrontation so as to prick the conscience of an outraged nation. Injuries and fatalities would very likely accompany this struggle, but King was seeking drama, not bloodshed. By carefully stage-managing events at Selma, by combining disruption with prudence, he hoped to appeal to the larger audience of the public and the more specific one of the President and lawmakers in Washington, D.C.

King's troops marched along the trail blazed by SNCC and local black activists in Selma. In 1963, two SNCC field-workers had established a beachhead in the town and conducted a voter registration drive that led to the formation of the Dallas County Voters League (DCVL). This indigenous association was headed by Reverend Frederick Reese. A high school teacher and Baptist clergyman, Reese felt strongly that black educators should take an active role in the freedom struggle. Dependent on white school boards and county administrators for their livelihood, many teachers had refrained from becoming actively involved in the movement. Reese believed that his colleagues had both a personal and professional obligation to seek to become registered voters and challenge those who tried to thwart them; otherwise, they could not properly fulfill their responsibility of instructing their pupils in exercising the duties of citizenship.

Amelia P. Boynton joined Reese as a prime mover behind the creation of the Voters League. The widow of the county's black agricultural extension agent, Mrs. Boynton was an independent businesswoman who operated an employment and insurance agency in

Selma. Along with her husband, she had actively taken part in civil rights efforts and was especially concerned with efforts to increase black voter registration. Herself an enrolled voter, Boynton was well aware of the discriminatory treatment most blacks suffered. She knew of one official who could barely pronounce the words "constitutionality" and "interrogatory" on a literacy test administered to a black teacher. After the applicant interrupted the clerk to read the words correctly, "the registrar turned red with anger" and flunked her. Boynton had originally invited SNCC into the county to aid the DCVL in mobilizing blacks against such injustices.

Spearheaded by Reverend Reese and Mrs. Boynton, the league sponsored voter registration workshops to encourage blacks to enroll. In the autumn of 1963, together with SNCC, it held a "Freedom Day" rally at the county courthouse that spurred more than 300 blacks to make an attempt to sign up to vote. Instead, the applicants met resistance from the board of registrars and from Sheriff Clark and his deputies, who tried to prevent the would-be enrollees from receiving food and water as they stood for hours waiting on line to enroll. Throughout the following year, SNCC continued to organize voter registration drives in Dallas County but met with scant success.

At the same time, the federal government tackled the registration problem in its usual fashion. Justice Department lawyers had filed suits to restrain Clark from interfering with voter registration activities, and in November 1963, they won a ruling barring county registrars from using the literacy test to discriminate against black applicants. However, this decree failed to deter officials from engaging in biased practices against prospective black voters, and additional legal action to stop them proved unsuccessful. To make matters worse, a local judge issued an injunction blocking the Voters League from conducting mass meetings. By 1965, after several years of frustrating litigation, less than 400 Dallas County blacks had managed to register to vote. Acknowledging this failure, Attorney General Nicholas Katzenbach complained of "the inadequacy of the judicial process to deal effectively and expeditiously with a problem so deep-seated and so complex."

The inability of the federal courts to remedy unfair registration practices was matched by the unwillingness of the executive branch to protect suffrage workers from harassment. Adhering to the policy of his predecessors, Johnson refused to deploy federal marshals to Dallas County to safeguard voter registration workers from the menace of Sheriff Clark and his deputies. The chief executive preferred to leave law enforcement under the control of local authorities, barring a total breakdown of public order. In a similar manner, the Justice Department refused to instruct FBI agents to offer relief when they saw the constitutional rights of suffragists under attack. For example, on Freedom Day, October 7, 1963, the FBI merely observed and took notes as peaceful protesters were pushed around and arrested by Sheriff Clark and his men on the steps of the U.S. courthouse. Observing this scene firsthand exasperated Howard Zinn. "For all the good the federal officials did," the historian and adviser to SNCC bitterly commented, "[Alabama Governor] George Wallace might have been President of the United States."

Despite the racist intimidation and the failure of the national government to check it, blacks in Selma refused to retreat. SNCC had helped galvanize the community behind the struggle for political empowerment and set in motion forces for liberation that could not be easily turned back. SNCC's executive secretary, James Forman, celebrated Freedom Day as "the day when a century of Southern fear and terror... had not been able to stop the forward thrust of a people determined... to be free." Nevertheless, SNCC's efforts had sputtered, and local black leaders called in civil rights reinforcements. Their immediate goal was to secure help in registering residents of their own and surrounding counties; nonetheless, in late 1964, when the Dallas County Voters League invited King and the SCLC to Selma, it opened the way for the enfranchisement of the majority of blacks throughout the South.

The second day of the new year brought King to Selma to shape the kind of crisis that would force the federal government to crack white southern interference with black voting. During January and February 1965, the SCLC mobilized blacks in a march to the courthouse, where they would petition to register. At first, a moderate white faction in Selma, represented by the city's director of public safety, Wilson Baker, kept Sheriff Clark and his troops in line. This group, which had taken over political control of the city, believed that brutal suppression of black protest would generate unfavorable publicity and endanger new opportunities for business and civic development. "[T]he social, economic, and industrial complexion of this community," the editor of Selma's newspaper commented, "has suddenly and simultaneously arrived at a point from which there can be no turning aside." Restraint more than racial reform was uppermost on their minds, as Baker declared in referring to the demonstrators: "If we can only get the bastards out of town without getting them arrested, we'll have 'em whipped." Patience, however, was a virtue Clark did not possess, and he soon ordered the arrest of scores of peaceful black protesters.

His tough posture did not deter Selma's blacks; it only united them further. When usually cautious middle-class African-American teachers joined Reverend Reese on a march to the courthouse, they raised black solidarity to a new height. Though the educators did not wind up in jail, on February 1, Martin Luther King, Jr., did. Imprisoned for four days, King directed his aides from his cell to pressure President Johnson "to intervene in some way." Upon his release, he met personally with the chief executive and received assurances that a voting rights bill was in preparation.

Meanwhile, the SCLC attempted to hasten delivery of this promised congressional legislation. In mid-February a night march in neighboring Perry County resulted in the first fatality of the Selma suffrage campaign. In conjunction with the Perry County Civic League, the SCLC had convened a mass meeting and attempted to conduct a peaceful rally, only to come under siege from city, county, and state police. While trying to shield his mother from a beating by a state trooper, twenty-six-year-old Jimmie Lee Jackson was shot in the stomach and later died. Several reporters, including Richard Valeriani of the National Broadcasting Company, were also injured in the melee, thereby ensuring that this police riot received unfavorable publicity from the national media. A series of protests continued throughout the month, and King pledged, "We are going to bring a voting bill into being in the streets of Selma."

In the aftermath of Jackson's shooting, the SCLC began to conceive of dramatically expanding the demonstrations into a march from Selma to Montgomery, fifty miles away. Following the murder, blacks in Perry County discussed the possibility of carrying Jackson's body to Montgomery and depositing it on the steps of the state capitol. "We had to do something," Albert Turner, one of the local leaders recalled, "to point out to the nation the evils of the system." After Jackson's burial, the SCLC picked up on the idea and planned a mass march from Selma to Montgomery to begin on Sunday, March 7. With King having returned to Atlanta that day, one of his aides, Hosea Williams, and the chairman of SNCC, John

Lewis, led 600 protesters over the Edmund Pettus Bridge toward the capital city. Before they could get across, however, state troopers and Clark's posse charged into the procession, lobbed tear gas canisters, and clubbed and chased the marchers back to town. Mrs. Boynton, who had previously been roughed up by the sheriff, was knocked unconscious in the assault. "The horses...were more humane than the troopers; they stepped over fallen victims," she wryly remarked.

This display of raw aggression finally provided the SCLC with the provocative incident it needed to mobilize public opinion and secure federal intervention. Television cameras vividly recorded the events of "Bloody Sunday," and the American Broadcasting Company interrupted its network premier showing of the film *Judgment at Nuremburg*, the story of the Nazi war trials, to present footage of the Fascist-style behavior here at home.

Throughout this period, King and other civil rights leaders held several meetings with the President and urged him to introduce legislation immediately to outlaw literacy requirements for voter registration and to authorize the assignment of federal registrars. Johnson intended to support a suffrage measure, but he had several options from which to choose, including taking the slow route of a constitutional amendment. The escalating racial conflict in Selma prompted the chief executive to scuttle any proposal that did not move swiftly to dismantle discriminatory registration barriers. A

Alabama state troopers, wearing gas masks, attack John Lewis on "Bloody Sunday" in Selma. (UPI/Bettmann Newsphotos)

growing coalition of lawmakers in both political parties called for quick congressional action, and outside of Dixie, civil rights sympathizers held a wave of protests in support of the Selma marchers. In the nation's capital hundreds of marchers demanded that Washington come to the aid of the suffragists, and a contingent from SNCC dramatically mounted a sit-in at the Justice Department to push it in the same direction. Meanwhile, the demonstrations in Alabama and the national outcry they engendered pushed President Johnson to accelerate his legislative timetable, dictated the selection of the most potent legislative option, and created the favorable political climate to guarantee its passage.

Even before the President had an opportunity to move forward, King and his followers precipitated a new crisis. They rescheduled the pilgrimage to Montgomery for March 9, despite the issuance of a federal court decree postponing it. King had not violated a federal judicial order before, but in this instance he was ready to proceed to show that racist violence could not be used to derail the civil rights movement. President Johnson sent to Selma his personal emissary, LeRoy Collins, former governor of Florida and director of the federal Community Relations Service, who carried on negotiations separately with the marchers and the state police and successfully defused the crisis. Accordingly, the protesters walked to the end of the bridge, knelt in prayer, and turned back, while the troopers calmly monitored the situation. This peaceful resolution did not prevent a group of whites from killing one of the returning marchers, the Reverend James Reeb, a white minister from Boston. Brutally beaten while he walked the streets of Selma, Reeb soon died from his wounds.

After federal Judge Frank M. Johnson lifted his ban, the parade finally began on March 21, two weeks after Bloody Sunday. By that time, Governor George C. Wallace refused to furnish protection for the marchers, forcing Johnson to federalize the Alabama National Guard for that purpose. Their presence generally deterred violence but could not prevent one further slaying of a white civil rights volunteer, Mrs. Viola Liuzzo of Detroit, as she rode in her car with a black companion en route to Montgomery to pick up returning marchers. The deaths of Liuzzo and Reeb especially shocked northern whites, including the President.

In the meantime, this renewed round of demonstrations produced the long-awaited presidential proposal on voting rights. On March 15, in a magnificent address to a joint session of Congress televised to an audience of 70 million Americans, Johnson praised the Selma demonstrators as freedom fighters and admonished Congress to allow "no delay, no hesitation, no compromise with" passage of remedial legislation to aid their cause. In one eloquent and memorable moment, he adopted the language of the civil rights movement and promised, "We shall overcome." Two days later, the administration measure reached the halls of Congress.

The Selma struggle had developed along two different fronts. Local movement leaders in Dallas County desired above all to unclog the registration process in their community. As its top priority, the DCVL hoped to place blacks on the voter lists and welcomed any action that brought significant modifications in biased registration procedures. When a federal judge instructed the enrollment board to cease administering literacy tests and to start processing black applicants at a speedier rate, the Voters League considered it a substantial step toward reaching its major goal. In contrast, the SCLC looked beyond the immediate arena and focused on obtaining national legislation to enfranchise blacks throughout the region. King and his aides argued "that if Selma Negroes gained [the right to vote] under special court order or through community agreement...this would not satisfy SCLC." Nevertheless, the grassroots goal and the broader civil rights aim remained intertwined in support of extending the ballot; only the tactics differed. In the end, the voting rights bill, forged as a result of the Selma campaign, gave each side what it desired.

Johnson's suffrage plan took the forceful approach recommended by civil rights proponents. Instead of a constitutional amendment, the chief executive asked Congress simply to pass legislation that suspended literacy tests, authorized the attorney general to dispatch federal registrars and observers to recalcitrant counties, and empowered the Justice Department to clear in advance changes in state electoral rules that might unfairly burden black voters. Johnson's lawyers had designed these provisions to enforce suffrage expansion through the administrative machinery of the executive branch rather than by the judiciary, where equal voting rights had been stalled for so long. Consequently, the measure contained an automatic triggering mechanism devised to snare only those states and localities that employed a literacy test and in which less than a majority of those eligible had registered to vote or had voted in the presidential election of 1964. As a result of this formula, Alabama, Georgia, Louisiana, Mississippi, South Carolina, Virginia, and sections of North Carolina would come under federal supervision.

Introduced in March, the voting rights bill encountered relatively little difficulty in Congress, and by early August it had become law. The final version followed closely the outline of Johnson's recommendation and also adopted a provision allowing the affected jurisdictions to escape coverage once they proved to the federal district court in Washington, D.C., that they had not employed a discriminatory test or device for the previous five years. In addition, the lawmakers issued a finding that the poll tax infringed upon the right to vote, and they directed the attorney general to initiate litigation, which resulted the following year in the removal of the levy in the four southern states that still required it in nonfederal elections. (The Twenty-fourth Amendment, ratified in 1964, had eliminated the franchise fee in all national elections.)

This landmark legislation emerged in such powerful shape for a variety of reasons. The President displayed a strong commitment to the bill and exercised firm leadership in guiding it through the legislature. His aides worked diligently to round up key votes and keep supporters in line at critical moments. Johnson helped win over to his position the Senate Republican leader, Everett Dirksen of Illinois, which guaranteed bipartisan backing for the administration's version of the measure. The President's task was made easier because of the favorable climate of opinion created by Reverend King's handling of the Selma episode. Southern whites found it increasingly difficult to defend the brutal opposition to black suffrage in Alabama, and their congressional representatives failed to mount their customary fierce challenge to the legislation. A Gallup Poll taken during the march to Montgomery reported that 76 percent of the nation favored a voting rights bill; in the South a surprising 49 percent of the sample indicated approval compared with 37 percent in opposition. Democratic Representative Hale Boggs of Louisiana summed up the sentiment of forty of his colleagues from the South who voted for the legislation: "I . . . support this bill because I believe the fundamental right to vote must be a part of this great experiment in human progress under freedom which is America."

The Voting Rights Act resulted in the reenfranchisement of the majority of southern blacks. Within four years after its passage, approximately three-fifths of southern black adults had registered to vote. The most striking gains occurred in the deep South, where resistance to the suffrage had been most harsh. In Mississippi, black registration leaped from 6.7 percent in 1964 to 59.4 in 1968. Similarly, black enrollment in Alabama jumped from 23 percent to 53 percent. In Dallas County, the scene of the Selma demonstrations, the number of registered blacks soared from less than 1,000 to over 8,500 within months after the suffrage law took effect.

The combination of federal power and grassroots activism helped generate the stunning rise in black political participation. The suspension of literacy requirements removed the major obstacle to black registration, and most of the new voters were signed up by local officials who complied with the law. In hard-core areas where blacks still encountered difficulty in securing the ballot, federal examiners intervened to place the applicants' names directly on the rolls. The greatest opportunities for success occurred when federal registrars operated in localities that also experienced voter registration drives. The presence of civil rights organizations laid the basis for progress by building solidarity among blacks and providing them with the strength to confront those risks involved in challenging white segregationists. The freedom movement bound people together in collaborative projects and broke down some of the helplessness they felt when facing the burdens of discrimination alone. As Mary King, a SNCC staff member, has written about political organizing in Mississippi: "If blacks failed individually they succeeded collectively, because of the learning and experience gained."

However potent the law, the federal government expected the civil rights groups themselves to register the bulk of disfranchised blacks. "Legislation is not self-implementing," the NAACP's Roy Wilkins acknowledged. "There is work to be done." The new law challenged civil rights proponents to undertake a "tedious, unglamorous task" that required "more recruits, more money and more dedication." After 1965, all of those resources were in short supply as the days of large demonstrations and widespread national support for the civil rights movement drew to a close.

To register additional voters, the Southern Regional Council once again formed a Voter Education Project. From 1966 to 1968, this second VEP funded and coordinated over 200 suffrage drives throughout the South. Not only did it help underwrite the costs of well-established groups like the NAACP in conducting enrollment campaigns, but the Atlanta-based group also injected money into the efforts of local civic associations, many of which had been spawned or nurtured by the civil rights movement. These projects attempted to empower blacks, individually and collectively, who had not previously felt a sense of political worth. To combat generations of political helplessness, they embarked on programs of basic education to teach lessons fundamental to expressing first-class citizenship. Vernon Jordan, the director of VEP, explained the problem: "Too many of these people have been alienated from the political process for too long a time...and so we have to...teach them what a local government is, how it operates, and try to relate their votes to the things they want."

RISE OF BLACK POWER

Heightened racial consciousness, instilled through the freedom struggle and boosted by the Voting Rights Act, swelled even further with the emergence of "black power." A concept that embodied racial pride and solidarity, it partially grew out of the positive experiences of the freedom struggle. The collective engagement of blacks against Jim Crow and disfranchisement through boycotts, sit-ins, freedom rides, voter registration drives, and other political activities fostered self-respect and a feeling of political efficacy. Men and women, boys and girls, who had long been relegated to the sidelines of southern politics, became active agents in reclaiming first-class citizenship and in transforming the structures of oppression. The Montgomery bus boycott, for example, did more than withhold "patronage from the bus; it...[restored] dignity to the patrons," as Joseph Lowery, an SCLC official, noted. He explained, "prior to the bus boycotts, the determination of our freedom rested with the courts. With the bus boycott, *we* determined it."

The notion of black power also arose from some of the negative consequences of the civil rights struggle. Resistance to racism spawned it, and disillusionment with white liberals nurtured it. The failure of the federal government to protect civil rights workers and the willingness of liberal whites to compromise the Mississippi Freedom Democratic Party's convention challenge in 1964 outraged many black activists. Furthermore, within the South, the constant exposure to violence and harassment faced by black and white civil rights organizers produced enormous tensions between them. Under these circumstances, even the most well-meaning white volunteers were perceived by their black comrades as guilty of paternalism. Middle-class, college-educated whites who journeyed to the South for a march or a voter registration campaign often had superior skills and resources compared to the blacks they worked beside. Their efforts, no matter how unself-conscious or helpful, were sometimes perceived as perpetuating white dominance. "Look at these fly-by-night freedom fighters bossing everybody around," a black SNCC member bitterly commented during the 1964 Mississippi Freedom Summer about white students who could soon return to their comfortable northern campuses.

The black power slogan first gained notoriety in June 1966, on a march initiated by James Meredith to mobilize black Mississippians to register to vote in the wake of passage of the Voting Rights Act. Soon after the pilgrimage through the Magnolia State had begun, Meredith, whose admission to the state university had sparked a riot in 1962, was shot and wounded. Rising to take up his cause, leaders of SCLC, SNCC, and CORE set out to complete the trek. Along the way, Stokely Carmichael, the chairman of SNCC, pointed out the new direction toward which many blacks were turning. At a stop in Greenwood, Mississippi, he declared that blacks should concentrate on gaining political control over their own communities. Deemphasizing integration and moral appeals to the consciences of whites, Carmichael proclaimed: "The only way we gonna stop them white men from whippin' us is to take over. We been saying freedom for six years and we ain't got nothin'. What we gonna start saying is Black Power."

Stokely Carmichael was a movement veteran who had grown up in New York City. A senior at the prestigious Bronx High School of Science when lunch counter sit-ins swept the South in 1960, Carmichael joined in demonstrations against Jim Crow. The following year he rode the buses as a freedom rider, was arrested in Mississippi, and served a jail sentence in the state prison at Parchman. In the early sixties, Carmichael attended Howard University and together with several other students formed the Nonviolent Action Group (NAG), an affiliate of SNCC. As a student he was influenced by his reading of Marx and by contact with Malcolm X, the influential Black Muslim minister, whom he invited to speak at Howard. His campus views matured and grew more militant by virtue of

From left to right, Floyd McKissick of CORE, Martin Luther King, Jr., of SCLC, and Stokely Carmichael of SNCC on the last leg of the Meredith march into Jackson. (Bob Fitch/Black Star)

his experiences on SNCC battlefields in the Mississippi delta and the Alabama black belt. In May 1966, the articulate and charming twenty-four-year-old Carmichael became chairman of SNCC, replacing John Lewis and signaling a change in direction of the organization toward black nationalism.

The chant of black power voiced both cultural and political aspirations. More of a rallying cry than a systematic program, black power expressed the dual message of racial unity and group self-determination. Heavily influenced by his activities as a SNCC fieldworker in Mississippi and Alabama, Carmichael saw the key to liberation in the political organizing of black communities. His personal experiences in the South found reinforcement in his identification with the African struggle against European colonialism.

Moreover, Carmichael's reading of America's multiethnic history taught him the necessity for minority groups to develop "their own institutions with which to represent their communal needs within the larger society."

In collaboration with Charles V. Hamilton, a political scientist who had taught at Tuskegee Institute, Carmichael attempted to clarify his views by publishing *Black Power: The Politics of Liberation in America*. Combining the moral outrage and toughened perspective of an embittered SNCC veteran with the scholarly analysis of an academic social scientist, this 1967 book rejected integration and criticized the values of white middle-class society as "antihumanist" and "racist." Denying that black power was merely "racism in reverse," the authors argued that blacks had no intention of turning whites into second-class citizens on the basis of their skin color. Instead, Carmichael and Hamilton espoused self-determination and self-identity as the goals of black power: "full participation in the decisionmaking processes affecting the lives of black people, and recognition of the virtues in themselves as black people." Acknowledging the predominance of race throughout American history, they contended that blacks could not end discrimination on a color-blind, individual basis but could only do so by organizing their own communities around common group concerns. For the present, they ruled out coalitions with whites, including some former allies; however, once blacks had developed independent bases of political and economic power, Carmichael and Hamilton held open the possibility of creating biracial alliances based on mutual interest. Yet if the authors intended their message to be interpreted as problack rather than antiwhite, they refused to soothe white sensibilities by guaranteeing that the outcome of black power would be nonracist. "The final truth," they asserted without apology, "is that white society is not entitled to reassurances, even if it were possible to offer them."

The rhetoric of black power produced divisions within the civil rights movement, but its substance evoked widespread appeal among blacks. Julian Bond, the communications director of SNCC, considered black power the logical outgrowth of the freedom struggle. He traced its lineage "from the courtroom to the streets in favor of integrated facilities, from the... backwoods roads in quest of the right to vote, from the ballot box to the meat of politics, the organization of voters into self-interest units." Dr. King, who participated with Carmichael on the Meredith march, disapproved of the antiwhite connotations of the phrase and the inflammatory remarks that frequently accompanied it. However, he applauded attempts "to build racial pride and refute the notion that black is evil and ugly." As King had expressed many times, most recently in Selma, the ballot offered a critical tool for exhibiting pride and achieving equality. Blacks of more radical persuasions shared this view. Malcolm X, the charismatic black nationalist leader whose ideology differed in most respects from King's, agreed with him that if blacks were fully permitted to exercise their constitutional right to vote they "would sweep all of the racists and segregationists out of office...[and] would change the entire political structure of the country."

The controversial black power concept had a mixed impact on black political development. On the one hand, it helped to splinter the civil rights coalition and hastened the decline of two of its most innovative components, SNCC and CORE. Having started out firmly committed to interracial cooperation, they became increasingly disillusioned with white liberals and the prospect of blacks gaining their freedom under white leadership. To the extent that whites had a continuing place in the movement, it was to work within their own communities to combat racist attitudes. As these two groups applied black power principles to their organizations and white participation dwindled, they lost considerable institutional and financial backing. Increasingly isolated from mainstream civil rights groups as well as from whites, by the end of the decade SNCC had virtually disappeared and CORE was in serious disarray. Their deterioration deprived blacks, especially in the South, of the kind of imaginative leadership that had rallied many local communities to organize for freedom. Much work remained to be done in registering voters and summoning them to political action, and the departure of these important organizations from the scene made those tasks more difficult.

On the other hand, burgeoning racial pride among African-Americans was instrumental for black political mobilization. Following successful completion of the legislative struggle to obtain the suffrage, political activists had to convert the disfranchised into actual voters. Collective action had demonstrated the power of an oppressed group to reshape its political world, and the racial esteem that developed convinced blacks that politics was as much their business as whites'. Traditionally, individuals with little income and education had a low rate of political participation. Concentrated disproportionately at the bottom end of the socioeconomic scale, blacks nonetheless became politically involved at a level above that predicted from their backgrounds. "Organization, with an emphasis on group consciousness and a sense of group efficacy," according to one political scientist, accounted for the difference. In Mississippi, where the black registration figure soared in the years following passage of the Voting Rights Act, a black observer touring the Magnolia State remarked upon the transformation in this way: "It is so good to realize that we are casting aside the feelings of inferiority and shame and realizing what a strong people we are."

The expanded electoral mobilization of blacks further stimulated their interest in competing for public office. This was especially true in areas with a large number of blacks among the eligible voters, where the chances of electing a black candidate seemed high. Just as acquisition of the ballot furnished a necessary step toward advancing first-class citizenship, so did the election of blacks serve as a badge of equality. The running of black candidates both reflected racial pride and presented a stimulus to further black political mobilization. The election of a black to a post in a rural county in Mississippi, the winner asserted, "will give the Negro race the feeling... like they can progress, and this in itself [will make] more people run for public office."

As southern blacks began competing for a growing number of political positions, they were most successful at the local level. Because blacks remained a clear minority of the state and national electorates, their greatest chances for success came in those towns and counties in which they constituted a majority of the voting-age population. A decade after enactment of the Voting Rights Act law nearly 50 percent of black elected officials held municipal government posts. The largest number of black officials sat on city councils, and about three-fifths of those were in small towns with a population of less than 5,000. This same pattern held true for southern black mayors, approximately 66 percent of whom presided over municipalities with under 5,000 residents.

A raised racial consciousness accounted for much of the support for turning whites out of office and replacing them with blacks; however, part of the explanation stemmed from practical political considerations. In most places in the South, especially where blacks were in the majority, few whites were initially willing to support black candidates or enter into alliances with them. Without white collaboration, blacks had little choice but to go it alone. In Greene County, Alabama, in the rural black belt, a leader of the group of blacks who took control of the government explained the futility of constructing an interracial coalition: "We wanted the government to be polka dot, but the whites wouldn't cooperate, so we had to make it all chocolate."

In a similar manner, blacks constituted a majority of the population in Lowndes County, Alabama, and sought to branch out on their own. After the 1965 Selma-to-Montgomery march, Stokely Carmichael had remained in Lowndes County to help in the political mobilization of the black community. Under the tutelage of SNCC, local blacks formed the independent Lowndes County Freedom Organization (LCFO) to compete against the white-dominated Democratic party. "To me," John Hulett, LCFO's chairman remarked, "the Democratic primaries...are something like a gambler who carries a marked card around in his pocket and every now and then has to let somebody win to keep the game going." Choosing the black panther as its insignia, an emblem of fierce racial pride, at the end of the decade LCFO succeeded in electing Hulett to the most critical county office of sheriff.

These triumphs were repeated elsewhere. In Hancock County, Georgia, blacks comprised about 75 percent of the residents and had only recently made inroads in challenging total white domination of their government. In 1964, local black leaders formed the Hancock County Democratic Club to promote voter registration and political education. A combination of civil rights organizing and the passage of the 1965 Voting Rights Act succeeded in enfranchising a majority of Hancock's black electorate. In 1966, this paid off in the election of three blacks to county posts, and two years later blacks captured two of the three seats on the powerful county commission.

Much of the success of black political efforts here could be attributed to John McCown. A civil rights veteran, he had worked with the SCLC and the Georgia Council on Human Relations. In Hancock he built upon the previous voter registration drives of the County Democratic Club and expanded its endeavors to secure federal poverty program benefits for blacks. Riding the crest of expanded black enrollment, in 1968 he became one of the two blacks to win election to the county commission and, for the first time, a black became a probate judge, the most important official at the courthouse. McCown had managed to construct a potent political organization that reduced black fears of participation and provided economic incentives to vote. His message appealed to black pride. "Instead of trying to change the heart of the lady at the welfare department," he declared, "it's better to get in a position to be her boss."

Severe tensions accompanied the transfer of power from whites to blacks, however. The Ku Klux Klan paraded through the streets on election eve, and assorted threats were hurled at black candidates. Once in office, McCown upset whites even further with his vigorous attempts to desegregate public schools and generate black economic development. In addition, McCown's abrasive manner offended whites, and in 1971 relations between the races plummeted to a new low in what was called "the Hancock County arms race." Sparta, the county seat with an all-white government, began to stockpile machine guns, allegedly to protect its residents. In response, the black-controlled county commission ordered its own cache of machine guns and sponsored the formation of a "hunting club." The confrontation ended only with the intervention of Governor Jimmy Carter, who negotiated an uneasy truce between the protagonists.

Nevertheless, verbal sniping continued for the next several years during which McCown was indicted for misusing federal funds. The turbulence finally ended after the outspoken McCown was killed in a plane crash in early 1976. A controversial figure was gone, but black political power remained. Even with McCown's tragic death blacks still controlled sixteen of eighteen positions in the government of Hancock County.

In other places blacks who gained political power found some whites willing to cooperate. In 1966, in Macon County, Alabama, the site of historic battles over black reenfranchisement, Lucius Amerson defeated the white incumbent for sheriff. Though Amerson won with solid grassroots black support, he declined to espouse the rhetoric of black power. Upon taking office, he received support from influential whites, including the probate judge and members of the Tuskegee City Council and County Commission. The chairman of the latter body, Allen Parker, helped promote interracial goodwill among officials and labored to enlarge county employment opportunities for blacks. "The public attitude... has changed

tremendously," Sheriff Amerson declared, "and has helped destroy
...the feeling that existed among Negroes as well as whites that a
Negro couldn't get cooperation from the white community."

The Macon County model pointed to the direction in which
black politics would head. Most black officials recognized the necessity of forming coalitions with whites to broaden their power
base. Only at the local level, where blacks were in the majority,
could they afford to ignore whites; and even there, the blacks had
to take whites into account to obtain needed economic resources.
The towns and hamlets where most black officials operated were
impoverished and depended on funds from state and national governments for internal improvements. Outnumbered in these arenas, as a fact of political life they needed to enter into alliances with
white lawmakers. Thus, black politicians who first obtained office
on the basis of appeals to racial pride nonetheless were compelled
to make common cause with whites to achieve their racial aims.

Black Mississippians were also torn between separatist and coalitionist tendencies. For them the civil rights struggle had meant a
way not only to secure the right to vote but also to obtain a fair
share of political power. Toward these ends, they had created the
Mississippi Freedom Democratic Party to stimulate voter registration and gain control of the instrumentality that dominated political
affairs in the state. Though interracial in conception—Ed King, the
white minister at Tougaloo College was one of its founders—in
practice the Freedom party reflected black consciousness and supported the election of black candidates whenever possible. "We
want to be on the ground level, where the decisions are made
about us," explained Bob Moses. "We don't want to [be] mobilized
every four years to vote. We want to be in the actual running of
things."

This strategy of encouraging independent black political action
clashed with the coalitionist approach of the NAACP. Since the
campaign to oust Theodore Bilbo from the Senate after World War
II, the NAACP had actively struggled to tear down the Magnolia
Curtain of racism draped across the state. During the 1950s and until his assassination in 1963, Medgar Evers, along with leaders like
Amzie Moore, Aaron Henry, and Hartman Turnbow, had kept
alive the voter registration efforts that SNCC and its allies would
build upon. The NAACP had collaborated with SNCC in launching
the MFDP and its 1964 convention challenge; however, after that

event the two groups drifted apart. Alarmed by the growing black power perspective of its rival, the older association chose to join with white moderates and labor leaders to seek national Democratic party recognition for their state's interracial coalition. In 1968, their protest proved successful, and a biracial Loyalist Democratic group supplanted the MFDP, which soon disbanded, as the chief vehicle for party reform among blacks and whites in the state.

The Democrats expanded black representation in party affairs not only in Mississippi but throughout the South. Wary of the formation of militant, predominantly black Democratic factions in Mississippi and Alabama, they sanctioned the claims of more moderate, interracial delegations, which pressed for seating at the 1968 convention. In addition, the party adopted far-reaching affirmative action guidelines that required "representation of minority groups on the national convention delegation in reasonable relationship to the group's presence in the population of the state." The results were striking. In 1972, at the Democratic presidential nominating meeting, 56 percent of the delegates from Mississippi were black, and in the delegations representing states covered by the Voting Rights Act, the proportion of blacks equaled or exceeded the percentage of blacks in the population.

Although they disdained political separatism, coalitionists tacitly supported their own version of black power as a form of voting power. Charles Evers, who succeeded his brother, Medgar, as the NAACP's field agent in Mississippi and who mounted several campaigns for political office in the state, urged blacks to "control the ballot of the county... control the entire county where we are predominant. We don't holler Black Power—but watch it." The NAACP and its black opposition did not disagree so much over ends—political parity for blacks—but over the means to attain it. Each side could have agreed with the view expressed by a black Mississippian who remarked: "Power is invested in the ballot, and that's why the white man worked like hell to keep you away from it."

Both the coalition and separatist courses significantly increased black office-holding in the years following adoption of the Voting Rights Act. In 1964, fewer than 25 black elected officials governed in the South, but by the end of the decade the figure had soared to nearly 500. In 1970, the number of elected blacks climbed still higher—to over 700.

Besides yielding these impressive gains, black ballots also helped elect more moderate white officials. In Dallas County, Alabama, shortly after the Voting Rights Act went into effect, newly enfranchised blacks remedied a long-standing political grievance and helped vote Sheriff Jim Clark out of office. In his place they installed Wilson Baker, the Selma law enforcement chief who had vainly tried to forestall violence against civil rights protesters in his city. In 1966, though blacks were not yet strong enough at the polls to beat the segregationist gubernatorial candidate, Lurleen Wallace, running as a surrogate for her husband, George, four years later blacks elsewhere joined with white majorities to elect moderate governors in Arkansas, Florida, Georgia, and South Carolina. Racist demagoguery in southern election campaigns was fast becoming a relic.

Despite these successes, southern blacks still encountered a variety of roadblocks to political equality. The formal impediments to voter registration had mainly disappeared, but white officials continued to devise techniques to hamper blacks who had managed to enroll for the suffrage. In 1971, white politicians in Mississippi ordered the reregistration of voters in approximately thirty counties, in many of which a large number of blacks had only recently enrolled. In other sections of the deep South, local registrars conducted business at inconvenient hours that failed to accommodate the schedules of working-class blacks, and they functioned exclusively at county courthouses too far away for many rural blacks easily to reach.

RACIAL POLARIZATION

As blacks reentered the political arenas of the South, mobilized their forces, and competed for office, the nation witnessed a sharp rise in racial polarization. Even at the height of the freedom struggle, many white Americans sympathized with black integrationist goals but disliked the movement's aggressive, confrontational tactics. In 1963, 64 percent of the whites polled in a nationwide survey had expressed the view that blacks were pushing too quickly for equality. The following year blacks rioted in the northern ghettos of Harlem, Rochester, Jersey City, and Philadelphia, and over the remainder of the decade violent uprisings spread to some 300 cities, involving a half-million blacks. The riots consumed millions of dollars in property damage and resulted in 50,000 arrests, 8,000 injuries, and 250 deaths, mostly of blacks. In 1967, in Detroit alone, 43 people were killed, 2,000 were wounded, and 5,000 were burned out of their homes.

The riots reflected both the reawakening of black consciousness and the continued awareness of unresolved grievances. Civil rights battles, while fought primarily in the South, inspired blacks everywhere to identify with the cause of liberation. Though rejecting nonviolence as a tactic, the rioters had taken pride in the willingness of their southern black brothers and sisters to stand up collectively to white racism. In the midst of the conflagration in Detroit, a looter explained what drove him into the streets. In words very much reminiscent of black protesters in the South, he explained that he was looking for "respect as a man, as a first-class citizen."

Outside the South, the law did not require segregation or promote disfranchisement; yet African-Americans faced systematic racial discrimination that deprived them of full equality. They had the right to vote and the right to enter public accommodations, but those who dwelled in squalid ghettos lacked decent housing, employment, and evenhanded police protection. Some notable economic improvements had occurred during the 1960s. Median black family income climbed to 61 percent of that earned by whites, the percentage of black families living below the poverty level diminished to 30 percent, and the unemployment rate for married black males dropped to 4 percent by mid-decade. However, these gains did not keep pace with rising black expectations stimulated by the civil rights struggle. Through rioting, many blacks sought to deliver a message of protest to white Americans that focused attention on the seriousness of their plight. They turned to extralegal methods because conventional political channels had failed to resolve their complaints.

The riots yielded mixed results. Many cities responded by seeking ways to relieve the miserable social conditions that fueled the disorders. They took out "riot insurance" by setting up programs to provide job training, recreational facilities, slum clearance, and more effective communication between police and the residents they served. At the same time, city and state governments also devised more punitive measures and put a good deal of their resources into riot control by beefing up their defense arsenals with expensive and powerful weapons.

This latter response mirrored the growing antagonism of whites toward black protest demands. Appalled by the violence and lawlessness, many whites called for a restoration of public order, severe punishment of rioters, and withdrawal of funding for poverty projects that appeared to reward antisocial behavior. Although civil rights leaders such as Dr. King and Roy Wilkins denounced violence, others like SNCC's Stokely Carmichael fanned the flames of discord. Carmichael and his black power associates were not responsible for the spontaneous eruptions that swept over American cities, but their inflammatory rhetoric scared and angered whites. "When you talk about black power," the SNCC chairman declared following a riot in Cleveland, "you talk of building a movement that will smash everything Western civilization has created." This type of provocative statement in tandem with the ghetto riots helped reinforce the menacing connotation that black power had assumed.

The rise of the Black Panther party (BPP) strengthened this image. Adopting the trademark of the Lowndes County Freedom Organization, Huey P. Newton and Bobby Seale, who had met each other in college, formed the organization in October 1966 in Oakland, California. In contrast to the LCFO, the Panthers were not a political party mainly interested in contesting elections. Along with Eldridge Cleaver, a thirty-one year-old ex-convict and writer who had spent most of his adult life in prison, they denounced capitalism and regarded the ghettos as an exploited colony within the United States. Blending black nationalism and Marxist-Leninist doctrines, the BPP considered itself as the revolutionary vanguard leading the urban masses in the destruction of "the machinery of the oppressor." In the ghetto this meant the police—"the military arm of our oppressors"—which residents frequently saw not as protectors but as the guardians of their misery and the agents of brutality. In fact, most of the summer riots had been sparked by incidents of excessive police force and charges of brutality. The Panthers responded by taking up arms for self-defense and patroling their neighborhoods to keep watch over the police. In 1967, a bloody confrontation between Newton and the police left one officer dead and the Panther founder wounded and placed under arrest. The next year, another shootout in Oakland killed a BPP official.

Often lost amidst this violence was the broader political program the Panthers advocated. In its original platform, the BPP demanded jobs for the unemployed, decent housing for the poor, and a greater voice for blacks in determining decisions affecting their communities. Working toward these goals, in Oakland and in cities such as Chicago, where they set up chapters, the Panthers instituted free breakfast and health care programs to improve neighborhood conditions. They conducted classes in black history and warned against the dangers of drug use, seeking to build racial pride in young black children and to instill confidence in their ability to reshape their lives.

Initially the Panthers put greater emphasis on community organizing than on electoral politics. Their battle cry of "power to the people" called for local control of economic and political institutions based upon armed struggle; nevertheless, by the late 1960s the Panthers had added the ballot as a weapon in its arsenal. Unlike some other black nationalist groups, the BPP formed alliances with white radicals and competed with them for political office in common cause against class as well as racial exploitation. By then, however, the militant actions of the party brought the weight of local, state, and federal governments upon the group, seriously damaging its efforts. Led by the FBI, whose director viewed the Panthers as "the greatest threat to the internal security of the country," government agents infiltrated the group, provoked internal dissension, and shot and jailed its followers. By the end of the decade, the police had killed over a score of Panthers and arrested some 750.

Meanwhile, such strife and the media attention it attracted had fueled a reactionary white backlash against additional civil rights reforms. No one played on the anxieties of whites better than did George Wallace. Having whipped up the antagonism of southerners against desegregation, the Alabama governor transported his racist messages to the North, where they received a favorable reception from those whites who feared that black progress came at their expense. Wallace exploited class as well as racial tensions. He catered to blue-collar workers and excoriated "left-wing theoreticians, briefcase totin' bureaucrats, ivory tower guideline writers, bearded anarchists, smart alleck editorial writers and pointy headed professors." The racial disturbances of the sixties propelled Wallace's presidential ambitions. In 1964, he tested out his antiestablishment, racist appeals by campaigning for the Democratic presidential nomination. His candidacy eventually fizzled, but not before he showed surprising strength among disgruntled white voters in Indiana, Maryland, and Wisconsin.

The increasing bitterness of racial tensions was reflected at every governmental level. In 1966, the Georgia legislature refused to seat Julian Bond as a duly elected representative from Atlanta. Bond had offended lawmakers by supporting SNCC's opposition to the Vietnam war and calling for alternatives to the military draft. A year later, Congress rejected the credentials of Adam Clayton Powell, who had easily won reelection from Harlem. Powell had embraced black power doctrines during the 1960s, but it was financial and ethical improprieties that got him into trouble. In each case, blacks saw white legislators as practicing a double standard of justice and acting unnecessarily harshly. The U.S. Supreme Court ultimately ruled in favor of Bond and Powell and restored their positions to them.

The politics of black power also aggravated racial discord in Ocean Hill–Brownsville, a section of Brooklyn, New York, populated by low-income, poorly educated African-Americans and Puerto Ricans. In 1967, under a plan sponsored by the New York City Board of Education in cooperation with the Ford Foundation, the United Federation of Teachers (UFT), and local community groups, Ocean Hill–Brownsville became part of an experimental project in school decentralization. Community activists had complained that the school system was failing to educate their children. Pointing accusing fingers at both insensitive bureaucrats and teachers, the overwhelming majority of whom were white, they called for sweeping educational reorganization to help address the needs of ghetto students. The proposal that was adopted fell short of their objectives, but it did establish school decentralization and called for the election of parents and other community residents to serve alongside teachers on a district governing board.

The experiment resulted in some positive achievements. Communitywide elections gave parents a powerful voice in their children's education that was used to introduce new programs emphasizing racial pride and instilling self-worth—two ingredients often absent from the classrooms and corridors of ghetto schools. As more minority teachers, parents, and paraprofessionals became involved in school affairs, students responded enthusiastically. One pupil recalled her excitement over seeing more black faces: "I mean you felt more accepted. You weren't an outsider in your own school. They were part of your environment. I mean they were Black. You can identify with them and they can identify with you."

However, the children soon got caught up in a power struggle between their parents, the teachers union, and the central school board. The Ocean Hill–Brownsville governing council, dominated by community residents, and the chief administrator of the district, Rhody McCoy, wanted greater community control over finances and personnel than the union and central board would allow. Albert Shanker, the president of the UFT, favored community participation, but demanded that teachers' job rights be protected. In the spring of 1968, the local governing agency unilaterally ordered the transfer of thirteen teachers and seven administrators out of the district, precipitating a confrontation with the union and central board over the issue of due process. When the matter was not resolved over the summer, the UFT took almost 54,000 teachers out on strike in September.

The controversy raged from Labor Day to the middle of November, driving a deep wedge between former allies in the civil rights coalition. Those like Shanker and his union followers who had supported the principle of school integration contended that the Ocean Hill–Brownsville experiment had deteriorated into black separatism. McCoy and his allies, many of whom were influenced by a growing emphasis on black consciousness, charged that the union constituted a racist obstacle to educational reform and black self-determination. Although the two sides did not divide strictly along racial lines—the community board hired a majority of white teachers as replacements for the strikers, and influential black activists such as Bayard Rustin supported the union—the conflict exacerbated racial tensions. The dispute turned even uglier and more divisive when charges of anti-Semitism surfaced. Most union members were Jewish, and they were angered by intemperate remarks made by some militants. After an inflammatory memo referring to Jews as "money changers," "bloodsucking exploiters," and "Middle East murderers" was distributed in two schools, the UFT made the already tense situation even worse by reprinting and circulating the missive to thousands of Jews throughout the city. For its part, the local governing board denied charges of anti-Semitism, pointing out that about half the teachers it hired were Jewish. Still, its measured response to the most vicious displays of anti-Semitism failed to settle the nerves of apprehensive Jews.

When the nearly two-month-old strike finally ended, the local school district was placed under state supervision and the union won reinstatement of the dismissed teachers and a new contract guaranteeing employee safeguards. At the same time, the state legislature enacted a measure that decentralized all New York City school districts, but it balanced local participation with limited autonomy for community governing boards. The educational establishment had prevailed, and had proved itself powerful enough to resist radical change. Overall, the political fallout from the dispute poisoned relations between blacks and Jews and between black power advocates and liberal labor leaders, and left the civil rights alliance and the electoral coalition behind it badly frayed.

Black militancy and white backlash also delayed passage of new civil rights legislation. In 1966, the Johnson administration proposed a package that attacked discrimination in housing and offered federal protection for civil rights workers. The former provision applied equally throughout the entire nation, thereby hitting whites in the North close to home. As the target of civil rights assaults expanded beyond the South, whites offered greater resistance. In 1966, a presidential aide complained "that it would have been hard to pass the emancipation proclamation in the atmosphere prevailing this summer." The hostile political atmosphere continued through the fall congressional elections, as Republicans increased their representation in the House by forty-seven seats.

Yet white backlash was not strong enough to kill the civil rights measure. Though President Johnson was deeply disturbed by the outbreak of riots and perceived them as the product of conspiratorial black nationalist forces, he did not retreat from supporting his latest civil rights proposals. He attempted to strike a balance between appearing not to reward the lawless actions of the rioters and backing measures that addressed what he considered to be the legitimate demands of traditional civil rights groups like the NAACP. In this way he could underscore, as one of his aides put it, that "law abiding citizens, black and white, should have and will have the safety and protection of their government." At the same time, he could strengthen the position of his moderate civil rights allies at the expense of their more militant critics. Joining with the NAACP and the Leadership Conference on Civil Rights, a coalition of reform lobbyists, the Johnson administration kept up the legislative pressure; in April 1968, Congress finally passed a civil rights act that featured the controversial fair housing provision. Reflecting the uneasy temper of the times, Congress also enacted a punitive antiriot measure aimed at prosecuting roving black agitators.

This hard-earned legislative victory could not restore unity to the civil rights forces. SNCC and CORE continued down their separatist paths and had little interest in a bill that aimed to promote integration. The SCLC continued to retain its interracial ideals, but broke with the President over his policy of escalating the war in Vietnam. In challenging the administration over this issue, Dr. King parted from his allies in the NAACP and Urban League, who remained loyal to Johnson. King's assassination on April 4, 1968, during the final deliberations on the Civil Rights Act, aided its passage as a tribute to the slain martyr, but also badly weakened the organization that relied heavily on his style of charismatic leadership. In addition to these internal strains that fractured the movement, the Johnson administration greatly accelerated its disintegration from without. The FBI had relentlessly investigated and harassed Dr. King and directed a clandestine counterintelligence program that succeeded in undermining black power groups such as the Panthers.

THE NIXON ADMINISTRATION AND BENIGN NEGLECT

While Johnson struggled to reinforce civil rights moderates at the expense of black radicals, the frustrations of military stalemate in Vietnam combined with antiwar protests at home prompted him not to run for another term as chief executive. The candidates who sought to succeed him guaranteed that African-Americans would remain faithful to the party of the President who had achieved more for civil rights than any of his predecessors. Johnson passed the Democratic standard on to his vice-president, Hubert H. Humphrey, the liberal stalwart who first led the charge, back in 1948, to swing Democrats behind a strong civil rights platform.

Humphrey's chief opponents did not offer black voters much of an alternative. Though once a firm advocate of the civil rights cause, the GOP nominee, Richard M. Nixon, had charted a political route that moved him away from the search for black ballots toward those of conservative white southerners. In this respect he had stiff competition from George Wallace, who ran on the American Independent party ticket and whose demagogic rhetoric and obstructionist actions had hampered black racial advancement.

Two black candidates competed as independents. Eldridge Cleaver, the Black Panther, was nominated by the Peace and Freedom party, a political formation of predominantly white leftists originating in California. The comedian Dick Gregory, who had assumed an active role in the civil rights movement, mounted a campaign that the political scientist Manning Marable concluded was "marked more by political satire than actual political content." Neither candidate had any chance of winning, but each served as an outlet for disaffected black nationalists and white radicals.

In his second bid for the White House, Nixon enthusiastically embraced a southern strategy that would ensure the victory that had narrowly eluded him in 1960. He pursued the same segment of white voters in Dixie that had backed Barry Goldwater in 1964. Besides resurrecting economic positions that attacked the big-spending social welfare programs of Johnson's Great Society, he played on the racial antipathies of conservative white southerners. Speaking out against busing to promote school desegregation, he voiced approval for freedom-of-choice plans that operated to retard full-scale desegregation. In obtaining the Republican nomination over another conservative aspirant, Governor Ronald Reagan of California, he associated himself with Senator Strom Thurmond of South Carolina, the 1948 Dixiecrat candidate, who had subsequently converted to the GOP. The alliance between the two was cemented by their agreement that, if elected, Nixon would slow down school desegregation and voting rights enforcement in the South.

In taking this stand Nixon hoped to undercut potential southern white support for Wallace. The Alabama governor delivered a populist message that echoed the economic and social discontent of working-class whites. To distinguish himself from Nixon and to appeal to a lower-income constituency than that attracted to well-to-do Republicanism, Wallace charged that there was not a "dime's worth of difference between the two major parties." He hammered away on the theme of "law and order," code words that expressed hostility toward black militants, antiwar demonstrators, and the liberal establishment that presumably "coddled" them.

Vice-President Humphrey represented that establishment, and only he actively campaigned for black votes. In a chaotic nominating convention racked by antiwar protests, the Democrats awarded unprecedented delegate representation to black southerners and ensured that their influence would expand even further in the future. On the campaign trail, Humphrey blasted Nixon and Wallace for exploiting "fear and tensions that grip significant portions of our people." Instead of a society dedicated to "opportunity and justice," he warned that his opponents would usher in "a fractured and separated society—black against white, rich against poor, comfortable against leftout."

As expected, Humphrey's rivals found a fertile field for their views in the South. The Voting Rights Act had greatly expanded the size of the black electorate in the region, but in the years immediately following its passage had also led to an upsurge in the number of whites registering to vote. Whites constituted some 60 to 70 percent of the newly enrolled electorate. In addition, demographic shifts laid the foundation for white defections from candidates of the national Democratic party, who were considered too liberal. The influx into the sunbelt of white northerners, many of whom had previously voted Republican, boosted the constituency for the growth of the GOP in the traditionally one-party South. Furthermore, as the South became more urbanized, Republicans drew increasing support from middle- and upper-class whites whose economic interests tied them more closely to the GOP's outlook.

Neither in the South nor elsewhere in the nation were black votes abundant enough to offset white abandonment of the Democrats. Though Humphrey received 88 percent of black ballots, southern whites overwhelmingly lined up behind his opponents. The Democratic candidate received only 31 percent of southern votes, most of them blacks, a figure that was nineteen points behind Johnson's in 1964. Nixon and Wallace divided Dixie's white electorate, each capturing five states and leaving Texas to Humphrey. The GOP contender obtained the support of 35 percent of the region's electorate, a share only slightly larger than Wallace's 34 percent. The Alabama governor cut into Democratic support in the North—working-class whites provided half his total votes—and nationally Wallace obtained 13.5 percent of the ballots cast, the strongest performance by a third-party contestant since 1924. Overall, Democratic defections also helped propel Nixon into the White House. The Republican winner garnered 301 electoral votes and a plurality of 43.4 percent of the popular votes.

President Nixon attempted to deliver on his southern campaign strategy. As Ethel Payne, a black journalist, noted shortly after his election, "Mr. Nixon has no debt to pay black voters." He tried to lift the burden of civil rights enforcement off the South by extending it to the North. The President told reporters, "we finally have in this country what the South has wanted and what the South deserves, a one nation policy." However evenhanded this approach sounded, it aimed to weaken civil rights implementation. The Justice Department's Civil Rights Division would be spread too thin with a staff insufficient in size to monitor and litigate against racial discrimination everywhere in the country. Moreover, many critics believed that in expanding civil rights coverage outside the South, Nixon strategists hoped that disgruntled northern politicians would join southerners in opposing strict enforcement of such controversial desegregation remedies as school busing.

Soon after entering the Oval Office, Nixon sought to reverse policy on school integration of fifteen years' standing. In 1969, for the first time since the historic *Brown* decision, federal lawyers appeared in court to support a southern state, Mississippi, in attempting to postpone the implementation of a desegregation plan. Subsequently, the chief executive affirmed his backing for "a truly desegregated public school system" through improvements in the quality of education, rather than by "buying buses, tires, and gasoline to transport young children miles away from their neighborhood schools."

At the same time, the Nixon administration looked to overhaul the provisions of the Voting Rights Act in order to relieve pressure on the South. Most of the important features of the statute were due for renewal after five years, and civil rights advocates favored a simple extension of the law. As with school integration, the President wanted to reshape the measure so that it would extend to the North. Consequently, his attorney general, John Mitchell, requested Congress to scrap the automatic triggering and preclearance sections and in their place authorize the Justice Department to initiate litigation against suffrage discrimination anywhere in the country. The attorney general would be empowered to seek suits halting the imposition of new voting restrictions and to send federal examiners to enforce court orders. Also, the law would suspend the use of literacy tests in the North as well as the South. "Voting rights is not a regional issue," Mitchell asserted. "It is a nationwide concern for every American which must be tested on a nationwide basis."

Civil rights supporters derided the proposal. They viewed the administration bill as a subterfuge to cripple a law that had proved successful. Having experienced the pitfalls of relying on courts to protect black voting rights, they vigorously opposed a return to the judicial approach. After five years, blacks still encountered suffrage problems in the South, and civil rights proponents wanted attention to remain focused on that region. Clarence Mitchell, the chief lobbyist for the NAACP, attacked the Nixon administration's offering as "a sophisticated, a calculated, incredible effort... to make it impossible for us to continue on the constitutional course that we have followed... in protecting the right to vote."

In general, the Nixon administration did not succeed in curbing civil rights advances. Though blacks had lost political clout within the White House, they still retained influence before the Supreme Court and in Congress. In 1969, the high tribunal rebuked the administration for stalling desegregation in Mississippi, and in *Alexander v. Holmes County Board of Education* it ordered an immediate end to dual school systems. Two years later, the justices sanctioned busing as a remedy for fashioning interracial schools in districts that had practiced segregation by law. Disappointed with the ruling in *Swann v. Charlotte-Mecklenburg Board of Education*, Nixon subsequently requested Congress to pass legislation limiting the use of busing, but the proposal failed. By the middle of the decade, southern schools surpassed those in the North as the least segregated in the country. In the South, 47.1 percent of black students attended schools with a white majority compared with 42.5 percent of northern blacks who did so.

With respect to political rights also, Congress and the courts checked the Nixon administration's racial options. In 1970, lawmakers renewed the Voting Rights Act with its original provisions intact. Literacy tests were again suspended for five years, though Nixon got his way in applying this to the entire country. In addition, the legislation extended the franchise to eighteen-year-olds. The following year when the attorney general tried to interpret the preclearance provision in a manner that narrowed its operation, Congress stepped in to frustrate him. In the meantime, the Supreme Court defined the scope of the Voting Rights Act very broadly. Beginning in 1969, it decreed that the statute was not only directed toward voter registration but was also meant to include "all actions to make a vote effective." In a series of decisions the judiciary empowered federal authorities to strike down electoral rules that had the purpose or effect of diluting the strength of black ballots. The conversion from single-member districts to at-large elections, the expansion of municipal boundaries through annexation of largely white areas, and reapportionment plans that produced racially gerrymandered districts were regulations of this type.

Given the judicial mandate and under the watchful eyes of Congress, the Nixon administration satisfactorily fulfilled its constitutional obligation to protect black enfranchisement. Whereas White House policymakers may have wished to slow down implementation of the Voting Rights Act, career service lawyers in the Justice Department carried out their enforcement duties in a highly professional manner. Many of these attorneys had held their positions since the Johnson era, and they took their cues from the court and the legislature. Consequently, as William E. Leuchtenburg has noted, "much of the positive activity under the Nixon Administration came not because of the enterprise of Nixon and his immediate aides, but rather from the momentum developed by the federal bureaucracy, a momentum no president can easily halt."

Congress also contained a sufficient amount of procivil rights strength to block the chief executive's attempt to appoint conservative southerners to the Supreme Court. In 1969, the Senate rejected the nomination of Clement Haynsworth from Strom Thurmond's South Carolina. A federal judge whose opinions in racial cases had aroused the concern of civil rights groups, Haynsworth was defeated after months of bitter and protracted debate. The next year, the President sent up the name of G. Harrold Carswell to fill the vacancy and was similarly rebuffed. The Florida jurist appeared much less qualified than Haynsworth, a judgment inadvertently rendered by one of his defenders. Even if Carswell "were mediocre, there were a lot of mediocre judges and people and lawyers," Republican Senator Roman Hruska of Nebraska declared. "They are entitled to a little representation, aren't they, and a little chance?" Hearing praise like this, a majority of lawmakers turned down the nominee.

In other areas affecting black advancement, the Nixon administration ranged between moderation and affirmative action. In 1970, one of Nixon's top counselors on domestic affairs, Daniel Patrick Moynihan, a former aide in the Johnson administration, advised the President: "The time may have come when the issue of race could benefit from a period of 'benign neglect'.... The forum has been too much taken over by hysteria, paranoids, and boodlers on all sides.

We may need a period in which Negro progress continues and racial rhetoric fades." Accepting this reasoning, the chief executive attempted to encourage economic self-help as the key to racial equality. In conservative fashion, Nixon promoted black capitalism as the cornerstone of black power. Cleverly expropriating his critics' rhetoric, he contended that despite their stridency and seemingly anticapitalist tones, the militants' ideas more clearly resembled "the doctrines of free enterprise than... those of the welfare thirties—terms of 'pride', 'ownership', 'private enterprise', 'capital', 'self-assurance', 'self-respect'."

To expand minority business opportunities, the President increased funding to the Small Business Administration and the Minority Business Enterprise in the Commerce Department. In 1969, minority firms received $8 million in federal contracts; four years later, they were getting $242 million. Similarly, during this period government aid to minority enterprises leaped from $200 million to $472 million. For the mass of blacks who were destined to remain employees and not employers, the President established the "Philadelphia Plan," which required construction workers' unions involved in federal contracts to sign up and retain a fixed proportion of black apprentices. Befitting his economic philosophy, Nixon's major innovative foray into the field of affirmative action shrewdly shifted the obligation of meeting equal opportunity guidelines away from management and onto organized labor.

BLACK CAUCUSES AND CONVENTIONS

By the end of Nixon's first term, blacks sought new ways to increase their influence. While the legislative and judicial branches of the federal government overrode the executive, black politicians organized to boost their leverage in Congress and shape the direction of public policy. In 1969, Representative Charles Diggs, Jr., a Detroit Democrat, organized the eight other black members of the House of Representatives into an informal committee to work with congressional leaders on civil rights and social welfare issues. Two years later, the Congressional Black Caucus (CBC) was officially formed, and functioned as a lobbying group along the lines of other special-interest blocs in the legislative branch. Though it made policy recommendations to expand benefits for blacks, the caucus succeeded mainly in joining with white liberal lawmakers in waging defensive actions to preserve strong enforcement of suffrage legislation and rescue civil rights programs from conservative assault. In addition, the formation of the CBC inspired black elected officials at the state and local levels to establish similar groups, such as the National Conference of Black Mayors, to present a black perspective on policy matters crucial to minorities.

Though not an official member of the CBC, which consisted solely of House lawmakers, Senator Edward Brooke of Massachusetts became its ally. At a time when the overwhelming majority of African-Americans preferred the Democratic party, Brooke was a Republican who belonged to the GOP's moderate-to-liberal wing. Elected in 1966, from a state with less than a 3 percent black population, the former state attorney general declared: "I can't serve just the Negro cause. I've got to serve all the people of Massachusetts." Nevertheless, as the nation's highest-ranking black elected official, Brooke attempted to press upon the White House his concern for civil rights and other items on the CBC agenda during the years his party held the presidency. He had actively campaigned for Nixon in 1968, but his enthusiasm waned as the President tried to put his southern strategy into practice. Consequently, Senator Brooke joined those of his colleagues who successfully thwarted much of Nixon's effort in that direction.

In the face of the Nixon administration's calculated retreat in many areas of civil rights, the most ambitious attempt to unite black political leaders came with the 1972 National Black Political Convention in Gary, Indiana. The meeting grew out of a call by the CBC for the development of "a national black agenda and the crystallization of a national black strategy for the 1972 elections and beyond." The caucus wound up not giving the conference its official endorsement, but individual members did attend. With some cracks in the foundation of unity already surfacing, convention planners emphasized the need for racial solidarity to "transform black political potential into power commensurate with the number of blacks in the United States." The more than 3,500 delegates who attended the sessions from March 10 to 12 adopted a comprehensive set of recommendations for black political and economic empowerment and created the National Black Political Assembly as an independent force for exerting pressure on white political institutions.

Stressing "unity without uniformity," the meetings were presided over by Diggs, Gary Mayor Richard Hatcher, and Amiri Baraka, the poet and black nationalist. The convention secured agreement on most of the items constituting a national black agenda. It approved resolutions calling for increased black congressional representation, community control of schools, a national health insurance program, and a guaranteed minimum annual income. Moreover, the delegates felt exhilarated by the very act of gathering together to shape a political course for African-Americans to follow. "I guess the strongest image I have about Gary," an organizer for the Mississippi Freedom Democratic Party remembered, "is the fact that black people were able to mobilize, black people from all walks of life, from all different states, to this one focal point."

However, the highly prized unity failed to last. The convention was torn by divisions between racial integrationists and cultural nationalists and between those who proposed forming a third political party and those who defended working within the existing two-party system. Tensions peaked, however, over the issues of school desegregation and support of the Palestine Liberation Organization, a revolutionary group opposed to Zionism and the state of Israel. When the convention voted to endorse black control of neighborhood schools instead of busing and its promotion of integration and to recognize the right of self-determination for Palestinians, integrationists and supporters of Israel vigorously condemned the resolutions. Succeeding meetings of the Black Political Assembly attracted progressively fewer delegates, black nationalists came to dominate them, and black elected officials abandoned them.

The attempt in Gary to forge black political unity collapsed under the weight of clashing political and ideological interests. Without solid support from established electoral leaders, Representative Shirley Chisholm of Brooklyn, New York, made a futile bid to compete in the Democratic presidential primaries in 1972. Her fellow members of the CBC, along with other prominent black Democrats, refused to line up behind her candidacy and instead chose to support the various leading white contenders for their party's nomination. Blacks played a large role at the Democratic National Convention, which nominated Senator George S. McGovern of South Dakota, the coauthor of the convention's newly reformed antidiscriminatory delegate selection rules.

In selecting the liberal McGovern, the Democrats infuriated

those who had found the candidacy of George C. Wallace attractive. The primary season had witnessed the explosive presence of Governor Wallace, who vowed to shake the "eyeteeth out" of the Democratic party. Running a staunchly antibusing campaign aimed at exploiting the white backlash, the Alabama governor defeated ten rivals for the Democratic presidential nomination to capture a victory in Florida with 42 percent of the vote. Wallace's win accurately gauged the mood of the white electorate, as Sunshine State voters passed a nonbinding referendum against forced busing. Fresh from this success, Wallace went on to pile up wins in the normally friendly southern states of Tennessee and North Carolina. The governor delighted crowds with his antielitist rhetoric: "If the pseudointellectuals think it is good to bus little children backwards and forwards...the average man doesn't, and there are more of them than there are [of] the pseudos." Northern voters also responded enthusiastically to this message, and Wallace triumphed in Michigan and Maryland and scored strong second-place finishes in Wisconsin, Pennsylvania, and Indiana. Tragedy struck while he was speaking in Maryland, as an assassin's bullet left him alive but paralyzed from the waist down. Unable to continue campaigning actively, the governor saw his powerful bid for the presidential nomination effectively come to an end.

Even without a Wallace candidacy, the results of the 1972 election suggested the sharpening polarization of the electorate along racial lines. Taking his cue from the Alabamian, the President repeated his own opposition to busing, called for a moratorium on additional court-ordered busing until July 1973, and vowed to "end segregation in a way that does not result in more busing." Winning 60.8 percent of the popular vote, Nixon attracted the vast portion of the southern white electorate that supported Wallace and collected the electoral votes of the entire South. Indeed, in his landslide victory, Nixon carried every state except Massachusetts and predominantly black Washington, D.C. Ironically, African-Americans demonstrated a high degree of the now seemingly elusive racial solidarity in giving the losing candidate more than 85 percent of their ballots.

From the vantage point of state and local arenas, black political progress appeared brighter. Although much remained to be done, following Nixon's reelection the number of black elected officials in the nation stood at over 2,600. Very impressively, the number of minority officeholders in the South climbed to nearly 1,200, up from approximately 875 a year earlier. The rate of increase in black electoral victories was slowing down, but some notable triumphs had occurred. In Selma, Alabama, the civil rights veterans Amelia Boynton and Frederick Reese led five blacks to win half the seats on the city council. Despite the continued existence of racism in more sophisticated forms, a local black leader contended that "by and large things have improved." Elsewhere in the South in 1972, two blacks, Andrew Young of Atlanta, Georgia, and Barbara Jordan of Houston, Texas, were elected to the U.S. House of Representatives. For the first time in seventy years blacks from the former Confederate states sat in Congress.

By the time the Watergate scandal pushed Richard Nixon into retirement, southern blacks had managed to make steady political gains within their communities. At the end of 1974, over 1,500 blacks held public office in the South. This figure included an additional congressman from Memphis, Tennessee, Harold Ford, and a growing number of black state legislators. Of the ninety-four who occupied legislative seats, about forty-eight were elected in 1974 alone, largely as a result of reapportionment ordered by federal courts and the Department of Justice. Birmingham, Alabama, once the most violently racist of all the major cities in the South, counted fifteen blacks in its state legislative delegation. In addition, black ballots continued to serve as an important element in the biracial Democratic party coalition that elected white Dixie moderates to governor's mansions and the U.S. Senate.

Reflecting the growing number of black elected officials, the Joint Center for Political Studies was founded in 1970 and has continued in operation to the present. According to Eddie N. Williams, its president since 1972, the Joint Center grew out of the assumption "that the civil rights movement as we knew it in the '60s was dead, that a new thrust was needed in the '70s, and that there was a great deal to be gained by developing that thrust along the lines of political participation by the citizen and the elected official." Working closely with the Congressional Black Caucus and associations of state and local black officeholders, the nonprofit, nonpartisan group conducts research on policy issues of special concern to black Americans and provides technical assistance to minority officials. The information gathered by this "black think tank" is disseminated largely through its monthly newsletter, *Focus*; a variety of research publications; workshops and educational seminars; and *The National Roster of Black Elected Officials*, which appears annually.

A decade after passage of the 1965 Voting Rights Act, black political influence was widespread but fragile. Renewed in 1970, the suffrage law was becoming a permanent fixture on the American scene. Under the vigilance of the federal government and civil rights groups, many of the impediments to black political participation were being eliminated. With registration of the majority of eligible blacks, attention shifted to making the most effective use of their ballots. Having won reenfranchisement, southern blacks strived to mobilize their communities in the competition for full electoral representation.

Chapter 5

The New Black Politicians: From Protest to Empowerment

CIVIL RIGHTS AND THE PROMISE OF ELECTORAL POLITICS

In February 1965, when demonstrations still constituted the central tactic of the freedom struggle, Bayard Rustin forecast the direction in which the civil rights movement would head. A seasoned veteran in the battle for racial justice, Rustin had participated in pioneering freedom rides challenging segregated transportation facilities in the 1940s, served as an adviser to Martin Luther King during the Montgomery bus boycott of the mid-1950s, and in August 1963, had helped organize the celebrated March on Washington for Jobs and Freedom. His civil rights activities had been built around protest, but looking ahead to the future he saw a shift taking place. "Direct action techniques," Rustin observed, "are being subordinated to a strategy calling for the building of community institutions or power bases." As the black struggle evolved from achieving equality of opportunity to obtaining equality of results, Rustin contended that political power, more than the moral force of nonviolent protests, would best fulfill the aims of the struggle.

Few civil rights proponents doubted the wisdom of organizing blacks to increase their political leverage. Although after the summer of 1964 militants increasingly questioned the value of forming coalitions with white liberals and labor unionists, as Rustin urged, they did agree with his premise that blacks needed greater power to reshape economic and political institutions that perpetuated their subordination, even after legal rights were attained. During the 1966 Meredith march through Mississippi, Stokely Carmichael emphatically told a crowd of blacks along the route: "If you don't have power, you're begging. We're going to take over and get black sheriffs and black tax assessors." SNCC, the group he led, had helped construct the Mississippi Freedom Democratic Party precisely for the purposes of gaining black control over political decisions affecting their own communities and influencing public policy in the South and the nation.

For different but related reasons, this preference for political solutions also appealed to white liberals. Presidential allies of the civil rights movement had expressed concern about the disruptive effects of demonstrations in provoking confrontations between the races. President Kennedy sought to steer black discontent off the streets and into courthouses, legislative halls, and voting booths. Along with his successor, Lyndon Johnson, he emphasized the right to vote as the chief instrument for blacks to resolve their grievances through regular electoral channels. As black protest took a violent course with the outbreak of urban riots in the mid-1960s, the Johnson administration prescribed the franchise and the election of black officials as an antidote to extremism. "There is more power in the ballot than there is in the bullet," the chief executive declared, "and it lasts longer." White House aides expected black officeholders to counteract the influence of "civil rights kooks" within their communities by offering responsible leadership.

Black elected officials also appealed to conservative whites. Although President Nixon had attempted to blunt enforcement of the Voting Rights Act, at the same time he recognized the value of the growing number of black officeholders who benefited from the measure. When a group of black elected officials visited the nation's capital in September 1969, the President ordered his staff to roll out "the red carpet" for the delegation. According to Leon Panetta (the chief civil rights officer in the Department of Health, Education, and Welfare), the Republican chief executive, like his Democratic predecessors, believed that "elected people were something special." Of all black leaders they "were most worth listening to" because they "clearly represented a constituency." Furthermore, some conservatives suggested that black involvement in government, either as voters or as officeholders, might help calm public unrest. John Patterson, who in the late 1950s had beaten George Wallace for governor of Alabama by outcampaigning him as a segregationist, a decade later came to see the merit of black political participation. "When you allow the nigra to participate in government," Patterson declared in 1966, "you can demand that he obey the law and stay off the streets, but deny him participation... and you can't make any demands on him at all."

In the post-Voting Rights Act era, blacks who competed for and obtained electoral positions understood the responsibility that had been placed upon them. As one officeholder succinctly put it, he and his elected colleagues represented "the last great white hope for peace in this land." As long as blacks sought to achieve their racial goals within the conventional political system, they conferred legitimacy on the ruling order and devalued other more disruptive tactics, from protest marches to riots. And as long as black candidates did not find their way unfairly blocked in seeking elective posts, they renewed faith in the possibility of minority advancement in peaceful and orderly fashion. But, if their bids for representation were thwarted, the black journalist Chuck Stone noted, "the comparative moderation of the political process will be increasingly disavowed by young blacks as a meaningless exercise in the quest for power."

However, African-Americans competed for political office for reasons other than defusing potential racial strife. Rather, they hoped to build upon the legal rights secured through the protest struggle and use them to continue the pursuit of first-class citizenship. "There's an inherent value in officeholding," a black political aspirant in South Carolina asserted. "A race of people excluded from public office will always be second class." Successful black candidates were expected by their constituents to close the gap between the promise of equality and the reality of the inferior conditions they still endured. "As the black politician returns to the scene of politics from years of deprivation," Fannie Lou Hamer declared, "he must restore the democratic principles of shared local control and responsiveness to human needs." From this perspective black elected officials were regarded as saviors of their people and, at the very least, they had the obligation to perform in a manner that advanced the material interests of the communities they represented.

The civil rights movement had served as a valuable training ground for the emergence of black politicians. John Lewis, a former chairman of SNCC, who later became a congressman from Atlanta, pointed out that, like himself, "a great many of the people that you see being elected are people that come from the civil rights movement." In the wake of passage of the 1965 Voting Rights Act most blacks who rose to office in Alabama and Mississippi had participated in some aspect of the freedom struggle. Whether through joining in a voter registration drive, marching in a demonstration, signing a petition, or housing a civil rights worker, black candidates had taken the first step toward political liberation. For those who engaged in such efforts, entry into the electoral arena constituted a natural extension of their commitment to toppling the hurdles to black equality. As they made the journey from protest to electoral politics, black officeseekers usually carried with them the same concern for helping the oppressed escape from poverty and injustice that had brought them into the movement in the first place. "Virtually every black candidate who runs in the South," one observer remarked, campaigns "with the hope of improving the lot of black people in his community."

In addition to the civil rights movement, President Johnson's Great Society programs paved the way for black electoral competition. Although the funds allocated to fight the "war on poverty" were insufficient to win an unconditional victory, they greatly increased the economic resources available for political organizing. Antipoverty agencies fostered the development of local leaders who gained valuable experience in exercising power and in establishing a political base from which to operate. Through the Economic Opportunity Act of 1964 blacks obtained representation on community governing boards, which furnished training in building necessary political skills, such as bargaining and negotiation. The Community Action Programs (CAPs) decreed that the poor have "maximum feasible participation" in designing and implementing policies directly affecting their welfare. Their presence on antipoverty governing boards, which allocated large sums of money, hampered the traditional control by white mayors over lucrative patronage rewards. Fighting back, the mayors managed to obtain a congressional cutback of the programs within a few years. Despite the controversy raised, the CAPs helped empower the previously disfranchised in many towns and cities in the South as well as the North. "The pro-

cess of election and service on community poverty boards," the political scientist Robert C. Smith has concluded, "provided a useful
socialization experience for blacks in urban politics."

One of the poverty program's recruits who successfully graduated to elective office was Johnny Ford of Tuskegee. The son of a
VA hospital employee, Ford had grown up in the town during the
heyday of the civil rights movement, before heading off to college
in Tennessee. He wound up in New York City in the mid-1960s
and found a job as a counselor in Brooklyn's impoverished Bedford-
Stuyvesant ghetto. In 1968, he hopped aboard the presidential
bandwagon of Senator Robert Kennedy as a staff member, and after
the senator's assassination he decided to return to his Alabama
hometown. "I've long felt that the South is the real frontier of this
nation," he remarked about his decision to move back to Dixie. In
1969, the twenty-eight-year-old Tuskegee native became director
of Macon County's Model Cities program, which garnered millions
of dollars in federal revenue. From this position he campaigned for
mayor and, in 1972, defeated the white incumbent, thereby becoming the city's first black to hold this top executive office.

For many others, however, making the adjustment from civil
rights to electoral politics was neither automatic nor easy. The two
activities involved different tactics and talents. Though demanding
a substantial degree of organization, mass demonstrations depended a good deal on emotional appeals and highly charged targets to rally people. They tended to be episodic and often lapsed
quickly after resolution of a particular crisis. In contrast, competition for public office, as a political scientist has observed, "is more
mundane and requires both long-term political skills and the ability
to consistently draw the black electorate." Candidates had to get
elected by spending long hours trying to register voters, campaigning door to door, and shepherding large numbers of people to the
polls. Robert Clark, the first black elected to the Mississippi legislature since Reconstruction, explained the challenge: "Just because
some folks hear you talk at a rally don't mean they're gonna vote for
you. You got to go campaign, talk to 'em, make 'em know you want
each vote."

The transfer of black politics from the streets to city halls,
county courthouses, and legislative chambers frequently had a
moderating effect on its practitioners. Once elected, black politicians had to master the techniques of making deals and forging
compromises, often settling for solutions hammered more out of

pragmatism than principle. Despite the humanistic concerns they often brought to their jobs, black elected officials had to accommodate to the constraints imposed upon them by the traditional political system they entered. Illustrating the aphorism that "politics makes strange bedfellows," some black officials collaborated with powerful whites whose past record on civil rights had been deplorable in order to pry loose economic rewards for their communities. In this vein, during the 1970s Mayor Ford of Tuskegee supported George Wallace in exchange for the benefits that the Alabama governor could deliver. Ford explained the practical considerations that guided him: "It's business with me—no emotion. What you must do is penetrate the system and, once within the system, learn how it works. And then work it well."

Most blacks who successfully entered politics did not abandon their civil rights concerns, but their movement into the electoral mainstream weakened some of the radical impulses of the civil rights era. The experience of the Mississippi Freedom Democratic Party was a case in point. The organizers of the MFDP conceived of the group as representing economically dispossessed sharecroppers and domestic workers. In 1968, when the biracial Loyalist delegation from Mississippi gained the authorized seats at the national convention, moderate whites and blacks had replaced many of the original Freedom Democrats. Mrs. Fannie Lou Hamer "felt disgusted" with the newcomers because they "didn't know what suffering is and don't know what politics is about." By the end of the 1970s, this Loyalist faction traded its national recognition for incorporation with the mostly white Democratic regulars, who controlled the party apparatus in the state. Little remained of the original spirit or membership of the MFDP by the time of fusion. Although unity accorded blacks formal sanction as political partners within the Democratic party, the progressive vision of the early civil rights militants had been tempered in the process.

The admission of blacks into electoral politics in places like Mississippi and Alabama did not displace former civil rights activists so much as it elevated into greater prominence one layer of the black leadership strata. During the height of the freedom struggle, battle zones throughout the deep South had attracted the most radical elements in the movement to brave the dangers of brutal repression. Field-workers from SNCC and CORE had recruited leaders predominantly among poor blacks and built a strong lower-class following in the hope of changing both political and economic relations in the region. The success of the movement in restoring voting rights and in encouraging competition for office-holding cleared the way for the emergence of middle-class blacks to assume a larger role in electoral politics. Equipped with greater educational skills and financial resources, they had the necessary advantages to construct political organizations and wage time-consuming campaigns. The political scientist Lester Salamon, who studied Mississippi very closely, noted one important effect of the transformation of the civil rights crusade: "As the danger of Movement involvement has subsided, the leadership...has shifted from the sharecroppers and small farmers who spearheaded the battle for political rights to the black professionals and businessmen who generally stayed in the background until the ball got rolling."

This changing source of leadership should not obscure the positive consequences that the civil rights movement had on altering the structure of black politics. Before the era of reenfranchisement, black political leaders who represented their communities usually derived authority from prominent whites. "Clientage politics," as Martin Kilson termed it, linked blacks personally to powerful whites who delivered minimal welfare rewards within the rigid system of segregation. Considering the "overwhelming preponderance of political, social and economic power of the white majority," Everett C. Ladd concluded, "it is hardly surprising that the decision of influential whites as to which of the 'eligible' Negroes were to be leaders was accepted by Negroes themselves." The extension of the suffrage, the racial esteem that accompanied it, and the mobilization that followed it broke the stranglehold of whites over selecting black political leaders and setting their agendas. According to Louis Martin, the noted black journalist and adviser to Presidents Kennedy and Johnson, the Voting Rights Act ushered in a new breed of minority politician who understood "that political power is generated in the black precincts and does not come from the hands of the great white father."

OBSTACLES TO OFFICE-HOLDING

Blacks stood the best chances of winning election to office where they outnumbered whites, primarily at the local level. Because bloc voting generally characterized the conduct of elections between the races, blacks needed to comprise a clear majority of the population in order to triumph. The size of the black population was one of the most important resources black communities possessed in electing members of their race to represent them. As Albert Karnig and Susan Welch found, black candidates usually lost as the black population grew proportionately larger, winning only when it reached a majority. Before that point, the growing percentage of blacks posed a threat to whites, who closed ranks against minority-group candidates. Once blacks obtained a majority, they had the raw strength to overcome white opposition.

Still, in many black-majority areas of the South, in order to win blacks needed to comprise at least 60 percent of the population, a figure that indicated an effective voting-age majority. In many places, demographic shifts had resulted in a black population with a disproportionate share of children and the elderly, the former not old enough to vote and the latter less inclined to do so. Migration from rural locales to the cities of the South and North had thinned the ranks of the adults most likely to cast a ballot. Moreover, the continued economic dependency of poor blacks on white employers and creditors as well as the persistence of racial discrimination and of fear and apathy meant that a simple population majority did not always guarantee black electoral success. Old habits died hard and some blacks could be expected to vote for whites because of the deference they had paid them in the past, others may have done so as a consequence of jealousies and rivalries within the black community itself, and some retained a reasoned measure of fear that casting a ballot could still lead to reprisals.

In addition, blacks had to contend with electoral rules that diluted the power of their ballots and hampered them from electing members of their own race. The most significant of these were at-large election requirements. Such arrangements, in which candidates were chosen by voters throughout a wide jurisdiction, frequently resulted in the election of whites and the exclusion of blacks. Even if blacks constituted 40 percent of the total population of a municipality, for instance, in an at-large contest they almost certainly failed to elect members of their race in proportion to their numerical presence in the community. In switching to elections by ward or single-member districts, black residents greatly enhanced their opportunity to elect black candidates in closer approximation to their strength in the overall electorate. Given the typical concentration of black residents in distinct subdivisions of a city, single-member district elections virtually assured that minorities could maximize their votes and select representatives of their own choosing.

Furthermore, with whites firmly in control of every state legislature, they could reapportion districts to weaken the black vote. Racial gerrymandering kept to a minimum the number of blacks who won election to state houses. For example, in 1971 three adjacent parishes [counties] in Louisiana each had a black population majority. However, when incumbent lawmakers redrew district lines for the state House of Representatives, they refused to form a black-majority district. Instead, they combined two of the black parishes with two predominantly white areas to form a white-majority parish and submerged the remaining black parish within a white-majority district. On the municipal level, white officials attempted to preserve their power by annexing adjacent territory in which a sufficient number of whites lived to once again put blacks in the minority. These sundry practices were often disguised as color-blind regulations, and indeed, at-large elections had first come into existence during the wave of Progressive reform at the turn of the century. Whatever their origins, their continued operation in the South, reinforced by the heritage of racial bias, deprived blacks of an equal opportunity to determine the outcome of elections.

This question of determining what constituted a fair share for minority representation proved especially controversial. Many white liberal allies of the civil rights movement were satisfied with a suffrage solution that removed unfair obstacles to minority registration and provided blacks with an equal opportunity to go to the polls and cast their ballots in a situation free from intimidation. They viewed the ballot from an individualistic perspective and rejected any notion that particular groups, however historically disadvantaged they might have been, were entitled to a share of representation proportionate to their percentage in the population. Accordingly, the federal government should do no more than protect individual black voters from invidious forms of discrimination rather than ensure that black ballots resulted in the election of black officeholders. Suffrage reformers had sought to make the black franchise equal in value to that of whites and then let blacks compete for political power in conventional ways. "If blacks...are able to form political alliances, to have their interests considered by elected officials through threat of political action, and are generally able to secure through their ballots the benefits of citizenship," one white observer remarked, "they are effectively participating in the political process."

Black leaders and their civil rights supporters generally saw the matter differently. They contended that the Voting Rights Act and the expanded registration accompanying it did not confer actual political equality or power. To them the ballot derived importance not principally as a color-blind instrument but as a race-conscious tool to advance the collective goals of Afro-American communities. Ultimately, blacks aimed to make government more responsive to their needs, and in theory it was possible to obtain greater influence over political affairs by backing white candidates who competed for their votes. However, in reality most blacks preferred representation by other blacks, who they believed reflected their aspirations. Feelings of pride and self-respect were also at stake. The civil rights struggle had succeeded in reawakening group consciousness among blacks, fostering the desire to see members of their own race attain positions of electoral leadership. Short of claiming a right to proportional representation, civil rights stalwarts considered the ratio of black officeholders to the percentage of minorities in the population as a convenient yardstick to measure political equality.

Although the 1965 Voting Rights Act dealt with the right to register to vote and not with the ability to win elections, it did recognize the plight of African-Americans in group-centered terms. The law addressed current black disfranchisement by locating its organic roots in the past, and attempted to remedy patterns of racial discrimination against a persecuted group rather than correct specific acts of bias suffered by individuals. The lawmakers devised a statistical formula that automatically identified the presence of racial bigotry and empowered the federal government to challenge the consequences of previously injurious practices. Employing a type of affirmative action, the statute compensated southern blacks for the discriminatory treatment they had received by suspending literacy exams and allowing blacks to register on the same basis as had whites in the past.

The federal courts helped resolve the issue by limiting the operation of at-large elections in the South. Holding back from declaring at-large contests constitutionally invalid, the judiciary nonetheless struck down electoral systems that hampered participation by minorities and constricted their possibilities for holding office. To gauge whether a particular at-large electoral plan was impermissible, judges considered a "totality of circumstances." They looked for a history of racial bias that had excluded blacks from gaining equal access to the electoral process and evaluated whether current electoral institutions perpetuated discriminatory practices of the past. To this end, the courts were less concerned about the original purposes behind the adoption of the election rules and were more interested in ascertaining the effect on black representation. This standard of judgment applied throughout the 1970s and boosted black officeholding in those jurisdictions mandated by the bench to discard their at-large procedures.

Cases from Texas and Louisiana, in 1973, established the precedents. In the Lone Star State blacks challenged the 1970 reapportionment of the state House of Representatives for creating multimember districts in Dallas and Bexar (San Antonio) Counties that diluted minority voting power. Only two blacks had ever been elected to the state legislature from Dallas and only five Mexican-Americans had represented Bexar County. In *White v. Regester*, the Supreme Court ordered the creation of single-member districts after examining a combination of factors that effectively reduced black electoral opportunities. Accordingly, it discovered a history of racial discrimination and black underrepresentation: the failure of the white-dominated Democratic party organization to nominate black candidates; the waging of racist campaigns; and the operation of electoral rules that handicapped African- and Mexican-Americans from winning at-large elections.

Following up this decision, a lower federal court overturned the at-large system of electing members to the school board and police jury in East Carroll Parish, Louisiana. Although constituting a majority of the population of this parish, blacks comprised only 46 percent of enrolled voters, having been barred from registering from 1922 to 1962. Though blacks had managed to win three of twelve contested seats since the initiation of at-large elections in 1968, the court found that the electoral system prevented Afro-American voters from achieving more effective representation. The judges acknowledged that barriers to black participation had been removed, but they concluded that "the debilitating effects of these impediments do persist." In rendering its opinion in *Zimmer v. Mc-Keithen*, the judiciary looked at the "totality of circumstances" in uncovering racial bias that denied blacks equal access to the political process. A governmental jurisdiction violated the rights of black voters if it consistently failed to slate blacks to run for office, if its elected officials declined to respond to the interests of their black constituents, and if it adopted procedures that heightened the effects of past racial bias by submerging black voters within large electoral districts and requiring that winning candidates receive a majority rather than a plurality of the votes cast. (Given the prevalence of racial bloc voting, the majority-vote rule hurt blacks particularly where they did not constitute a majority of registered voters.)

These rulings were reinforced by the Justice Department. Under the preclearance section of the Voting Rights Act, the attorney general possessed the authority to reject suffrage changes that had the purpose or effect of discriminating against blacks. This provision pertained only to electoral rules adopted or altered since November 1964. Challenges against procedures fashioned before that date required litigation and were adjudicated as discussed above. Nevertheless, the Civil Rights Division of the Justice Department took its legal cues from the judiciary and refused to sanction switches from single-member districts to at-large elections that weakened the potency of black votes. Along with the courts, Justice Department watchdogs scrutinized reapportionment, redistricting, and annexation plans that potentially minimized opportunities for black representation.

HIGH HOPES, LIMITED REWARDS

As the judicial and executive branches cleared sundry obstacles to minority political participation, southern blacks continued their slow but steady progress in winning public office. In 1976, blacks held 1,847 elected positions in the South, and four years later, the figure rose to 2,457. Despite these successes, blacks remained underrepresented in the proportion of offices they won. In 1980, of the more than 32,350 elected officials in the jurisdictions originally covered by the Voting Rights Act, about 5 percent were black. This share trailed far behind the proportion of the black population in the region, which ranged from 18.9 percent in Virginia to 35.2 percent in Mississippi. Moreover, in approximately one-quarter of the black-majority counties no blacks had been elected, a condition that also existed in nearly half the counties with a black population over 20 percent.

The substantial number of blacks who did triumph managed to reap important rewards for their constituents. Though the situation varied from place to place, from rural villages and towns to major urban areas, in general black elected officials delivered tangible benefits that had been long denied to their communities. Routine services, such as garbage collection, paved streets, police and fire protection, and recreational facilities, were upgraded and extended to black residents. Wherever possible, black public officials sought to increase the number of government jobs available through affirmative action programs that awarded contracts to minority businesses and employment to minority workers. They also avidly pursued and obtained federal government grants to fund capital investment for economic development and to expand the distribution of health care and social welfare projects in their locales.

The election of blacks pried open access to governmental structures that had been the exclusive domain of whites. Since the late nineteenth century, the disfranchisement of black southerners had made them the object of political attention; however, in regaining the ballot and recovering positions in government, they returned as active political agents. In so doing, black elected officials joined in the formulation and execution of policies, and brought to the attention of their white colleagues issues of special concern to blacks that previously had been ignored. To the extent that knowledge is power, black representatives gained vital information to help shape decision-making and protect the interests of their constituents. "No matter what happened," a black city council member in Florida declared, his white counterparts "knew I was listening to everything that went on."

In addition to these material improvements, blacks gained critical psychological advantages from their empowerment. The presence of black candidates and officeholders stimulated increased black political mobilization, as African-Americans turned out with pride to vote for one of their own. This revived sense of self-esteem was aptly voiced by Fannie Lou Hamer. When blacks still sat on the political sidelines, Mrs. Hamer remarked, "some white folks

...would drive past your house in a pickup truck with guns hanging up on the back and give you hate stares." This changed as blacks approached the center of the electoral arena, she pointed out, and "those same people now call me Mrs. Hamer, because they respect people who respect themselves." Furthermore, these feelings of respect and dignity were carried forth by black politicians, who served as valuable role models, especially for the younger members of their communities.

With political reemancipation came raised expectations of what black representatives could accomplish. Because they had been systematically excluded from political participation, southern blacks prized the ballot in the belief that it would advance the goals of their race as a whole and not merely benefit a few. The president of the Savannah, Georgia, branch of the NAACP explained: "Black officeholders...must be individuals who serve at the pleasure of the black community." Accordingly, black constituents placed demands on their representatives that exceeded the ordinary requirements of the job. Edith Ingram, elected the probate judge of Hancock County, Georgia, in 1968, described the myriad services she performed for the people who regularly came to her office, many of whom were on public assistance:

> I have to write checks for them, pay bills, buy groceries, take them to the doctors, balance checkbooks, certify them for welfare, make doctors' appointments, read letters, answer letters and fix loan papers for houses. A good 85 percent to 90 percent of the work that we do is non-office related work, but these people have no one else to depend on—they trust us, so we do it.[1]

Indeed, many black officials discovered what Richard Arrington found out when he became mayor of Birmingham: "There are the expectations of the black community that expects you to do more than you can do."

Though black officials exerted increasing influence and shared authority, their power was limited in a variety of ways. With a relatively small number of exceptions, black elected officials in most cities and counties of the South and the nation were in the minority

---

[1]Ingram is quoted in Lawrence J. Hanks, *The Struggle for Black Empowerment in Three Georgia Counties* (Knoxville: University of Tennessee Press, 1987), pp. 69–70.

and could not deliver political dividends without the cooperation of white colleagues. In such situations minority officeholders had to walk a delicate tightrope in balancing the concerns of their constituents with the need to bargain with their fellow white officials who represented opposing interests. Based on personal experience, State Senator Leroy Johnson of Atlanta stated the problem: "Your position in the black community has to take on a veneer of militancy, but...you have to be willing to negotiate, to compromise, in order to be effective."

Even in those areas where blacks came to control the majority of government posts, they often lacked the economic resources to affect significantly the material conditions of the impoverished population. Although the poverty rate among black families declined over the course of the 1970s, from 41 percent to 30 percent, the percentage of poor blacks was more than four times the white figure of 7 percent. At the end of the decade black families earned 57 percent of the income of that of whites. This represented a slight improvement over the economic situation that existed when the Supreme Court outlawed school desegregation in *Brown*, but marked a downswing from the 60 percent level that prevailed in the years immediately following Johnson's Great Society. Blacks also experienced a higher incidence of unemployment than did whites, and the joblessness of young black male adults reached depression-era levels.

Lowndes County, Alabama, highlighted the gap between political and economic power. Directed by LCFO, black political participation did improve living conditions, largely through the acquisition of outside federal and foundation grants and the election of a sheriff who attempted to dispense a more evenhanded brand of justice than in the past. But blacks continued to suffer from a disproportionate burden of economic distress. Their median family income rose slightly in comparison with that of white residents, from a ratio of 33 percent to 41 percent. However, their median family income of $7,443 lagged way behind the national average of $18,350 earned annually by whites. Expressing this predicament, the black Sheriff John Hulett remarked: "Until people become economically strong, political power alone won't do."

Though economic prospects remained as bleak for most blacks elsewhere throughout the country, a small but growing segment of African-Americans saw their fortunes rise. Expanding opportunities resulting from desegregation and affirmative action programs swelled the size of the black middle class. By the late 1970s, the share of black workers occupying middle-class positions stood at 33 percent, a jump from 13 percent in 1960. For two-income families in which both husbands and wives worked, blacks had just about achieved parity with whites. From this group, with its access to superior economic resources and educational skills, black political leaders emerged. Following reenfranchisement, the representatives of this class, more so than those of lower-income blacks, succeeded in penetrating the structures of electoral office-holding that traditionally had been reserved for whites.

The ascent to power of that class during the 1970s reflected a complex picture of black political development. Themselves only recently risen from the bottom rungs of the economic ladder, middle-class black politicians tended to identify with the plight of their less fortunate brethren. Moreover, the newly acquired wealth of black middle-class families was not fully secure because their prosperity rested more heavily than that of whites on the combined incomes of working wives as well as working husbands and on earnings derived from public sector jobs and those protected by affirmative action regulations. Consequently, they were vulnerable to downswings in the economy and fluctuations in the political climate, especially in a conservative direction. Under these circumstances and because they were products of the same emancipatory forces that shaped the racial consciousness of poor blacks, these middle-class leaders often shared with the former mutual concerns associated with race.

Yet the interests of these politicians also cut across racial lines and embraced concerns they held in common with their middle- and upper-class white colleagues. Urban black politicians, especially in cities that sought to attract economic investment on a large scale, joined with moderate white businesspeople and their representatives to promote lucrative downtown redevelopment projects that favored buildings over ordinary people. In the process, black businesspeople, professionals, and white-collar workers benefited from attempts to revitalize the economy of their cities, whereas poor residents gained little from the private-sector, low-wage service jobs that accompanied urban renewal, and often suffered dislocation as a result of "urban removal." As a result, the black middle class reaped substantial rewards, while considerable poverty persisted among a sizable portion of the black population, a situation that occasioned observers to speak of the appearance of a permanent black underclass.

The "new South" interracial coalition did produce progress, albeit unevenly. The alliance of middle-class black politicians with white corporate and financial elites made sense during the 1970s when American cities were suffering from internal decay and a shrinking tax base. The flight of middle-class whites to the suburbs left behind the poor, who required a large share of public services but who could not afford to fund them. In striking a partnership with influential white civic leaders, black politicians sought to plug the drain on the depleted treasuries they had inherited upon assuming office. They did manage to attract new industries and jobs, and at the very least their presence at the governmental helm assured that consideration would be given to black concerns as never before. The election of blacks to high public office, according to the political scientist Peter Eisinger, meant that "black interests, *as they are defined by black administrators*, have proved as central as the interests of white capital in the establishment of economic development goals" (emphasis in original).

BLACK WOMEN OFFICEHOLDERS

Although the majority of black elected officials were men, the 1970s saw a rapid rise of black women officeholders throughout the nation. In 1975, black women comprised 15 percent of all Afro-American elected officials, a total of 530 out of 3,503 officeholders. Four years later the proportion of all black elected officials who were female had jumped 59 percent, and black females held 882 of 4,607 positions. By comparison, the figures for black men elected to public office increased from 2,973 to 3,725, a growth rate of 25 percent. Like their male counterparts, black women were most likely to hold government posts at the municipal and county levels and to represent areas with a predominantly black population.

The growing number of black women politicians reflected the impact of the civil rights movement. Black women had played a crucial, though often unsung, role in the freedom struggle. The top leadership positions were usually held by men and individuals such as Martin Luther King, Roy Wilkins, and Stokely Carmichael were most easily identified by the public; but women both initiated and provided grassroots support for the civil rights protests that transformed the South and the nation. Without the courage, commitment, and vision of Rosa Parks, Jo Ann Robinson, Ella Baker, and Fannie Lou Hamer, to name a few, together with the legions of ordinary housewives and workers who boycotted, marched, sat in, and went to jail, a widespread freedom struggle could not have been launched and sustained. As with men, in recruiting large numbers of women to its ranks, the civil rights movement inspired pride and encouraged standards of political participation that carried over to the electoral arena. Not coincidentally, by the end of the 1970s a majority of elected black women (51 percent) resided in the South, the primary battlefield and proving ground of the civil rights struggle and the region in which grassroots female leadership first flourished.

Black female politicians owed some of their success to the expanding opportunities generally available to women. Between 1975 and 1981, the number of all female officeholders soared from 7,089 to 16,585, with most of these positions concentrated in local government. The proportion of women holding seats on county governing boards more than doubled, from 456 to 1,205; and from 1971 to 1981, the number of women state legislators tripled, from 293 to 908. By the end of the 1970s, a thousand women were serving as mayors of towns and cities throughout the United States. This extraordinary growth spurt can be attributed in part to the very low level of female office-holding at the beginning of the seventies. Nevertheless, these electoral accomplishments also owed much to the development of the feminist movement during the 1960s and 1970s. Itself influenced by the civil rights struggle, the women's movement raised an awareness of gender discrimination, provided an egalitarian ideology to challenge it, and stimulated women to attack the barriers blocking their full and active participation as citizens.

The relationship of black women to feminism was complicated by race. Although sympathetic with its liberationist goals, black women activists tended to identify more closely with black men in the fight against racial oppression than with white women, whose skin color was the same as the male agents of blacks' exploitation. Whatever male chauvinism black women experienced within civil rights ranks did not stop them from displaying their considerable talents alongside men and developing their skills even further. The importance of black women within the political culture nurtured by the civil rights movement can be seen in the relative figures for black and white female officeholders. Black women constituted a higher percentage of black elected officials than did white women of white officials. In 1979, 18 percent of all black state legislators but only 10 percent of white lawmakers were female.

At the same time, these figures showed that neither black nor white women had reached parity with men. In recognition of both their growing achievements and the distance yet to be closed, women of the two races joined together within the National Women's Political Caucus. Formed in 1971, the group promoted racial and ethnic diversity in its membership, challenged racism as well as sexism, and worked for a broad range of political and social reforms of special interest to women.

The importance of the civil rights struggle in serving to empower black women can be glimpsed in the life of Unita Blackwell. A resident of Mayersville, Mississippi, a tiny delta town of 500 people, Mrs. Blackwell was a housewife in her early thirties when she first encountered SNCC workers in the area. Impressed with the group's dedication and concern for developing local leadership, she gravitated toward SNCC and heeded its message: "If you all go and register to vote this is the way to help yourself." It took Blackwell three tries before the county registrar allowed her to register in 1964, and by then she was actively engaged with SNCC in the Freedom Summer campaign and in the creation of the Mississippi Freedom Democratic Party. A member of the MFDP contingent that failed to win recognition at the 1964 Democratic National Convention, she returned four years later to gain a seat on the revamped biracial delegation from the Magnolia State. After Mayersville became incorporated in 1976, Mrs. Blackwell was chosen its first mayor. In 1980, she became cochair of the state Democratic party, the organization that had excluded her on account of race sixteen years earlier. Her success illustrates the connection between the civil rights movement and electoral politics, as well as the strength and perseverence of the black women who contributed to the freedom struggle.

BLACK MAYORS IN ATLANTA AND TUSKEGEE

While noteworthy breakthroughs were occurring among women and in small towns like Mayersville, perhaps more than any other major city in the South, Atlanta, Georgia, reflected the changing currents of black political development in the years following passage of the Voting Rights Act. Characterized by a tradition of electoral activity that succeeded in dismantling discriminatory suffrage obstacles and in stimulating voter registration, black Atlantans already enjoyed a significant measure of influence in municipal politics during the 1960s. This "black Mecca" of Dixie, with its distinguished churches, independent businesses, and institutions of higher learning, had attracted and nurtured a resilient black middle class that included the family of the Reverend Martin Luther King, Jr. Its economic, political, and religious chieftains had allied themselves with white business and civic leaders, who ruled the city with a combination of racial benevolence and paternalism. The kind of racist rhetoric that infected political discourse elsewhere in the South was kept to a minimum, as white candidates campaigned for black ballots to ensure their victories.

Nevertheless, white politicians did not consider the black electorate as an equal governing partner, and they made vital decisions affecting their city without consulting the black community or adequately taking into account the impact of decisions upon it. In 1968, when city officials failed to solicit black advice in the creation of a metropolitan rapid transit system, disgruntled minority voters helped defeat the proposal in a referendum. The plan subsequently passed, but only after blacks were included in a policy-formulating capacity. Furthermore, under white control, urban renewal had meant revitalization of the central business district at the expense of the needs of low-income black neighborhoods.

The transition from moderate black influence to substantial black power began to occur in 1969. That year, white civic leaders split in their choice for mayor, and black voters swung the election to Sam Massell by giving him over 90 percent of their ballots. (He received only a quarter of the white votes.) At the same time, blacks won the post of vice-mayor, four seats on the Board of Aldermen, and an additional two seats on the school board. Mayor Massell's administration subsequently fractured its black base of support. Shortly after taking office, the chief executive faced a disruptive strike by predominantly black sanitation workers. Massell upset black leaders, including his vice-mayor, Maynard Jackson, in settling the dispute to the disadvantage of the strikers. However, the mayor attempted to patch up his coalition by rehiring the workers and appointing a black to head the Sanitation Department.

During the remainder of his term, black politicians devoted their energies to obtaining an increased share of government services and benefits for their constituents and to ensuring that existing programs were administered fairly.

In 1973, black Atlantans were ready to exert a greater measure of control over their city and to reshape the biracial coalition that had governed in the past. They had demographic forces on their side. During the 1960s the composition of the population had shifted in favor of blacks. Over the course of that decade, the proportion of black Atlantans had increased nearly 37 percent, while that of whites had fallen by 20 percent. In 1970, blacks comprised a 51 percent majority of the city's residents, and three years later they used this numerical advantage to elect Maynard Jackson, who defeated Massell in a racially charged campaign to become Atlanta's first nonwhite mayor. Having guessed that the bulk of the black votes would go to his opponent, Massell reversed his previous campaign form to appeal for white support. Proclaiming Atlanta "Too Young To Die," he suggested that the city would decay under black rule. The *Atlanta Constitution* frowned upon this approach and commented that the incumbent appeared to be "running for mayor of a South African city which practices apartheid rather than the mayor of a fully integrated American city."

Massell's strategy misfired, and Jackson captured 59 percent of the total ballots cast. The heated battle lured to the polls a larger proportion of blacks (67 percent) than whites (55 percent). Jackson received an overwhelming 95 percent of the black vote and, although the electorate generally divided along racial lines, he received 17 percent of the white vote. Together with the mayor's post, blacks won half the seats on the city council and gained a slim one-vote margin on the school board. These victories followed the previous year's election to Congress of Andrew Young, a former assistant to Dr. King. Young had a reputation as a skillful peacemaker and conciliator, and in a district only two-fifths black, he obtained 53 percent of the vote. Nearly every black and about one-quarter of the whites who went to the polls supported the civil rights activist. The triumphs of Jackson and Young demonstrated the arrival of black elected officials as a dominant force in Atlanta politics, but they also indicated that whites still retained significant influence in shaping the outcome of electoral competition.

Only thirty-five-years old when he became mayor, Jackson belonged to a family of distinguished men and women. His relatives included politicians and preachers, a professor and a performer. His father was a Baptist minister who once ran for a seat on a local school board in Texas. His great-great-grandfather founded the Wheat Street Baptist Church in Atlanta, and his grandfather organized the Georgia Voters League. Jackson's mother had earned a doctorate in French and taught at Spelman College in Atlanta and North Carolina Central University in Durham. One of his aunts, Mattiwilda Dobbs, was a highly acclaimed opera singer. A graduate of Martin Luther King's alma mater, Morehouse College, Jackson obtained a law degree from North Carolina Central and returned to Atlanta to work as an attorney handling cases for low-income clients. The assassinations of Dr. King and Senator Robert F. Kennedy in 1968 helped persuade him to embark on a political career. "I decided the solution to the country's problems had to be in politics," he remarked, "not in violence." He aimed high in his first campaign in 1968, competing for the U.S. Senate seat from Georgia held by Herman Talmadge. Jackson lost by a wide margin, but his strong showing in Atlanta, where he outpolled the popular incumbent, encouraged him to run for vice-mayor in 1969. Four years later, he succeeded in capturing city hall.

Once in office as mayor, Jackson helped deliver important rewards. He reorganized the police department, appointed a black to head the new agency, and increased the number of Afro-American law enforcement officers. Subsequently, the city experienced a decline in black complaints of police brutality. The mayor also embarked on a vigorous affirmative action program that resulted in the black share of Atlanta's public work force climbing from 42 percent in 1972 to 51 percent five years later. During this period, the share of contracts awarded by the city to minorities jumped from 2 to 13 percent. In addition, Mayor Jackson instituted a plan giving black firms 25 percent of the contracts for work to expand Atlanta's international airport.

Though Jackson disturbed white business and civic leaders with many of these policies and with an aggressive personal style they found abrasive, he could hardly afford to ignore them. To promote urban redevelopment and economic expansion, the mayor needed the resources and expertise white corporate executives and financiers could provide. "Blacks have the ballot box," an Atlanta newspaper editor admitted, "and whites have the money." When a sanitation strike tied up the city in 1977, Jackson treated it even more harshly than had his white predecessor. In a move that could only have pleased influential whites, the mayor took a hard-line stance against the work stoppage for higher wages, rejected union demands, and fired the offending strikers. Before he became mayor, Jackson had supported striking garbage workers; however, as official head of the city he placed sound business management practices and fiscal responsibility ahead of the needs of poor wage earners. He also heeded white demands to remove his controversial law enforcement chief, and replaced him with a more acceptable black.

The assumption of political power by Mayor Jackson and other black officials improved the overall position of Atlanta's nonwhite population, though it left many nagging problems unsolved. As one scholar has concluded, these accomplishments "often in the face of considerable opposition...represent...a more equitable share for the black community within existing priorities." Still, black leaders did very little to restructure those priorities, which continued to place the poor at a disadvantage. By 1980, 6 percent of black households earned at least $35,000, and more black Atlantans had incomes in excess of $50,000 than was true for minority residents anywhere else in the South. At the same time, however, this premier

Maynard Jackson, smiling after his victory as Atlanta's first black mayor. (UPI/Bettmann Newsphotos)

city had a high incidence of black poverty—25 percent of black families earned less than $5,000 a year. Overall, one-third of black families lived below the poverty line, compared with 7 percent of whites. Indeed, the diversity of Atlanta's population, reflected in its class structure, sometimes made it difficult for blacks to unite on behalf of efforts to relieve severe impoverishment. For example, during the 1977 sanitation strike, moderate black leaders rallied around the mayor against the demands of workers. In cities like Atlanta, as black political affairs progressed, they became more complicated and pragmatic—pointing to the distance traveled since the height of the civil rights movement with its moral clarity and solidarity.

Much of this complexity can likewise be seen in the experience of Tuskegee, Alabama. During the 1970s, Mayor Johnny Ford pursued a vigorous policy of obtaining outside money for economic development. At a time when the Nixon administration was dismantling the apparatus of Lyndon Johnson's War on Poverty, the Tuskegee mayor managed to secure over $30 million in federal and state grants and an additional $30 million from other funding sources. Much of Ford's success as a fund-raiser derived from his pragmatic brand of politics. This former campaign aide of Senator Robert Kennedy endorsed Nixon's reelection in 1972, explaining that he wanted to back a winner and have access to power. "It's paying off," he remarked in 1973. "Other places may be losing Federal funds because of cuts, but not Tuskegee. I've prevented that."

The Ford regime directed its efforts to improving basic public services and generating local financial growth. His administration created a new sewage system and expanded police protection. Municipal officials designed an industrial park to attract firms into the area, to serve as the centerpiece of the town's economic revitalization, and to provide jobs for area residents. Plans were prepared for the construction of an oil refinery, a dog-racing track, and an experimental tomato farm.

Unfortunately, many of these efforts failed to produce the anticipated results. Only the racetrack scheme materialized, while the industrial park failed to lure necessary private capital from investors. Although Ford continued to work with willing white leaders, more than half the white population fled Tuskegee, taking with them valuable economic assets that potentially could have benefited the town's growth. In addition, charges of corruption involving black officials, though unproven in most instances, hampered their ability to carry out several of the projects. As in Atlanta, the economic gains flowed to the black middle class rather than to those at the lower end of the economic scale. In 1980, the median income of black families was $10,423, the highest in the black-belt section of the state. Yet the percentage of blacks living in poverty was three times greater than that of whites, and over the decade the median income level in comparison with that of whites had actually dropped from 63 to 60 percent. Black politicians had not found sufficient resources or fashioned an adequate agenda to meet the needs of Tuskegee's most impoverished residents.

These drawbacks notwithstanding, the fruits of black political office-holding in the 1970s cannot be gauged simply in quantitative terms. In Tuskegee, reenfranchisement had empowered blacks to secure a significant measure of control over their lives. No longer did they have to endure the humiliation inflicted by white officials who sought to keep them from registering and who arbitrarily devised gerrymandering plans to limit the effectiveness of their votes. Black Tuskegeeans and their Macon County neighbors experienced the pride that comes when the barriers to treatment as first-class citizens are shattered. A government that for generations had been directed by and for whites came to represent the majority of the people it ruled. Political equality did not necessarily translate into economic equality, nor did individual opportunity guarantee that all members of the exploited group would derive benefits equally. But Tuskegee blacks had unprecedented access to a government that had previously excluded them, they more easily identified with governing officials, and they no longer felt so restrained within the tight physical and psychological confines of white supremacy. This experience of liberation meant a great deal to a retired VA hospital worker who had spent most of his life under vastly different circumstances. "Everything's better," he explained. "In the old days, before black elected officials ran the county, most black people steered clear of white enclaves. They used to arrest you over there if you went through, but not anymore."

BLACK RULE IN CLEVELAND AND GARY

While southern blacks were expanding their political power and leverage, their northern counterparts also extended their influence within the electoral arena. These regional pursuits of political equality were both distinct and interconnected. Black northerners, many of whom had migrated from the South during the periods surrounding the First and Second World Wars, generally faced a less rigid Jim Crow system than existed in Dixie. The residential and school segregation they encountered usually was reinforced by custom rather than by explicit laws. This was particularly true following World War II, when northern whites responded to anti-Fascist democratic ideology and removed some of the racially biased obstacles blocking minority advancement. Discrimination unquestionably remained embedded in northern institutions and practices, but they operated more subtly than in the South.

At the same time, given the freer space that they found in urban centers above the Mason-Dixon line, black northerners had greater access to political representation than did disfranchised or partially enfranchised southern blacks. In cities like Chicago and New York blacks sat on municipal councils and represented their districts in state legislatures and Congress. When not electing candidates of their own race, blacks cast their ballots to shape the outcome of local and national elections that pitted whites against each other. This type of electoral clout had helped nudge presidents and lawmakers since Franklin D. Roosevelt's time to add civil rights to the national agenda.

Nevertheless, black northerners lacked fully developed political strength. Their votes counted and frequently served as the balance of electoral power, but they did not share with whites an equal voice in their governance. In northern cities, political machines advanced the interests of an assortment of white ethnic groups that had arrived there in large numbers before transplanted blacks did. Though political bosses organized blacks as a constituency within their machines, the bosses kept the blacks on the periphery of real power and did virtually nothing to tackle the problems of racism and economic deprivation that pervaded the ghetto. Black politicians served as intermediaries between party organizations and their communities, and occasionally delivered material benefits—patronage jobs, intervention with law enforcement officials, handouts of food for the holidays—but they reflected the unequal power relationships between the races. Even where blacks constituted an integral component of the political machine, such as in Chicago, their leaders provided representation without disturbing the entrenched political and economic structures that perpetuated black subordination.

This form of quasi representation, bereft of independent power, depended on white patrons as the source of authority and dispenser of rewards. Unlike generations of white ethnic groups that had penetrated and captured control of urban political machines as an integral part of their upward economic and social mobility, African-Americans faced unparalleled obstacles in taking the same route to success. Though immigrants also encountered discrimination from whites whose forebears had preceded them to these shores, the newcomers nevertheless shared, in common with the existing residents, the privilege of skin color that relatively quickly lowered barriers to acceptance and assimilation. Blacks, however, could claim no such bond, and by virtue of their race faced uncommon prejudice that kept them on the outside of dominant political institutions. They alone had to wage a fierce struggle merely to obtain the right to vote and other elementary features of citizenship that white Americans from many ethnic backgrounds took for granted.

The new politics that emerged after 1965 increasingly thrust blacks onto center stage as agents of social change and group advancement. Black northerners took pride in the valiant struggles of the southern civil rights movement, which prompted community leaders to turn their attention to the more subtle problems of political and economic discrimination. Civil rights battles in the North focused on securing adequate jobs, quality housing and education, and impartial police protection rather than on Jim Crow and disfranchisement; but, as in the South, black northerners demanded respect and equal treatment in practice as well as in theory. The emancipationist ideology of the freedom movement joined with the social welfare programs of Johnson's War on Poverty to heighten black consciousness of oppression and the possibilities for overcoming it. The Voting Rights Act inspired northern blacks, and after 1970 eliminated literacy tests in the region. More and more black northerners successfully exercised their electoral muscle as had other ethnic minorities before them.

Yet egalitarian ideals and government programs were not enough. With shifting demographic patterns on their side, the number of blacks in the populations of urban centers rose, and they became serious contenders for public office. In the 1950s and 1960s whites had moved out of the inner cities and into the surrounding suburbs to seek a more comfortable lifestyle, one "uncontaminated" by the presence of incoming black migrants. These pilgrimages produced a sharp upswing in the black proportion of the urban population. In those areas in which blacks approached or actually became a majority of the population they had the most success in dethroning whites from the leadership of dominant political organizations.

Events in Cleveland, Ohio, and Gary, Indiana, demonstrated the changing configuration and complexity of black political development in the North. Between 1930 and 1965, the city of Cleveland lost about 300,000 of its white residents, while the number of blacks increased by over 200,000. As a result of this reshuffling, blacks constituted 34 percent of the total population and composed a slightly higher 40 percent of the city's registered voters. Many of the newly enrolled blacks had signed up during registration drives sponsored by the Democratic party in preparation for the 1964 campaign against the conservative Republican, Barry Goldwater. Thus, although blacks remained a minority of Cleveland's electorate, they held a large enough portion of the ballots to position themselves to compete for the most important post of mayor.

Until 1965, black voters had thrown their support behind white Democratic mayoral candidates. In 1961 and 1963, they had helped elect Ralph Locher and gained ten of thirty-three seats on the city council. Black politicians usually posed little challenge to white rule and chose to consolidate their power within their own districts. They had not developed the idea of uniting black communities around common issues in order to advance the racial goals of their constituents throughout the city. This situation began to alter after the mayor and his administration angered black leaders in their handling of disputes concerning school desegregation, employment practices, and police-community relations. The efforts of local chapters of national civil rights groups, such as the NAACP and CORE, along with a local coalition known as the United Freedom Movement, managed to increase black participation in protest and electoral activities and to raise expectations about the possibilities of running a black candidate for mayor against Locher. Indeed, as William Nelson and Philip Merranto observed, black leaders began to view "electoral politics...as an extension of the movement; a shortcut to the civil rights goals of housing, education, welfare."

In 1965, Carl Stokes launched a challenge to the mayor that fell short of success but pointed up the chance for future victory. Stokes had grown up in Cleveland's black ghetto, served in the armed forces, and obtained a law degree. He entered municipal government in the late 1950s with an appointment as a city prosecutor, and he first won a seat to the Ohio House of Representatives in 1962. Three years later, after his reelection, Stokes ran for mayor against three white candidates, including the incumbent. Though black Democratic elected officials stuck with Mayor Locher, Stokes won a whopping 85 percent of the minority electorate. With black officeholders lined up behind the Democratic organization, Stokes depended on grassroots groups and volunteers to conduct his campaign. Though he lost, his presence as a candidate succeeded in boosting black turnout at the polls to a record high level. Within two years black participation at the ballot box had leaped from 57 percent to 72 percent.

Given the population figures, Stokes's solid base of support in the black community alone was not enough for victory. He needed white allies. In his losing bid, Stokes had garnered 3 to 5 percent of white votes, but he required considerably more to win. The black aspirant looked to white business leaders for backing, and they saw in him an opportunity to heal the city's worsening racial conflicts. In 1966, a bloody riot in the Hough section of the city left four dead and hundreds wounded. Mayor Locher reacted to the violence with a tough law-and-order policy that emphasized more police firepower than programs to deal with the underlying ills that had sparked the uprising. The mayor set the tone for his tough approach by refusing to meet with the visiting Martin Luther King, Jr., or with local black leaders. When Stokes decided again to challenge Locher in 1967, he not only had blacks behind him, but he also attracted white businesspeople who believed that his election might calm racial tensions that posed a threat to their long-range plans for economic development of the city.

In his second try, in 1967, Stokes emerged victorious to become the first black mayor of a major American city. He patched together a winning coalition consisting of the overwhelming majority of blacks and enough whites to put him ahead. The black candidate reassured whites that he wanted "to get the Negro question out of the way." Once that happened, he asserted, "then we can talk about issues. I'm telling the people my election would not mean a Negro takeover." At the same time, Stokes ran as a black candidate as well as a candidate who happened to be black. "In 1965 when I ran," he declared, "they whispered that I was a Negro. They don't have to whisper today. I am a Negro. I am proud of it. I intend to remain one."

This strategy paid off in the 1967 campaign. First, he defeated Mayor Locher for the Democratic nomination by winning 96 percent of the black vote and 15 percent of the white. This contest again brought out black voters in record numbers, and their turnout at the polls exceeded that of whites by 15 percent. Next, in the general election Stokes defeated his Republican opponent, Seth Taft, by a slender margin of 50.3 to 49.7 percent. Black turnout was even higher than it had been in the primary, and Stokes captured 95 percent of the votes cast. He also slightly increased his backing among whites by gaining 20 percent of their ballots. In doing so, he

Carl Stokes campaigning for votes in downtown Cleveland.
(UPI/Bettmann Newsphotos)

had the support of white business leaders, including the publishers of the city's major newspapers. In contrast, Cleveland's working-class ethnic voters deserted him, thereby abandoning their traditional Democratic allegiances in harsh response to the riots and with the feeling that the fruits of black protest came at their expense.

Stokes's victory gave blacks a unique sense of pride, much the same way as the civil rights struggle in the South had empowered disfranchised blacks. "Stokes was a symbol...for black progress," a city councilman recalled. "You would see old people walking to the polls and perhaps they never voted a day in their lives." He underscored further the stark break from the past that had occurred for blacks: "They considered politics a white man's business. We could have councilmen and judges, but they never dreamed that day would come when a black man would be mayor of the town."

Unfortunately, the hopes generated by the election of Stokes went largely unfulfilled. The mayor did deliver a variety of benefits to his black constituents. His administration built public housing for poor blacks, set up child-care centers and health facilities in minority neighborhoods, and provided funds to stimulate black business enterprise. However, his two terms in office witnessed continuous conflicts with whites, especially city workers, and ongoing fragmentation among blacks. A series of scandals rocked the administration, which was also plagued by several strikes by municipal employees that paralyzed the city and fostered discontent. Contrary to the expectations of his white backers, Stokes's installation in city hall was not sufficient to forestall further racial disturbances, though he did have a calming influence when violence again flared in 1968.

The end of his second term saw the black electorate fractured and whites united. The split among blacks was particularly disappointing, and in 1971, upon Stokes's retirement, this division resulted in the election of a white Republican mayor. The grassroots organizations that had united around Stokes to place him in office collapsed, greatly lowering black morale and political participation. During the 1970s, the number of registered black voters decreased by 20,000 and voter turnout declined drastically—from 75 percent to 48 percent. Blacks still had access to city government, and Carl Stokes's brother, Louis, represented them in Congress, but the promise of a reshaping of municipal politics along progressive lines withered.[2]

Meanwhile, in Gary, Indiana, black political development followed a similar pattern as in Cleveland but proved to be more durable. In this midwestern home of U.S. Steel, by the late 1960s blacks comprised about 55 percent of the city's population. As whites flocked to the suburbs during the previous decade, Gary's black population rapidly expanded into a majority. Nevertheless, in 1967, whites accounted for 52.3 percent of the city's registered voters compared with 47.7 percent for blacks. Up to that time, the black electorate had thrown its clout behind the local Democratic machine, keeping its leaders in office. For instance, in 1963, two-thirds of the mayor's votes came from blacks, leaving whites to make up only a third of the winning total. In return for this support, black machine functionaries obtained patronage and other spoils; however, the dire economic conditions of their constituents living in the ghettos showed little improvement.

As in Cleveland, civil rights protests of the early 1960s helped alter the structure of black politics in Gary. Community activists engineered direct-action demonstrations to challenge unfair racial practices that the dominant machine organization failed to address. These drives mobilized many blacks who previously had been politically inactive, especially those in lower-income brackets, and heightened their desire to use the electoral arena to advance racial objectives. Community leaders looked to loosen the hold of the machine on blacks and substitute in its place a political organization directed by blacks and aimed at raising the poor quality of housing, education, and law enforcement that plagued many inner-city neighborhoods.

The leadership for this assault on the established order came from Richard G. Hatcher. A lawyer and county prosecutor, Hatcher had been active in local civil rights efforts. He served as adviser to the NAACP youth group, provided counsel for a number of local protest associations, and in 1963, headed the Gary contingent to the march on Washington. That same year, he won a seat on the city council with the backing of the Democratic machine. He soon established his independence from party chieftains and lost the

[2]Not until 1989 did Cleveland elect its second black mayor, Michael Smith.

plentiful patronage plums they had for distribution to the party faithful. Hatcher also broke with tradition by using his position to promote the broad civil rights aims of the black community. In one of his major accomplishments, he directed the battle to obtain a pathbreaking fair housing law for the city.

In 1967, while Carl Stokes was mounting an insurgent campaign in Cleveland, Hatcher launched his own bid for mayor of Gary. Divorced from the machine, including those black politicians customarily in its service, he set up a dynamic, grassroots organization of volunteers. Crisscrossing black neighborhoods, Hatcher's workers played upon the racial pride that had been blossoming and delivered the message that the time had arrived to elect a black mayor. They waged an intense drive to boost black voter registration, and over a seven-month period succeeded in enrolling an additional 2,200 names. Though black registration still lagged slightly behind that of whites, the Hatcher candidacy and the hard work behind it managed to stimulate 3,000 more blacks than whites to turn out at the polls. In his Democratic primary contest against two whites, including the incumbent mayor, Hatcher won by capturing about 70 percent of the black vote, while the white electorate split its ballots between his rivals.

The black nominee also prevailed in the general election, where he faced a single white opponent, the Republican Joseph Radigan. Though the candidate of his party, Hatcher failed to receive the endorsement of the regular Democratic organization, which remained deeply suspicious of his independence. Machine leaders not only withheld their backing, but they orchestrated attempts to purge the voter registration lists of 5,000 black names. This chicanery was blocked by the intervention of the Justice Department and issuance of a federal court injunction restoring the names. On election day, Hatcher eked out a slim victory of 1,389 votes, approximately 51 percent of the total cast. He garnered an astounding 96 percent of the black electorate, and owed his triumph to the very high turnout of blacks at the polls. A greater percentage of blacks than whites participated, 76 percent to 72 percent, and in addition to his solid black base of support, he obtained 14 percent of the white ballots. Though opposed by most whites, Hatcher scored particularly well in predominantly liberal Jewish districts.

Both Hatcher's candidacy and the determined organizing efforts on his behalf contributed to the victory of Gary's first black mayor.

The campaign mobilized many blacks who had felt themselves outside of the electoral process. "People for the first time really began to see how important a vote was," a Hatcher supporter acknowledged, "and that they could control a way of life." Having obtained office, the mayor initiated programs directed at relieving long-neglected problems in the black community. His administration undertook to construct public housing, encouraged affirmative action hiring plans, and recruited blacks for government employment. These benefits underscored for many blacks the connection between electoral politics and minority-group advancement and promoted in Gary's black residents both pride and confidence in government authority. Moreover, unlike the experience in Cleveland, Hatcher succeeded in solidifying black organizational support behind him and won reelection throughout the next two decades.

Black mayoral candidates also fashioned winning coalitions elsewhere by combining solid black support with a small but sufficient minority of white backers. Such was the situation in Detroit. Though the Motor City had a history of racial strife dating back to the 1943 race riot, it also had a tradition of biracial labor activism, black militancy, and liberal reform. By 1965, Detroit counted two blacks, Charles C. Diggs, Jr., and John Conyers, in its congressional delegation, and one African-American sat on the city council. During much of the 1960s the city had been run by Mayor Jerome Cavanagh, a white liberal whose generally enlightened administration was tarnished by the explosion of racial violence in 1967. The urban rebellion helped contribute to white flight to the suburbs. By the end of the decade, blacks comprised 43 percent of Detroit's population. In 1969, Richard Austin, a black accountant and chair of the Wayne County Board of Supervisors, ran for mayor but narrowly lost to his white opponent by a margin of 1 percent. Nevertheless, three blacks were elected to the nine-member city council. (The following year, Austin won election as Michigan's secretary of state.)

In 1973, Coleman Young attempted to become Detroit's first black mayor. During World War II, he had served as a second lieutenant in the Army Air Corps. While in the military, Young was arrested along with 100 black soldiers for trying to integrate an officers' club in Indiana. On the heels of the publicity generated by the protest, the Army desegregated this establishment. After finishing his tour of duty, he returned home to work as a union organizer in the automobile industry. However, his left-wing sympathies during the 1940s and 1950s made him the target of both conservative politicians and the powerful, anti-Communist United Automobile Workers. Nevertheless, he demonstrated remarkable political resiliency. By the 1960s, Young had survived the anti-Communist postwar backlash and moved into the electoral arena as a Democratic state senator and party leader still championing liberal and labor causes.

By the time he ran for mayor, in 1973, Young had an advantage that was not available to Austin four years earlier: The number of black registered voters exceeded that of whites. In the nonpartisan primary, he competed in a field of nineteen candidates. No one received a majority, and Young finished second to John Nichols, the white police commissioner. In the runoff contest against Nichols, who symbolized law and order to whites and police brutality to blacks, Young insisted that he would not engineer a black takeover and pledged "to field a team that has balance—racially, ethnically and politically." From the 1.5 million people who went to the polls, he hammered out a slim winning margin of 14,000 votes by mobilizing the overwhelming majority of the black electorate and obtaining about 8 percent of the white ballots.

Though Afro-American mayors of major cities usually emerged when blacks approached or reached a majority of the population, the election of Tom Bradley in Los Angeles was a notable exception. In a city with only a 15 percent black electorate, Bradley defeated the longtime incumbent, Sam Yorty, in a contest filled with racial bitterness. A former UCLA track star, policeman, and lawyer, Bradley served as a city councilman during the 1960s, representing a district that was two-thirds nonblack. Having lost the Democratic mayoral primary to Yorty in 1969, four years later Bradley fashioned a "coalition of conscience" to triumph over his rival with 56 percent of the vote. In 1973, he captured city hall by gaining 95 percent of black ballots, a bare majority of the Chicano (Mexican-American) electorate, and nearly half the white vote—running particularly well among liberal Jews. A source of pride to the black community in a city that was predominantly white, Bradley succeeded in convincing the electorate that his election was a sign of racial progress and an alternative to black radicalism. "The American dream is often verbalized," he asserted, "but it would really have meaning all over the country if a black who believed in the system, who worked and prepared himself for new opportunities, was able to achieve that kind of victory."

THE NEW CHALLENGE

These victories along with those in Cleveland and Gary marked the dawning of a new era in black urban politics. For more than a decade after 1967, black mayors took control of city halls in prominent urban areas both in the North and the South. As municipalities acquired black majorities, constructed political organizations to rally the previously disfranchised portion of the electorate, and marshaled economic resources to wage effective campaigns, black candidates triumphed in Newark, Washington, D.C., Oakland, Birmingham, and New Orleans. The appearance of black mayors and other elected officials directly opened up government to African-Americans on a more equal basis than ever before. In 1974, 1,593 blacks occupied elected positions outside of the South; six years later the number jumped to 2,455. Although black political leaders made mistakes and problems of poverty seemed as intractable to them as to their white predecessors, black officials demonstrated that white monopoly control of public affairs could be broken. Henceforth, blacks in towns and cities throughout the nation staked their claim to an equal partnership with whites in governance.

They faced a difficult task, however. In many of the cities in which they ascended to power, blacks inherited a multitude of severe financial problems that limited their options for action. Much of the situation was beyond their command. During the 1970s, structural flaws in the economy produced both recession and inflation that drained tax revenues away from maintaining basic city services, let alone expanding them. Major urban areas teetered on the brink of bankruptcy and needed to be rescued by infusions of state and federal funds. Low-wage foreign competition in the production and distribution of manufactured goods hurt American industry and resulted in plant closings and unemployment in many of the urban locations dominated by black chief executives. Furthermore, the continued migration of whites to the suburbs and the parallel movement of a rising black middle class out of the inner cities left behind an increasingly poor population of blacks unable to contribute to the upkeep of their communities.

In addition, black mayors were hampered in other ways. Those seeking improvements for their constituents often found their efforts slowed by entrenched municipal government employees whose jobs were protected by civil service codes. As a result, changes in personnel to implement new directions in policy could occur only slowly at best and at worst could be thwarted by unsympathetic bureaucrats. Moreover, many issues could not be handled through local initiatives. Cities depended on state and federal governments for funds, but growing conservatism in the 1970s deprived them of political allies to fill crucial material needs. Into the void stepped large corporate investors and financial developers, who in return for their economic assistance steered many municipal projects toward enterprises that created jobs and housing for middle- and upper-class residents to the detriment of the poor.

Despite this sometimes dismal picture, African-Americans still found pursuit of electoral power worthwhile. Throughout the nation, a substantial segment of the black electorate benefited from the tangible improvements that increased political strength brought. After 1965, opportunities for public employment and distribution of municipal services had far less to do with skin color than at any time during American history. Furthermore, black empowerment meant much more than could be calculated in dollars and cents. It provided a source of political agency for blacks, breaking down habits of nonparticipation ingrained through generations of racial discrimination. To the extent that the members of any group of people, white or black, male or female, could exert control over their lives in an increasingly complex and technological society, African-Americans had joined the ranks of first-class citizens and helped shape the political landscape of the country.

Chapter 6

Progress and Poverty: Politics in a Conservative Era

The movement of blacks into positions of influence and power in local and state governments, however impressive the gains, was not enough to produce genuine racial equality. Many of the problems blacks encountered were national in scope and required national attention and resources to remedy. Furthermore, the laws placed on the statute books as a result of the civil rights struggle needed federal enforcement, and in the case of the Voting Rights Act, periodic renewal. The economic misery that plagued so many African-Americans demanded solutions beyond the purview of local politicians. The burdens inflicted by chronic unemployment, inflation, and inadequate housing and health care traversed municipal, county, and state boundary lines and became the responsibility of officials in Washington. Unless blacks and their white allies could shape public policy in the nation's capital to deal with these concerns, the benefits of political empowerment would remain incomplete.

As the fruits of black political mobilization began to ripen during the 1970s, they matured in a climate less nurturing to their continued growth. Black southerners had regained their right to vote with the flowering of liberal reform in the mid-1960s; yet within a decade the nation had moved in a conservative direction that posed serious threats to hard-earned civil rights and social programs and to the initiation of new ones. In the wake of disillusionment over the Vietnam war and racial strife in American cities, Richard Nixon and other conservatives had risen to prominence by deemphasizing racial justice, promising a return to law and order, and pledging economic retrenchment. In this gloomy environment, African-Americans looked to engage their foes in the national arena in which the vital policies affecting their welfare were forged. The preservation and expansion of electoral victories in local black communities throughout the nation depended on winning battles in Washington to sustain them.

While much needed to be done before blacks achieved the economic equality to accompany their recently gained civil and political rights, in an age of federal retrenchment they were largely forced to fight defensive operations. Although they did wage new skirmishes for racial advancement, civil rights proponents spent much of their creative energies guarding against rollbacks in existing programs. During the Nixon administration, civil rights advocates had successfully petitioned Congress and the courts to maintain strict enforcement of the Voting Rights Act and school desegregation decisions. A bipartisan coalition of moderate and liberal lawmakers, reinforced by determined civil rights lobbyists, ensured that landmark suffrage legislation remained intact and defeated administration-sponsored attempts to circumvent court-ordered busing. On the economic front, the Republican chief executive managed to terminate some of his predecessor's Great Society programs and trim others by turning funding over to the states. But even in this area, in 1973 Congress acknowledged the plight of the poor by adopting the Comprehensive Employment and Training Act (CETA), which provided public service jobs and manpower training to those out of work.

BLACK POLITICAL INFLUENCE AND THE FORD ADMINISTRATION

When the Watergate scandal forced Nixon to resign, in 1974, Vice-President Gerald Ford stepped in to serve out Nixon's term. A staunch conservative and a veteran of some twenty-five years in the House of Representatives, Ford had given qualified support to civil rights legislation. As a lawmaker from Grand Rapids, Michigan, Ford routinely voted for passage of civil rights bills extending the suffrage to blacks and challenging racial discrimination in public accommodations and housing. However, in compiling this record he had, like President Nixon, embraced those proposals only after making concerted efforts to soften their impact. As a congressman in 1970, he had lined up behind the chief executive in favor of replacing key provisions of the Voting Rights Act with a version that would have removed much of the weight of enforcement from the white South. His stance in opposition to school busing reflected Nixon's, as well as that of his white constituents who decried imposing this means of remedying racial imbalance in neighborhood schools.

Nevertheless, upon succeeding the disgraced Nixon on August 9, 1974, Ford assumed a conciliatory posture that was absent from his predecessor's final days in office. To restore confidence in the presidency and to bind the wounds inflicted by the Watergate debacle, he sought to reassure some of those who felt most estranged from the White House. These gestures followed earlier attempts "to clear the air" with black leaders while he was still vice-president. As Ford later recalled it, disturbed that "the Nixon Administration had closed the door to minorities, particularly blacks," he hoped they would see him as "point man...for dealing with the government; that there was at least one man in the Administration who would listen to them." Unfortunately, when he tried to follow up these meetings by submitting recommendations for action, Nixon's staff ignored him. Within a week of becoming President, he summoned to the Oval Office members of the Congressional Black Caucus, whose chairman, Charles Rangel of New York, called the conference "absolutely, fantastically good."

A short time later, President Ford had sufficient opportunity to show the sincerity of his intentions. Very much on the minds of black lawmakers and civil rights advocates was the upcoming renewal of the Voting Rights Act, whose key provisions were due to lapse in August 1975. For the third time in ten years, Congress had to debate the merits of federal protection of the suffrage and decide whether forceful supervision should continue into the future and for how long. Though southern blacks had taken notable strides in gaining entry to the electoral arena, their political strength was still fragile and depended on continued oversight from Washington to reach its full potential. Remembering the nation's abandonment of the freed slaves at the end of Reconstruction a century earlier, modern-day civil rights supporters worried about the harm that another premature federal withdrawal would cause to the Second Reconstruction's enfranchised blacks.

President Ford appeared to agree with their concern. He okayed the Justice Department's recommendation to extend the Voting Rights Act for an additional five years, thereby choosing not to repeat Nixon's unsuccessful attempt to fasten controversial amendments to it. Acknowledging that southern blacks had made great progress in the decade since passage of the law, the Ford administration noted that the number of black elected officials remained disproportionately low and that evidence of racial discrimination in registration and voting persisted. In taking this position, the chief executive further endeared himself to civil rights advocates by invoking the memory of Dr. King and linking it to the renewal campaign. On January 14, 1975, Ford commemorated the anniversary of the slain minister's birthday by recalling King's leadership in enacting the original suffrage law, which, he remarked, "has helped to open our political process to full citizen participation" and must be "safeguarded."

Boosted by the President and with solid bipartisan congressional backing, the renewal measure headed for sure passage. Compared with previous battles, the current deliberations took place in an atmosphere of relative harmony. Neither the administration nor the liberals disagreed over preserving what had become the most important provision of the statute—the section-five requirement for the covered states to clear changes in their electoral laws with the Justice Department before they took effect. There were differences over the length of time desired for extension—the White House favored five years and civil rights lawmakers advocated ten—and the President was reluctant to add to the bill a liberal-sponsored measure to grant language minorities the same protection guaranteed to oppressed racial groups. Nevertheless, unity rather than discord characterized the congressional proceedings. Joseph Rauh, the civil rights attorney who had pleaded the case of the Mississippi Freedom Democratic Party in 1964, summed up the feeling of reformers: "I guess one of the happiest things for us is the broad consensus that has grown up behind extending the Voting Rights Act."

Though southern lawmakers did not abandon their customary opposition to the suffrage bill, they lacked both the passion and strength to mount an effective challenge to it in 1975. Accepting the political reality that the legislation was going to pass in some form, they tried to revive the Nixon administration strategy of expanding coverage of section five nationwide. Moreover, opponents concentrated their energy on designing provisions to make it easier for the southern states to remove themselves from the act's penalties. Their arguments failed to persuade their legislative colleagues. A proposal for a ten-year extension sailed through the House, and the Senate displayed an unusual enthusiasm for agreement by voting to impose cloture to terminate debate even before southern legislators had the opportunity to wage a filibuster.

Despite this overwhelming show of support, the final outcome became unexpectedly enmeshed in controversy. While the Senate discussed the measure, President Ford suddenly backed away from his firm endorsement of the bill and suggested enlarging its scope to include the entire nation. In offering this last-minute proposal, Ford seemed to be heeding the calls of southern members of his party to take such action. With Republicanism on the rise in Dixie—Goldwater and Nixon had made significant inroads in the once solid Democratic South's presidential vote—the GOP leader looked to the region to help gain his party's nomination and win election in his own right in 1976. His about-face drew a barrage of criticism from civil rights supporters, Democrats and Republicans alike, who charged that his puzzling position confused the issue and put the entire bill in jeopardy. However, Ford's political calculation turned into an empty gesture as the chief executive once again reversed his field. Fearing that his intervention would stall passage of the bill's special provisions before their expiration, the President withdrew his objection to enactment of the original measure. As the presidential fog lifted from the Capitol, both chambers of Congress approved a modified seven-year extension by wide margins.

This victory demonstrated the increasing leverage of southern blacks upon their national representatives. The South's trio of black legislators, Barbara Jordan of Texas, Andrew Young of Georgia, and Harold Ford of Tennessee, were expected to cast their votes for the bill (as were the thirteen black lawmakers from the North); but it was a matter of considerable surprise that 69 of 105 of their white colleagues from the region joined them on the final tally. In the Senate, where Edward Brooke, the Massachusetts Republican, sat as the lone black, 13 of 24 southerners lined up behind the measure.

Reflecting the changing pattern of partisan affiliation in Dixie, the party of Abraham Lincoln and the party of Jefferson Davis were trading places. As conservative whites jumped to the Republicans and northern transplants brought their GOP allegiances to the region, Democrats in the South were coming to rely more heavily on the growing black electorate for support at the polls. Though southern Democratic lawmakers did not embrace liberal economic positions that would have benefited African-Americans, they had little difficulty in backing a suffrage law that created the very constituency they needed to help keep them in power. This shifting arithmetic led southern Democrats and Republicans to calculate differently. In the House, two-thirds of the southern Democratic bloc supported extension of the Voting Rights Act in contrast to nearly two in three Dixie Republicans who opposed it. A Louisiana lawmaker expressed the sentiments of his fellow Democrats: "We found that the sky did not fall under the 1965 Voting Rights Act, that things worked pretty well in the South, the deep South of the old Confederacy, which readjusted their [sic] patterns of voting, readjusted their attitudes toward all people."

In the end, the Ford administration chose to follow the new consensus on voting rights that had developed, but in the more controversial area of school busing the administration pursued the old course laid out by President Nixon. Supreme Court decisions sanctioning busing generated substantial opposition among whites in the North as well as the South. Building upon this hostility, in 1972 the Nixon administration had introduced congressional legislation instructing the judiciary to try to retain the neighborhood school concept and to use busing only as a last resort. The bill passed the House only to die in the Senate. The chief executive kept the measure alive during the remainder of his abbreviated term, and after Ford replaced him, Congress finally approved the proposal. This action delighted the new chief executive, who declared: "I have consistently opposed forced busing to achieve racial balance as a solution to quality education." Furthermore, these words gave encouragement to antibusing opponents such as those in Boston who militantly protested against court-ordered desegregation. Launching school boycotts, holding marches, and fomenting violence, these foes of busing succeeded in plunging the city into turmoil for several years during the mid-1970s.

These attacks notwithstanding, the practical effect of the legislative measure was minimal, because Congress did not have the authority to curtail courts from enforcing the constitutional rights of minority students through busing. In fact, during the Nixon-Ford years nearly 50 percent of black pupils attended desegregated schools in the South, a figure higher than that in the North. And, despite the resistance in Boston, the judiciary remained firm in enforcing its busing decrees. In addition, civil rights lobbyists and their congressional allies defeated a more serious threat to busing than the bill Ford had signed into law. They succeeded in turning back attempts to end court-ordered busing altogether by way of a constitutional amendment, passage of which would have required a two-thirds vote of Congress before ratification by the states.

Beyond salvaging the influential Voting Rights Act and retaining some degree of enforcement of school desegregation, African-Americans saw their efforts toward greater racial advancement stall. Blacks used political power to sustain their legal rights of citizenship, but they had far less success in shaping the agenda that would have addressed their economic needs. With fiscal conservatism emerging as the dominant theme in Washington and throughout the country, social programs to stimulate employment, extend health insurance, and furnish housing, which would have aided the working class and poor of both races, realistically did not stand much of a chance. Moreover, the growing inflationary spiral of the mid-1970s, together with rising unemployment—"stagflation," as economists labeled it—brought to a virtual halt the economic gains blacks had been experiencing since the heyday of the civil rights movement a decade before. In 1975, the median income of black families had inched up to 61 percent of whites', but having reached this peak, it immediately began sliding even further away from full equality. Without renewed federal commitment to tackling their economic problems, blacks managed only to fight a rearguard political battle to maintain the status quo.

THE ELECTION OF JIMMY CARTER

The presidential election of 1976 offered dim prospects for meaningful change. The Republican incumbent's performance in civil rights matters, after getting off to a good start, had come to disappoint blacks. Much of the goodwill Ford had created by supporting extension of the Voting Rights Act eroded in his clumsy handling of the bill at its final stage before passage. In addition to his antibusing stand, Ford's position against federal aid to rescue financially troubled cities from bankruptcy upset black activists. They criticized the President for his callousness in allowing major urban centers of the North, which contained substantial black populations, to cut back on municipal social services rather than helping them preserve these programs through an infusion of funds from Washington. In the wake of the riots in the late 1960s and the flight of whites to the suburbs, the cities had become associated increasingly with the presence of impoverished racial minorities whose problems white Americans preferred to ignore. After Ford rejected New York City's plea for relief in 1975, M. Carl Holman, a long-time civil rights advocate and director of the Urban Coalition, contended that many blacks believed New York "would never have been dealt with like that if it had been seen as a city of Wasps [white Anglo-Saxon Protestants]."

Nor had the Democratic presidential nominee identified himself closely with the cities and their black residents. The former governor of Georgia, Jimmy Carter had presided over a largely rural and small-town state. He brought a brand of New South progressivism to the statehouse in Atlanta that emphasized honesty and efficiency in government, streamlining the budgetary process, and upgrading the public education system, which ranked near the bottom in the country. Accordingly, this political and economic modernization fostered an environment hospitable to business investment and growth. In 1976, Carter secured his party's presidential nomination by effectively campaigning in the primaries as an "outsider" from Washington, an image that in the post-Watergate era garnered widespread appeal from an electorate disillusioned with national politicians. Weary of "imperial presidents," either of the activist Republican or the Democratic variety, Americans saw merit in the kind of low-expectation approach to government offered by Carter. A self-described conservative in fiscal affairs, the Georgian fit in well with the mood of economic retrenchment and frugality that voters wanted in the nation's capital.

Although Carter's record as governor did not hold out much promise for the extension of costly programs to reduce black poverty, his racial views provided a bit more encouragement for black advancement. However, the case in his favor was hardly clear-cut. Carter had been born and raised in Plains, Georgia, and returned there to live after completing a career in the Navy. During the 1950s and 1960s, he accepted the rigid segregationist practices and nearly total disfranchisement that characterized his home area in southwest Georgia. Never a negrophobe, he did not actively condone Jim Crow so much as he made very little effort to eradicate it. Yet unlike many of his neighbors, this peanut farmer refused to join the White Citizens Council or other states' rights groups opposed to desegregation, and on one occasion in the mid-1960s, he even waged a losing battle to open up his Baptist church doors to black congregants. Nevertheless, elected governor in 1970, he roundly criticized court-ordered busing and endorsed a constitutional amendment to prevent it. He also developed close ties with George Wallace, who he thought had the best chance of defeating Nixon in 1972, and when George McGovern instead of Wallace won the Democratic nomination that year, Carter unsuccessfully tried to extract a pledge from him to relax enforcement of the Voting Rights Act in the South.

While in office, the Georgia governor balanced these positions with others that won black support. In an era when black voters were becoming critical to the election of white Democratic party officials, new South politicians like Carter (and even some old-style segregationists like Wallace) discarded the racist rhetoric of the past and abandoned irresponsible opposition to the laws of the land that compelled desegregation. The changes wrought by the civil rights movement had made a distinct impression upon Carter, and he accepted them with both a "sense of relief" and "secret gratitude." In effect, the struggle for black equality had also freed many whites from the shackles of racism that kept the South locked into economic and political backwardness. In 1971, Governor Carter had proclaimed the start of a new day: "I say to you quite frankly that the time for racial discrimination is over. No poor, rural, weak, or black person shall ever have to bear the additional burden of being deprived of the opportunity for an education, a job, or simple justice." He matched the symbolism of his eloquent rhetoric with some substance. During his administration, the governor arranged to desegregate the walls of the state capitol by hanging a portrait of Dr. King alongside paintings of distinguished white Georgians, a ceremony that ended with the singing of the powerful civil rights anthem "We Shall Overcome." Moreover, Carter doubled the number of blacks working in state government, increased black appointments to middle-management positions, and signed into law the state's first open-housing measure.

This overall performance won Carter the staunch backing of Dr. King's family and some of the martyred civil rights leader's top associates. Congressman Andrew Young of Atlanta, a King confidant, became an early booster of the governor for the Democratic presidential nomination in 1976. He was joined by the Reverend Martin Luther King, Sr., who remarked that he had "never met a finer person than Governor Carter." Though other black civil rights leaders-turned-politicians, such as Julian Bond, declined to endorse him, Carter held on firmly to his King-Atlanta connections.

The strength of this attachment was sorely tested during the primaries. In Indianapolis, appearing before a largely white audience, Carter reiterated his opposition to racial discrimination at the same time as he defended those "who are trying to maintain the ethnic purity of their neighborhoods." He further stated his disapproval of the government's deliberately "trying to break down an ethnically oriented community...by injecting into it a member of another race." These comments smacked of the kind of rhetoric that George Wallace had skillfully employed as a presidential candidate in whipping up a white backlash among ethnic groups fearful that black advances would come at their expense. Carter survived this episode by apologizing for any misunderstanding his statement might have caused, which satisfied most black leaders. Representative Young and "Daddy" King rallied around Carter and forgave him for making "a slip of the tongue that does not represent his thinking."

This reaffirmation of support enabled Carter to attract the bulk of black votes in winning crucial primary contests, which carried him to the Democratic National Convention as the frontrunner. There he heard the stirring keynote speech of Representative Barbara Jordan of Houston, the first black to receive the honor of delivering this prestigious address. In 1967, as a first-term Texas state senator, Jordan had come to the attention of President Lyndon Johnson, who invited her to the White House to participate in a strategy session concerning fair-housing legislation. She impressed the President, as well as her colleagues in the Texas legislature, by combining a concern for civil rights with hardheaded legislative pragmatism. Elected to Congress in 1972, Jordan quickly rose to prominence as perhaps the most eloquent member of the House Judiciary Committee in its televised investigation of the Watergate-related impeachment charges against President Nixon. Chosen to rally the Democratic faithful at the 1976 nominating convention, she declared that her very presence on the podium showed "that the American dream need not forever be deferred." The assembled delegates who heard these words and who subsequently nominated Carter for President included 323 blacks comprising 10.6 percent of the convention members. (In contrast, blacks comprised only 3 percent of the GOP convention delegates who chose Ford as their candidate.) The Democratic reform initiative launched in 1964 was evidenced most vividly in the Mississippi contingent, which contained the highest ratio of blacks to whites of any delegation at the gathering.

Throughout the nomination process and in the subsequent general election campaign, Carter successfully reached out to blacks. A devout Baptist, he avidly cultivated black support by speaking in black churches and delivering a message his listeners could relate to. Churches had traditionally functioned as key institutions in the political life of black communities, and Carter knew how to tap into their emotional style and felt comfortable in the role of a preacher presenting a sermon. He stressed the themes of redemption and compassion, brotherhood and love, justice and equality, and linked them personally and directly to Dr. King. "I sometimes think that a Southerner of my generation," the Georgian remarked, "can most fully understand the meaning and impact of Martin Luther King's life. He and I grew up in the same South." As Carter's biographer, Betty Glad, concluded, more than any substantive program the candidate offered, blacks responded to him out of "nostalgia for the rhythms and religion of rural Christianity."

Indeed, black ballots proved pivotal in Carter's triumph over Ford. The Georgian eked out a very tight victory over the incumbent, gaining a bare 50 percent of the popular vote and capturing 297 electoral votes to Ford's 241—the closest margin since 1916. In patching together a coalition of states from his native South, the Midwest, and the Northeast, Carter secured a whopping 90 percent of the black vote. His strongest support came from the southern black electorate, which gave him 92 percent of its ballots. The

Representative Barbara Jordan of Texas delivering the keynote address at the 1976 Democratic National Convention. (AP/Wirephoto)

huge vote that Carter obtained from blacks helped him secure all but one state (Virginia) in the South, where Ford otherwise received about 55 percent of the total white southern vote. When Mississippi, which only a decade before had barred nearly all blacks from the franchise, swung into the Democratic column, Andrew Young gleefully declared: "I knew that the hands that picked the cotton finally picked the president." Nationally the governor piled up 5.2 million black votes, more than triple his slender popular vote margin of 1.7 million.

Blacks flocked to Carter for a variety of reasons. On a personal level, his southern Baptist religious fervor and regional heritage appealed to blacks not only in the South but also to those whose roots extended back to Dixie. Carter credited the civil rights movement with transforming both himself and the South, a message that earned him widespread support from former leaders of that struggle. The key endorsements of Reverend King and Congressman Young, Julian Bond noted, "made Carter legitimate in the eyes of blacks all over the country." Furthermore, Carter ran extremely well among blacks because of his party label. Polls revealed that the Georgian scored heavily with traditional Democrats, and no group exceeded the loyalty exhibited by black Democrats in recent presidential elections. The party of FDR's New Deal and LBJ's Great Society had even greater attraction in 1976, when the unemployment rate under the Republicans had risen to 8 percent and was substantially higher among adult black males.

The important contribution African-Americans made to Carter's triumph stood in sharp contrast to the mood of despair felt by many blacks in that bicentennial-year celebration of the Declaration of Independence. Carl Holman detected "a dangerous cynicism," especially among young blacks, who demanded more than the civil rights victories of the past that had brought liberty without equality. "There's a great feeling of being out of it—outsiders in your own country—which was a feeling they began to lose in the sixties," Holman asserted. "And it's come back double-barrelled now." Even before the 1960s ended, the country's urban ghettos had exploded as rioters violently expressed their bitterness in the streets rather than calmly at the polls. Between 1968 and 1972, the black turnout of eligible voters fell. The decline was especially pronounced in the North, where the ballot did not hold the same attraction for blacks as it did for those southerners who had fought a long, difficult struggle to regain the franchise. The traumas of Vietnam and Watergate had heightened this alienation, but the frustration of many African-Americans emerged even stronger from the unwillingness of political leaders to grapple with the continuing crises of joblessness, poor health, and substandard housing that gripped black communities. "There is," the political scientist Samuel D. Cook declared in 1976, "a groping for direction, issues, priorities, funds, organization, inspiration, affirmation, protest, and movement."

Yet such assessments did not tell the whole story, as many blacks showed signs that they were not ready to give up on the political system. Since 1972, the number of blacks registered to vote had grown by three quarters of a million. Civil rights groups such as the NAACP had joined with labor unions, the Democratic party, and the Voter Education Project to mount active enrollment campaigns to sign up new voters. In the South, blacks narrowed the registration gap between the races from over 40 percent in the mid-1960s to about 11 percent a decade later. Equally as impressive, registered blacks turned out for the 1976 presidential election in growing numbers. This contest brought to the polls about 64 percent of enrolled black voters nationwide, surpassing the 58 percent participating in 1972. The upswing in the rates of black registration and turnout as well as the impact of the minority vote in determining Carter's victory convinced many African-Americans that they were still heading in the right direction. No one was more optimistic than John Lewis, the former chairman of SNCC and director of VEP. "I wish—Lord, how I wish," he commented after the election, "Martin [Luther King] were alive today. He would be very, very happy. Through it all, the lunch counter sit-ins, the bus strike, the marches and everything, the bottom line was voting."

AFFIRMATIVE ACTION AND BAKKE

Having helped elect a President, blacks expected their faith in the electoral system to be suitably rewarded. Not only did they desire to obtain the traditional spoils of victory—jobs and appointments—but they also sought to influence the setting of a public policy agenda that recognized the special needs of their communities. In President Carter they acquired increased access to top-level government positions, but they fell short in steering his administration along a course that would lead to bold new programs.

The President recruited an impressive array of blacks to Washington. Patricia R. Harris, former ambassador to Luxembourg and chair of the Credentials Committee at the 1972 Democratic National Convention, entered the Cabinet as secretary of housing and urban development. An undergraduate at Howard University in 1943, Harris had participated in an early sit-in demonstration to desegregate a cafeteria in the District of Columbia. The chief executive staffed the Justice Department with Solicitor General Wade McCree, a Harvard-trained federal judge from Michigan, and Assistant Attorney General for Civil Rights Drew Days III, a Yale Law School graduate who had previously handled cases for the NAACP Legal Defense Fund. He chose Clifford Alexander, Jr., an adviser to President Johnson, as secretary of the Army. Carter, who on the campaign trail had showered praise upon the civil rights movement, appointed several individuals who had played significant roles in that struggle. He selected Andrew Young, one of Dr.

King's closest advisers in the SCLC, for the Cabinet-level post of ambassador to the United Nations. From SNCC the President tapped John Lewis to operate Volunteers in Service to America (VISTA), the domestic equivalent of the Peace Corps. (This agency was a division of ACTION, whose associate director was Mary King, a white SNCC organizer.) Named as assistant secretary of labor, Ernest Green twenty years earlier, in 1957, had been part of the courageous group of black students that defied a menacing mob to desegregate Central High School in Little Rock, Arkansas. By the end of Carter's term in office the list of his black appointees had expanded to include 15 ambassadors, 30 federal judges, over 50 sub-Cabinet officials, 110 members of advisory boards and commissions, and 25 members of the White House staff.

Aside from the recognition they conferred, these appointments did not produce bold initiatives in civil rights policy. The most challenging opportunity arose over affirmative action, and the Carter administration acted cautiously. This issue sharply divided the races. Most whites objected to any preferential treatment—reverse discrimination as they saw it—that placed them at a disadvantage in hiring and in admission into graduate and professional schools. They considered any program that established a fixed number of positions, or quotas, for minorities as a violation of the principle of equal opportunity. In stark contrast, the majority of blacks took the opposite position. African-Americans argued that on the basis of past discrimination, the effects of which still persisted, they were entitled to compensatory treatment. In their view, this meant the establishment of flexible goals, not quotas, to recruit qualified minorities until a level was reached that indicated they were competing equally. The controversy posed a thorny political hazard for Carter because it split two key elements of his electoral coalition: blacks and Jews. Victims of discriminatory quotas in the past, Jewish-Americans deplored any attempt to resurrect quotas even for the purpose of including, rather than excluding, certain groups of people.

The President attempted to walk a fine line on this matter. Having made earnest efforts to increase minority employment in his administration, the chief executive readily acknowledged that blacks suffered from the impact of racial bias, past and present, and pledged "to root out those last vestiges of discrimination in government and set a pattern for the private sector." He disapproved of quotalike regulations that limited access to employment, however, and believed that minorities would benefit in the long run from racially impartial hiring and admission standards.

In this respect, President Carter reflected the position of most white Americans. A 1972 survey had indicated that 82 percent of whites opposed affirmative action plans that favored blacks over equally qualified whites. Nevertheless, 77 percent of those polled approved of the creation of job-training programs for blacks. Like Carter, the overwhelming majority of respondents differentiated between "legitimate" compensatory programs that allowed minority groups an opportunity to compete on an equal level with whites and "unfair" policies that supposedly granted one group preferential treatment over another. These attitudes were hardened by the economic situation of the 1970s, which heightened competition for increasingly scarce jobs and spaces in graduate and professional schools. The decade's economic cycle of recession coincidental with inflation—that is, stagflation, as noted earlier—together with the outpouring into the marketplace of the postwar baby-boomers made whites much less hospitable to racial advancement than in the 1960s, when jobs and educational opportunities were more plentiful.

African-Americans generally considered affirmative action from a much different perspective. Having only recently regained their legal right to equality, blacks resented being told to forget their unfortunate history of racial discrimination and to make it on their own without due compensation from the government and the private sector. They refused to believe that such relief could be termed "reverse discrimination" when whites still retained firm control over economic and political power in society. Besides, to blacks racial bias was not so much an individual matter of discrimination as an institutional one allowing whites on the whole to continue to preserve their long-standing advantages. African-Americans argued that they would have a very difficult time in ever catching up to the mass of white Americans who had inherited the legacy of superior educational and employment benefits solely on the basis of their skin color. Thus, they contended that "benign" racial classifications were legitimate and proper.

Their arguments received some sanction in the courts. In 1971, the Supreme Court ruled in *Griggs v. Duke Power Company* that "neutral" employment tests were invalid if they perpetuated the effects of prior discriminatory employment practices. The justices found the results of such bias to exist when blacks failed to hold jobs in rough proportion to their percentage in the general population. Yet the issue was far from settled. In 1974, the high tribunal in *DeFunis v. Odegaard* had the opportunity to decide the fate of an affirmative action plan adopted by the University of Washington Law School that applied different entrance standards for blacks and whites. However, because the white plaintiff who charged discrimination had already been admitted to the law school while the suit was pending, the court declared the litigation moot, left the admissions plan intact, and managed to duck the controversial question for the time being.

The issue again surfaced at the medical school of the University of California, Davis, and forced the Carter administration to take action. The university had set aside a designated number of spaces for minority students in order to guarantee their selection. Alan Bakke, a rejected white applicant, sued to gain admission and overturn this procedure. After Bakke won in a lower court, the university appealed to the Supreme Court, where the Justice Department intended to file a brief in opposition to the school's affirmative action plan. Reflecting White House thinking, government lawyers premised their arguments on the principle that "racial classifications favorable to minority groups are presumptively unconstitutional."

Before the department could complete its brief, civil rights advocates inside and outside the administration managed substantially to revise the government's handiwork. Ironically, the original draft that critics found unacceptable had been written under the supervision of Carter's two top black attorneys, McCree and Days. In opposition stood Joseph Califano, the secretary of health, education, and welfare, who was white, and several black officeholders such as Ambassador Young and Eleanor Holmes Norton, the director of the Equal Employment Opportunity Commission. Taking their concerns to the President, they warned him, in Young's words, that the "Bakke case is perceived as a betrayal of the black community by the judicial system." At the same time, the Congressional Black Caucus applied additional pressure on the chief executive and informed him that the Justice brief "irretrievably undermined public and private affirmative action programs." In the wake of these maneuvers, Carter's lawyers, led by McCree and Days, redrafted the brief along lines suggested by its critics. The final version softened the department's antiquota position, supported university guidelines that took race into account for admission, and suggested that the case be returned to the California judiciary for rehearing. Although the Supreme Court agreed that racial criteria generally were a legitimate consideration in designing affirmative action programs, in this instance it upheld the claim of unfair discrimination and ordered Bakke's matriculation into the medical school.

This episode demonstrated the strengths and exposed the limitations of black political influence during the Carter years. Because the President had had the sensitivity and had felt a political obligation to appoint blacks to important posts in his administration, they were well-placed during the Bakke affair to correct Carter from making, what Califano called, "the most serious mistake...in domestic policy to date." Yet having helped shape this crucial policy matter, black officials and their white allies could not control the ultimate outcome of the decision. The Supreme Court took care of that, and its increasingly conservative orientation, reflecting appointments to the bench made by Nixon, confined affirmative action within narrow boundaries. Though civil rights sympathizers sat on the high tribunal, most notably Thurgood Marshall, the former chief counsel of the NAACP, they did not constitute a majority. Nevertheless, their presence on the court, like that of blacks in the Carter administration, modestly advanced civil rights goals so long as they did not stray too far from the center of the judicial and political spectrum.

The same situation applied in Congress. Throughout the late 1970s the Black Caucus and its white liberal allies made little progress with the majority of lawmakers who believed their constituents demanded fiscal restraint and would not tolerate massive spending to relieve economic distress. For example, the Black Caucus rallied behind a measure aimed at relieving the problem of unemployment, which was disproportionately high among blacks. Before Congress, in 1978, enacted a "full employment" bill sponsored by Senator Hubert Humphrey of Minnesota and Representative Augustus Hawkins, a black Democrat from California, conservative lawmakers had turned it into a hollow proposal.[1] Even worse, a national health plan offered by Senator Edward Kennedy of Massachusetts that would have been of great benefit to blacks went unpassed.

Given their optimistic expectations of President Carter, blacks had reason to feel disappointed with his performance. The President, who had campaigned for the White House as a Washington outsider, failed to establish effective relations in dealing with Congress. In this post-Watergate era, the task of leading lawmakers in a more activist, progressive direction would have severely challenged any chief executive, but Carter proved unwilling and unable to marshal his resources toward that end. He had promised the electorate competence, efficiency, and integrity—to restore character and decency to the Oval Office—not new programs for social reform. Further, the slimness of his victory did not furnish a mandate or provide him with the incentive to pursue bold domestic ventures. Still, he might have channeled some of the enthusiasm and energy he displayed in promoting his policy of human rights abroad into efforts at extending civil and economic rights at home. His liberal critics waited in vain for him to guide the nation morally and politically "to an understanding of the demands and subtleties of civil rights in the late 1970s and 1980s."

For black Americans Carter compounded his leadership difficulties by his handling of a controversy surrounding Ambassador Young. The outspoken delegate to the United Nations had become the most visible black representative in the Carter administration. To blacks the former civil rights leader and Atlanta congressman was a source of great pride, but to whites he demonstrated the inability of the chief executive to exercise his presidential authority firmly. The U.N. diplomat had received a great deal of publicity for his comments denouncing the racism both of America's friends and foes abroad as well as for extolling one of the nation's enemies, Cuba, for combating colonialism in Africa. Indeed, Young had served as a forceful advocate within the administration against apart-

---

[1]The original bill had called for a reduction of unemployment to 4 percent within five years and authorized the federal government to provide "last resort" jobs to reach this target. Instead, the final version relied primarily on the private sector to create jobs and attempted to set a brake on federal spending by establishing a goal of 3 percent inflation within five years.

heid in South Africa and for establishing closer ties with newly independent African states. In August 1979, after it became known that Young had held an unauthorized meeting with agents of the Palestine Liberation Organization (PLO), an action contrary to Carter's Middle East policy, the ambassador was forced to resign. The appointment of another black, Donald F. McHenry, to succeed Young only partially repaired the damage to Carter's image in the black community.

In addition, the Young incident once again inflamed tensions between two of the most loyal elements of the Democratic coalition: blacks and Jews. Despite their long history of cooperation within the civil rights movement, since the late 1960s issues concerning affirmative action and the Middle East had strained relations between the groups. Jewish organizations had thrown their considerable weight behind Bakke's challenge to racial quotas, and black activists had called for recognition of a Palestinian homeland, a position they held as an act of solidarity with nonwhite, exploited people and one which they regarded as even handed. Blacks considered support for Bakke's case as inimical to their economic advancement, and Jews viewed deliberations with the PLO as a threat to the security of Israel. Proponents from each side worked to defuse the hostility, but events such as those prompting Young's departure heightened the conflict. Shortly after the U.N. ambassador left his job, tempers again flared. When Jesse L. Jackson, the director of People United to Save Humanity (PUSH)[2] and a former colleague of Young's in the SCLC, met with and embraced Yasser Arafat, the leader of the PLO, he occasioned a barrage of criticism from Jewish organizations.

THE ELECTION OF RONALD REAGAN

Troubled by these political splits, African-Americans had even more to worry about in the hard times that had befallen many residents of their communities. Between 1975 and 1980, the median income of blacks compared with whites dropped three points to 58 percent. The proportion of blacks without jobs hovered around 14 percent, double the rate for whites. That figure was bad enough,

[2]The name was later changed to People United to Serve Humanity.

but the 40 percent rate of unemployment for black teenagers, more than twice that of white youths, was even worse. The incidence of poverty among blacks was also greater than for whites, and the situation was deteriorating. In 1980, 33 percent of blacks compared with 10 percent of whites were impoverished. Much of their plight stemmed from the rise of single-parent families headed by women. At the end of the decade, 40 percent of black families lived in such households, and half of them experienced poverty. These deplorable conditions were aggravated by the spiraling inflation of the late 1970s, and the suffering continued as Afro-American activists could get neither the President nor Congress to exert sufficient leadership to mount a forceful attack on black problems.

Nonetheless, blacks did not abandon their quest for political power. While stalemated in the national arena, they continued their efforts at the local level. The greatest progress came in the South, where the civil rights movement served as a catalyst for political change. By 1980, over 50 percent of all black officeholders, nearly 2,500, resided in Dixie. In 1979, Richard Arrington won election as mayor of Birmingham, the scene of some of the most vicious racial strife during the freedom struggle. In the North and West, black mayors occupied city halls in major urban areas such as Detroit, Gary, Newark, and Los Angeles; and in the nation's capital, Marion Barry, an early leader of SNCC, ran the municipal government. On the down side, the annual rate of increase in the number of black elected officials was on the decline, falling from 13.5 percent in 1977 to 6.6 percent three years later. Moreover, blacks held only about 1 percent of the available elected positions in the nation overall, though they made up over 11 percent of the population. In the Voting Rights Act states of the South, where the minority population reached as high as 35 percent in Mississippi, blacks composed only 5 percent of elected officials.

The prospects for improvement did not appear too bright as the presidential election of 1980 took place. The Democrats renominated Carter after he beat back a challenge from Senator Kennedy, but his chances had been severely damaged by the inability of his government to bring a halt to galloping inflation and to obtain the release of fifty-three American hostages held in Iran since November 1979. However limited the incumbent's accomplishments in civil rights, a Carter victory offered greater hope for black advancement than did a win by his Republican opponent. Ronald Reagan, the former governor of California and opponent of the 1964 Civil Rights Act, held the states' rights philosophy of the right wing of his party and promised to reduce the federal commitment to civil rights enforcement and the Great Society economic programs that had benefited blacks substantially. He launched his campaign in the South with an appearance in Philadelphia, Mississippi, the location of the murders of three civil rights workers during the 1964 Freedom Summer, by pledging to "restore to state and local governments the powers that properly belonged to them." These views reflected Reagan's close ties with southern Republicans who had replaced the Democrats in the region as the fiercest opponents of civil rights measures.

Unlike in 1976, the black vote did not save Carter from defeat. Though Reagan won only 51 percent of the popular vote, he overwhelmed his Democratic rival in the electoral column with 489 votes. The incumbent received 41 percent of the popular vote total, with most of the remaining 8 percent going to Congressman John Anderson of Illinois, a liberal Republican running as an independent. Blacks cast the bulk of their ballots for Carter (estimates ranged from 85 to 90 percent), but their votes could not overcome the GOP contender's margins of victory in key industrial states of the Northeast and Midwest and in every southern state except Carter's home territory of Georgia. In spite of their lopsided support for the Democrat, black enthusiasm for Carter had waned. Whereas the turnout of the total voting-age black population was almost 4 percent higher than in 1976, the turnout of eligible registered voters was lower by nearly 3 percent. Because the number of black registrants had increased over the past four years, the percentages meant that many of those who had signed up to vote chose not to cast their ballots (see Table 2).

The elections not only thrust a conservative Republican into the White House, but they also spelled defeat for several prominent liberal Democrats in the Senate. Control of the upper chamber shifted to the GOP, which secured a net gain of twelve seats for a total of fifty-three. Among the losers were Gaylord Nelson of Wisconsin, Birch Bayh of Indiana, Frank Church of Idaho, and George McGovern of South Dakota, all of whom had been counted on as civil rights supporters in the past. The new Senate included an additional four Republicans from the South, which mirrored the improved GOP fortunes in the region in presidential and statewide

Table 2   Estimated National Black Voter Registration and Turnout in 1976 and 1980 Presidential Elections

	1976	1980
Voting-age population	15,398,000	16,967,000
Number registered	9,024,800	11,400,000
Number of voters	5,784,872	7,000,000
Turnout of registered voters, percent	64.1	61.4
Turnout of voting-age population, percent	37.6	41.3

SOURCE: Joint Center for Political Studies, *The Black Vote: Election '76* (Washington, D.C., 1977), 11; and Eddie N. Williams, "Black Political Progress in the 1970s: The Electoral Arena," in Michael B. Preston, Lenneal J. Henderson, Jr., and Paul Puryear, eds., *The New Black Politics* (New York: Longman, 1982), 103.

elections. Perhaps as distressing to black reformers as the upsurge of conservatism in the Senate, the Republican majority resulted in the selection of Strom Thurmond of South Carolina as chair of the powerful Judiciary Committee. Though Thurmond had made some accommodations to the black electorate that had swelled in his state since his Dixiecrat bid for the presidency in 1948, he still favored a sharp curtailment in federal spending and a relaxation of civil rights laws in the South.

On a slightly more encouraging note, the elections saw a net increase of one member in the Congressional Black Caucus, bringing its total to eighteen. Losing one nonvoting delegate seat from the Virgin Islands, the caucus picked up two new representatives from Los Angeles and Chicago. Another two seats passed from one black to another, while the rest were retained by incumbents. (Two years earlier Senator Edward Brooke of Massachusetts had lost his reelection bid for a third term.) Overall, the Democrats kept their majority in the House, 243-192, though the Republicans gained thirteen new legislators. At state and local levels, black officeholders grew by 2.6 percent to 5,020, still a modest figure but markedly higher than the 1,185 officials who had held office in 1969.

THE REAGAN ASSAULT AND HARD TIMES

Reagan's first term witnessed an expected assault on the racial front. The President set the tone of his administration in his appointment policy. Although he selected a black, Samuel Pierce, to sit in his Cabinet as secretary of housing and urban development, the chief executive disappointed black Republicans by falling short of reaching the number of top-level minority appointments made under Carter. Not merely the quantity but the ideological bent of the appointments troubled civil rights proponents. In making selections the President picked individuals who shared his concern that civil rights programs be limited in scope and not be used to practice "reverse discrimination."

Signaling this shift in direction was his handling of the Commission on Civil Rights. He turned this respected, independent investigative agency, operating since 1957 as a strong advocate for bold racial policies, into an organization that trumpeted the administration's retreat from affirmative remedies to combat the effects of racial bias in employment and education. To preside over this change, Reagan selected Clarence Pendleton as chair of the commission. A black Democrat turned Republican, Pendleton had worked for the Model Cities Program and served as executive director of the Urban League branch in San Diego, California. Despite his background, Pendleton denounced the notion that "all minority progress comes out of a civil rights or social service gun." He opposed busing and affirmative action as "bankrupt" policies, and argued that the "only way for blacks to get a real piece of the action is to get out there and compete in the marketplace and not rely solely on handouts and political favoritism."

As a defender of the free enterprise system and an opponent of restrictive federal regulation, the chief executive sought to weaken government enforcement of affirmative action plans for hiring minorities. Though Reagan intensely disliked compensatory programs, the Supreme Court had upheld, with qualifications, the principle of affirmative action in *Bakke* and in a series of cases following it. As recently as 1980, the high tribunal sustained congressional legislation requiring that at least 10 percent of all federal funds for public works projects go to minority contractors in order to rectify past discrimination. The Reagan administration tried to confine the impact of such rulings. The administration narrowed the coverage of its affirmative action guidelines to exclude federal vendors with less than 250 employees whereas previously the regulations had applied to firms with a minimum of 50 workers. According to the secretary of labor, the new standard exempted 75 percent of federal contractors. In a similar vein, William Bradford Reynolds, the assistant attorney general in charge of the Civil Rights Division, signaled an even further pullback from the concept of affirmative action as a legitimate means of promoting the constitutional rights of exploited groups. Reynolds opposed policies that entitled blacks and other minorities to benefits strictly on the basis of their race. Under his direction, the Justice Department office chiefly responsible for civil rights enforcement sought to provide employment relief only to individuals who could prove they had personally suffered from discrimination.

The Reagan administration also damaged civil rights interests by attempting to reverse a long-standing policy concerning racial discrimination in education. Since the 1960s, private academies had sprouted in the South as a refuge for white students fleeing court-ordered desegregation of public schools. In 1970, after the judiciary refused to allow segregated private academies the benefit of a federal tax exemption, the Internal Revenue Service promulgated regulations to carry out that decree. However, in January 1982, the President instructed the IRS to restore tax-exempt status to private schools like Bob Jones University, a religious institution in South Carolina that admitted blacks but banned interracial dating between coeds. The President agreed with the university's claim that removal of the tax exemption interfered with the First Amendment freedom of the school to practice its religious beliefs. Reagan's order, which nonetheless smacked of racism, also stemmed from his conservative opposition to government interference with private enterprise and to the establishment of coercive guidelines for mandating racial quotas in schools. After influential lawmakers and civil rights lobbyists fired a heavy round of criticism against Reagan's proposal, the President backed off. The Supreme Court eventually decided the issue against Reagan's position by approving the original IRS ruling denying tax exemptions to private schools that engaged in racial discrimination even if the policy conflicted with their religious practices.

The major political battle between Reagan and his civil rights opponents occurred over renewal of the Voting Rights Act. For black Americans this landmark law had come to represent one of the last vestiges of federal commitment to racial advancement in an era of diminishing expectations, and they considered the measure essential for continuing to open up government to minority participation. As the Reagan administration slashed the budget with deep cuts in social programs, critics looked to the power of the ballot as a crucial means of challenging these reductions. "The only real safety net that minorities and the poor can rely on is their capacity to influence the political system," remarked Eddie N. Williams, the president of the Joint Center for Political Studies. Toward that end, the suffrage statute had effectively eliminated the major barriers to voter registration, but its enforcement machinery was still necessary to combat a new generation of obstacles—at-large elections, racial gerrymandering, discriminatory annexations—that diluted the strength of minority ballots cast at the polls.

With the act due for renewal in 1982, with Reagan in the White House, and with Republicans in control of the Senate, the bill's supporters took the precaution of starting their efforts a full year in advance. In addition to undertaking the customary fight to retain the special provisions requiring prior federal clearance of electoral changes and keeping designated jurisdictions from escaping coverage prematurely, the suffragists pursued a new challenge. In 1980, in a slim 5-to-4 decision, the Supreme Court ruled that in suits involving at-large election procedures, civil rights litigants had to prove that a municipality deliberately intended to weaken the vote of minorities. This opinion, in *City of Mobile v. Bolden*, posed a particular problem for blacks because most of the disputed at-large rules had been passed at the turn of the century, and their framers had usually couched their intentions in racially neutral language and in the spirit of reform. In contrast to this burdensome standard of proof, black plaintiffs and their attorneys wanted courts to judge the legality of at-large elections by their effect in permitting or denying blacks the opportunity to choose members of their own race to represent them. Thus, suffrage proponents wanted Congress to amend the Voting Rights Act to direct the judiciary to make discriminatory result as well as intent the standard for proving electoral bias.

The Reagan administration took a position on renewal that conformed with its opposition to race-conscious affirmative action remedies. In October 1981, after the House passed a ten-year-extension proposal containing a provision for an "effects" test in vote dilution suits, the President sought to persuade the Republican-dominated

Senate to modify it. The administration and its supporters charged that the bill's result-minded approach would promote proportional representation, which the President warned "would come down to whether all of society had to have an actual quota system" of minority elected officials. Echoing this view, the foes of "preferential treatment" portrayed themselves as standing for the true meaning of civil rights: the "color-blind ideal of equal opportunity for all."

Defenders of the measure denied any design to impose racial quotas on the electoral system. In contrast to the administration's, their view of equal opportunity allowed, indeed required, the government to take racial considerations into account in order to overcome the current effects of past discrimination. They believed that the Constitution safeguarded individual as well as group rights within the political process. The suffrage coalition, composed of the Congressional Black Caucus and civil rights, liberal, and labor groups, insisted that the bill did not sanction proportional representation or quotas, but only enabled the courts to consider whether certain rules had an unfair impact in lowering the chances for minorities to elect candidates of their own race. A civil rights attorney from Atlanta thought it inappropriate to raise the issue of proportional representation, "just as it is also pretty irrelevant to talk about any realistic opportunity within the existing electoral system because black voters had always been shut out, pure and simple."

From this clash of arguments, the Senate hammered out a compromise. Within the Republican majority, a contingent of racial moderates was not willing to abandon blacks, especially in their quest for something so basic to democracy as the right to vote. Led by Robert Dole of Kansas, the upper chamber agreed to an effect-oriented approach that permitted the courts to examine the "totality of circumstances" resulting in the denial of equal electoral opportunity for minorities. In practice, this reestablished the judicial standard in operation before the *Mobile* decision. At the same time, the lawmakers specifically rejected proportional representation as a valid remedy and affirmed their commitment to the Voting Rights Act by renewing it for another twenty-five years, the longest extension to date.

The final outcome illustrated that despite recent setbacks, blacks still commanded political influence in preserving hard-earned fundamental rights of citizenship. This was particularly evident in the South. With most southern senators refusing to join the filibuster waged by Jesse Helms, a North Carolina Republican, the obstructionist ploy failed miserably. Only four senators from Dixie, three Republicans and one independent, steadfastly declined to approve the measure, and even Strom Thurmond saw fit to cast his first vote ever in favor of a civil rights law. The expanded black electorate in the South, which served as a crucial balance of power in sending legislators to Washington, once again swayed the majority of the region's congressional lawmakers to stand behind the suffrage law. Given this overwhelming mandate, President Reagan signed the bill, praising it as proof of "our unbending commitment to voting rights."

Nevertheless, like Nixon before him, Reagan supported the principle of enfranchisement while attempting to weaken its implementation. Though the Justice Department continued to enforce the statute in conformity with the general policy outlines established by previous administrations, Assistant Attorney General Reynolds interpreted his responsibilities narrowly in clearing electoral procedures submitted by the South. He attempted to raise the standard for demonstrating racial discrimination and to shift the burden of proving it from state and local officials onto the victims. However, as was the case during the Nixon years, civil rights activists successfully persuaded both Congress and the Supreme Court to hold the Justice Department to strict enforcement of the law.

The Reagan administration's policies had a more devastating effect on the economic well-being of blacks than on their political clout. During his first two years in office, Reagan adopted anti-inflationary, budget-slashing programs that succeeded in bringing prices under control at the expense of rising unemployment. African-Americans suffered disproportionately. In 1982, over 17 percent of the black work force could not find jobs, compared with 8.6 percent for whites. The ratio of black families living in poverty jumped from 32.4 percent to 35.7 percent, about three times the figure for impoverished whites. Black poverty continued to be associated with female-headed households: 56 percent of black women (compared with 36 percent of white women) who headed families fell below the subsistence level. The last two years of Reagan's first term brought a measure of economic recovery, but blacks still suffered harshly. Unemployment fell to about 14 percent, and the proportion of the poverty-stricken declined to just under 34 percent. These "improvements," however, did not enable black families to close the gap between their income and that of white families. By the mid-1980s, black families earned a median income of 57.6 percent of whites', a ratio about the same as at the beginning of the decade.

Although part of the deterioration in black material conditions could be attributed to structural defects affecting the American economy in general, the Reagan administration exacerbated the problems. Drastic cuts in or outright elimination of job programs like CETA; reductions in food stamp distribution, health services, and welfare eligibility; and the removal of guaranteed student loans punched holes in the "safety net" of federal assistance to low-income workers and the poor. For instance, rollbacks in educational support were reflected in the decline in black matriculation in four-year colleges from 10.4 percent in 1978 to 9.2 percent in 1984. Not surprisingly then, a 1982 public opinion survey revealed that 85 percent of blacks believed the Reagan administration was going too far in slicing government spending for social welfare programs. In contrast, only 37 percent of whites shared this view.

The President's fiscal policies also accentuated class divisions within the black community. During the 1970s, expanding opportunities arising from desegregation and affirmative action programs had swelled the size of the black middle class, at the same time as the number of poor black families increased. While the share of black families earning more than $50,000 annually nearly doubled—from 4.5 percent in 1970 to 8.8 percent—by the mid-1980s, the number of black households with incomes under $10,000 comprised 30.3 percent of the total, a leap of 11 percent. To achieve middle-class status, black families depended on two wage earners and employment in public-sector jobs to a greater degree than did white middle-class households. The recession and budget cuts of Reagan's first two years in office hurt both the poor who relied on declining welfare assistance and middle-class families dependent upon government employment. But the economic recovery after 1982 mostly aided middle-class blacks who had the skills and educational background to take advantage of the new job openings.

In stark contrast to the majority of African-Americans and their elected representatives, some middle-class black professionals and businesspeople endorsed Reagan's conservative brand of government retrenchment and free-market economics. Such notable intellectuals as Thomas Sowell, an economics professor at Stanford University, lent their voices to the attack on affirmative action and welfare programs. Like Reagan, they blamed the enduring poverty in black communities on New Deal–Great Society liberalism. According to their viewpoint, these programs reduced individual incentive to find jobs and fostered out-of-wedlock births and single-parent households. These black "neoconservatives" charged established black political and civil rights leaders with perpetuating this cycle of government dependency and called upon African-Americans to help themselves by adopting traditional values of individual initiative, competition, and hard work. Agreeing that black communities should do more to solve their own problems, their opponents responded to this criticism by accusing Reagan's conservative supporters of blaming the victims for the social ills resulting from generations of systematic racism and economic exploitation in the United States.

HAROLD WASHINGTON, CHICAGO, AND THE POLITICS OF RENEWAL

In the political arena, blacks had been struggling to gain greater electoral power in their communities since the early days of the civil rights movement. In the decade and a half following passage of the 1965 Voting Rights Act, black politicians had been striving to put into practice many of the goals of the freedom struggle. Much remained to be done. The damaging impact of the Reagan retrenchment helped reenergize blacks at the local level to seek to gain a fair share of the scarce economic resources available. At the same time, the black electorate looked forward to the possibility of challenging Reagan's reelection and moving the White House in a progressive direction more compatible with their interests and needs.

The city of Chicago provided an excellent opportunity for blacks to lead the way in revitalizing Afro-American politics. Since the New Deal, blacks had served as clients of the Democratic machine that ran the "Windy City," an arrangement that afforded them some influence in municipal affairs without any real power. Their elected leaders, such as Congressman William Dawson, had faithfully delivered the black vote for the organization's candidates and in return received the spoils of patronage and access to city hall. Their constituents obtained the benefits typically conferred by political machines, but these token rewards for their loyalty failed to make up for city officials neglect of widespread problems of poor housing, inferior education, and lack of police protection. In fact, black collaboration with the dominant white machine had not prevented Chicago's neighborhoods and schools from becoming among the most segregated in the nation.

For two decades following his election as mayor, in 1955, Richard J. Daley, the "Boss," displayed the power of the machine to manage black politics and stifle challenges to its rule. Daley, who had first won victory largely on the strength of black votes, operated a kind of "plantation politics" that treated blacks as subjects rather than equal ruling partners and placed white interests ahead of black concerns. One of his black critics who successfully broke from the machine described the mayor as a "plantation master ...who keeps his darkies loyal to him by doling out small political favors...[and] is playing the same old 'divide and conquer' game his forefathers experienced when they made some slaves 'house servants' and kept others out in the field." In the mid-1960s, when civil rights leaders launched a determined attack on racial discrimination in housing and education, Daley drew upon his black machine loyalists to help outmaneuver the insurgents. Even Martin Luther King, Jr., who, in 1966, had been invited by local civil rights leaders to direct the campaign against racism, proved little match for the "Boss" and his entrenched black political allies.

However, during the 1970s black Chicagoans showed increasing signs of independence from machine domination. In 1972, a disgruntled black electorate aided in the defeat of the incumbent state's attorney, Edward V. Hanrahan, a law-and-order candidate. A few years earlier he had authorized a raid against the militant Black Panthers that left two of their leaders dead and four wounded under questionable circumstances. Black voters also successfully challenged the Daley organization in several congressional and aldermanic contests. The greatest chance for blacks to declare their political independence came only after the death of Mayor Daley, in 1976. In a special election to choose Daley's successor, black voters lined up behind the machine-picked candidate, but three years later over 60 percent cast their ballots for Jane Byrne, who ran without the Democratic organization's backing against the incumbent.

These encouraging signs notwithstanding, blacks still remained subject to the effects of machine rule. The organization had depended on low levels of black participation so that its ward heelers and precinct captains could most effectively control those who bothered to show up at the polls. Furthermore, by placing the party's interests above the needs of the minority community, machine politicians discouraged many blacks from seeing how their electoral participation might make a difference in improving their lives. In 1977, only 27.5 percent of eligible blacks turned out to vote for mayor despite the candidacy of an antimachine black, State Senator Harold Washington. Two years later, the black turnout scarcely climbed to 34 percent. Racial polarization compounded blacks' problem. In elections that pitted the races against each other, black contestants stood very little chance of attracting white votes to achieve a winning margin.

For blacks the Byrne administration proved to be a severe disappointment. Once installed in power, the mayor made her peace with the Democratic regulars and dashed any hope of reform. Instead, she tried to diminish the voting strength of blacks on the city council, and replaced black appointees on municipal boards with whites. Although blacks had contributed to her mayoral victory, she calculated that her chances for reelection were greater if she mobilized white ethnic voters, who had long supported the Democratic organization. These moves galvanized black activists to oppose the mayor. In June 1982, they mounted a well-publicized and highly coordinated boycott of Byrne's ChicagoFest, a summer festival and exposition designed to promote local business. This successful display of unity encouraged blacks to transform their protest activities into an electoral movement challenging the mayor at the polls. One of the boycott's organizers, the Reverend Jesse Jackson, of Operation PUSH, expressed the anger of blacks who felt neglected by city hall politicians: "We are not bound by Chicago plantation politics. We must aggressively use our dollars and our votes."

Merging protest and electoral politics, Chicago blacks struggled for empowerment with a fervor reminiscent of the civil rights era. As they had in the South during the 1960s, voter registration drives rallied blacks around a common battle for freedom. The task was much bigger than getting people to exercise their civic responsibility of voting; it aimed, as one black leader asserted, "to accomplish a dramatic shift in the political scales in favor of those who have been ignored, used, and abused for too long." Showing the way, an alliance of groups representing Chicago's poorest, most politically disfranchised neighborhoods emerged to conduct voter enrollment campaigns. People Organized for Welfare and Employment Rights (POWER), an organization originally established to protest cutbacks in state welfare funding, spearheaded the registration drives by operating in public assistance offices and unemployment centers. More than 200 community groups helped get their message across to congregations in black churches and to audiences listening to "soul" stations on the radio. Largely as a result of this impressive grassroots coalition, by the fall of 1982 around 150,000 blacks had added their names to the suffrage lists. Moreover, this community-wide campaign succeeded in bringing up the enrollment of eligible blacks to just over 86 percent, a figure that exceeded the 78 percent registration rate for whites.

This surge in enrollment placed blacks in a strong position to unseat Mayor Byrne in her bid for reelection in 1983. By this time, the black population had grown to 40 percent in the city; Hispanics constituted another 12 percent of its residents. As in other places with a large Afro-American population, black Chicagoans entertained serious hopes for electing a member of their race as mayor. Owing once again to a formidable display of community organizing and group solidarity, blacks chose a consensus candidate to compete for city hall. Under the direction of Chicago Black United Communities, over 30,000 blacks had participated in surveys to determine who they desired to run. From what amounted to a carefully planned but informal plebiscite, Harold Washington emerged as the top choice from over ninety prominent names.

Washington commanded respect for his extensive political experience. A graduate of Northwestern University Law School, he had served as a member of the Illinois legislature and as a representative in Congress. Once an ally of the Daley machine, he had broken away to establish strong credentials as an independent reformer who spoke out for liberal, consumer, and civil rights causes. Elected to Congress in 1980, he fought for extension of the Voting Rights Act and battled against the Reagan administration's spending cuts for jobs and welfare assistance. In 1977, Washington had run in the Democratic primary for mayor, but with the black electorate poorly mobilized, he received only 11 percent of the total vote. Heartened by the outpouring of new registrants in 1982 and convinced that this time he had a chance to win, the congressman agreed to run. In doing so, he reminded blacks that after years of giving white candidates their votes without receiving an adequate share of power in return, the point had arrived when "it's our turn." Though constructing his campaign on a solid black foundation, Washington fully realized that he needed progressive white and Hispanic votes to win in a city where blacks composed a minority of the population.

Against all odds and predictions, Washington won a narrow victory in the Democratic primary against two prominent white contenders. In addition to Byrne, the congressman faced Richard M. Daley, the son of the former mayor, who considered himself his fa-

Harold Washington campaigning for mayor of Chicago in 1983.
(AP/Wide World Photos)

ther's rightful successor. In this three-way contest, Washington captured 37 percent of the ballots to 33 percent for the incumbent and 30 percent for the heir of the "Boss." The white vote divided nearly evenly between Byrne and Daley, while the congressman garnered nearly 85 percent of the black votes. The victor benefited from the outpouring to the polls of newly registered blacks. In 1983, the turnout of blacks in the primary soared to 64 percent of the voting-age population, up from 34 percent in the previous Democratic mayoral race. Approximately 56 percent of Washington's black voters reported that they had registered during the massive enrollment drives of the year before. Though the white turnout rate had also grown since 1979, it had fallen five percentage points behind that of blacks. The winner also secured about 12 percent of the Hispanic and 4 percent of white ballots cast, but their combined votes amounted to slightly less than his margin of victory. Thus, Washington won on the strength of unprecedented support from blacks and the close split in the white vote for his opponents.

Customarily, the winner of the Democratic primary in Chicago was a sure bet to triumph over the Republican in the general election, but when that winner was black all wagers were off. As the earlier contest had shown, the electorate in Chicago voted mainly along racial lines. In a city where whites comprised over 53 percent of the registered voters, unless Washington made greater inroads among whites and Latinos than he had in the primary, he stood a good chance of losing. This was especially true in a showdown with a single white opponent around whom the majority white electorate could unite.

The Republican candidate, State Representative Bernard Epton, made Washington's character and race the dominant campaign issues. Hammering away at Washington's ethics, the GOP nominee attacked his rival's record, which included a conviction for income tax evasion and a suspension of his law license. By the usual standards of Chicago's political morality these indiscretions, for which Washington acknowledged his mistakes, were relatively minor. However, most whites were willing to abandon their party's nominee more so on the basis of his skin color than his ethical transgressions. One of the many Democratic officials who defected from Washington justified his decision in this way: "The people in my area just don't want a black mayor—it's as simple as that." Epton's campaign supporters fed on this racial animosity by adopting the

slogan "Epton For Mayor. Before It's Too Late," and by passing out
handbills warning in vulgar language that a takeover of city hall
would spell doom for Chicago. These negative comments prompted
Washington to respond in kind, and he attacked Epton's integrity,
his cozy legislative relationship with private insurance companies,
and his emotional stability. At the same time, the congressman took
the higher road in urging reform-minded white voters to join his
campaign assault against the Democratic machine.

On election day, Washington won with a fraction over 50 percent of the votes cast in the closest mayoral clash since 1919. As
expected, the voting was polarized by race. The Democratic nominee owed his victory to the nearly unanimous backing (99.5 percent) he received from blacks, which accounted for approximately
77 percent of his total vote. Not only did Washington's candidacy
attract solid black approval, but it also succeeded in mobilizing an
extraordinarily high black turnout of 73 percent of the voting-age
population, surpassing the white figure of 67 percent. In contrast,
Epton obtained 95 percent of his ballots from whites, and the Republican candidate won over eight out of ten white Democrats. The
victor scored poorly among the city's Irish, Italian, and Polish voters, the mainstays of the Daley machine, who deserted the black
Democratic candidate in droves to back Epton. Their racial fears
and animosities were strong enough to override their traditional
ethnic allegiances to whoever triumphed in the Democratic primary. "They responded to Washington's race rather than to his partisan affiliation," Dianne Pinderhughes concluded. "They became
whites, as opposed to Americans of European descent."

There were key exceptions to the racial division at the polls that
helped cement Washington's slender 46,000-vote victory. The triumphant mayor-elect captured almost three-quarters of the Hispanic vote. The more than 45,000 votes marked a stunning jump six
times greater than the number he had garnered in the primary. In
addition, Washington won a small but sufficient portion of whites to
his side. About 12 percent of those who participated provided more
than double the number of white ballots cast for him in the Democratic primary. A large share of these votes came from liberal Jews
who put race and religion aside (Epton was Jewish) and welcomed
Washington's reform message.

Washington captured the mayor's office, but he did not immediately gain control over the city government. Democrats on the

municipal council outnumbered Washington supporters and brawled them to a stalemate. These heated battles reminded one journalist of "Mississippi in 1964, where the Freedom Democratic Party challenged the segregationist regulars." After court-ordered redistricting left the pro- and anti-Washington factions at equal strength, the mayor was able to cast tie-breaking votes in his favor. Like other black mayors in major cities throughout the country, Washington recognized that he needed the cooperation of influential white civic leaders in order to govern, and he brought them into his ruling partnership with blacks, Latinos, and reformers to replace the old party stalwarts.

The mayor promoted the financial development of Chicago, which most profited the city's elites, while at the same time he did not neglect minority economic concerns. He initiated a vigorous affirmative action program in municipal hiring and in awarding government contracts, which aided black businesspeople and professionals. Also, he continued to work to relieve the plight of working-class and poor blacks, who had constituted the backbone of his candidacy and election. Though many problems lingered, the reform mayor took significant steps to increase the availability of low-income housing and provide such public services as health care and police protection more equitably than in the past.[3]

Much of the pattern in Washington's election was repeated in the victory of W. Wilson Goode as the first black mayor of Philadelphia, in May 1983. Goode had compiled a strong record as chair of the Pennsylvania Public Utility Commission and as managing director of Philadelphia. In a city in which blacks comprised 40 percent of the population, he competed in the Democratic primary against the former mayor, Frank Rizzo, the darling of the city's white ethnic groups, who had inflamed racial passions during his two previous terms in office. Surprisingly, this contest did not witness the bitter racial rhetoric of the Chicago campaign. In beating Rizzo with 53 percent of the votes, Goode did slightly better than Washington had against Epton. He galvanized black voters into

[3]In 1987, Mayor Washington won reelection to a second term, but shortly thereafter, he suffered a fatal heart attack. His death occasioned a power struggle in the city council to choose a successor. The black alderman Eugene Sawyer was selected, largely with white support, while the majority of black legislators favored another candidate, Timothy Evans. In 1989, the effects of this battle still divided the Sawyer and Evans forces within the black community, which led to the election of Richard M. Daley as mayor.

turning out in high numbers. He received 98 percent of their ballots, and secured a small but slightly higher proportion of white crossover support than his Chicago counterpart. Having won the mayoral nomination in this largely Democratic city, the black candidate went on to victory with 55 percent of the vote in the general election against two white candidates. Yet Goode encountered strong racial sentiment against him. The election returns indicated that white ethnic voters in the City of Brotherly Love were just as strongly opposed to Goode as were their ethnic cousins in Chicago to Mayor Washington.

The racial consciousness and solidarity tapped by Washington and Goode in their respective campaigns also were evident in the heightened efforts of blacks throughout the nation to become politically engaged. The victories in Chicago and Philadelphia convinced many blacks that their votes could make a difference. In addition to such positive reinforcement, African-Americans had an increased incentive to vent their negative feelings toward the Reagan administration at the ballot box. The success of the civil rights coalition in strengthening the Voting Rights Act against White House opposition focused renewed attention on the franchise as a key instrument in forwarding black interests.

Spurred on by anti-Reagan sentiments and rearmed with a powerful suffrage weapon, the NAACP, VEP, SCLC, and other organizations stepped up attempts to enroll additional black voters. The largest increases came in the South, where such intensive drives had taken place for over two decades. From 1980 to 1984, black voter registration in the region climbed by 14 percent, with the greatest gains occurring in the Voting Rights Act states of Alabama (37 percent), North Carolina (28 percent), and Mississippi (20 percent). Furthermore, throughout the country black political participation rose in response to active campaigning by black candidates for office and to heated state and local contests in which white politicians cultivated black votes. In the off-year congressional elections of 1982, minority turnout jumped by nearly 6 percent, a notable increase over the figure in 1978. Reflecting this revived spurt of interest, the number of black elected officials nationwide grew by 8.6 percent between 1982 and 1983, the steepest rise in seven years.

One of those winners, Harvey Gantt, became mayor of Charlotte, North Carolina, in 1983. He forged a coalition of blacks and whites to emerge victorious in this white-majority city. His career underscored the close connection between the civil rights struggle and electoral politics. As a youth in neighboring South Carolina, Gantt had participated in the early sit-in protests and become the first black student to desegregate Clemson University, where he received a degree in architecture. His generation, he remarked, is "the group now that are becoming the mayors." Though he had come to substitute negotiations for demonstrations as his preferred tactic, Gantt did not forget the lessons of his previous struggles. "I'm...a believer," the mayor affirmed, "in taking the benefits brought about by...all the other direct-action kinds of things and molding them into long-term, institutional changes that would occur, systematic changes that have occurred in our society."

This political reawakening stemmed from the desire of blacks to continue the process of empowerment that had begun with the emergence of the civil rights movement. As economic conditions deteriorated in the late 1970s and early 1980s, black communities mobilized to obtain a greater share of electoral power in order to meet the unfulfilled material needs of their residents. Though successful in many towns and cities across the nation, for the most part they had been unable to check the wave of political conservatism in national affairs ushered in by the Reagan administration. Blacks and their liberal white allies did hold onto many of their civil rights gains through victories in Congress and the judiciary. But as long as Reagan remained in office, the powerful institution of the presidency would continue to order priorities in a manner that limited advances toward racial equality. At a time when African-Americans were flexing their political muscles locally, the goal of capturing the White House and reshaping its agenda became as natural as it was essential.

Chapter 7

In Search
of Legitimacy

In the four decades since the Second World War, African-Americans gradually, if not grudgingly, had won a considerable measure of acceptance for their reenfranchisement as full citizens of the United States. Where blacks gained public office, including those at the head of major cities throughout the country, whites generally endorsed the validity of their rule. Undoubtedly, the struggle for political empowerment produced legislative conflicts in Washington and fierce opposition both in the South and the North, as witnessed in Chicago, but, overall, white Americans acknowledged the principle of majority rule and the sanctity of free elections. Whites have largely recognized, that is, the legitimacy of black political representation as an extension of democratic values and the norms of fair play. Moreover, these basic tenets of the political culture received reinforcement from the nation's Cold War ideology, which contrasted American freedom with Soviet totalitarianism. Condemning the Soviet Union for stifling free elections abroad, the United States could not easily tolerate racist restrictions on ballot boxes on its own shores. Besides, federal enforcement of the Voting Rights Act kept in check the resistance of those whites who stubbornly refused to concede the legitimacy of black political power.

Both the considerable progress blacks had made in the electoral arena and their frustration with not having achieved a great deal more prompted black political leaders to focus their attention on the battle for the White House. Within the American political system perhaps nothing reflects the legitimacy of minority-group participation more than competition for the presidency. "The Presidential election is the centerpiece of the U.S. political process," the political scientist Mack H. Jones observed, "and therefore every

222

discrete political faction should be expected to use the quadrennial election in some way to advance its interests." To the extent that American political leaders set out broad agendas and debate specific policy objectives, they do so during presidential elections. The chief executive, the nation's highest elected official, plays the key role in focusing attention on a problem, in identifying a course of action to address it, and in rallying legislative and public support behind efforts to solve it. Not since Lyndon Johnson had an occupant of the Oval Office assigned a high priority to the needs of blacks and other exploited groups. Unless the presidency once again became a platform for the cause of racial equality, African-Americans would continue to find it hard to catch up politically and economically with other citizens.

Previously, the black electorate had wielded considerable influence in presidential elections and contributed significantly to the winning margins of Democratic nominees, most recently in the election of Jimmy Carter in 1976. Still, no black candidate had mounted a strong challenge for the top office in the land. Representative Shirley Chisholm of New York had actively campaigned in the Democratic presidential primaries in 1972, but her effort attracted scant support. Not only a black, she was also a woman in a nation that simply was unprepared to cast aside considerations of race and gender in selecting its chief executive. Having won reenfranchisement scarcely a few years before, blacks did not constitute a large enough bloc of voters to turn Chisholm's hopes into a serious bid. However, since the early seventies black political muscle had developed sufficiently to elect mayors of major metropolitan areas as well as a growing contingent of county, state, and national lawmakers.

By the middle of Reagan's first term, the possibility of a black presidential challenge began to take shape. Upset by the President's economic policies, which disproportionately raised the level of black unemployment and poverty, influential blacks joined together to map out a strategy to combat those worsening conditions. After several months of discussions, on June 20, 1983, a group of elected officials, known as the Black Leadership Family, sponsored the idea of an Afro-American presidential bid. The mayoral victory of Harold Washington earlier in the year heavily shaped their thinking. His candidacy had served to mobilize the black electorate in record numbers and at the same time attracted enough Latinos and whites to form a winning coalition. "We've got to be involved in mainstream political activity," Washington declared. "That's what's happening here in Chicago. And that's the lesson that's going out across the country."

In striving for the presidency, blacks naturally looked to compete within the Democratic party. Though black voters had occasionally supported moderate-to-liberal Republican candidates in local and statewide elections, since the formation of FDR's New Deal coalition they stood firmly behind Democratic presidential nominees. In 1980, blacks had accounted for about one-quarter of the ballots cast for Jimmy Carter and remained the most loyal element within the Democratic fold. The party of Roosevelt, Truman, Kennedy, and Johnson opened its doors to increased minority representation after 1964; however, many black Democrats believed increasingly that their party had come to take their votes for granted. Given their overwhelming support for Democratic standard-bearers, they expected to obtain more decision-making positions within the party and to fashion programs that more forcefully addressed black concerns. They also worried that Democratic officials, in the hope of recapturing the votes of white conservatives who had become Reagan Republicans, were seeking to modify their position at the expense of the black faithful. Thus, by contending for the Democratic presidential nomination, blacks hoped to boost their leverage within the party and help pick the candidate most sensitive to their interests.

JESSE JACKSON FOR PRESIDENT

With these considerations in mind, the Reverend Jesse L. Jackson chose to launch his candidacy for the presidency. He received inspiration from the example of fellow Chicagoan Harold Washington. The mayor's come-from-behind victory, Jackson concluded, "demonstrated that while some will join us if we assert ourselves, without such aggressiveness no one else will lead our fight for equitable representation." He questioned whether Democratic leaders sufficiently appreciated the contribution blacks made to their party's fortunes. In the case of Washington, top national Democrats, such as Walter Mondale and Edward Kennedy, did not enter his corner until after he had beaten his white rivals in the primary and faced only a Republican hurdle to the city's highest office. Jackson believed that his candidacy would test whether white leaders were ready to accept blacks on an equal basis or whether blacks would continue to play a "Harlem Globetrotter" role, giving the Democratic party "its soul, its excitement, its rhythm, its margin of victory, and yet not be allowed to set any policy."

Jackson's foray into electoral politics grew out of his involvement in the civil rights struggle of the 1960s. As a student at North Carolina Agricultural and Technical State University in Greensboro in the early sixties, Jackson had led demonstrations in the city that spawned the sit-in movement. Subsequently, he became a staff member of the SCLC, and established his base of operations in Chicago after Dr. King directed a desegregation campaign there. He headed SCLC's Operation Breadbasket, a project that applied economic pressure on white-owned businesses to open up job opportunities for blacks, and on April 4, 1968, he was part of King's entourage when the civil rights leader was assassinated in Memphis. In the early 1970s, he broke with King's designated successor, the Reverend Ralph D. Abernathy, and created Operation PUSH as his own organization to carry on the work he had begun with the SCLC.

Though Jackson had not held public office in Chicago, he actively participated in its political life and supported the reform forces opposing the Daley machine. At the 1972 Democratic convention, he was a coleader of the interracial group that successfully challenged the credentials and unseated the delegation headed by the Chicago boss. From his base of operations at PUSH, Jackson initiated economic boycotts, held voter registration drives, furnished campaign workers, and conducted a weekly radio broadcast that publicized concerns voiced by the black community. By linking protest with electoral politics and mobilizing local communities to shape national agendas, he carried on the tradition of the civil rights movement.

A minister himself, Jackson also reflected the close relationship between the black church and Afro-American politics. During the civil rights movement clergymen had opened their churches to mass meetings and voter registration drives and preached sermons that combined the themes of personal redemption through Christ with social justice through protest. The church was a critical component of the black liberation battle because it was one of the few institutions exclusively under black control and capable of reaching a mass audience. The Reverend Jackson underscored the historic importance of the church in reminding blacks "that we were not brought from Africa to be white people's slaves. But perhaps [we] were sent here by God to save the nation." His political mission received the endorsement of the National Baptist Convention, the largest black religious body in the country, whose president, T. J. Jemison, had led a pioneering bus boycott in Baton Rouge in 1953.

More than an electoral campaign, Jackson's candidacy resembled a civil rights crusade. It attracted campaign staff such as the Reverend C. T. Vivian, who like Jackson had fought in the front lines of the freedom struggle during the 1960s. Many of those who worked on his behalf did so in recognition "of the unfulfilled objectives of Martin Luther King and the civil rights movement and to warn... that the movement's earlier gains were in danger." And the candidate clearly tied his current challenge to past civil rights efforts. Shortly before announcing his intention to seek the presidency, at a rally honoring Dr. King and commemorating the twentieth anniversary of the march on Washington, Jackson revived the spirit of that historic occasion by proclaiming: "Our day has come. From slaveship to championship...[f]rom the outhouse to the courthouse to the White House, we will march on."

Just as blacks once marched to recover the right to vote, they responded to Jackson's campaign by descending on courthouses and registration offices to sign up for the ballot. Jackson stirred memories of civil rights days by embarking on a "Southern Crusade" for voter registration that built upon the intensive local efforts of civic groups and civil rights organizations, such as the NAACP, to enroll additional blacks. He also took every available opportunity to prod the Reagan Justice Department to enforce the Voting Rights Act more vigorously, and he even succeeded in cajoling Assistant Attorney General William Bradford Reynolds to travel to Mississippi and witness suffrage violations for himself. In one notable instance, the persistent Jackson persuaded the usually reticent Reynolds to join him in singing "We Shall Overcome" at a rally. In the eleven southern states some 695,000 new black voters registered between 1980 and 1984, (see Table 3), with a considerable share of them lured out by Jackson's appeal. One survey indicated that 67 percent of recent registrants attributed their interest in enrolling to the Jackson campaign.

Jesse Jackson, on the right, leading the procession at the 1983 march on Washington. Next to him, from right to left, are Walter Fauntroy, the Washington, D.C., delegate to Congress; Coretta Scott King, widow of the slain civil rights leader; and Joseph Lowery, president of the SCLC. (Jim Wilson/New York Times Pictures)

His roots deeply sunk into the soil of civil rights, Jackson ventured to cultivate the field of presidential politics. According to a member of his campaign staff, Jackson's "genius lay in linking nonelectoral forms of political mobilization and protest with traditional electoral politics." The minister's charismatic personality, his ability to arouse masses of blacks at rallies and voter registration drives, and his support network in churches throughout black communities furnished him with valuable resources to attract a substantial following. By a wide margin over any other contender, 51 percent of African-Americans rated him the most important black leader in the United States. However, the ability to mount effective protests and deliver inspiring oratory would not translate into

Table 3 Black Voter Registration in the South, 1968–1984[a]

	1968	1976	1980	1982	1984
Alabama	56.7	58.4	55.8	69.7	69.2
Arkansas	67.5	94.0	57.2	63.9	60.9
Florida	62.1	61.1	58.3	59.7	55.5
Georgia	56.1	74.8	48.6	50.4	49.8
Louisiana	59.3	63.0	60.7	61.1	62.5
Mississippi	54.4	60.7	62.3	64.2	68.2
North Carolina	55.3	54.8	51.3	50.9	59.7
South Carolina	50.8	56.5	53.7	53.9	49.8
Tennessee	72.8	66.4	64.0	66.1	67.1
Texas	83.1	65.0	56.0	49.5	59.1
Virginia	58.4	54.7	53.2	49.5	50.7
Total	62.0	63.1	55.8	56.5	58.5

[a]Estimated percentage of voting-age blacks registered.

SOURCE: The 1968 figures are from David Garrow, *Protest at Selma* (New Haven, Conn.: Yale University Press, 1978), 189. The remaining figures are from U.S. Department of Commerce, Bureau of the Census, *Statistical Abstract of the United States*, annual (Washington, D.C.), 1976, 406; 1981, 495; 1982–1983, 488; 1985, 253.

real victories at the ballot box without a campaign that reached out to a broad segment of the Democratic electorate and brought large numbers of voters to the polls. Furthermore, as a civil rights organizer Jackson could devise novel tactics aimed at producing social change from outside the conventional political system, but as an aspirant for his party's nomination he had to operate within the confines of the Democratic organization and play by its rules. Ballots, not ballyhoo, counted in electoral victories.

Jackson acknowledged these political realities and sought to expand his base beyond the black community. He tried to fashion a "rainbow coalition" that attracted the dispossessed of all races— poor whites, Latinos, Native Americans, and Asians, as well as blacks. He hoped to draw upon those elements of the Democratic party that felt locked out of the process of decision-making. Intending to shift the ideological tilt of the party toward the left, Jackson argued that it could win against the conservative and popular Reagan only by gaining the backing of the millions of Americans who felt disaffected and no longer bothered to cast a ballot. In 1980,

Reagan had won in sixteen states by a margin of victory of less than 5 percent. A Democratic candidate who enticed higher percentages of ordinarily nonparticipating blacks and whites to the voting booths, he argued, could improve the party's presidential outlook in 1984.

Working with an assortment of civil rights activists, community organizers, antinuclear advocates, feminists, and others who championed progressive social causes, Jackson devised a "rainbow" agenda to incorporate into the Democratic platform. In the manner of Dr. King, he attacked a host of ills—racism, militarism, and materialism—that plagued not only blacks but all Americans. Making peace a priority, Jackson criticized Reagan's aggressive Cold War policies and called for stepped-up negotiations with the Soviets, a pledge from the United States not to deploy nuclear weapons in a first-strike capacity, a revamped approach toward the Caribbean that emphasized diplomacy instead of military might to resolve disputes, firm opposition to apartheid in South Africa, and a solution to Middle Eastern hostilities that recognized the Palestinian right to a homeland. The candidate envisioned that peace abroad would foster economic justice at home. By reducing the military budget 20 percent, Jackson claimed, the United States could reallocate its financial resources to create jobs and assist the poor. He would replace Reaganism, with its tax advantages for the wealthy and its deregulation of large corporations, with an economics of compassion that favored working people and the impoverished.

According to Jackson, the key to these changes came through political empowerment of alienated Americans. Notwithstanding that many of his proposals were considered too radical for mainstream Democrats, the candidate reflected the traditional liberal position that the remedy to social and economic problems rested in the ballot. In this vein, he made vigorous enforcement of the Voting Rights Act central to his campaign. An electorate that was expanded to include more blacks, Latinos, and poor people would presumably enhance the election possibilities of candidates sympathetic to progressive goals. If that happened, Jackson foresaw a chain of events producing sweeping reforms throughout society. For example, responsive elected officials would pass the equal rights amendment, and "since 70 percent of all poor children live in a house headed by a women where there is no man," Jackson contended, "to enfranchise women is to protect children." Further-

more, he envisioned women workers allying themselves with organized labor to end state right-to-work laws that hampered union
organization. Thus, through beefed-up implementation of the Voting Rights Act, a measure originally crafted to help blacks, other
exploited groups in society would ultimately gain protection and
security.

Jackson's assault on the runoff primary fit in with this line of
thinking. Used chiefly in the South, this procedure required that
if no candidate received a majority of the vote on the first ballot, a
second contest be held between the two top contenders to determine the winner. This system had come into effect at the beginning
of the twentieth century during a period of one-party rule, when
victory in the Democratic primary was tantamount to election. It
was also part of a package of racially inspired laws that successfully
disfranchised black southerners. After blacks regained the right to
vote and began competing in Democratic primaries against a field
of white candidates, they often found their path blocked by the majority runoff requirement. A black officeseeker might gain a plurality in the first election, especially if whites split their votes among
several candidates, only to lose in a head-to-head contest with the
remaining white opponent, as the electorate divided along racial
lines. Where blacks comprised a minority of the voters their
chances of winning a second primary were slim. Keeping in mind
that candidates such as Harold Washington might not have won if
they had had to survive a runoff primary, Jackson urged the elimination of this practice.

In addition, he wanted to change Democratic party rules that
hampered minority contestants like himself in pursuing the presidential nomination. The Democrats required that primary candidates obtain at least 20 percent of the vote cast in a congressional
district to gain a single delegate to the national convention. In only
86 of 425 congressional districts did the black population reach 25
percent of the total, barely enough to aid a black aspirant. Consequently, Jackson sought to convince Democratic leaders to lower
the threshold requirement to no more than 15 percent, but they
failed to agree. The unwillingness to revise this rule meant that a
candidate might not achieve delegate strength approximating his or
her primary vote. As it later turned out, Jackson obtained 18 percent of the popular vote, but his share of convention delegates
amounted to only 10 percent.

Although the "rainbow" alliance had a distinctly black hue, Jackson's support among blacks was far from unanimous in 1984. A Gallup poll revealed that 59 percent of black Democrats preferred Jackson, but a hefty 34 percent favored Walter Mondale, Carter's vice-president, who had strong ties to the liberal-labor wing of the party. Those black politicians most closely linked to national Democratic affairs were less likely to back Jackson, the acknowledged outsider, than an established white candidate like Mondale, who had compiled a good record on civil rights as a senator from Minnesota. They believed that defeating Reagan was the most important goal in 1984, and that the quixotic Jackson certainly had no chance of doing so. Black mayors, such as Coleman Young of Detroit, Richard Arrington of Birmingham, and Andrew Young of Atlanta, along with the heads of national civil rights groups, declined to endorse the Chicago minister. "A black candidacy," the president of the Urban League declared, "would be a counterproductive retreat into emotional symbolism at the expense of realistic coalition efforts better suited to meeting black needs." In contrast, Jackson tended to generate greater enthusiasm from local black officials and community leaders who had few ties to the national Democratic party apparatus or the power brokers who ran it. Furthermore, he appealed most strongly to younger blacks, whose attachment to the Democrats did not date back as far as that of their elders.

Black opposition to Jackson also stemmed from issues of personality and power. The flamboyant candidate had a reputation for self-promotion, for failing to act as a team player while grabbing headlines to advance his own interests. A prominent black California legislator, Willie Brown, expressed the view of many of those who had doubts about him: "You can't teach Jesse anything. He never has been disciplined." Along with Andrew Young, many members of Dr. King's family and immediate staff refused to endorse their former SCLC associate, who, they believed, had rushed too quickly and indiscreetly to assume the mantle of leadership following the death of the martyred King. Moreover, some black officials who had successfully made the transition from civil rights to electoral politics resented Jackson's attempt to run for the presidency from outside an elected power base. They considered him an interloper, a shrewd protest leader, who threatened their hard-earned leverage within Democratic party circles and challenged their authority within their own electoral constituencies. Black politics had developed to the point at which its practitioners fought the same kind of "turf battles," as Adolph Reed calls them, as their white counterparts.

The rift among blacks was minor compared with the conflict between Jackson and Jewish voters. Next to African-Americans, Jews had been the staunchest supporters of Democratic presidential aspirants. Moreover, Jews had provided more support than the members of other white ethnic groups for black mayoral candidates, such as Carl Stokes, Richard Hatcher, and Harold Washington. Their devotion to liberalism and civil rights notwithstanding, since the late 1960s many Jews had broken with blacks over issues concerning affirmative action and the Palestinian-Israeli struggle (see Chapter 6). Unfortunately, Jackson's 1984 campaign damaged relations between these past allies even further. In an off-the-record remark to a black journalist, Jackson referred to Jews as "Hymies" and to New York City, the home of some 3 million of them, as "Hymietown." When his unguarded comments appeared in a news story in the *Washington Post*, the candidate first denied making them and then apologized, regretting any pain he may have caused and repudiating anti-Semitism.

Even had Jews been inclined to forgive Jackson's slip of the tongue, and most did not appear so willing, the substantive matter of Israel still troubled them. Jackson defended the survival of the Jewish nation, but he also called for the creation of a Palestinian state on territory Israel had captured in a war with its Arab enemies in 1967. This policy, which struck Jackson as evenhanded and essential for peace in the Middle East, was totally unacceptable to most Jewish leaders in its recognition of the radical Palestinian Liberation Organization. Extremists in the Jewish community viciously attacked Jackson for what they regarded as his anti-Semitic views, called him a "goddamn dirty Nazi," and picketed his appearances. Aggravating the situation, Minister Louis Farrakhan, the head of the Nation of Islam (the Black Muslims) and an outspoken Jackson defender, labeled Judaism "a gutter religion." Though Jackson denounced this inflammatory remark, he declined to repudiate Farrakhan himself. The candidate explained that he believed in the principle of redemption as embodied by Jesus and that he had tried to reach out and convert people with whom he disagreed, including white segregationists such as George Wallace and Orval Faubus.

"Isn't it better," he asked, to bring black militants "inside where we can at least talk to them, perhaps even change them?" Jackson knew that many blacks who were not Muslims, especially those living in impoverished urban ghettos, felt the same anger that separatists like Farrakhan expressed. Consequently, he attempted to walk a very fine political line between blacks and Jews in handling this emotional incident.

In effect, the candidate had to stick with his black base of support, his particular source of strength, whatever the risk of offending Jews and other whites. This fact of political life ensured him representation at the 1984 national convention, but guaranteed his defeat. Indeed, in a field crowded with seven white candidates, Jackson made a respectable showing by running third behind Mondale and Senator Gary Hart of Colorado. He won over 3.5 million primary votes, which included victories in Louisiana and the District of Columbia. He gained a plurality of the popular vote in South Carolina, his birthplace, and in Virginia, and carried forty-six congressional districts and seven major cities. In two of them, Atlanta and Philadelphia, Jackson triumphed without the backing of their black mayors, who endorsed Mondale. Ignoring the reservations of some of their political leaders, the overwhelming majority of blacks cast their ballots for Jackson. His figures among blacks ranged from a low of 50 percent in Alabama, where Birmingham Mayor Arrington supported Mondale, to a high of 87 percent in New York.

In contrast, the black candidate picked up only a fraction of the white electorate during the primaries. He averaged a slim 5 percent of the white vote, recording his greatest share, 9 percent, in California. Jackson tended to run slightly higher among whites in states containing the lowest percentages of blacks in the population—a clue that racial perceptions significantly affected voters. Although the evidence is fragmentary, it points to the conclusion that a hard-core one-fifth of whites were unwilling to vote for a black presidential candidate, and a substantial majority of the white electorate were not ready to support one as controversial as Jackson. Even many sympathetic white liberals refused to vote for him because they "felt left out." Believing that Jackson had not forged a true rainbow coalition, they faulted him for concentrating too heavily on solidifying his black support. A white Jackson adviser acknowledged that poor coordination and mistrust "inhibited the campaign's ability to reach out beyond its black core." Nevertheless, Jackson did attract more than three-quarters of a million white votes, which constituted about 22 percent of his total ballots. Given the preponderance of the white majority in the electorate, this showing fell far short of building the winning biracial coalition a minority presidential candidate needed.

Realistically, the black minister never had a chance of obtaining the 1984 Democratic nomination. Though linking together a network of grassroots groups and a dedicated staff to guide their activities, Jackson lacked both an experienced national organization and the funds to operate it. The candidate raised only about $4 million in contributions, with an average donation of $27. This broke down to an expenditure of 99 cents for each vote he won, compared with the $3 per vote the more prosperous Mondale campaign could afford to spend. Starved for adequate resources, Jackson did not have the political capital necessary to defeat entrenched party leaders with their access to superior sources of money and talent. These deficiencies, in turn, reinforced the direction of his strategy. To conserve expenses and deploy personnel efficiently, Jackson had to focus on the black electorate, thereby reducing the possibility that his message would get across to potential white supporters. Without this backing, the rainbow coalition appeared monochromatic.

Yet Jackson accomplished a good deal of what he had set out to achieve. He succeeded in mobilizing unprecedented black political participation. In the South alone, his candidacy sparked 150,000 blacks to add their names to the enrollment lists, and throughout the country black registration reached the level of that of whites. Nationally, about 20 percent of his supporters had decided to vote for the first time in their lives, and in Dixie black voter turnout in the Democratic primaries actually surpassed the rate for whites. He also inspired other blacks to run for office, including a woman in Dallas County, Alabama, who remarked that Jackson "made black people feel they could make a difference." Having a black candidate as a serious contender for the presidency was a source of great racial pride and revived some of the feeling of the civil rights movement that politics could be a tool for social change. "For those who did not have an opportunity to participate in the 'March on Washington', or in Selma," the Reverend Jackson told his campaign followers, "God has provided you another opportunity."

Besides coaxing blacks out to the polls, Jackson's efforts opened the way for future presidential challenges. It brought large numbers of black activists into the electoral process and gave them an inside view of how to conduct a national campaign. They became intimately familiar with Democratic party rules and learned valuable lessons about fund-raising, media relations, and the myriad tasks of preparing a candidate to stump through the country in search of support. Drawing upon the metaphor of baseball, California Assemblyman Willie Brown concluded that Jackson had become the "Jackie Robinson of American politics," and predicted that "a whole lot of little leaguers in many cities and counties" would someday join Jackson in rising up to the political big leagues. The nomination contest had bestowed increased legitimacy on the notion of a black competing for the White House. Lucius Barker, a political scientist and Jackson delegate from Missouri, commented that "Jackson is the first black person to really become a *national political* leader in terms of national *presidential* politics" (emphasis in original). Jackson had communicated to white Americans that blacks were interested in and capable of contesting for the presidency and that they could offer leadership for millions of citizens distressed by the lingering problems of economic inequality, racial injustice, and Cold War hostilities exacerbated during the Reagan regime. "[W]e might have learned," the historian John Hope Franklin observed about Jackson's performance, "that it was conceivable that a black man had the qualities to be President." Though the Chicago clergyman had not triumphed in the usual sense, he did earn respect for himself and gained recognition for the political aspirations of African-Americans.

Despite these achievements, the Jackson forces had only a slight impact on the 1984 Democratic national platform. Blacks comprised 18 percent of the representatives in attendance and most of them were pledged to the Reverend Jackson. However, with Mondale firmly in charge, they proved no match for the majority of delegates who rejected the main planks of the "rainbow platform." They did manage to come away with one compromise, convention endorsement of affirmative action goals and timetables, but the convention remained silent on the subject of controversial quotas. Mondale easily won the nomination with 2,191 votes compared to 1,200 for Senator Hart and 465 for Jackson (higher than his actual number of delegates, which totaled 384). The former vice-president counted some prominent blacks on his side. Indeed, he tapped Mayor Andrew Young to speak against Jackson's proposal to curb runoff primaries, an action that engendered a barrage of boos and catcalls from most black delegates. Nor did the black contingent feel much better about the selection of Congresswoman Geraldine Ferraro of New York as Mondale's running mate. Jackson backers applauded the choice of a woman, but they regretted that a black female had not been seriously considered for the number-two spot.[1] Still, Jackson did gain a minor concession. The party agreed to establish a fairness commission to investigate complaints about the discriminatory operation of its rules on selecting convention delegates, and the group eventually dropped the threshold vote a candidate had to receive from 20 to 15 percent. (At the same time, it minimized the effect of this change by increasing the number of "superdelegates," party leaders chosen outside the primary and caucus system, who could attend the convention.)

Putting aside his disappointment, Jackson lined up behind the national ticket. Considerable sentiment existed among blacks for the Chicago minister to run as an independent, but he declined. Instead, he showed Democratic chieftains that he could play by the rules and abide by the outcome of party decisions. No longer a civil rights leader exclusively, Jackson had to act like a politician who needed to mend his fences in preparation to do battle another day.

He went a long way in that direction by delivering a stirring, emotional address to the convention. Affirming his political commitment to the Democratic party and to his social mission "to feed the hungry; to clothe the naked; to house the homeless; to teach the illiterate; to provide jobs for the jobless; and to choose the human race over the nuclear race," Jackson called for a coalition of "Red, Yellow, Black, and White" to join together in defeating Reagan in common pursuit of these goals. Toward this end, he attempted to heal the wounds of discord that had festered between blacks and Jews during the campaign. Recalling their mutual sacrifices sealed in blood in the civil rights era and their shared victim-

---

[1]Although white female delegates to the Democratic Convention were delighted with the choice of Ferraro, black female representatives were dismayed that no woman from their ranks came under consideration. In August 1984, they expressed their disappointment by forming the National Political Congress of Black Women as a means of exerting independent leverage.

ization as scapegoats throughout history, the Reverend Jackson denounced racism and anti-Semitism and urged Jewish-Americans and African-Americans to "turn to each other and not on each other, and choose higher ground." Without erasing all the bruised feelings, this powerful speech did have a soothing effect. Vic McTeer, a black delegate from Mississippi, where Fannie Lou Hamer and the Freedom Democrats had been denied representation twenty years before, felt much of his anger over the Democrats' treatment of Jackson subside after he saw white members of his delegation respond to the address with tears in their eyes and with hands reaching out to clasp those of blacks.

THE REAGAN LANDSLIDE AND THE STRUGGLE FOR BLACK POLITICAL SURVIVAL

Although Jackson's rhetoric touched deep emotions within Democrats at the convention and the millions watching on television, it could not save the party from defeat. Mondale chose not to assign Jackson a prominent role in his campaign, preferring instead to chase after the votes of traditional white Democrats who had defected to Reagan in 1980. Even the Mondale-loyalist Andrew Young griped about the neglect of blacks and called the candidate's advisers "smart-assed white boys and they think they know it all." Jackson dutifully made appearances for the ticket, but even if he had been used more heavily it would have made little difference. Surpassing his performance in 1980, the Republican chief executive won by a landslide. Reagan captured 59 percent of the popular vote and swept 525 of 538 electoral votes, taking every state except Mondale's home territory of Minnesota and the predominantly black District of Columbia. Losing 91 percent of the black ballots cast did not prove much of a handicap for the incumbent, because 66 percent of white voters, up from 55 percent in 1980, enthusiastically backed him. While Jesse Jackson had been mounting voter registration drives among blacks, the Republicans had been busily engaged in escorting new voters into their party. In fact, 60 percent of those citizens voting for the first time selected Reagan over Mondale.

The 1984 election returns indicated the enduring significance of race in determining presidential preferences. The polarization in black and white support for the two contenders continued a thirty-two-year trend. Starting with Eisenhower's victory in 1952, only one Democrat, Lyndon Johnson, had received a majority of white votes. This stood in sharp contrast to the mass of black voters who opposed every Republican challenger during that same period. Conventional wisdom attributed the polarization to Jackson; yet if the black minister's candidacy heightened it did not cause this racial divide. Though Jackson's campaign prompted some whites to jump to the Republicans, the large majority of them simply favored extending the term of a very popular chief executive whose administration had begun to restore economic recovery and national pride. Reagan's financial measures further split blacks from whites in making their presidential choices, as class reinforced racial concerns. Disproportionately harder hit by unemployment and poverty, and still trailing behind whites in average yearly earnings, most blacks found relatively little comfort in the Reaganomic policies aimed at boosting the fortunes of the middle and upper classes. Not surprisingly then, in the South, which had the largest income gap between the races, polls showed 57 percent of whites praising Reagan's economic performance and 87 percent of blacks objecting to it. Consequently, on election day over 70 percent of southern white voters cast their ballots for the Republican.

Despite the huge Reagan victory, blacks did not find the election completely discouraging. In the South, the black turnout rate grew by 5.3 percent from that of four years before. This increase reflected an even higher rise in the percent of blacks registered since 1980. Indeed, in Louisiana and Georgia the pace of black enrollment exceeded that of whites. Nationally, the upsurge in participation narrowed the differences between white and black registration (3.3 percent) and turnout (5.6 percent) to their lowest points in the post-World War II period. A higher proportion of the total voting-age black population in the country cast their ballots in this presidential election than in the previous one. On the down side, however, the percentage of those who were registered and actually voted had declined slightly. This situation suggested that the Jackson Democratic primary campaign had helped swell the pool of available voters, but that the subsequent contest between Reagan and Mondale dampened their enthusiasm. The President's conservatism and the challenger's failure to excite African-Americans kept many blacks at home.

Black participation produced mixed results. While Reagan retained the White House and the Republicans held onto their control of the Senate, the Democrats picked up one vote in the upper chamber and maintained their majority in the House. Black votes provided the winning margins for Democratic senators in Alabama, Illinois, and Michigan as well as for seven members in the House. Black candidates did not fare so well. Though the number of blacks serving in state legislatures increased slightly, the Congressional Black Caucus suffered a net reduction of one seat. In addition to this loss, six black congressional candidates who were considered as having a chance of winning went down to defeat. As usual, black officeseekers tended to run strongest at the local level. In 1984, the greatest annual increases occurred in the election of black county officials and mayors, especially in the South, the scene of Jackson's most intensive political efforts in mobilizing black voters. Yet, as Thomas Cavanagh, a political scientist and researcher for the Joint Center for Political Studies, suggested, "most of the black-majority districts may already have black incumbents, making future gains more difficult to achieve."

The second Reagan administration proved no more promising to Afro-American political advancement than did the first. Given the partisanship of the black vote, the President had little incentive to modify his previous course. Nevertheless, the Republican administration went further in antagonizing blacks than even its opponents had expected. In the aftermath of Reagan's reelection, the Justice Department indicted eight long-time civil rights activists in Alabama on criminal charges that were viewed as an attempt to roll back black political power. The government contended that the accused had engaged in vote fraud by improperly soliciting and casting absentee ballots in the heart of the state's black-belt area. Convictions on these felony charges could result in heavy fines and lengthy prison terms.

The cases originated in the region surrounding Selma, where blacks had encountered the greatest resistance to enfranchisement during the civil rights years. Through the efforts of such local leaders as Albert Turner of Perry County, a former SCLC staff member and an organizer of the historic 1965 suffrage march to Montgomery, and Spiver Gordon, a city councilman in nearby Greene County, blacks had won a total of 138 offices and gained control of five county commissions, five school boards, and nine towns. Though the Voting Rights Act had enabled blacks to constitute a majority of the electorate in those rural locations, whites managed to retain substantial influence. They continued to wield economic clout in those counties, which were among the poorest in the state, and they converted their superior financial resources into victories at the polls. Whites held onto the reins of government in five counties and in thirty-three towns and occupied the top positions of voter registrar, district attorney, and circuit judge. In the fierce political struggles that ensued, absentee ballots often counted as the margin of victory in determining the outcome of elections and thus had been a serious bone of contention for years. Each side charged the other with manipulating these ballots and with engaging in fraud by signing up people without their knowledge and voting in their names and those of individuals who no longer resided in the black belt.

Complicating this interracial conflict, blacks also divided among themselves. Increasingly, black candidates began to vie against each other for office, and in such instances the white minority played a balance-of-power role in deciding the winners. In this section of Alabama, with its history of bigotry and disfranchisement, black leaders eyed suspiciously white attempts to exploit rivalries between black factions. They charged that whites collaborated with disgruntled blacks as a subtle means of reasserting their political hegemony. As a matter of fact, John Kennard, the black tax assessor of Greene County, who had won election with white backing, initiated the complaints of absentee ballot fraud against his black opponents. Kennard, who had been in grade school during the heyday of the freedom struggle in the 1960s and had gone on to graduate from the University of Alabama, headed a group of young insurgents that sought to challenge the rule of blacks identified with the civil rights movement who had governed the county since 1970. Although as a youth he had joined in demonstrations and marches, he felt that the time had come for a change in leadership and strategy. "All this stuff about 'We Shall Overcome' was in the sixties," Kennard asserted and bluntly rejected the "philosophy among the old-line black leadership that there's something evil and demonic and a master plan in the white community to enslave us."

Conservative whites took advantage of these generational and ideological splits within the black community. Local white Alabamians joined Kennard in persuading the Reagan Justice Department to file charges against Albert Turner and his allies in Perry and Greene counties. The complainants were looking ahead to the upcoming 1986 elections, which featured the bid for another term by Senator Jeremiah Denton, a Republican who had opposed renewal of the Voting Rights Act in 1982. Involved in a close contest with his Democratic opponent, Representative Richard C. Shelby, Denton thought his chances would be stronger if black leaders came under attack and the black electorate felt discouraged from going to the polls. The Republican administration insisted that it was not acting out of political or racial motives and argued that it was merely seeking to punish one group of blacks for committing fraud against other blacks.

Federal prosecutors denied that they were deliberately intimidating black voters by bringing these suits, but the targets of these trials thought otherwise. They accused Washington of selective enforcement, pointing out that it had not responded in the past to similar complaints filed by blacks against whites. Furthermore, the "black-belt eight" contended that the federal government used heavy-handed tactics in investigating the cases, especially in rounding up for questioning those blacks who had signed the controversial ballots. Many of them were elderly and infirm, and their interrogation by federal agents revived memories of the not-so-distant past when blacks could not register to vote or paid a heavy penalty for doing so.

Ignoring cries of protest from civil rights organizations and the Congressional Black Caucus and their white allies, the Reagan administration persisted in its Alabama prosecutions but obtained only partial success. In the case of three defendants, including Albert Turner, an interracial jury failed to return a guilty verdict. Other trials resulted in hung juries, though several of the accused later pleaded guilty to lesser misdemeanor counts. Only in the case of Spiver Gordan did an all-white jury decide to convict, and even then he was acquitted on most of the charges. Whatever the intention of the Reagan administration, it failed to curtail the determination of Alabama blacks to exercise their franchise: in 1986, the latter won a measure of revenge by pouring out at the polls and contributing to the defeat of Senator Denton.

THE RESURGENCE AND RESHAPING OF THE CIVIL RIGHTS COALITION

Meanwhile, blacks had salvaged another victory against the Reagan administration shortly before the 1986 congressional elections. Blacks emerged triumphant as they once again bolstered electoral politics with protest to further their goals. Groups of blacks and their white supporters, many of them prominent individuals, took turns picketing the South African embassy in Washington for more than a year, which resulted in arrests on a daily basis. Their persistence and the surrounding publicity generated by the demonstrations had a positive impact on Congress. In mid-September, a bipartisan coalition of lawmakers passed a bill imposing moderate economic sanctions on South Africa. Later that month, President Reagan vetoed this popular legislative measure, which sought to apply punitive action against a nation whose institutions rested on racial oppression and minority rule. In doing so, the chief executive rejected this central item on the black political agenda, an expression of solidarity with a brutally persecuted people of color living on the continent to which African-Americans traced their roots. The civil rights movement had cracked the edifice of apartheid and disfranchisement that existed in the American South, and most Americans supported proposals to aid in overcoming these evils in southern Africa. Though the sanctions bill approved by Congress fell short of totally embargoing economic trade with and investment in the racist regime, it went too far for the President, who preferred to dismantle apartheid through a policy of "constructive engagement" that emphasized voluntary persuasion rather than coercion. On October 2, 1986, a month before the legislative elections, the Senate joined the House to register its disagreement with Reagan's approach and repass the bill over his veto. Representative Lynn Martin, an Illinois Republican, echoed the sentiments of more than two-thirds of her colleagues in overriding the President: "The vote matters not because of what it says about South Africa. It matters because of what it says about America."

This victory helped whet the appetite of disgruntled blacks throughout the South and the nation to use the off-year congressional elections to communicate their discontent with the White House. The existence of considerable Republican support for South African sanctions did not sufficiently offset general black hostility to Reagan's GOP administration. The Democrats recaptured control of the Senate by a margin of fifty-five to forty-five seats. According to the Joint Center for Political Studies, Democrats in California and Nevada gained only a minority of white votes but won by obtaining a huge share of black ballots. The same situation prevailed in four contests in the deep South—Alabama, Georgia, Louisiana, and North Carolina—where black voters tipped the winning balance in favor of Democratic challengers. In two other states, Florida and Maryland, blacks helped expand what otherwise would have been slight victory margins. They did so there by turning out to vote at a rate equaling or surpassing that of whites. Overall, blacks still lagged behind whites in turnout by 7 percentage points, but this marked a significant improvement over the gap of 11 percent in the 1982 off-year congressional elections.

Although the results of these elections demonstrated the rising strength of black political influence in the South since passage of the Voting Rights Act, they also indicated its limits. The triumphant candidates in Dixie gained the overwhelming portion of black ballots, between 80 and 90 percent, and a substantial minority of the white electorate, around 40 percent. Victory depended upon holding onto the bulk of the black electorate while at the same time luring enough white Reagan Democrats into a biracial coalition. Calculating this political arithmetic, successful southern Democrats ran as moderates, very carefully adjusting their messages to attract both liberal blacks and conservative whites. After winning his senatorial election, John Breaux of Louisiana pledged "to remember that he could never have won without the black vote." Nevertheless, the question remained of how responsive Democrats like Breaux would be to black concerns when they also had to consider the political risks of alienating their volatile white supporters. Many southern whites answered with caution. A Raleigh, North Carolina, newspaperman warned: "If black political leaders read too much into the returns of 1986 and do not fashion their agenda with an eye toward winning the next election, they could contribute to a rupturing of the Democratic coalition of which they are a vital part."

The election outcome also suggested that while blacks were continuing to advance politically, they could not afford to ignore the power of the white electorate. Though blacks secured four additional seats in the House of Representatives, pushing their total to a record high of twenty-three members, two of these gains were significantly shaped by the decisions of white voters. In Mississippi, Mike Espy became the first black candidate since Reconstruction to represent his state in Congress. The delta district Espy served contained a slight black voting-age majority, but on two previous occasions another black contestant, state legislator Robert Clark, had failed to win sufficient support from white voters and lost. In 1986, Espy defeated the incumbent Republican by generating a large black turnout in his behalf, nearly doubling his share of white votes to 12 percent, and keeping a significant bloc of whites from voting against him. Many whites who disliked his opponent but could not bear to cast a ballot for a black candidate simply stayed away from the polls, thereby indirectly contributing to Espy's slender 2.3 percent margin of victory.

In the case of the election of Congressman John Lewis from Atlanta, white voters played an even more direct role. This contest pitted Lewis, the former chairman of SNCC, against his old civil rights comrade, Julian Bond, in the Democratic primary. In this black-majority district, 87 percent of whites threw their support to Lewis, who triumphed while receiving only 40 percent of black ballots. This election reversed the traditional positions of each race at the polls. Previously, when blacks comprised a minority of the electorate, they had lined up behind the white candidate considered the most racially moderate in the field and swung the election in his or her favor. Now the white minority helped elect Lewis, who they perceived as more temperate than Bond. Elsewhere, in the black-majority city of New Orleans the winning black mayor, Sidney Barthelemy, also failed to win a majority of black votes, but clinched victory by capturing ample support from whites. These triumphant officials faced the delicate task of representing black concerns without offending the segment of the white electorate that had tipped the balance of power in their favor. At the same time, they had to repair splits within the black community that had opened from these intraracial clashes for power, which constituted a natural step in the evolution of black politics.

Although increased competition for public office sometimes proved divisive, blacks generally remained united in their unfinished goal of achieving racial equality. Despite the growing economic stratification within the black polity, middle-class black politicians still tended to identify with the plight of their less fortunate constituents from whom they were only recently removed. "Even those blacks who have 'made it' economically," Thomas Cavanagh reported, "are more likely to support the views of poor blacks than those of well-to-do whites." Having benefited from civil rights and affirmative action remedies, they most assuredly did not want to see those gains weakened or terminated. Public opinion surveys indicated that in contrast with whites most blacks favored compensatory federal programs to reverse the economic and social effects of past racial discrimination. Thus, so long as the United States had not become a color-blind society, race persisted as a crucial category for determining political choices.

Black solidarity, reinforced by expanding political clout, brought some notable legislative victories in the final two years of the Reagan era. With Democrats once again in control of both houses of Congress and with several newly elected senators owing their victories to blacks, the prospects for challenging the administration's conservative policies improved. This was especially true when issues involved basic civil rights matters and avoided controversial affirmative action or big spending measures. The defeat of Robert Bork's nomination to the Supreme Court vividly testifies to this point. A legal scholar and federal judge who had served as solicitor general during Nixon's final Watergate days, Bork had distressed blacks and their white allies by his long history of outspoken opposition to numerous pieces of civil rights legislation and accompanying liberal judicial opinions. Denying any racist motives, Bork had reached these judgments on constitutional grounds and propounded a conservative legal philosophy in harmony with the President's. Whatever the source of Bork's views, civil rights advocates contended that the nominee's ideas fell outside of the judicial mainstream, and they considered him a formidable threat to the advances so recently made. They further believed that his appointment to the high bench would forge a clear majority against extending any future benefits.

The administration and its opponents engaged in a vigorous lobbying campaign to rally public and congressional support for their respective sides. With Democrats having replaced Republicans in control of the crucial Senate Judiciary Committee, Bork's foes succeeded in using the hearings to generate resistance to the nomination. An interracial coalition of civil rights organizations, liberal and labor groups, and proabortion feminist organizations, all of which found Bork's positions detrimental to their respective causes, convinced the committee to issue a negative report on the candidate. The full Senate concurred with this recommendation, and the critical votes to deny the appointment came dramatically from southern Democrats. In a new version of the "solid South," fifteen of sixteen Democratic senators from the region voted against the judicial nominee. Though not entirely unsympathetic to Bork's legal reasoning, these moderate and conservative lawmakers were also mindful that this legal scholar aroused deep indignation from their black constituents. The 1986 elections had only recently underscored the political importance of the black electorate and the danger of ignoring its interests. "When the blacks stay with the Democrats," a senior Democratic officeholder in Mississippi remarked, "we can just about win, but when they leave, we can't." To many southern senators, the political risks of supporting the controversial Bork were too great, and they hesitated to stir up past racial animosities. As Senator Richard C. Shelby of Alabama, a moderate conservative who owed his election to black voters, declared: "In the South, we've made a lot of progress. We do not want to go back and revisit old issues."[2]

The revitalized civil rights forces in Washington won another important victory over the President's opposition that also reflected a concern with halting any retreat from hard-earned civil rights gains. Specifically, the One-Hundredth Congress reversed the President in his refusal to restore protections that had been recently whittled down by the Supreme Court in the case of *Grove City College v. Bell*. In 1984, the high tribunal had ruled that under the 1964 Civil Rights Act the federal government could not completely cut off funds to a college for practicing discrimination in some but not all of its activities. In other words, federal sanctions had to be applied on a selective basis specifically against an offending program without penalizing the entire educational institution. This decision represented a setback from the previously expansive interpretation of the law, and the Reagan administration heartily endorsed it. The case involved discrimination against women by Grove City College in Pennsylvania, but its legal reasoning also applied to racial minorities. Subsequently, civil rights and women's groups persuaded lawmakers to pass legislation restoring government authority to remove federal funds from institutions that permitted any discrimination under their auspices. After Reagan vetoed the bill, on March 22, 1988, moderate Republicans, as they had on the South Africa issue, joined the Democratic majority in furnishing the two-thirds vote necessary to override the President. In doing so, Congress expressed its broad agreement for preserving the full scope of the valued Civil Rights Act, which legislators had battled so hard to place on the books in the first place.

While blacks displayed their influence in Washington, they continued to flex their political muscle at the state and local levels. In

---

[2]This civil rights victory was diminished by the eventual confirmation of Judge Anthony M. Kennedy, a conservative considered to have a more flexible judicial temperament than Bork's but who nonetheless has consistently voted with the conservative bloc.

addition to playing significant roles in deciding the outcome of close elections between white candidates, they boosted the number of blacks holding office. In 1987, there were over 6,600 black elected officials throughout the nation, a rise of 4.1 percent from the year before. For the first time black politicians broke through the barriers that had kept governments lily-white in seventy-one locales. Among those significant victories was the election of a black candidate as a supervisor (commissioner) in Fannie Lou Hamer's Sunflower County, Mississippi; the election of the father of one of the young girls killed in the 1963 bombing of a church in Birmingham to a seat on the Jefferson County Commission; and further north, in Baltimore, Maryland, the election of a black as mayor. In addition, black incumbents triumphed as mayors in Atlanta, Birmingham, Chicago, Detroit, Los Angeles, and Philadelphia; and in cities such as Gary and Newark, black challengers defeated the reigning black chief executives.

Nationally, however, African-Americans still held only 1.5 percent of elected posts. Though minority office-holding continued to grow steadily, it did so very slowly. As blacks began to fill the available positions in places where they constituted a majority of the population, the opportunities to add to the total number of black officials diminished. There was room for some improvement as the judiciary ordered local governments to convert from at-large to single-member district elections, thereby creating new black-majority jurisdictions. Nevertheless, in many villages and towns in the rural South, blacks had yet to crack white political domination, which was reinforced through tradition and economic dependency. Furthermore, because they were a minority of the population in most cities, in every state, and throughout the nation, blacks needed to attract greater white support to expand their representation. As the 1980s drew toward a close, Afro-American candidates generally had failed to establish these winning biracial coalitions. Blacks did not occupy any state governor's mansion or hold any U.S. Senate seat, and only some thirteen held statewide offices.

JESSE JACKSON AND THE RAINBOW REVIVAL

With this mixed record in the background, Jesse Jackson once again sought to expand the horizon of black political opportunity by competing for the 1988 Democratic presidential nomination. This time he was less interested in the symbolism of merely running than he was in actually obtaining the top prize. In this pursuit, he stood upon an even firmer base of black support than in his previous campaign. A poll taken a year before the Democratic convention showed that 67 percent of blacks preferred Jackson as their first choice for the nomination, whereas no more than 3 percent of those surveyed favored any one of his potential rivals. Unlike 1984, there was no white candidate in the field who had the liberal credentials of a Mondale or his proven dedication to civil rights. Nor did any aspirant have the former vice-president's close ties to the national party establishment that pulled many black politicians away from Jackson in his first campaign. Under these circumstances and given the substantial backing Jackson commanded among rank-and-file black Democrats, the Chicago minister experienced much less opposition to his candidacy from black leaders this time around. Most notably, former opponents such as Mayor Richard Arrington of Birmingham; Willie Brown, speaker of the California Assembly; and Congressman John Lewis hopped aboard his bandwagon. Some, such as Mayor Coleman Young of Detroit, remained unconvinced, but others, such as Andrew Young, though still not endorsing Jackson, at least stayed neutral.

Yet if Jackson had a realistic chance to improve his performance in contending for the nomination, he had to do more than solidify his black foundation of support. "It's very easy to finish third," Alan Dershowitz, a Harvard Law School professor, said of Jackson's 1984 standing, "if you're black in America, and you're a black candidate seeking a black constituency." To place second and especially first, Jackson had to reach beyond the approximately 20 percent of the Democratic electorate that was securely his. Accordingly, he attempted to broaden his appeal among whites and nonblack minorities, such as Hispanics and Native Americans, and draw a fuller range of colors into his rainbow coalition than he had in 1984. He moved in this direction by bringing in some experienced white political consultants to serve alongside his trusted black confidants. Bert Lance of Georgia, who had helped engineer Jimmy Carter's successful 1976 campaign; John White, former chair of the Democratic National Committee; Ann Lewis, past head of the liberal Americans for Democratic Action; and Jim Hightower, the agricultural commissioner of Texas, were among those Jackson relied on for counsel. Underscoring his commitment to an expanded biracial coalition, he selected Assemblyman Brown to chair his national organization, and picked Gerald Austin, a white political operative who served as campaign manager for Governor Richard Celeste of Ohio, to oversee the organization's day-to-day affairs. The increased visibility of Austin and other nonblacks, Jackson calculated, "tells other people that *they* are welcome" and would raise "the comfort level" for whites.

Jackson aimed his message at diverse segments of the American electorate. He continued to trumpet many of the themes that identified him most closely with black and progressive white concerns: affirmative action, sanctions against South Africa, federally guaranteed full employment, opposition to Reagan's Central American policies, and support for evenhanded treatment of Israeli and Palestinian positions in the Middle East. However, he abandoned or downplayed other issues that had been associated with his previous campaign. No longer did he focus his attack on runoff primaries and party rules establishing a minimum threshold for winning convention delegates, procedures that had a disproportionately negative impact on black and other minority candidates. In general, he attempted to extend the appeal of his progressive agenda to moderate and conservative Democrats who, during the past two decades, had defected from the party or had been turned off to the political system altogether. Jackson explained: "Last time my rhetoric was sufficient to do what I had to do—open up the process, demand room for progressive-thinking people, register new voters. You know there's a right wing and a left wing, and it takes both to fly a plane. My concern is about 85 million voters in neither wing: they're in the belly of the plane."

Jackson raised economic and social issues designed to rally the disaffected behind him. He hammered away at Republican policies that cost factory workers their jobs and lost family farmers their mortgages. Speaking in the language, minus the racism, of white populists of the past, Jackson attacked the "economic violence" that wealthy corporations and their representatives in Washington had perpetrated on the economically disadvantaged. Addressing himself to black and white victims of financial privilege and corporate greed, he asked for the "small fish" to join against the "barracudas." He wrapped this message in a patriotic banner by calling for a "reinvestment in America" that would halt plant closings, stop foreclo-

Jesse Jackson, flanked by some of his rivals for the Democratic party presidential nomination, appears at a candidate forum in October 1987. From left to right stand Senator Albert Gore of Tennessee, Congressman Richard Gephardt of Missouri, Jackson, Democratic party chair Paul Kirk, Jr., Governor Bruce Babbitt of Arizona, Senator Paul Simon of Illinois, and Governor Michael Dukakis of Massachusetts. (UPI/Bettmann Newsphotos)

sures, and create domestic jobs. Furthermore, he highlighted his long-standing concern with the danger of drugs ("Down with dope. Up with hope."), a matter middle-class Americans felt extremely worried about.

These themes struck some responsive chords among white voters. As he hopscotched around the country campaigning in the Democratic primaries and caucuses, he wooed many whites who would not have considered voting for him in 1984. In early April, a *USA Today* poll revealed that 32 percent of whites were more willing to back Jackson on this occasion than four years earlier. Jim Hightower of Texas noted the newfound appeal of Jackson as he espoused his brand of populism: "He is transcending the fact that he is a black candidate. He is gaining white support... from the kind of people who like Willie Nelson—the sort of redneck, lower middle-class constituency that is out there, and, since Bobby Kennedy and George Wallace, hasn't been voting that much." In one survey, taken in August 1987, 16 percent of rural whites selected Jackson as either their first or second choice for the top spot on the Democratic ticket. Furthermore, Jackson's approach encouraged his rivals for the nomination to shape their campaigns around similar issues dealing with drugs, education, health care, and protection for blue-collar workers threatened with layoffs and farmers endangered by foreclosures. Commentators observed that Jackson's popularity had risen as he moved into the party mainstream, but the Chicago minister could equally claim that he had pulled the Democratic center in his progressive direction.

Still, Jackson was stuck with several political liabilities that posed severe problems for him. His position on the Israeli-Palestinian conflict continued to cause him difficulties with Jewish-American voters. He tried to allay the fears of this important segment of the Democratic electorate by pledging to maintain strong U.S. support for the defense of Israel, whose security, he insisted, would not be jeopardized by carefully negotiating recognition of a Palestinian homeland. Jackson also avoided a repetition of the unfortunate "Hymie" incident, and he distanced his campaign from the controversial Muslim minister, Louis Farrakhan. This second time around, Jackson's attempts at reconciliation did bring some Jews into his camp. Indeed, his own campaign manager, Gerald Austin, was a Jew who had once been disturbed by the Hymie remark, but now had come to believe that Jackson meant no offense in using the term. However, most of Austin's coreligionists did not forgive Jackson so easily, and instead many apparently agreed with Mayor Edward Koch of New York City that Jews would be "crazy" to vote for Jackson.

Besides his specific problem with Jews, the Chicago civil rights leader generally had trouble convincing whites to endorse him. Whereas many of them thought that Jackson did not have sufficient political experience or that elements of his rainbow platform were too liberal, others indicated that they would not vote for him under any circumstance. Jackson was viewed unfavorably by 38 percent of Democrats, and even if he captured his party's nomination, polls showed him gaining only 27 percent of the total white vote. Personal perceptions and ideology undoubtedly influenced these views, but so too did the fact that Jackson was a black candidate and, therefore, to some extent unacceptable to many whites. The primary contest in West Virginia rudely demonstrated this point when a local resident bluntly informed reporters: "[I] ain't voting for no nigger." Most whites did not display such candor, and though it is difficult to disentangle racial concerns from other factors that generated opposition to Jackson, one may reasonably conclude that race came into play. As a black Jackson supporter lamented after New York's divisive primary: "In the South, if they didn't like you, they told you. In the North, they are just as racist, and just as prejudiced, but they're just a little smoother." Like his populist predecessors before the turn of the century, the black candidate had difficulty in forging an interracial alliance behind common class grievances.

In spite of these drawbacks, Jackson achieved some notable successes in the primaries and caucuses. He ran stronger than in 1984 among both black and white electorates and out of a field of six white candidates, including several state governors, U.S. senators, and a congressman, he finished second to Governor Michael Dukakis of Massachusetts. Gathering nearly 7 million votes, Jackson won over 1,200 delegates, three times the 1984 number. He scored impressive triumphs in the South by winning primaries in Alabama, Georgia, Louisiana, Mississippi, and Virginia, together with the caucus in South Carolina, his native state. In this region, blacks composed from 33 to 46 percent of the Democratic electorate, and they cast over 90 percent of their votes for Jackson. At the same time, the black candidate beat his rivals by lifting his share of the white vote to 10 percent, up from 4 percent in 1984. Overall, in the former Confederate states Jackson received 28 percent of the popular vote to edge out his closest competitors, Dukakis (27 percent) and Senator Albert Gore of Tennessee (25 percent). This showing was remarkable, particularly in a section of the country that until very recently had deprived its black citizens of the right to vote.

In the rest of the country (that is, outside of the South), where blacks generally constituted a smaller proportion of the population and the Democratic electorate, Jackson did surprisingly well. He astonished most political pundits and purveyors of conventional wisdom by winning the Michigan caucus. Forty percent of his total vote came from whites. In addition to capturing black-majority Detroit, despite the opposition of Mayor Young, he won in several predominantly white cities. In a state with a slumping automobile industry and strong blue-collar union membership, his condemnation of plant closings and corporate irresponsibility gained a large following. In this instance, his populist rhetoric was well-received. In addition, his personal magnetism, combined with a defense of old-fashioned values stressing the importance of family, upward mobility, and the danger of drugs, prompted many whites to shift, as Jackson put it, "from racial battleground to economic common ground and moral higher ground."

Elsewhere Jackson showed growing support among whites, as his share of the vote greatly exceeded the percentage of blacks in the voting-age population. He came in first in Alaska and Delaware, and finished second by gaining between 20 and 29 percent of the total vote in Connecticut, Indiana, Maine, Maryland, Minnesota, Missouri, Montana, Nebraska, New Mexico, Ohio, Pennsylvania, Vermont, and Wisconsin. He did even better in securing between 30 and 39 percent of the vote in Arizona, California, Colorado, Hawaii, Illinois, Kansas, New Jersey, New York, Oregon, and Washington. Although he finished second in the three-way, state-wide contest in New York, Jackson triumphed in New York City with 46 percent of the votes and a coalition of blacks, Hispanics, and progressive whites behind him (see Table 4).

Nevertheless, Jackson fell considerably short of his goal. After peaking in Michigan, he lost in nearly all of the remaining primary and caucus elections. Following the bruising New York contest, Governor Dukakis emerged as the clear front-runner, and the field narrowed down to the Massachusetts governor and the Chicago clergyman. Jackson trailed behind his remaining rival in the ensuing head-to-head battles, especially as the white majority rallied around Dukakis. For all of his efforts over the previous four years in diminishing white opposition and even converting nonblacks to his candidacy, Jackson could not persuade a sufficient number of whites to back him. Whatever their racial views, many white Democrats appeared to harbor sincere doubts as to Jackson's electability. They believed Jackson's views were too far to the left of the political mainstream, and would not bring back to the fold conservative Democrats who had voted for Reagan. Anthony Lewis of the *New York Times* spoke for many of those who found Jackson appealing but a sure loser: "When I hear liberals talking about their exhilaration at the Jackson candidacy, their delight at its populist character, I worry. That sounds like the gushy liberalism that has

Table 4 Percentage of Votes Won by Jesse Jackson in Democratic Primaries, 1984 and 1988[a]

	Black voting-age population[b]	1984	1988
Alabama (p)	22.9	19.6	43.6[c]
Alaska (c)	3.4	10.6	34.6[c]
Arizona (c)	2.5	15.7	37.8
California (p)	7.1	19.6	35.2
Colorado (c)	3.2	4.2	33.6
Connecticut (p)	6.0	12.0	28.3
District of Columbia (p)	65.8	67.3[c]	80.0[c]
Georgia (p)	24.3	21.0	39.8[c]
Hawaii (c)	1.9	4.2	35.0
Illinois (p)	12.9	21.0	32.3
Kansas (c)	4.8	3.3	30.8
Louisiana (p)	26.6	42.9[c]	35.5[c]
Maine (c)	0.3	0.4	26.8
Maryland (p)	20.8	25.5	28.7
Michigan (c)	11.7	16.7	53.5[c]
Mississippi (p)	31.0	26.9	44.4[c]
Nebraska (p)	2.6	9.1	25.7
New Jersey (p)	11.0	23.6	32.9
New Mexico (p)	1.7	11.9	28.1
New York (p)	12.4	25.6	37.1
North Carolina (p)	20.3	25.4	33.0
Ohio (p)	9.2	16.4	27.5
Oregon (p)	1.2	9.5	38.1
Pennsylvania (p)	8.1	16.0	27.3
South Carolina (c)	27.3	25.0	54.8[c]
Tennessee (p)	14.2	25.3	20.7
Texas	11.1	16.4(c)	25.0(p)[d]
Virginia	17.5	26.7(c)	45.1(p)[c]
Vermont (p)	0.2	7.8	25.7[d]
Washington (c)	2.4	3.0	34.6
Wisconsin (p)	3.2	9.9	28.2

(p) represents a primary and (c) a caucus election.

[a]Primaries in which Jackson obtained at least 25 percent of the vote in either one or both years. Absent from the table is Puerto Rico, where Jackson won the primary with 29 percent of the vote in 1988.

[b]Percentage black of total voting-age population in 1980.

[c]Jackson victories.

[d]Texas and Vermont also had caucuses, and Jackson won both with 40 percent and 46 percent of the vote, respectively.

SOURCE: The Democratic primary election results are taken from *Congressional Quarterly Weekly* (June 16, 1984), 1443, and (July 9, 1988), 1894. The caucus totals, also, are from *Congressional Quarterly Weekly* (June 2, 1984), 1317, and (June 4, 1988), 1524. The figures on voting-age population are drawn from U.S. Department of Commerce, Bureau of the Census, *Statistical Abstract of the United States, 1984* (Washington, D.C.: Government Printing Office, 1984), 263.

got the Democratic Party out of touch with reality before: the reality of the need to win the center."

This hard-nosed perception of Jackson carried over to the decision not to select him as the vice-presidential candidate. Instead, Dukakis chose Senator Lloyd Bentsen of Texas as his running mate. In making this choice the Massachusetts governor sought to revive the "Boston-Austin axis" that had produced victory for John Kennedy and Lyndon Johnson in 1960. Bentsen was a moderate to conservative Democrat whose views on many domestic and foreign policy issues diverged from those of the more liberal Dukakis. In balancing the ticket geographically and ideologically, Dukakis hoped to forge a winning majority by prying loose Reagan Democrats and returning them to his column. Blacks decried this strategy because they believed that it took their votes for granted and it slighted the Reverend Jackson. They contended that the minister had earned a place on the ticket through his strong showing in the primaries. Jackson was similarly offended, but by the time the Democrats gathered at their convention in July, he had come around to endorsing Dukakis and Bentsen.

Although African-Americans did not get their first choice for either spot on the ticket, they did significantly increase their representation at the 1988 Democratic convention. Of those in attendance, 962, or 23 percent, were black. This constituted a one-third increase over the number of black delegates who had sat at the previous convention and comprised the highest number ever to participate in the party's quadrennial meeting. Together with Jackson's white delegates they succeeded in obtaining a few platform concessions on educational and health care issues as well as a pledge not to fund the military operations of antigovernment rebels in Central America. They also lent their support to Jackson in gaining a personal commitment from Dukakis to recruit additional blacks to his campaign staff and to policy-making positions within the party. Democratic chieftains also agreed to make some rule changes that Jackson had sought, including a reduction in the number of superdelegates chosen outside of the primary and caucus system.

The highlight for the Jackson delegates came with their candidate's prime-time television address to the convention and the nation. As he had in 1984, Jackson thrilled the audience with his vision of an America that "keeps hope alive" for all of its citizens, no matter how weak or humble, whatever their race, creed, or sex.

"We meet tonight at a crossroads, a point of decision," he remarked and went on to ask, "Shall we expand, be inclusive, find unity and power, or suffer division and impotence?" Jackson eloquently answered his own question by pointing out that Dukakis's Greek "foreparents came to America on immigrant ships. My foreparents came to America on slave ships. But whatever the original ships, we are both on the same side now."

Having failed in his bid for the nomination, Jackson nonetheless helped redefine victory. As the influential columnist David Broder noted: "For Jesse L. Jackson... 'winning' has meanings that cannot be captured in primary-election returns or exit-poll numbers." In a poignant illustration of the progress blacks had made, Jackson brought Rosa Parks with him onto the stage of the convention and introduced her to the thousands in the hall and the millions watching on television. Thirty-three years before, she had been arrested for challenging bus segregation in Montgomery, and now she stood beside a leading contender for the presidential nomination. Jackson also reminded the assemblage that only twenty-four years had passed since another group of Democrats had "locked out" Fannie Lou Hamer, Aaron Henry, and the Mississippi Freedom Democrats from taking their seats at the convention. Now Henry was listening to these words as a member of the Mississippi delegation, an interracial contingent headed by a black man, Ed Cole. Even the site of the meeting inspired thoughts of the momentous changes that had occurred. Jackson pointed out that this gathering in the capital of Georgia was taking place "in a state where governors once stood in school house doors." He further recalled that just over two decades before, in this city over which Andrew Young presided as mayor, the state legislature had barred the SNCC worker Julian Bond from assuming his seat in the legislature because of his objections to the Vietnam war. In this fashion, Jackson vividly connected his own journey as a legitimate contender for the presidency to the triumphs and sacrifices of the civil rights movement in scores of black communities across the nation.

In countless ways, Jackson had become a role model for young blacks who one day might also aspire to the nation's highest office. Certainly many African-Americans had dreamed that one day there would be a black president, but Jackson's candidacy gave new meaning to this hope. Shirley Chisholm's 1972 bid for the Democratic nomination had not attracted much support, even from

blacks, whereas Jackson's campaign had drawn a huge black following and considerable interest among whites. Although those who
were older might not see a black president in the White House in
their lifetime, they took great pride in what Jackson had already
achieved. "A five-year-old can look at the T.V. screen and see a
black man running for President and have it be credible," a Jackson
enthusiast explained. "Jesse has inspired a belief that nothing is un-
conquerable."

This contest also demonstrated that Jackson was more than a
candidate for blacks. His challenge helped transform the attitudes
of many whites, and sometimes in a startling manner. In Texas, for
example, a white man seeking to have his photograph snapped
alongside Jackson mentioned to the candidate that he had marched
in Selma. After Jackson retorted that it was nice to be with him
again, the fellow replied: "No, you don't understand. I marched
with the Klan. I just don't want to be on the wrong side of history
again." Although most whites did not experience a conversion this
dramatic, those marking their ballots for Jackson in some small way
reflected the changes that his candidacy represented. Not a winner
in the conventional sense, Jesse Jackson had taken a great stride in
gaining political acceptance for himself and for black Americans.

THE ELECTION OF GEORGE BUSH

The 1988 presidential election did little to address, let alone pose solutions for, the chronic political and economic problems of African-
Americans. The Democratic standard-bearer, Michael Dukakis, appealed to voters to judge his competence as an administrator and
not his political ideology. Accordingly, for most of the campaign he
soft-pedaled his views as a liberal—the dreaded L word his Republican rival, Vice-President George Bush, hurled against him as an
epithet. Though Dukakis did appoint some blacks to his staff, including Ronald Brown, a Jackson campaign aide, and though he recruited Jackson to speak for him, especially in the last weeks of the
contest, he did not elevate the special concerns of the black community to the forefront of his political agenda. He set the tone early
when he delivered a speech in Philadelphia, Mississippi, mention-
ing civil rights in passing but omitting any reference to the three
Freedom Summer workers who were killed there a quarter-century

earlier. Taking note of this omission, *The New York Times* aptly commented: "Ignoring the South's often painful, sometimes proud progress in race relations is a peculiar way to profess leadership."

The GOP ticket of Bush and Senator Dan Quayle of Indiana offered no real alternative, as it pledged to extend Reagan administration policies that 79 percent of blacks found objectionable. In fact, blacks had comprised a scant 2.7 percent of the Republican National Convention delegates who chose their standard-bearers and the Reaganomic platform upon which they ran. If Dukakis could be faulted for sins of omission, Bush was guilty of premeditated racial assault. In shades of vintage George Wallace and Richard Nixon, Bush revived the theme of law and order by casting blacks in the image of criminals. Through highly provocative television ads, he attacked Governor Dukakis for granting a prison furlough to Willie Horton, a black inmate in Massachusetts, who escaped from the program and raped a white woman. The Republican candidate never referred to the color of Horton's skin, but he did not have to; the medium vividly conveyed this message for him. As Michael Kinsley, the editor of the *New Republic*, pointed out, whether Bush and his advisers were racially motivated was irrelevant. "Hortonism taps into a thick vein of racial paranoia that is a quarter-inch below the surface of the white American consciousness."

Given the choice of having Dukakis neglect them or Bush insult them, African-Americans chose to vote for the Democrat. Nearly 90 percent of the black electorate cast their ballots for the Massachusetts governor, about the same proportion supporting Democratic presidential nominees over the past two decades. Nevertheless, blacks appeared to approach the ballot box with slightly less enthusiasm than in recent years, as their turnout at the polls dropped by about 5 percent of those eligible to participate. (Overall, the white turnout also declined.) In major cities such as Chicago, Detroit, Cleveland, New York, and Philadelphia, the black vote fell an even larger 10 percent. While blacks continued to line up behind the Democratic hopeful, whites preferred the GOP contender. Bush received around 60 percent of white votes. Though he did not score as well as Reagan, the Republican President-elect won 54 percent of the popular votes and 426 electoral ballots.

Though blacks and Democrats failed to vault their candidate into the White House in 1988, they did better in extending their political power elsewhere. The Congressional Black Caucus added its first representative from New Jersey, and the Democrats gained five seats in the House and one in the Senate. At the state level, the Democrats increased their number by twenty-nine legislators, halting the trend toward the Republican party that was taking place throughout the 1980s. One of the black incumbents gaining reelection to the House, Mike Espy of Mississippi, did so in impressive fashion. Espy, who had triumphed with a bare 52 percent of the vote in 1986, walloped his Republican opponent by winning 65 percent of his district's electorate. He improved his performance by sweeping the black vote and obtaining an amazing 40 percent of the ballots from his white constituents. The House also saw Espy's colleague, William H. Gray of Pennsylvania, reach an important milestone in his selection as chairman of the Democratic Caucus. In securing this position, Gray became the first black representative to fill a prestigious leadership job in Congress. (The following year, he became House majority whip, ranking third in the Democratic chain of command in the lower chamber.) Moreover, after the election the Democratic National Committee selected Ronald Brown, who had steered Jackson's convention forces and later counseled Dukakis during the campaign, to the post of party head.

In addition, the election returns confirmed the continuing gains made by women of color. Although the annual growth rate was slowing down, between 1979 and 1988 the number of black female elected officials nearly doubled to a figure of 1,625. In the process, the gap between black male and female officeholders had narrowed. In 1979, there were about four times as many black men as women holding elected posts; a decade later the ratio stood at approximately three to one. Only one black woman, however, Cardiss Collins of Illinois, sat in the House of Representatives (a drop from a high of four in 1975). The majority of women still served in municipal governments and local school boards. Paralleling this upsurge in office-holding was the higher voter turnout rate of black females than males. Black women had not yet caught up with men in obtaining public office, but they had surpassed black males by about seven percentage points in going to the polls (see Table 5).

The 1988 elections underscored the difficulties and possibilities facing African-Americans. Staying exceedingly loyal to the Democrats and obtaining new bases of influence, they nonetheless felt that the party welcomed their presidential support but followed a

Table 5   Black Elected Officials in the United States, 1975–1988

	Number of males	Number of females	Percent male increase	Percent female increase
1975	2,973	530		
1976	3,295	684	10.8	29.1
1977	3,529	782	7.1	14.3
1978	3,660	843	3.7	7.8
1979	3,725	882	1.8	4.6
1980	3,936	976	5.7	10.6
1981	4,017	1,021	2.0	4.6
1982	4,079	1,081	1.5	9.7
1983	4,383	1,223	7.5	13.1
1984	4,441	1,259	1.3	2.9
1985	4,697	1,359	5.8	10.8
1986	4,942	1,482	5.2	9.1
1987	5,117	1,564	3.5	5.5
1988	5,204	1,625	1.8	3.9

SOURCE: Joint Center for Political Studies, *National Roster of Black Elected Officials* (Washington, D.C., 1988), 17.

strategy to attract conservative white voters. Surveys indicated that the strength of their partisan attachment to the Democrats was weakening, particularly among younger blacks coming of political age after the peak of the civil rights movement. At the same time, the Republicans showed some signs of trying to entice disaffected black Democrats to their ranks. Below the presidential level a number of Republicans had already fashioned winning coalitions with the black electorate. For example, New Jersey's governor, Thomas Kean, had won office with 60 percent of the black vote; and George Voinovich attracted 85 percent of black ballots in his victory as mayor of Cleveland. Even President Bush recognized the need to refashion the unflattering image left by his predecessor. Putting aside the offensive rhetoric from his campaign, he called for a "kinder and gentler America" and, in a highly publicized gesture, met with Jesse Jackson to discuss how to bring that about. Yet, until the Republicans offered more than soothing words and proposed meaningful alternatives to the policies of the Reagan administration, they had little chance of significantly improving their standing among nonwhite voters.

Chapter 8

Still Running for Freedom

KEEPING HOPE ALIVE

By the end of the 1980s, the future of black politics appeared unsettled. To an extent unfathomable in 1941, African-Americans exerted considerable influence in local and national affairs; yet old patterns of discrimination still lingered. The process of empowerment had moved ahead in many areas, but not at the same rate and often in a halting fashion. Furthermore, the increased measure of acceptance gained by Jesse Jackson in his presidential bids did little to wipe out opposition to black political equality in many places where racism had traditionally flourished and where it continued to operate, albeit in more subtle forms.

The notable achievements of the civil rights struggle often obscure the political dilemmas that continue to perplex African-Americans and their allies at the end of the 1980s. Unquestionably, blacks constitute a powerful force in the electorate. By 1988, they comprised 11.2 percent of the nation's registered voters, a figure comparable to the proportion of blacks in the nation's population; they had narrowed the enrollment gap between the races to a slight 1 percent; and their rate of turnout at the polls trailed that of whites by only 4 percent. Yet their political impact remained circumscribed. Holding a mere 1.4 percent of elected positions, blacks saw their chances for victory drop off as they competed for higher office. Although only 3 percent of whites declared themselves unwilling to vote for a black candidate in a local school board election, the figure jumped to 18 percent for a black presidential aspirant. Many blacks believed their electoral clout was further limited because the Democrats took them for granted and the Republicans virtually ignored them. They had loyally contributed around 90 percent of their ballots to Democratic presidential candidates since 1964, but as Dukakis's selection of Bentsen suggested, the party deliberately shaped its strategy with mainstream white voters, not blacks, in mind.

In addition, questions remained as to whether conventional electoral politics could resolve the fundamental economic problems experienced by blacks and other impoverished Americans. These were problems that resulted not from individual acts of bigotry but from the enduring presence of discrimination deeply embedded in fundamental institutions throughout the centuries.

Economic inequality imposed a heavy burden on African-Americans. Notwithstanding the gains achieved by the middle class, the majority of blacks had made little progress in catching up with whites. Twenty years after a presidential commission warned that the United States was "moving toward two societies, one black, one white—separate and unequal," the median family income of blacks relative to whites was heading downward. From 60 percent of the earnings of whites in 1968, the figure had dropped even lower, to 56 percent by 1988 (see Table 6). The proportion of blacks out of work was more than double that of whites, and the percentage of blacks living below the poverty line tripled that of whites. A visit to any of the inner-city ghettos that had experienced rioting in the 1960s revealed that little had changed since then; per-

Table 6   Median Family Income (current dollars), 1960–1987

	White	Black	Black-to-White Percentage
1960	$ 5,835	$ 3,230	55.4%
1965	7,251	3,993	55.1
1970	10,236	6,279	61.3
1975	14,268	8,779	61.5
1980	21,904	12,674	57.9
1985	29,152	16,786	57.7
1987	32,274	18,098	56.1

SOURCE: U.S. Department of Commerce, Bureau of the Census, *Statistical Abstract of the United States, 1989* (Washington, D.C.: Government Printing Office, 1989), 445.

haps conditions had even worsened. Scholars and journalists wrote increasingly about the phenomenon of the black underclass in those depressed areas, a growing group "that is slipping further and further behind the rest of society." People with little education, they no longer bothered to seek work, lived in poverty and despair, were hooked on drugs, and were virtually unaffected by the presence of blacks governing their city halls. This gloomy picture did not do justice to the millions of blacks in those communities who were working hard to raise their families, struggling to make ends meet, and striving to keep narcotics out of their neighborhoods. Nevertheless, the situation was desperate enough to alarm blacks and whites interested in achieving equality in fact as well as in law.

For Jesse Jackson or any other Afro-American leader seeking progressive social change, the challenge remains to develop black political resources and shape them into instruments to lessen economic disparities between the races. The success of the black middle class has heralded the breakdown of legal barriers to economic opportunity that accompanied desegregation, but the persistence of substantial black poverty and unemployment attests to the cleavage between electoral expectations and material rewards. By committing themselves to the ballot as a central tool for emancipation, blacks, implicitly if not explicitly, accepted the ground rules of the American political system. Consequently, black politicians have softened the more radical, communitarian side of reenfranchisement and empowerment, as envisioned by the Student Nonviolent Coordinating Committee. As a result, they have become part of the dominant political culture whose values have improved the lot of the black middle class while leaving the plight of lower-class blacks largely unaltered.

The increased legitimacy that Jesse Jackson gained for black political aspirations marked a new beginning and not an end. African-Americans could build on the political freedom they had so gallantly achieved during the second half of the twentieth century. They had learned the hard way that empowerment was an ongoing struggle and that genuine participation in community and governmental affairs involved more than the acquisition of formal constitutional rights. It also demanded collective action and the assertion of group pride to sustain the belief among ordinary people that they could exert greater control over their lives despite historic obstacles. The civil rights movement had reawakened racial consciousness, which in turn nurtured subsequent struggles for political power, such as those waged by the Reverend Jackson. Whatever else they obtained in the process, the quest for first-class citizenship revived in blacks feelings of self-respect and "somebodyness," qualities so essential in pursuing the struggle for freedom that will no doubt take many varied forms in the years ahead.

As blacks and their white allies looked toward the future, they could take some comfort from the past. Notwithstanding the limitations of the suffrage as an instrument of liberation, the political emancipation of blacks made a critical difference. The civil rights movement, combining protest with electoral politics, succeeded in transforming individuals and communities through collective struggle. It is inappropriate to figure black political advancement strictly on a cost-accounting basis, as a story recounted by SNCC's Bob Moses poignantly shows. He told of a woman he remembered working with in Mississippi, Mrs. Hazel Palmer, who had not been elected to any office or gained material success by objective standards. But that was beside the point. "[I]t didn't matter that she did not make it in any other way that society thinks people make it," Moses insisted. "But she had won something in her spirit that no one could take away from her." The Mrs. Palmers of the South became empowered to stand up in their communities and affirm their rights as first-class citizens and active political agents. This freedom of the mind will be difficult to take away and may serve as perhaps the most valuable legacy bequeathed to future generations of African-Americans in their attempt to obtain the unfulfilled promises of racial equality.

LOOKING TOWARD THE FUTURE

Disappointed with the performances of the two major parties in addressing their problems, African-Americans have been considering the option of pursuing an independent political course. A poll taken in 1986 revealed that 53 percent of blacks favored a black candidate like Jesse Jackson running for the presidency as an independent. Considering the structural biases of the political system in discouraging third parties and the danger of isolating blacks even further from the electoral majority, the prospect of a black-led party successfully competing for the White House appears remote. However, political theorists, such as Ronald W. Walters of Howard University, have suggested that while remaining within the two-party system, blacks could pursue an "independent-leverage" strategy. Based on group solidarity, collective interests, and the threat of withholding their votes, they would negotiate for increased programmatic benefits in return for their support. Such an approach would require a high degree of organizational cohesion and discipline not only from the mass of black voters but also from their leaders, many of whom are now tied into established political party structures. Nevertheless, it is clear that blacks must develop tough bargaining strategies to compete for power against the other interests arrayed in their partisan coalitions.

If blacks remain within the Democratic orbit, as they most likely would for the foreseeable future, they will have to forge coalitions that extend to them a greater share of political power. Along with progressive whites, Hispanics, and other minorities, they must find a way to broaden the party's foundation of support to include the millions of Americans who felt alienated from the system. The attempts of Mondale and Dukakis to outbid their conservative opponents for the same old votes did not work. Without an expansion of the electorate to embrace potential voters more inclined to favor government efforts against poverty and discrimination, the Democrats and their black supporters will probably continue to finish second in contests for the highest office in the land.

Blacks and their allies will also have to find a way to reconnect politics and protest, national and local struggles. The civil rights movement had made electoral progress possible, and without a revival of its energy and vision routine black political participation will not be sufficient to remove the blockades to genuine equality. The Jackson campaigns marked a start toward merging the forces seeking social change with the practitioners of conventional politics. The challenge ahead is to sustain this alliance and build a movement around it. The history of the civil rights struggle demonstrated that the quest for liberation arose not from any single individual but from collective action. Like Martin Luther King, the charismatic Jesse Jackson served as an agent for a larger network of blacks and whites pressing for freedom. Like their predecessors in the civil rights movement, African-Americans have to continue to organize their communities, devise innovative strategies to apply constant pressure on their representatives, and carry their demands from the towns and cities where they reside to the nation's capital, where power is ultimately wielded. The culmination of the civil rights movement in the achievement of political equality requires nothing less.

EPILOGUE

The entry of blacks into positions of political power has occurred relatively late enough to guarantee that the supply of victorious firsts will not be exhausted for some time. A year after Jesse Jackson's 1988 presidential run came to an end, the Democratic voters of New York City elected an African-American, David Dinkins, as their candidate for mayor. Because this triumph happened in the nation's largest city, the center of the media universe, it assumed greater significance than if it had come to pass virtually anywhere else. Yet surely as noteworthy as the event itself was the fact that it had taken New York more than twenty years to follow the examples set by Cleveland and Gary. In addition, since 1973, Los Angeles, the leading city on the West Coast, could brag about having an African-American mayor. In 1989, the city known as the Big Apple, which prefers to establish the fashionable trends, finally had caught up with its urban counterparts throughout the rest of the country.

Jackson's 1988 campaign had pointed the way toward victory. The civil rights minister, though losing the state to Governor Dukakis, carried New York City with slightly over 40 percent of the vote. In doing so, he exposed the vulnerability of Ed Koch, the incumbent mayor completing his third term. Elected in 1976, Koch confronted a desperate financial crisis and helped engineer the city's recovery. However, his administration was marred by a series of scandals involving close political associates, and his flamboyant personality offended many constituents. Among the most upset were blacks and other minorities who believed that the mayor's programs to restore the city's fiscal health ignored, or even aggravated, the condition of the most impoverished residents of their communities. To make matters worse, in 1988, Koch exacerbated tensions between blacks and the city's large Jewish population by attacking the Reverend Jackson as anti-Semitic, reminding voters that the presidential candidate had termed New York City "Hymietown" during the 1984 campaign. Despite the mayor's bitter opposition, Jackson managed to line up solid black support with sufficient backing from Hispanics and liberal whites to emerge ahead of his two opponents in the city. (Koch allied himself with Senator Albert Gore, who came in third.)

Encouraged by Jackson's strong showing, Dinkins, the president of the borough of Manhattan since 1985, challenged Koch's bid for an unprecedented fourth term. Born in Trenton, New Jersey, in 1927, Dinkins served in the Marines and, in 1950, graduated from Howard University with a degree in mathematics. A year later he moved to Harlem and decided to become an attorney. Following his graduation from Brooklyn Law School, in 1956, he pursued a career in politics and served as Democratic party district leader, state assemblyman, and city clerk, a position he held for ten years before winning election as chief executive of Manhattan. A pensive, soft-spoken individual, Dinkins had a talent for listening carefully before acting and for playing the role of conciliator. He would need to draw upon those skills to forge a winning coalition in a city where blacks constituted less than a quarter of the electorate. His critics called Dinkins indecisive, but almost all agreed that in the rough-and-tumble world of New York City politics, he remained a gentleman—"a political Bill Cosby," as one newspaper dubbed him.

Although neither Koch nor Dinkins sought to attack the other along racial lines, the Democratic mayoral contest took place against a backdrop of growing racial animosities. Trouble had been brewing for some time. The stress of daily life in a city as large as New York strained the limits of racial toleration. The twin problems of crime and drug abuse, nurtured by poverty, took on racial overtones and fostered mutual suspicion. In 1984, when Bernhard Goetz shot four black youths who he believed were trying to rob him on a subway train, many whites regarded him as a hero, a kind of real-life Lone Ranger. The situation grew worse as a number of disturbing incidents followed. On December 20, 1986, a gang of whites attacked three blacks after they entered a pizza parlor in the predominantly white section of Howard Beach, Queens. In trying to make his escape, one of the blacks was struck by a car and killed. A little more than two years later, in April 1989, a white female jogger running in Central Park was raped, beaten, and left for dead by a roving band of black and Hispanic teenagers. Racial friction again reached a peak during the primary campaign for mayor. On

August 23, 1989, four black youths ventured into the mainly white neighborhood of Bensonhurst, Brooklyn, to inquire about purchasing a used car. They were assaulted by a mob of whites, one of whom fired a gunshot that killed sixteen-year-old Yusuf Hawkins. Racial demonstrations followed this tragic incident.

Dinkins won the Democratic primary, but the outcome of the election reflected sharp racial cleavages. In a field of one black and three white candidates, Dinkins gained about 50 percent of the vote and Koch came in second with 42 percent. The nature of their support was markedly different. Blacks constituted 56 percent of Dinkins's total vote, while whites composed 34 percent, and Hispanics 8 percent. In contrast, 89 percent of Koch's vote came from whites, 7 percent from Hispanics, and only 2 percent from blacks. As expected Dinkins ran strongest in New York's minority communities. He captured more than 90 percent of black ballots and a slight majority of Hispanic votes. On the other side, 70 percent of whites stuck with Koch. One of his supporters from Bensonhurst, a community Koch carried by a margin of nearly seven to one, explained her vote for the incumbent: "I'm afraid to have a black mayor."

However, what impressed most observers was not the racial polarization of the electorate but the relative success Dinkins had in attracting white crossover voters. This minority of whites, about 30 percent, constituted a critical element of Dinkins's winning margin of victory. The Manhattan borough president scored twice as well among whites as Jesse Jackson had in 1988. His 25 percent share of Jewish votes was also an improvement over that of Jackson, and was noteworthy because it came against Koch, himself a Jew. Most whites believed that Dinkins would help heal the city's racial wounds, and according to one exit poll 60 percent of whites expected Dinkins to treat both races fairly. In sampling a cross section of the entire electorate, another survey reported that 91 percent said Dinkins displayed sensitivity to peoples' needs compared with only 7 percent who thought Koch did so. The impact of the Bensonhurst murder was difficult to measure precisely. Though most voters cited other issues as more important in making up their minds, the Bensonhurst killing probably encouraged a greater number of blacks to go to the polls and reinforced the feeling among whites that Dinkins could help defuse similar racial conflicts in the future. As one of his black supporters remarked: "Dinkins projects the kind of personality that's not threatening to whites and is acceptable to blacks."

Nevertheless, Dinkins had a tough battle in the general election. Successful in uniting Democratic party leaders, most notably Mayor Koch, behind him, Dinkins still had to keep the white Democratic rank and file in line. In a city where Republicans were outnumbered five to one, the Democratic nominee normally was a shoo-in. However, Dinkins's Republican opponent, Rudolph Giuliani, a former federal prosecutor, waged a fierce campaign to lure white Democrats away from their traditional fold. Besides attacking Dinkins for financial improprieties, Giuliani appealed to racial fears. Behind the moderate Dinkins, he warned, stood the more controversial figure of Jesse Jackson waiting to call the shots.

Dinkins won by a narrow margin of two percentage points—the closest mayoral election since 1905. Despite substantial defections by white Democrats, he held onto 30 percent of the white electorate, including between 33 and 40 percent of Jews. Dinkins ran extremely well among minority voters, gaining more than 90 percent of black ballots and nearly 70 percent of Hispanic votes. Notwithstanding this breakthrough victory, those figures showed the continuing role of racial considerations in determining electoral choices. Yet looked at from a different perspective, the results also demonstrated Dinkins's success in attracting a genuine multiracial coalition. Of the mayor's total vote, approximately 50 percent came from blacks, 30 percent from whites, and 17 percent from Hispanics—a "gorgeous mosaic," as Dinkins called it.[1]

If recent history can serve as an accurate guide, Dinkins will find his job as mayor a difficult challenge, filled with high expectations that may be difficult to satisfy. Most likely, African-Americans and Hispanics will receive more appointments to city government and minority businesses will obtain a greater share of municipal contracts. Mayor Dinkins already serves as a source of pride for

---

[1]Election Day also saw another landmark victory. L. Douglas Wilder, the Democratic lieutenant governor of Virginia, became the first black to be elected governor in the nation's history. In a contest characterized by negative campaigning, but in which the race issue remained in the background, Wilder defeated his Republican opponent by a mere 7,000 votes out of nearly 2 million cast. Race still mattered, however. Many whites who voted for the rest of the statewide Democratic ticket declined to support Wilder, accounting for the closest gubernatorial contest in Virginia's history.

Campaigning for mayor of New York City, David
Dinkins stands under a statue of George
Washington on the steps of Federal Hall in lower
Manhattan. (AP/Wide World Photos)

many black New Yorkers. "When Martin Luther King was alive we
had somebody to look up to," a resident of Brooklyn's Bedford-
Stuyvesant area declared. "Now the black community is lost. David
Dinkins will help a lot." At the same time, however, the plight of
the impoverished and the homeless and the problems of crime and
drugs will remain beyond the grasp of even the most compassionate
occupant of city hall to solve. The mayor will face an entrenched
municipal bureaucracy resistant to change, powerful corporate developers, tough-minded union leaders, and a shortage of revenue to
address issues that are national in scope. Furthermore, Dinkins will
have to strike the delicate balance of responding to the special

needs of minority communities without losing the necessary economic and political support of the white majority. Whatever solutions ultimately work, they must involve a readjustment of domestic priorities and a federal commitment that combines the economic realism of the New Deal's battle against the depression with the moral urgency of the civil rights struggle against racism.

Winning an election, especially for the first time, is rich in symbolism, but cannot be an end in itself. David Dinkins and other Afro-American elected officials, together with their nonblack allies, must somehow find ways to govern effectively and deliver the substantive benefits necessary to improve their constituents' lives. Otherwise, the promise of electoral politics as a means of achieving racial equality will remain unfulfilled.

Bibliographical Essay

The entries noted in the following pages are meant to be a select list of the works upon which this study is primarily based. A full citation appears only at the first referral to the source. My main purpose is to provide the reader with a guide to the available published literature and the themes that they raise; therefore, manuscript sources are omitted. I have made a few exceptions in noting unpublished doctoral dissertations and conference papers that were of particular help.

PREFACE

A very useful discussion that distinguishes between the civil rights movement and the black freedom struggle and calls for a focus on local communities is presented in Clayborne Carson, "Civil Rights Reform and the Black Freedom Struggle," in *The Civil Rights Movement in America*, Charles W. Eagles, ed., University Press of Mississippi, Jackson, Miss., 1986, 19–32.

CHAPTER 1

Two anthologies that furnish a background for the general study of Afro-American history and black politics are Darlene Clark Hine, ed., *The State of Afro-American History: Past, Present and Future*, Louisiana State University Press, Baton Rouge, 1986, and Michael B. Preston, Lenneal J. Henderson, Jr., and Paul Puryear, eds., *The New Black Politics: The Search for Political Power*, Longman, New

York, 1982. Useful surveys on the civil rights movement and on black politics can be found in Matthew Holden, *The Politics of the Black "Nation,"* Chandler, New York, 1973; Manning Marable, *Black American Politics; From the Washington Marches to Jesse Jackson*, Verso, London, 1985; Milton D. Morris, *The Politics of Black America*, Harper & Row, New York, 1975; Hanes Walton, Jr., *Invisible Politics: Black Political Behavior*, State University of New York Press, Albany, 1985; Lucius J. Barker and Jesse J. McCrory, Jr., *Black Americans and the Political System*, Winthrop, Cambridge, Mass., 1976; Harvard Sitkoff, *The Struggle for Black Equality, 1954–1980*, Hill & Wang, New York, 1981; and Rhoda Lois Blumberg, *Civil Rights: The 1960s Freedom Struggle*, Twayne, Boston, 1984.

W. E. B. Du Bois, *The Souls of Black Folk*, New American Library, Chicago, 1973, demonstrates the importance of the ballot as a key weapon for black liberation. On the influence of the New Deal on the development of black political strategies, there are two excellent monographs: Harvard Sitkoff, *A New Deal for Blacks*, Oxford University Press, New York, 1978, and Nancy J. Weiss, *Farewell to the Party of Lincoln: Black Politics in the Age of FDR*, Princeton University Press, Princeton, 1983. The impact of World War II is covered most extensively in Neil A. Wynn, *The Afro-American and the Second World War*, Holmes & Meier, New York, 1975, and in several surveys of life in general on the home front. Among them are Richard Polenberg, *War and Society: The United States, 1941–1945*, J. B. Lippincott, Philadelphia, 1972, and John Morton Blum, *V Was for Victory: Politics and Culture During World War II*, Harcourt, Brace, Jovanovich, New York, 1976. Richard M. Dalfiume, "The 'Forgotten Years' of the Negro Revolution," *Journal of American History*, 55 (June 1968): 90–106, is a seminal article on the origins of the civil rights struggle; Harvard Sitkoff, "Racial Militancy and Interracial Violence in the Second World War," *Journal of American History*, 58 (December 1971): 661–681, explores the moderating influence white liberals had on the development of black protest; Lee Finkle, "The Conservative Aims of Militant Rhetoric; Black Protest During World War II," *Journal of American History*, 60 (December 1973): 692–713, extends Sitkoff's analysis to the black press; and Peter J. Kellogg, "Civil Rights Consciousness in the 1940s," *The Historian*, 42 (November 1979): 18–41, notes the transformation of liberal thinking toward support of racial equality. Dominic J. Capeci, Jr., has examined outbreaks of racial violence and the response of the federal government in *Race Relations in Wartime Detroit: The Sojourner Truth Housing Controversy of 1942*, Temple University Press, Philadelphia, 1984, and "The Lynching of Cleo Wright: Federal Protection of Constitutional Rights during World War II," *Journal of American History*, 72 (March 1986): 859–887. Herbert Garfinkel, *When Negroes March*, Atheneum, New York, 1969, investigates A. Philip Randolph, the March on Washington Movement, and the FEPC; and Allen M. Winkler, "The Philadelphia Transit Strike of 1944," *Journal of American History*, 59 (June 1972): 73–89, comments on the FEPC's efforts in resolving racial strife during a labor dispute. Jervis Anderson, *A. Philip Randolph: A Biographical Portrait*, Harcourt Brace Jovanovich, New York, 1972, provides a flattering account of the labor leader and protest innovator. Catherine A. Barnes, *Journey from Jim Crow: The Desegregation of Southern Transit*, Columbia University Press, New York, 1983, covers wartime challenges to segregated transportation and shows the continuity of those efforts with later civil rights struggles. Jules Tygiel, *Baseball's Great Experiment: Jackie Robinson and His Legacy*, Vintage, New York, 1983, is a social history of the racial integration of America's premier sport. August Meier and Elliott Rudwick, *CORE: A Study in the Civil Rights Movement, 1942–1968*, Oxford University Press, New York, 1973, details the emergence of a major civil rights group, which pioneered direct-action forms of protest that would become popular in the 1950s and 1960s.

The long legal struggle of blacks to topple the white primary as a means of gaining access to the most meaningful elections in the South is amply described in Darlene Clark Hine, *Black Victory: The Rise and Fall of the White Primary in Texas*, KTO Press, Millwood, N.Y., 1979, and Steven F. Lawson, *Black Ballots: Voting Rights in the South, 1944–1969*, Columbia University Press, New York, 1976. The battles against the poll tax are discussed in Hollinger F. Barnard, ed., *Outside the Magic Circle*, University of Alabama Press, University, Ala., 1985, which is the autobiography of Virginia Foster Durr, a leading southern white liberal reformer; and in a scholarly study by Frederic D. Ogden, *The Poll Tax in the South*, University of Alabama Press, University, Ala., 1958. The attempts of southern blacks and their allies to use their restored ballots in the postwar period were first chronicled by Henry Lee

Moon, *Balance of Power: The Negro Vote*, Doubleday, Garden
City, N.Y., 1948, and more recently by Robert Korstad and Nelson
Lichtenstein, "Opportunities Found and Lost: Labor, Radicals, and
the Early Civil Rights Movement," *Journal of American History*,
75 (December 1988): 786–811, and by Patricia Sullivan, "The Voting Rights Movement in South Carolina during the 1940s" paper
presented at meeting of the Southern Historical Association, Houston, Tex., 1985. Mississippi and the significance of the Bilbo episode are presented in James W. Silver, *Mississippi: The Closed Society*, Harcourt, Brace, & World, New York, 1966, and in Lawson,
Black Ballots. Detailed studies of black politics in local communities are contained in C. C. Bacote, "The Negro in Atlanta Politics,"
Phylon, 25 (December 1955): 333–350; Everett Carll Ladd, Jr., *Negro Political Leadership in the South*, Atheneum, New York, 1969
[Winston-Salem]; Korstad and Lichtenstein, "Opportunities Found
and Lost" [Winston-Salem]; and William H. Chafe, *Civilities and
Civil Rights*, Oxford University Press, New York, 1981 [Greens-
boro]. Focused at the national level, Harvard Sitkoff, "Harry Truman and the Election of 1948: The Coming of Age of Civil Rights in
American Politics," *Journal of Southern History*, 37 (November
1971), analyzes the pivotal balance of power wielded by northern
black voters in Truman's presidential victory and its implications for
the future.

CHAPTER 2

Historians are in general agreement that President Truman fur-
thered the civil rights agenda of African-Americans, but they remain divided as to how effective and determined he was in achieving those goals. William Carl Berman, *The Politics of Civil Rights
in the Truman Administration*, Ohio State University Press, Columbus, Ohio, 1970, and Barton J. Bernstein, "The Ambiguous
Legacy: Civil Rights," in *Politics and Policies of the Truman Administration*, Barton J. Bernstein, ed. Quadrangle, Chicago, 1970:
269–314, take a critical view of Truman's performance and find fault
with his leadership as well as with liberalism in general. A more
favorable view of the President and his civil rights accomplishments
is presented by Donald McCoy and Richard T. Reutten, *Quest and
Response: Minority Rights and the Truman Administration*, Uni-

versity of Kansas Press, Lawrence, Kans., 1973, and by Robert J. Donovan, *Conflict and Crisis: The Presidency of Harry Truman, 1945–1948*, Norton, New York, 1977. For additional insights into the Truman presidency by a contemporary civil rights leader, see Walter White, *A Man Called White*, Viking, New York, 1948. Nancy J. Weiss, *Farewell to the Party of Lincoln: Black Politics in the Age of FDR*, and Harvard Sitkoff, "Harry Truman and the Election of 1948," both cited in Chapter 1, also offer judicious comments on the political dimensions of civil rights.

Postwar political developments in black communities are treated in Hugh D. Price, *The Negro in Southern Politics: A Chapter of Florida History*, New York University Press, New York, 1957; four works cited for Chapter 1 [Ladd, *Negro Leadership*; Moon, *Balance of Power*; Korstad and Lichtenstein, "Opportunities Found and Lost"; Chafe, *Civilities and Civil Rights*; and Bacote, "Atlanta Politics"]; Alton Hornsby, Jr., "The Negro in Atlanta Politics, 1961–1973," *Atlanta Historical Bulletin*, 21 (Spring 1977): 7–33; David J. Garrow, ed., *The Montgomery Bus Boycott and the Women Who Started It: The Memoir of Jo Ann Gibson Robinson*, University of Tennessee Press, Knoxville, Tenn., 1987; and J. Mills Thornton, "Challenge and Response in the Montgomery Bus Boycott of 1955–56," *Alabama Review*, 33 (July 1989): 163–235. The comments of William H. Chafe concerning the negative effects of anti-Communism on racially progressive labor unions appear in *The Unfinished Journey: America Since World War II*, Oxford University Press, New York, 1986. Adam Fairclough, "The Preachers and the People: The Origins and the Early Years of the Southern Christian Leadership Conference, 1955–1959," *Journal of Southern History*, 52 (August 1986): 403–440, notes the linkages between electoral and protest politics. Aldon D. Morris, *The Origins of the Civil Rights Movement*, Free Press, New York, 1984, offers a sociological perspective on the community structures that spawned black political protest. Doug McAdam, *Political Process and the Development of Black Insurgency*, University of Chicago Press, Chicago, 1982, also provides a sociological view, on a national as well as a regional scale, of the political resources that shaped the direction of the civil rights movement. The impact of the *Brown* decision in shaping racial politics in the South and the nation is beautifully chronicled in Richard Kluger, *Simple Justice*, Knopf, New York, 1975. The hostile reactions on the part of white political, economic, and social leaders in challenging the landmark opinion are dealt with perceptively by Numan V. Bartley, *The Rise of Massive Resistance*, Louisiana State University Press, Baton Rouge, 1970, and Neil R. McMillen, *The Citizens' Council: Organized Resistance to the Second Reconstruction, 1954–1964*, University of Illinois Press, Urbana, Ill., 1971.

A number of works have examined the impact of the accelerating civil rights struggle on national politics. Robert Frederick Burk, *The Eisenhower Administration and Black Civil Rights*, University of Tennessee Press, Knoxville, Tenn., 1984, offers a well-balanced, but ultimately unfavorable, portrayal of President Eisenhower's handling of civil rights matters, a view that is shared by most writers on the subject. One account that accords more credit to Eisenhower than has customarily been granted is Michael Mayer, "With Much Deliberation and Some Speed," *Journal of Southern History*, 52 (February 1986): 41–76. A sometimes fond but mostly harsh assessment of Eisenhower's role, written by one who served the administration, appears in E. Frederick Morrow, *Black Man in the White House*, Coward-McCann, New York, 1963. Roy Wilkins, with Tom Matthews, *Standing Fast*, Viking, New York, 1982, is the memoir of a prominent civil rights leader who found Eisenhower's leadership sadly lacking. The contrasts in style of the two most notable black politicians of this period, Adam Clayton Powell and William Dawson, are analyzed in James Q. Wilson, "Two Negro Politicians: An Interpretation," *American Journal of Political Science*, 4 (November 1960): 360–369. Gary W. Reichard, "Democrats, Civil Rights, and Electoral Strategies in the 1950s," *Congress and the Presidency*, 13 (Spring 1986): 59–81, traces Democratic party strategies toward black voters during the 1950s. Both regional and national assessments of the impact of the black vote on partisan politics at middecade are contained in a special issue of the *Journal of Negro Education*, 26 (Summer 1957), and in Chandler Davidson, *Biracial Politics: Conflict and Consensus in the Metropolitan South*, Louisiana State University Press, Baton Rouge, 1972. My own *Black Ballots* (cited for Chapter 1) also covers these issues.

The story of the Macon County and Tuskegee struggle, both patient and courageous, has found a historian worthy of its merit. Robert J. Norrell, *Reaping the Whirlwind: The Civil Rights Movement in Tuskegee*, Vintage, New York, 1985, carefully and sympathetically charts racial politics on both sides of the color line in this community identified with Booker T. Washington. Three earlier studies that provide useful accounts of the *Gomillion* case and the related boycott are Harry Holloway, *The Politics of the Southern Negro: From Exclusion to Big City Organization*, Random House, New York, 1969; Lewis Jones and Stanley Smith, *Voting Rights and Economic Pressure*, Anti-Defamation League, New York, 1958; and Bernard Taper, *Gomillion v. Lightfoot*, McGraw-Hill, New York, 1962.

CHAPTER 3

For nearly two decades after its publication, David L. Lewis, *King: A Critical Biography*, Praeger, New York, 1970 [republished as *King: A Biography*, University of Illinois Press, Urbana, Ill., 1978], was the standard interpretation of the nation's best-known civil rights leader. In the late 1980s, three enormously valuable studies appeared, which draw upon manuscript records that were not available to Lewis and on extensive interviews. David Garrow has written more thoroughly about King's career than any other contemporary scholar. His early studies, *Protest at Selma: Martin Luther King and the Voting Rights Act of 1965*, Yale University Press, New Haven, Conn., 1978, and *The FBI and Martin Luther King, Jr.*, Norton, New York, 1981, paved the way for the encyclopedic *Bearing the Cross: Martin Luther King, Jr., and the Southern Christian Leadership Conference*, William Morrow, New York, 1986. Adam Fairclough, *To Redeem the Soul of America: The Southern Christian Leadership Conference and Martin Luther King, Jr.*, University of Georgia Press, Athens, Ga., 1987, offers thoughtful interpretations of King, the organization he led, and the larger movement. Taylor Branch, *Parting the Waters: America in the King Years, 1954–1963*, Simon & Schuster, New York, 1988, places King within the larger black religious culture from which he emerged. Very helpful in discussing the Crusade for Citizenship program is Aldon Morris, *Origins of the Civil Rights Movement* (New York, 1984). The sketch of Fred Shuttlesworth was drawn primarily from Morris. Howell Raines, *My Soul Is Rested: Movement Days in the Deep South Remembered*, Putnam, New York, 1977, provides a revealing collection of interviews with prominent and not so well-known leaders and opponents of the civil rights movement. For additional interviews, along with a narrative of the freedom struggle that emphasizes the roles played by plain, though extraordinary, people, consult Juan Williams, *Eyes on the Prize: America's Civil Rights Years, 1954–1965*, Viking, New York, 1987. Other major civil rights groups that engaged in direct-action protests and political organizing in southern communities have also received detailed treatments. On SNCC, see the work of Howard Zinn, a historian who participated as an adviser to the organization, *SNCC: The New Abolitionists*, Beacon Press, Boston, 1964, and that of Clayborne Carson, *SNCC and the Black Awakening of the 1960s*, Harvard University Press, Cambridge, Mass., 1981, which is the most judicious treatment of the subject. The camaraderie born out of the fierce battles waged by this vanguard organization is reflected in the insightful accounts offered by three former staff members: James Forman (executive secretary), *The Making of Black Revolutionaries*, Macmillan, New York, 1972; Cleveland Sellers (program director), with Robert Terrell, *The River of No Return: The Autobiography of a Black Militant and the Life and Death of SNCC*, William Morrow, New York, 1973; and Mary King (assistant communications director), *Freedom Song: A Personal Story of the 1960s Civil Rights Movement*, William Morrow, New York, 1987. Joe Sinsheimer, "Never Turn Back: An Interview With Sam Block," *Southern Exposure*, 15 (Summer 1987): 37–50, furnishes a poignant firsthand account from a SNCC organizer from Mississippi. On CORE, see Meier and Rudwick, *CORE* (cited for Chapter 1), the standard work on the subject. James Farmer, *Lay Bare the Heart: An Autobiography of the Civil Rights Movement*, Arbor House, New York, 1985, provides a moving account of the organization and its operation from the perspective of one of its founders. The NAACP still has not been the focus of a scholarly monograph for the years since World War II. However, this period is seen through the eyes of its executive director, Roy Wilkins, in his memoir, *Standing Fast* (cited for Chapter 2).

The performance of the Kennedy administration is rated very highly in Carl Brauer, *John F. Kennedy and the Second Reconstruction*, Columbia University Press, New York, 1977. Another favorable study of Kennedy, by his chief civil rights adviser, can be found in Harris Wofford, *Of Kennedys and Kings: Making Sense of the Sixties*, Farrar, Straus & Giroux, New York, 1980. A sensitive portrayal, it describes the difficulties a civil rights advocate close to

Martin Luther King, Jr., faced in trying to shape government policy. Much more critical of the Kennedy administration are Victor Navasky, *Kennedy Justice*, Atheneum, New York, 1971, a trenchant analysis of the Justice Department, and Pat Watters and Reese Cleghorn, *Climbing Jacob's Ladder: The Arrival of Negroes in Southern Politics*, Harcourt, Brace, & World, New York, 1967, which finds Kennedy's implementation of voting rights programs sadly lacking. A balanced and mildly critical assessment of the Kennedy administration's handling of the desegregation of interstate transportation appears in Barnes, *Journey from Jim Crow* (cited for Chapter 1). A comparison of the styles and accomplishments of Kennedy and Johnson in furnishing presidential leadership is offered by Tom Wicker, *JFK and LBJ: The Influence of Personality Upon Politics*, Penguin, Baltimore, 1970. The political maneuvering behind the enactment of the 1964 civil rights law is detailed in Charles Whalen and Barbara Whalen, *The Longest Debate: A Legislative History of the 1964 Civil Rights Act*, New American Library, New York, 1986. I have previously reviewed the literature and historiographical opportunities for research on Johnson's civil rights policies in "Civil Rights," in *Exploring the Johnson Years*, Robert A. Divine, ed. University of Texas Press, Austin, Tex., 1981: 93–125.

The struggle of black Mississippians for political liberation is best analyzed by John Dittmer, "The Politics of the Mississippi Movement, 1954–1964," in *The Civil Rights Movement in America*, Charles W. Eagles, ed. University Press of Mississippi, Jackson, Miss., 1986: 65–93. The same volume includes comments on Dittmer's essay by Neil McMillen as well as essays and commentaries on various aspects of the freedom struggle. Joseph Sinsheimer, "COFO and the 1963 Freedom Vote: New Strategies for Change in Mississippi," *Journal of Southern History* 55 (May 1989): 217–244, perceptively discusses community organizing and political development surrounding the conduct of symbolic mock elections. These activities set the stage for the 1964 Mississippi Freedom Summer. The events of that campaign and its impact on the volunteers is analyzed from a sociological perspective in Doug McAdam, *Freedom Summer*, Oxford University Press, New York, 1988. The strains placed on black and white workers are described by Allen J. Matusow, "From Civil Rights to Black Power: The Case of SNCC, 1960–1966," in *Twentieth-Century America: Recent Interpretations*, Barton J. Bernstein and Allen J. Matusow, eds., Harcourt,

Brace, Jovanovich, New York, 1972: 494–519. Elizabeth Sutherland, ed., *Letters from Mississippi*, McGraw-Hill, New York, 1965 compiles the writings of the highly reflective summer participants. The challenge at the Democratic convention, which climaxed Freedom Summer, is documented and analyzed in Leslie Burl McLemore, "The Mississippi Freedom Democratic Party: A Case Study of Grass-Roots Politics," Ph.D. diss. (University of Massachusetts, 1971). For a listing of a variety of works on the same subject, see Jennifer McDowell and Milton Loventhall, eds., *Black Politics: A Study and Annotated Bibliography of the Mississippi Freedom Democratic Party*, Center for the Study of Political Science, San Jose, Calif., 1971. The legal response by the Johnson administration to the widespread brutality against the summer workers, including the murder of three of them in Philadelphia, Mississippi, receives critical treatment in Michal Belknap, *Federal Law and Southern Order: Racial Violence and Constitutional Conflict in the Post-Brown South*, University of Georgia Press, Athens, Ga., 1987. The strategy of President Johnson and the Democratic party in dealing with the black vote in 1964 is the topic of an unpublished essay by Mark Stern of the political science department of the University of Central Florida: "The 1964 Presidential Election: Partisan Shifts and the Southern Black Vote," in my possession.

The continuing story of the Tuskegee struggle appears in Robert J. Norrell, *Reaping the Whirlwind* (cited for Chapter 2). Some useful data on Birmingham is furnished by Harry Holloway, *Politics of the Southern Negro* (cited for Chapter 2). The diverse relationships between civil rights activists and southern white business leaders in fourteen communities are discussed in original essays prepared for a volume edited by Elizabeth Jacoway and David R. Colburn, *Southern Businessmen and Desegregation*, Louisiana State University Press, Baton Rouge, 1982. Colburn has also written a book-length study that ably traces the origins of a community's struggle and the impact the civil rights movement had upon it in *Racial Change and Community Crisis: St. Augustine, Florida, 1877–1980*, Columbia University Press, New York, 1985.

CHAPTER 4

The voting rights struggle in Selma is detailed in Garrow, *Protest at Selma*; Fairclough, *To Redeem the Soul of America*; Forman, *Mak-*

ing of Black Revolutionaries; Zinn, *SNCC*; and Clayborne Carson, *In Struggle* (all cited for Chapter 3). The local actors and politics of the Selma movement are fleshed out in Charles E. Fager, *Selma, 1965*, Charles Scribner's Sons, New York, 1974; J. Mills Thornton, "Municipal Politics and the Course of the Civil Rights Movement" (paper delivered at the Conference on New Directions in Civil Rights Studies, University of Virginia, May 1988); Stephen L. Longenecker, *Selma's Peacemaker: Ralph Smeltzer and Civil Rights Mediation*, Temple University Press, Philadelphia, 1987; Sheyanne Webb and Rachel West Nelson, *Selma, Lord, Selma*, University of Alabama Press, University, Ala., 1980; and from interviews contained in Williams, *Eyes on the Prize*, and Raines, *My Soul Is Rested* (cited for Chapter 3). The legal precedents leading to passage of the Voting Rights Act and the legislative battle itself are discussed in Charles V. Hamilton, *The Bench and the Ballot: Southern Federal Judges and Black Voters*, Oxford University Press, New York, 1973; Lawson, *Black Ballots* (cited for Chapter 1); and in President Lyndon B. Johnson's memoirs, *The Vantage Point: Perspectives of the Presidency, 1963–1969*, Holt Rinehart Winston, New York, 1971. For similar conclusions about the federal government's caution in implementing the 1965 law, see my *In Pursuit of Power: Southern Blacks and Electoral Politics, 1965–1982*, Columbia University Press, New York, 1985, and Howard Ball, Dale Krane, and Thomas P. Lauth, *Compromised Compliance: Implementation of the 1965 Voting Rights Act*, Greenwood Press, Westport, Conn., 1982. Mary King's *Freedom Song* (cited for Chapter 3) notes the nontangible rewards of political organizing.

The development of black power and its theoretical application to electoral strategies in the South appear in the classic work of Stokely Carmichael and Charles V. Hamilton, *Black Power: The Politics of Liberation in America*, Vintage Books, New York, 1967. Matusow, "From Civil Rights to Black Power" (cited for Chapter 3), places the issue in historical perspective and offers a critique of the approach. Joyce Ladner, a sociologist and SNCC veteran, offers very useful insights into different conceptions of black power in "What Black Power Means to Negroes in Mississippi," in *The Transformation of Activism*, August Meier, ed. Aldine, Chicago, 1970: 131–154. For examinations into the effects of racial awareness on black voting behavior, see Sidney Verba, Norman Nie, and Jae-on Kim, *Participation and Political Equality*, Cambridge University Press, Cambridge, Engl., 1978, and Richard D. Shingles, "Black Consciousness and Political Participation: The Missing Link," *American Political Science Review*, 75 (1981): 76–91. The Meredith march, during which the slogan of black power was first publicized, is treated in Milton Viorst, *Fire in the Streets: America in the 1960s*, Simon & Schuster, New York, 1979; Cleveland Sellers, with Robert Terrell, *The River of No Return*; Carson, *In Struggle*; David Garrow, *Bearing the Cross: Martin Luther King, Jr., and the Southern Christian Leadership Conference* (all cited for Chapter 3); and Lawson, *Pursuit of Power*. Martin Luther King, *Where Do We Go from Here?: Community or Chaos*, Harper & Row, New York, 1967 offers a sensitive account by one of the central participants in the march about the controversy over black power. The comment of Malcolm X on the use of the ballot is quoted in Manning Marable, *Race, Reform, and Rebellion: The Second Reconstruction in Black America, 1945–1982*, University Press of Mississippi, Jackson, Miss., 1984, which provides a provocative and informative synthesis of the larger black freedom struggle.

Case studies of black power in operation in southern politics are found in works dealing with Lowndes County, Alabama, and Hancock County, Georgia. For the former see Hardy T. Frye, *Black Parties and Political Power: A Case Study*, G. K. Hall, Boston, 1980; Andrew Kopkind, "The Lair of the Black Panther," *New Republic*, 155 (June 18, 1966): 10–13; Kopkind, "Lowndes County, Alabama: The Great Fear Is Gone," *Ramparts*, 13 (April 1975): 8–12; and John Corry, "A Visit to Lowndes County, Alabama," *New South*, 27 (Winter 1972): 28–36. On Hancock County, see the critical account by John Rozier, *Black Boss: Political Revolution in a Georgia County*, University of Georgia Press, Athens, Ga., 1982, and the more favorable scholarly appraisal by Lawrence J. Hanks, *The Struggle for Black Political Empowerment in Three Georgia Counties*, University of Tennessee Press, Knoxville, Tenn., 1987. Firsthand accounts of the efforts of black candidates to gain office are compiled in Julian Bond, ed., *Black Candidates: Southern Campaign Experiences*, Voter Education Project, Atlanta, Ga., 1968. William M. Simpson, "The 'Loyalist' Democrats of Mississippi: Challenge to a White Majority, 1965–1972," Ph.D. diss. (Mississippi State University, 1974), describes the transformation of the insurgent movement in the Magnolia State. For case studies of successful black political organizing and campaigning in Mississippi, see Minion K. C. Morrison, *Black Political Mobilization: Leadership, Power, and Mass Behavior*, State University of New York Press, Albany, 1987. The efforts of the Democratic party to increase minority access to its affairs are detailed in William J. Crotty, *Decision for the Democrats: Reforming the Party Structure*, Johns Hopkins University Press, Baltimore, 1979, and Byron E. Shafer, *Quiet Revolution: The Struggle for the Democratic Party and the Shaping of Post-Reform Politics*, Russell Sage Foundation, New York, 1983.

The subjects of black power, the ghetto explosions, and the white backlash are dealt with in Joe R. Feagin and Harlan Hahn, *Ghetto Revolts*, Macmillan, New York, 1973; James W. Button, *Black Violence: Political Impact of the 1960s Riots*, Princeton University Press, Princeton, N.J., 1978; and Marshall Frady, *Wallace*, New American Library, New York, 1975. Robert H. Wiebe, "White Attitudes and Black Rights from *Brown* to *Bakke*," in *Have We Overcome?*, Michael V. Namorato, ed., University Press of Mississippi, Jackson, Miss., 1979: 147–171, discusses the changing shape of white public opinion during this period. The story of the Black Panther party from the perspective of its leaders is told in Huey P. Newton, with J. Herman Blake, *Revolutionary Suicide*, Harcourt Brace Jovanovich, New York, 1973; Bobby Seale, *Seize the Time*, Random House, New York, 1970; and Robert Scheer, ed., *Eldridge Cleaver: Post-Prison Writing and Speeches*, Random House, New York, 1969. The Ocean Hill–Brownsville controversy is detailed in Diane Ravitch, *The Great School Wars*, Basic Books, New York, 1974; Robert G. Weisbrot and Arthur Stein, *Bittersweet Encounter: The Afro-American and the Jew*, Negro Universities Press, Westport, Conn., 1970; and Jonathan Kaufman, *Broken Alliance*, Charles Scribner's Sons, New York, 1988. Henry Hampton and Steve Fayer with Sarah Flynn, *Voices of Freedom*, Bantam, New York, 1990, contains an oral history of the school crisis. Allen Matusow, *The Unraveling of America: A History of Liberalism in the 1960s*, Harper & Row, New York, 1984, and Todd Gitlin, *The Sixties: Years of Hope, Days of Rage*, Bantam, New York, 1987, comment on the influence of the Panthers on white radicals. Philip S. Foner, ed., *The Black Panther Speaks*, Lippincott, Philadelphia, 1970, provides a documentary collection of the organization. The complex history of the Detroit uprising is told in painstaking detail and in balanced fashion in Sidney Fine, *Violence in the Model City: Race Relations, the Cavanagh Administration, and the Detroit Race Riot of 1967*, University of Michigan Press, Ann Arbor, Mich., 1989. On the efforts against Julian Bond and Adam Clayton Powell, see John Neary, *Julian Bond: Black Rebel*, Morrow, New York, 1971; Andy Jacobs, *The Powell Affair, Freedom Minus One*, Bobbs-Merrill, Indianapolis, 1973; Kent M. Weeks, *Adam Clayton Powell and the Supreme Court*, Dunellen, New York, 1971; and P. Allan Dionesopoulos, *Rebellion, Racism, and Representation: The Adam Clayton Powell Case and Its Antecedents*, Northern Illinois University Press, De Kalb, Ill., 1970.

The election of 1968 is covered in Lewis Chester, Godfrey Hodgson, and Bruce Page, *An American Melodrama*, Dell, New York, 1969, and William L. O'Neill, *Coming Apart: An Informal History of America in the 1960s*, Quadrangle, New York, 1971. The changing outlines of southern politics, especially the drift toward presidential Republicanism, are portrayed in a number of impressive works by political scientists. See Earl Black and Merle Black, *Politics and Society in the South*, Harvard University Press, Cambridge, Mass., 1987; Alexander P. Lamis, *The Two-Party South*, Oxford University Press, New York, 1984; and Harold W. Stanley, *Voter Mobilization and the Politics of Race: The South and Universal Suffrage, 1952–1984*, Praeger, New York, 1987. Two historians who have provided a sophisticated examination of evolving political trends in Dixie are Numan V. Bartley and Hugh D. Graham, *Southern Politics and the Second Reconstruction*, Johns Hopkins University Press, Baltimore, 1975. Each of these works owes a great debt to V. O. Key's classic, *Southern Politics in State and Nation*, Vintage Books, New York, 1949. Monroe Lee Billington, *The Political South in the Twentieth Century*, Charles Scribner's Sons, New York, 1975, is a useful text for historical background on the changes that have taken place. Jody Carlson, *George C. Wallace and the Politics of Powerlessness*, Transaction Books, New Brunswick, N.J., 1981, analyzes the Wallace campaigns for the presidency from 1964 to 1976.

On the Nixon administration, consult the President's own account, *RN: The Memoirs of Richard Nixon*, Grosset & Dunlop, New York, 1978, as well as the work of one of his chief political aides who dealt with the South, Harry S. Dent, *The Prodigal South Returns to Power*, John Wiley, New York, 1978. More negative assessments of Nixon's performance are found in Richard Harris, *Justice: The Crisis of Law, Order, and Freedom in America*, Dutton, New York, 1970; Leon E. Panetta and Peter Gall, *Bring Us Together: The Nixon Team and the Civil Rights Retreat*, Lippincott, Philadelphia, 1971; William E. Leuchtenburg, "The White House and Black America: From Eisenhower to Carter," in *Have We Overcome?* Namorato, ed., 121–145; and my *In Pursuit of Power* and "E Pluribus Unum: Civil Rights and National Unity," in *American Choices: Social Dilemmas and Public Policy Since 1960*, Robert H. Bremner, Gary W. Reichard, and Richard J. Hopkins, eds. Ohio State University Press, Columbus, Ohio, 1986: 35–73. Gary Orfield, *Congressional Power: Congress and Social Change*, Harcourt Brace Jovanovich, New York, 1975, offers a sharp appraisal of the 1970 Voting Rights Act extension.

The efforts to form independent black political interest groups have received some treatment. Marguerite Ross Barnett, "The Congressional Black Caucus: Illusions and Realities of Power," in *The New Black Politics: The Search for Political Power*: 28–55, Preston, Henderson, and Puryear, eds. (cited for Chapter 1), offers a useful overview of the operation of black congressional lawmakers. A wide variety of organizational attempts are described by Martin Kilson, "The New Black Political Class," in *Dilemmas of the New Black Middle Class*, Joseph R. Washington, ed. (n.p., 1980): 81–100. The Gary convention is discussed in Marable, *Race, Reform, and Rebellion*; Vincent Harding, *The Other American Revolution*, Center for Afro-American Studies, University of California, Los Angeles, 1981; and Ronald W. Walters, *Black Presidential Politics in America: A Strategic Approach*, State University of New York, Albany, 1988. The early years of the Joint Center for Political Studies are recounted by Alex Poinsett, "'The Joint': D.C. Center for Political Studies Backs Up Elected Officials," *Ebony*, 28 (April 1973): 124–132.

CHAPTER 5

Bayard Rustin's challenging analysis appears in "From Protest to Politics: The Future of the Civil Rights Movement," *Commentary*,

39 (February 1965): 25–31. On the transition of blacks from protesters to candidates, see my *In Pursuit of Power* and Bond, *Black Candidates*, which are cited for Chapter 4; Ladd, *Negro Leadership* (cited for Chapter 1); Albert K. Karnig and Susan Welch, *Black Representation and Urban Policy*, University of Chicago Press, Chicago, 1980; Chuck Stone, *Black Political Power in America*, Dell, New York, 1970; Jason Berry, *Amazing Grace: With Charles Evers in Mississippi*, Saturday Review Press, New York, 1973; Leonard A. Cole, *Blacks in Power: A Comparative Study of Black and White Elected Officials*, Princeton University Press, Princeton, N.J., 1976; Lester M. Salamon, "Leadership and Modernization: The Emerging Black Political Elite in the American South," *Journal of Politics*, 35 (August 1973): 615–646; Robert C. Smith, "The Changing Shape of Urban Black Politics, 1960–1970," *The Annals of the American Academy of Political and Social Science*, 439 (September 1978): 16–28; Paul Jeffrey Steckler, "Electing Black Candidates to Office in the South," *The Urban Lawyer*, 17 (Summer 1985): 473–487; Jack Bass and Walter DeVries, *The Transformation of Southern Politics: Social Change and Political Consequence Since 1945*, Basic Books, New York, 1976; Bette Woody, *Managing Crisis Cities: The New Black Leadership and the Politics of Resource Allocation*, Greenwood Press, Westport, Conn., 1982; and Martin Kilson, "Political Change in the Negro Ghetto, 1900–1940's," in *Key Issues in the Afro-American Experience*, vol. 2, Nathan I. Huggins, Martin Kilson, and Daniel Fox, eds. Harcourt Brace Jovanovich, New York, 1971: 167–192. The politics of the Community Action Program of the War on Poverty are discussed in Matusow, *The Unraveling of America* (cited for Chapter 4). For a profile of Tuskegee's Johnny Ford, see Marshall Frady, *Southerners: A Journalistic Odyssey*, New American Library, New York, 1980.

The best overview of the issue of at-large versus single-member district elections is provided by the essays contained in Chandler Davidson, ed., *Minority Vote Dilution*, Howard University Press, Washington, D.C., 1984. The Washington Research Project, *The Shameful Blight: The Survival of Racial Discrimination in Voting in the South*, Washington Research Project, Washington, D.C., 1972, catalogues the sundry forms of franchise abuse that persisted after passage of the Voting Rights Act. For the argument that the federal government has exceeded statutory and constitutional boundaries in seeking to maximize minority voting strength by applying affirmative action principles, see Abigail M. Thernstrom, *Whose Votes Count? Affirmative Action and Minority Voting Rights*, Harvard University Press, Cambridge, Mass., 1987, and Katharine I. Butler, "Denial or Abridgement of the Right to Vote: What Does It Mean?" in *The Voting Rights Act: Consequences and Implications*, Lorn S. Foster, ed. Praeger, New York, 1985: 44–59.

The performance of black elected officials is discussed and evaluated in Hanks, *Black Empowerment* (cited for Chapter 4); Margaret Edds, *Free At Last: What Really Happened When Civil Rights Came to Southern Politics*, Adler & Adler, Bethesda, Md., 1987; Peter K. Eisinger, *The Politics of Displacement: Racial and Ethnic Transition in Three American Cities*, Academic Press, New York, 1980; Rufus P. Browning, Dale Rogers Marshall, and David H. Tabb, *Protest Is Not Enough: The Struggle of Blacks and Hispanics for Equality in Urban Politics*, University of California Press, Berkeley, Calif., 1984; James W. Button, *Blacks and Social Change*, Princeton University Press, Princeton, 1989; and Paul Jeffrey Stekler, "Black Politics in the New South: An Investigation of Change at Various Levels," Ph.D. diss. (Harvard University, 1982). The black middle class has received extensive treatment in L. Bart Landry, *The New Black Middle Class*, University of California Press, Berkeley, Calif., 1987, and the underclass has been analyzed by William Julius Wilson, *The Truly Disadvantaged: The Inner City, the Underclass, and Public Policy*, University of Chicago Press, Chicago, 1987.

There remains to be written a systematic study of the role of black women in the civil rights movement and electoral politics. The best place to obtain data on black female officeholders is the Joint Center of Political Studies, *The National Roster of Black Elected Officials*, published annually. The center started keeping statistics on black women officeholders in 1975. Other sources of useful information are Susan M. Hartmann, *From Margin to Mainstream: American Women and Politics Since 1960*, Knopf, New York, 1989; Paula Giddings, *When and Where I Enter: The Impact of Black Women on Race and Sex in America*, Bantam, New York, 1984; and Sara Evans, *Personal Politics: The Roots of Women's Liberation in the Civil Rights Movement and the New Left*, Vintage, New York, 1980. For a discussion and analysis of Unita Blackwell, see Minion K. C. Morrison, *Black Political Mobilization* (cited for Chapter 4).

Mack H. Jones, "Black Political Empowerment in Atlanta: Myth and Reality," *The Annals of the American Academy of Political and Social Science*, 439 (September 1978): 90–117, offers a critical assessment of the impact of black mayors in Atlanta; and Edds, *Free At Last*, and Eisinger, *The Politics of Displacement*, provide more favorable evaluations. For background on Maynard Jackson, see Fred Powledge, "Profiles: A New Politics In Atlanta," *New Yorker*, 49 (December 31, 1973): 28–40, and Peter Ross Range, "Capital of Black-Is-Beautiful," *New York Times Magazine*, April 7, 1974, 28–29, 68–78. Edds, *Free At Last*, and Robert J. Norrell, *Reaping the Whirlwind* (cited for Chapter 2) offer complementary and balanced views on Tuskegee and Macon County. The discussions of Cleveland and Gary are based largely on the thorough case study by William E. Nelson, Jr., and Philip J. Meranto, *Electing Black Mayors: Political Action in the Black Community*, Ohio State University Press, Columbus, Ohio, 1977. For additional information on Cleveland, see Kenneth G. Weinberg, *Black Victory: Carl Stokes and the Winning of Cleveland*, Quadrangle, Chicago, 1968. On other victorious mayors, see Wilbur C. Rich, *Coleman Young and Detroit Politics*, Wayne State University Press, Detroit, 1989, which is a favorable if uneven treatment. It can be supplemented by Fine, *Violence in the Model City* (cited for Chapter 4); Eisinger, *The Politics of Displacement*; and Korstad and Lichtenstein, "Opportunities Found and Lost" (cited for Chapter 1). Tom Bradley has yet to find a scholarly biographer, but background information can be compiled from the sketch in *Current Biography* (1973): 53–55. Appearing too late to be helpful in this study but nonetheless useful for others to consult is Jimmie Lewis Franklin, *Back to Birmingham: Richard Arrington, Jr., and His Times*, University of Alabama Press, Tuscaloosa, 1989.

CHAPTER 6

President Ford offers his version of his efforts to work with blacks in *A Time to Heal*, Harper & Row, New York, 1979. He does not, however, explain his maneuvering on the Voting Rights Act extension. I examine the renewal of that legislation in my book *In Pursuit of Power* (cited for Chapter 4). Jack Bass and Walter DeVries, *The Transformation of Southern Politics*, as cited for Chapter 5, provides valuable data on the shift in southern Democratic support for the suffrage act. A thorough review of various aspects of the busing controversy is furnished by Gary Orfield, *Must We Bus? Segregated Schools and National Policy*, Brookings Institution, Washington, D.C., 1978. A comprehensive and eloquent treatment of the Boston struggle from the perspective of three diverse families is J. Anthony Lukas, *Common Ground*, Knopf, New York, 1985. In contrast with Boston, efforts to desegregate the schools through busing went more smoothly in Charlotte, North Carolina, and this story is chronicled in Frye Gaillard, *The Dream Long Deferred*, University of North Carolina Press, Chapel Hill, N.C., 1988.

On the 1976 presidential election and the political mood of African-Americans, see Elizabeth Drew, *American Journal: The Events of 1976*, Random House, New York, 1977; Samuel DuBois Cook, "Democracy and Tyranny in America: The Radical Paradox of the Bicentennial and Blacks in the American Political System," *Journal of Politics*, 38 (August 1976): 276–294; Kandy Straud, *How Jimmy Won: The Victory Campaign from Plains to the White House*, Morrow, New York, 1977; Jules Witcover, *Marathon: The Pursuit of the Presidency, 1972–1976*, Viking Press, New York, 1977; and the Joint Center for Political Studies, *The Black Vote: Election '76*, Joint Center for Political Studies, Washington, D.C., 1977. Barbara Jordan relates her story in her memoir coauthored with Shelby Hearon, *Barbara Jordan: A Self-Portrait*, Doubleday, Garden City, N.Y., 1979. President Carter defends his policies in *Keeping the Faith: Memoirs of a President*, Bantam, New York, 1982. On his gubernatorial record, see the laudatory account of Gary Fink, *Prelude to the Presidency: The Political Character and Legislative Leadership Style of Governor Jimmy Carter*, Greenwood Press, Westport, Conn., 1980. For the presidential years, Betty Glad, *Jimmy Carter: In Search of the Great White House*, Norton, New York, 1980, offers a favorable, but well-balanced, contemporary assessment. Louis Martin, the veteran black journalist, Democratic party operative, and Carter aide offers a glowing comment in "Carter Accomplishments in Civil Rights," *Focus*, 8 (December 1980): 7–8. A highly critical portrayal of Carter's civil rights performance, especially compared to Lyndon Johnson's, from a man who served both presidents is Joseph Califano, *Governing America: An Insider's Report from the White House and the Cabinet*, Simon & Schuster, New York, 1981. The Carter administration's twists and turns on the *Bakke* case are described by Califano and in studies by J. Harvie Wilkinson III, *From Brown to Bakke: The Supreme Court and School Integration 1954–1978*, Oxford University Press, New York, 1981, and Alan P. Sindler, *Bakke, DeFunis, and Minority Admissions: The Quest for Equal Opportunity*, Longman, New York, 1978. Relations between blacks and Jews receive historical treatment in Robert Weisbrot and Arthur Stein, *Bittersweet Encounter* and Weisbrot's *Israel in the Black American Perspective*, Greenwood Press, Westport, Conn., 1985. Jonathan Kaufman, *Broken Alliance* (cited for Chapter 4), is a sensitive work by a journalist focusing on the people involved in several of the episodes that heightened tensions between the two groups.

The rise of Ronald Reagan to the presidency is lucidly portrayed by the *Washington Post* columnist Lou Cannon in *Reagan*, Putnam, New York, 1982. Details of black voting in the 1980 elections are furnished in Milton Morris, "Blacks and the 1980 Presidential Election," *Focus* (October–November 1980): 3–4, 8. Critical evaluations of the Reagan administration's performance on equal opportunity and affirmative action programs are contained in Harrell R. Rodgers, Jr., "Fair Employment Laws for Minorities: An Evaluation of Federal Implementation," in *Implementation of Civil Rights Policy*, Charles S. Bullock III and Charles M. Lamb, eds. Brooks/Cole Publishing, Monterey, Calif., 1984: 93–117; Hanes Walton, *When the Marching Stopped: The Politics of Civil Rights Regulatory Agencies*, State University of New York Press, Albany, 1988; and Tinsley Yarbrough, "The Reagan Administration, the IRS, and Discriminatory Private Schools" (paper presented at Southern Political Science Association annual meeting, Birmingham, Ala., 1983). The Eddie Williams quote on the importance of the vote to counteract Reagan's budget-slashing effects on the poor appears in "Perspective," *Focus*, 9 (May 1981): 2. I trace the events surrounding renewal of the Voting Rights Act in 1982 in my *In Pursuit of Power*. For different views of the Reagan administration's enforcement of the landmark suffrage law, compare Frank Parker, "Retreat on Voting Rights?" *Focus*, 14 (May 1986): 4–5, 7, and Abigail M. Thernstrom, "Voting Rights' Trap," *New Republic*, 193 (September 2, 1985): 21–23, as well as her *Whose Votes Count? Affirmative Action and Minority Voting Rights* (cited for Chapter 5). The economic crisis among blacks and the growing class distinctions are reviewed in "The State of the Union: One Nation or Two?" *Focus*, 10 (March 1982): 6; Andrew F. Brimmer, "Black Economic Progress," *Focus*, 13 (April 1985): 6, 8; and Andrew Hacker, "American Apartheid," *New York Review of Books* (December 3, 1987): 26–33. A discussion of black neoconservatives appears in Salim Muwakkil, "New Issues Reviving Dominant Arguments," *In These Times* (November 13–19, 1985): 3, 6. Thomas Sowell, *Race and Economics*, D. McKay Co., New York, 1975, and his *Civil Rights: Rhetoric or Reality?*, Morrow, New York, 1984, are two of the most notable works that reflect the thinking of black conservatives.

The Chicago mayoral election has already captured a good deal of scholarly investigation. For a background of black politics in Chicago, see the classic, James Q. Wilson, *Negro Politics: The Search For Leadership*, Free Press, New York, 1965. A more recent account that challenges Wilson's model of black political behavior is Dianne M. Pinderhughes, *Race and Ethnicity in Chicago Politics: A Reexamination of Pluralist Theory*, University of Illinois Press, Urbana, Ill., 1987. David Garrow, *Bearing the Cross: Martin Luther King and the Voting Rights Act of 1965* (cited for Chapter 3), and Alan B. Anderson and George W. Pickering, *Confronting the Color Line: The Broken Promise of the Civil Rights Movement in Chicago*, University of Georgia Press, Athens, Ga., 1986, offer accounts of Martin Luther King's campaigns for open housing and the grassroots struggle for racial equality in Chicago during the 1960s. William J. Grimshaw, *Black Politics in Chicago: The Quest for Leadership, 1939–1979*, Center for Urban Policy, Loyola University, Chicago, 1980, briefly surveys black politicians and their changing relationship to the Democratic political machine. A first-hand account by an opponent of the Daley machine appears in Anna R. Langford, "How I 'Whupped' the Tar Out of the Daley Machine," in *What Black Politicians Are Saying*, Nathan Wright, Jr., ed. Hawthorn Books, New York, 1972: 3–31. On the election of Harold Washington, the most reliable account is Paul Kleppner, *Chicago Divided: The Making of a Black Mayor*, Northern Illinois University Press, De Kalb, Ill., 1985. Other useful works on this subject are Abdul Alkalimat, "Mayor Washington's Bid for Re-election," *Black Scholar*, 17 (November/December 1986): 2–39; Alkalimat and Doug Gills, "Black Power vs. Racism: The Election of Harold Washington," in *The New Black Vote: A Look at Four American Cities*, Rod Bush, ed. Synthesis Publications, San Francisco, 1984: 55–179; Michael Preston, "The Election of Harold Washington: Black Voting Patterns in the 1983 Chicago Mayoral Race," *PS*, 16 (Summer 1983): 486–488; Twiley W. Barker, "Political Mobilization of Black Chicago: Drafting a Candidate," *PS*, 16 (Summer 1983): 482–485; Manning Marable, "Harold Washington and the Politics of Race in Chicago," *Black Scholar*, 17 (November/December 1986): 14–23; Thomas E. Cavanagh, "How Washington Won Chicago," *Focus*, 11 (May 1983): 3, 7–8; David Moberg, "Washington Learns that Reform Comes Slowly," *In These Times* (January 28–February 3, 1987): 12–13; and Gerald McWorter, Doug Gills, and Ron Bailey, "Black Power Politics as Social Movement: Dialectics of Leadership in the Campaign to Elect Harold Washington Mayor of Chicago" (Afro-American Studies and Research Program, University of Illinois, June 1984). A very handy compilation of newspaper clippings and other sources related to the election can be found in Peoples College Press, *Black Power in Chicago: A Documentary Survey of the 1983 Mayoral Democratic Primary*, Chicago, 1983.

On the upsurge in black voter participation in the early 1980s, see Gracia M. Hillman, "Operation Big Vote: Crusade '82 Begins," *Focus*, 12 (January 1984): 8; "Largest Increases in BEOs Since 1976," *Focus*, 12 (January 1984): 8; and Adolph L. Reed, Jr., *The Jesse Jackson Phenomenon: The Crisis of Purpose in Afro-American Politics*, Yale University Press, New Haven, Conn., 1986. Harvey Gantt details his career and political philosophy in Laura Haessley, "We're Becoming the Mayors," *Southern Exposure*, 14 (March/April 1986): 44–52.

CHAPTER 7

The issue of legitimacy is discussed in Peter K. Eisinger, *The Politics of Displacement* (cited for Chapter 5). The importance of the presidency as a symbol of political legitimacy is noted from a critical perspective by Mack H. Jones, "A Black Presidential Candidate in

1984: More of the Same," *PS*, 16 (Summer 1983): 495–496, and from a more positive viewpoint by Lucius J. Barker, "Black Americans and the Politics of Inclusion," *PS*, 16 (Summer 1983): 500–507. Shirley Chisholm, *Unbought and Unbossed*, Avon Books, New York, 1971, is an autobiographical account of the Brooklyn lawmaker's political career before her unsuccessful campaign for the presidency, which she writes about in *The Good Fight*, Harper & Row, New York, 1973. On that race, see Stephan Lesher, "The Short, Unhappy Life of Black Presidential Politics, 1972," *New York Times Magazine*, June 25, 1972, 12–22. It is still too soon to have a first-rate biography of Jesse Jackson, but until one appears there are several helpful works on the subject. Unfortunately, most of these reflect the highly charged views that divide opinion about him. Barbara A. Reynolds, *Jesse Jackson: The Man, the Movement, the Myth*, Nelson-Hall, Chicago, 1975, offers much detail about Jackson's life and generally portrays the minister in an unflattering light. However, the author's negative conclusions apparently underwent modification in the wake of Jackson's bid for the presidency. Reynolds republished the book with a different title, *Jesse Jackson: America's David*, JFJ Associates, Washington, D.C., 1985, and although the text remains the same, she added a new introduction much more sympathetic to her subject. Thomas H. Landess and Richard M. Quinn, *Jesse Jackson and the Politics of Race*, Jameson Books, Ottawa, Ill., 1985, draws heavily on the Reynolds account to reach unfavorable conclusions about Jackson personally and professionally. A more scholarly but no less critical analysis of Jackson's attempt to jump from protest to electoral politics is presented by Adolph L. Reed, Jr., *The Jesse Jackson Phenomenon* (cited for Chapter 6). A more balanced account, by two reporters who covered Jackson's 1984 campaign, appears in Bob Faw and Nancy Skelton, *Thunder in America*, Texas Monthly Press, Austin, 1986. Elizabeth O. Colton, Jackson's press secretary, who resigned during the campaign, offers an inside account of the 1988 presidential bid that is critical of the candidate's personality but recognizes the importance of his cause [see *The Jackson Phenomenon: The Man, the Power, the Message*, Doubleday, New York, 1989]. The most sympathetic treatments of the Jackson bid are found in the wide-ranging work of a campaign aide, Sheila D. Collins, *The Rainbow Challenge: The Jackson Campaign and the*

Future of U.S. Politics, Monthly Review Press, New York, 1986, and of a scholar–Democratic convention delegate, Lucius J. Barker, *Our Time Has Come: A Delegate's Diary of Jesse Jackson's 1984 Presidential Campaign*, University of Illinois Press, Urbana, Ill., 1988. The participation of black voters in the primaries and general elections is analyzed in a series of publications sponsored by the Joint Center for Political Studies, Washington, D.C.: Thomas E. Cavanagh, *The Impact of the Black Electorate* (1984); Thomas E. Cavanagh and Lorn S. Foster, *Jesse Jackson's Campaign: The Primaries and Caucuses*, (1984); and Thomas E. Cavanagh, *Inside Black America: The Message of the Black Vote in the 1984 Elections* (1985). Hardy T. Frye, "Jesse Jackson and the Rainbow," *Socialist Review*, 17 (March-April, 1987): 55–80, and Marguerite Ross Barnett, "The Strategy Over a Black Presidential Candidacy," *PS*, 16 (Summer 1983): 489–491, provide an understanding of the divisions within black leadership circles on support for Jackson. The most recent collections of scholarly analyses of the Jackson campaign and its impact are Robert P. Steed, Laurence W. Moreland, and Tod A. Baker, eds., *The 1984 Presidential Election in the South: Patterns of Southern Party Politics*, Praeger, New York, 1986, in which see especially Harold W. Stanley, "The 1984 Presidential Election in the South: Race and Realignment," 303–335, for a summary conclusion; Laurence W. Moreland, Robert P. Steed, and Tod A. Baker, eds., *Blacks in Southern Politics*, Praeger, New York, 1987; and Lucius J. Barker and Ronald W. Walters, eds., *Jesse Jackson's 1984 Presidential Campaign: Challenge and Change in American Politics*, University of Illinois Press, Urbana, Ill., 1989.

The Reagan administration's prosecution of the voter fraud cases in the Alabama black belt is discussed in Margaret Edds, *Free At Last* (cited for Chapter 6); Sheila D. Collins, "Justice Department Undermines Act," *In These Times* (July 10–23, 1985): 5, 22; Allen Tullos, "Voting Rights Activists Acquitted," *Nation* (August 3, 1985): 78–80; and "Vote Fraud on Trial," *Newsweek* (November 25, 1985): 10. The results of the 1986 congressional contests are analyzed in Linda Williams, "1986 Elections: Major Implications for Black Politics," *Focus*, 14 (November-December 1986): 5–7, and Bill Minor, "Congressman Espy from Mississippi," *Southern Changes*, 8 (December 1986): 1–3. The effect of the black electorate on reshaping southern white Democratic politicians is discussed in Earl Black and Merle Black, *Politics and Society in the South*, and Alexander P. Lamis, *The Two-Party South* (both cited for Chapter 4). The increasing competition between black candidates for office and the pivotal balance of power role played by whites is discussed in a paper by Monte Piliawsky and Paul J. Stekler, "The Evolution of Black Politics in New Orleans: From Protest to Powerbrokers," in possession of author.

Information on Jackson's 1988 presidential bid was compiled concurrently with the campaign. Given the contemporary nature of the event, I had to rely on available newspapers and periodicals. Of particular importance in tracking this contest was *Focus*, published by the Joint Center for Political Studies, particularly the section called "Political Trendletter." In addition, from the popular press the following articles are worth noting explicitly: Doug Foster, "Interview with Jesse Jackson: He Thinks He Can Win," *Mother Jones* (October 1987): 27–45, and "Jackson's White Organizers," *Newsweek* (February 8, 1988): 26. In the *Village Voice*: "Jackson's Message" (March 21, 1988): 23–24; "Jackson's Big Takeoff" (April 11, 1988): 22; and Thulani Davis and James Ridgeway, "Jesse Jackson's New Math" (December 22, 1987): 20–25. Also, Joyce Purnick and Michael Oreskes, "Jesse Jackson Aims for the Mainstream," *New York Times Magazine*, November 29, 1987, 28–31, 34–36, 58–61; E. J. Dionne, "Black Residents of New York See a Campaign Tinged with Racism," *New York Times*, April 21, 1988, 12; Anthony Lewis, "The Jackson Reality," *New York Times*, March 31, 1988, A27; David Broder, "Jackson Becomes an Agent for Change," Raleigh *News and Observer*, May 2, 1988, 13A; Andrew Kopkind, "Is Jesse the Great White Hope?" *Nation* (December 26, 1987/January 2, 1988): 773, 790–791; Kopkind, "Jesse's Movement," *Nation* (April 2, 1988): 448–489; "For Jesse Jackson and His Campaign," *Nation* (April 16, 1988): 517, 519–522; and "Bad," *New Republic*, 198 (April 18, 1988): 7–9. The implications of the Willie Horton issue are discussed by Michael Kinsley, "GOP Knew Symbolic Value of a Black Rapist," *Tampa Tribune*, November 5, 1988, 15A. For an academic study published before the Jackson candidacies that is pessimistic about the possibilities of a biracial coalition of the dispossessed in the South to unite politically, see Robert Emil Botsch, *We Shall Not Overcome; Populism and Southern Blue-Collar Workers*, University of North Carolina Press, Chapel Hill, 1980.

CHAPTER 8

The Moses statement comes from a speech to the organizers training center (San Francisco, Calif., June 5, 1987), a copy of which was kindly furnished to me by Joseph Sinsheimer. For a similar point of view by a movement veteran and scholar, see Vincent Harding, *The Other American Revolution* (cited for Chapter 4). For suggestions on options open to black politicians and the electorate in the future, particularly concerning an independent strategy, see Ronald W. Walters, *Black Presidential Politics in America* (cited for Chapter 4); and Lorenzo Morris and Linda F. Williams, "The Coalition at the End of the Rainbow: The 1984 Jackson Campaign," in *Jesse Jackson's 1984 Presidential Campaign*, Barker and Walters, eds. (cited for Chapter 7).

Index